WARLORD OF MARS™

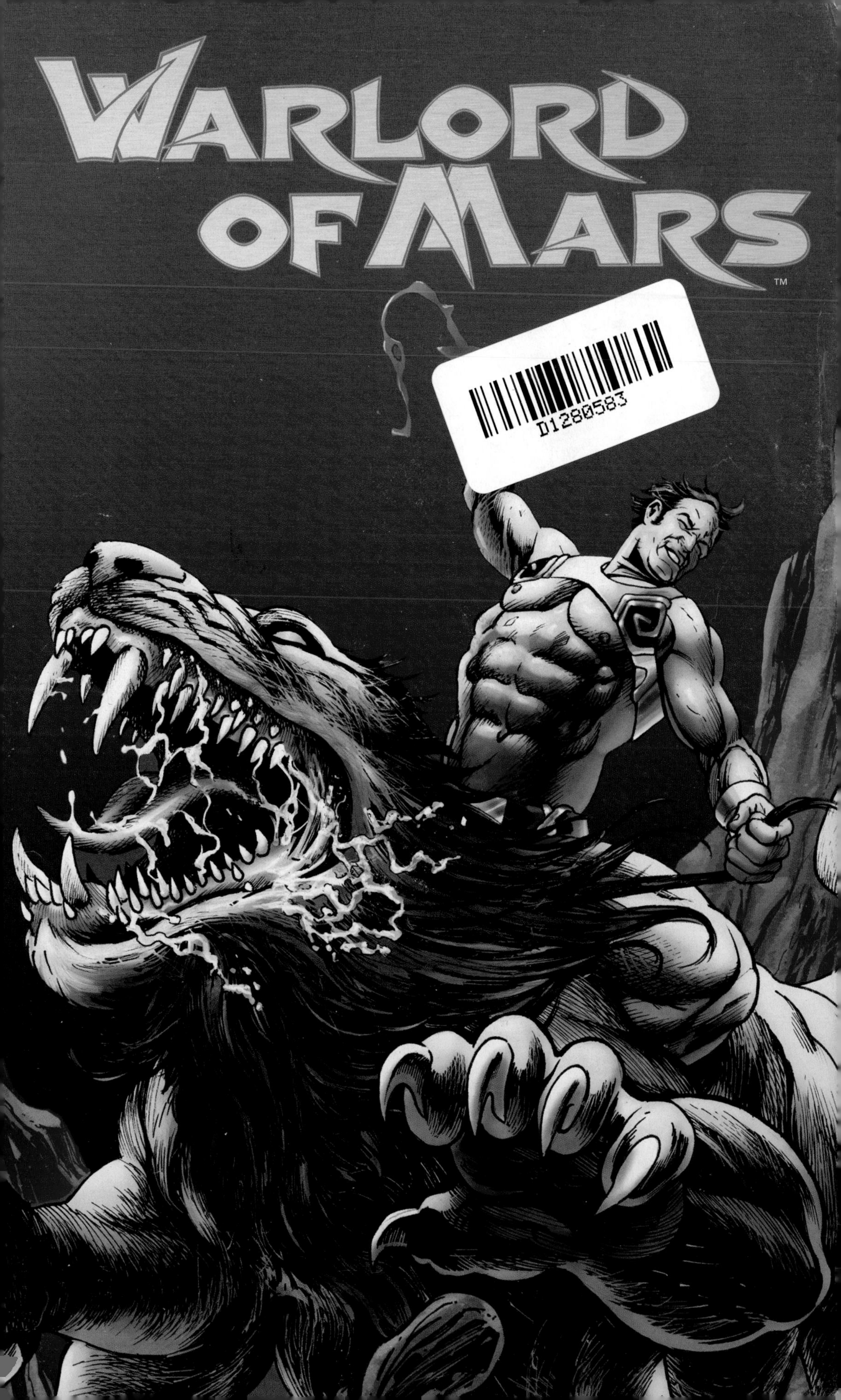

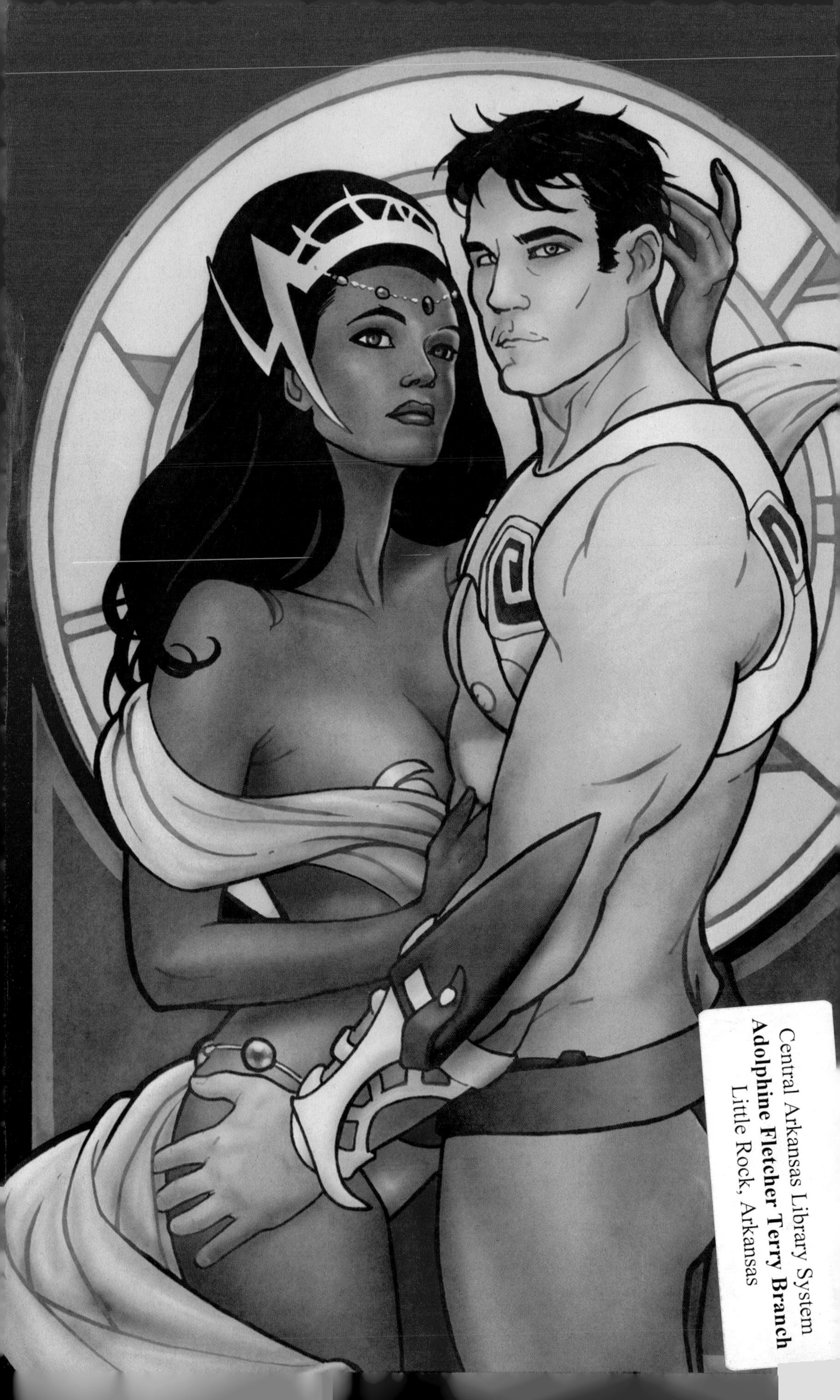

WARLORD OF MARS

written by
ARVID NELSON

illustrated by
STEPHEN SADOWSKI
LUI ANTONIO

colored by
ADRIANO LUCAS

lettered by
TROY PETERI

collection cover by
JOE JUSKO

based on the stories of
EDGAR RICE BURROUGHS

collection design by **JASON ULLMEYER**

This volume collects issues 1-9 of Warlord of Mars by Dynamite Entertainment

DYNAMITE
ENTERTAINMENT
WWW.DYNAMITE.NET

WARLORD OF MARS™ VOLUME 1. Contains materials originally published in Warlord of Mars #1-9. Published by Dynamite Entertainment. 155 Ninth Ave. Suite B, Runnemede, NJ 08078. Warlord of Mars is ™ and © 2011 Savage Tales Entertainment, llc. All rights reserved. DYNAMITE, DYNAMITE ENTERTAINMENT and the Dynamite Entertainment colophon are ® and © 2011 DFI. All names, characters, events, and locales in this publication are entirely fictional. Any resemblance to actual persons (living or dead), events or places, without satiric intent, is coincidental. No portion of this book may be reproduced by any means (digital or print) without the written permission of Dynamite Entertainment except for review purposes. The scanning, uploading and distribution of this book via the Internet or via any other means without the permission of the publisher is illegal and punishable by law. Please purchase only authorized electronic editions, and do not participate in or encourage electronic piracy of copyrighted materials. Printed in Canada

For information regarding press, media rights, foreign rights, licensing, and advertising e-mail: marketing@dynamite.net

NICK BARRUCCI   PRESIDENT
JUAN COLLADO   CHIEF OPERATING OFFICER
JOSEPH RYBANDT   EDITOR
RICH YOUNG   DIRECTOR BUSINESS DEVELOPMENT
JOSH JOHNSON   CREATIVE DIRECTOR
JASON ULLMEYER   SENIOR DESIGNER
JOSH GREEN   TRAFFIC COORDINATOR
CHRIS CANIANO   PRODUCTION ASSISTANT

First Edition   ISBN-10: 1-60690-206-7   ISBN-13: 978-1-60690-206-6   10 9 8 7 6 5 4 3 2 1

A note from E.R. Burroughs concerning this series

In submitting Captain John Carter's strange manuscript to you in graphic narrative form, I believe a few words relative to this remarkable personality will be of interest.

My first recollection of Captain Carter is of the few months he spent at my father's home in Virginia, just prior to the opening of the Civil War. I was then a child of but five years, yet I well remember the tall, dark, athletic man I called Uncle Jack.

He seemed always to be laughing; and he entered into the sports of the children with the same hearty good fellowship he displayed toward those pastimes in which the men and women of his own age indulged. His manners were perfect, and his courtliness was that of a southern gentleman of the highest type. His horsemanship was a marvel and delight even in that country of magnificent horsemen. We all loved him.

When the war broke out he left us, nor did I see him again for some fifteen years. When he returned it was without warning, and I was much surprised to note he had not aged apparently a moment. He was, when others were with him, the same happy fellow we had known of old, but at night, when he thought himself alone, I saw him sit for hours gazing up into the stars, his face set in a look of wistful longing and hopeless misery, at what I did not know until I read his manuscript years afterward.

He told us that he had been prospecting in Arizona part of the time since the war; and that he had been very successful was evidenced by the unlimited amount of money with which he was supplied. As to the details of his life during these years, he would not speak.

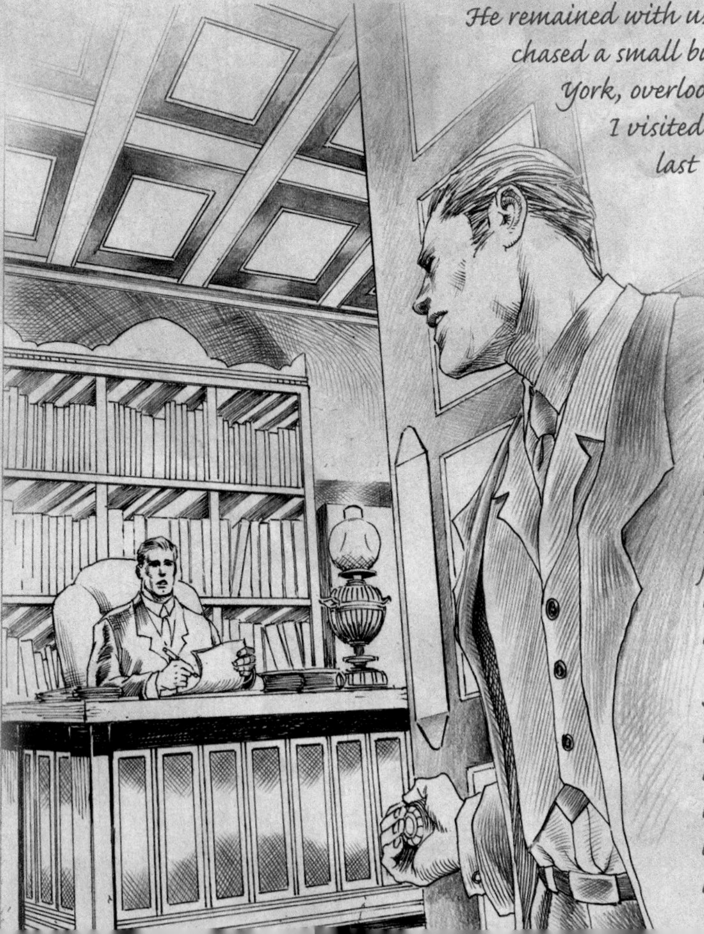

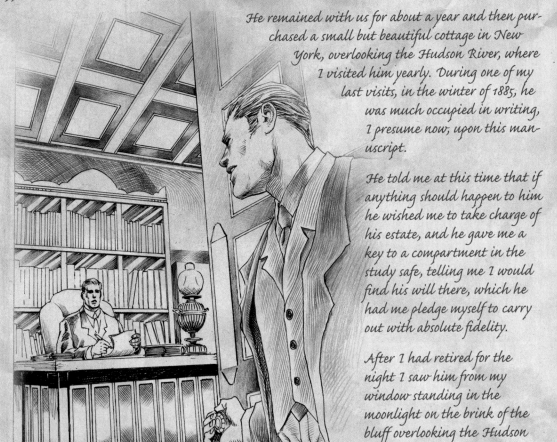

He remained with us for about a year and then purchased a small but beautiful cottage in New York, overlooking the Hudson River, where I visited him yearly. During one of my last visits, in the winter of 1885, he was much occupied in writing, I presume now, upon this manuscript.

He told me at this time that if anything should happen to him he wished me to take charge of his estate, and he gave me a key to a compartment in the study safe, telling me I would find his will there, which he had me pledge myself to carry out with absolute fidelity.

After I had retired for the night I saw him from my window standing in the moonlight on the brink of the bluff overlooking the Hudson with his arms stretched out to the heavens. I thought at the time that he was praying, although I never understood that he was in the strict sense of the term a religious man.

Several months after I had returned home from my last visit, I received a telegram from him asking me to come to him at once.

I arrived at the little station, about a mile from his grounds, on the morning of March 4, 1886, and when I asked the livery man to drive me out to Captain Carter's he replied he had some very bad news; the Captain had been found dead shortly after daylight. For some reason this news did not surprise me.

I found the watchman who had discovered him in his little study. He related the few details connected with the finding of the body, which he said had been still warm when he came upon it. It lay, he said, stretched full length in the snow with the arms outstretched above the head toward the edge of the bluff, and when he showed me the spot it flashed upon me that it was the identical one where I had seen him that other night, with his arms raised to the skies.

A local physician and the coroner's jury quickly reached a decision of death from heart failure. Left alone in the study, I opened the safe and withdrew the will. The instructions were peculiar indeed, but I have followed them to each last detail as faithfully as I was able.

He directed that I remove his body to Virginia without embalming, and that he be laid in an open coffin within a tomb which he previously had had constructed and which, as I later learned, was well ventilated. The instructions impressed upon me that I must personally see that this was carried out just as he directed, even in secrecy if necessary.

In addition to providing me with a lifetime income, his further instructions related to his manuscript, which I was to retain sealed and unread, just as I found it, until twenty-one years after his death.

A strange feature about the tomb, where his body still lies, is that the massive door is equipped with a single, massive spring lock which can be opened only from the inside.

Yours very sincerely,
Edgar Rice Burroughs.
March 4, 1907

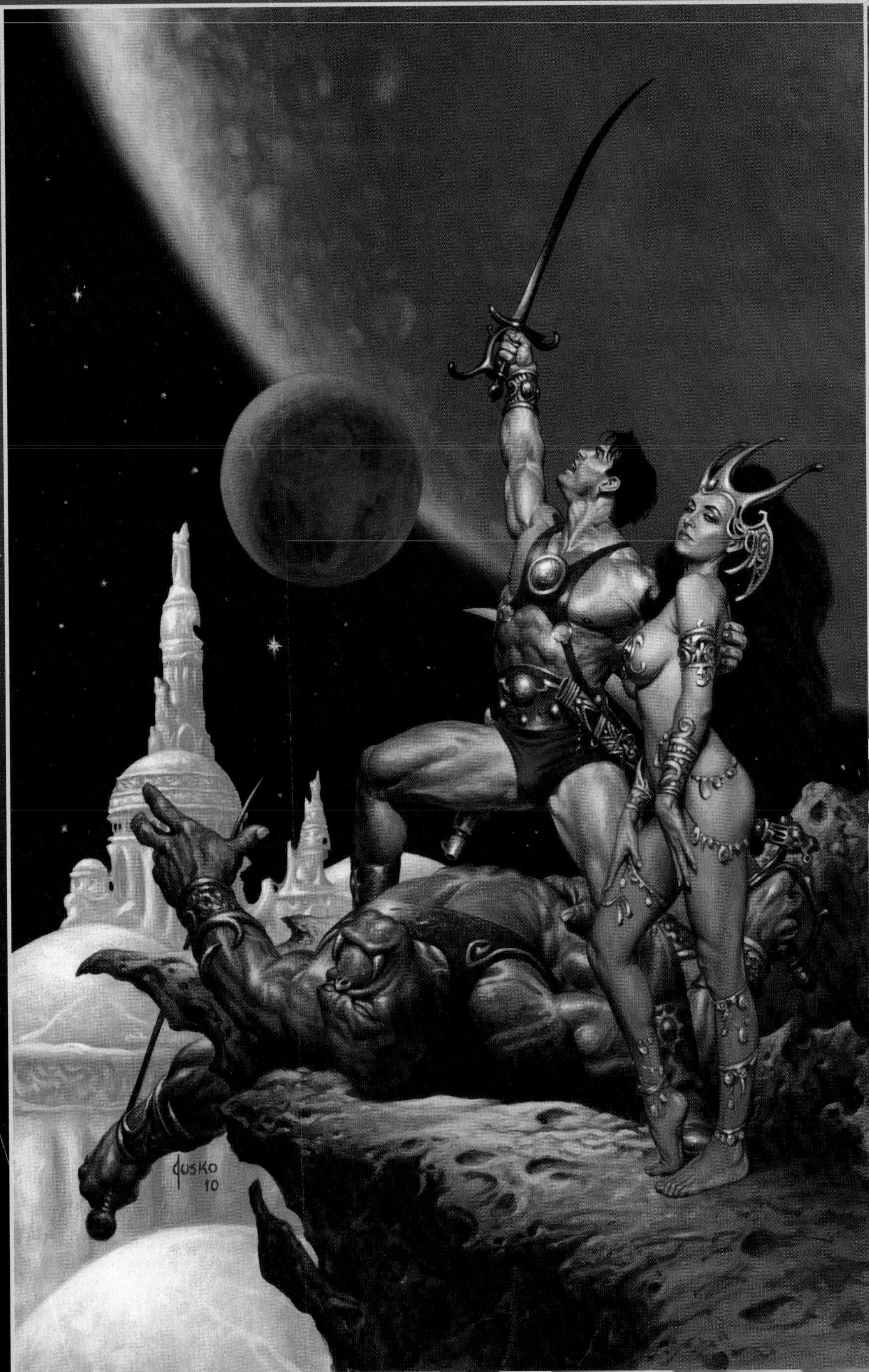

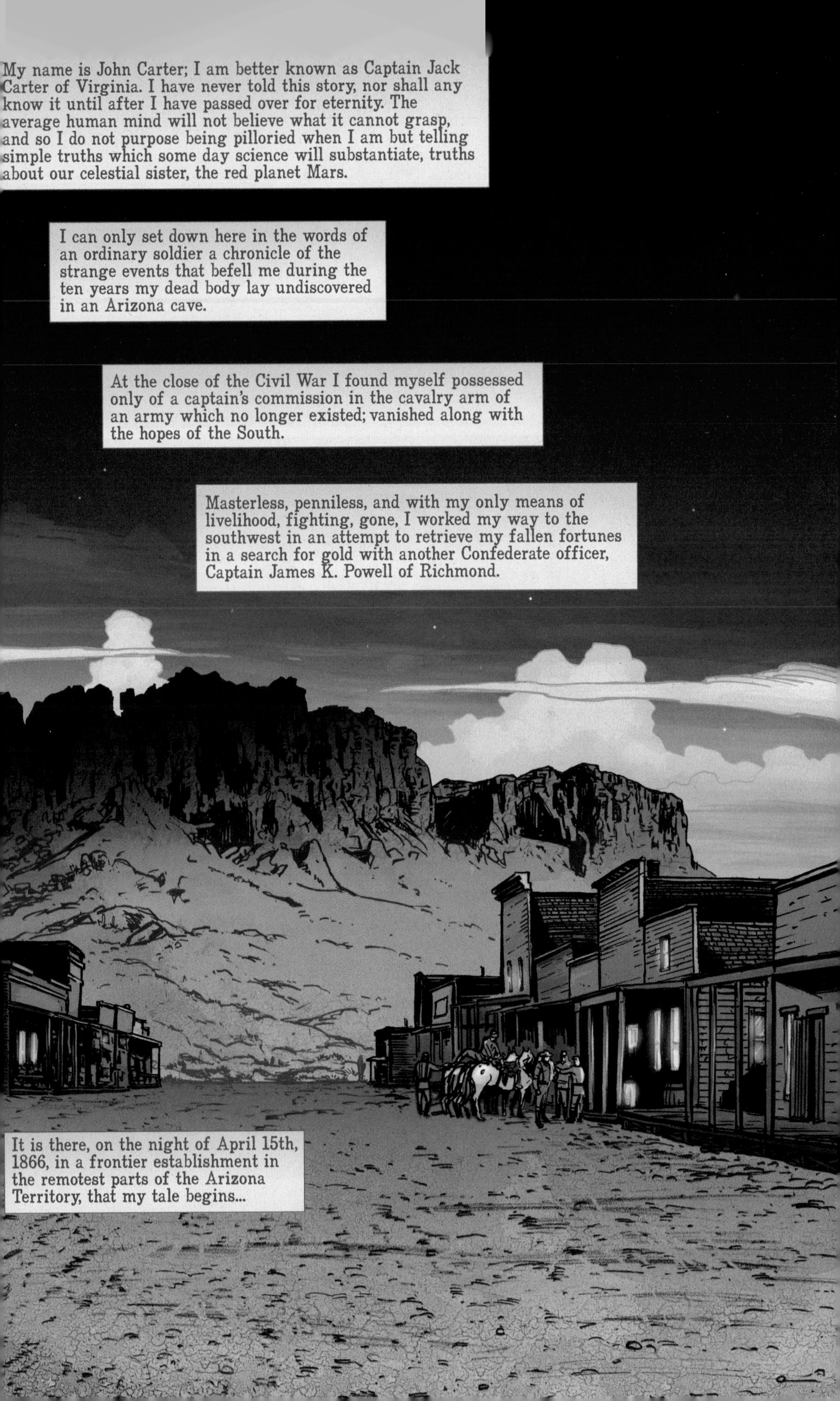
My name is John Carter; I am better known as Captain Jack Carter of Virginia. I have never told this story, nor shall any know it until after I have passed over for eternity. The average human mind will not believe what it cannot grasp, and so I do not purpose being pilloried when I am but telling simple truths which some day science will substantiate, truths about our celestial sister, the red planet Mars.
I can only set down here in the words of an ordinary soldier a chronicle of the strange events that befell me during the ten years my dead body lay undiscovered in an Arizona cave.
At the close of the Civil War I found myself possessed only of a captain's commission in the cavalry arm of an army which no longer existed; vanished along with the hopes of the South.
Masterless, penniless, and with my only means of livelihood, fighting, gone, I worked my way to the southwest in an attempt to retrieve my fallen fortunes in a search for gold with another Confederate officer, Captain James K. Powell of Richmond.
It is there, on the night of April 15th, 1866, in a frontier establishment in the remotest parts of the Arizona Territory, that my tale begins...

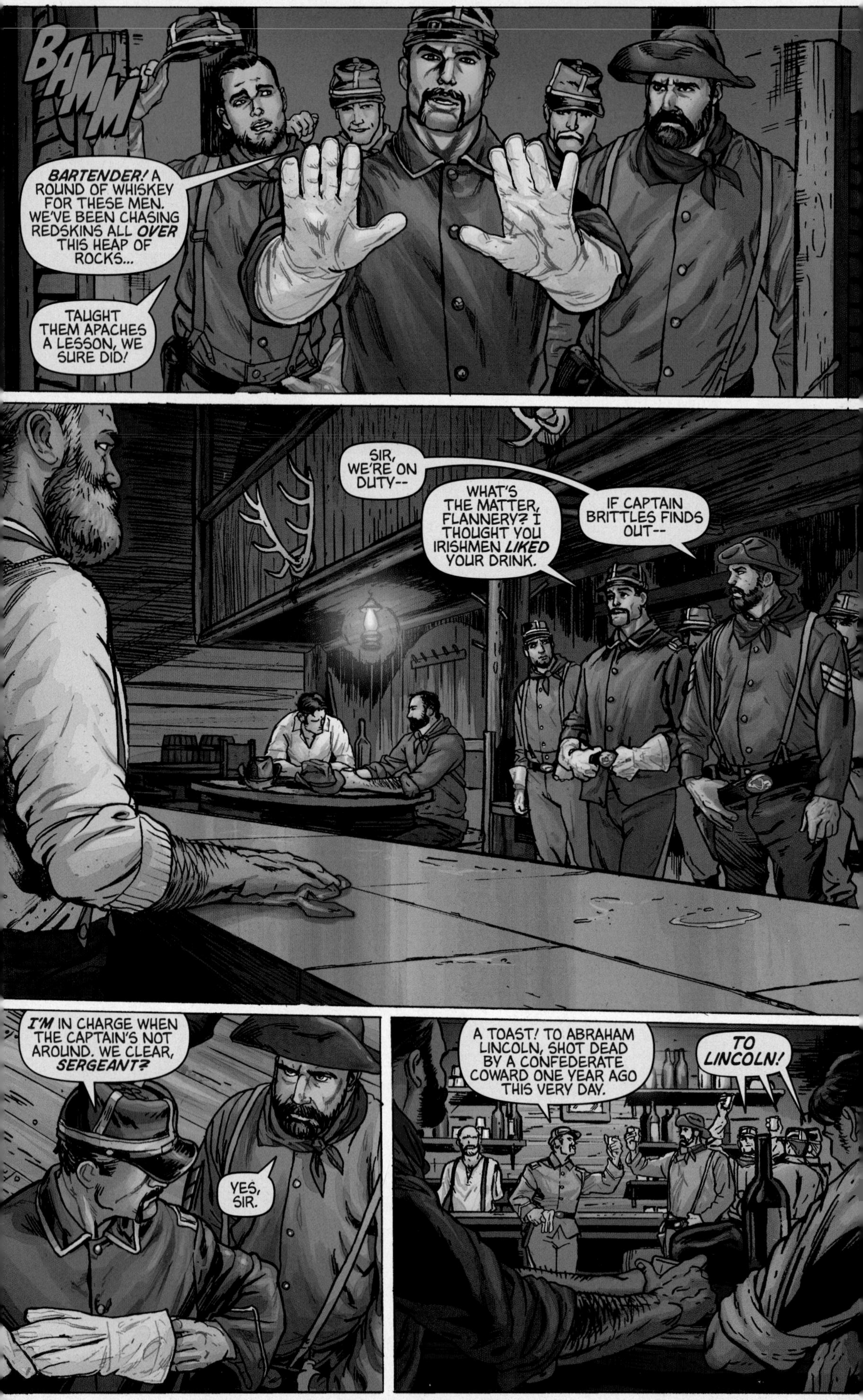
BAMM
BARTENDER! A ROUND OF WHISKEY FOR THESE MEN. WE'VE BEEN CHASING REDSKINS ALL OVER THIS HEAP OF ROCKS...
TAUGHT THEM APACHES A LESSON, WE SURE DID!
SIR, WE'RE ON DUTY--
IF CAPTAIN BRITTLES FINDS OUT--
WHAT'S THE MATTER, FLANNERY? I THOUGHT YOU IRISHMEN LIKED YOUR DRINK.
I'M IN CHARGE WHEN THE CAPTAIN'S NOT AROUND. WE CLEAR, SERGEANT?
YES, SIR.
A TOAST! TO ABRAHAM LINCOLN, SHOT DEAD BY A CONFEDERATE COWARD ONE YEAR AGO THIS VERY DAY.
TO LINCOLN!

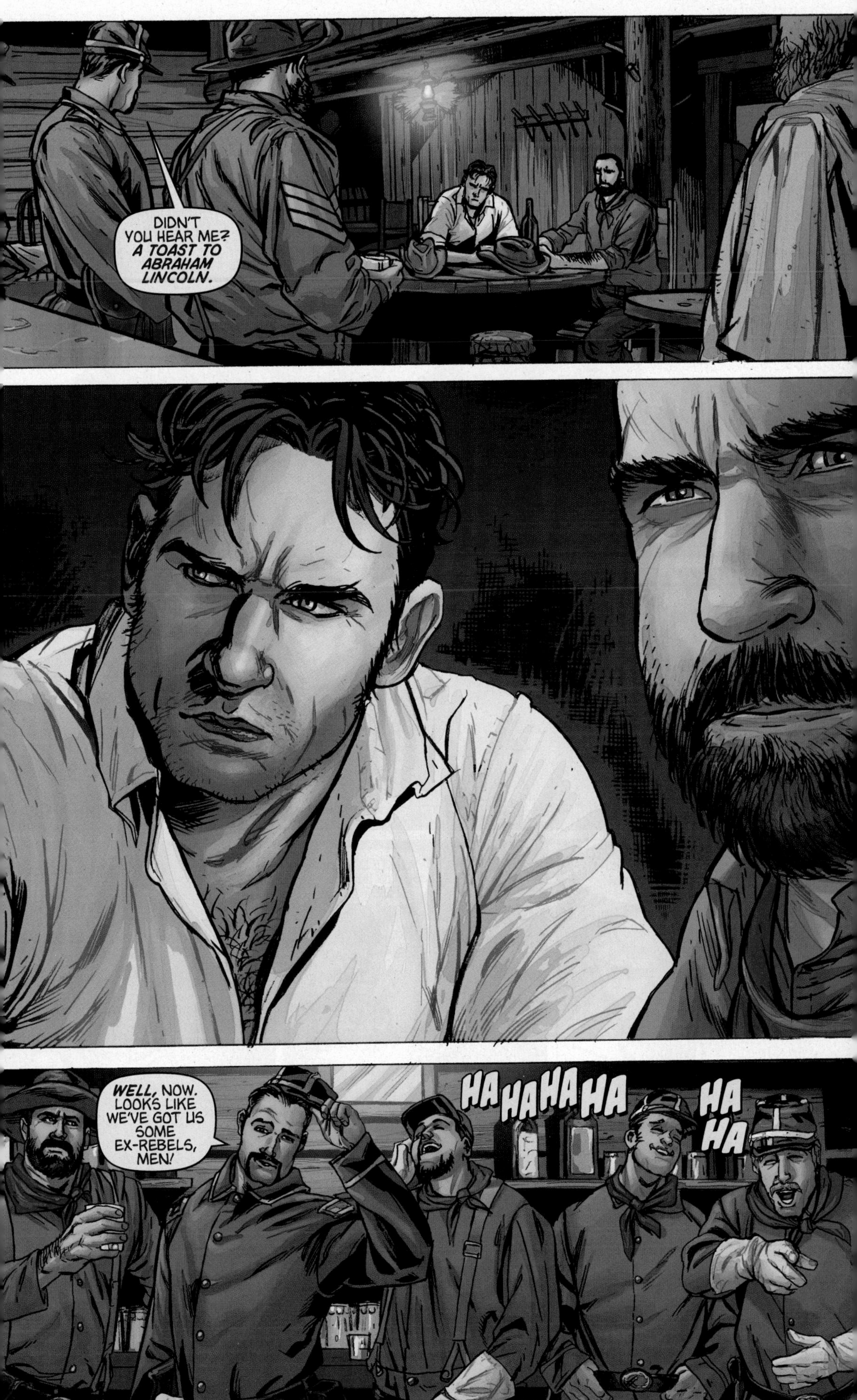

DIDN'T YOU HEAR ME? A TOAST TO ABRAHAM LINCOLN.
WELL, NOW. LOOKS LIKE WE'VE GOT US SOME EX-REBELS, MEN!
HA HA HA HA HA
HA HA

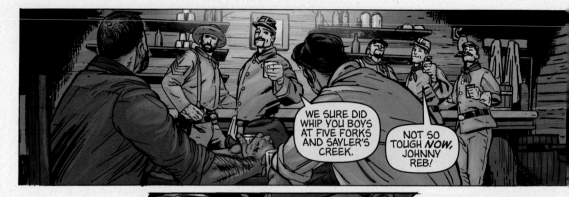

WE SURE DID WHIP YOU BOYS AT FIVE FORKS AND SAYLER'S CREEK.

NOT SO TOUGH *NOW*, JOHNNY REB!

SERGEANT FLANNERY, YOU ARE CORRECT. WE OUGHT TO SHOW... *RESPECT* FOR OUR VANQUISHED FOES.

SO I'M GOING TO BE BIG ABOUT THIS. I'M GOING TO GIVE YOU REBEL BOYS A CHOICE.

SMAK

YOU'RE EITHER GOING TO *DRINK* TO OUR DEPARTED COMMANDER-IN-CHIEF, OR YOU'RE GOING TO *HIGH-TAIL* IT OUT OF HERE.

WHAT'LL IT BE, JOHNNY REB?

I THINK THEY'S YELLOW.

NOT WORTH IT, CARTER.

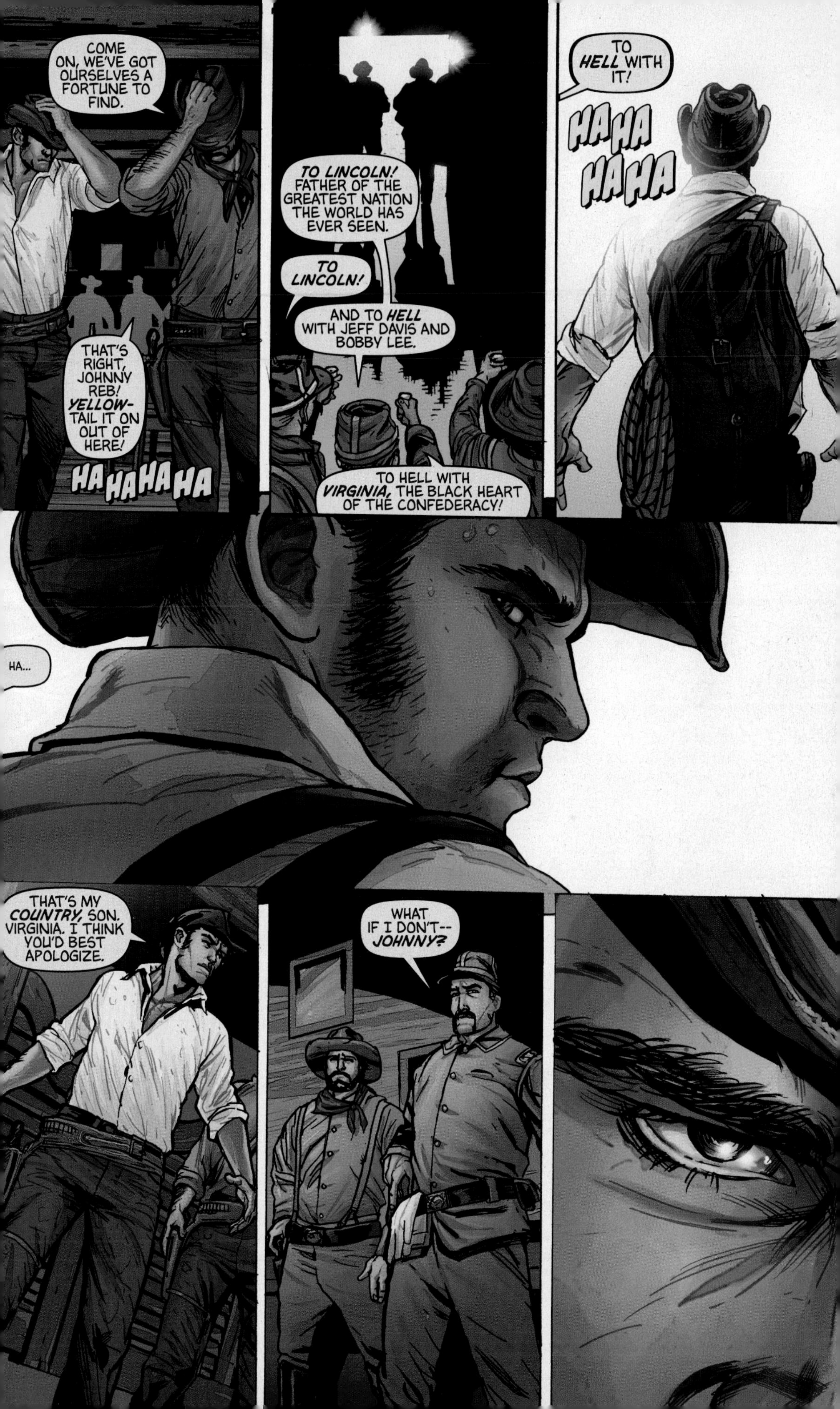
COME ON, WE'VE GOT OURSELVES A FORTUNE TO FIND.
THAT'S RIGHT, JOHNNY REB! YELLOW-TAIL IT ON OUT OF HERE!
HA HA HA HA HA
TO LINCOLN! FATHER OF THE GREATEST NATION THE WORLD HAS EVER SEEN.
TO LINCOLN!
AND TO HELL WITH JEFF DAVIS AND BOBBY LEE.
TO HELL WITH VIRGINIA, THE BLACK HEART OF THE CONFEDERACY!
TO HELL WITH IT!
HA HA HA HA
HA...
THAT'S MY COUNTRY, SON. VIRGINIA. I THINK YOU'D BEST APOLOGIZE.
WHAT IF I DON'T-- JOHNNY?

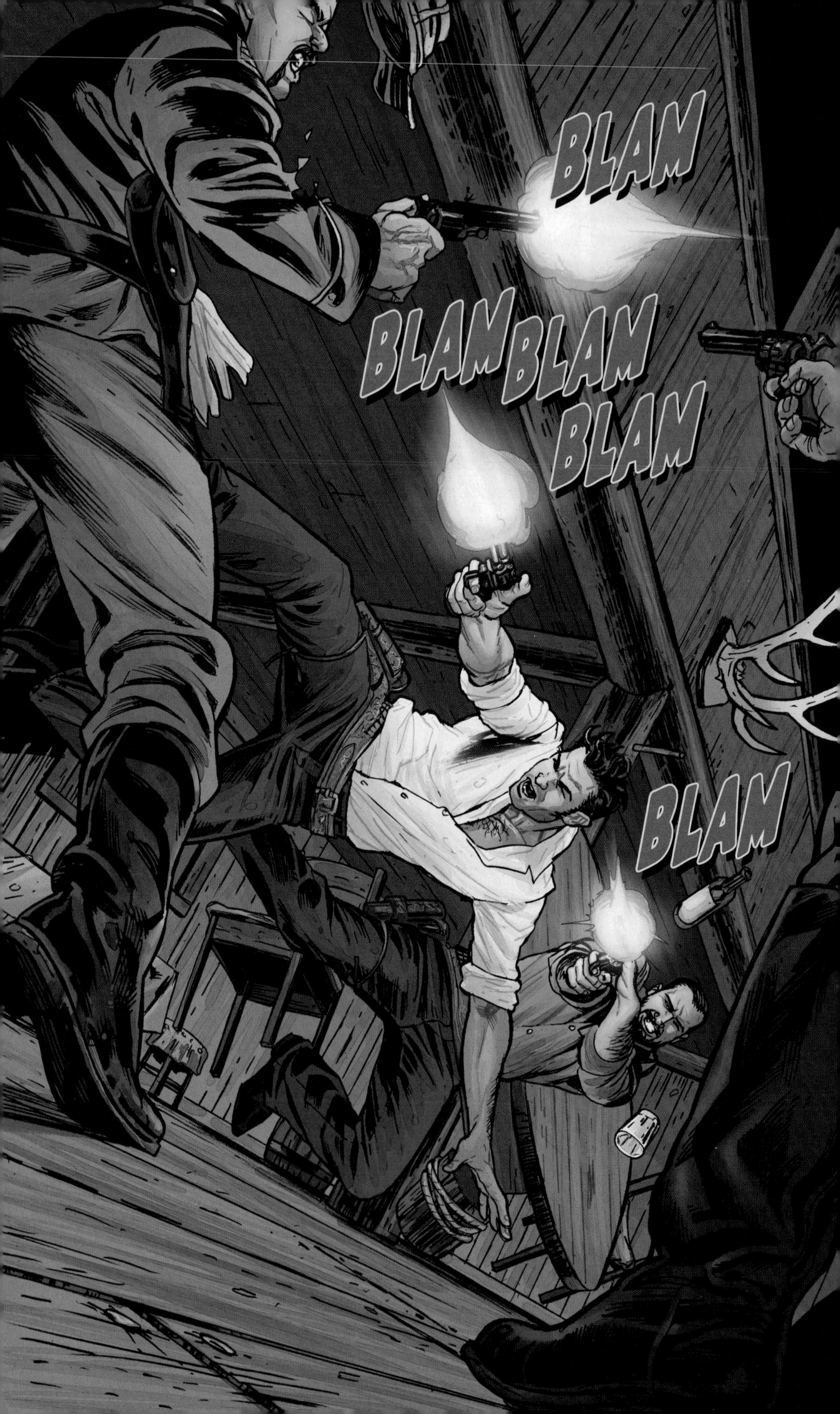
BLAM
BLAM BLAM
BLAM
BLAM

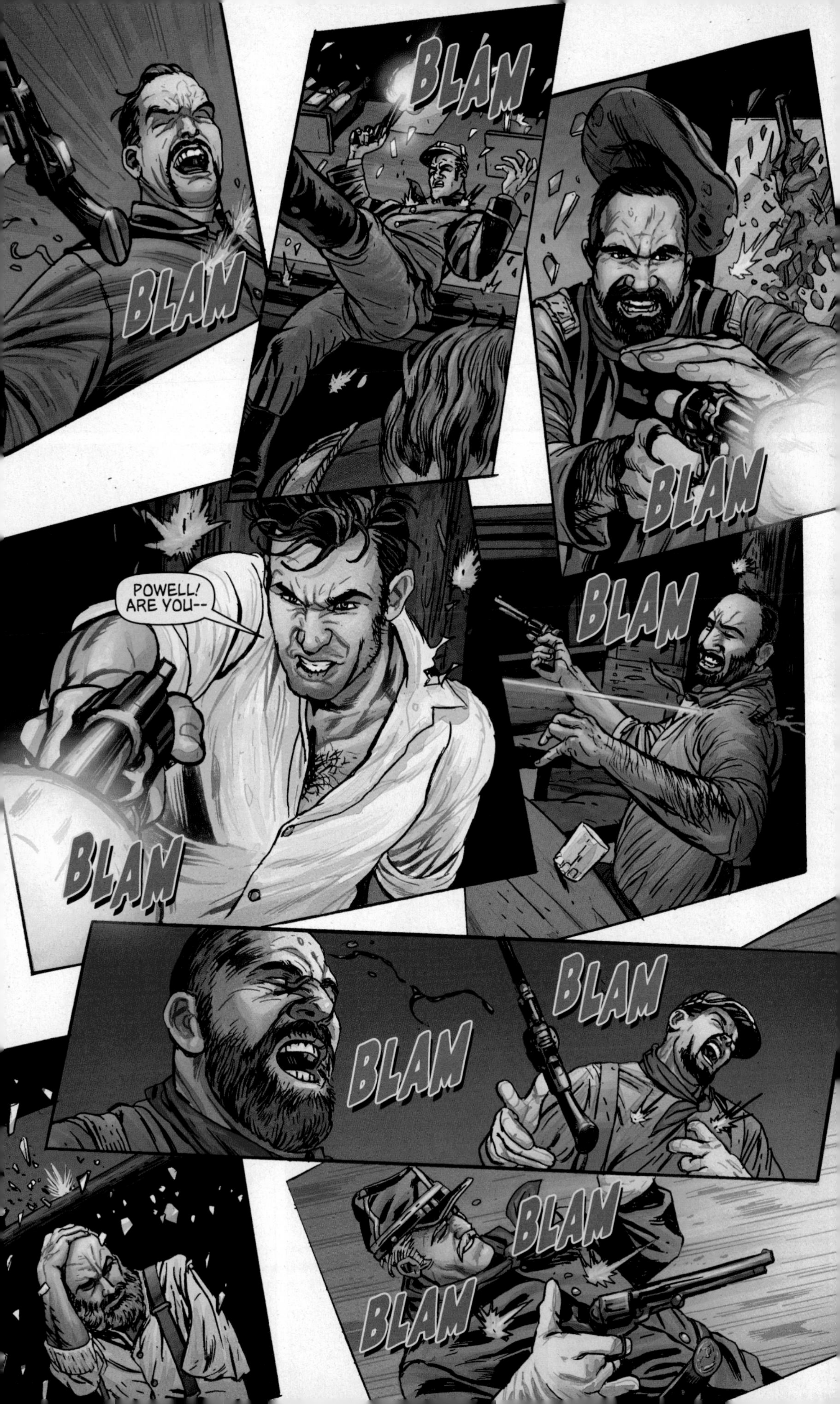
BLAM
BLAM
BLAM
POWELL! ARE YOU--
BLAM
BLAM
BLAM
BLAM
BLAM
BLAM

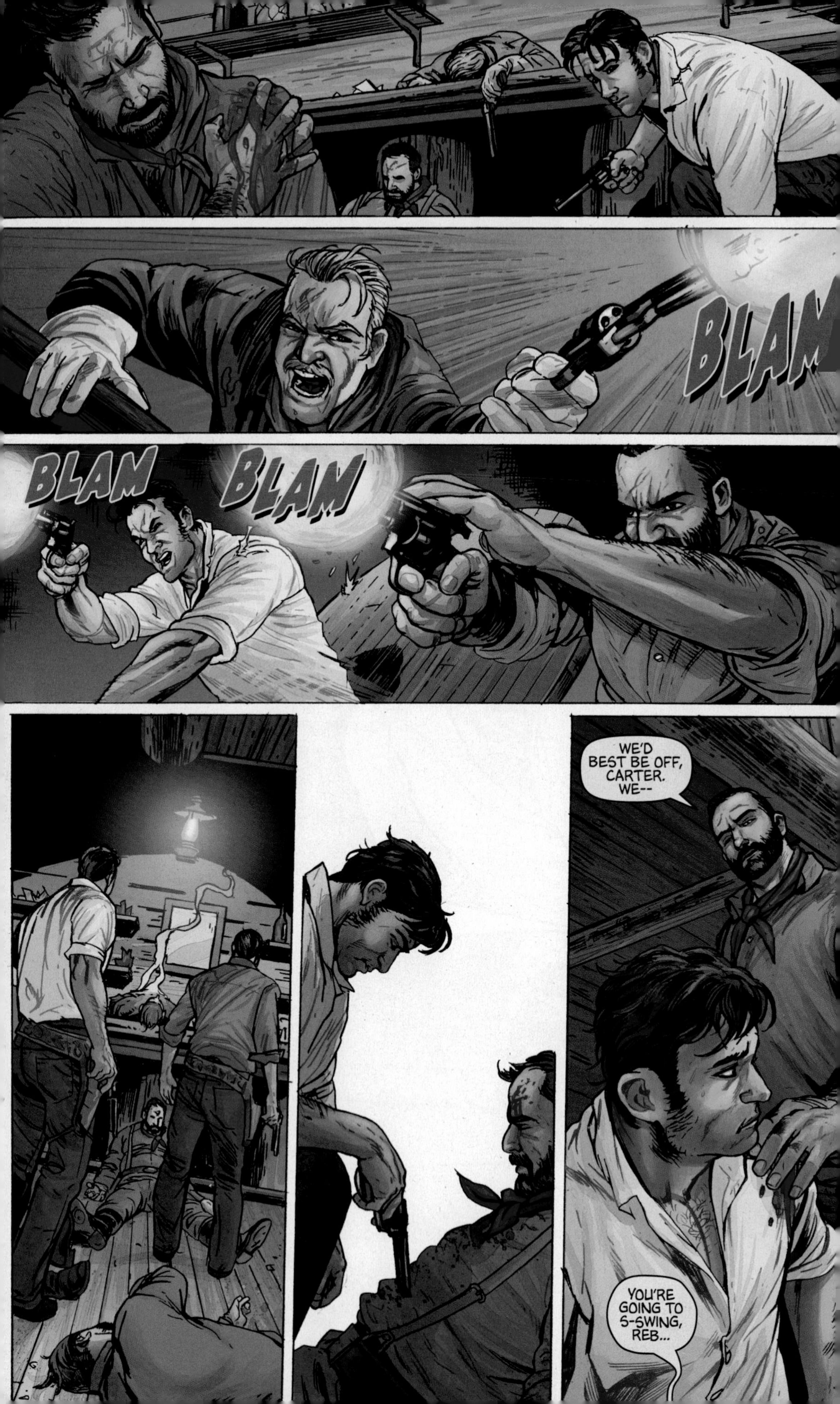
BLAM
BLAM
BLAM
WE'D BEST BE OFF, CARTER. WE--
YOU'RE GOING TO S-SWING, REB...

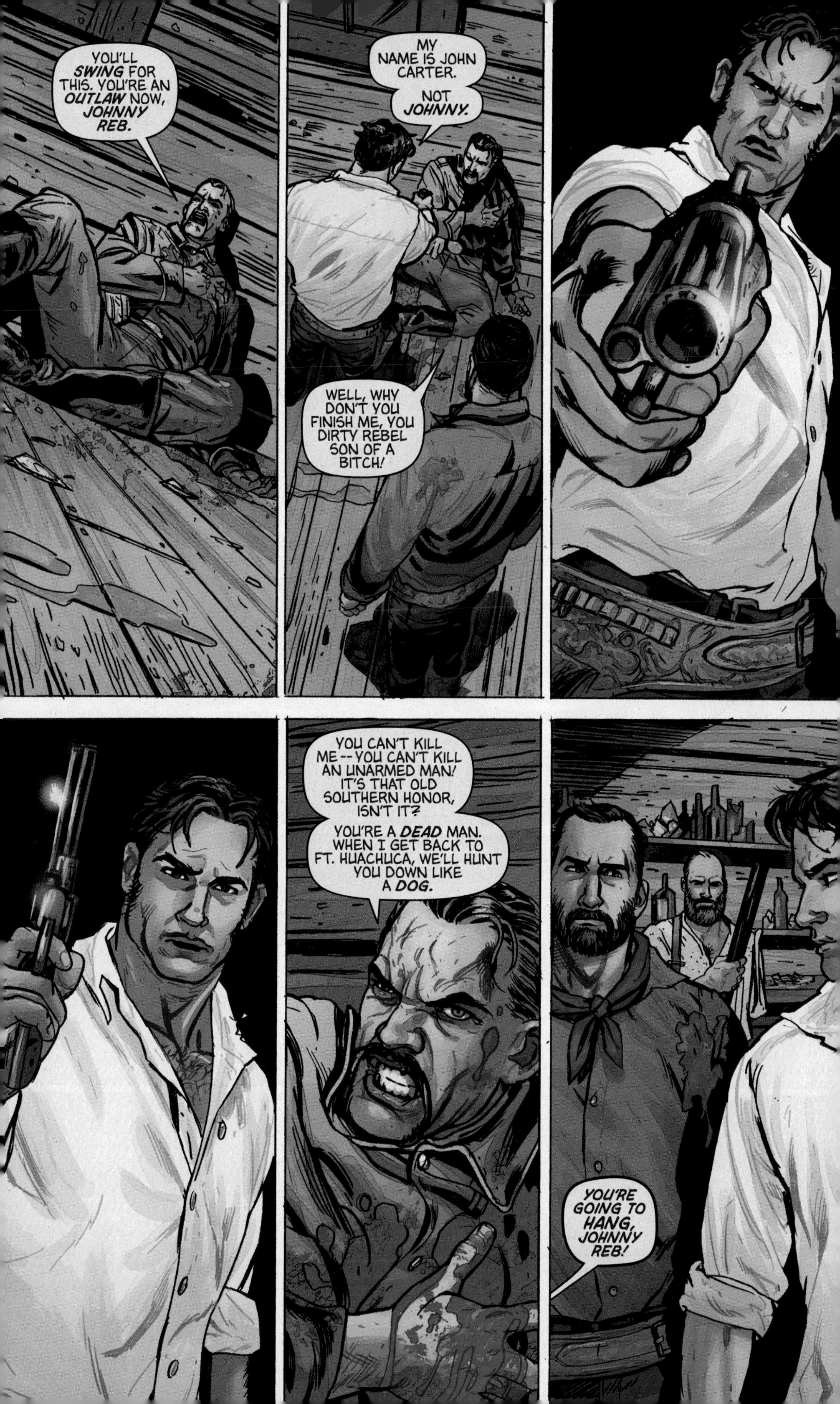
YOU'LL SWING FOR THIS. YOU'RE AN OUTLAW NOW, JOHNNY REB.
MY NAME IS JOHN CARTER.
NOT JOHNNY.
WELL, WHY DON'T YOU FINISH ME, YOU DIRTY REBEL SON OF A BITCH!
YOU CAN'T KILL ME--YOU CAN'T KILL AN UNARMED MAN! IT'S THAT OLD SOUTHERN HONOR, ISN'T IT?
YOU'RE A DEAD MAN. WHEN I GET BACK TO FT. HUACHUCA, WE'LL HUNT YOU DOWN LIKE A DOG.
YOU'RE GOING TO HANG, JOHNNY REB!

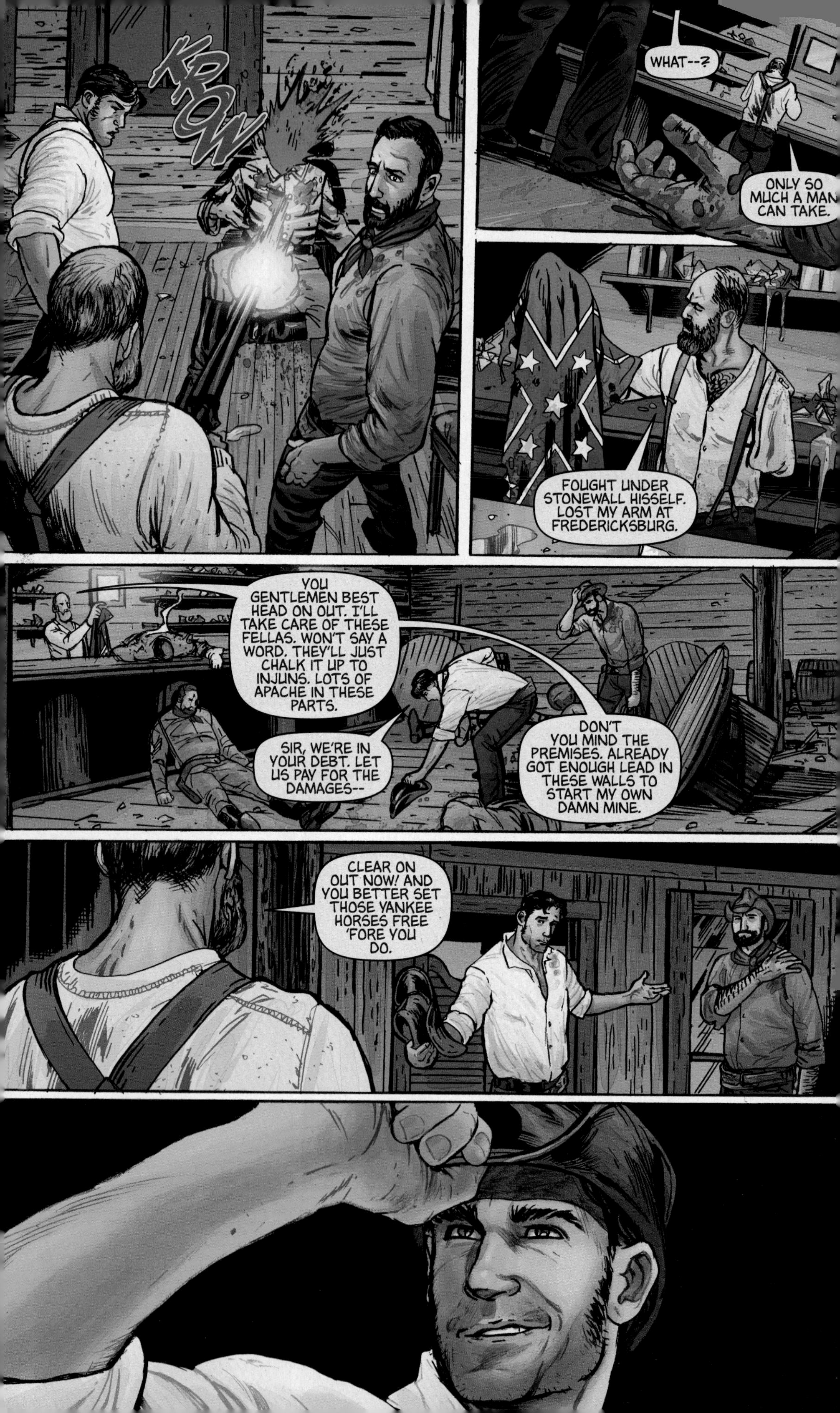
KROW
WHAT--?
ONLY SO MUCH A MAN CAN TAKE.
FOUGHT UNDER STONEWALL HISSELF. LOST MY ARM AT FREDERICKSBURG.
YOU GENTLEMEN BEST HEAD ON OUT. I'LL TAKE CARE OF THESE FELLAS. WON'T SAY A WORD. THEY'LL JUST CHALK IT UP TO INJUNS. LOTS OF APACHE IN THESE PARTS.
SIR, WE'RE IN YOUR DEBT. LET US PAY FOR THE DAMAGES--
DON'T YOU MIND THE PREMISES. ALREADY GOT ENOUGH LEAD IN THESE WALLS TO START MY OWN DAMN MINE.
CLEAR ON OUT NOW! AND YOU BETTER SET THOSE YANKEE HORSES FREE 'FORE YOU DO.

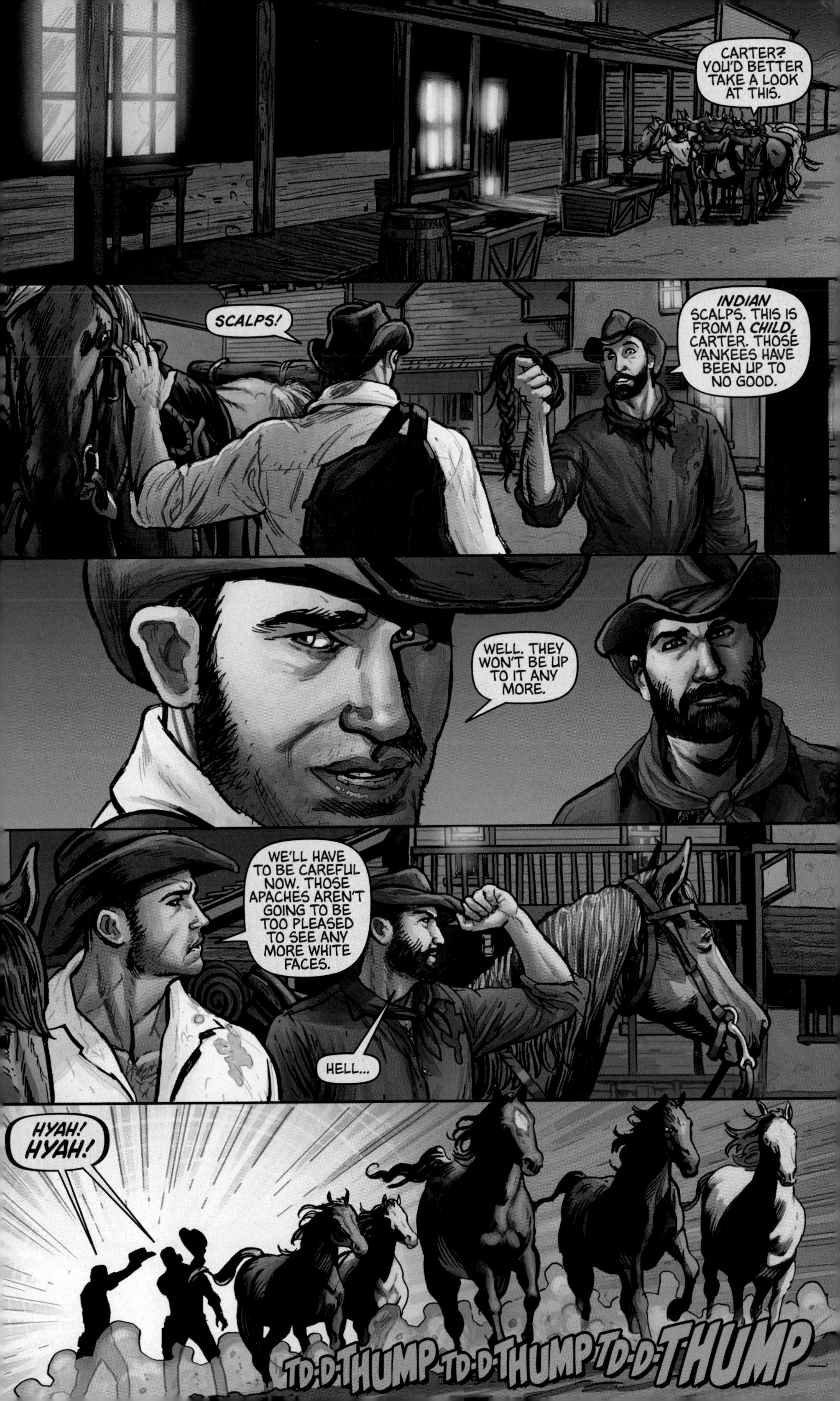

CARTER? YOU'D BETTER TAKE A LOOK AT THIS.
SCALPS!
INDIAN SCALPS. THIS IS FROM A CHILD, CARTER. THOSE YANKEES HAVE BEEN UP TO NO GOOD.
WELL. THEY WON'T BE UP TO IT ANY MORE.
WE'LL HAVE TO BE CAREFUL NOW. THOSE APACHES AREN'T GOING TO BE TOO PLEASED TO SEE ANY MORE WHITE FACES.
HELL...
HYAH! HYAH!
TD-D-THUMP TD-D-THUMP TD-D-THUMP

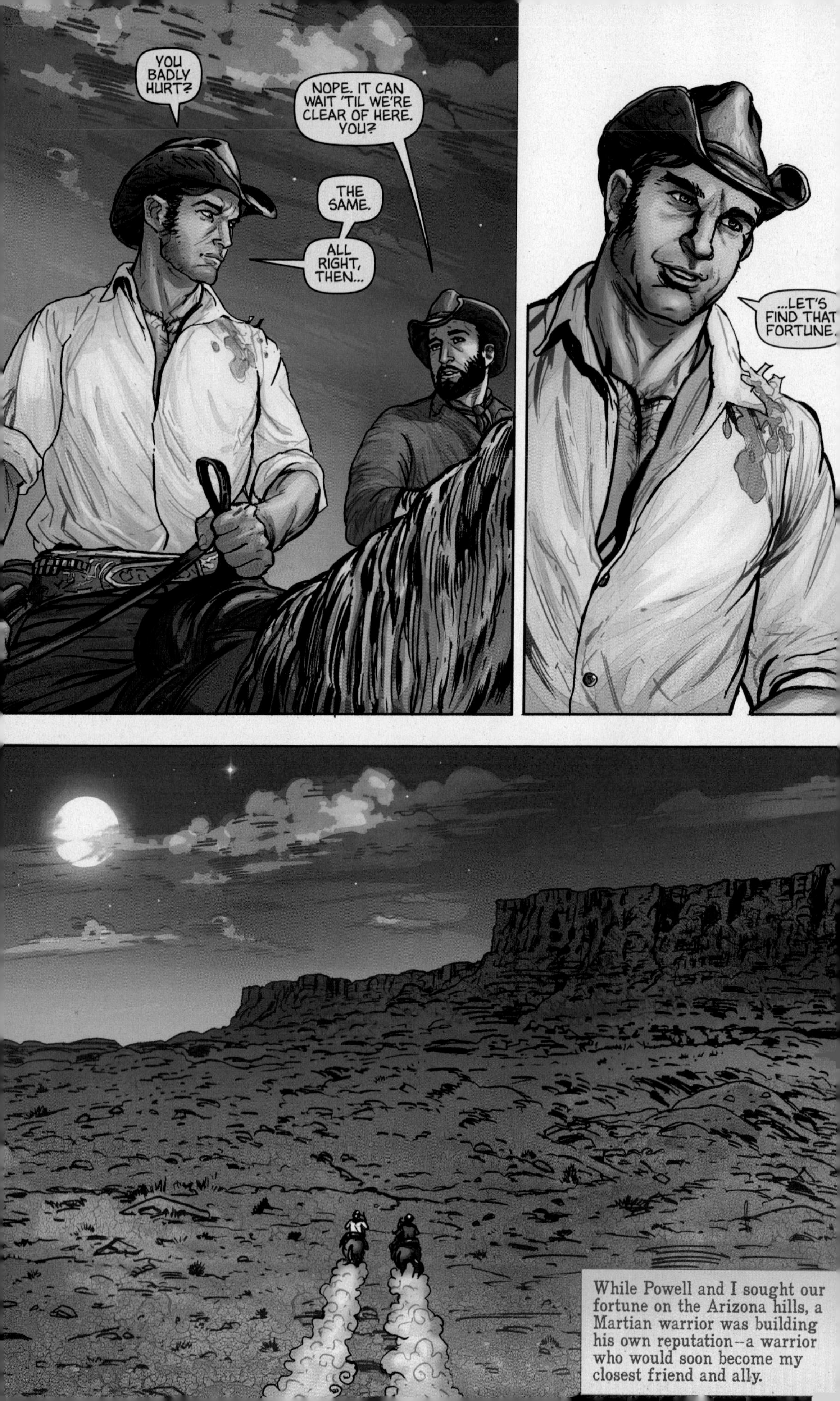
YOU BADLY HURT?
NOPE. IT CAN WAIT 'TIL WE'RE CLEAR OF HERE. YOU?
THE SAME.
ALL RIGHT, THEN...
...LET'S FIND THAT FORTUNE.
While Powell and I sought our fortune on the Arizona hills, a Martian warrior was building his own reputation--a warrior who would soon become my closest friend and ally.

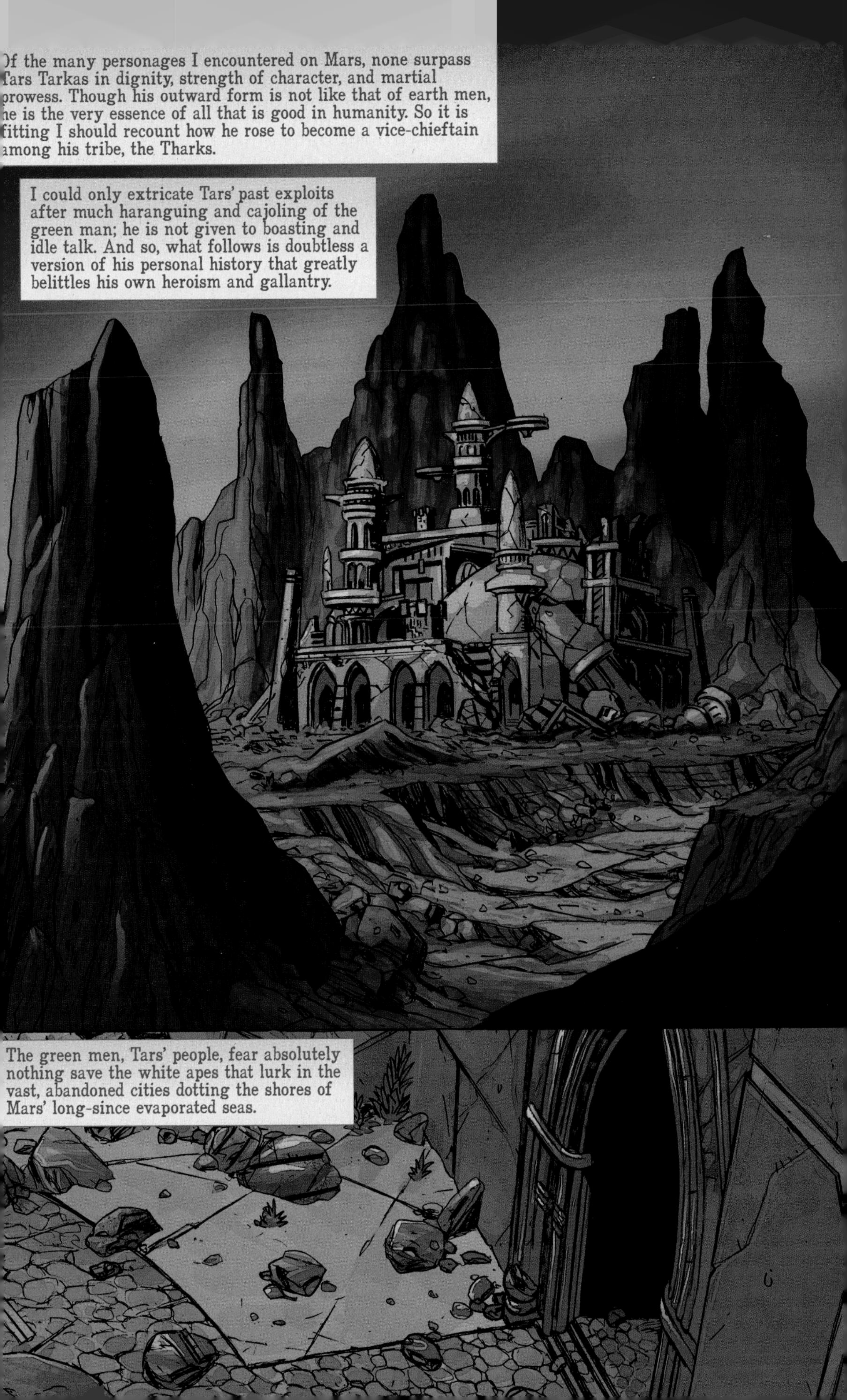
Of the many personages I encountered on Mars, none surpass Tars Tarkas in dignity, strength of character, and martial prowess. Though his outward form is not like that of earth men, he is the very essence of all that is good in humanity. So it is fitting I should recount how he rose to become a vice-chieftain among his tribe, the Tharks.
I could only extricate Tars' past exploits after much haranguing and cajoling of the green man; he is not given to boasting and idle talk. And so, what follows is doubtless a version of his personal history that greatly belittles his own heroism and gallantry.
The green men, Tars' people, fear absolutely nothing save the white apes that lurk in the vast, abandoned cities dotting the shores of Mars' long-since evaporated seas.

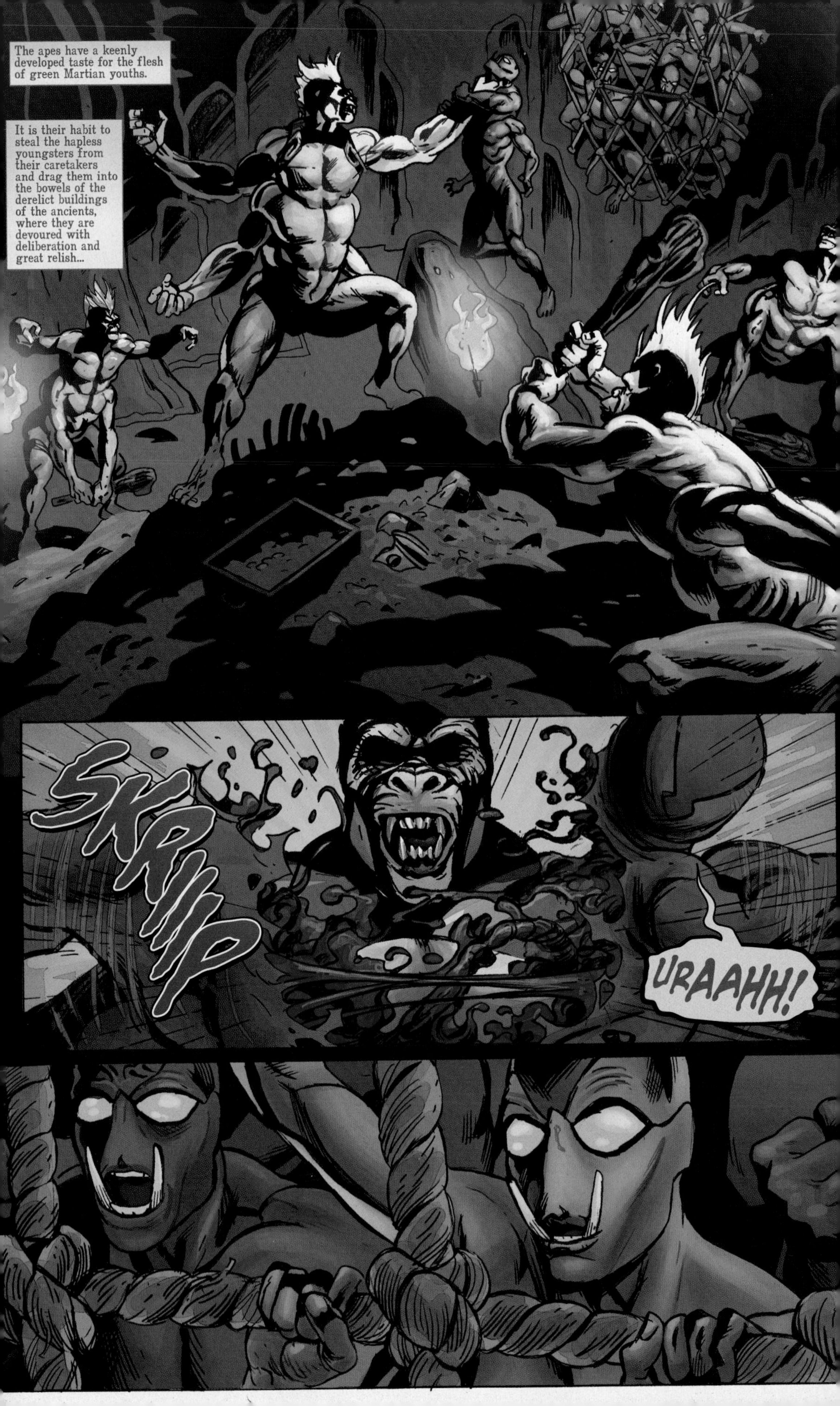
The apes have a keenly developed taste for the flesh of green Martian youths.
It is their habit to steal the hapless youngsters from their caretakers and drag them into the bowels of the derelict buildings of the ancients, where they are devoured with deliberation and great relish...
SKRIIIP
URAAHH!

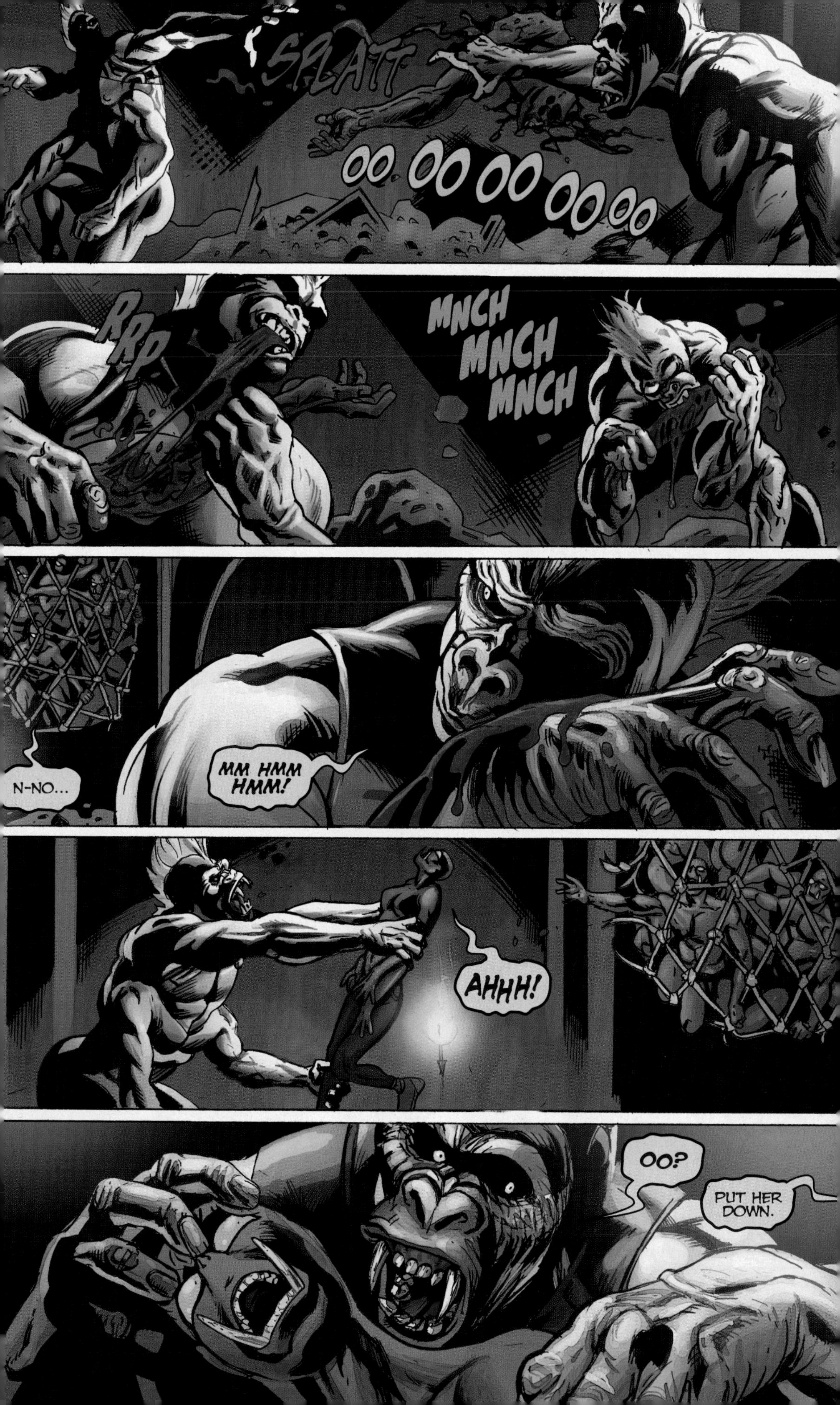
SPLATT
OO OO OO OO OO OO
RRRP
MNCH
MNCH
MNCH
N-NO...
MM HMM HMM!
AHHH!
OO?
PUT HER DOWN.

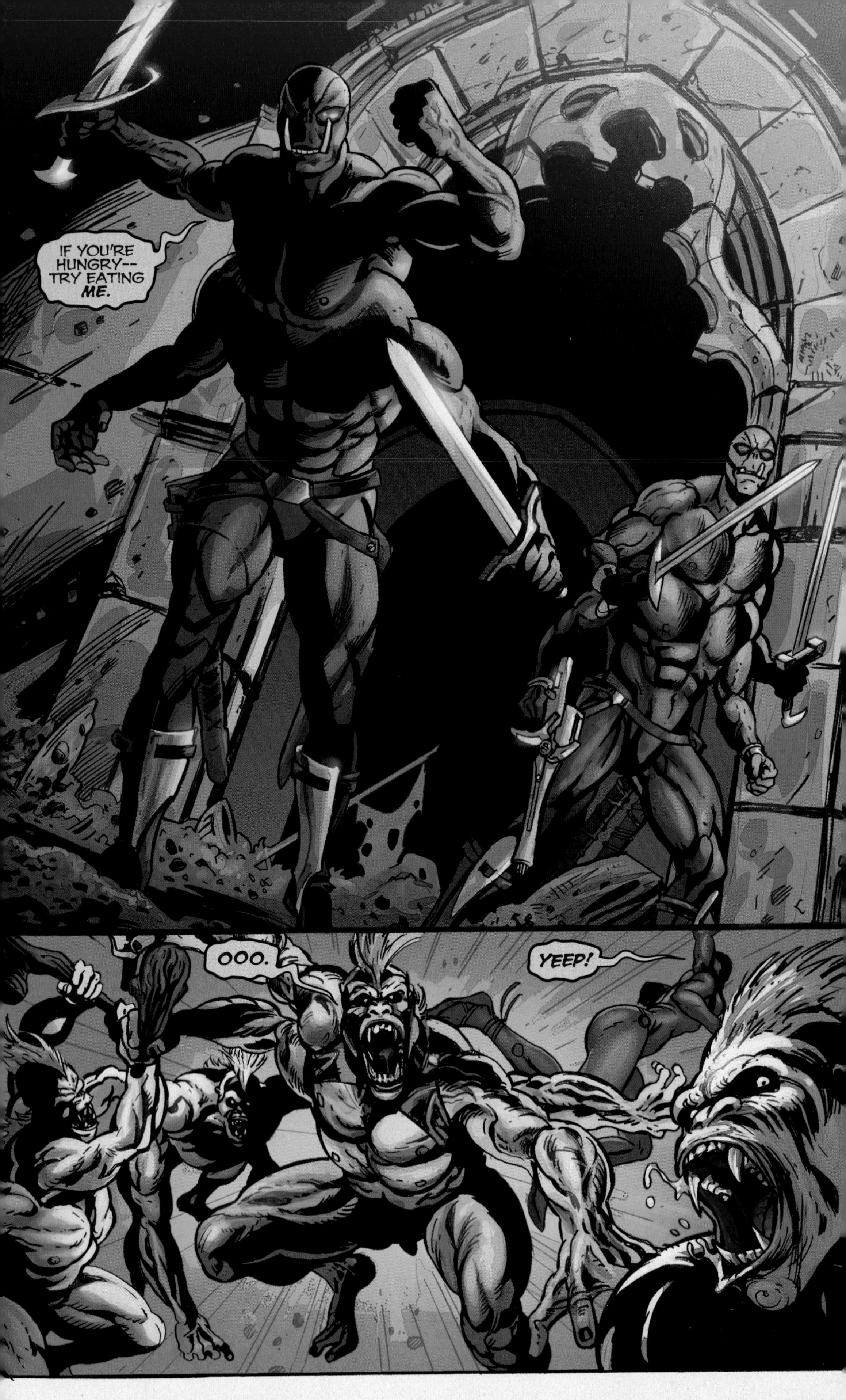
IF YOU'RE HUNGRY-- TRY EATING ME.
OOO.
YEEP!

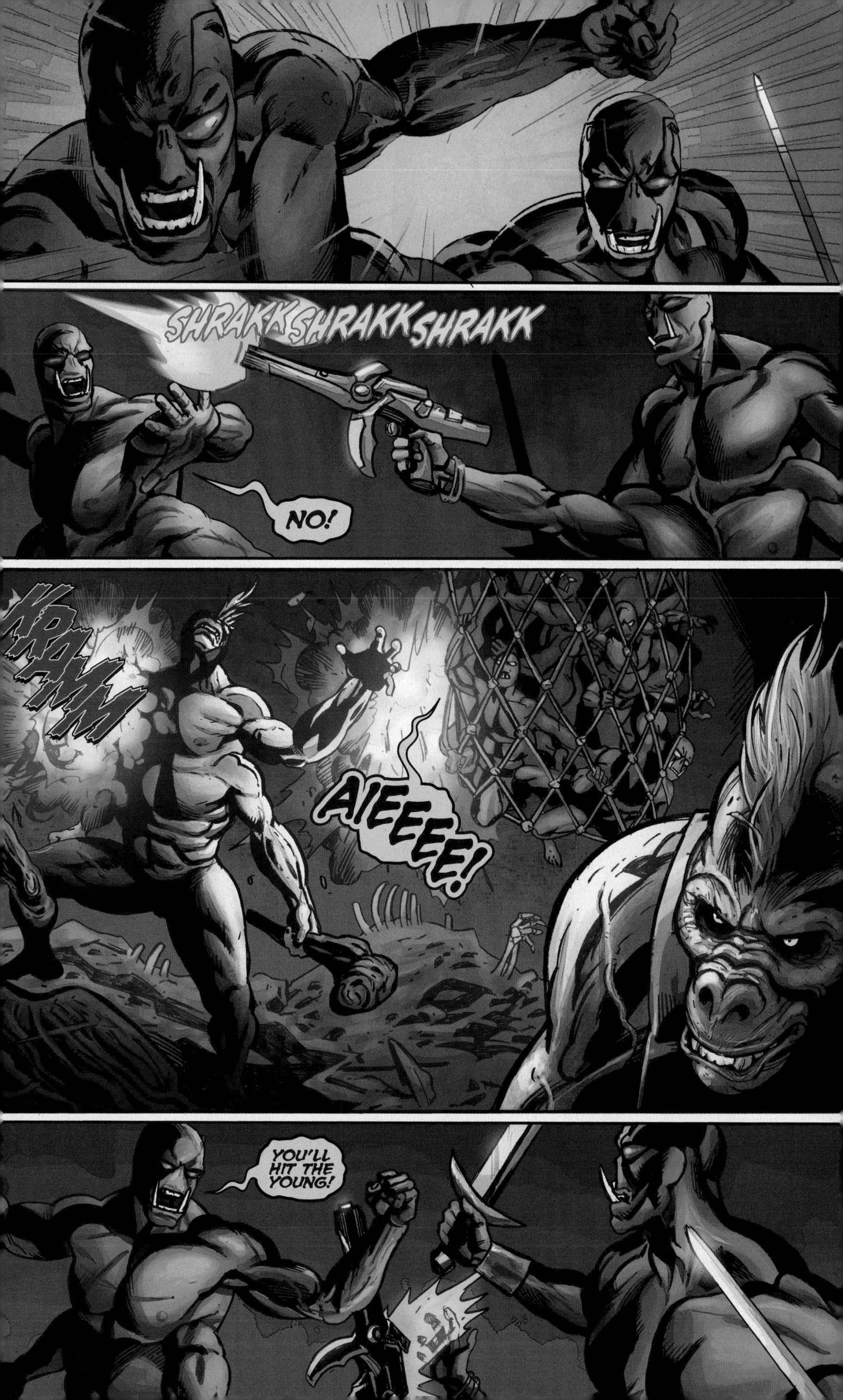

SHRAKK SHRAKK SHRAKK
NO!
KRAMM
AIEEEEE!
YOU'LL HIT THE YOUNG!

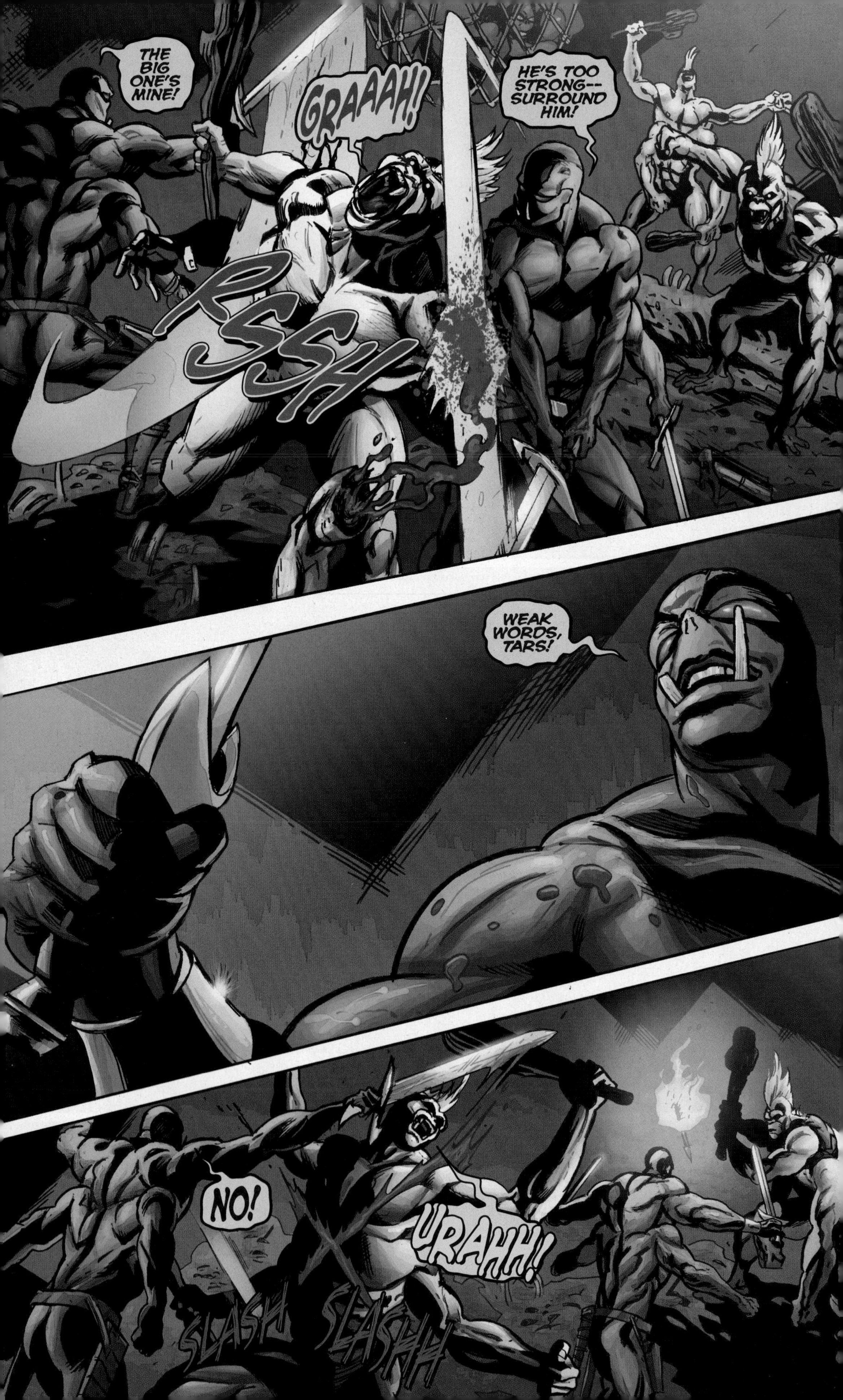
THE BIG ONE'S MINE!
GRAAAH!
HE'S TOO STRONG-- SURROUND HIM!
RSSH
WEAK WORDS, TARS!
NO!
URAHH!
SLASH SLASHH

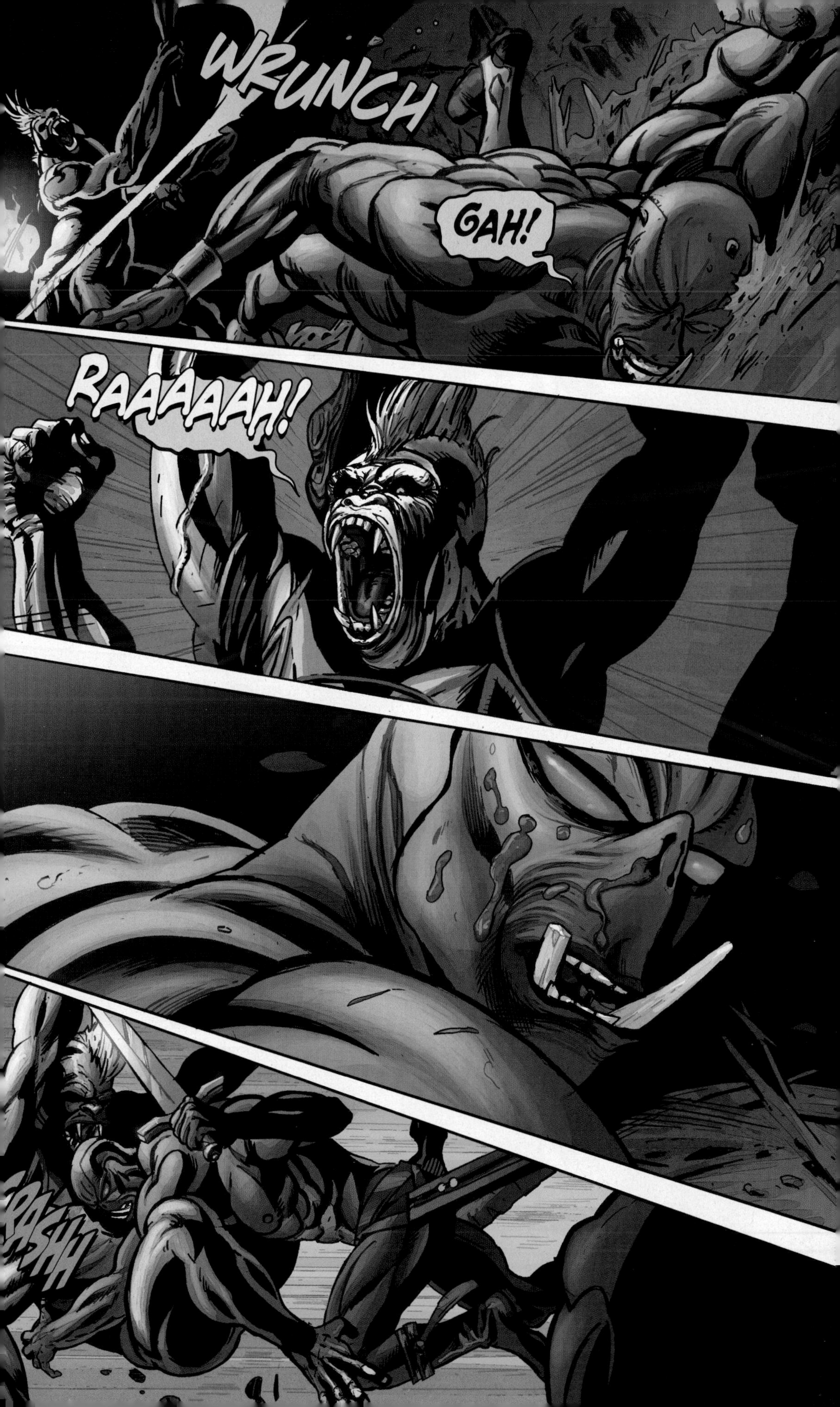
WRUNCH
GAH!
RAAAAAH!
RASHH

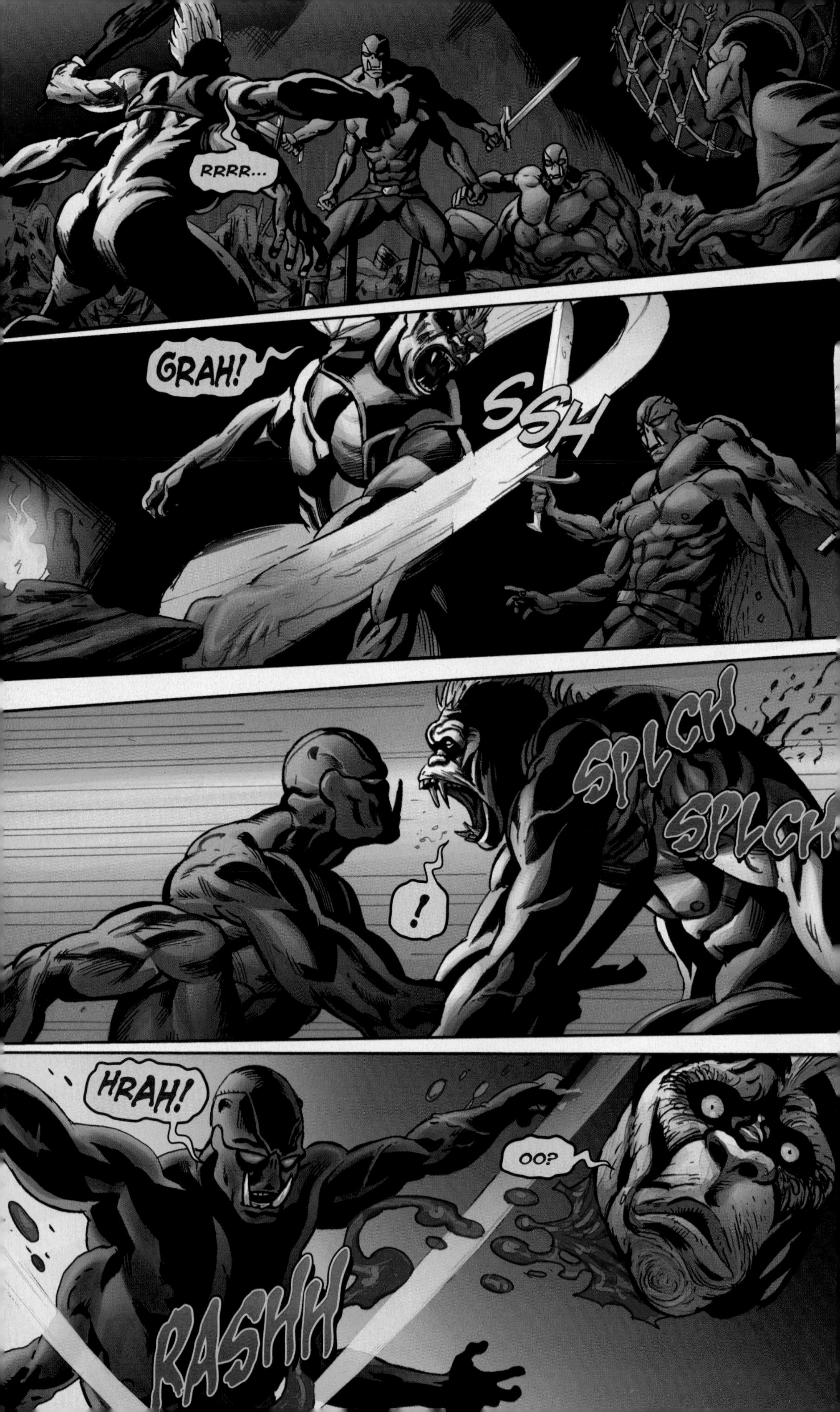
RRRR...
GRAH!
SSH
SPLCH
SPLCH
!
HRAH!
OO?
RASHH

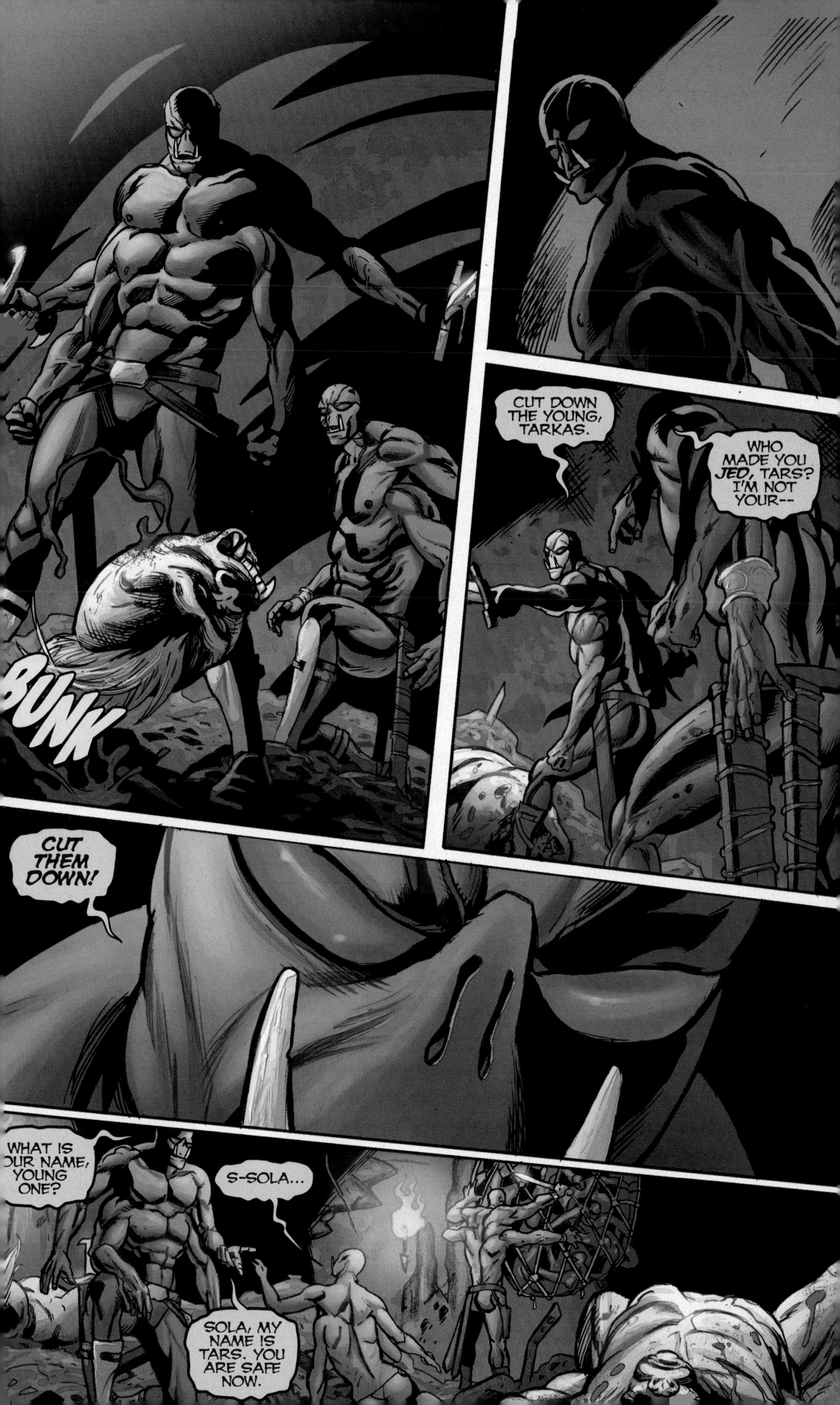
BUNK
CUT DOWN THE YOUNG, TARKAS.
WHO MADE YOU JED, TARS? I'M NOT YOUR--
CUT THEM DOWN!
WHAT IS OUR NAME, YOUNG ONE?
S-SOLA...
SOLA, MY NAME IS TARS. YOU ARE SAFE NOW.

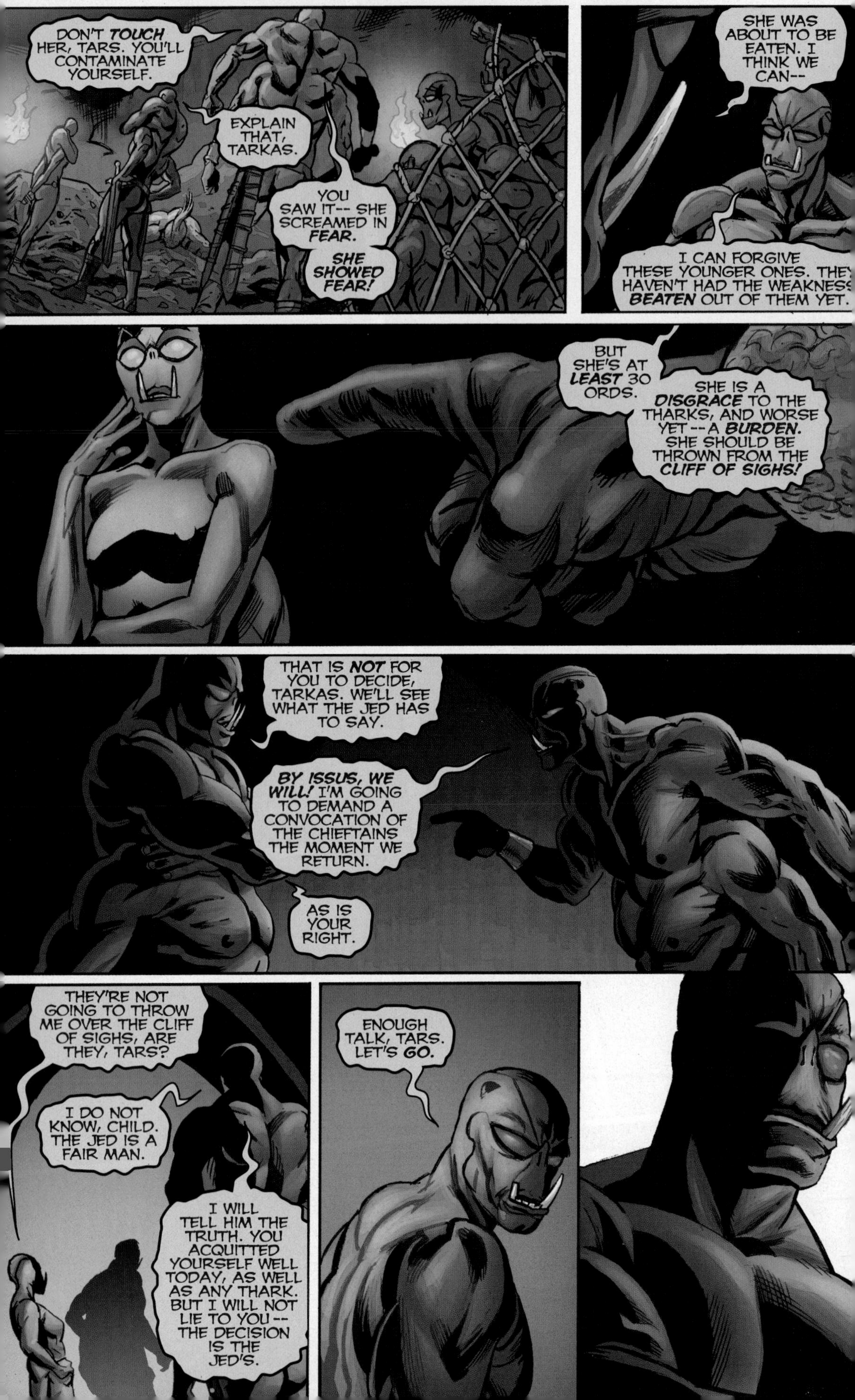
DON'T TOUCH HER, TARS. YOU'LL CONTAMINATE YOURSELF.
EXPLAIN THAT, TARKAS.
YOU SAW IT-- SHE SCREAMED IN FEAR.
SHE SHOWED FEAR!
SHE WAS ABOUT TO BE EATEN. I THINK WE CAN--
I CAN FORGIVE THESE YOUNGER ONES. THEY HAVEN'T HAD THE WEAKNESS BEATEN OUT OF THEM YET.
BUT SHE'S AT LEAST 30 ORDS.
SHE IS A DISGRACE TO THE THARKS, AND WORSE YET --A BURDEN. SHE SHOULD BE THROWN FROM THE CLIFF OF SIGHS!
THAT IS NOT FOR YOU TO DECIDE, TARKAS. WE'LL SEE WHAT THE JED HAS TO SAY.
BY ISSUS, WE WILL! I'M GOING TO DEMAND A CONVOCATION OF THE CHIEFTAINS THE MOMENT WE RETURN.
AS IS YOUR RIGHT.
THEY'RE NOT GOING TO THROW ME OVER THE CLIFF OF SIGHS, ARE THEY, TARS?
I DO NOT KNOW, CHILD. THE JED IS A FAIR MAN.
I WILL TELL HIM THE TRUTH. YOU ACQUITTED YOURSELF WELL TODAY, AS WELL AS ANY THARK. BUT I WILL NOT LIE TO YOU-- THE DECISION IS THE JED'S.
ENOUGH TALK, TARS. LET'S GO.

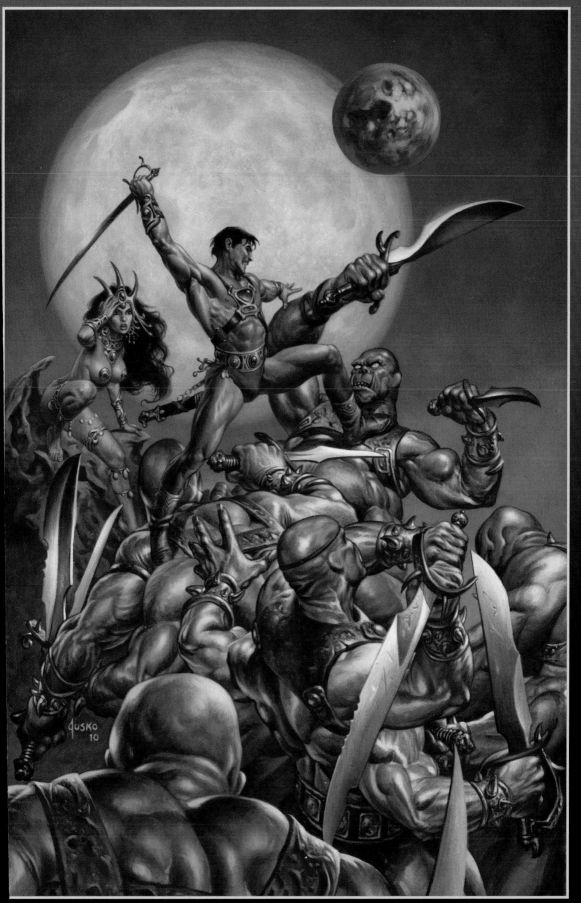

A TALE OF TWO PLANETS part two

Issue #2 cover by JOE JUSKO

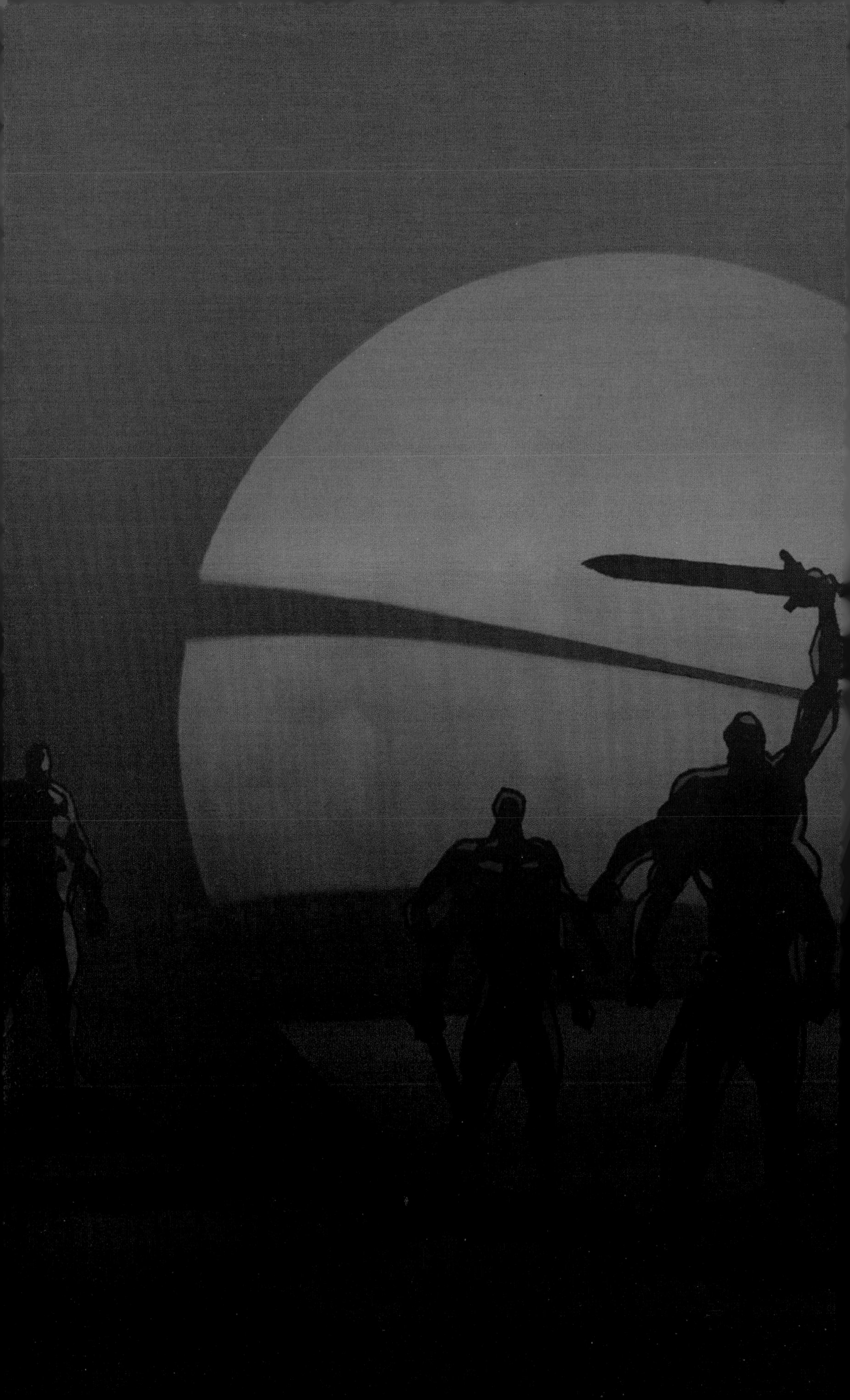

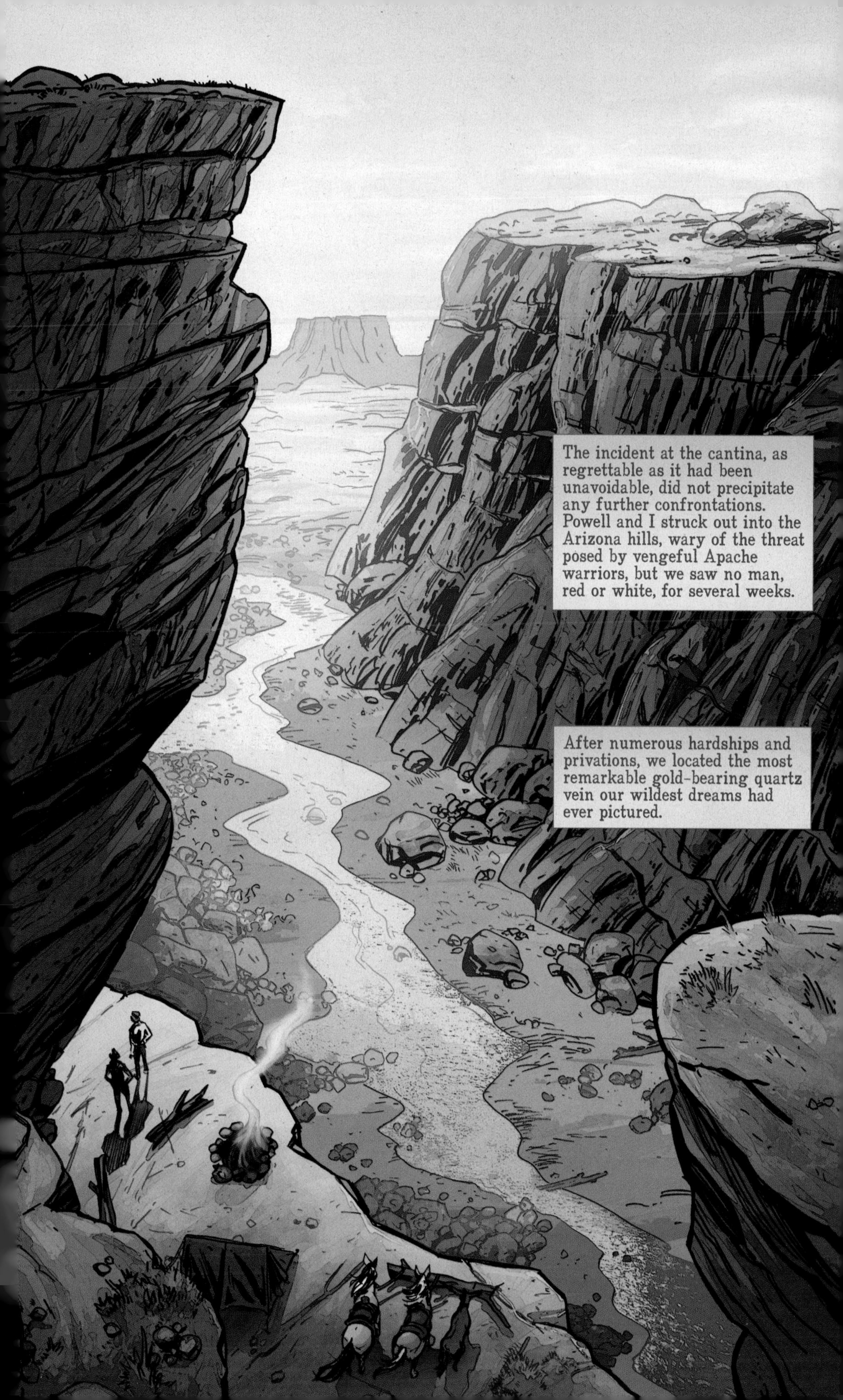
The incident at the cantina, as regrettable as it had been unavoidable, did not precipitate any further confrontations. Powell and I struck out into the Arizona hills, wary of the threat posed by vengeful Apache warriors, but we saw no man, red or white, for several weeks.
After numerous hardships and privations, we located the most remarkable gold-bearing quartz vein our wildest dreams had ever pictured.

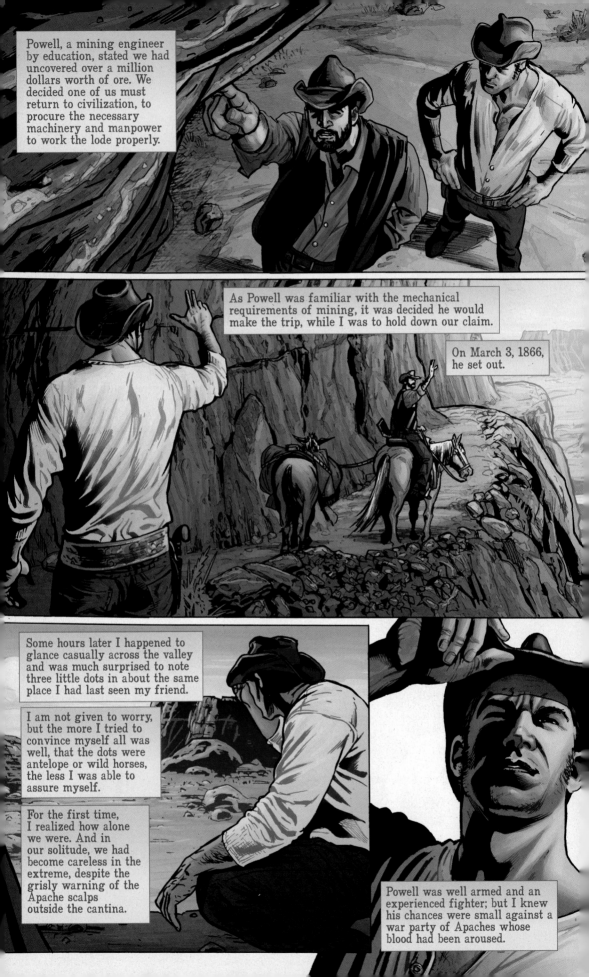

Powell, a mining engineer by education, stated we had uncovered over a million dollars worth of ore. We decided one of us must return to civilization, to procure the necessary machinery and manpower to work the lode properly.

As Powell was familiar with the mechanical requirements of mining, it was decided he would make the trip, while I was to hold down our claim.

On March 3, 1866, he set out.

Some hours later I happened to glance casually across the valley and was much surprised to note three little dots in about the same place I had last seen my friend.

I am not given to worry, but the more I tried to convince myself all was well, that the dots were antelope or wild horses, the less I was able to assure myself.

For the first time, I realized how alone we were. And in our solitude, we had become careless in the extreme, despite the grisly warning of the Apache scalps outside the cantina.

Powell was well armed and an experienced fighter; but I knew his chances were small against a war party of Apaches whose blood had been aroused.

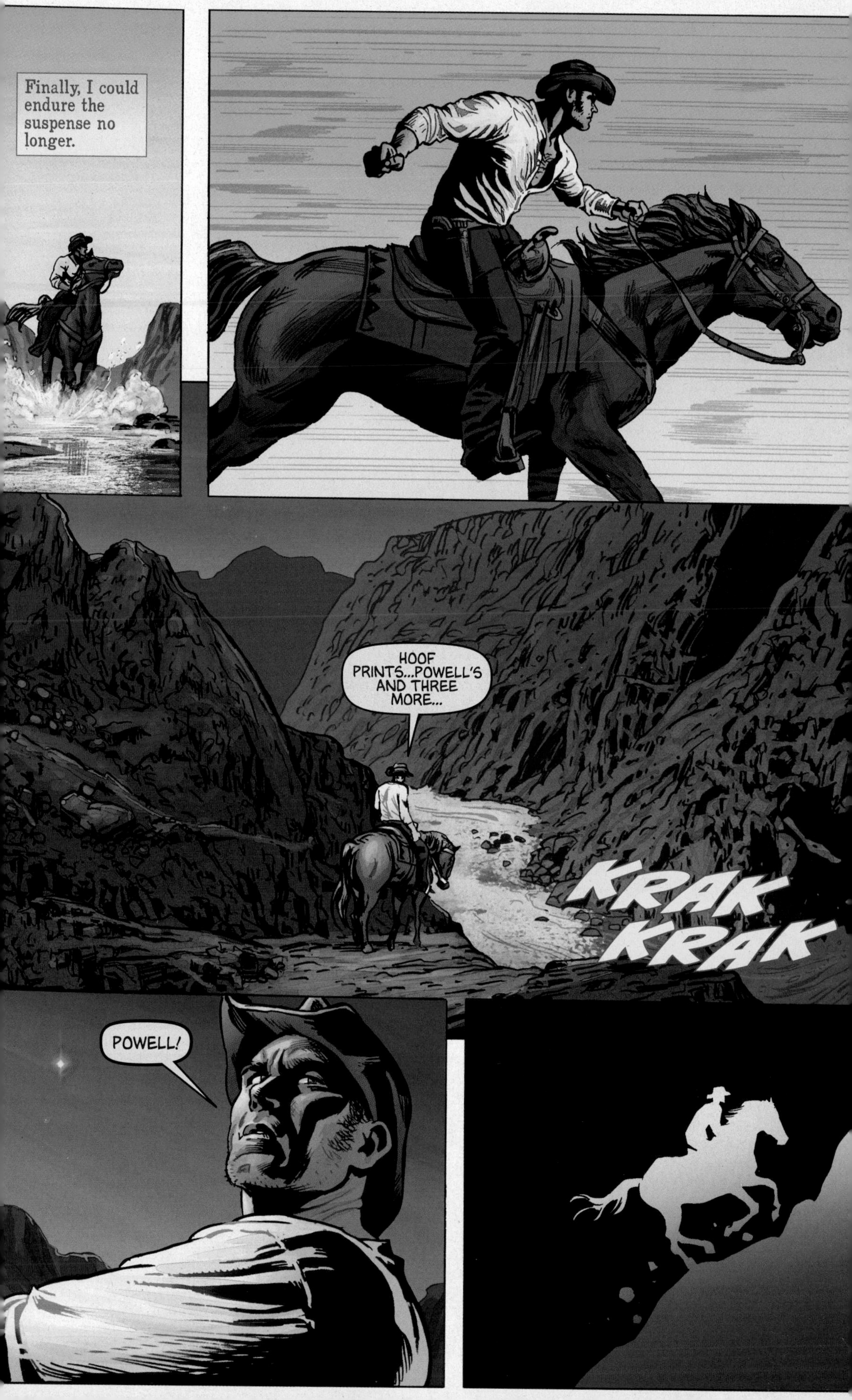

Finally, I could endure the suspense no longer.
HOOF PRINTS...POWELL'S AND THREE MORE...
KRAK KRAK
POWELL!

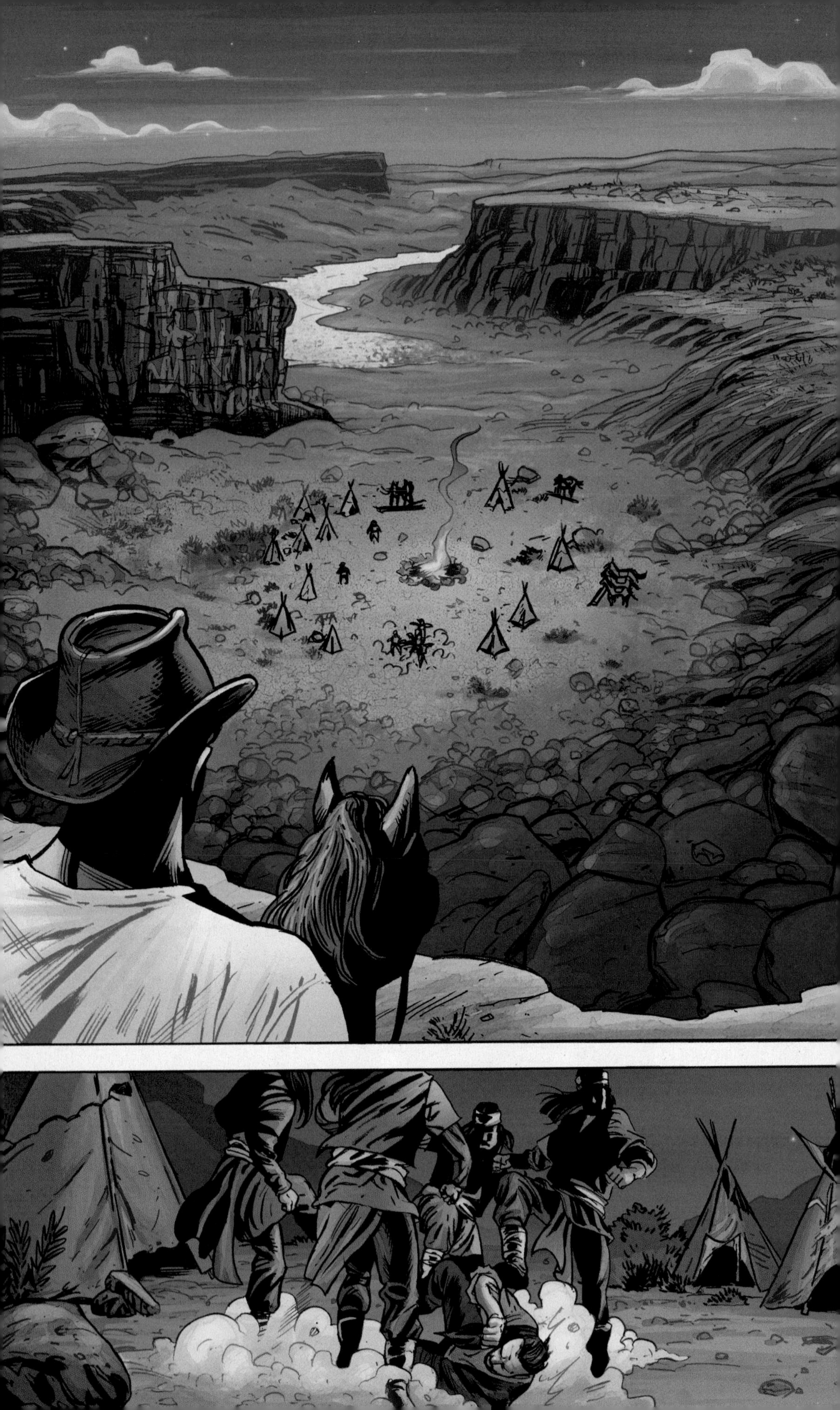

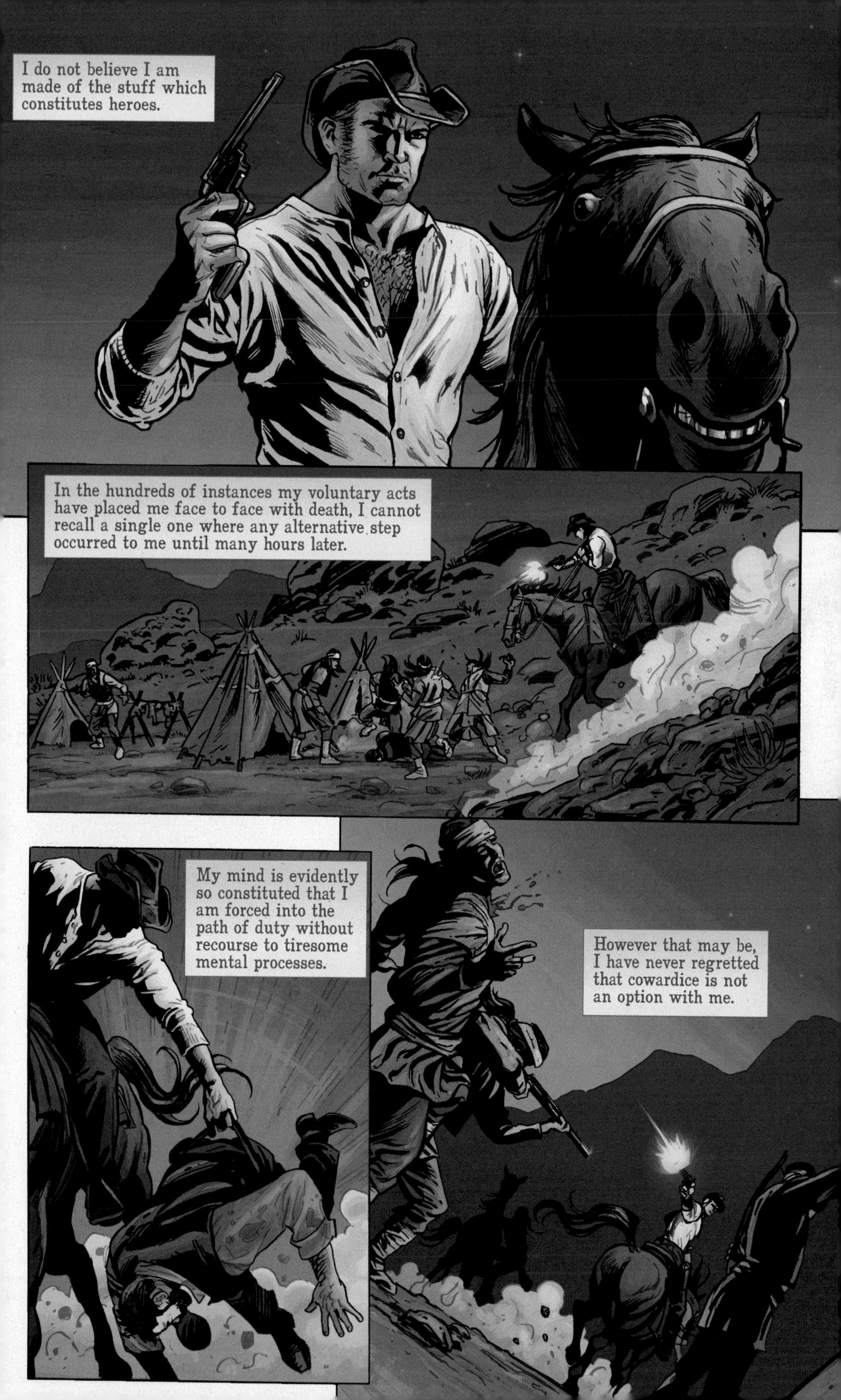
I do not believe I am made of the stuff which constitutes heroes.
In the hundreds of instances my voluntary acts have placed me face to face with death, I cannot recall a single one where any alternative step occurred to me until many hours later.
My mind is evidently so constituted that I am forced into the path of duty without recourse to tiresome mental processes.
However that may be, I have never regretted that cowardice is not an option with me.

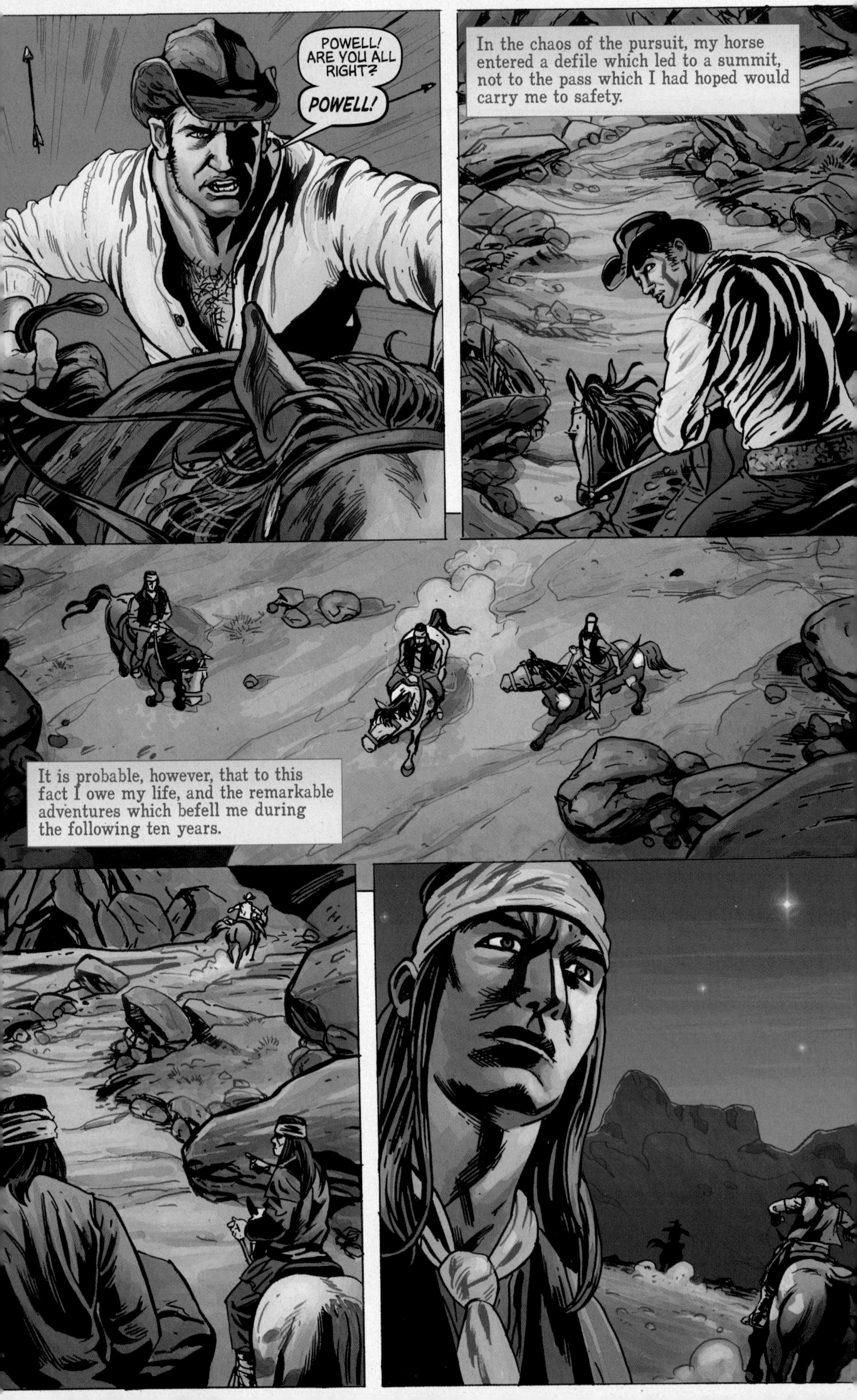

POWELL! ARE YOU ALL RIGHT?
POWELL!
In the chaos of the pursuit, my horse entered a defile which led to a summit, not to the pass which I had hoped would carry me to safety.
It is probable, however, that to this fact I owe my life, and the remarkable adventures which befell me during the following ten years.

THEY'RE TURNING AROUND? WHY DON'T THEY FINISH ME?

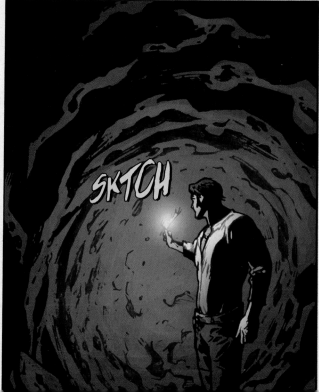

SKTCH

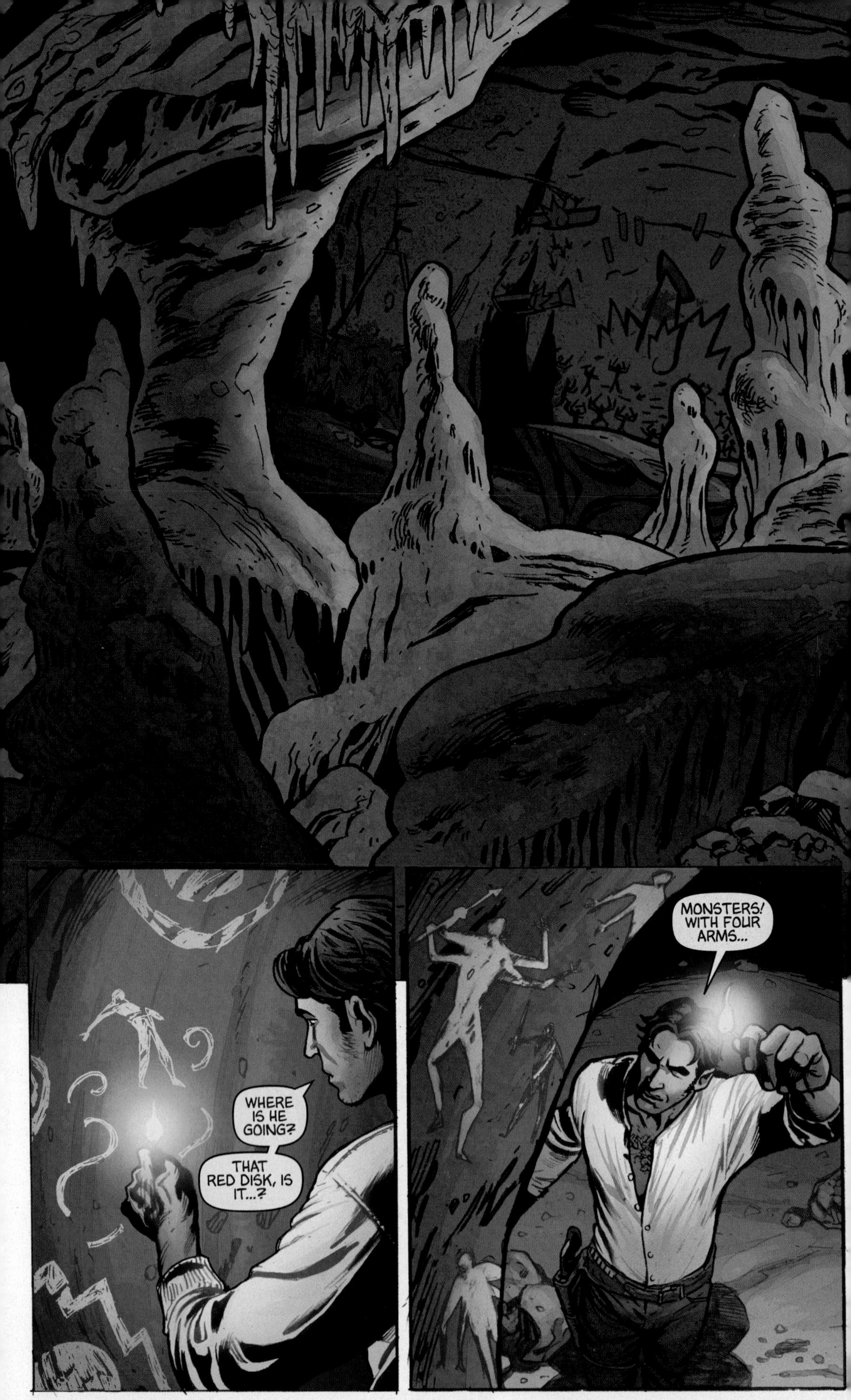
WHERE IS HE GOING?
THAT RED DISK, IS IT...?
MONSTERS! WITH FOUR ARMS...

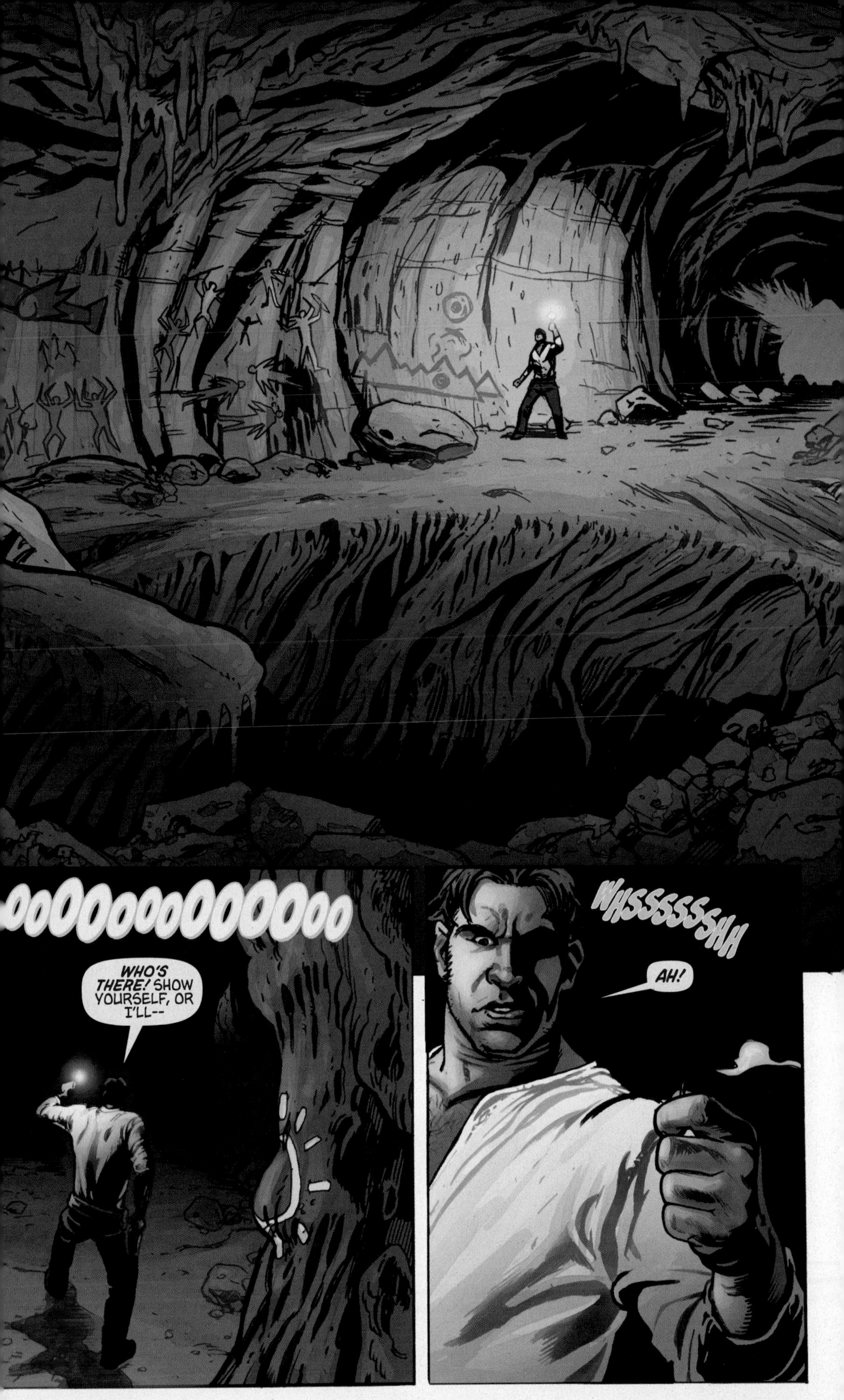

OOOOOOOOOOOOOOOO
WHO'S THERE! SHOW YOURSELF, OR I'LL--
WHSSSSSSSHH
AH!

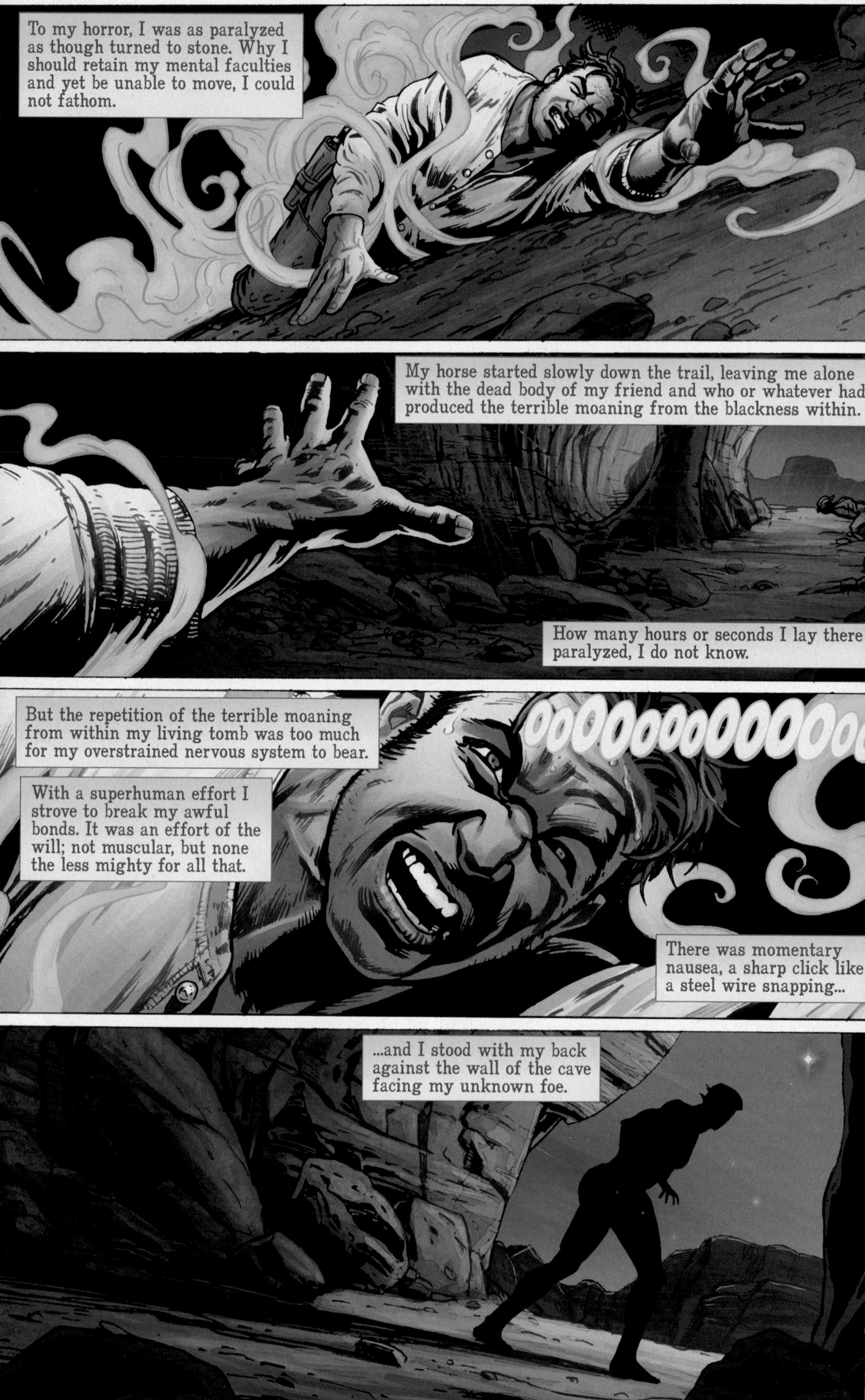
To my horror, I was as paralyzed as though turned to stone. Why I should retain my mental faculties and yet be unable to move, I could not fathom.
My horse started slowly down the trail, leaving me alone with the dead body of my friend and who or whatever had produced the terrible moaning from the blackness within.
How many hours or seconds I lay there paralyzed, I do not know.
But the repetition of the terrible moaning from within my living tomb was too much for my overstrained nervous system to bear.
With a superhuman effort I strove to break my awful bonds. It was an effort of the will; not muscular, but none the less mighty for all that.
OOOOOOOOOOOOOO
There was momentary nausea, a sharp click like a steel wire snapping...
...and I stood with my back against the wall of the cave facing my unknown foe.

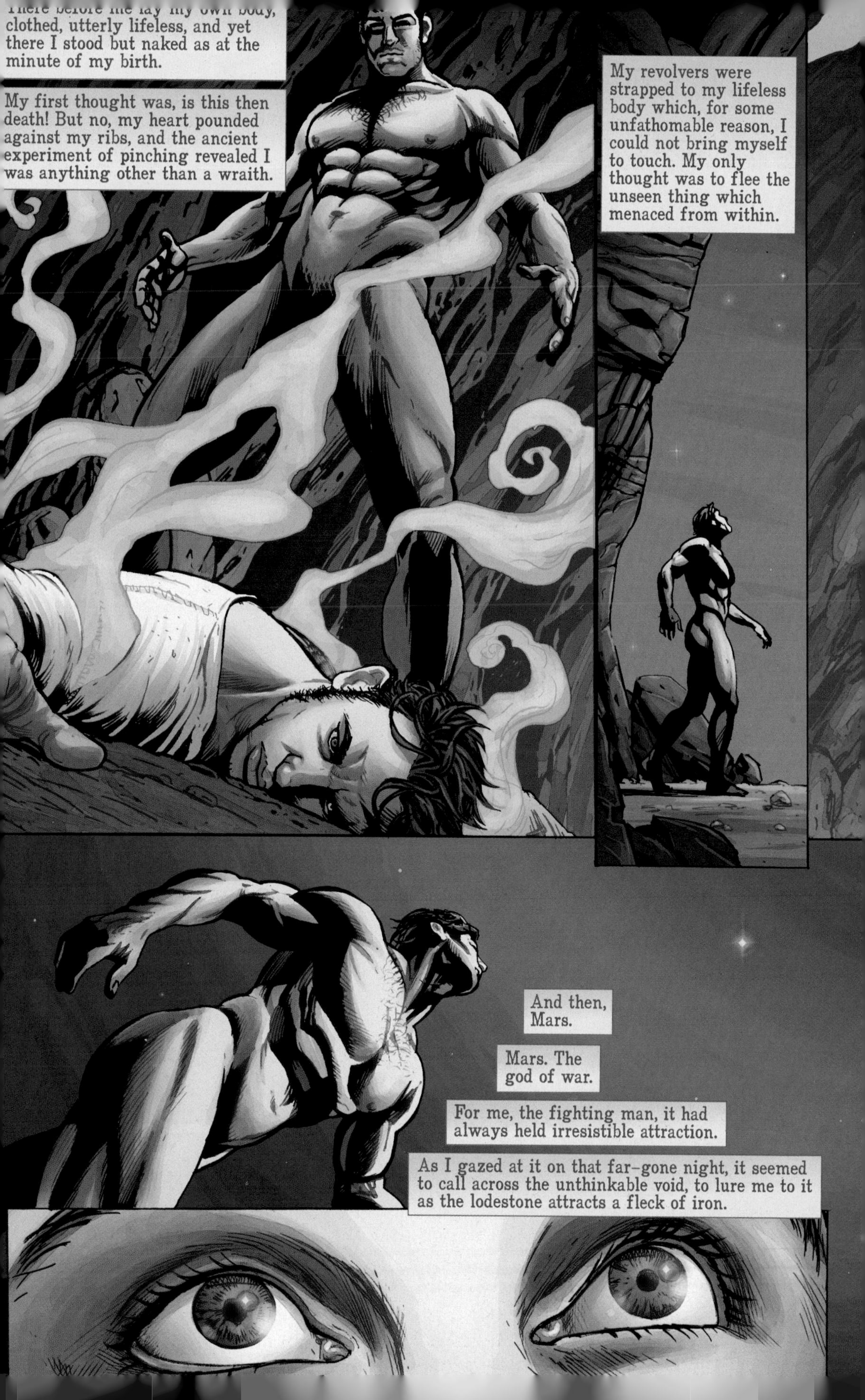
There before me lay my own body, clothed, utterly lifeless, and yet there I stood but naked as at the minute of my birth.
My first thought was, is this then death! But no, my heart pounded against my ribs, and the ancient experiment of pinching revealed I was anything other than a wraith.
My revolvers were strapped to my lifeless body which, for some unfathomable reason, I could not bring myself to touch. My only thought was to flee the unseen thing which menaced from within.
And then, Mars.
Mars. The god of war.
For me, the fighting man, it had always held irresistible attraction.
As I gazed at it on that far-gone night, it seemed to call across the unthinkable void, to lure me to it as the lodestone attracts a fleck of iron.

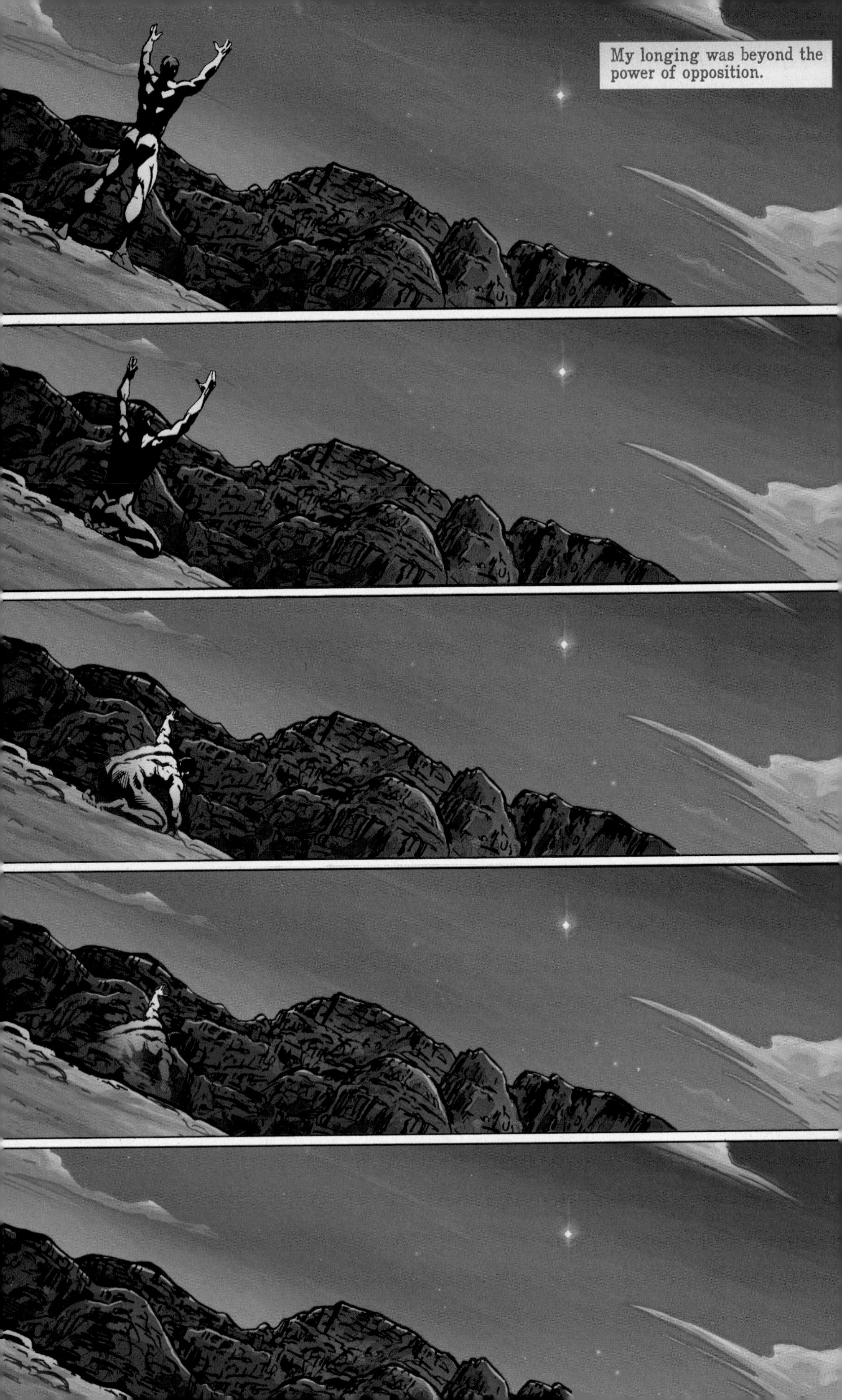
My longing was beyond the power of opposition.

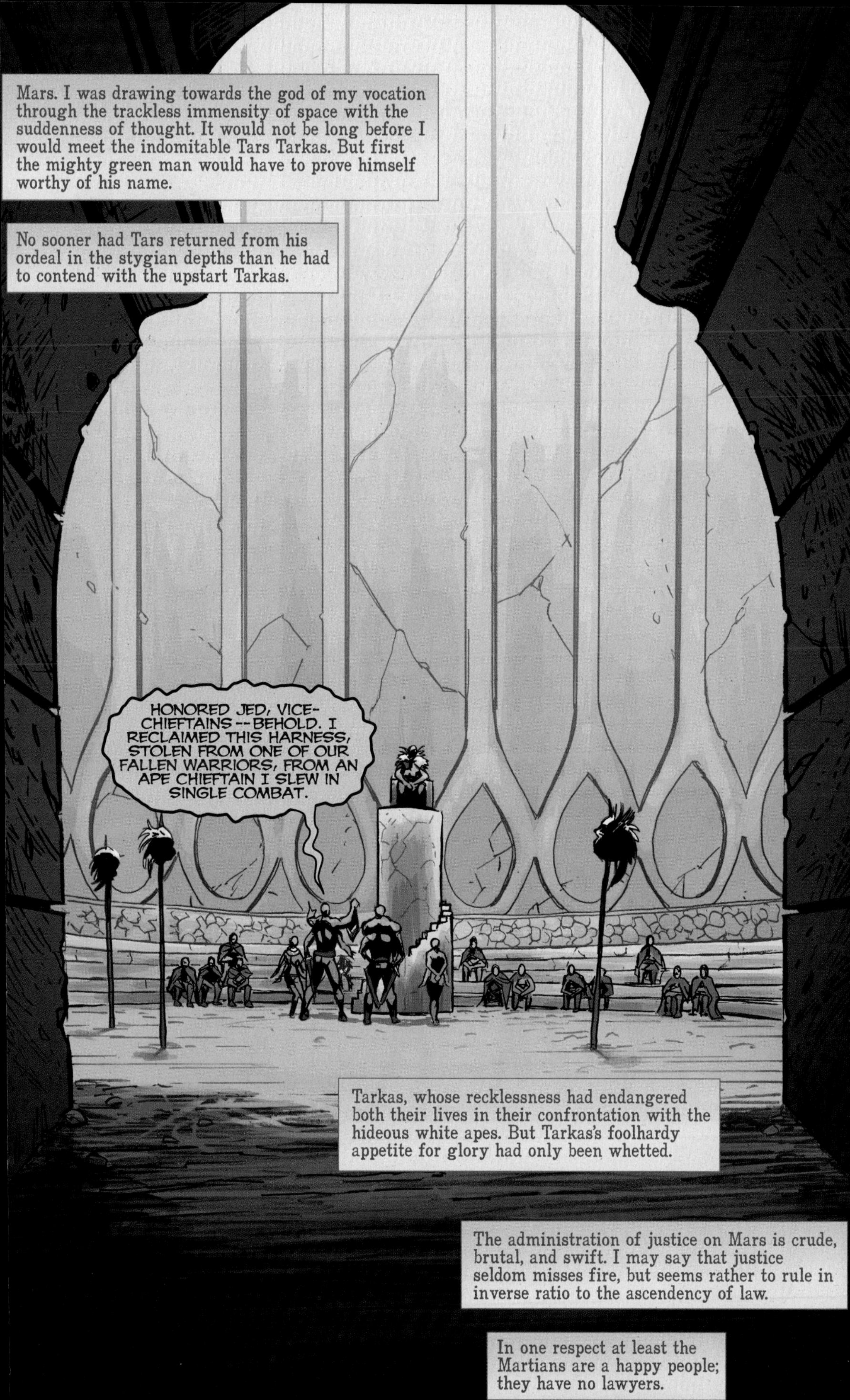
Mars. I was drawing towards the god of my vocation through the trackless immensity of space with the suddenness of thought. It would not be long before I would meet the indomitable Tars Tarkas. But first the mighty green man would have to prove himself worthy of his name.
No sooner had Tars returned from his ordeal in the stygian depths than he had to contend with the upstart Tarkas.
HONORED JED, VICE-CHIEFTAINS --BEHOLD. I RECLAIMED THIS HARNESS, STOLEN FROM ONE OF OUR FALLEN WARRIORS, FROM AN APE CHIEFTAIN I SLEW IN SINGLE COMBAT.
Tarkas, whose recklessness had endangered both their lives in their confrontation with the hideous white apes. But Tarkas's foolhardy appetite for glory had only been whetted.
The administration of justice on Mars is crude, brutal, and swift. I may say that justice seldom misses fire, but seems rather to rule in inverse ratio to the ascendency of law.
In one respect at least the Martians are a happy people; they have no lawyers.

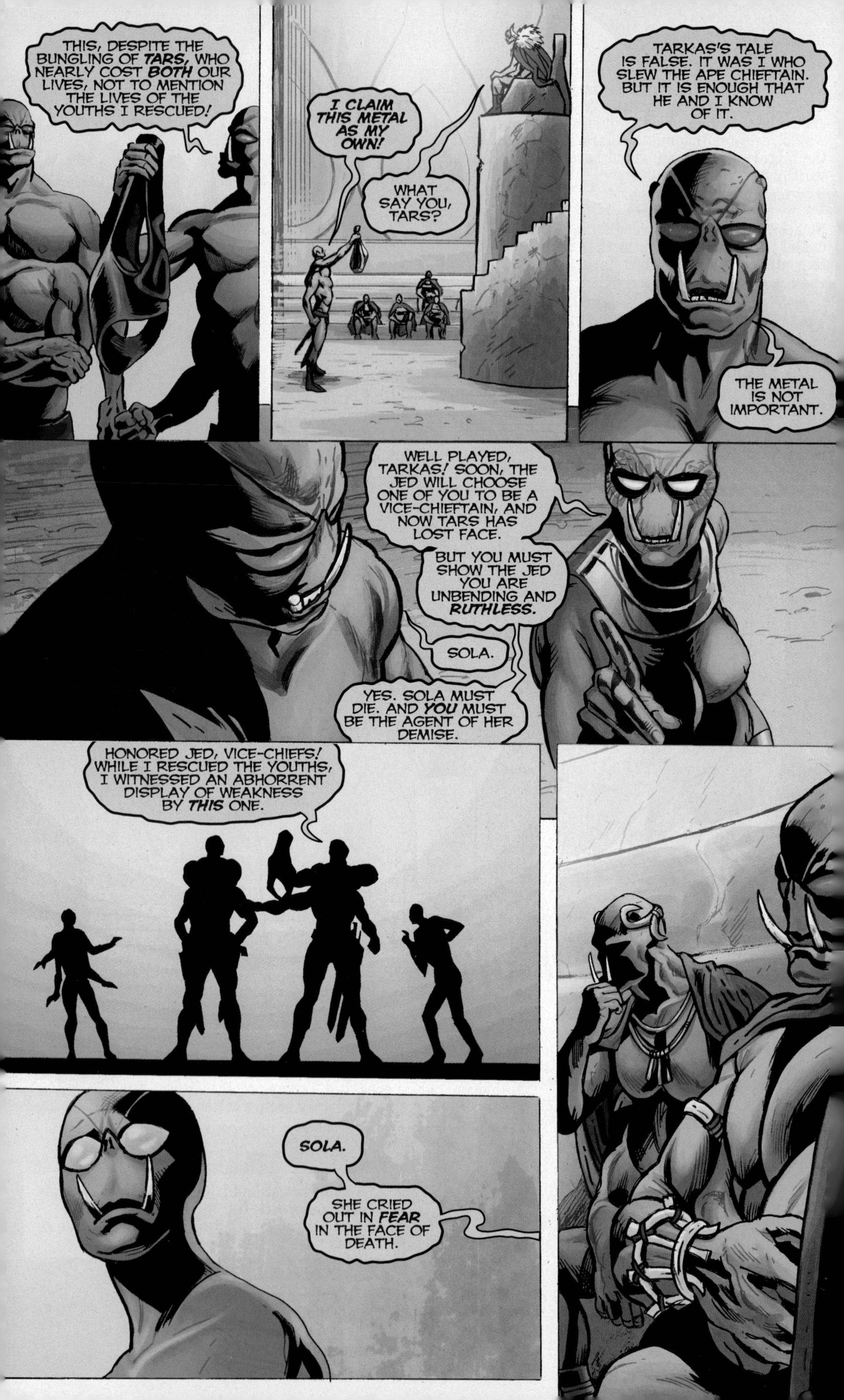
THIS, DESPITE THE BUNGLING OF TARS, WHO NEARLY COST BOTH OUR LIVES, NOT TO MENTION THE LIVES OF THE YOUTHS I RESCUED!
I CLAIM THIS METAL AS MY OWN!
WHAT SAY YOU, TARS?
TARKAS'S TALE IS FALSE. IT WAS I WHO SLEW THE APE CHIEFTAIN. BUT IT IS ENOUGH THAT HE AND I KNOW OF IT.
THE METAL IS NOT IMPORTANT.
WELL PLAYED, TARKAS! SOON, THE JED WILL CHOOSE ONE OF YOU TO BE A VICE-CHIEFTAIN, AND NOW TARS HAS LOST FACE.
BUT YOU MUST SHOW THE JED YOU ARE UNBENDING AND RUTHLESS.
SOLA.
YES. SOLA MUST DIE. AND YOU MUST BE THE AGENT OF HER DEMISE.
HONORED JED, VICE-CHIEFS! WHILE I RESCUED THE YOUTHS, I WITNESSED AN ABHORRENT DISPLAY OF WEAKNESS BY THIS ONE.
SOLA.
SHE CRIED OUT IN FEAR IN THE FACE OF DEATH.

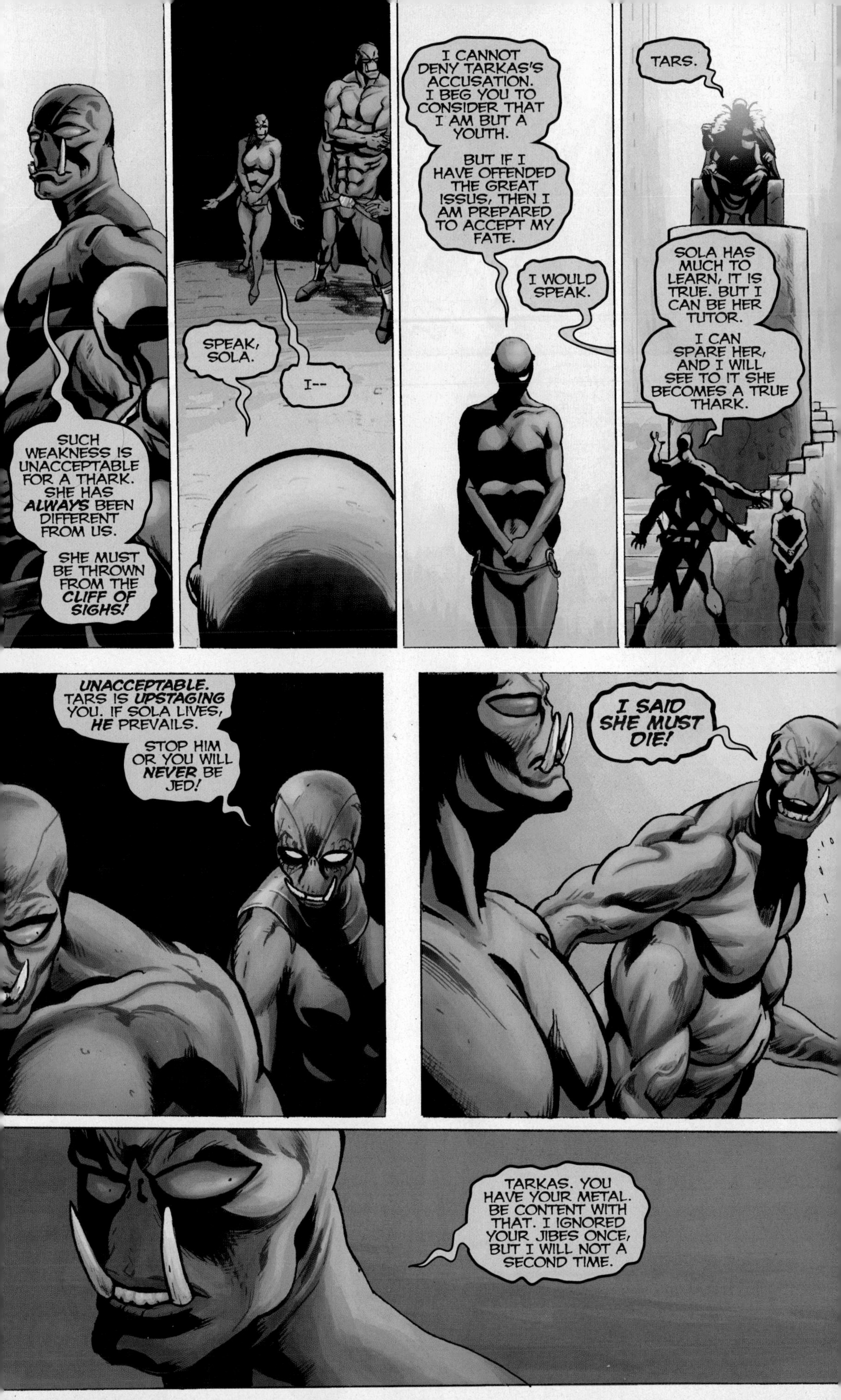
SUCH WEAKNESS IS UNACCEPTABLE FOR A THARK. SHE HAS ALWAYS BEEN DIFFERENT FROM US.
SHE MUST BE THROWN FROM THE CLIFF OF SIGHS!
SPEAK, SOLA.
I--
I CANNOT DENY TARKAS'S ACCUSATION. I BEG YOU TO CONSIDER THAT I AM BUT A YOUTH.
BUT IF I HAVE OFFENDED THE GREAT ISSUS, THEN I AM PREPARED TO ACCEPT MY FATE.
I WOULD SPEAK.
TARS.
SOLA HAS MUCH TO LEARN, IT IS TRUE. BUT I CAN BE HER TUTOR.
I CAN SPARE HER, AND I WILL SEE TO IT SHE BECOMES A TRUE THARK.
UNACCEPTABLE. TARS IS UPSTAGING YOU. IF SOLA LIVES, HE PREVAILS.
STOP HIM OR YOU WILL NEVER BE JED!
I SAID SHE MUST DIE!
TARKAS. YOU HAVE YOUR METAL. BE CONTENT WITH THAT. I IGNORED YOUR JIBES ONCE, BUT I WILL NOT A SECOND TIME.

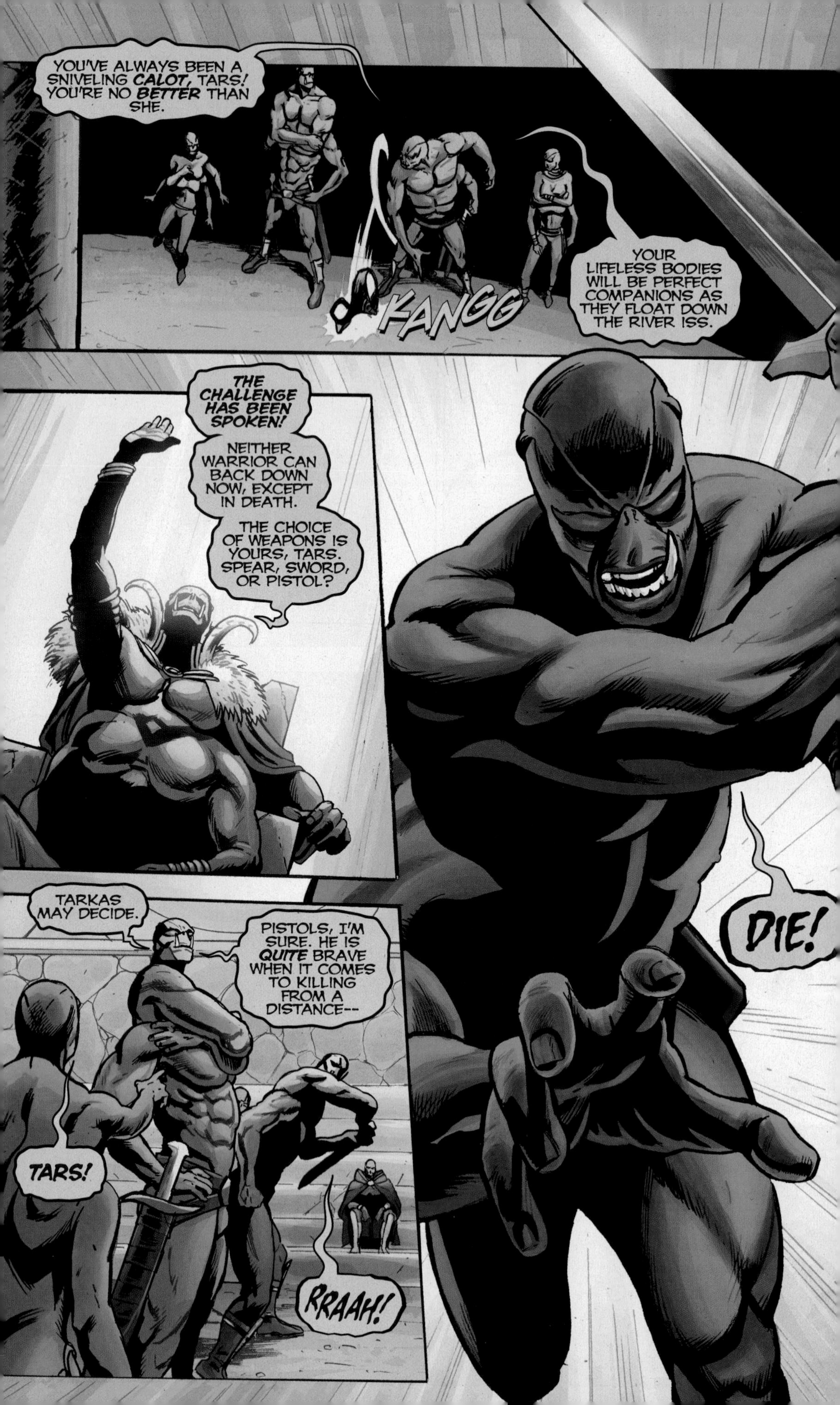
YOU'VE ALWAYS BEEN A SNIVELING CALOT, TARS! YOU'RE NO BETTER THAN SHE.
KANGG
YOUR LIFELESS BODIES WILL BE PERFECT COMPANIONS AS THEY FLOAT DOWN THE RIVER ISS.
THE CHALLENGE HAS BEEN SPOKEN!
NEITHER WARRIOR CAN BACK DOWN NOW, EXCEPT IN DEATH.
THE CHOICE OF WEAPONS IS YOURS, TARS. SPEAR, SWORD, OR PISTOL?
TARKAS MAY DECIDE.
PISTOLS, I'M SURE. HE IS QUITE BRAVE WHEN IT COMES TO KILLING FROM A DISTANCE--
TARS!
RRAAH!
DIE!

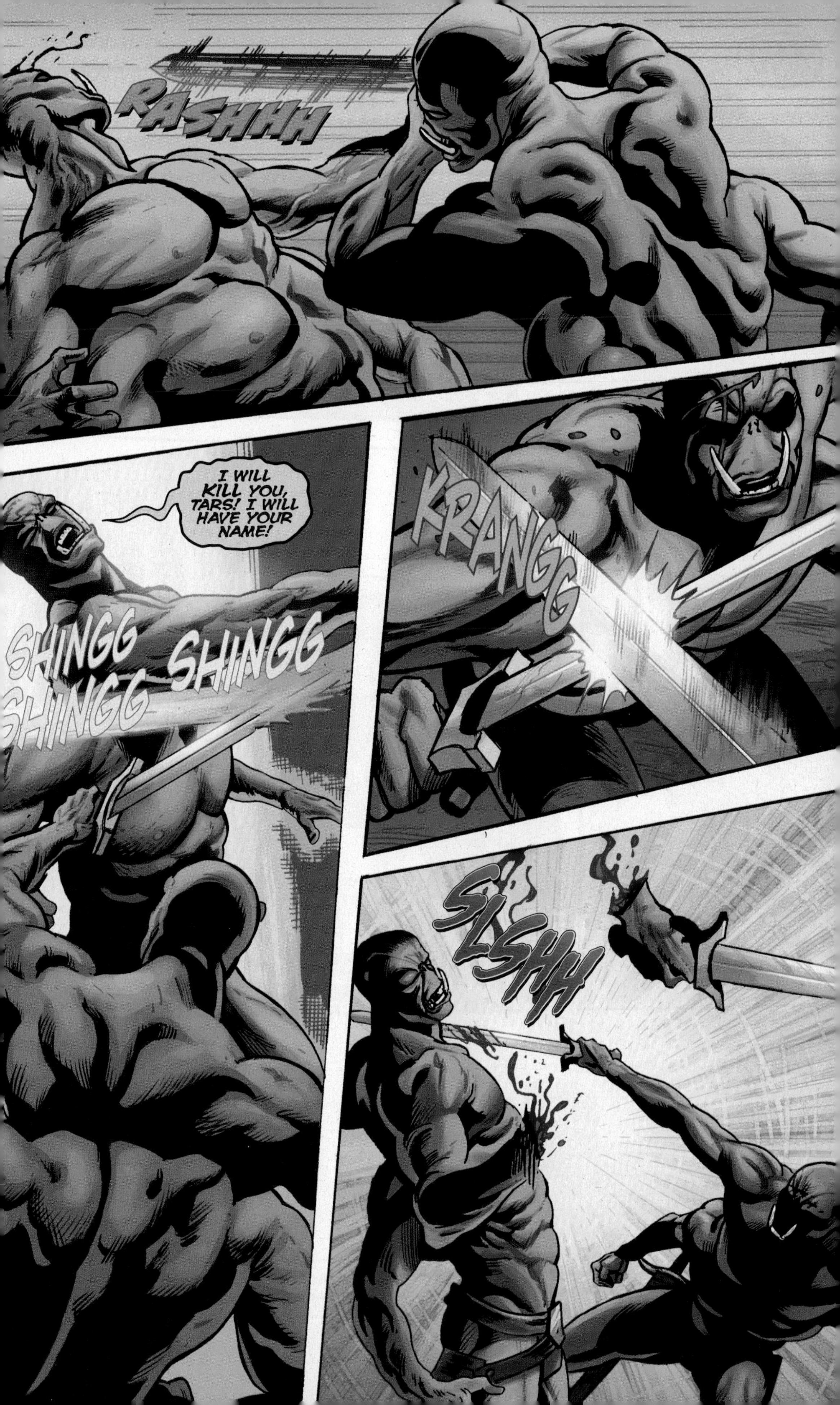

RASHHH
I WILL KILL YOU, TARS! I WILL HAVE YOUR NAME!
SHINGG
SHINGG
SHINGG
KRANGG
SLSHH

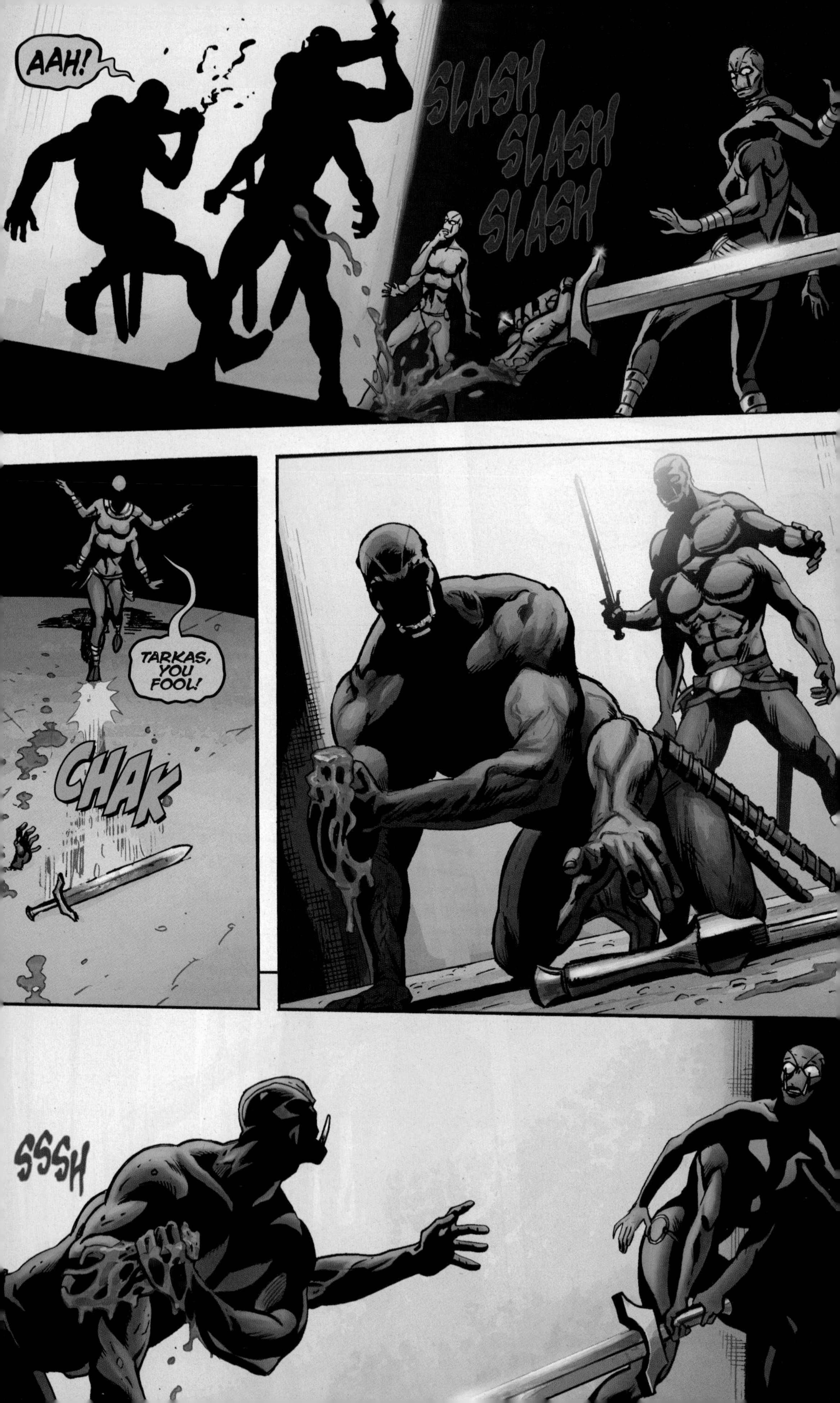
AAH!
SLASH
SLASH
SLASH
TARKAS, YOU FOOL!
CHAK
SSSH

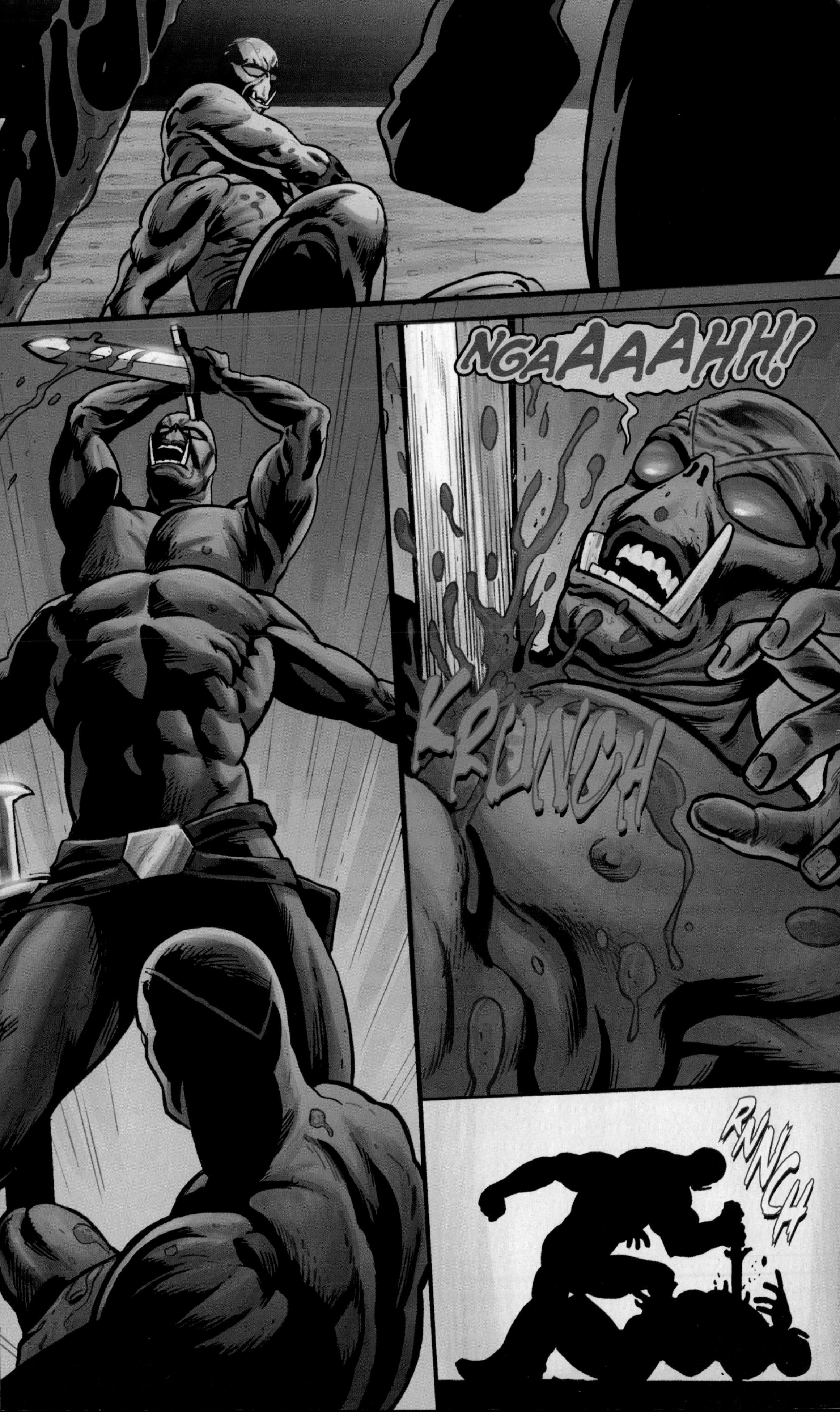
NGAAAAAHH!
KRUNCH
RNNCH

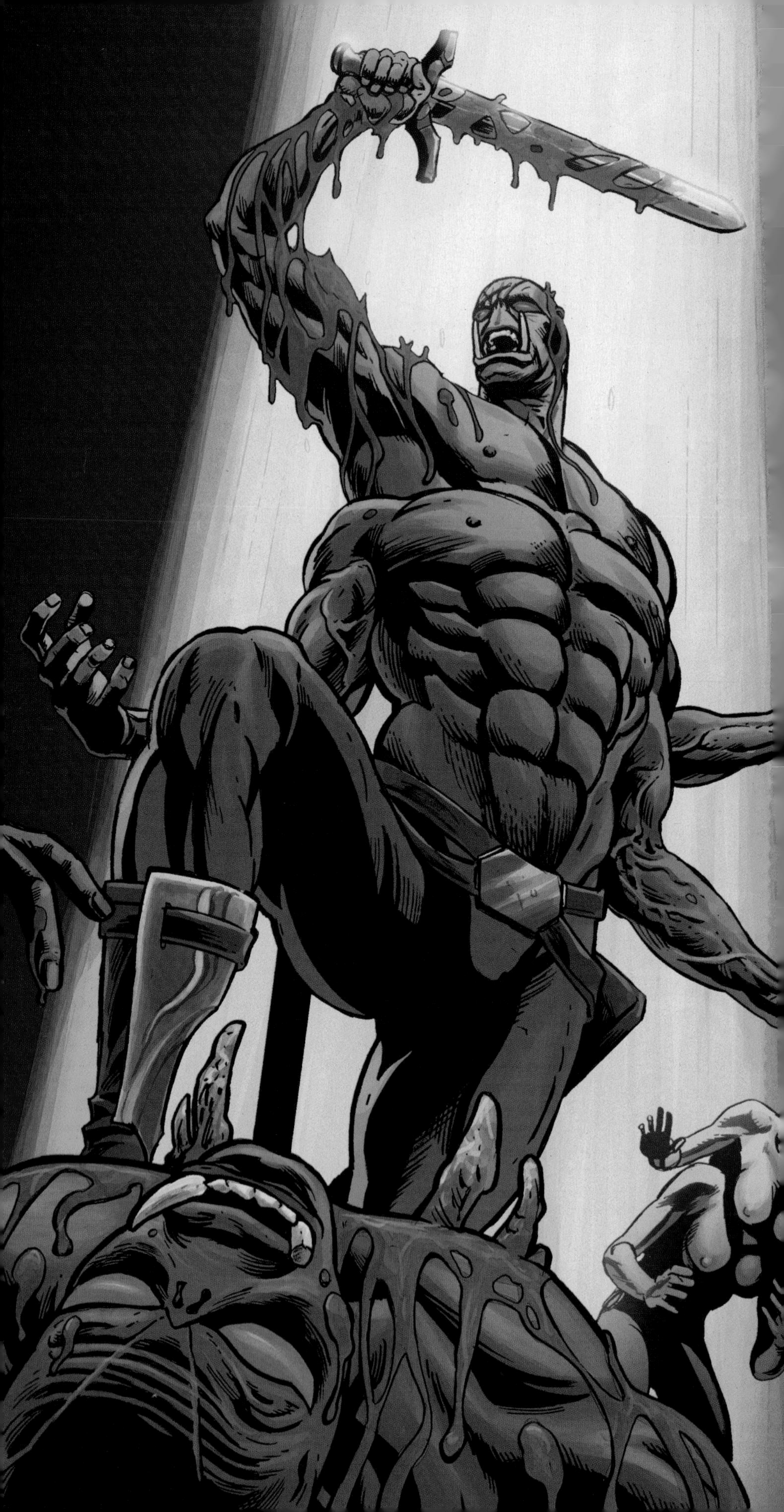

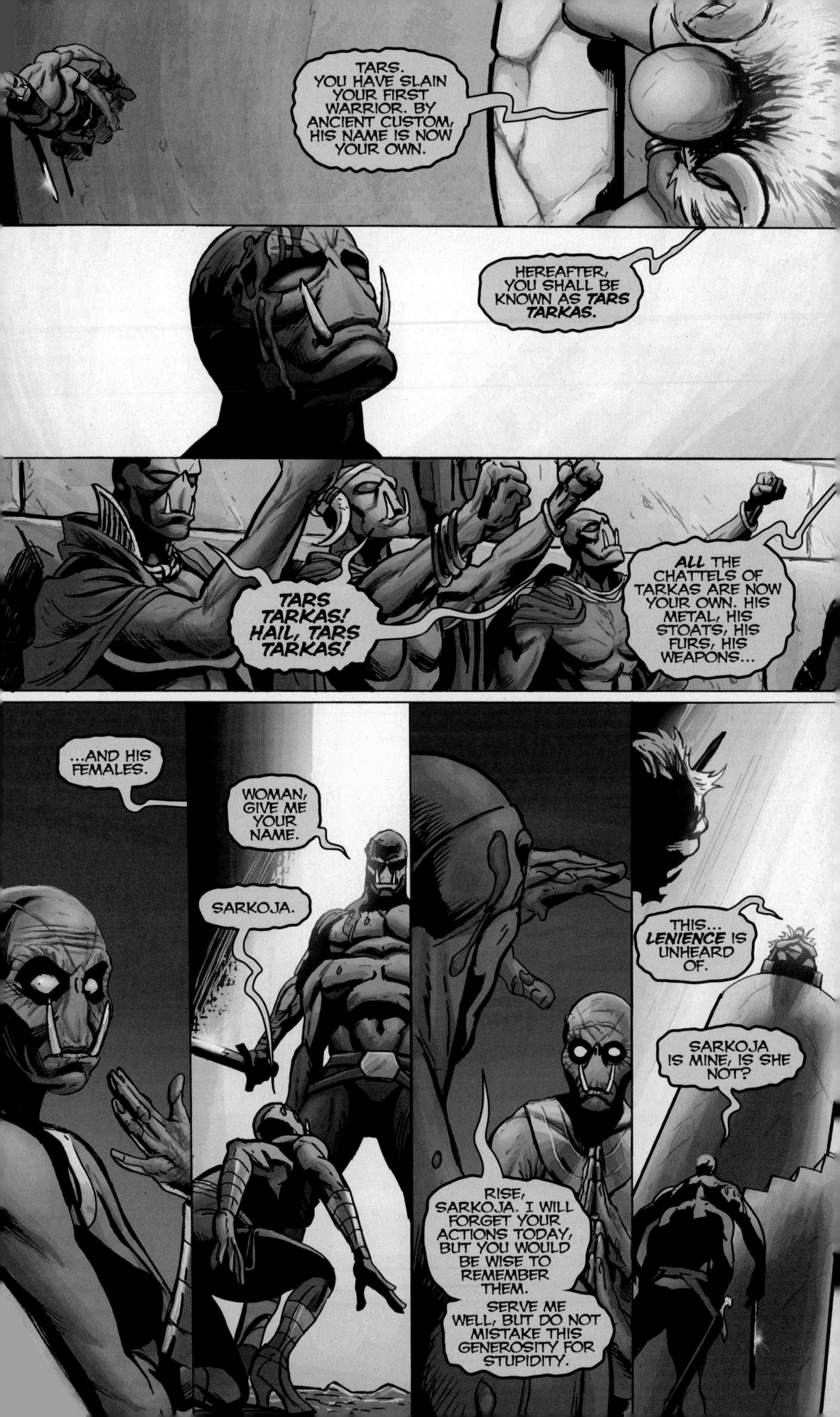
TARS. YOU HAVE SLAIN YOUR FIRST WARRIOR. BY ANCIENT CUSTOM, HIS NAME IS NOW YOUR OWN.
HEREAFTER, YOU SHALL BE KNOWN AS *TARS TARKAS.*
TARS TARKAS! HAIL, TARS TARKAS!
ALL THE CHATTELS OF TARKAS ARE NOW YOUR OWN. HIS METAL, HIS STOATS, HIS FURS, HIS WEAPONS...
...AND HIS FEMALES.
WOMAN, GIVE ME YOUR NAME.
SARKOJA.
RISE, SARKOJA. I WILL FORGET YOUR ACTIONS TODAY, BUT YOU WOULD BE WISE TO REMEMBER THEM.
SERVE ME WELL, BUT DO NOT MISTAKE THIS GENEROSITY FOR STUPIDITY.
THIS... ***LENIENCE*** IS UNHEARD OF.
SARKOJA IS MINE, IS SHE NOT?

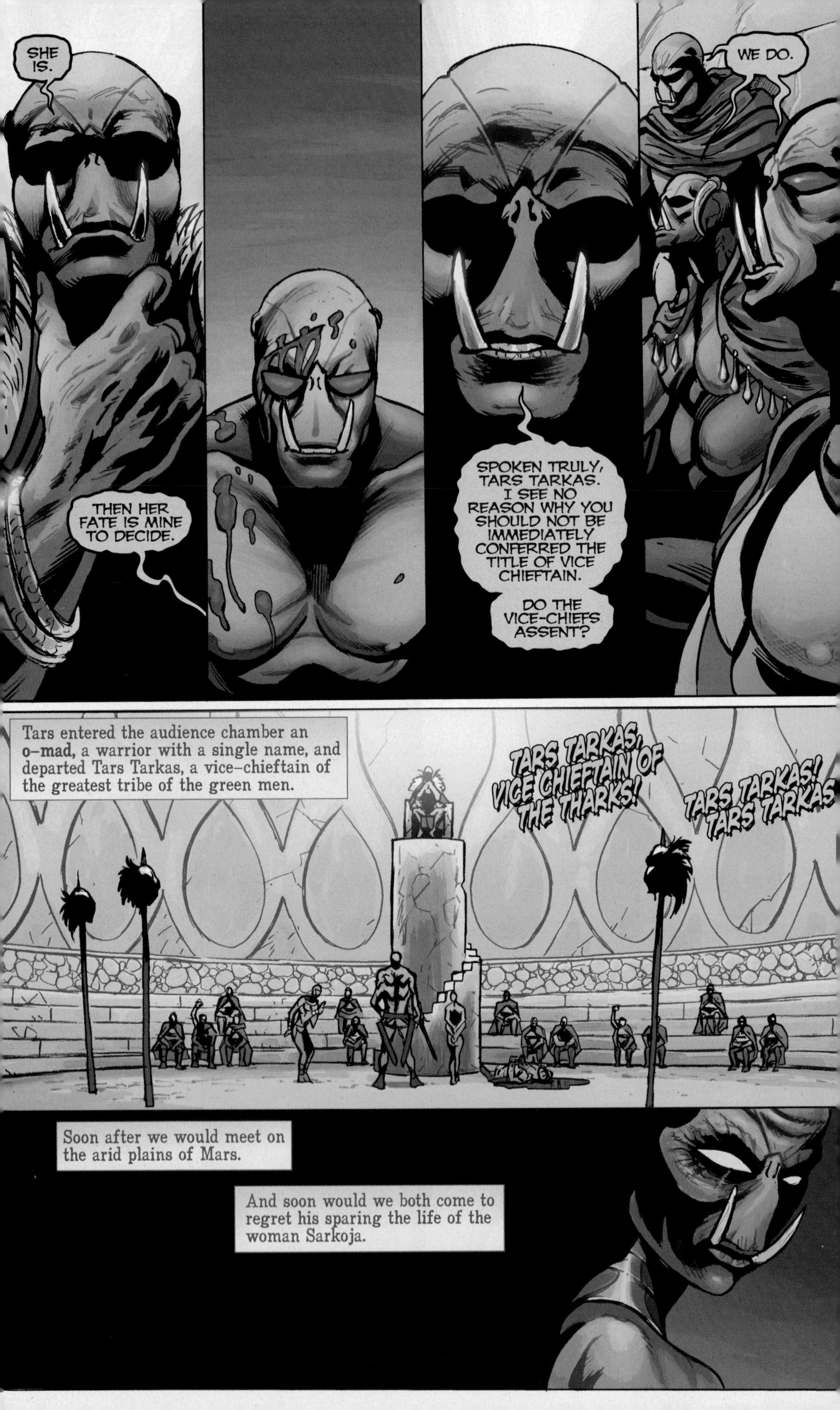
SHE IS.
THEN HER FATE IS MINE TO DECIDE.
SPOKEN TRULY, TARS TARKAS. I SEE NO REASON WHY YOU SHOULD NOT BE IMMEDIATELY CONFERRED THE TITLE OF VICE CHIEFTAIN.
DO THE VICE-CHIEFS ASSENT?
WE DO.
Tars entered the audience chamber an o-mad, a warrior with a single name, and departed Tars Tarkas, a vice-chieftain of the greatest tribe of the green men.
TARS TARKAS, VICE CHIEFTAIN OF THE THARKS!
TARS TARKAS! TARS TARKAS
Soon after we would meet on the arid plains of Mars.
And soon would we both come to regret his sparing the life of the woman Sarkoja.

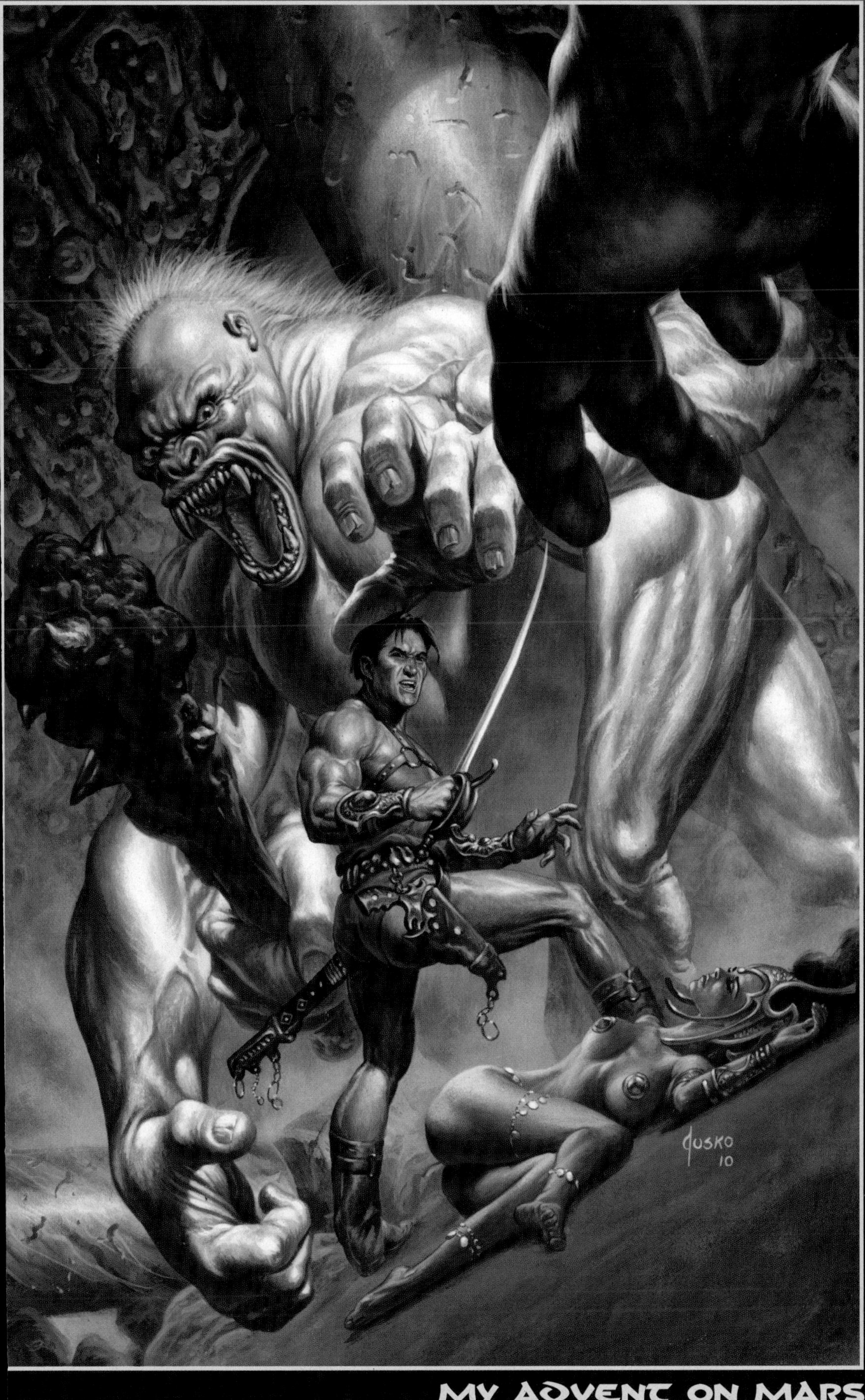
JUSKO
10

MY ADVENT ON MARS

Issue #3 cover by JOE JUSKO

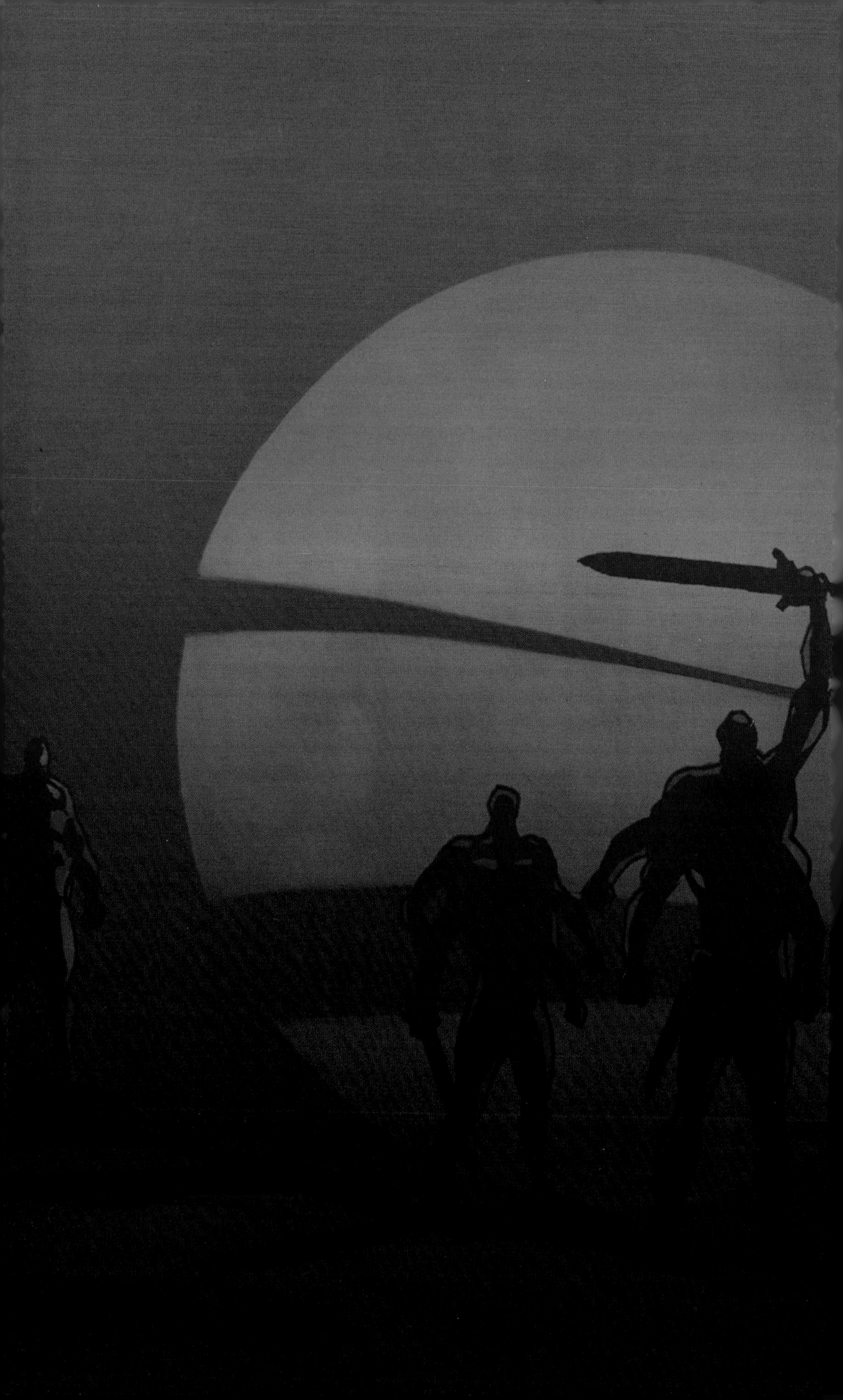

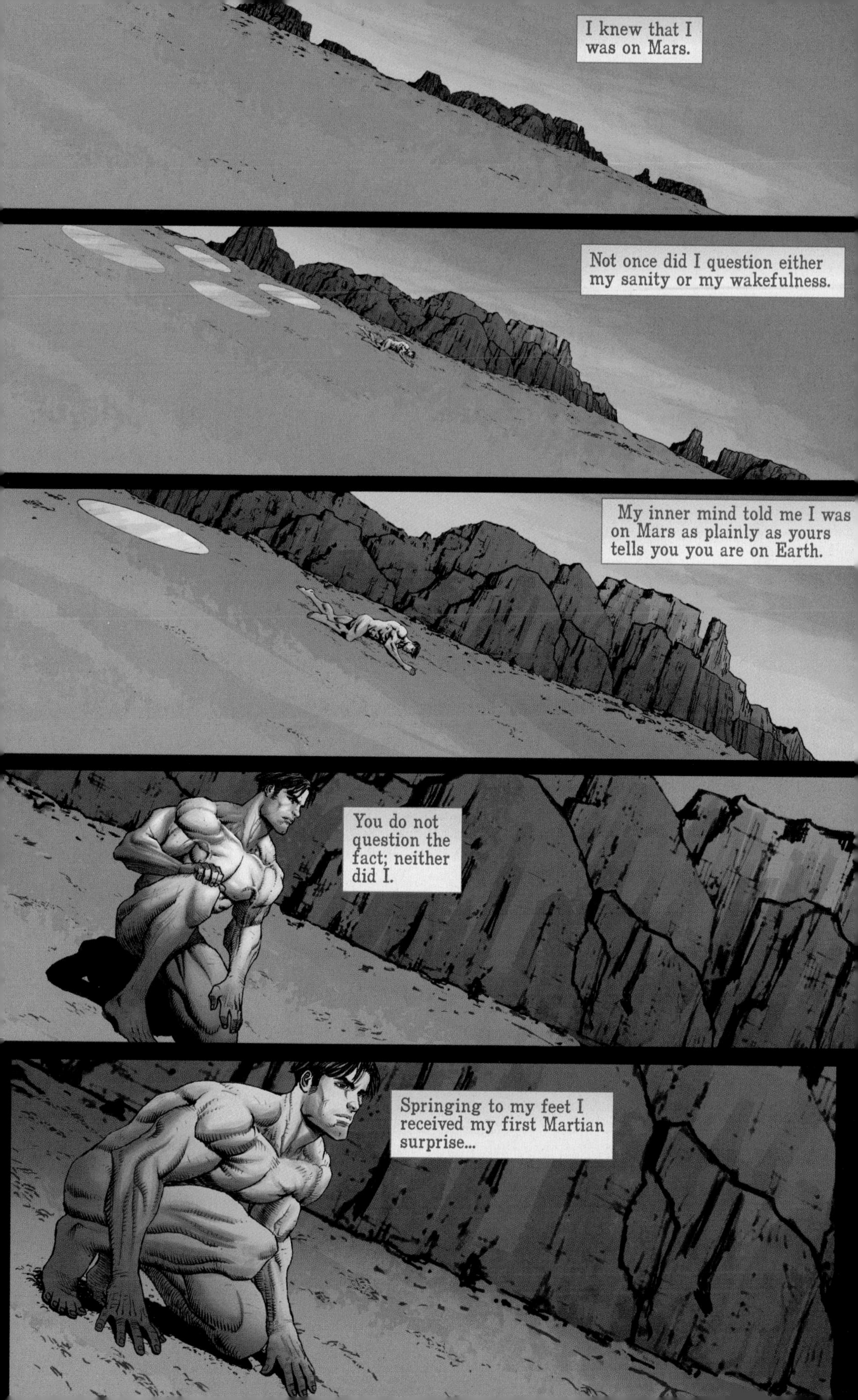
I knew that I was on Mars.
Not once did I question either my sanity or my wakefulness.
My inner mind told me I was on Mars as plainly as yours tells you you are on Earth.
You do not question the fact; neither did I.
Springing to my feet I received my first Martian surprise...

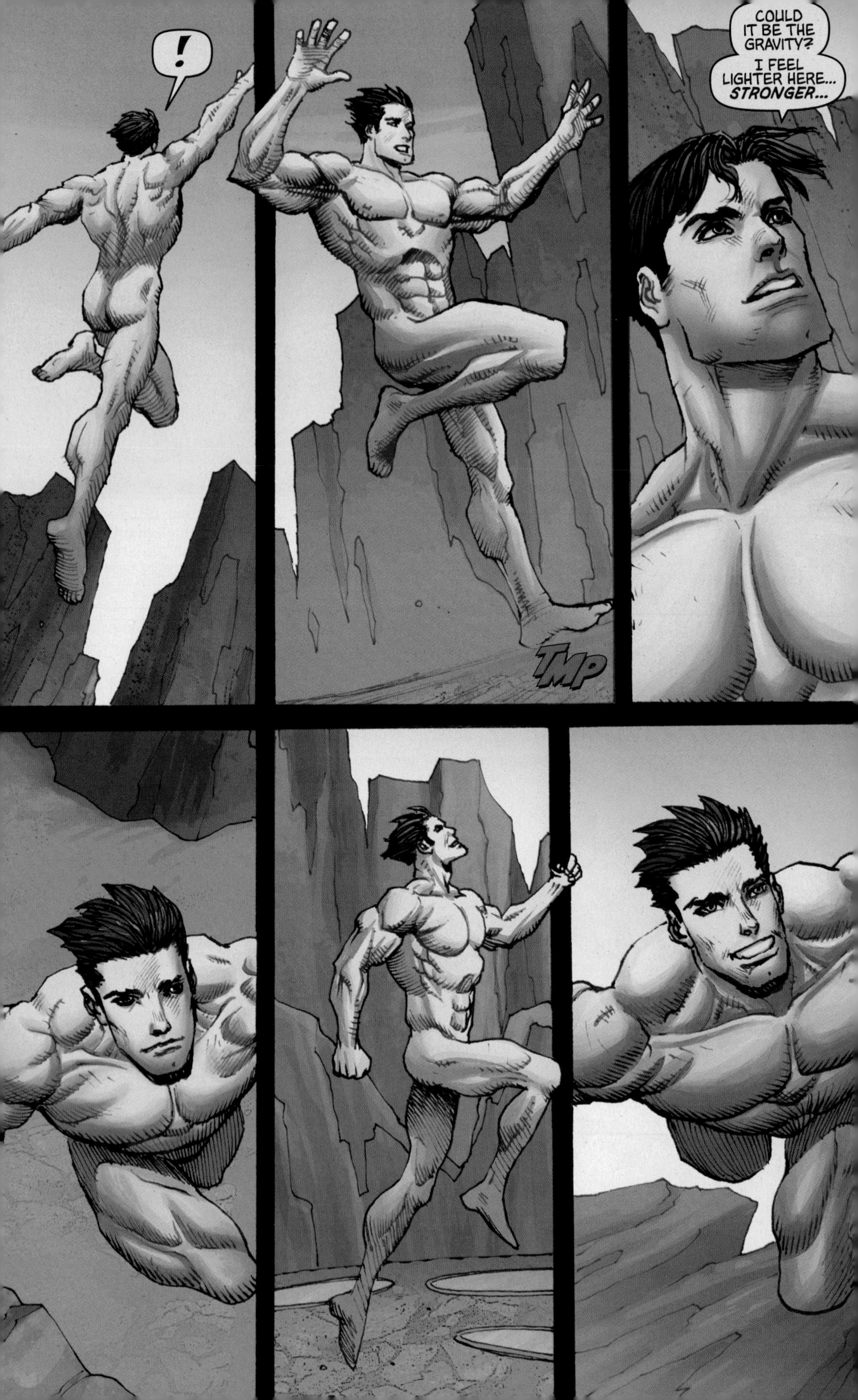
!
TMP
COULD IT BE THE GRAVITY?
I FEEL LIGHTER HERE... STRONGER...

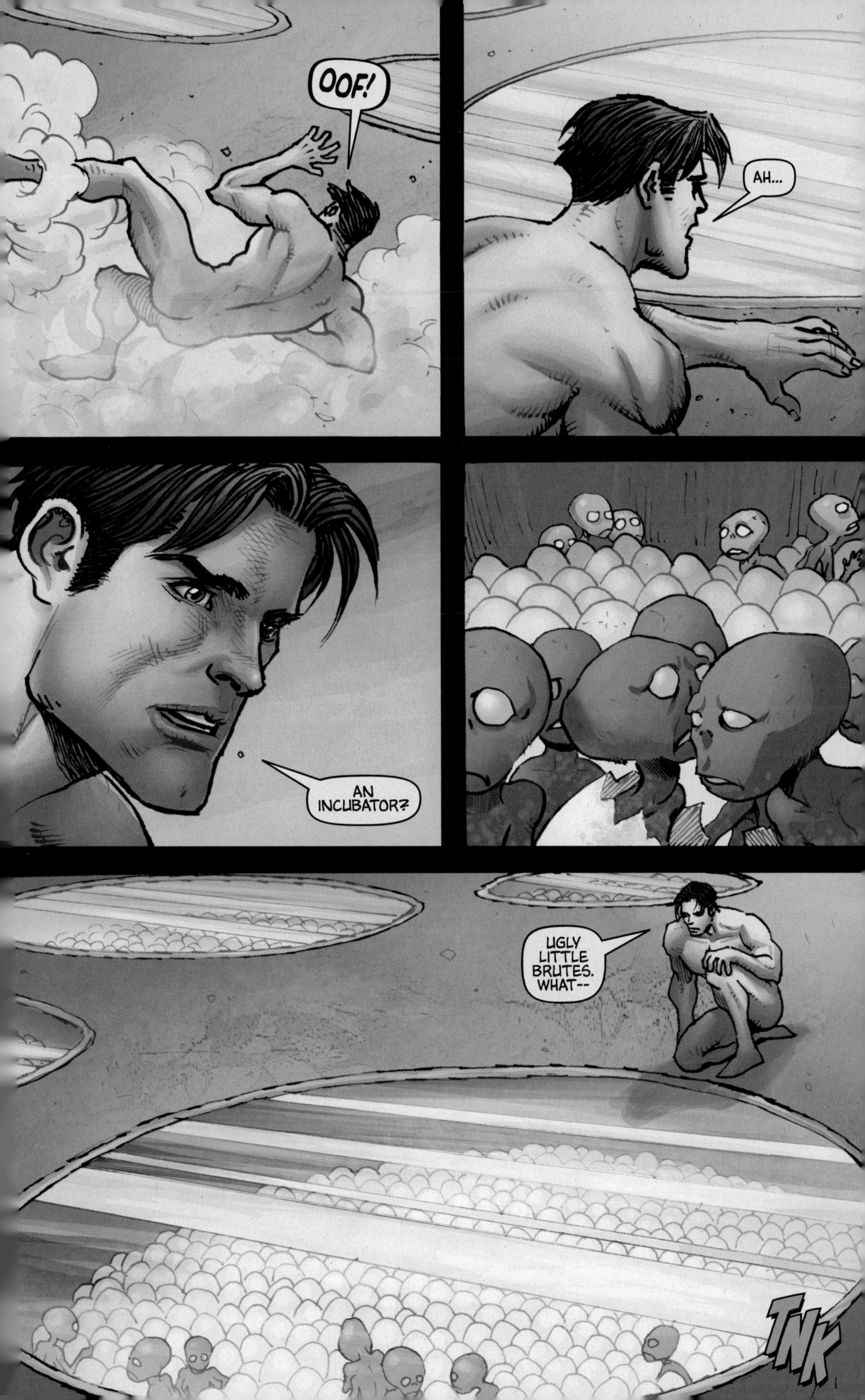
OOF!
AH...
AN INCUBATOR?
UGLY LITTLE BRUTES. WHAT--
TNK

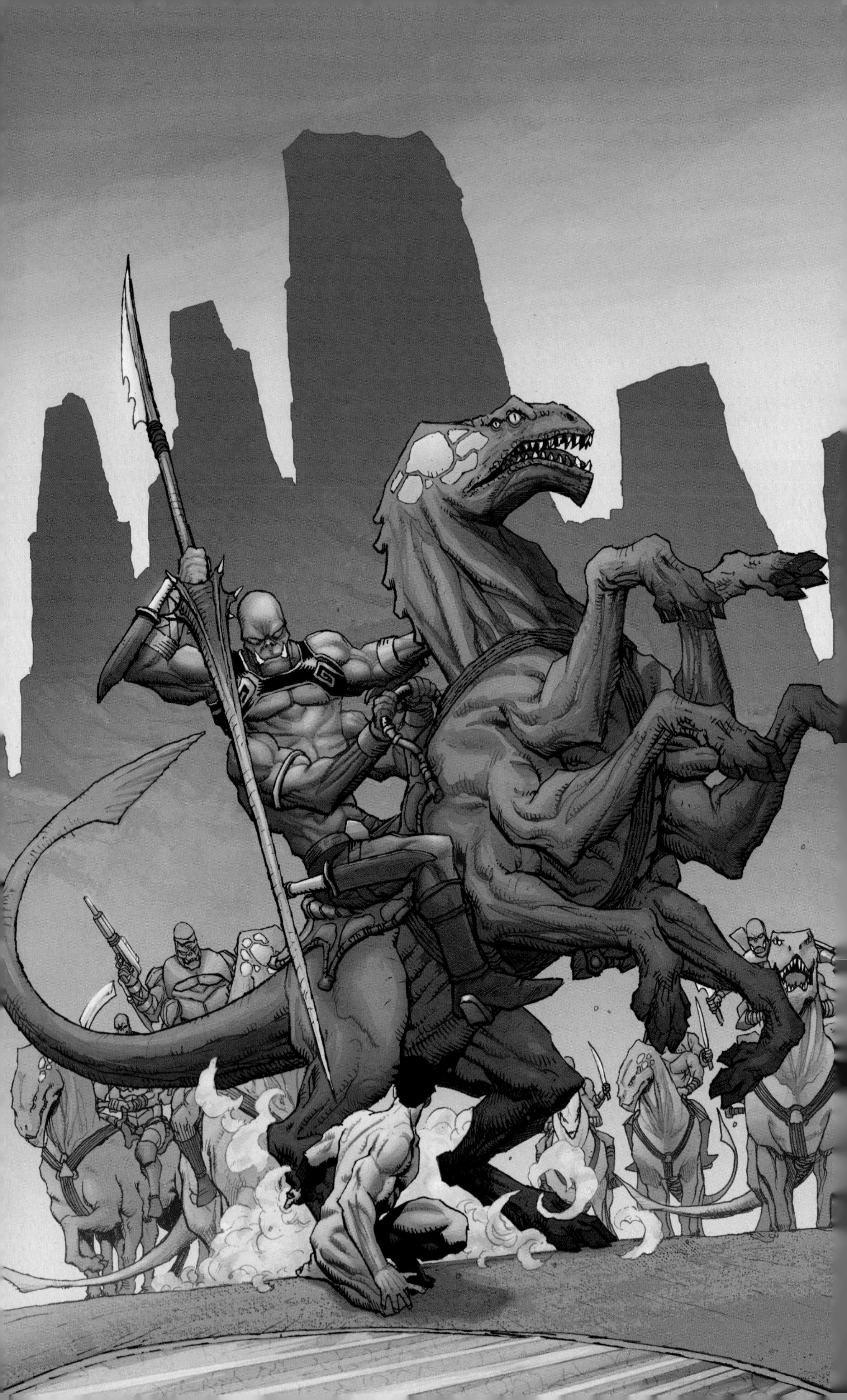

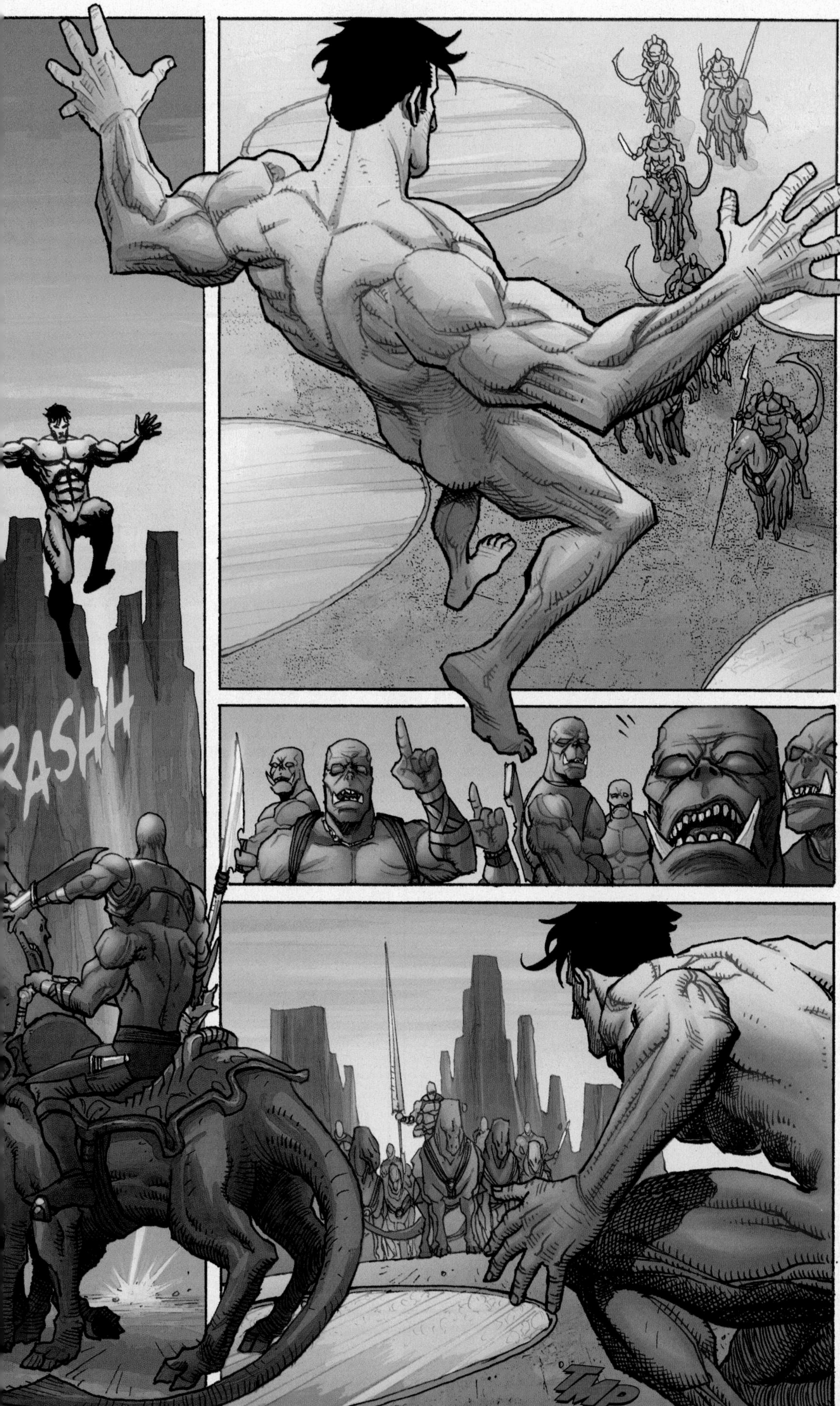
RASHH
TMP

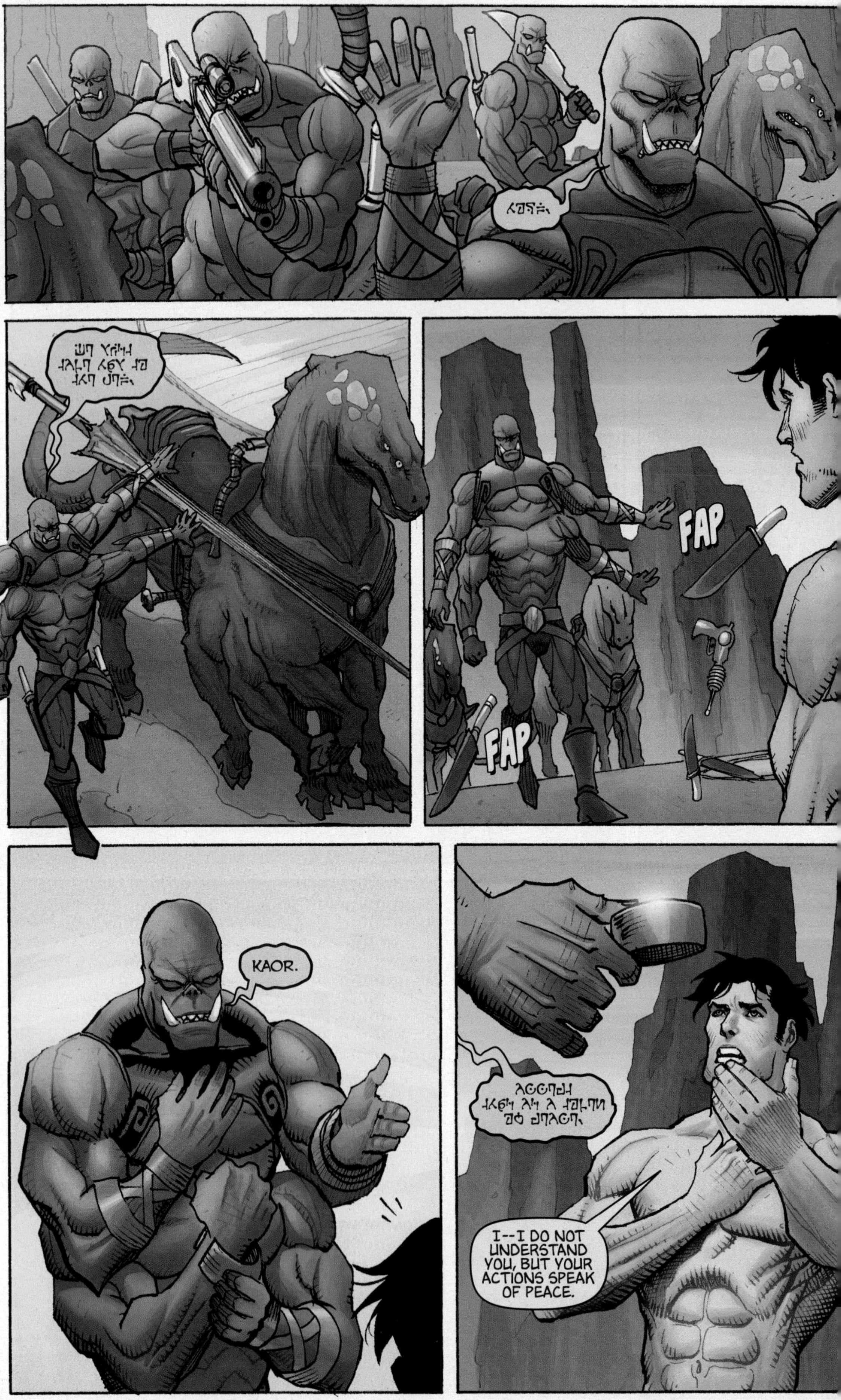
FAP
FAP
KAOR.
I--I DO NOT UNDERSTAND YOU, BUT YOUR ACTIONS SPEAK OF PEACE.

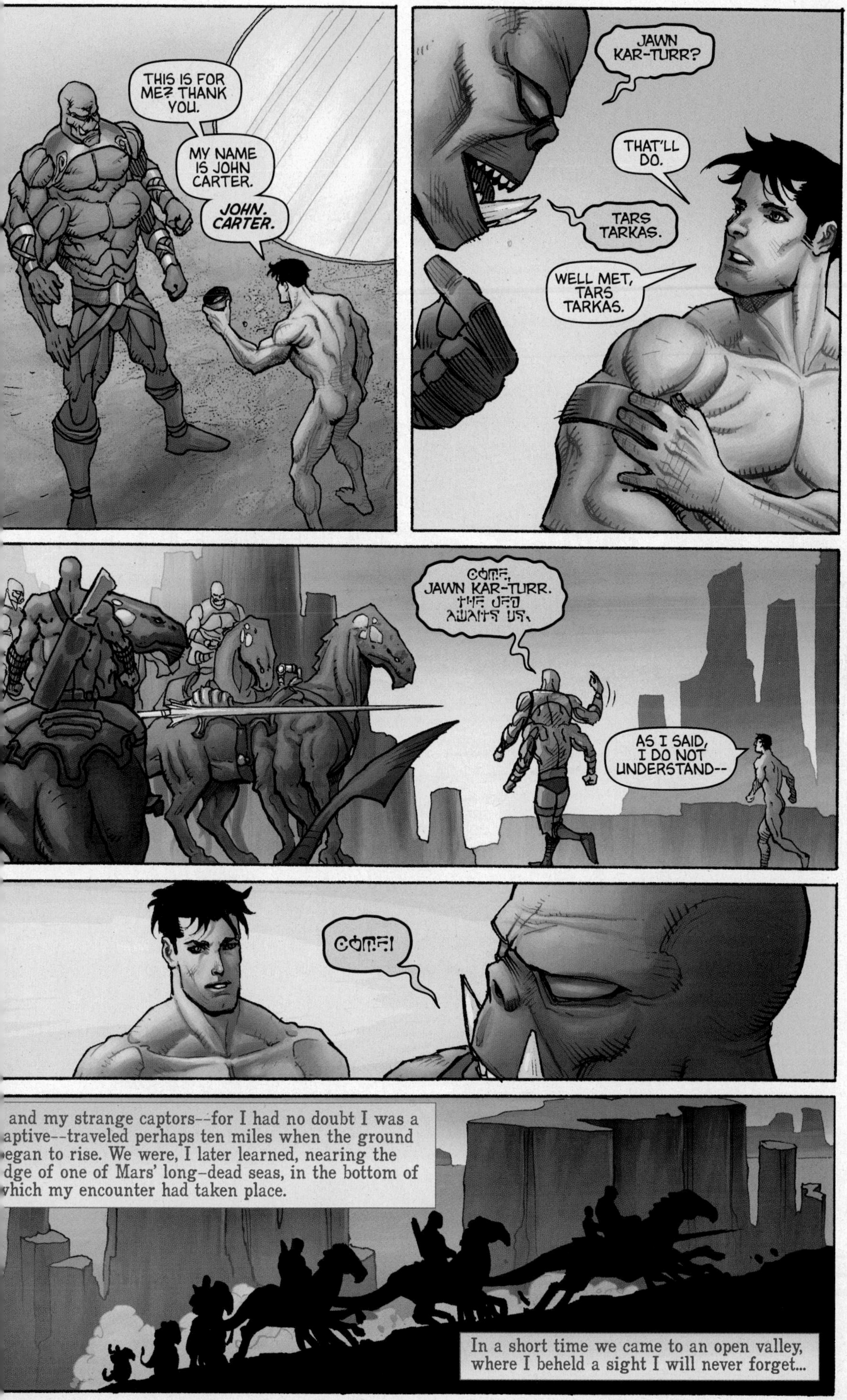

THIS IS FOR ME? THANK YOU.
MY NAME IS JOHN CARTER.
JOHN. CARTER.
JAWN KAR-TURR?
THAT'LL DO.
TARS TARKAS.
WELL MET, TARS TARKAS.
COME, JAWN KAR-TURR. THE JED AWAITS US.
AS I SAID, I DO NOT UNDERSTAND--
COME!
and my strange captors--for I had no doubt I was a aptive--traveled perhaps ten miles when the ground egan to rise. We were, I later learned, nearing the dge of one of Mars' long-dead seas, in the bottom of hich my encounter had taken place.
In a short time we came to an open valley, where I beheld a sight I will never forget...

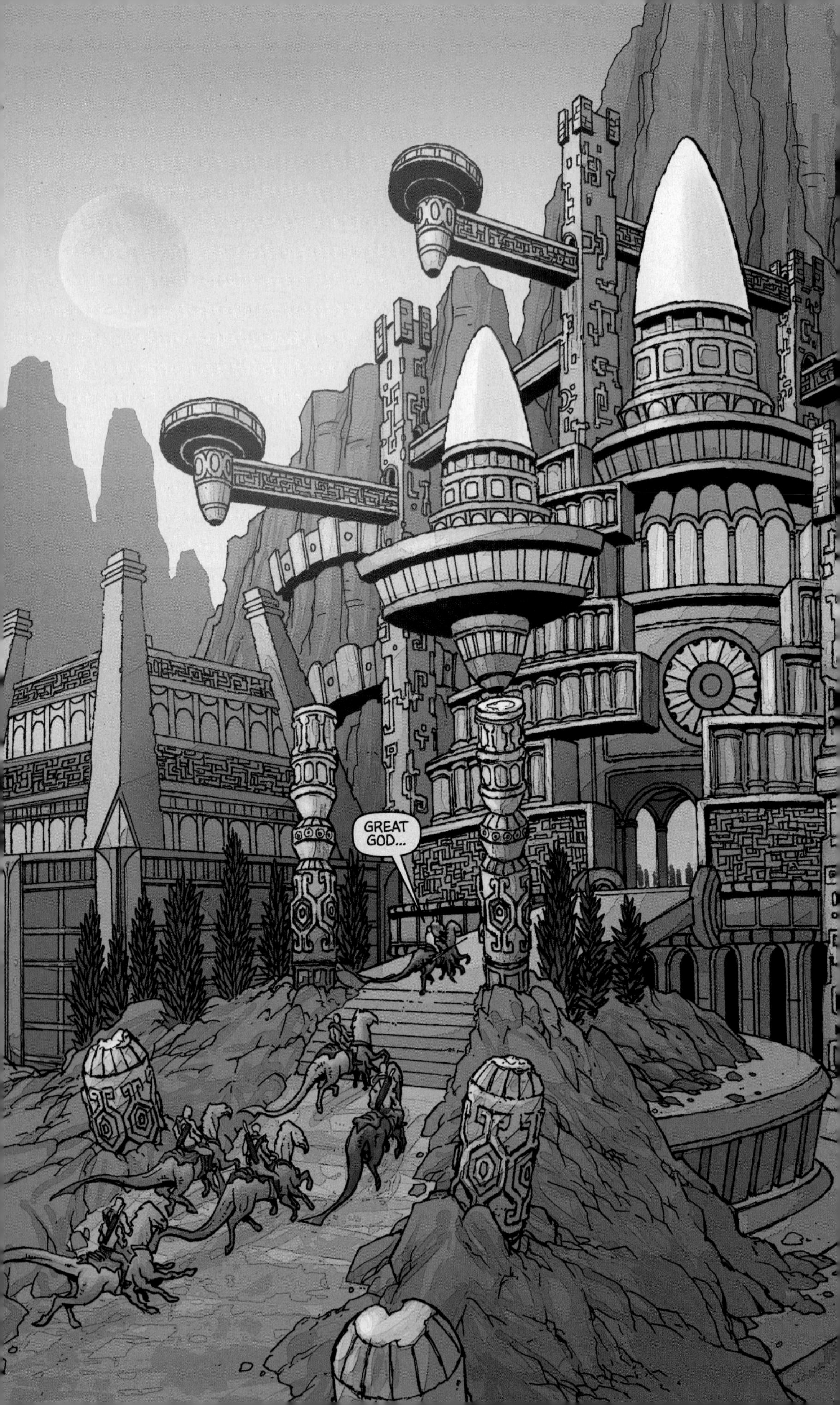
GREAT GOD...

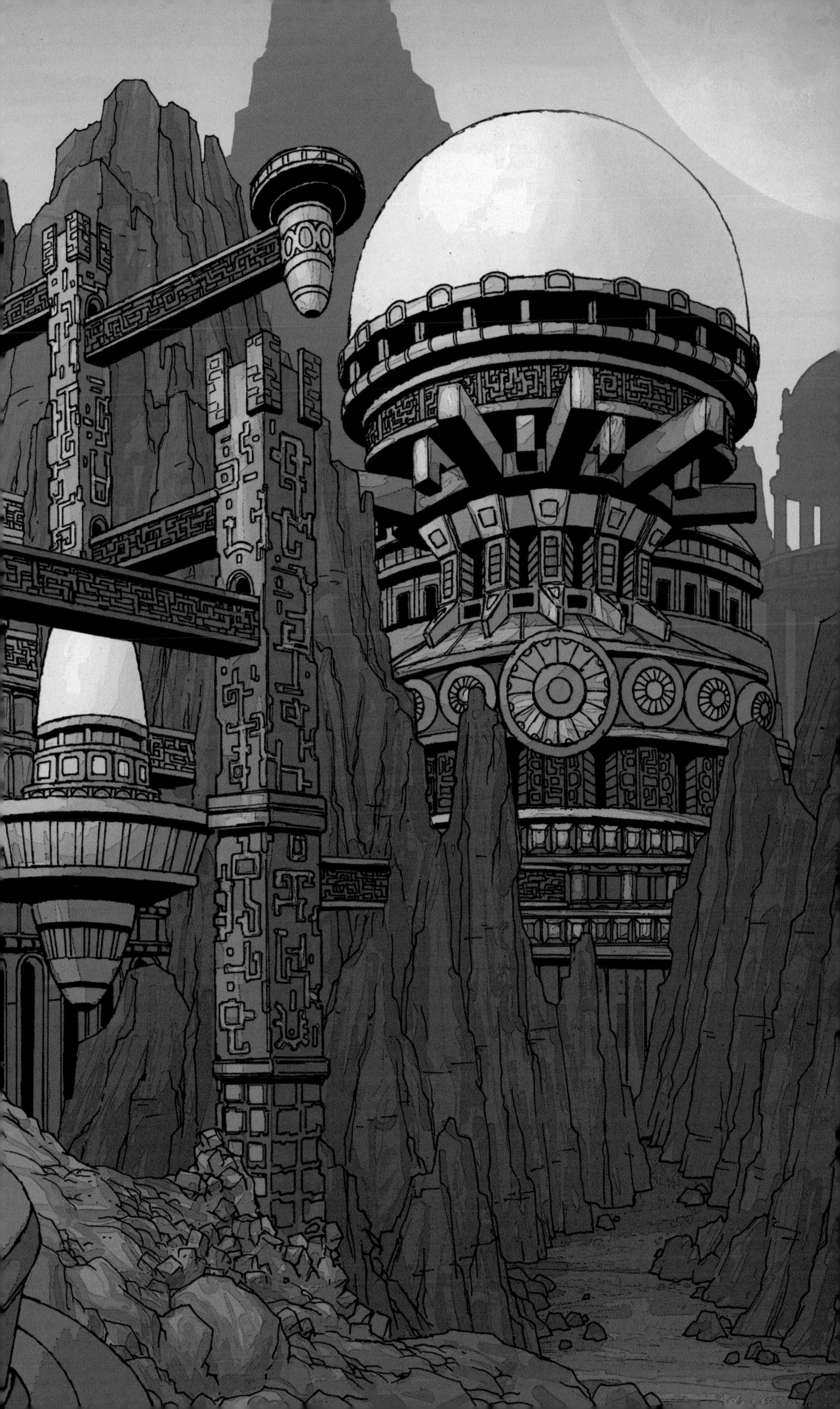

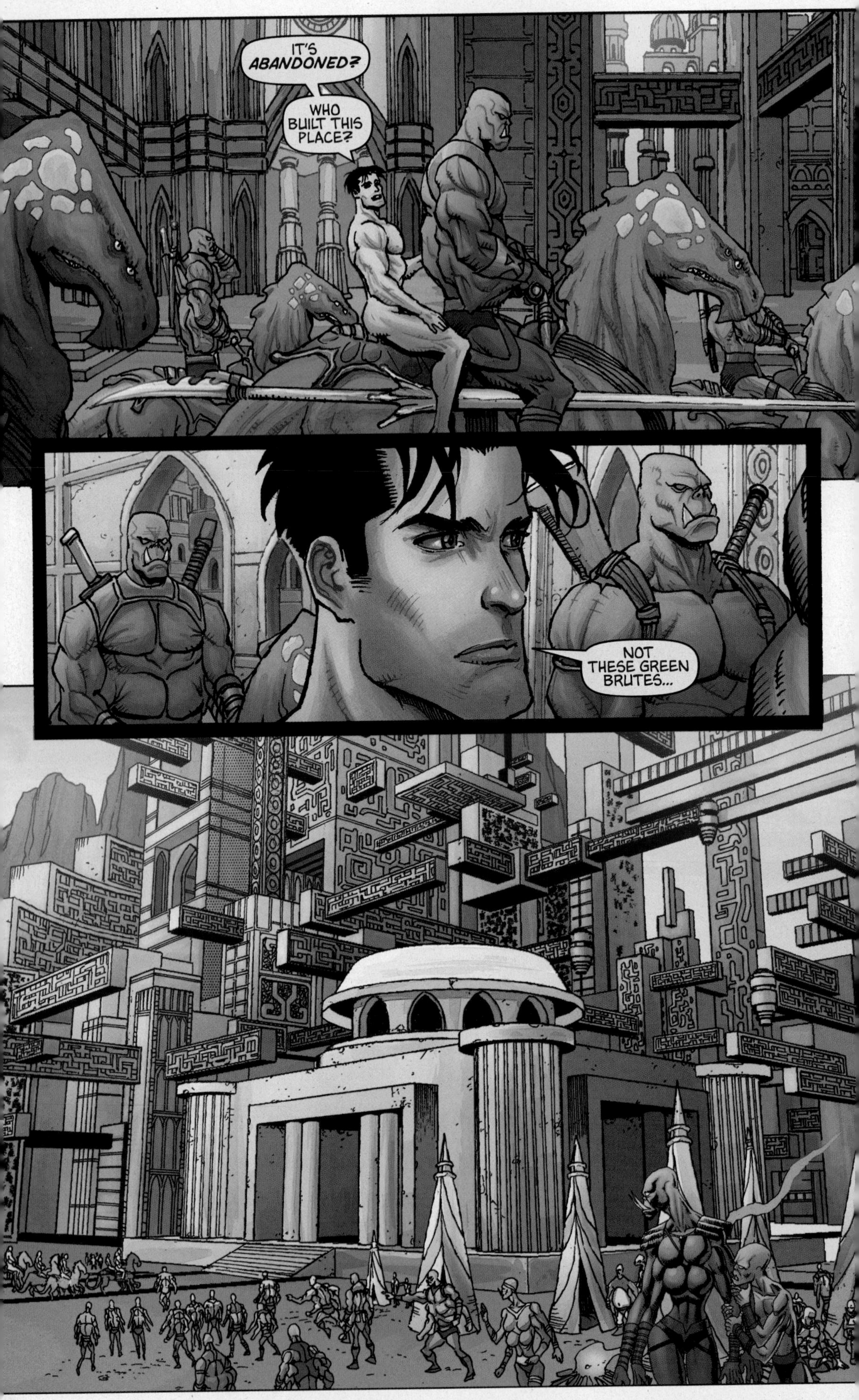
IT'S ABANDONED?
WHO BUILT THIS PLACE?
NOT THESE GREEN BRUTES...

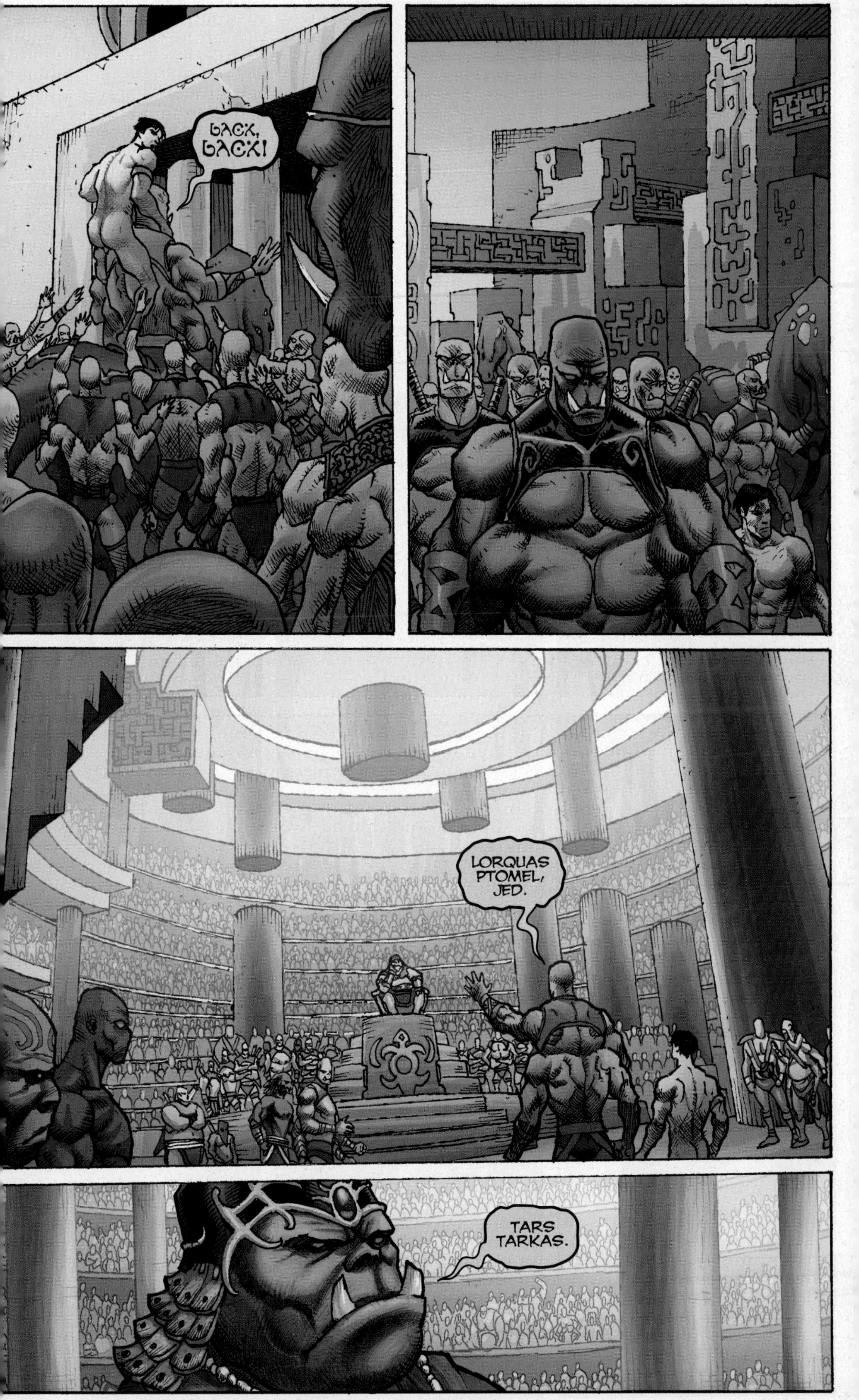
BACK, BACK!
LORQUAS PTOMEL, JED.
TARS TARKAS.

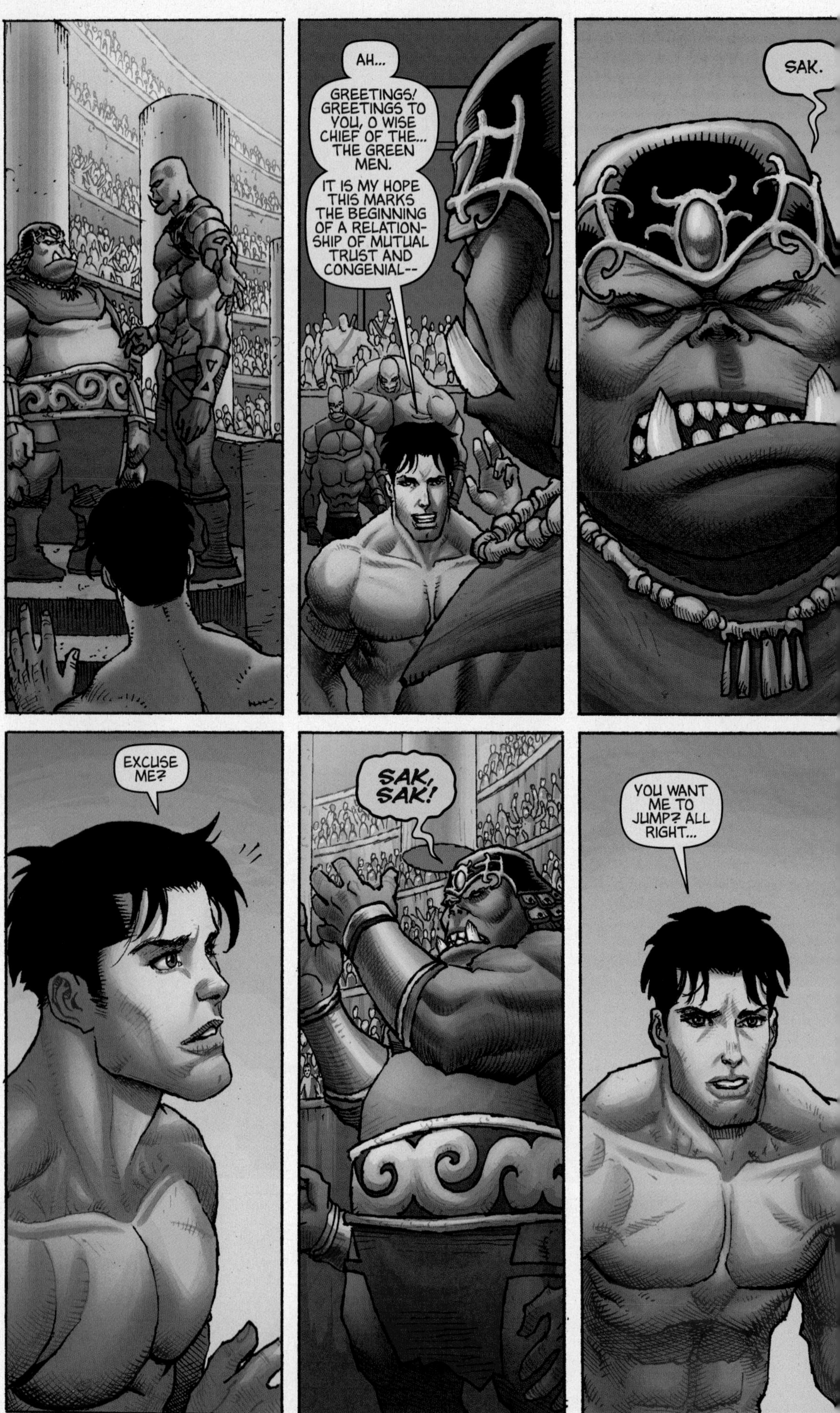
AH...
GREETINGS! GREETINGS TO YOU, O WISE CHIEF OF THE... THE GREEN MEN.
IT IS MY HOPE THIS MARKS THE BEGINNING OF A RELATIONSHIP OF MUTUAL TRUST AND CONGENIAL--
SAK.
EXCUSE ME?
SAK, SAK!
YOU WANT ME TO JUMP? ALL RIGHT...

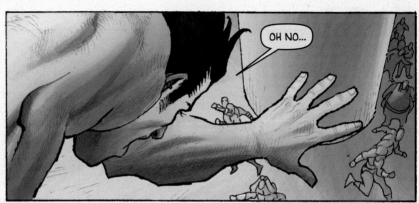

OH NO...

THWACK

HAAA HA HA!

ON YOUR FEET, PUNY MAN-THING!

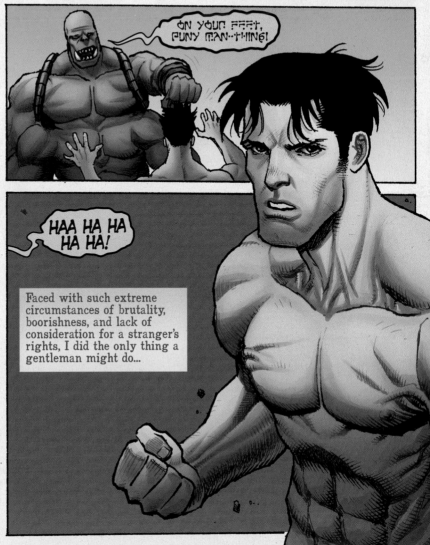

HAA HA HA HA HA!

Faced with such extreme circumstances of brutality, boorishness, and lack of consideration for a stranger's rights, I did the only thing a gentleman might do...

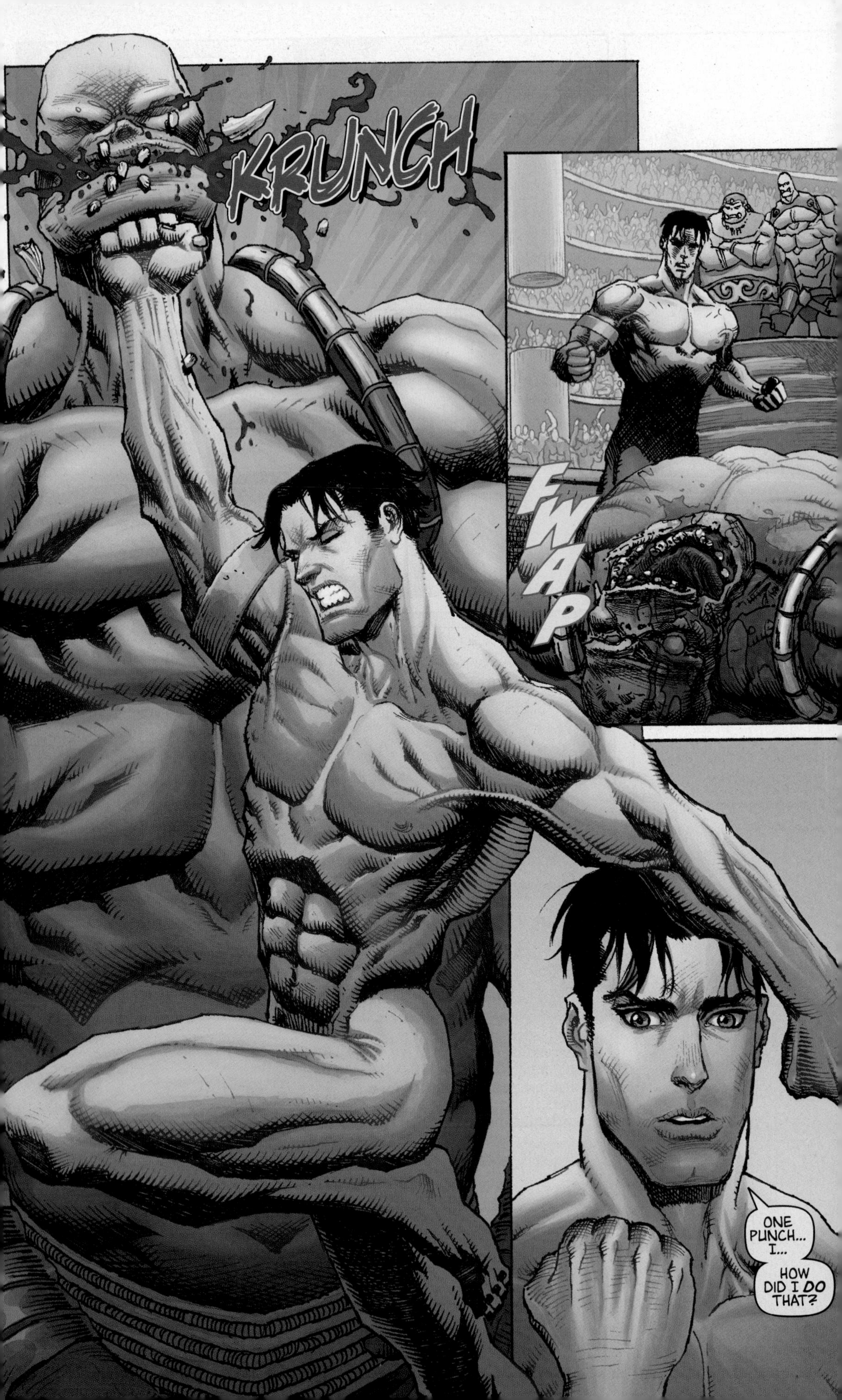
KRUNCH
FWAP
ONE PUNCH... I...
HOW DID I DO THAT?

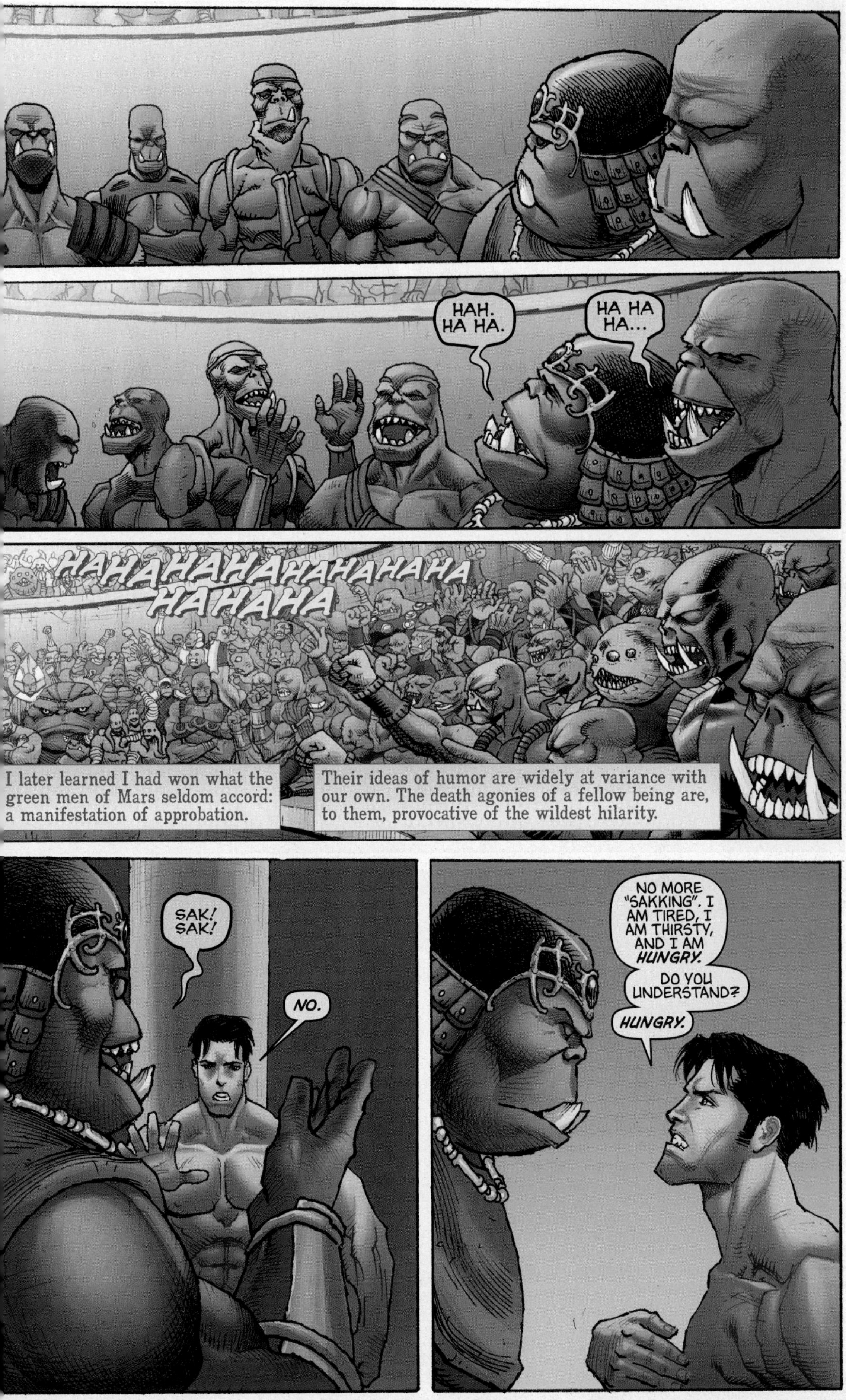
HAH. HA HA.
HA HA HA...
HAHAHAHAHAHAHAHA HAHAHA
I later learned I had won what the green men of Mars seldom accord: a manifestation of approbation.
Their ideas of humor are widely at variance with our own. The death agonies of a fellow being are, to them, provocative of the wildest hilarity.
SAK! SAK!
NO.
NO MORE "SAKKING". I AM TIRED, I AM THIRSTY, AND I AM HUNGRY.
DO YOU UNDERSTAND?
HUNGRY.

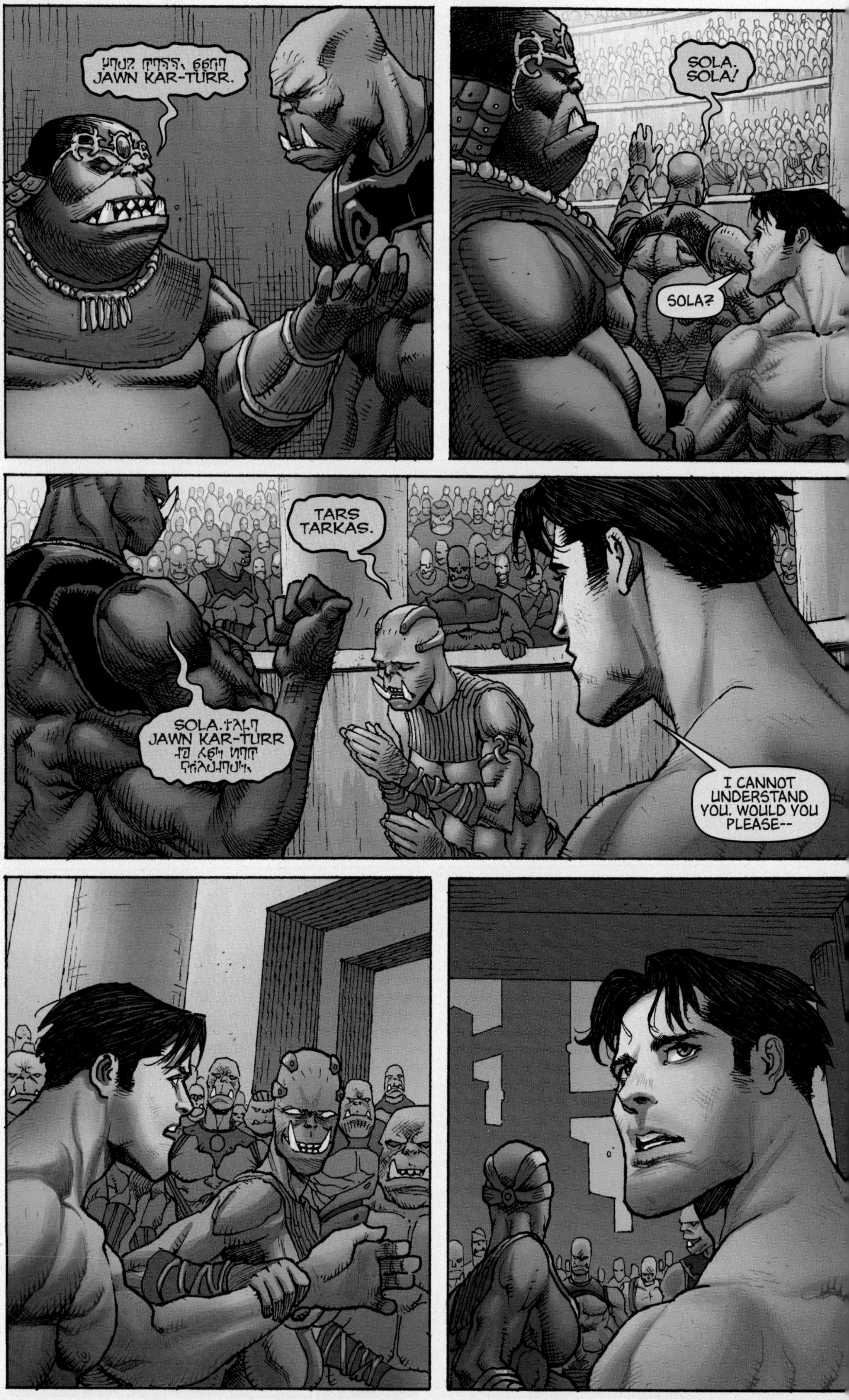
JAWN KAR-TURR.
SOLA, SOLA!
SOLA?
TARS TARKAS.
SOLA.
JAWN KAR-TURR
I CANNOT UNDERSTAND YOU. WOULD YOU PLEASE--

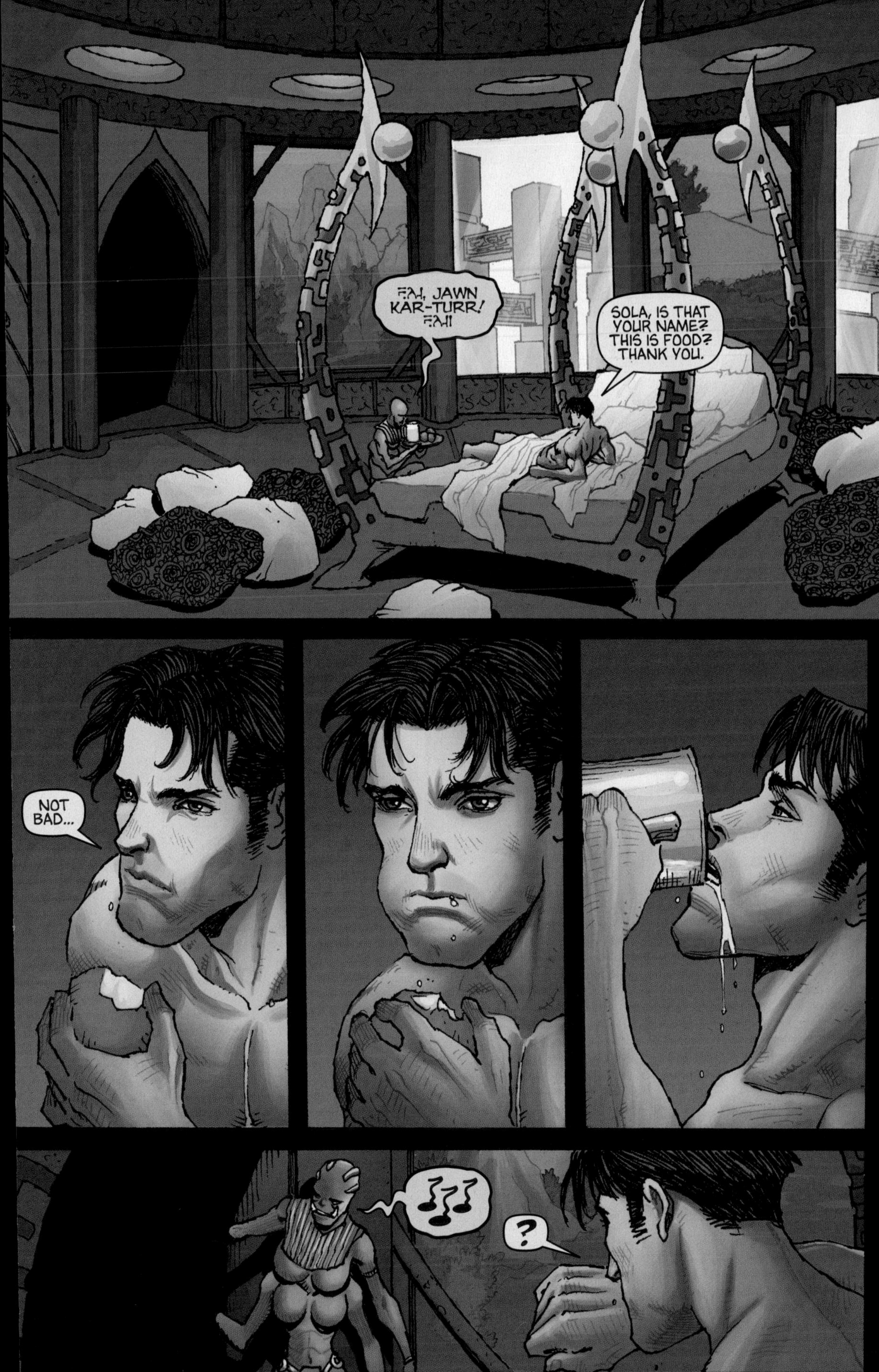

F'Λl, JAWN KAR-TURR! F'Λl
SOLA, IS THAT YOUR NAME? THIS IS FOOD? THANK YOU.
NOT BAD...
?

SﬁλUﬀ Ỵ6Ỵ,

At that moment, I did not know, nor did I care, if the strange beast represented a deadly threat to my person.

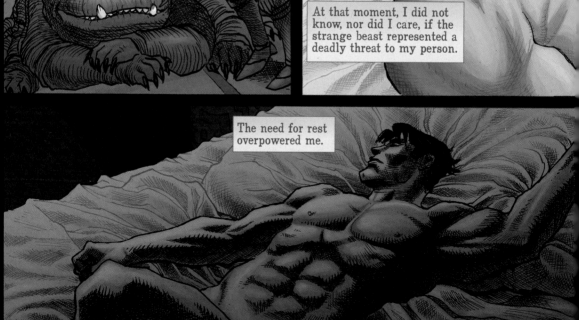

The need for rest overpowered me.

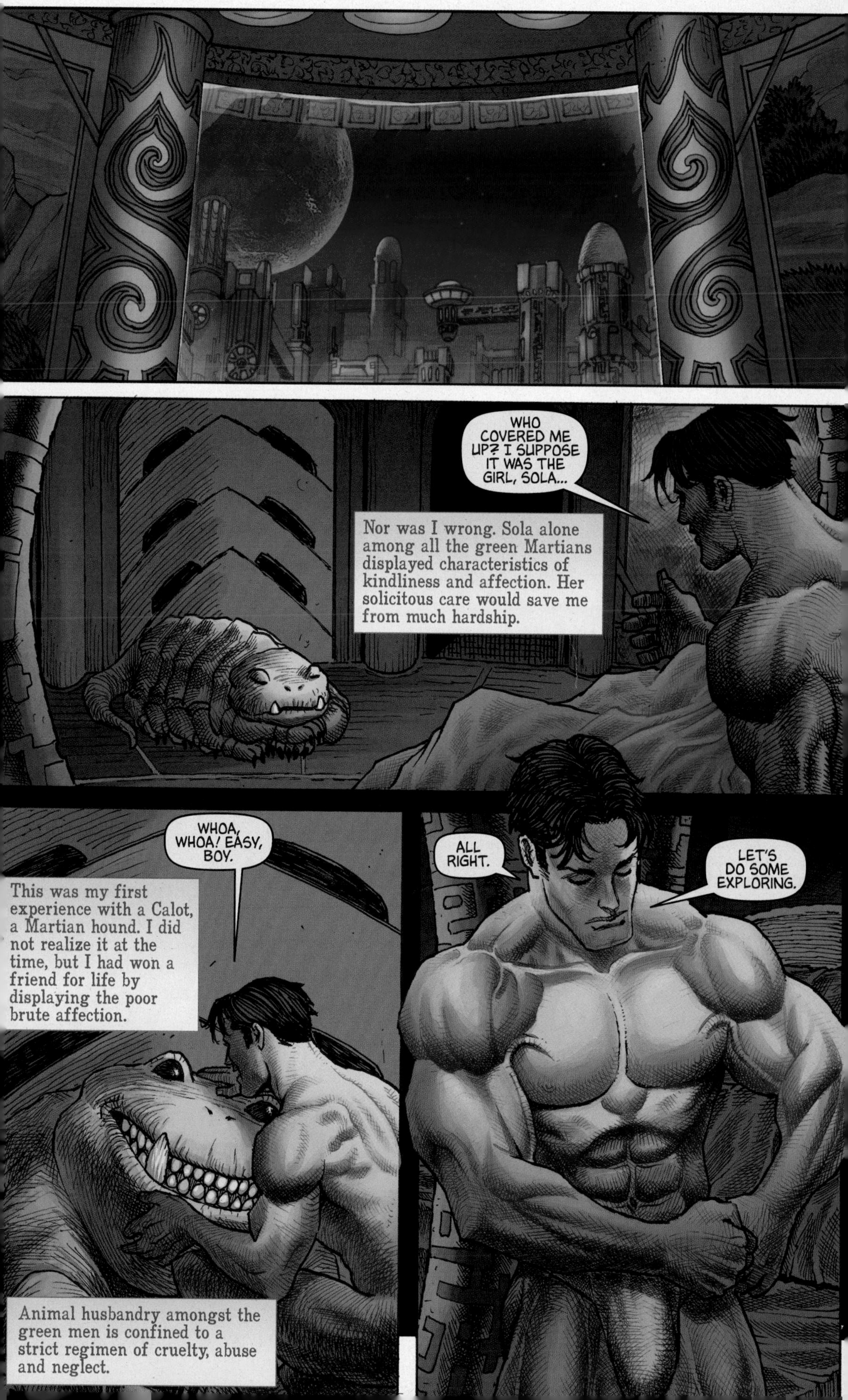
WHO COVERED ME UP? I SUPPOSE IT WAS THE GIRL, SOLA...
Nor was I wrong. Sola alone among all the green Martians displayed characteristics of kindliness and affection. Her solicitous care would save me from much hardship.
WHOA, WHOA! EASY, BOY.
This was my first experience with a Calot, a Martian hound. I did not realize it at the time, but I had won a friend for life by displaying the poor brute affection.
Animal husbandry amongst the green men is confined to a strict regimen of cruelty, abuse and neglect.
ALL RIGHT.
LET'S DO SOME EXPLORING.

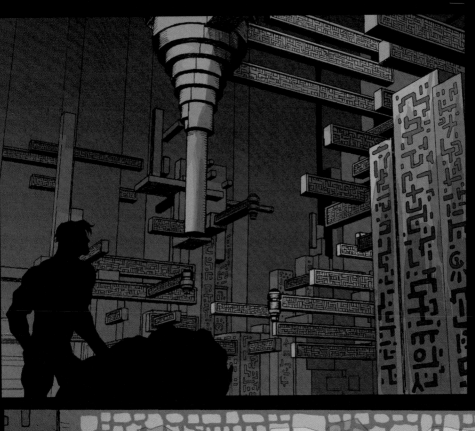

THERE IS ABSOLUTELY NO WAY THOSE GREEN HALF-BRUTES COULD HAVE CREATED THIS...

SO WHO DID?

AND WHERE DID THEY GO? THIS CITY WAS BUILT FOR CREATURES *MY* SIZE...

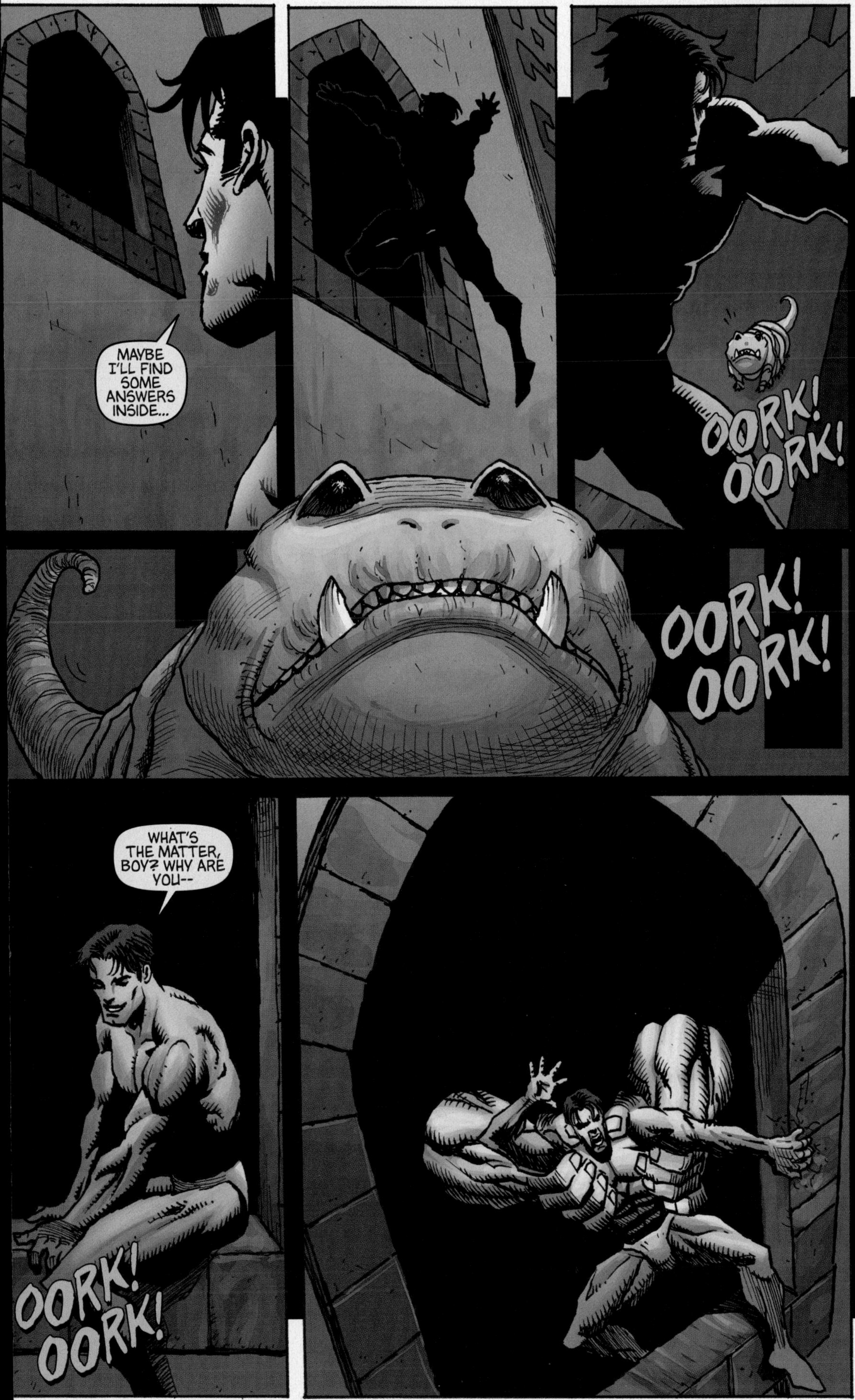
MAYBE I'LL FIND SOME ANSWERS INSIDE...
OORK! OORK!
OORK! OORK!
WHAT'S THE MATTER, BOY? WHY ARE YOU--
OORK! OORK!

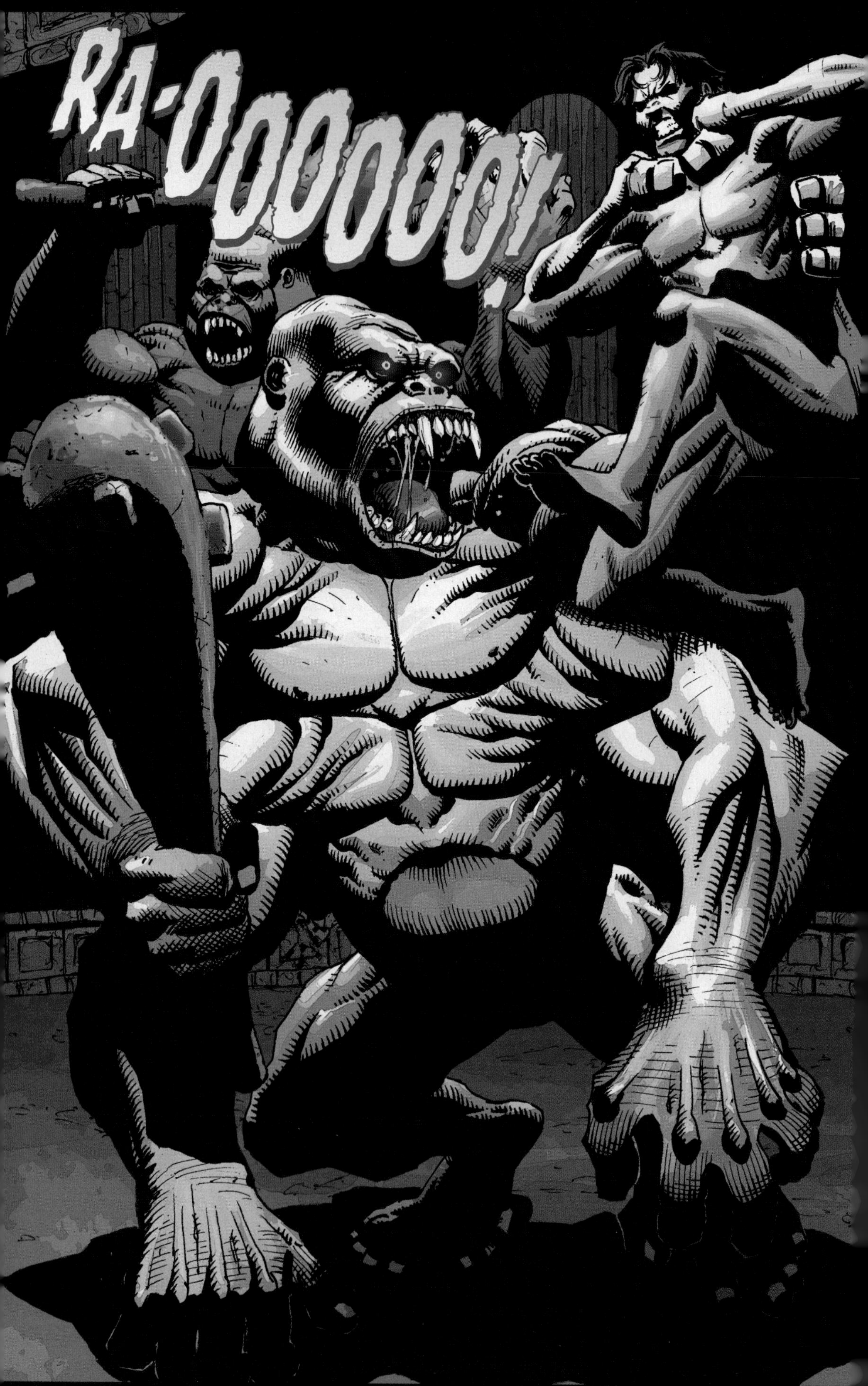
RA-OOOOOO!

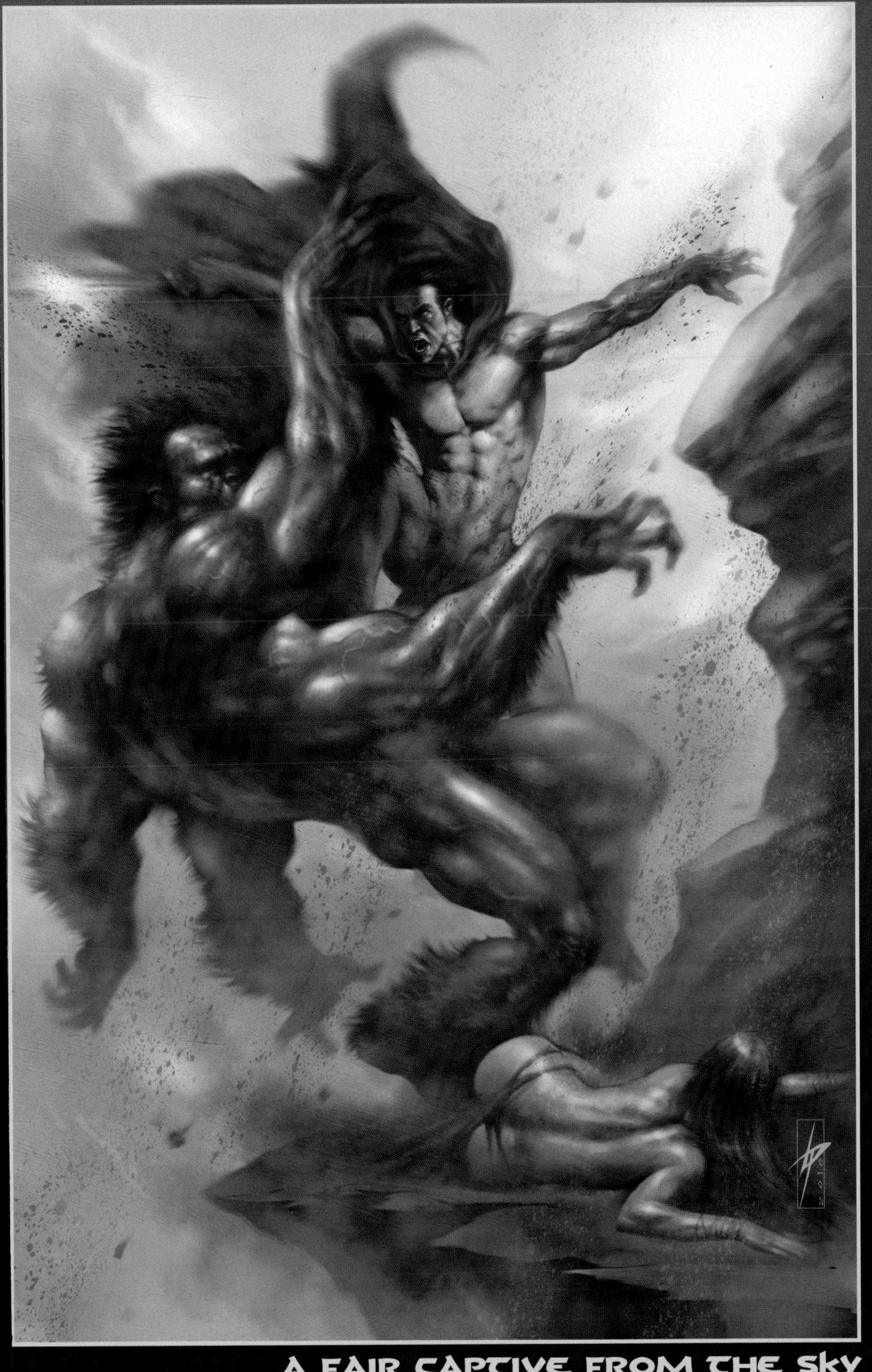

A FAIR CAPTIVE FROM THE SKY

Issue #4 cover by LUCIO PARRILLO

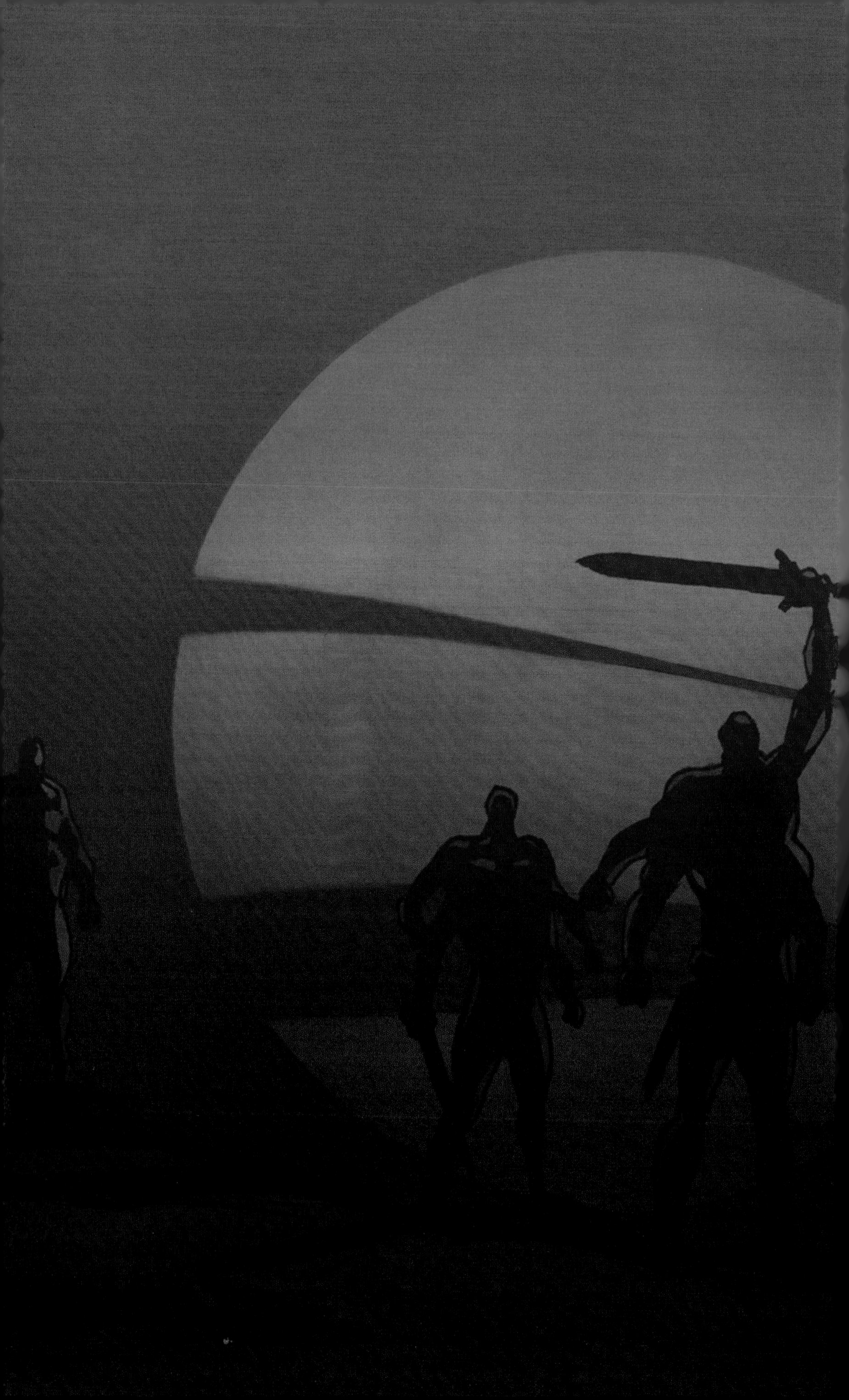

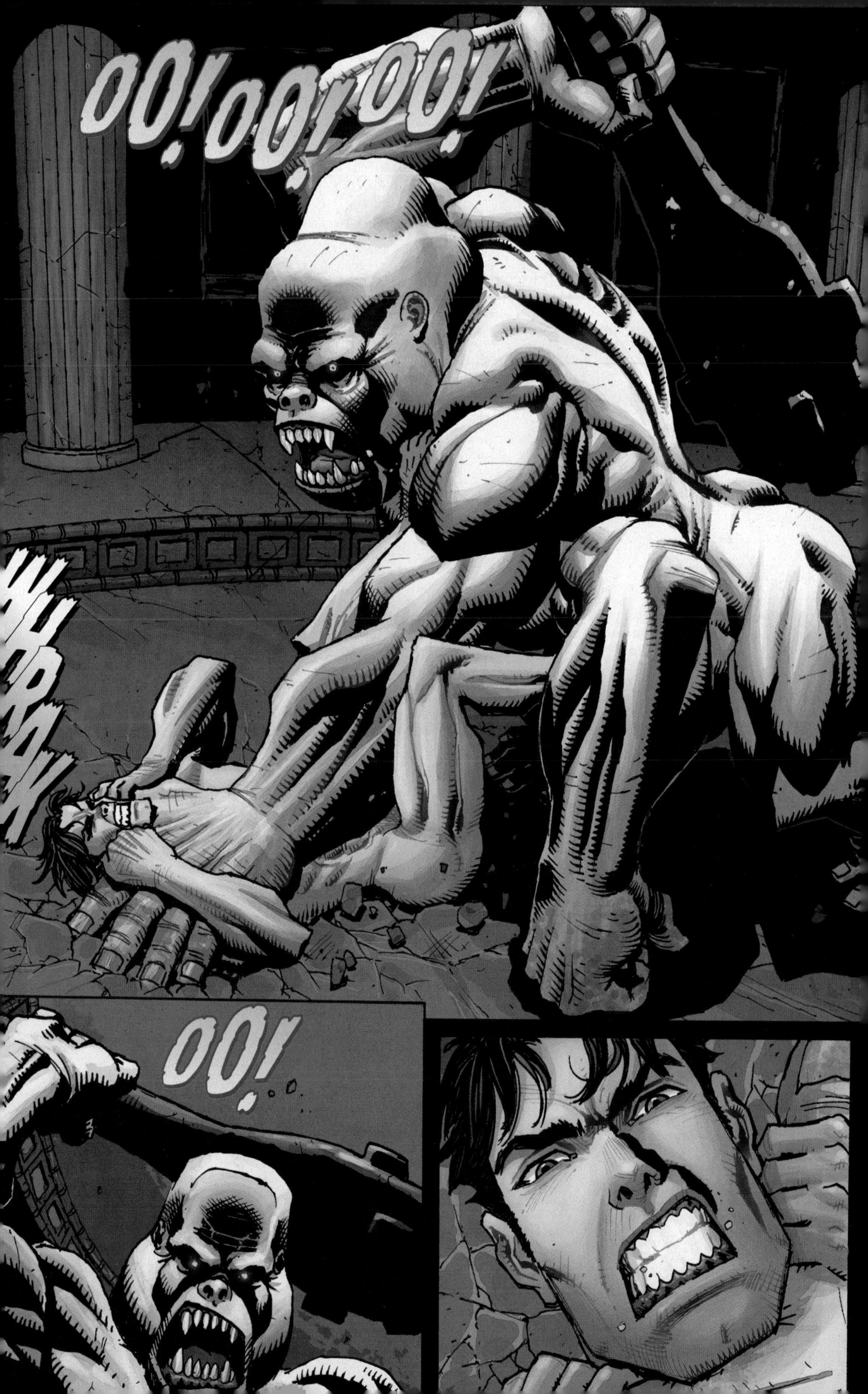
OO!OO!OO!
OO!

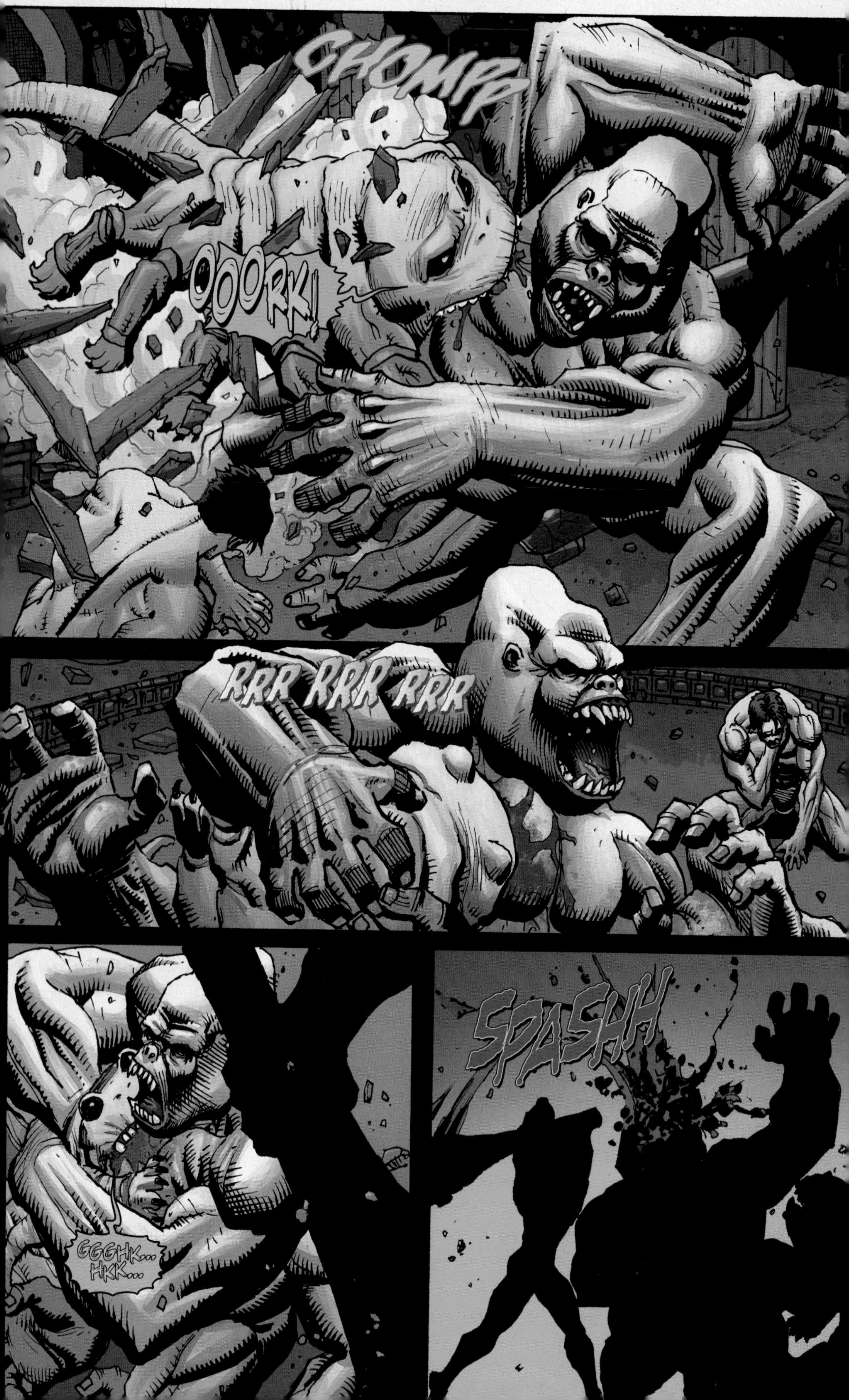
CHOMP
OOORK!
RRR RRR RRR
GGGHK... HKK...
SPASHH

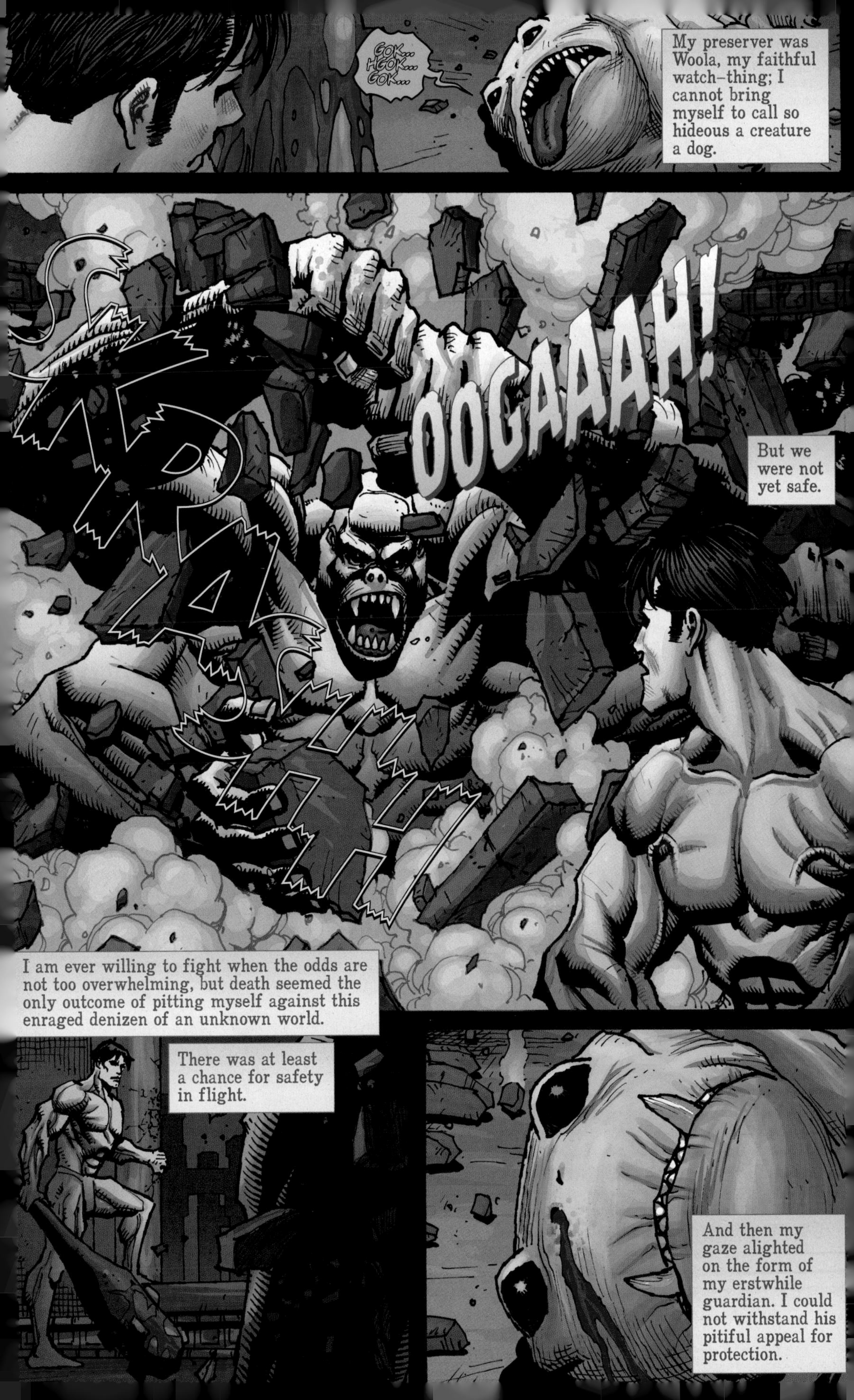
GOK... HGOK... GOK...
My preserver was Woola, my faithful watch–thing; I cannot bring myself to call so hideous a creature a dog.
OOGAAAH!
But we were not yet safe.
I am ever willing to fight when the odds are not too overwhelming, but death seemed the only outcome of pitting myself against this enraged denizen of an unknown world.
There was at least a chance for safety in flight.
And then my gaze alighted on the form of my erstwhile guardian. I could not withstand his pitiful appeal for protection.

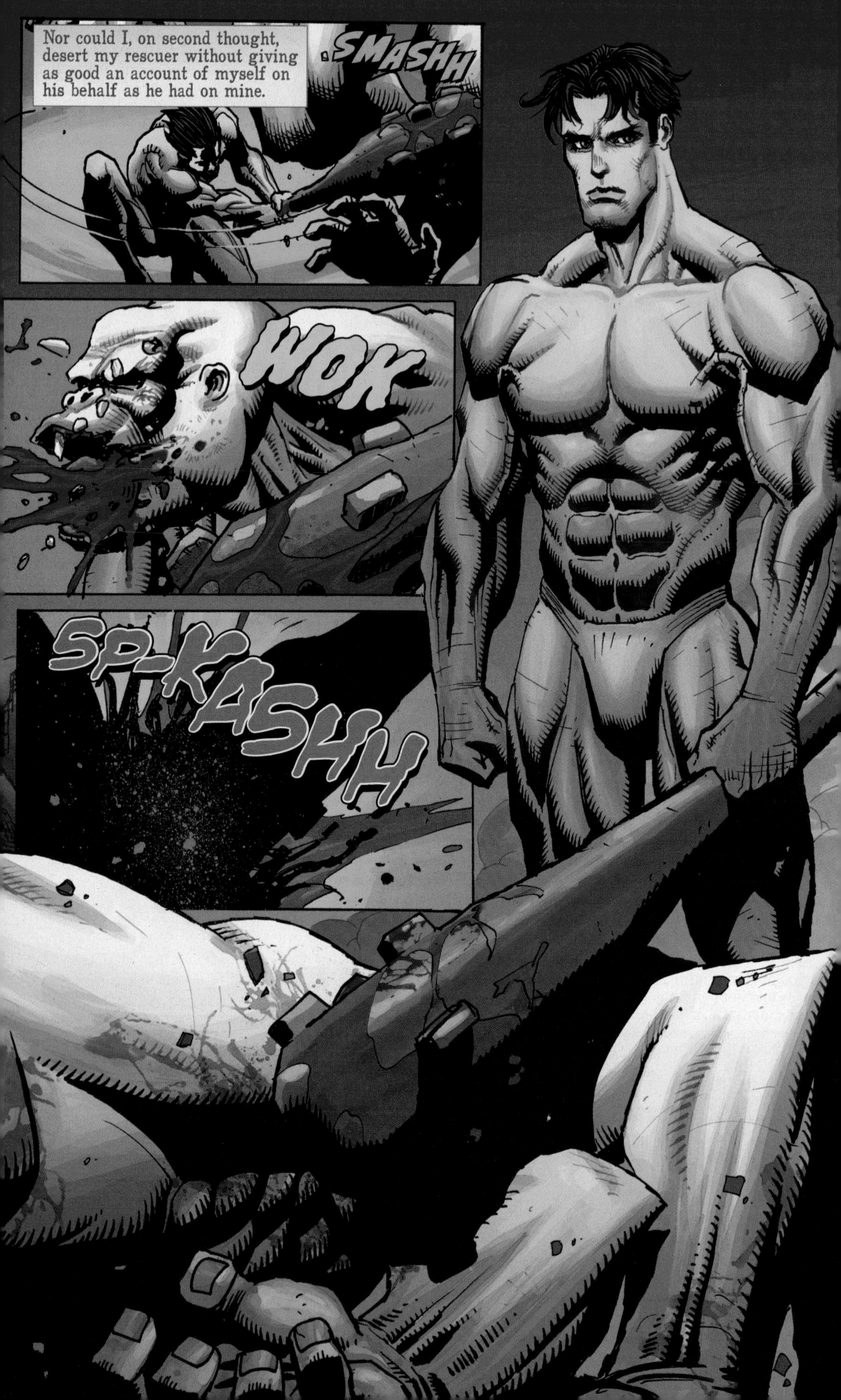

Nor could I, on second thought, desert my rescuer without giving as good an account of myself on his behalf as he had on mine.
SMASHH
WOK
SP-KASHH

Panel 1: TARS TARKAS!

HA HA HA HA HA

ᕗᑎᒪᕬᕬ ᓀᕐ᠇᠇, JAWN KAR-TURR.

Panel 2: HA HA HA HA HA

SOLA? I--

JAWN KAR-TURR! ᕬᑌᑎ ᓭᑐᕬ ᕬᓭᓭ ᑌᒣᒪᕬᒪᑎᐧ

Panel 3: WHAT ARE YOU GOING ON ABOUT?

Yᐧᑎᕬᑌ ᑌᑌᓀᓭᑎᐧᑎ, TARS TARKAS.

Sola, it seemed, had noted my absence and informed Tars Tarkas.

The encounter with the apes, together with my set-to with the Martian warrior the other day, placed me in high regard among the green people.

Devoid of all sentiments of friendship or love, they worship only physical prowess and bravery.

Sola was the only one whose face was not twisted in laughter.

ᐧᕬᒪᕬᕬ ᕬᐧᑎ.

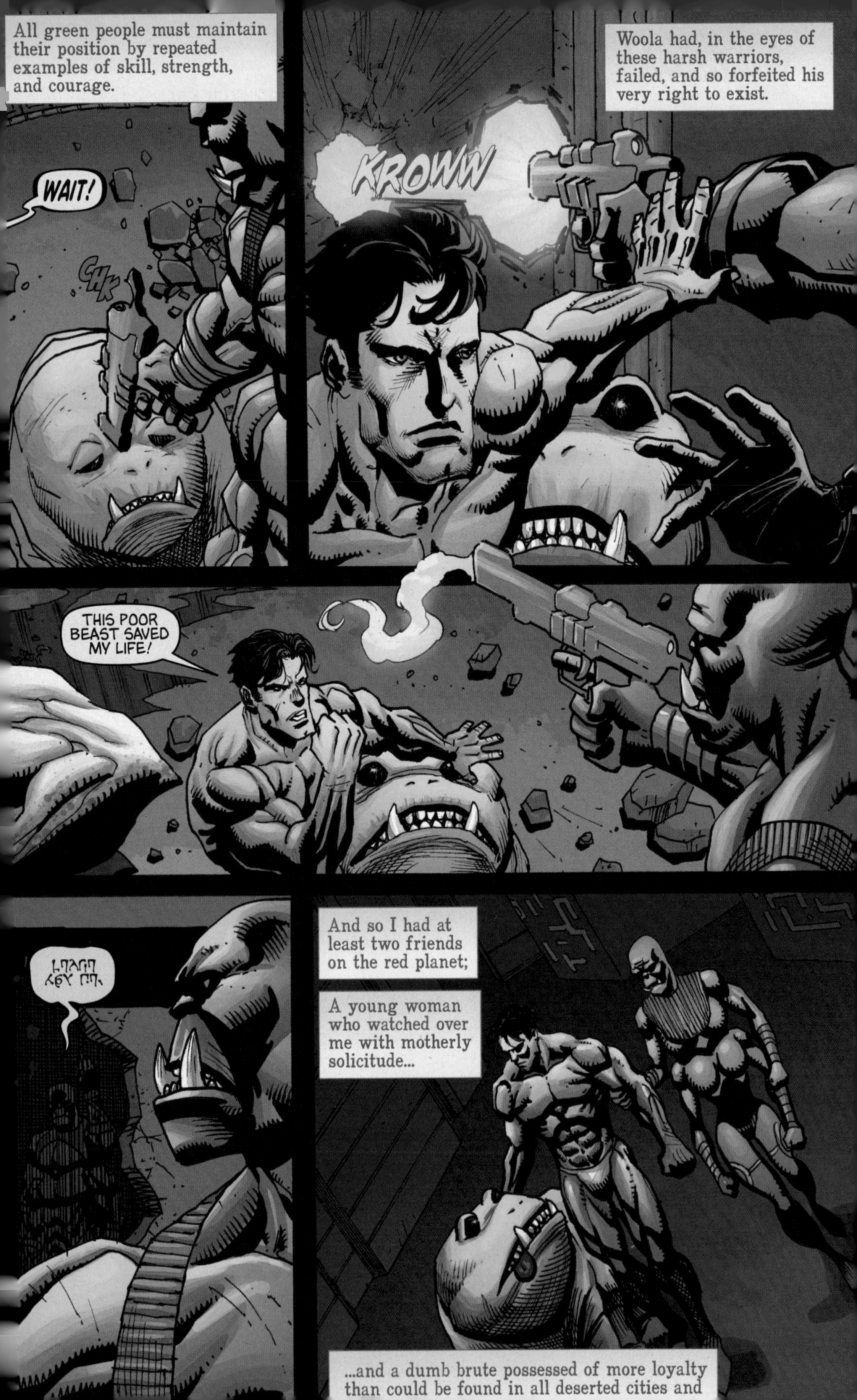
All green people must maintain their position by repeated examples of skill, strength, and courage.
WAIT!
CHK
Woola had, in the eyes of these harsh warriors, failed, and so forfeited his very right to exist.
KROWW
THIS POOR BEAST SAVED MY LIFE!
And so I had at least two friends on the red planet;
A young woman who watched over me with motherly solicitude...
...and a dumb brute possessed of more loyalty than could be found in all deserted cities and

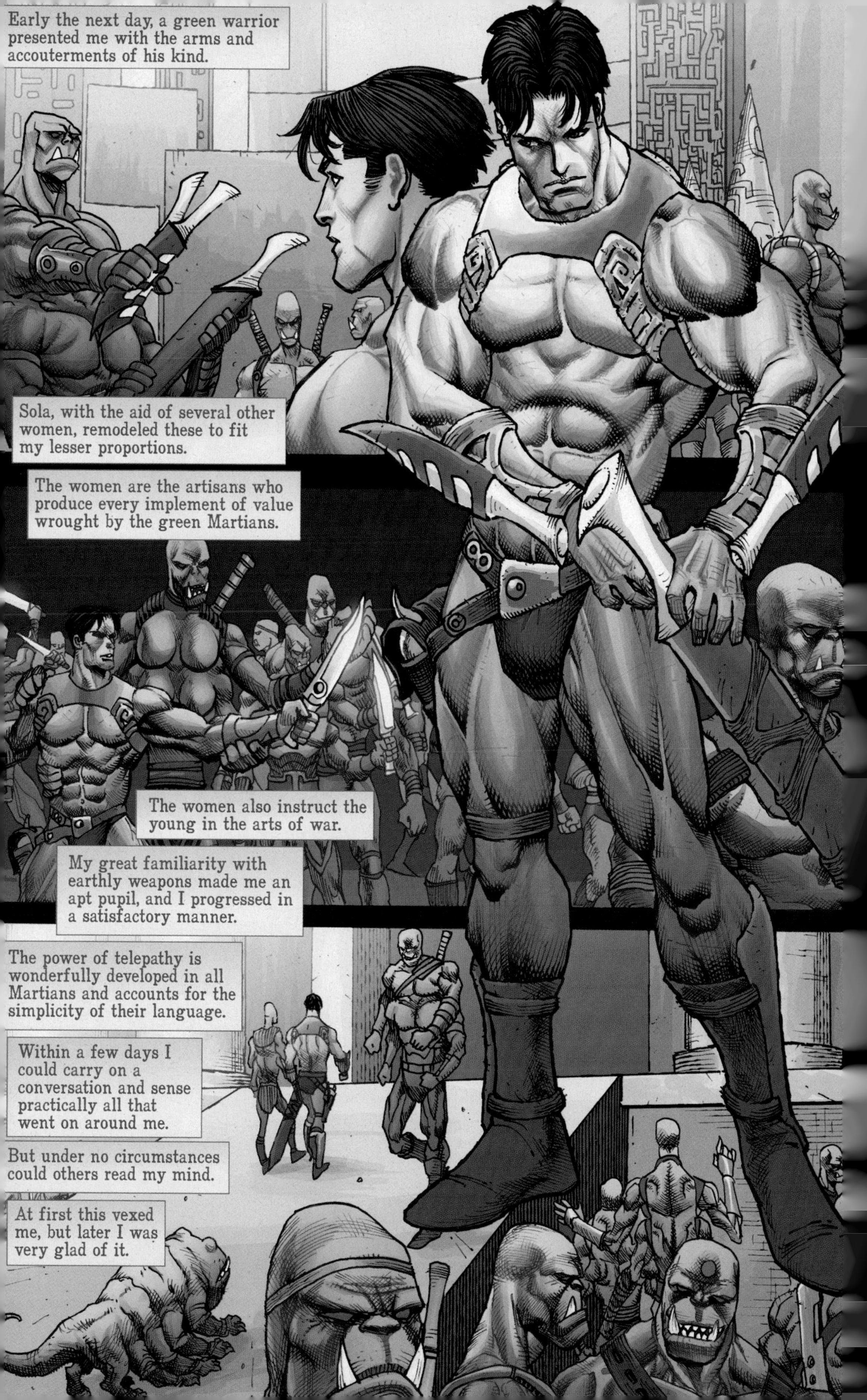
Early the next day, a green warrior presented me with the arms and accouterments of his kind.
Sola, with the aid of several other women, remodeled these to fit my lesser proportions.
The women are the artisans who produce every implement of value wrought by the green Martians.
The women also instruct the young in the arts of war.
My great familiarity with earthly weapons made me an apt pupil, and I progressed in a satisfactory manner.
The power of telepathy is wonderfully developed in all Martians and accounts for the simplicity of their language.
Within a few days I could carry on a conversation and sense practically all that went on around me.
But under no circumstances could others read my mind.
At first this vexed me, but later I was very glad of it.

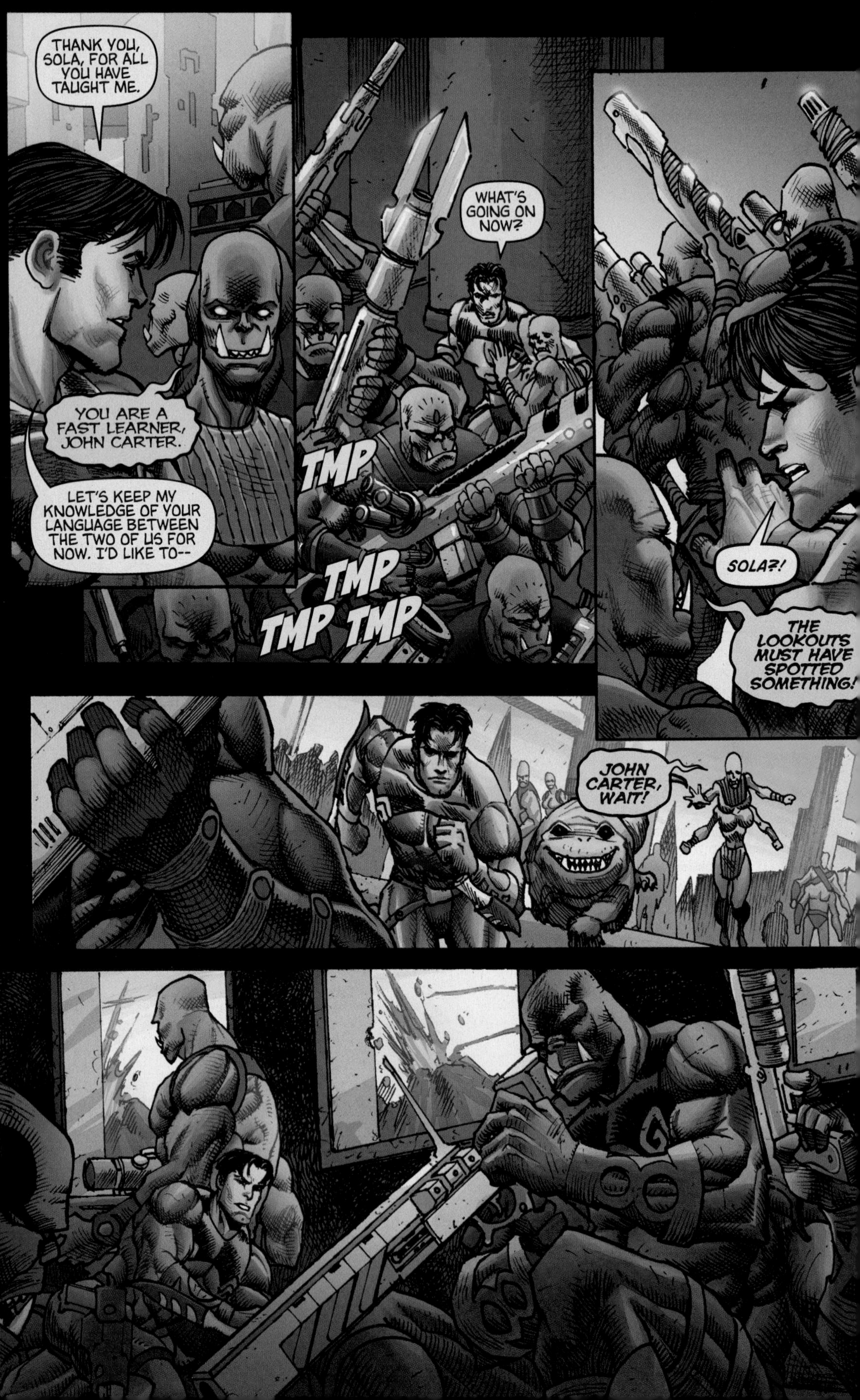
THANK YOU, SOLA, FOR ALL YOU HAVE TAUGHT ME.
YOU ARE A FAST LEARNER, JOHN CARTER.
LET'S KEEP MY KNOWLEDGE OF YOUR LANGUAGE BETWEEN THE TWO OF US FOR NOW. I'D LIKE TO--
WHAT'S GOING ON NOW?
TMP
TMP
TMP TMP
SOLA?!
THE LOOKOUTS MUST HAVE SPOTTED SOMETHING!
JOHN CARTER, WAIT!

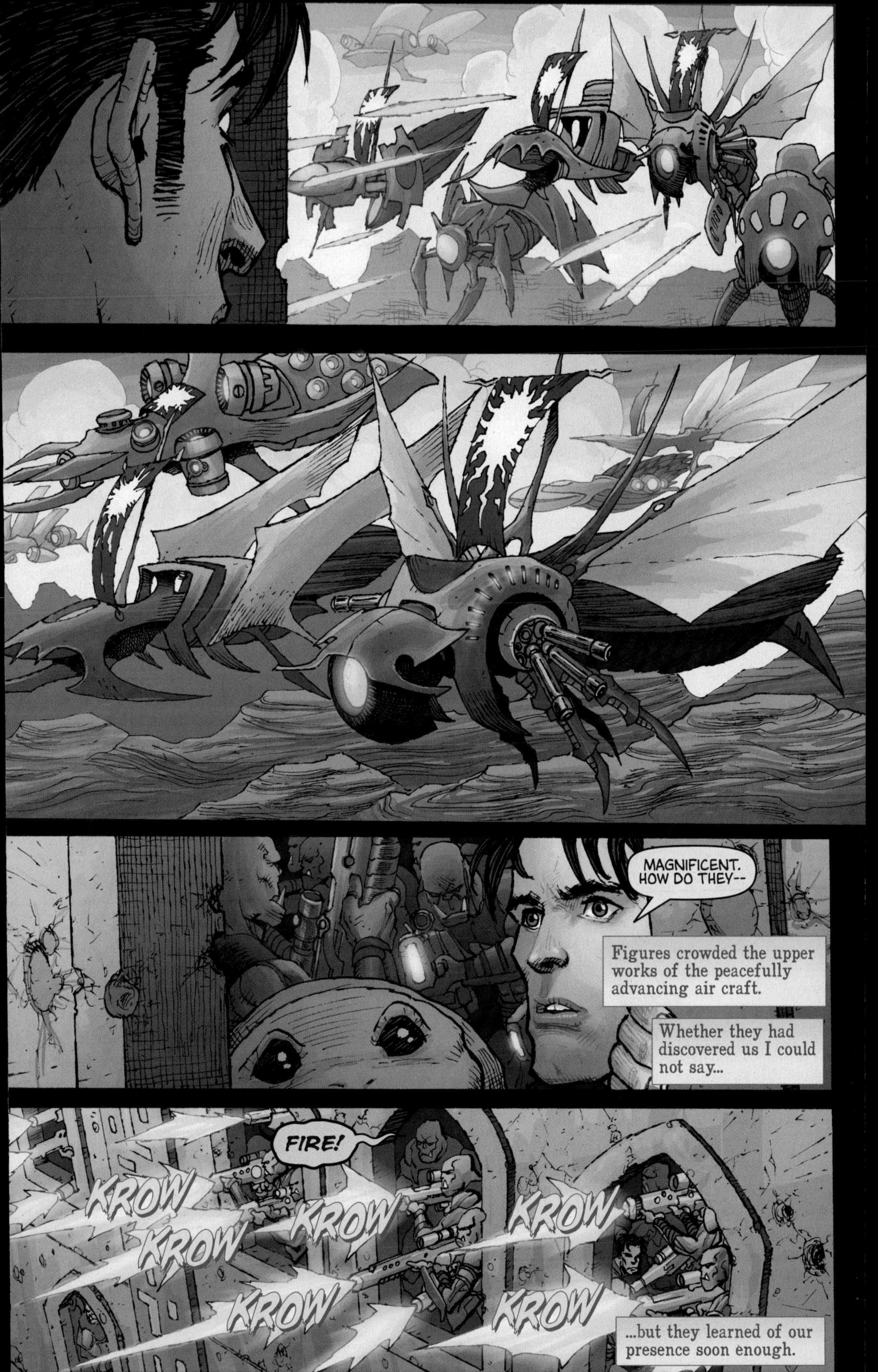
MAGNIFICENT. HOW DO THEY--
Figures crowded the upper works of the peacefully advancing air craft.
Whether they had discovered us I could not say...
FIRE!
KROW
KROW
KROW
KROW
KROW
KROW
...but they learned of our presence soon enough.

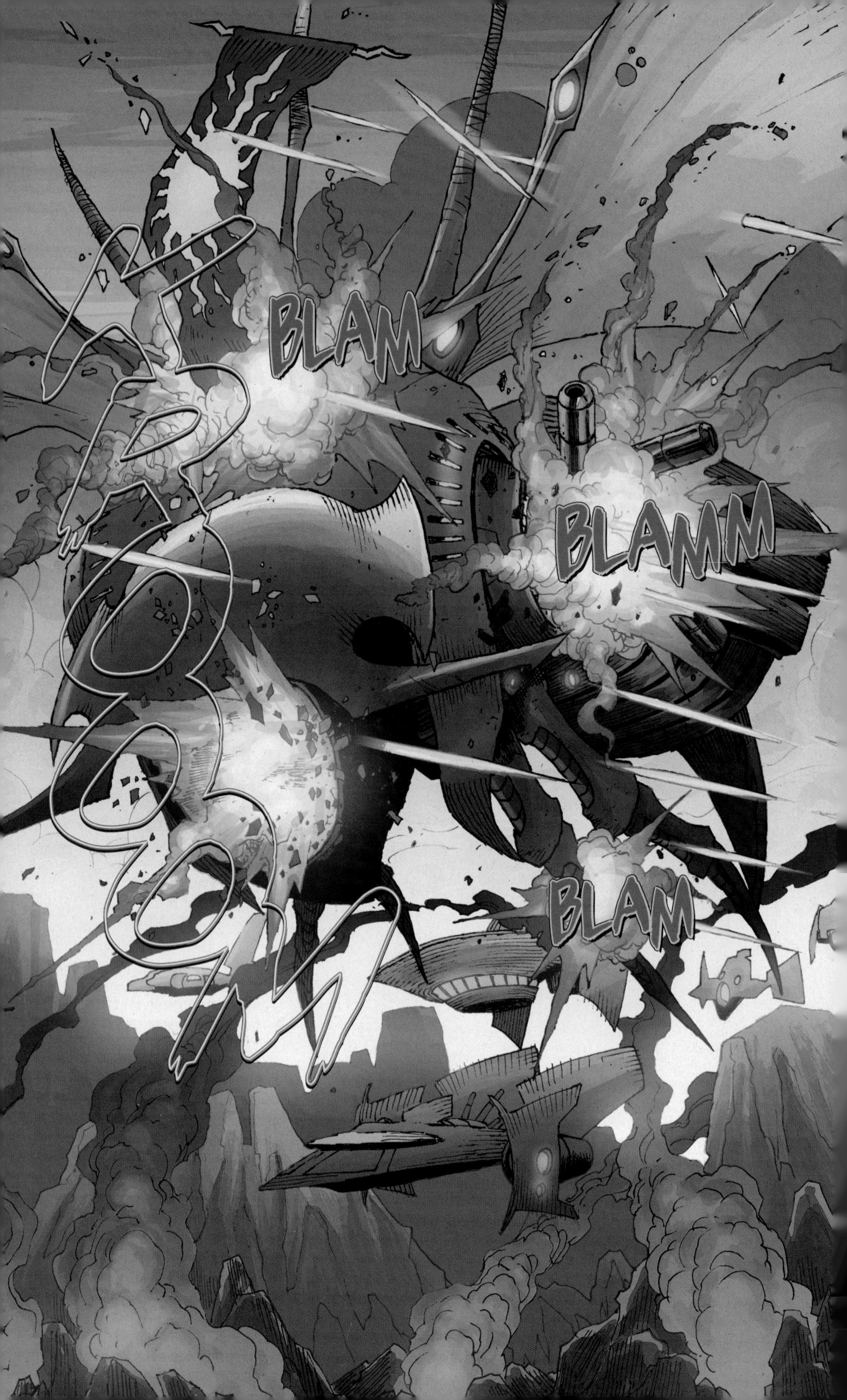
BLAM
BLAMM
BLAM

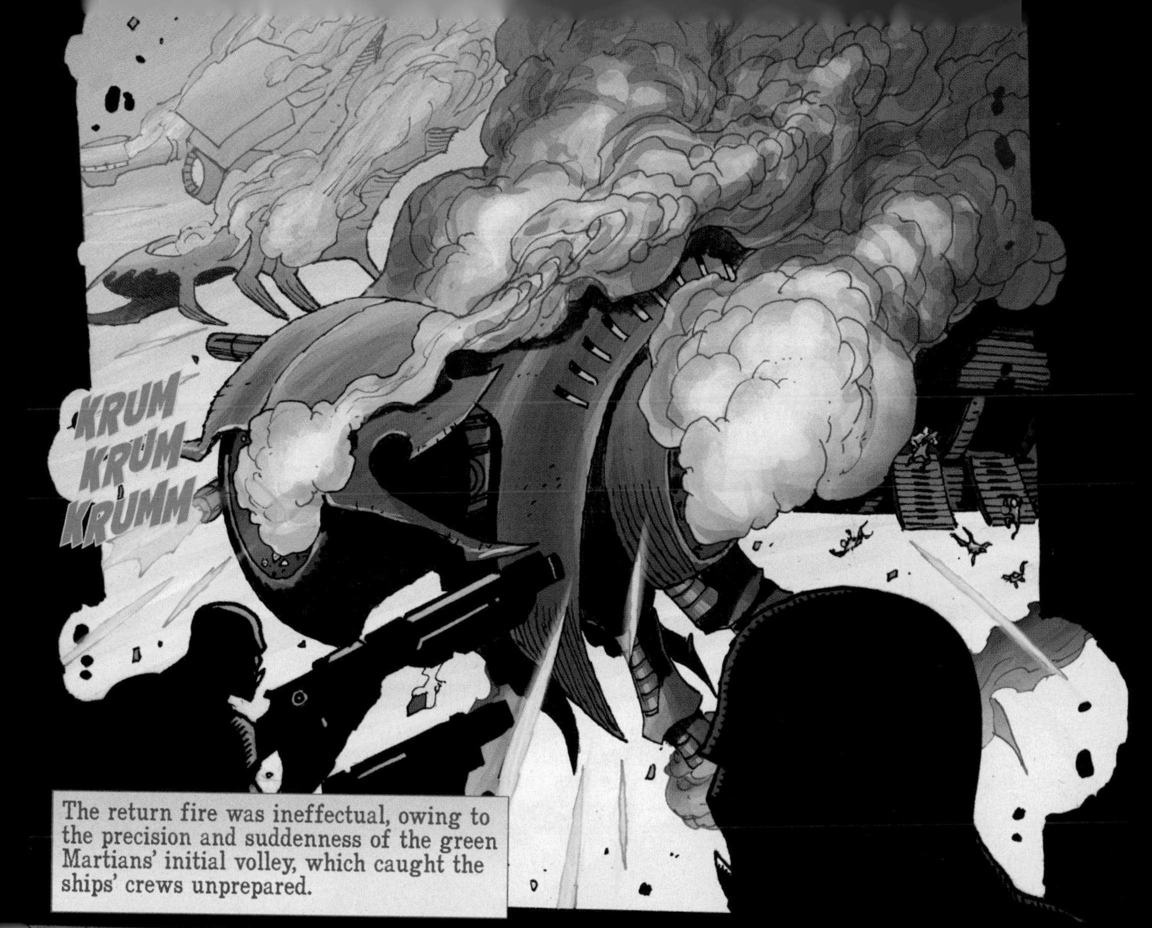
KRUM KRUM KRUMM
The return fire was ineffectual, owing to the precision and suddenness of the green Martians' initial volley, which caught the ships' crews unprepared.

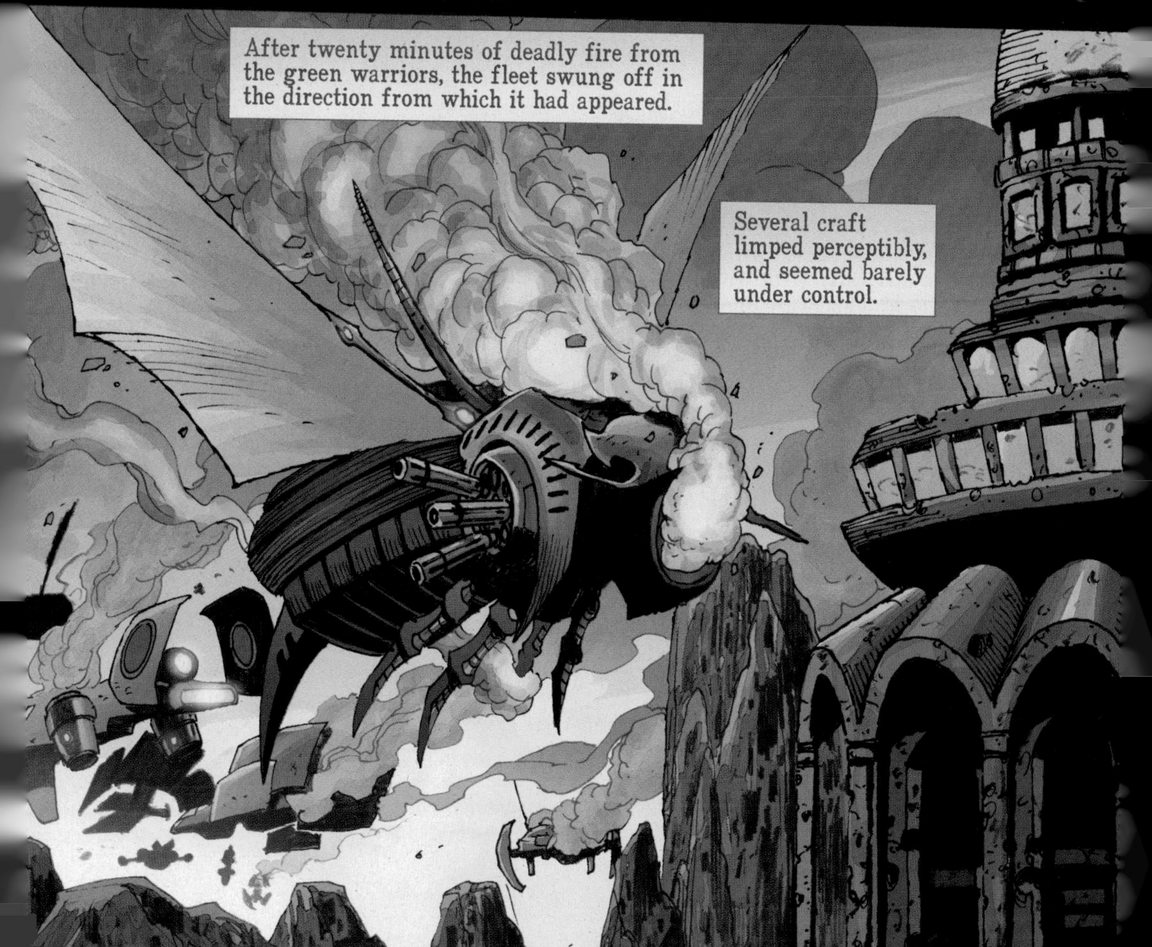
After twenty minutes of deadly fire from the green warriors, the fleet swung off in the direction from which it had appeared.
Several craft limped perceptibly, and seemed barely under control.

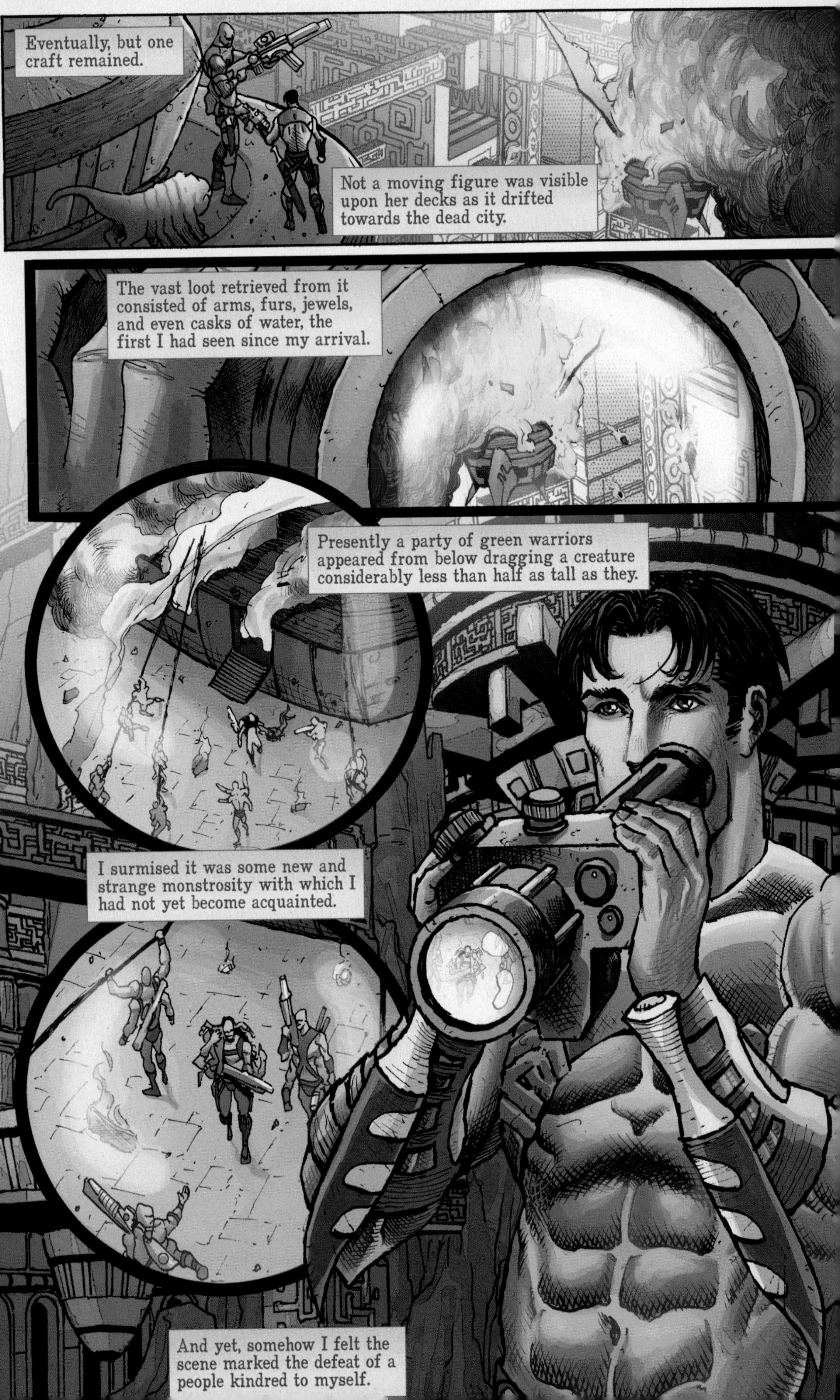
Eventually, but one craft remained.
Not a moving figure was visible upon her decks as it drifted towards the dead city.
The vast loot retrieved from it consisted of arms, furs, jewels, and even casks of water, the first I had seen since my arrival.
Presently a party of green warriors appeared from below dragging a creature considerably less than half as tall as they.
I surmised it was some new and strange monstrosity with which I had not yet become acquainted.
And yet, somehow I felt the scene marked the defeat of a people kindred to myself.

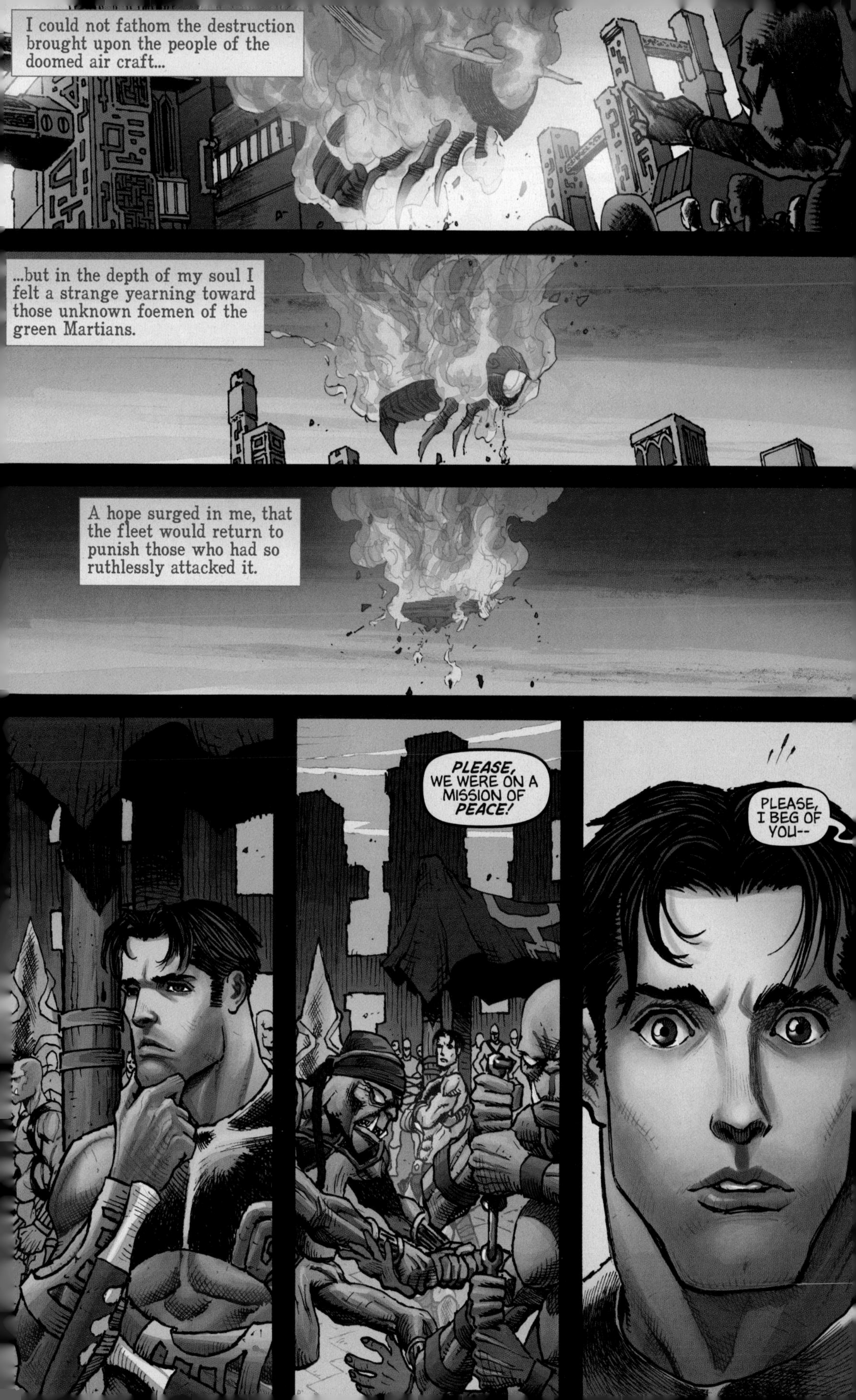
I could not fathom the destruction brought upon the people of the doomed air craft...
...but in the depth of my soul I felt a strange yearning toward those unknown foemen of the green Martians.
A hope surged in me, that the fleet would return to punish those who had so ruthlessly attacked it.
PLEASE, WE WERE ON A MISSION OF PEACE!
PLEASE, I BEG OF YOU--

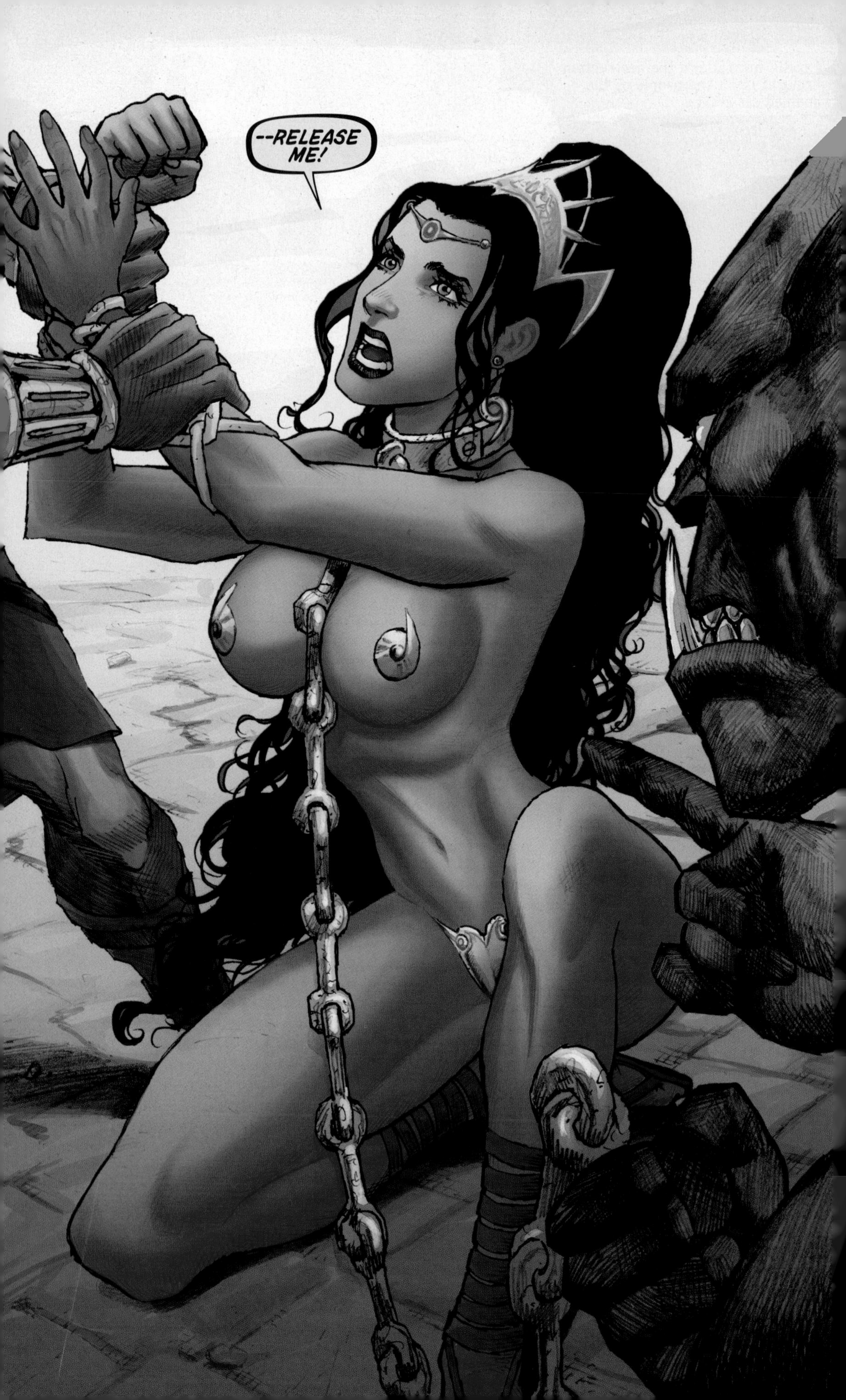
--RELEASE ME!

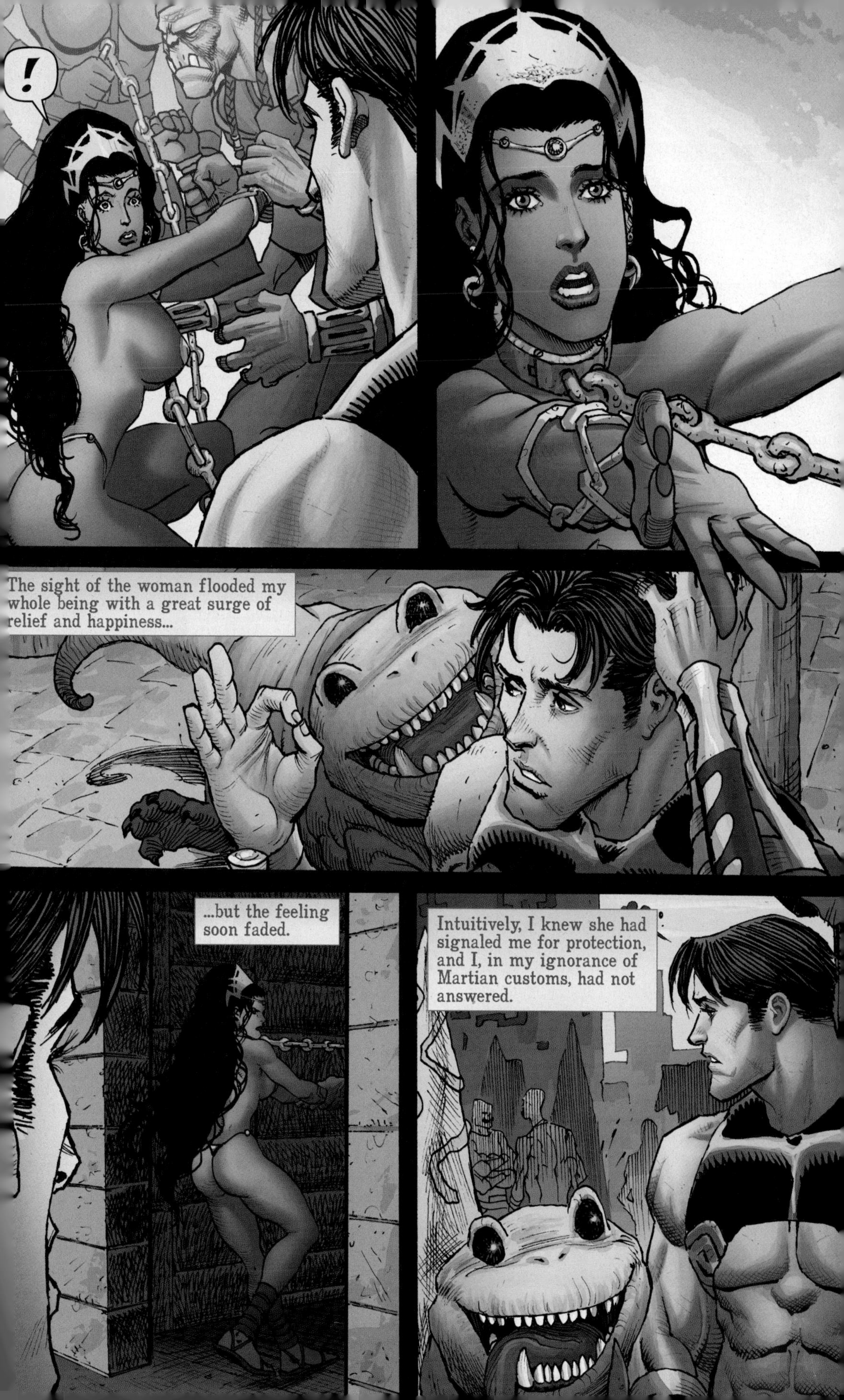
!
The sight of the woman flooded my whole being with a great surge of relief and happiness...
...but the feeling soon faded.
Intuitively, I knew she had signaled me for protection, and I, in my ignorance of Martian customs, had not answered.

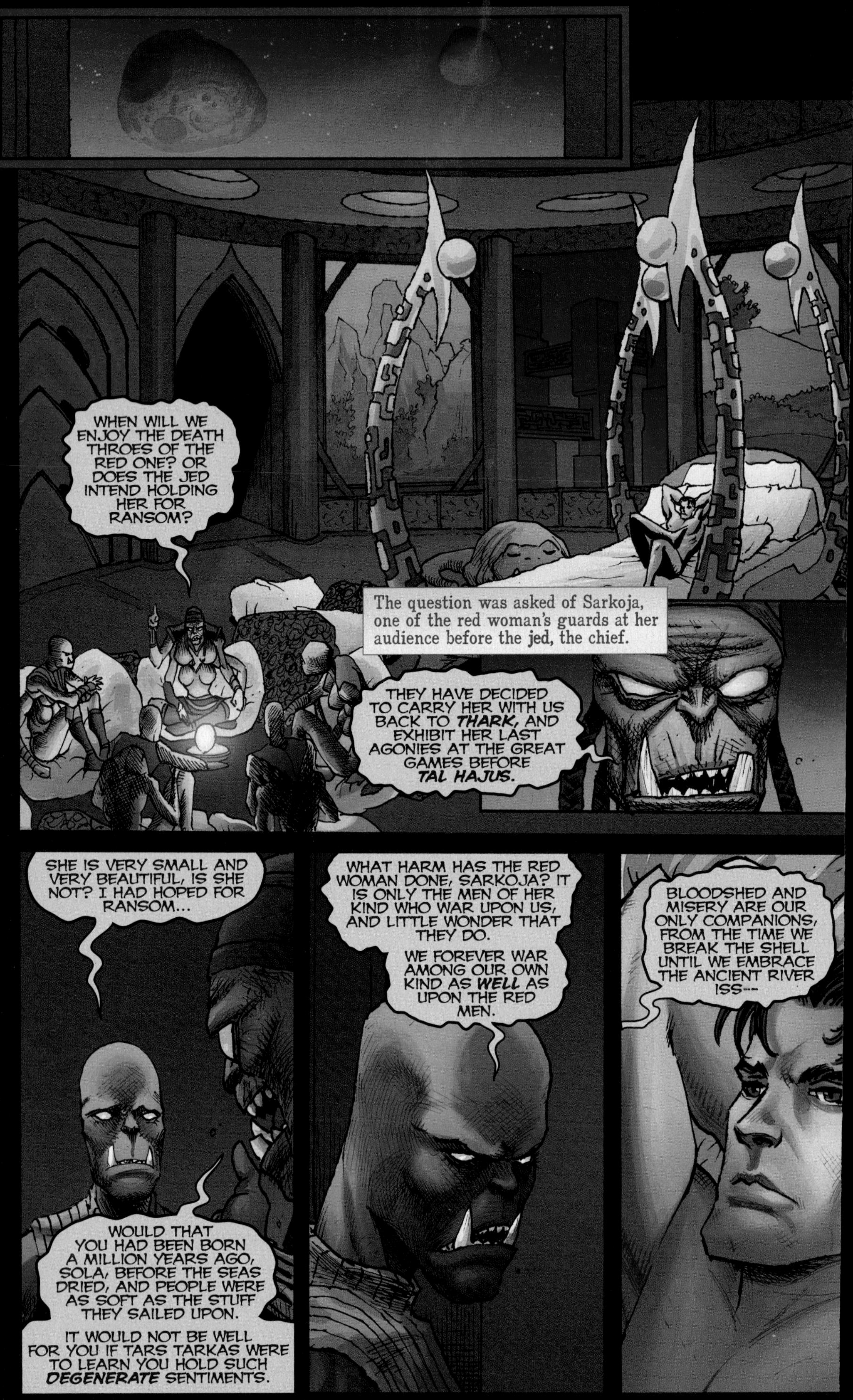

WHEN WILL WE ENJOY THE DEATH THROES OF THE RED ONE? OR DOES THE JED INTEND HOLDING HER FOR RANSOM?
The question was asked of Sarkoja, one of the red woman's guards at her audience before the jed, the chief.
THEY HAVE DECIDED TO CARRY HER WITH US BACK TO THARK, AND EXHIBIT HER LAST AGONIES AT THE GREAT GAMES BEFORE TAL HAJUS.
SHE IS VERY SMALL AND VERY BEAUTIFUL, IS SHE NOT? I HAD HOPED FOR RANSOM...
WOULD THAT YOU HAD BEEN BORN A MILLION YEARS AGO, SOLA, BEFORE THE SEAS DRIED, AND PEOPLE WERE AS SOFT AS THE STUFF THEY SAILED UPON.
IT WOULD NOT BE WELL FOR YOU IF TARS TARKAS WERE TO LEARN YOU HOLD SUCH DEGENERATE SENTIMENTS.
WHAT HARM HAS THE RED WOMAN DONE, SARKOJA? IT IS ONLY THE MEN OF HER KIND WHO WAR UPON US, AND LITTLE WONDER THAT THEY DO.
WE FOREVER WAR AMONG OUR OWN KIND AS WELL AS UPON THE RED MEN.
BLOODSHED AND MISERY ARE OUR ONLY COMPANIONS, FROM THE TIME WE BREAK THE SHELL UNTIL WE EMBRACE THE ANCIENT RIVER ISS--

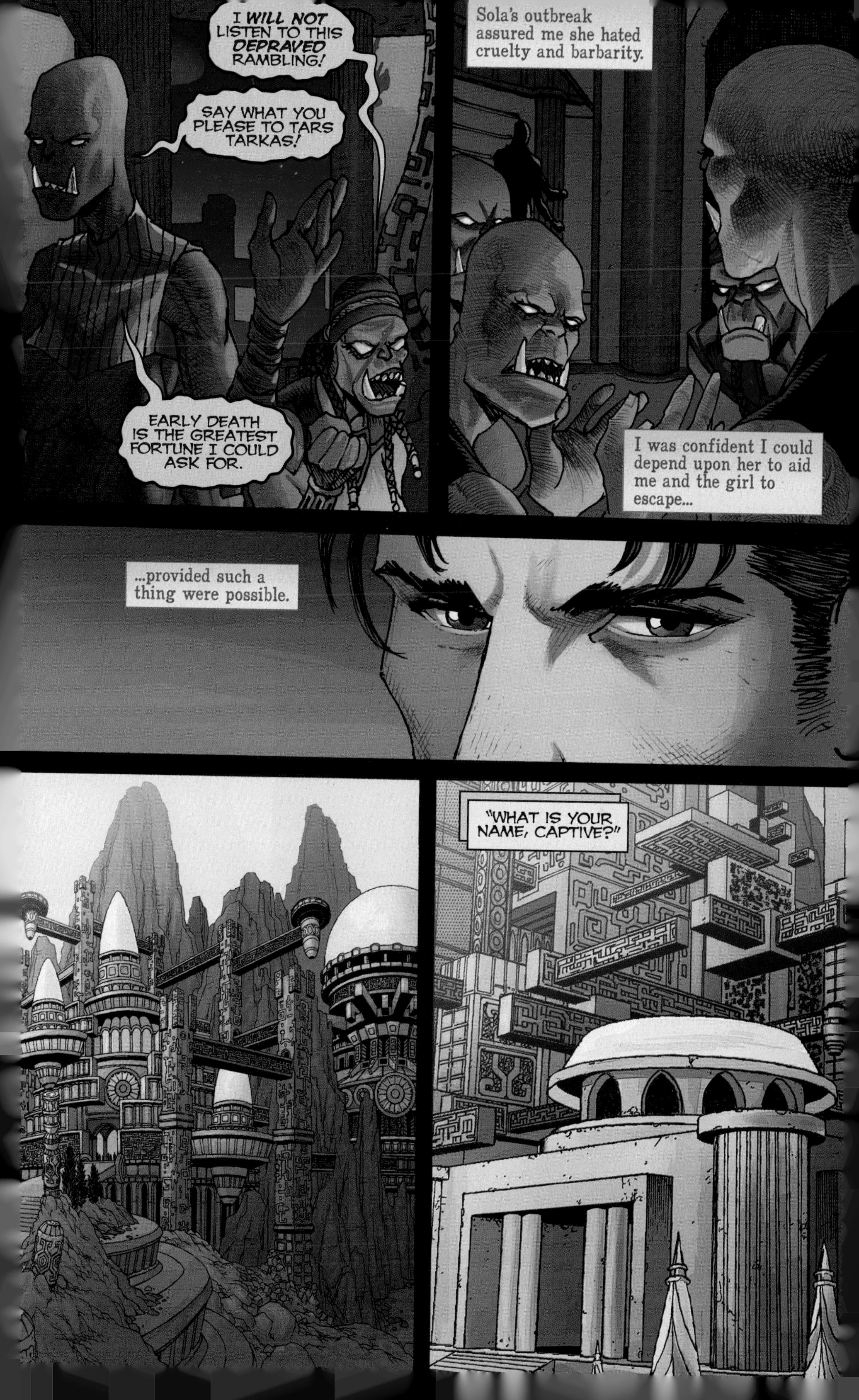

I WILL NOT LISTEN TO THIS DEPRAVED RAMBLING!
SAY WHAT YOU PLEASE TO TARS TARKAS!
EARLY DEATH IS THE GREATEST FORTUNE I COULD ASK FOR.
Sola's outbreak assured me she hated cruelty and barbarity.
I was confident I could depend upon her to aid me and the girl to escape...
...provided such a thing were possible.
"WHAT IS YOUR NAME, CAPTIVE?"

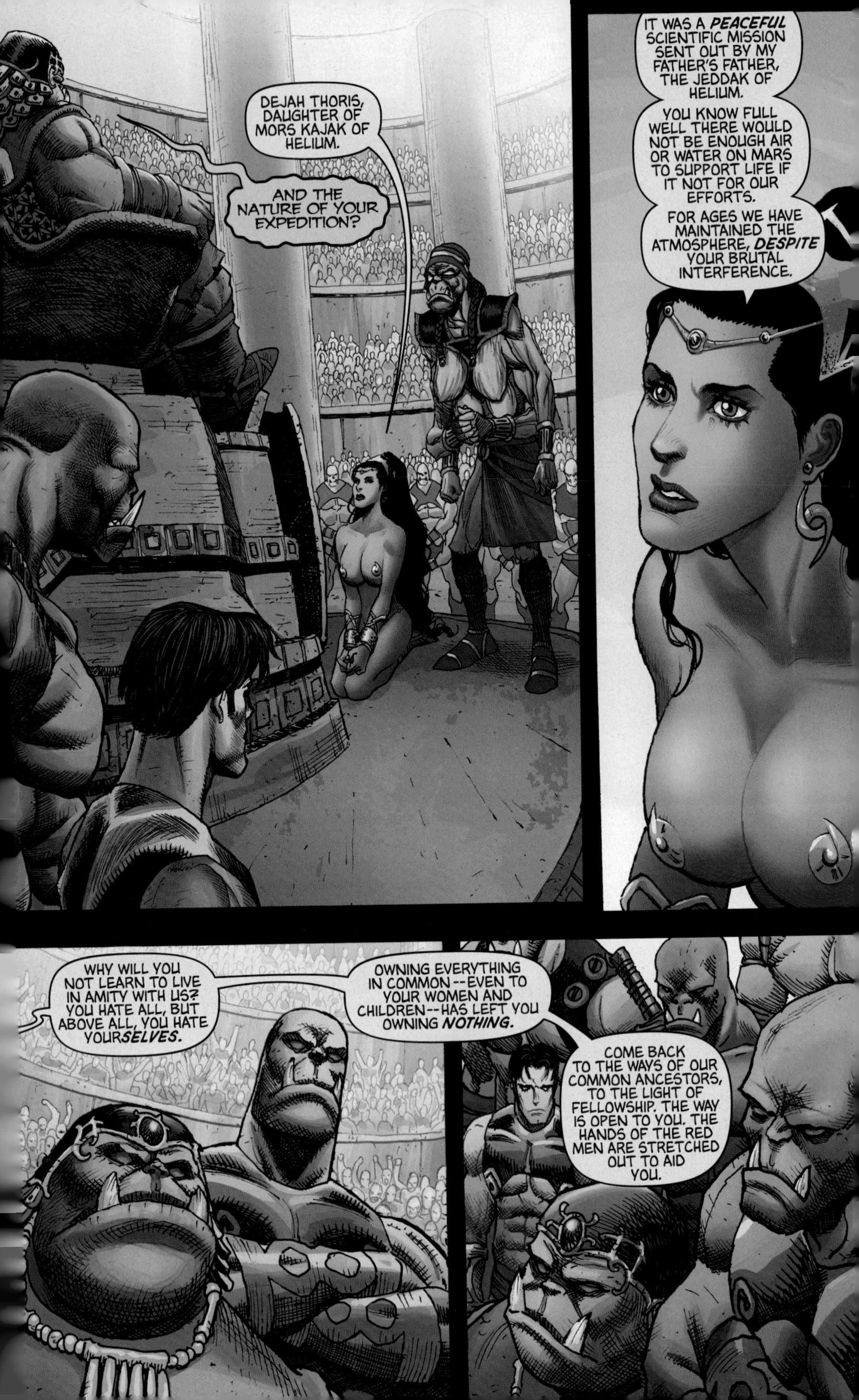
DEJAH THORIS, DAUGHTER OF MORS KAJAK OF HELIUM.
AND THE NATURE OF YOUR EXPEDITION?
IT WAS A *PEACEFUL* SCIENTIFIC MISSION SENT OUT BY MY FATHER'S FATHER, THE JEDDAK OF HELIUM.
YOU KNOW FULL WELL THERE WOULD NOT BE ENOUGH AIR OR WATER ON MARS TO SUPPORT LIFE IF IT NOT FOR OUR EFFORTS.
FOR AGES WE HAVE MAINTAINED THE ATMOSPHERE, *DESPITE* YOUR BRUTAL INTERFERENCE.
WHY WILL YOU NOT LEARN TO LIVE IN AMITY WITH US? YOU HATE ALL, BUT ABOVE ALL, YOU HATE YOUR*SELVES*.
OWNING EVERYTHING IN COMMON--EVEN TO YOUR WOMEN AND CHILDREN--HAS LEFT YOU OWNING *NOTHING*.
COME BACK TO THE WAYS OF OUR COMMON ANCESTORS, TO THE LIGHT OF FELLOWSHIP. THE WAY IS OPEN TO YOU. THE HANDS OF THE RED MEN ARE STRETCHED OUT TO AID YOU.

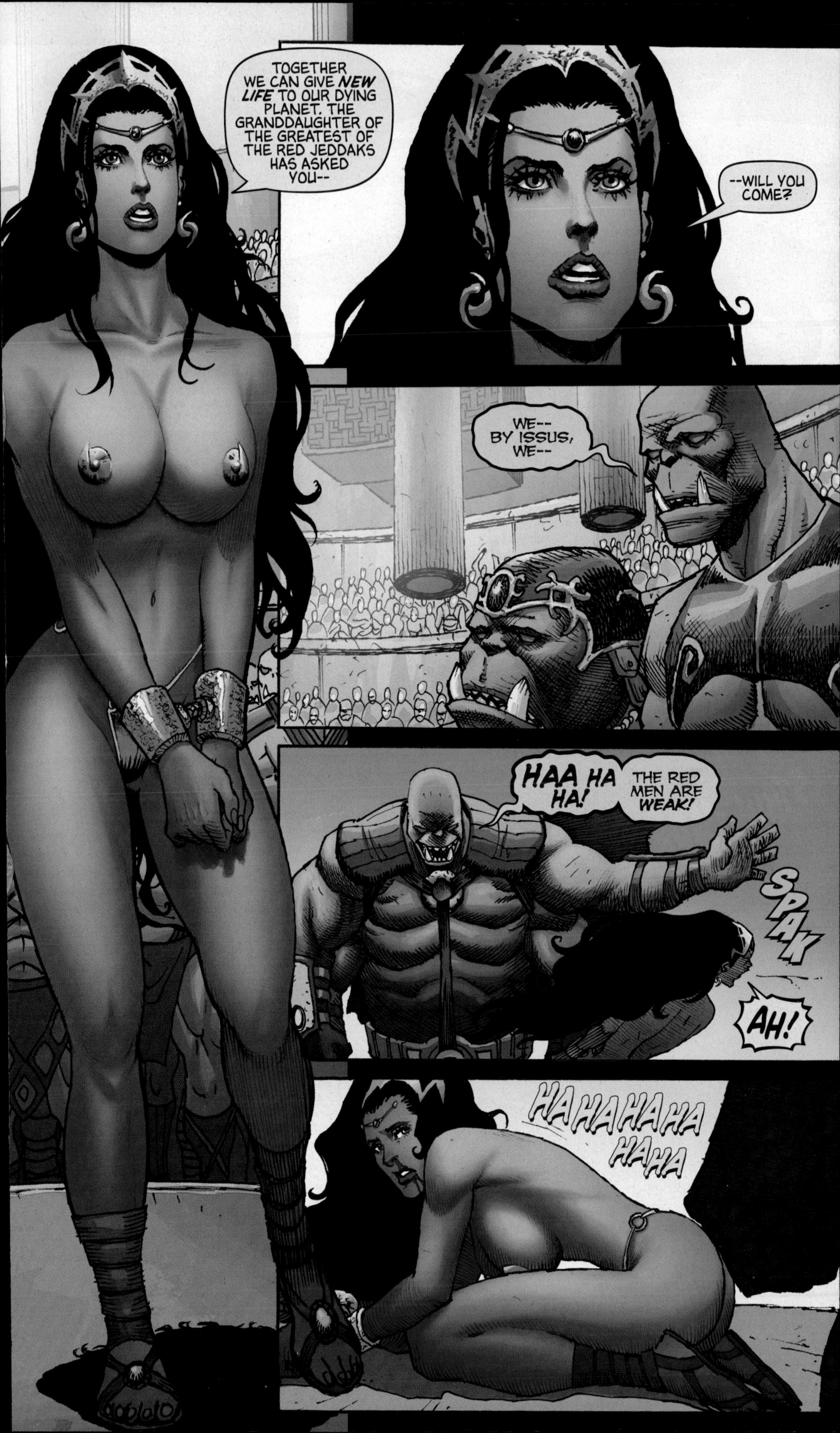
TOGETHER WE CAN GIVE NEW LIFE TO OUR DYING PLANET. THE GRANDDAUGHTER OF THE GREATEST OF THE RED JEDDAKS HAS ASKED YOU--
--WILL YOU COME?
WE-- BY ISSUS, WE--
HAAA HA HA!
THE RED MEN ARE WEAK!
SPAK
AH!
HAHAHAHAHA HAHA

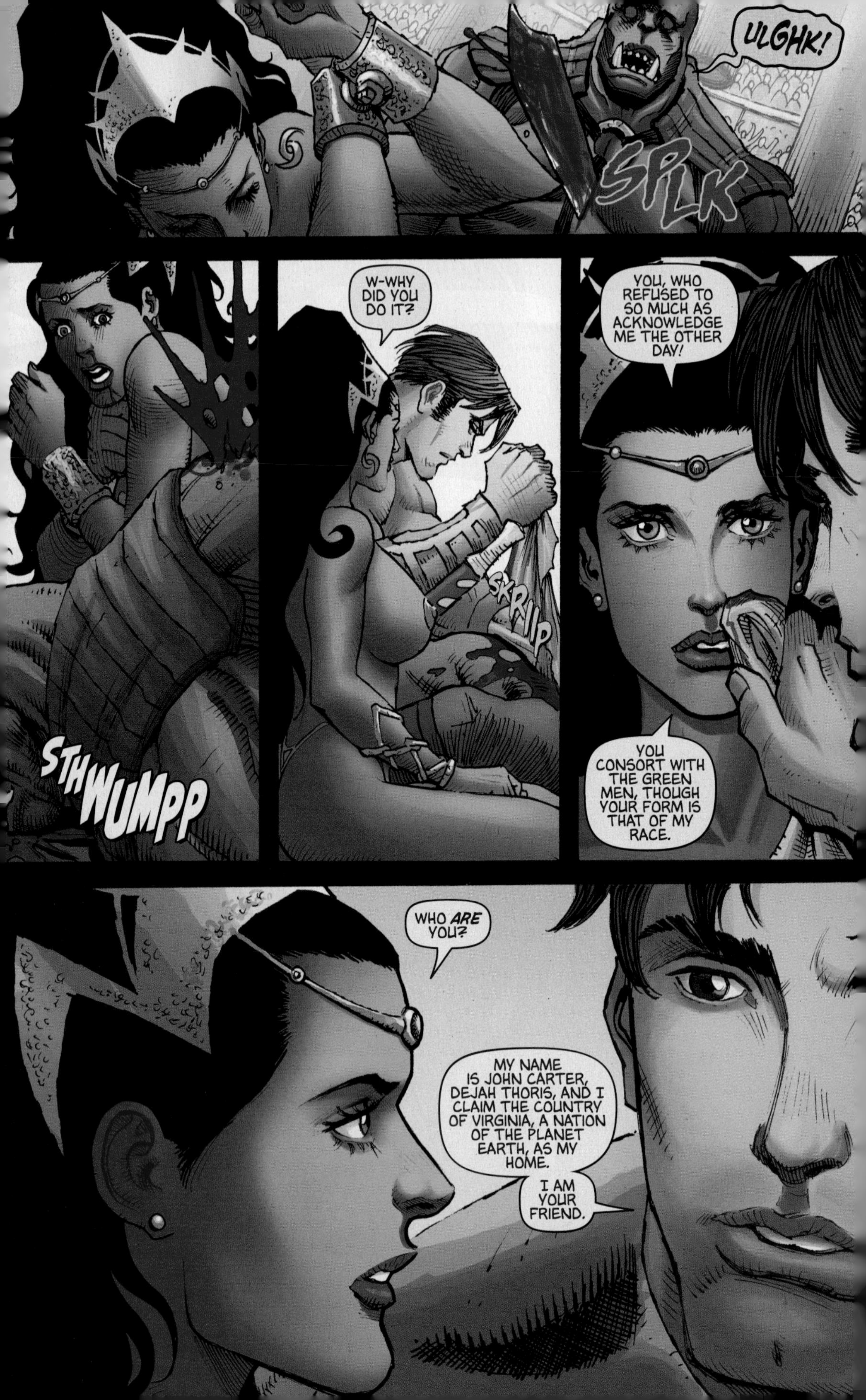
ULGHK!
SPLK
STHWUMPP
W-WHY DID YOU DO IT?
SKRIIP
YOU, WHO REFUSED TO SO MUCH AS ACKNOWLEDGE ME THE OTHER DAY!
YOU CONSORT WITH THE GREEN MEN, THOUGH YOUR FORM IS THAT OF MY RACE.
WHO *ARE* YOU?
MY NAME IS JOHN CARTER, DEJAH THORIS, AND I CLAIM THE COUNTRY OF VIRGINIA, A NATION OF THE PLANET EARTH, AS MY HOME.
I AM YOUR FRIEND.

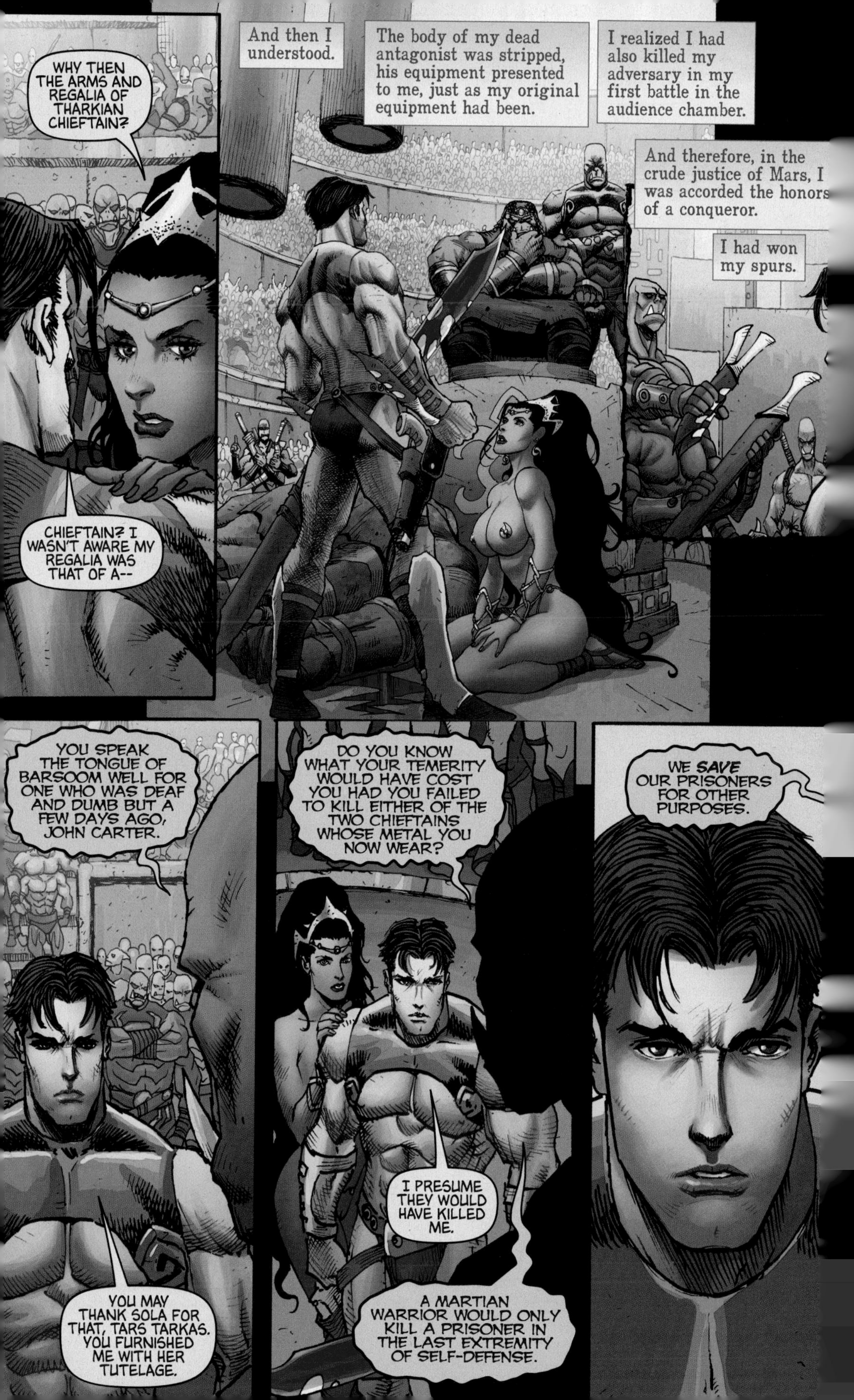
WHY THEN THE ARMS AND REGALIA OF THARKIAN CHIEFTAIN?
CHIEFTAIN? I WASN'T AWARE MY REGALIA WAS THAT OF A--
And then I understood.
The body of my dead antagonist was stripped, his equipment presented to me, just as my original equipment had been.
I realized I had also killed my adversary in my first battle in the audience chamber.
And therefore, in the crude justice of Mars, I was accorded the honors of a conqueror.
I had won my spurs.
YOU SPEAK THE TONGUE OF BARSOOM WELL FOR ONE WHO WAS DEAF AND DUMB BUT A FEW DAYS AGO, JOHN CARTER.
YOU MAY THANK SOLA FOR THAT, TARS TARKAS. YOU FURNISHED ME WITH HER TUTELAGE.
DO YOU KNOW WHAT YOUR TEMERITY WOULD HAVE COST YOU HAD YOU FAILED TO KILL EITHER OF THE TWO CHIEFTAINS WHOSE METAL YOU NOW WEAR?
I PRESUME THEY WOULD HAVE KILLED ME.
A MARTIAN WARRIOR WOULD ONLY KILL A PRISONER IN THE LAST EXTREMITY OF SELF-DEFENSE.
WE SAVE OUR PRISONERS FOR OTHER PURPOSES.

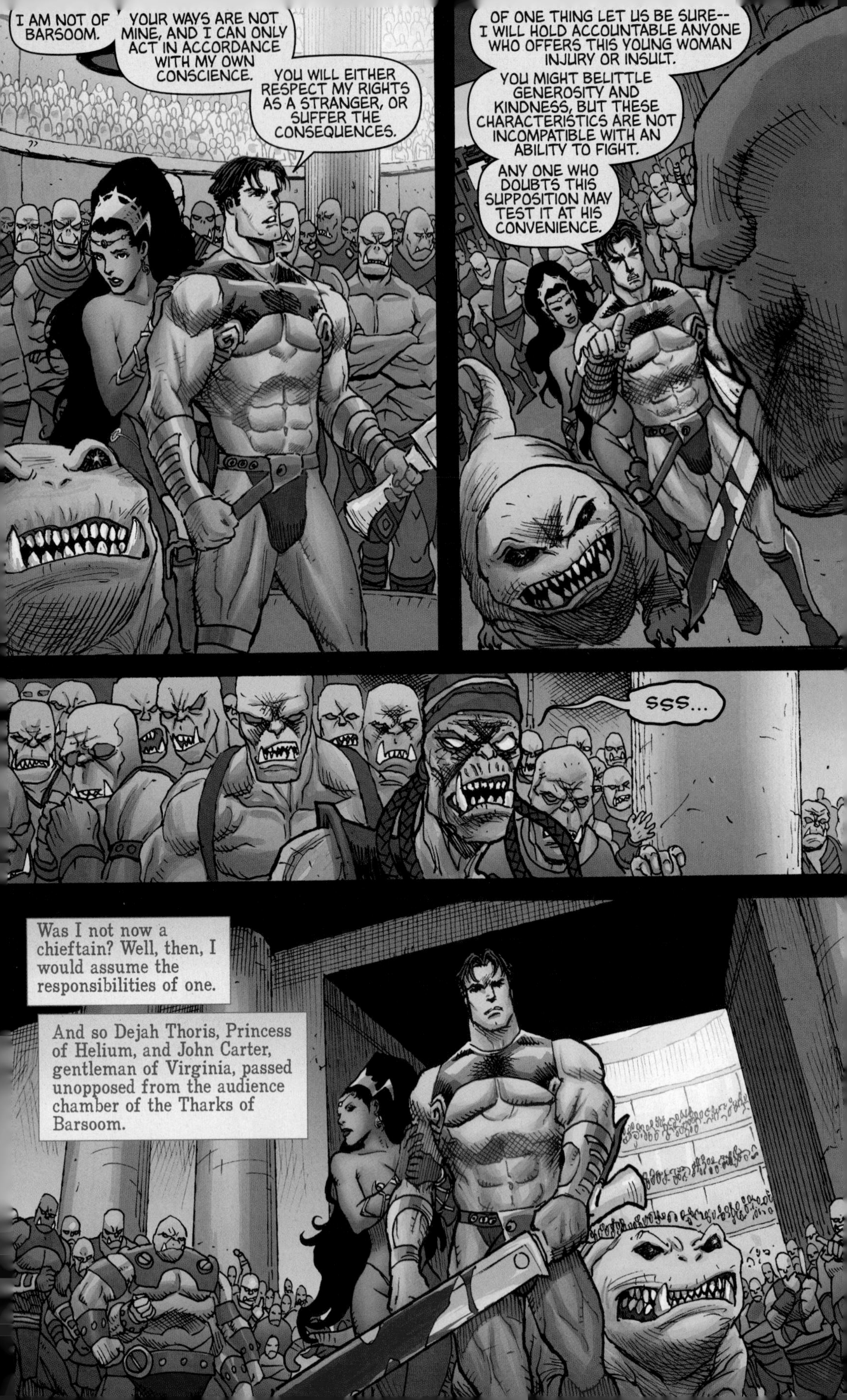
I AM NOT OF BARSOOM.
YOUR WAYS ARE NOT MINE, AND I CAN ONLY ACT IN ACCORDANCE WITH MY OWN CONSCIENCE.
YOU WILL EITHER RESPECT MY RIGHTS AS A STRANGER, OR SUFFER THE CONSEQUENCES.
OF ONE THING LET US BE SURE-- I WILL HOLD ACCOUNTABLE ANYONE WHO OFFERS THIS YOUNG WOMAN INJURY OR INSULT.
YOU MIGHT BELITTLE GENEROSITY AND KINDNESS, BUT THESE CHARACTERISTICS ARE NOT INCOMPATIBLE WITH AN ABILITY TO FIGHT.
ANY ONE WHO DOUBTS THIS SUPPOSITION MAY TEST IT AT HIS CONVENIENCE.
SSS...
Was I not now a chieftain? Well, then, I would assume the responsibilities of one.
And so Dejah Thoris, Princess of Helium, and John Carter, gentleman of Virginia, passed unopposed from the audience chamber of the Tharks of Barsoom.

WARLORD OF MARS

No. 5 ——————— 3.99

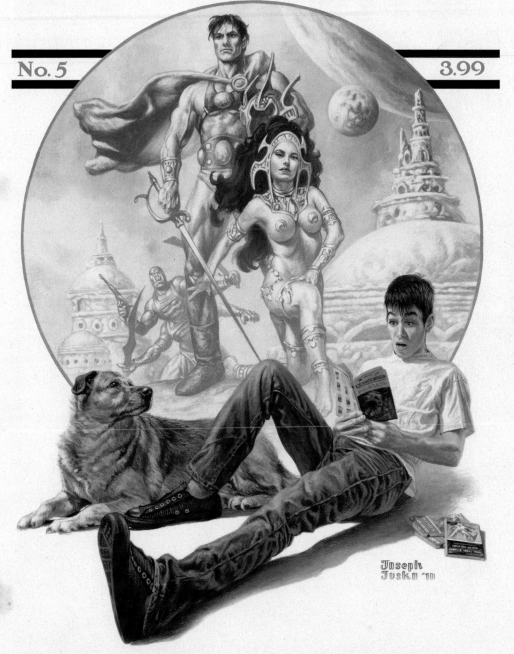

Arvid Nelson--Lui Antonio--Adriano Lucas--Troy Peteri

A DUEL TO THE DEATH

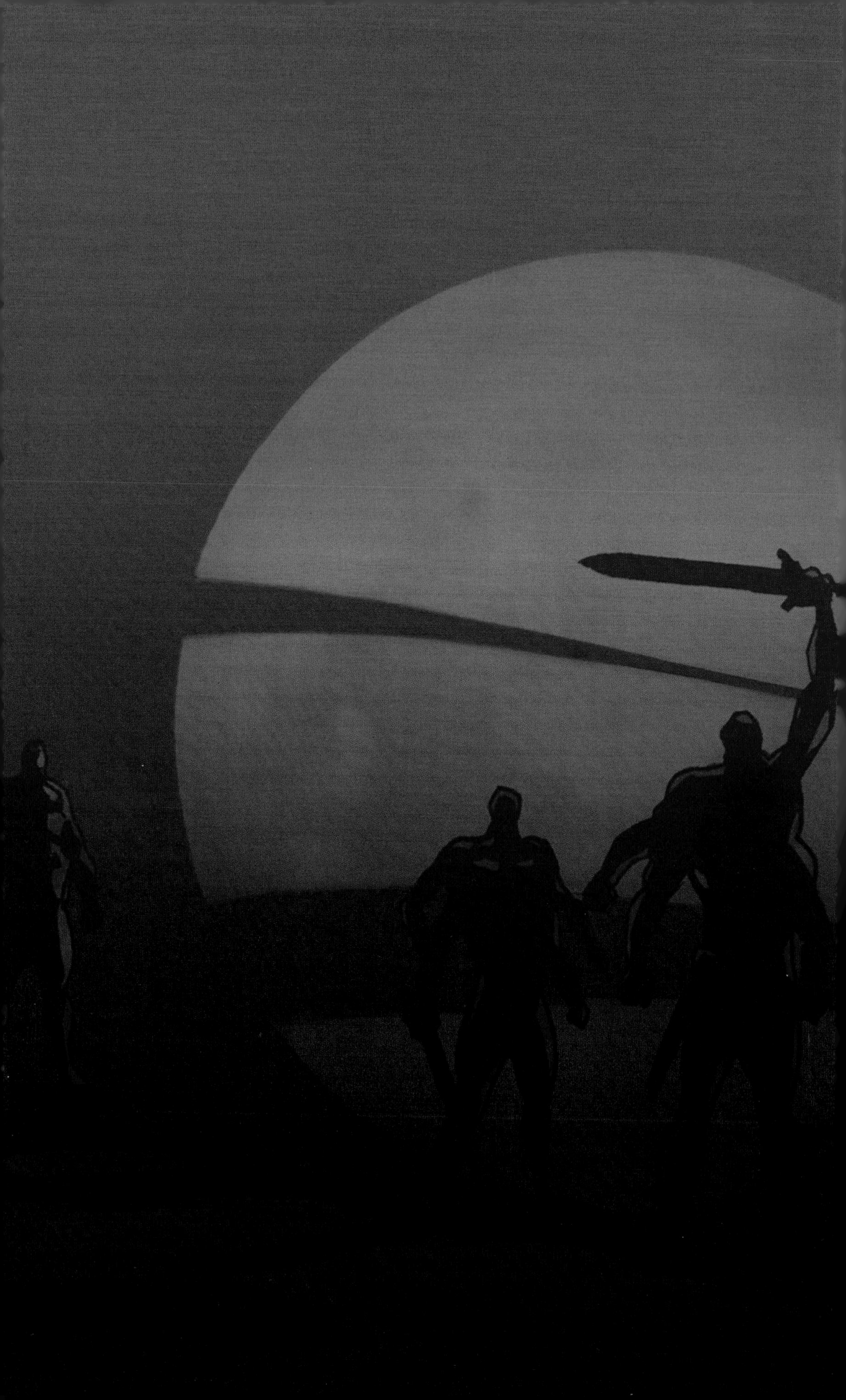

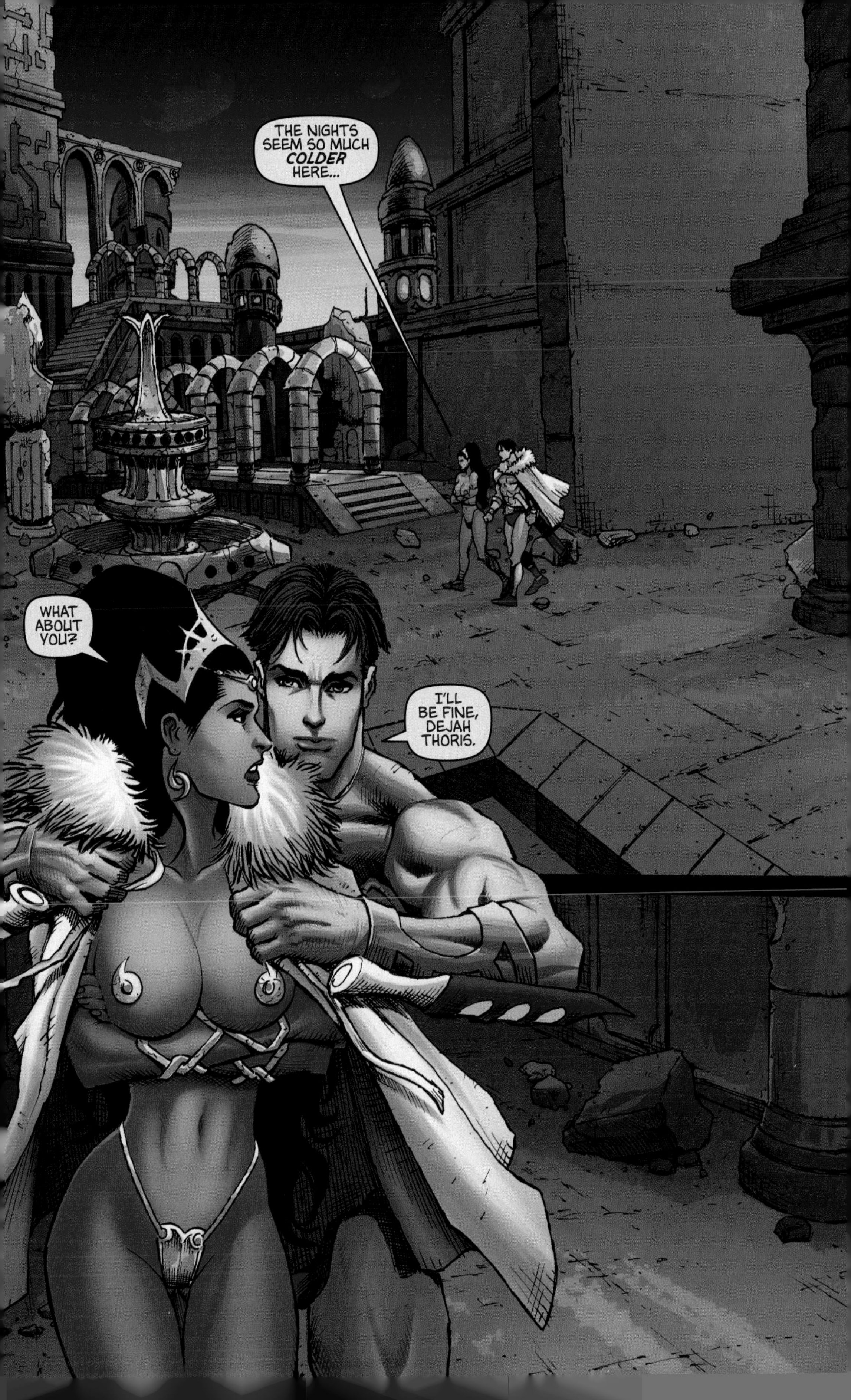
THE NIGHTS SEEM SO MUCH COLDER HERE...
WHAT ABOUT YOU?
I'LL BE FINE, DEJAH THORIS.

YOU HAVE GAINED QUITE AN ENTOURAGE, JOHN CARTER.

HAH.

YOU ARE A GREAT CHIEFTAIN AMONG THE GREEN MEN NOW!

AND YET, I'M STILL A PRISONER. WE BOTH ARE.

BUT I HAVE ENTRUSTED YOUR CARE TO SOLA, DEJAH THORIS. YOU WILL BE SAFE WITH HER.

THE OTHER FEMALE-- SARKOJA. SHE HATES ME. BUT SHE HATES YOU EVEN MORE.

I CAN DEAL WITH SARKOJA.

DON'T WORRY YOURSELF ABOUT THAT.

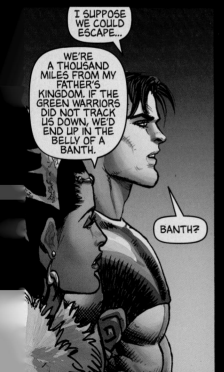

I SUPPOSE WE COULD ESCAPE...

WE'RE A THOUSAND MILES FROM MY FATHER'S KINGDOM. IF THE GREEN WARRIORS DID NOT TRACK US DOWN, WE'D END UP IN THE BELLY OF A BANTH.

BANTH?

THANK YOU, JOHN CARTER, FOR PROTECTING ME. FORGIVE ME FOR THE CRUEL THOUGHTS I HARBORED AGAINST YOU THESE PAST FEW DAYS.

IT'S NOTHING--

WHAT I CANNOT FATHOM IS THAT CLAIM TO BE NOT OF BARSOOM.

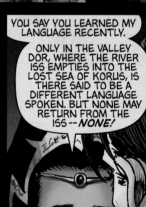

YOU SAY YOU LEARNED MY LANGUAGE RECENTLY.

ONLY IN THE VALLEY DOR, WHERE THE RIVER ISS EMPTIES INTO THE LOST SEA OF KORUS, IS THERE SAID TO BE A DIFFERENT LANGUAGE SPOKEN. BUT NONE MAY RETURN FROM THE ISS--NONE!

THEY WOULD KILL YOU HORRIBLY ANYWHERE ON BARSOOM IF THAT WERE TRUE!

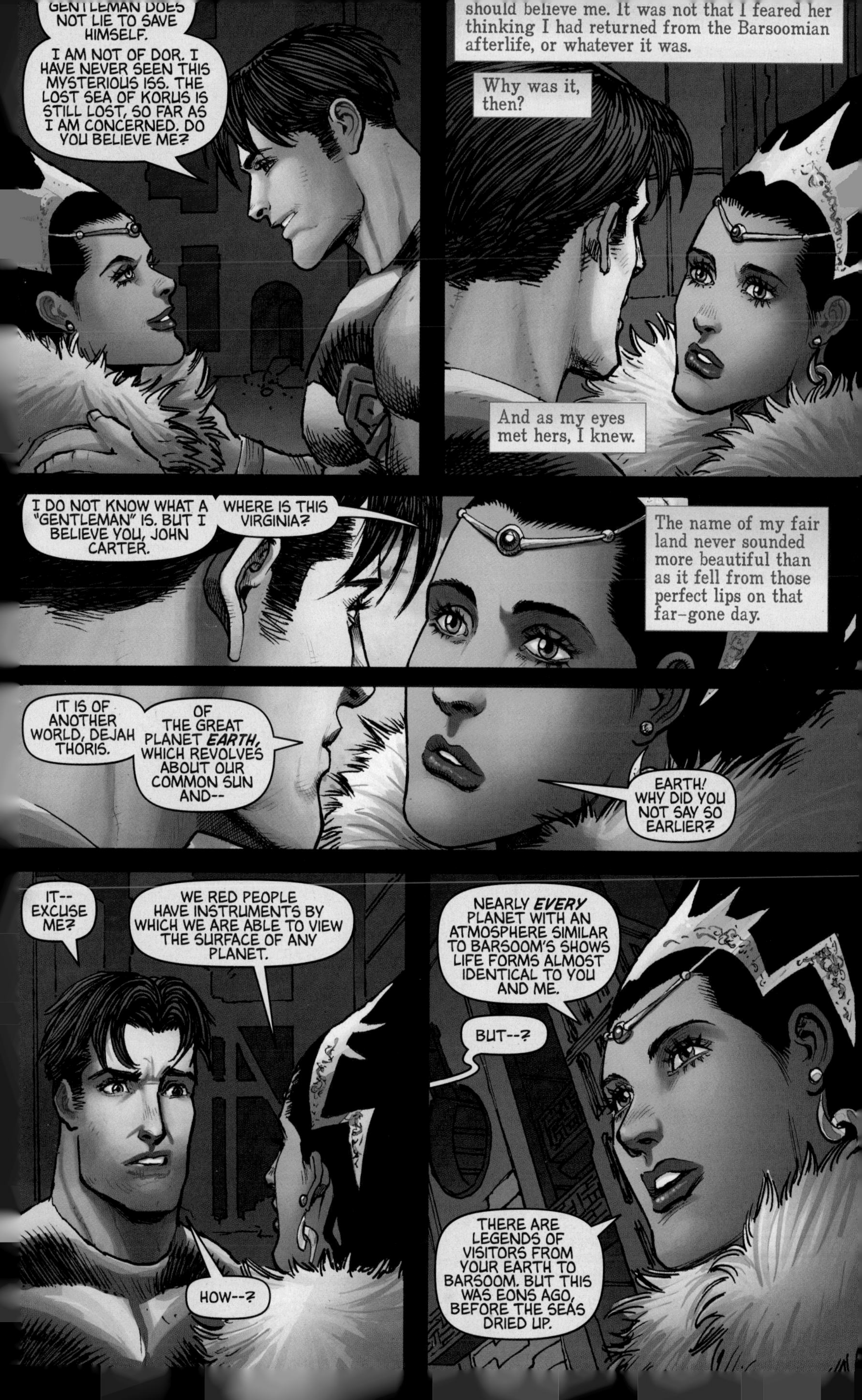
GENTLEMAN DOES NOT LIE TO SAVE HIMSELF.
I AM NOT OF DOR. I HAVE NEVER SEEN THIS MYSTERIOUS ISS. THE LOST SEA OF KORUS IS STILL LOST, SO FAR AS I AM CONCERNED. DO YOU BELIEVE ME?
should believe me. It was not that I feared her thinking I had returned from the Barsoomian afterlife, or whatever it was.
Why was it, then?
And as my eyes met hers, I knew.
I DO NOT KNOW WHAT A "GENTLEMAN" IS. BUT I BELIEVE YOU, JOHN CARTER.
WHERE IS THIS VIRGINIA?
The name of my fair land never sounded more beautiful than as it fell from those perfect lips on that far-gone day.
IT IS OF ANOTHER WORLD, DEJAH THORIS.
OF THE GREAT PLANET EARTH, WHICH REVOLVES ABOUT OUR COMMON SUN AND--
EARTH! WHY DID YOU NOT SAY SO EARLIER?
IT-- EXCUSE ME?
WE RED PEOPLE HAVE INSTRUMENTS BY WHICH WE ARE ABLE TO VIEW THE SURFACE OF ANY PLANET.
HOW--?
NEARLY EVERY PLANET WITH AN ATMOSPHERE SIMILAR TO BARSOOM'S SHOWS LIFE FORMS ALMOST IDENTICAL TO YOU AND ME.
BUT--?
THERE ARE LEGENDS OF VISITORS FROM YOUR EARTH TO BARSOOM. BUT THIS WAS EONS AGO, BEFORE THE SEAS DRIED UP.

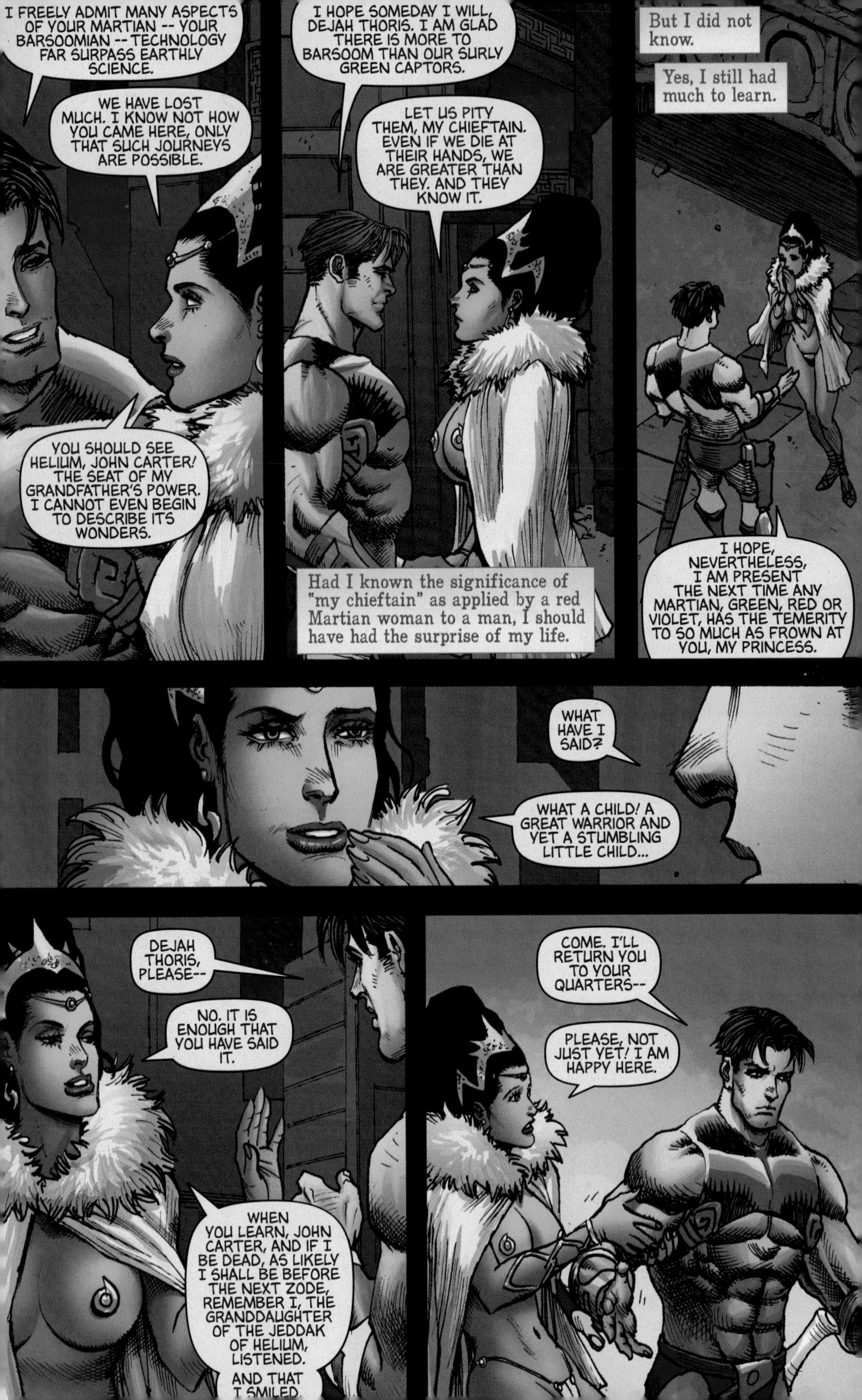
I FREELY ADMIT MANY ASPECTS OF YOUR MARTIAN -- YOUR BARSOOMIAN -- TECHNOLOGY FAR SURPASS EARTHLY SCIENCE.
WE HAVE LOST MUCH. I KNOW NOT HOW YOU CAME HERE, ONLY THAT SUCH JOURNEYS ARE POSSIBLE.
YOU SHOULD SEE HELIUM, JOHN CARTER! THE SEAT OF MY GRANDFATHER'S POWER. I CANNOT EVEN BEGIN TO DESCRIBE ITS WONDERS.
I HOPE SOMEDAY I WILL, DEJAH THORIS. I AM GLAD THERE IS MORE TO BARSOOM THAN OUR SURLY GREEN CAPTORS.
LET US PITY THEM, MY CHIEFTAIN. EVEN IF WE DIE AT THEIR HANDS, WE ARE GREATER THAN THEY. AND THEY KNOW IT.
Had I known the significance of "my chieftain" as applied by a red Martian woman to a man, I should have had the surprise of my life.
But I did not know.
Yes, I still had much to learn.
I HOPE, NEVERTHELESS, I AM PRESENT THE NEXT TIME ANY MARTIAN, GREEN, RED OR VIOLET, HAS THE TEMERITY TO SO MUCH AS FROWN AT YOU, MY PRINCESS.
WHAT HAVE I SAID?
WHAT A CHILD! A GREAT WARRIOR AND YET A STUMBLING LITTLE CHILD...
DEJAH THORIS, PLEASE--
NO. IT IS ENOUGH THAT YOU HAVE SAID IT.
WHEN YOU LEARN, JOHN CARTER, AND IF I BE DEAD, AS LIKELY I SHALL BE BEFORE THE NEXT ZODE, REMEMBER I, THE GRANDDAUGHTER OF THE JEDDAK OF HELIUM, LISTENED.
AND THAT I SMILED.
COME. I'LL RETURN YOU TO YOUR QUARTERS--
PLEASE, NOT JUST YET! I AM HAPPY HERE.

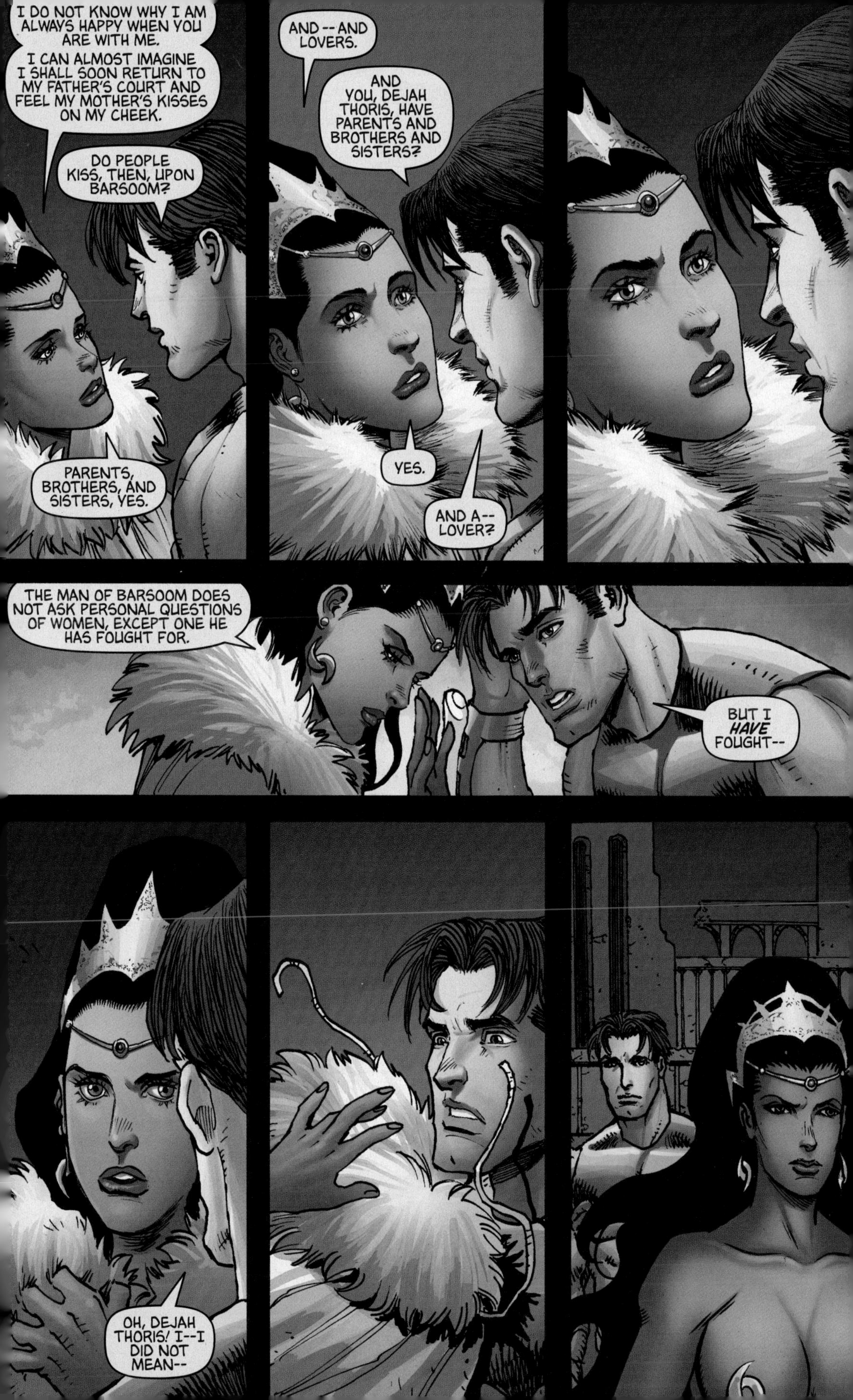
I DO NOT KNOW WHY I AM ALWAYS HAPPY WHEN YOU ARE WITH ME.
I CAN ALMOST IMAGINE I SHALL SOON RETURN TO MY FATHER'S COURT AND FEEL MY MOTHER'S KISSES ON MY CHEEK.
DO PEOPLE KISS, THEN, UPON BARSOOM?
PARENTS, BROTHERS, AND SISTERS, YES.
AND--AND LOVERS.
AND YOU, DEJAH THORIS, HAVE PARENTS AND BROTHERS AND SISTERS?
YES.
AND A--LOVER?
THE MAN OF BARSOOM DOES NOT ASK PERSONAL QUESTIONS OF WOMEN, EXCEPT ONE HE HAS FOUGHT FOR.
BUT I *HAVE* FOUGHT--
OH, DEJAH THORIS! I--I DID NOT MEAN--

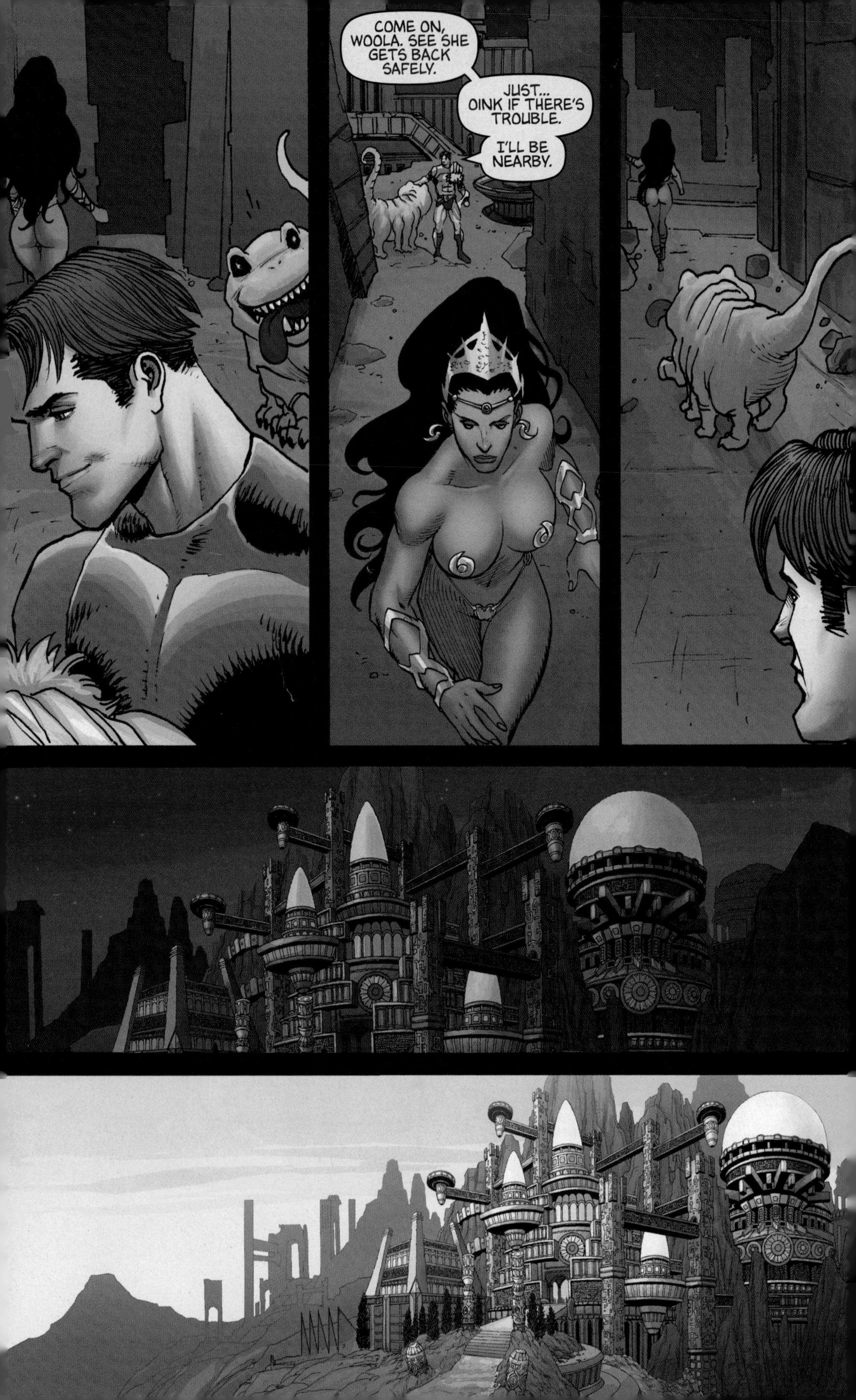
COME ON, WOOLA. SEE SHE GETS BACK SAFELY.
JUST... OINK IF THERE'S TROUBLE.
I'LL BE NEARBY.

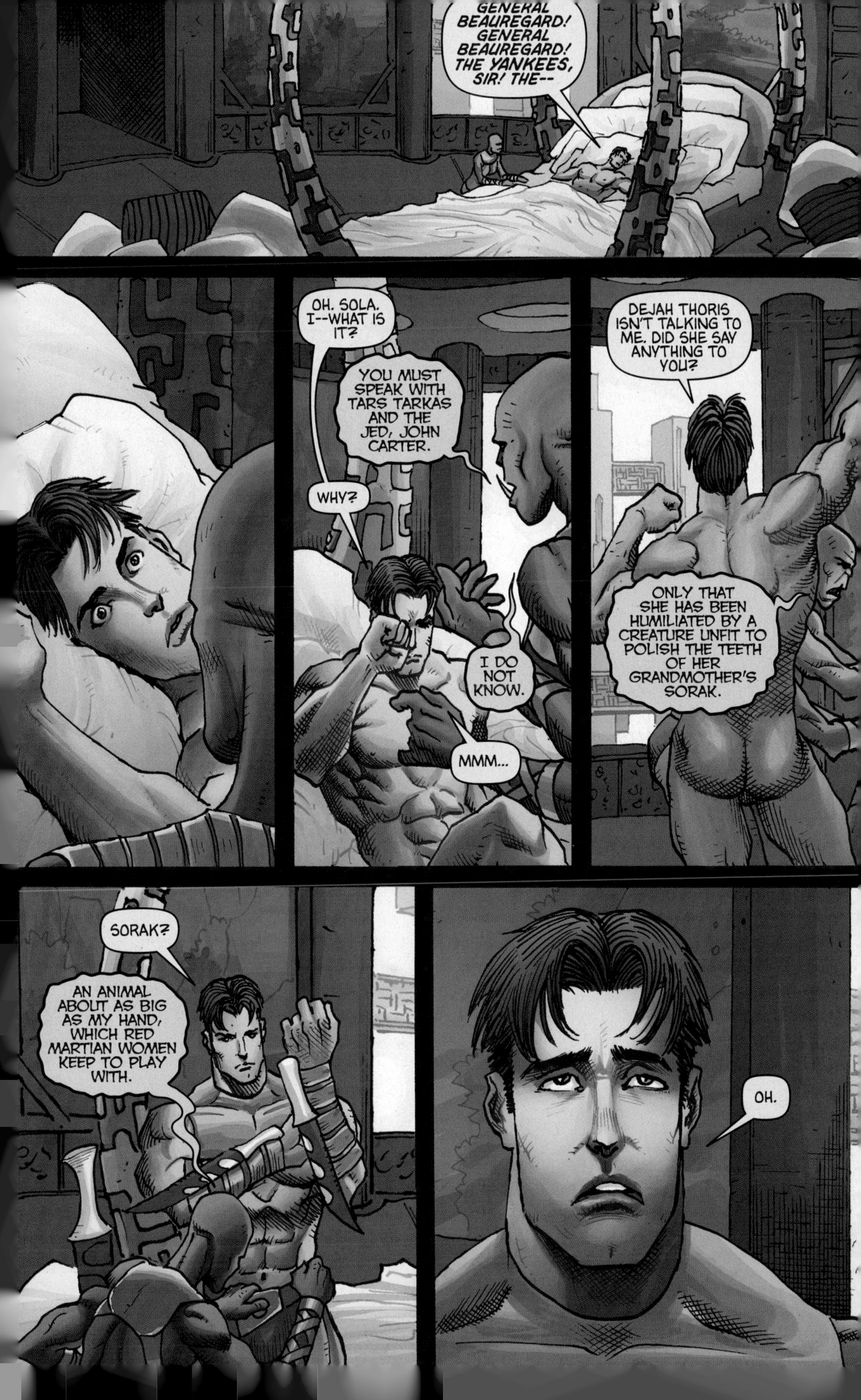
GENERAL BEAUREGARD! GENERAL BEAUREGARD! THE YANKEES, SIR! THE--
OH. SOLA. I--WHAT IS IT?
YOU MUST SPEAK WITH TARS TARKAS AND THE JED, JOHN CARTER.
WHY?
I DO NOT KNOW.
MMM...
DEJAH THORIS ISN'T TALKING TO ME. DID SHE SAY ANYTHING TO YOU?
ONLY THAT SHE HAS BEEN HUMILIATED BY A CREATURE UNFIT TO POLISH THE TEETH OF HER GRANDMOTHER'S SORAK.
SORAK?
AN ANIMAL ABOUT AS BIG AS MY HAND, WHICH RED MARTIAN WOMEN KEEP TO PLAY WITH.
OH.

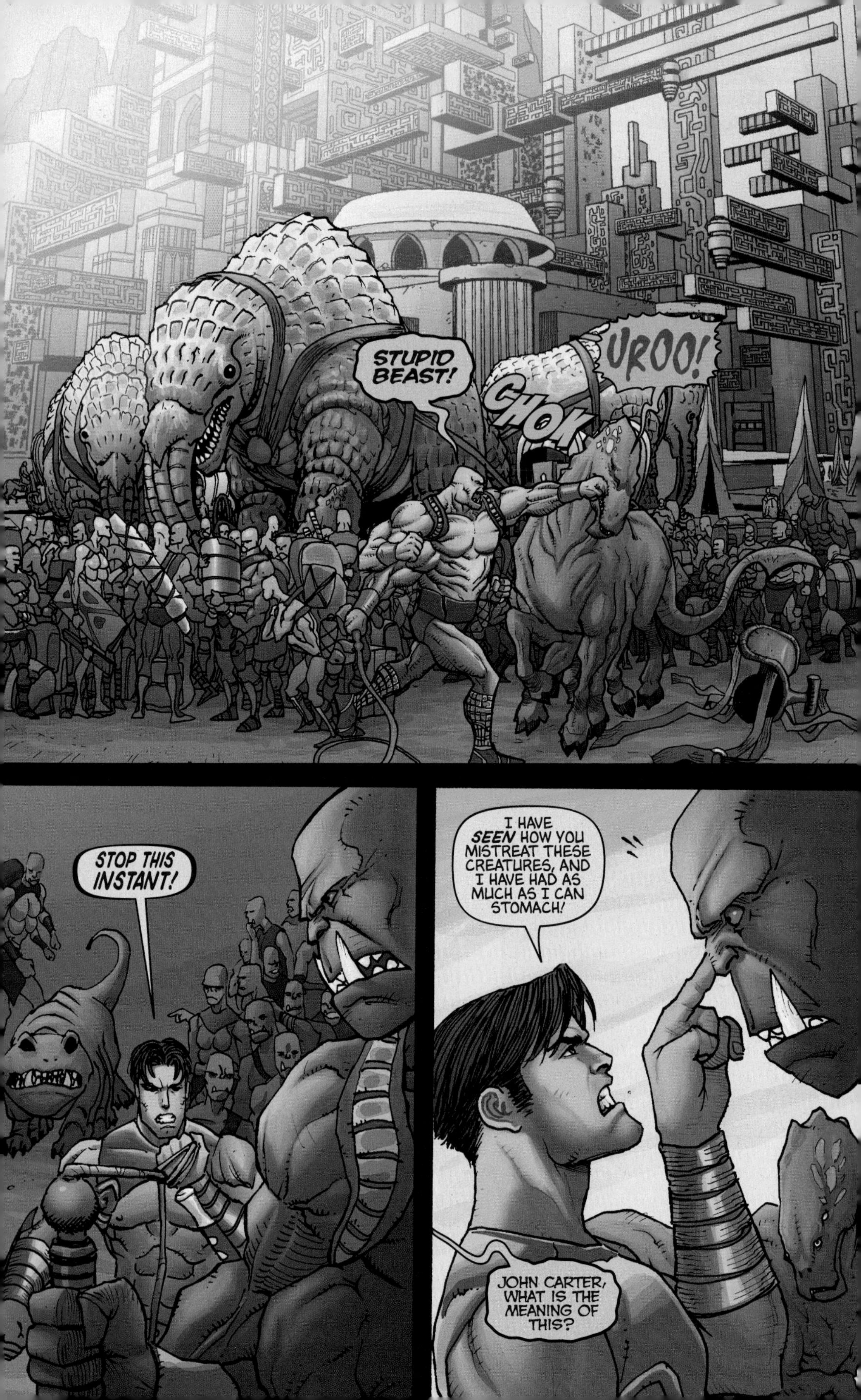
STUPID BEAST!
CHOK
UROO!
STOP THIS INSTANT!
I HAVE SEEN HOW YOU MISTREAT THESE CREATURES, AND I HAVE HAD AS MUCH AS I CAN STOMACH!
JOHN CARTER, WHAT IS THE MEANING OF THIS?

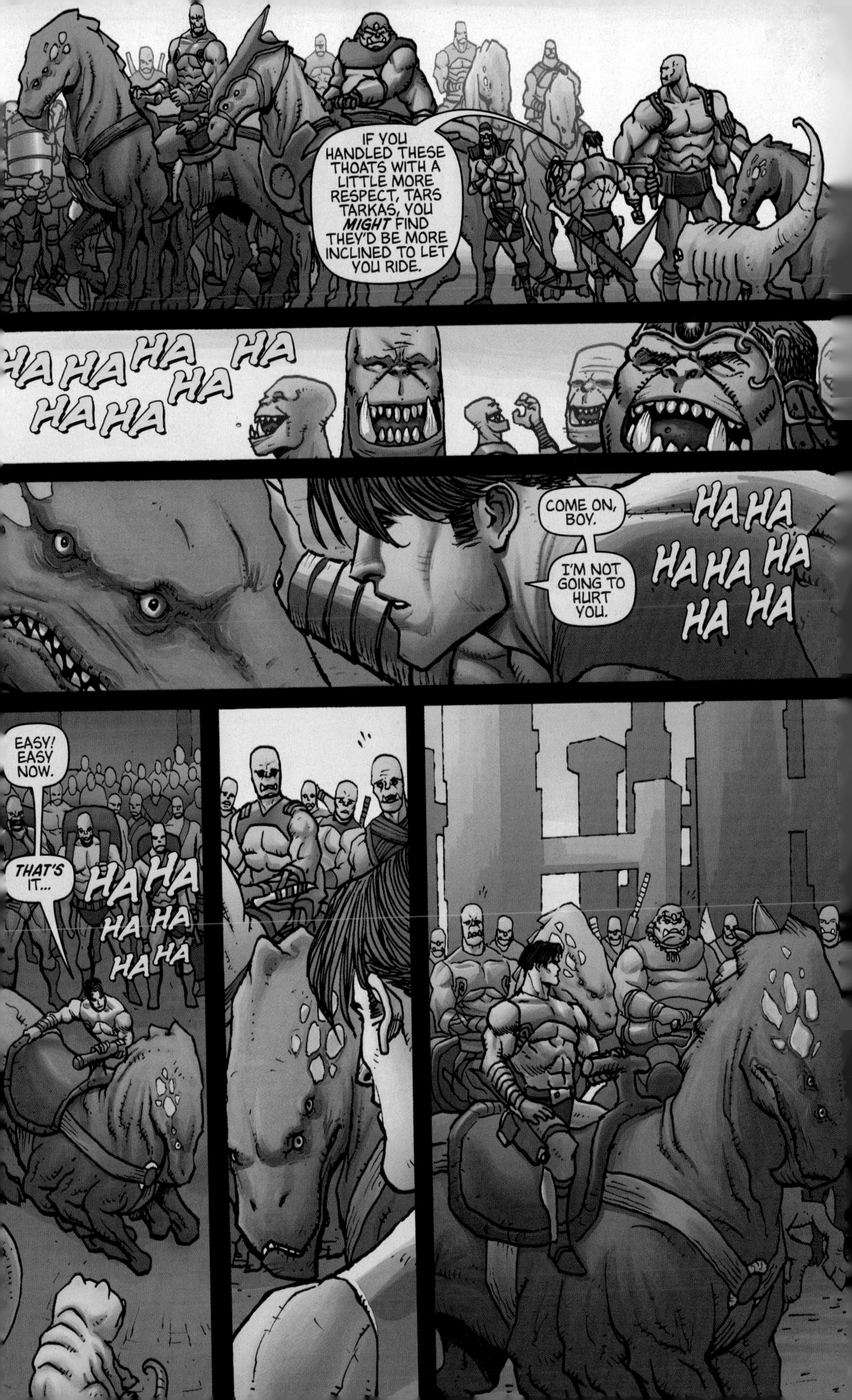
IF YOU HANDLED THESE THOATS WITH A LITTLE MORE RESPECT, TARS TARKAS, YOU *MIGHT* FIND THEY'D BE MORE INCLINED TO LET YOU RIDE.
HA HA HA HA HA HA HA
COME ON, BOY.
I'M NOT GOING TO HURT YOU.
HA HA HA HA HA HA HA
EASY! EASY NOW.
THAT'S IT...
HA HA HA HA HA HA

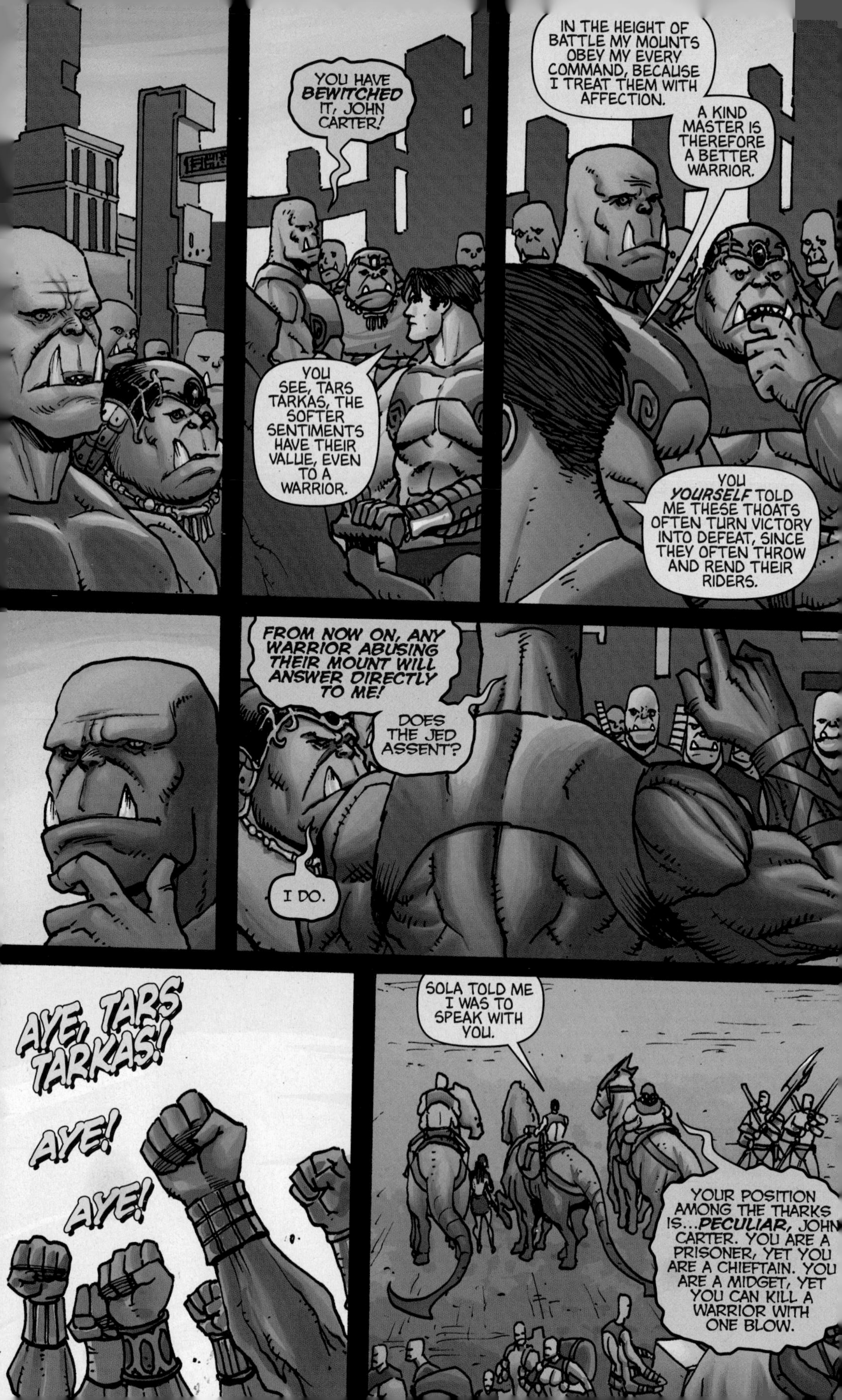
YOU HAVE *BEWITCHED* IT, JOHN CARTER!
YOU SEE, TARS TARKAS, THE SOFTER SENTIMENTS HAVE THEIR VALUE, EVEN TO A WARRIOR.
IN THE HEIGHT OF BATTLE MY MOUNTS OBEY MY EVERY COMMAND, BECAUSE I TREAT THEM WITH AFFECTION.
A KIND MASTER IS THEREFORE A BETTER WARRIOR.
YOU *YOURSELF* TOLD ME THESE THOATS OFTEN TURN VICTORY INTO DEFEAT, SINCE THEY OFTEN THROW AND REND THEIR RIDERS.
FROM NOW ON, ANY WARRIOR ABUSING THEIR MOUNT WILL ANSWER DIRECTLY TO ME!
DOES THE JED ASSENT?
I DO.
AYE, TARS TARKAS!
AYE!
AYE!
SOLA TOLD ME I WAS TO SPEAK WITH YOU.
YOUR POSITION AMONG THE THARKS IS...*PECULIAR,* JOHN CARTER. YOU ARE A PRISONER, YET YOU ARE A CHIEFTAIN. YOU ARE A MIDGET, YET YOU CAN KILL A WARRIOR WITH ONE BLOW.

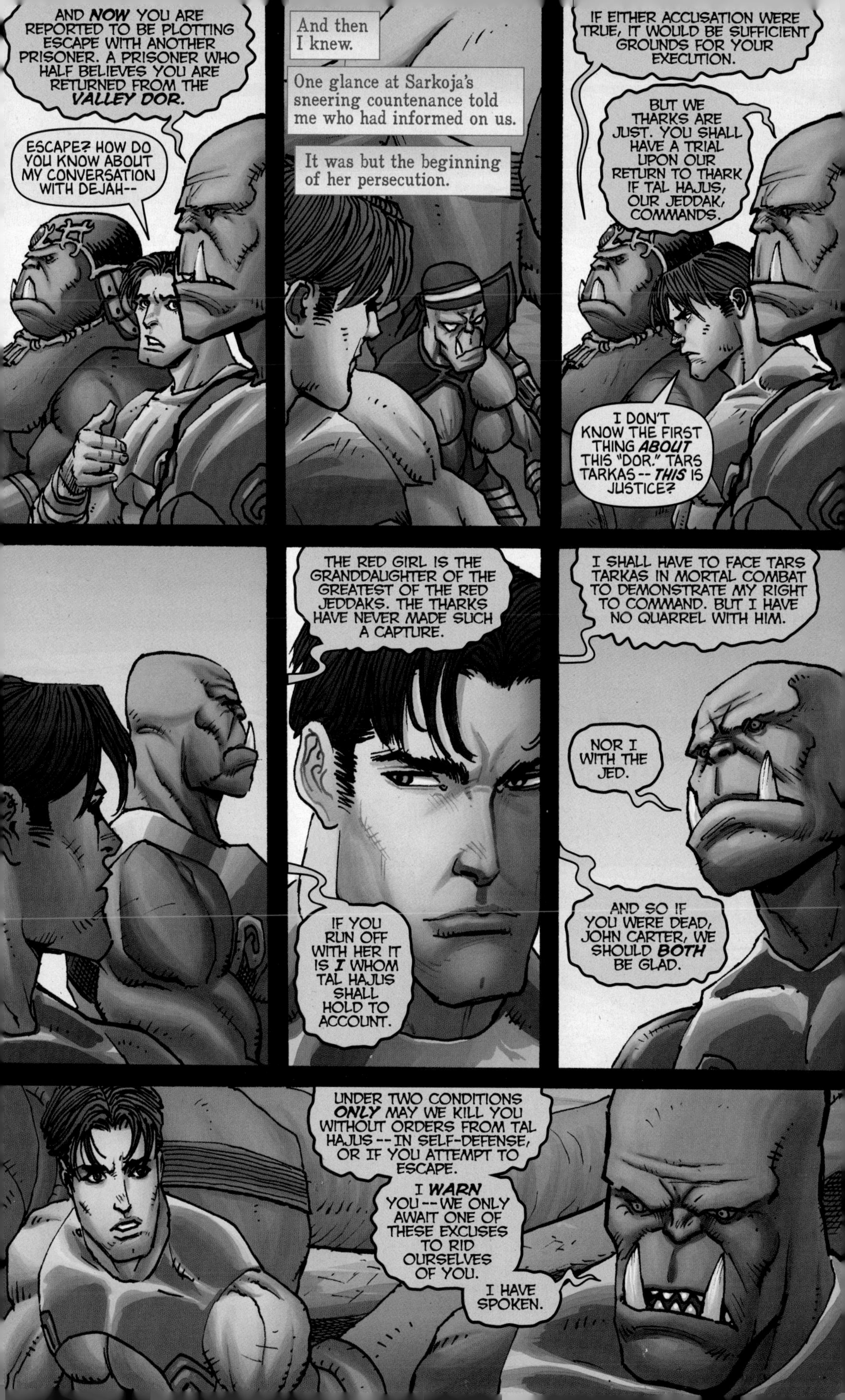
AND NOW YOU ARE REPORTED TO BE PLOTTING ESCAPE WITH ANOTHER PRISONER. A PRISONER WHO HALF BELIEVES YOU ARE RETURNED FROM THE VALLEY DOR.
ESCAPE? HOW DO YOU KNOW ABOUT MY CONVERSATION WITH DEJAH--
And then I knew.
One glance at Sarkoja's sneering countenance told me who had informed on us.
It was but the beginning of her persecution.
IF EITHER ACCUSATION WERE TRUE, IT WOULD BE SUFFICIENT GROUNDS FOR YOUR EXECUTION.
BUT WE THARKS ARE JUST. YOU SHALL HAVE A TRIAL UPON OUR RETURN TO THARK IF TAL HAJUS, OUR JEDDAK, COMMANDS.
I DON'T KNOW THE FIRST THING ABOUT THIS "DOR." TARS TARKAS -- THIS IS JUSTICE?
THE RED GIRL IS THE GRANDDAUGHTER OF THE GREATEST OF THE RED JEDDAKS. THE THARKS HAVE NEVER MADE SUCH A CAPTURE.
IF YOU RUN OFF WITH HER IT IS I WHOM TAL HAJUS SHALL HOLD TO ACCOUNT.
I SHALL HAVE TO FACE TARS TARKAS IN MORTAL COMBAT TO DEMONSTRATE MY RIGHT TO COMMAND. BUT I HAVE NO QUARREL WITH HIM.
NOR I WITH THE JED.
AND SO IF YOU WERE DEAD, JOHN CARTER, WE SHOULD BOTH BE GLAD.
UNDER TWO CONDITIONS ONLY MAY WE KILL YOU WITHOUT ORDERS FROM TAL HAJUS -- IN SELF-DEFENSE, OR IF YOU ATTEMPT TO ESCAPE.
I WARN YOU -- WE ONLY AWAIT ONE OF THESE EXCUSES TO RID OURSELVES OF YOU.
I HAVE SPOKEN.

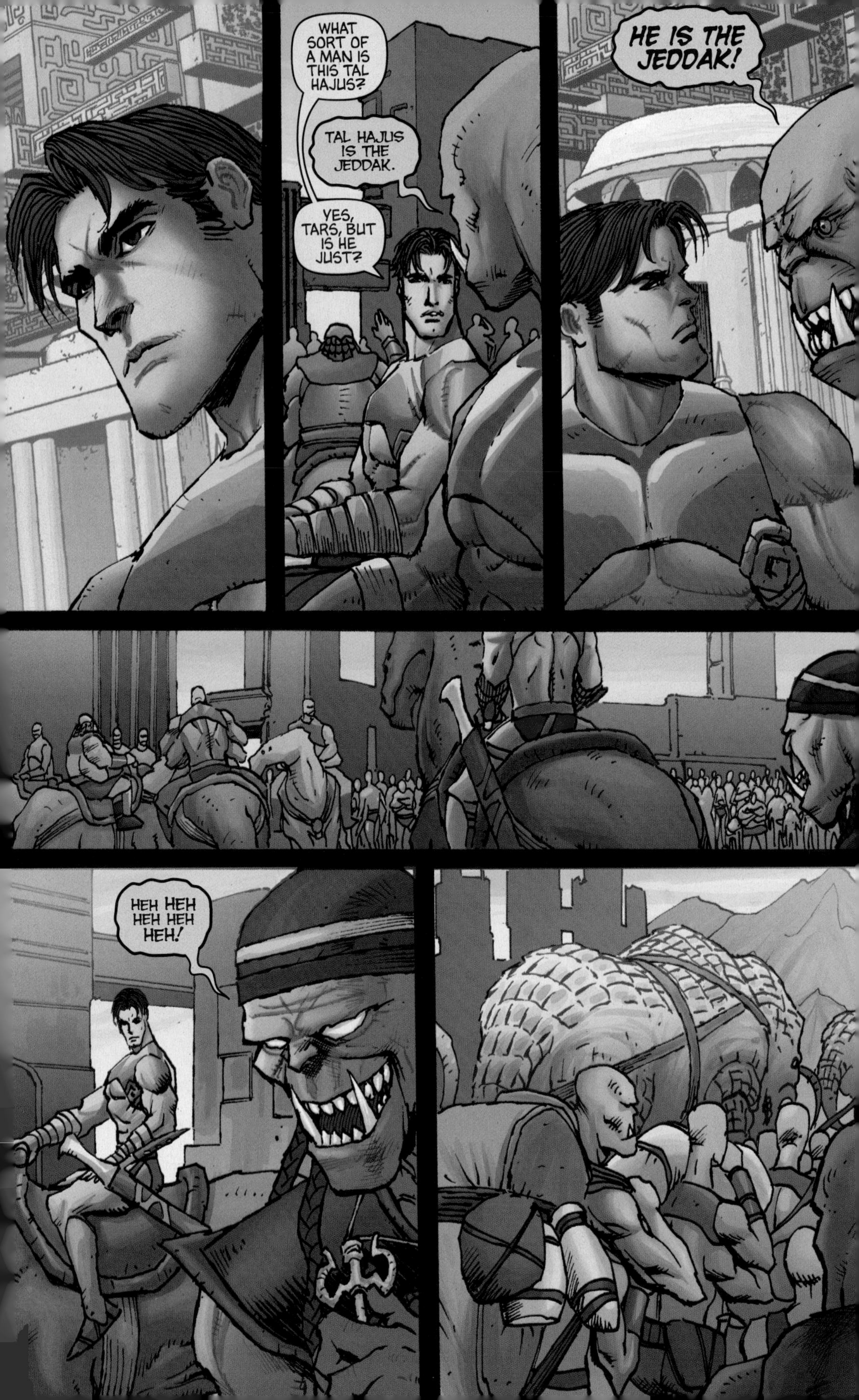
WHAT SORT OF A MAN IS THIS TAL HAJUS?
TAL HAJUS IS THE JEDDAK.
YES, TARS, BUT IS HE JUST?
HE IS THE JEDDAK!
HEH HEH HEH HEH HEH!

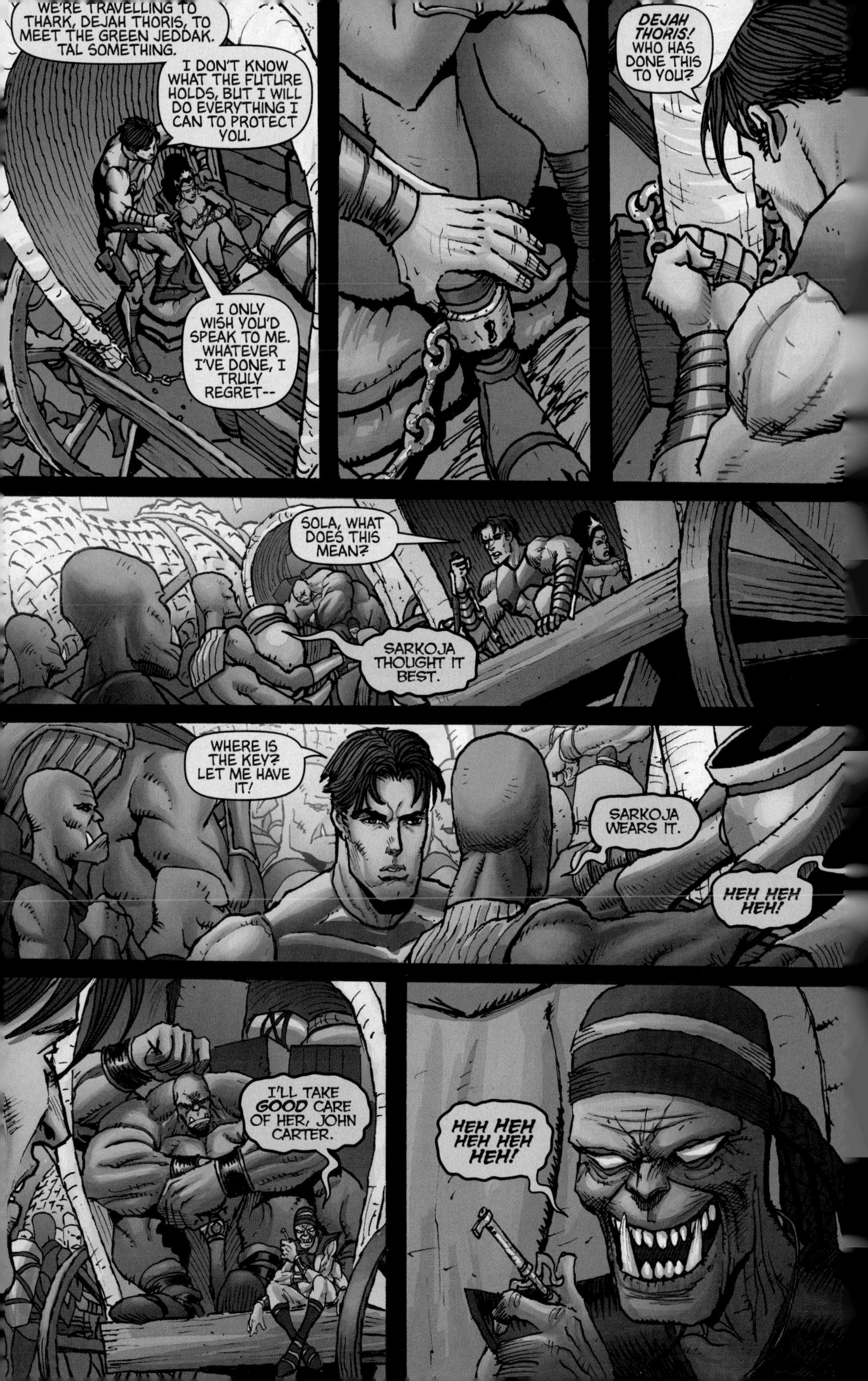
WE'RE TRAVELLING TO THARK, DEJAH THORIS, TO MEET THE GREEN JEDDAK. TAL SOMETHING.
I DON'T KNOW WHAT THE FUTURE HOLDS, BUT I WILL DO EVERYTHING I CAN TO PROTECT YOU.
I ONLY WISH YOU'D SPEAK TO ME. WHATEVER I'VE DONE, I TRULY REGRET--
DEJAH THORIS! WHO HAS DONE THIS TO YOU?
SOLA, WHAT DOES THIS MEAN?
SARKOJA THOUGHT IT BEST.
WHERE IS THE KEY? LET ME HAVE IT!
SARKOJA WEARS IT.
HEH HEH HEH!
I'LL TAKE GOOD CARE OF HER, JOHN CARTER.
HEH HEH HEH HEH HEH!

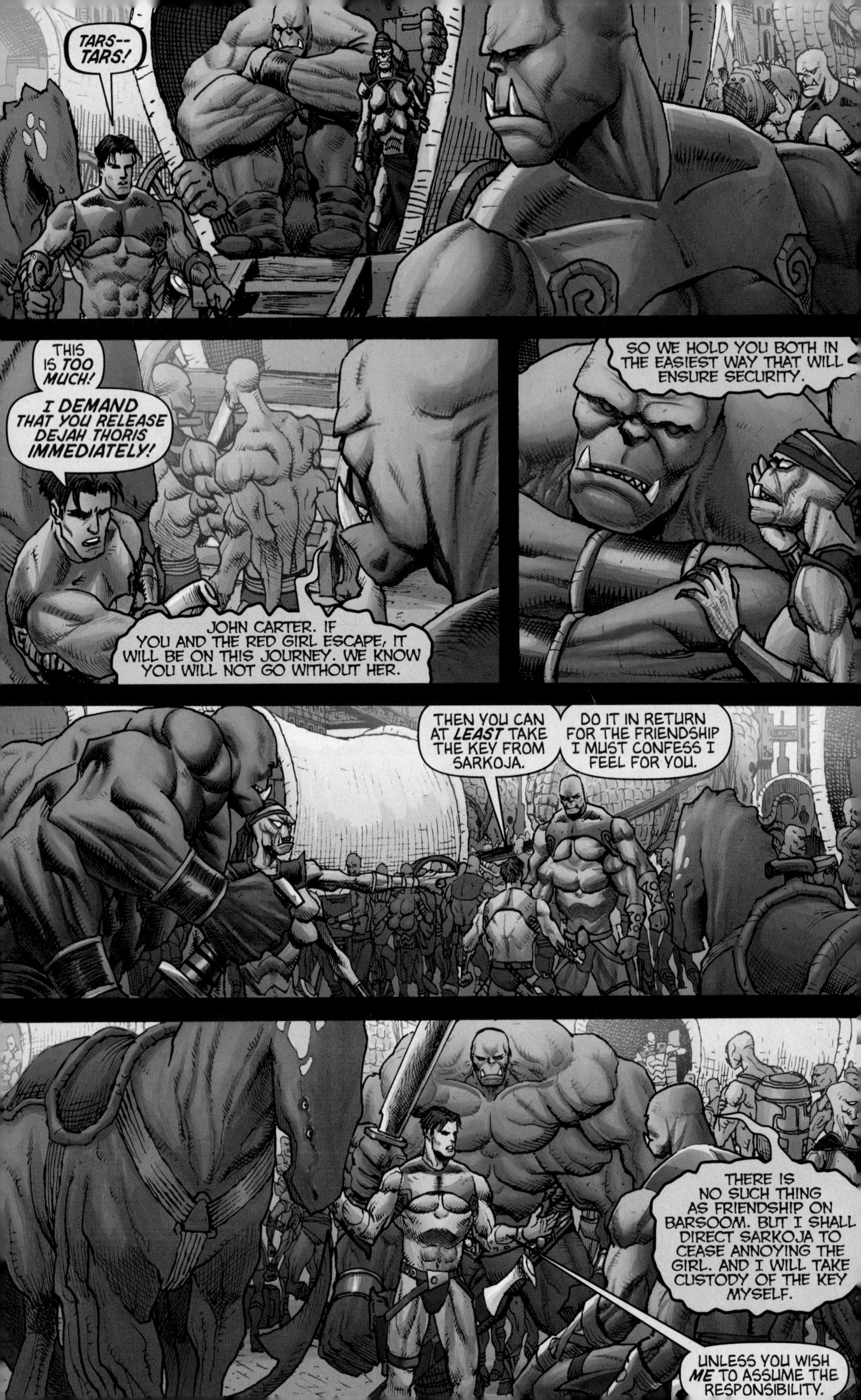
TARS-- TARS!
THIS IS *TOO MUCH!*
I DEMAND* THAT YOU RELEASE DEJAH THORIS *IMMEDIATELY!
JOHN CARTER. IF YOU AND THE RED GIRL ESCAPE, IT WILL BE ON THIS JOURNEY. WE KNOW YOU WILL NOT GO WITHOUT HER.
SO WE HOLD YOU BOTH IN THE EASIEST WAY THAT WILL ENSURE SECURITY.
THEN YOU CAN AT *LEAST* TAKE THE KEY FROM SARKOJA.
DO IT IN RETURN FOR THE FRIENDSHIP I MUST CONFESS I FEEL FOR YOU.
THERE IS NO SUCH THING AS FRIENDSHIP ON BARSOOM. BUT I SHALL DIRECT SARKOJA TO CEASE ANNOYING THE GIRL. AND I WILL TAKE CUSTODY OF THE KEY MYSELF.
UNLESS YOU WISH *ME* TO ASSUME THE RESPONSIBILITY.

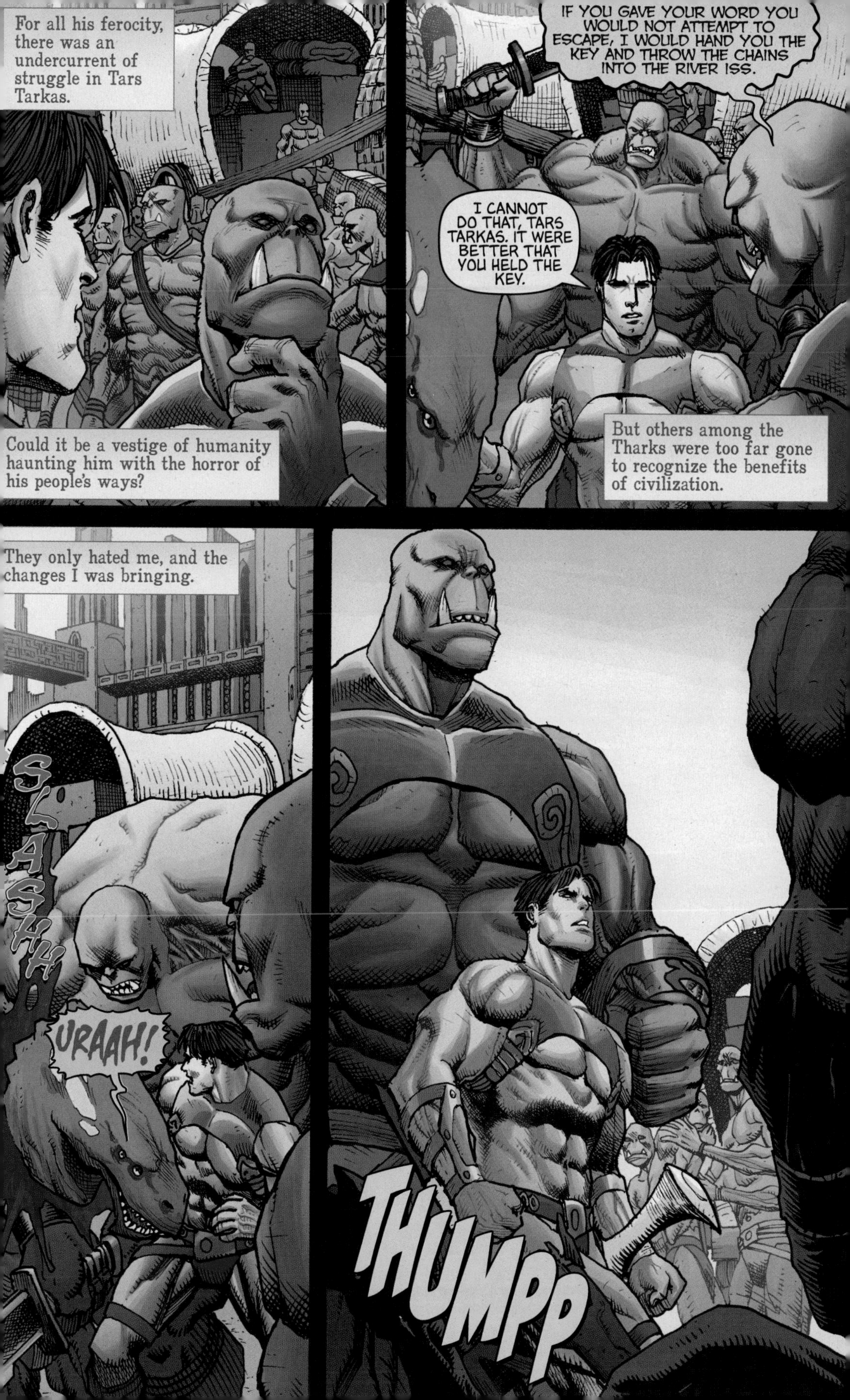
For all his ferocity, there was an undercurrent of struggle in Tars Tarkas.
Could it be a vestige of humanity haunting him with the horror of his people's ways?
IF YOU GAVE YOUR WORD YOU WOULD NOT ATTEMPT TO ESCAPE, I WOULD HAND YOU THE KEY AND THROW THE CHAINS INTO THE RIVER ISS.
I CANNOT DO THAT, TARS TARKAS. IT WERE BETTER THAT YOU HELD THE KEY.
But others among the Tharks were too far gone to recognize the benefits of civilization.
They only hated me, and the changes I was bringing.
SLASHH
URAAH!
THUMPP

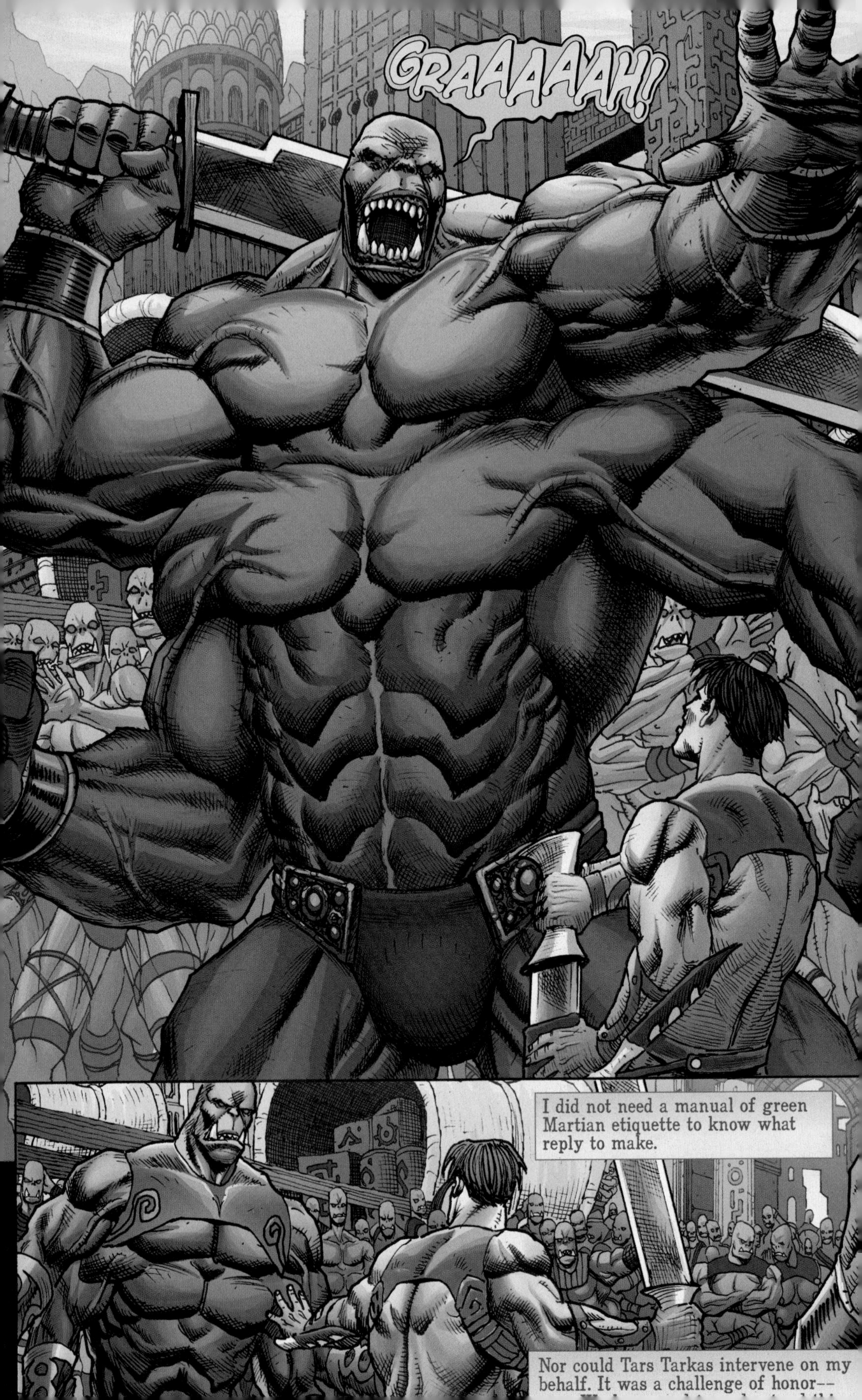
GRAAAAAH!
I did not need a manual of green Martian etiquette to know what reply to make.
Nor could Tars Tarkas intervene on my behalf. It was a challenge of honor--

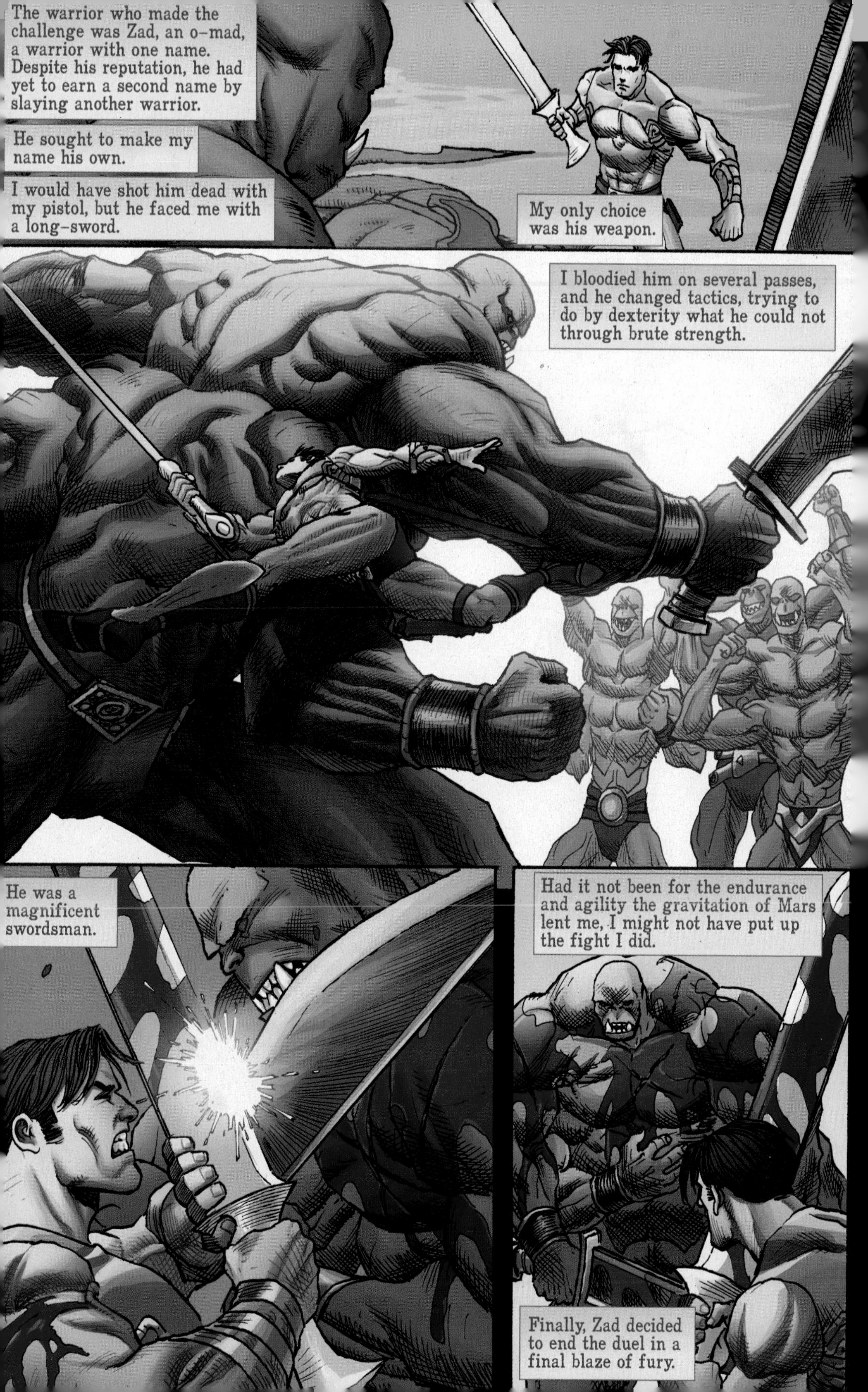
The warrior who made the challenge was Zad, an o-mad, a warrior with one name. Despite his reputation, he had yet to earn a second name by slaying another warrior.
He sought to make my name his own.
I would have shot him dead with my pistol, but he faced me with a long-sword.
My only choice was his weapon.
I bloodied him on several passes, and he changed tactics, trying to do by dexterity what he could not through brute strength.
He was a magnificent swordsman.
Had it not been for the endurance and agility the gravitation of Mars lent me, I might not have put up the fight I did.
Finally, Zad decided to end the duel in a final blaze of fury.

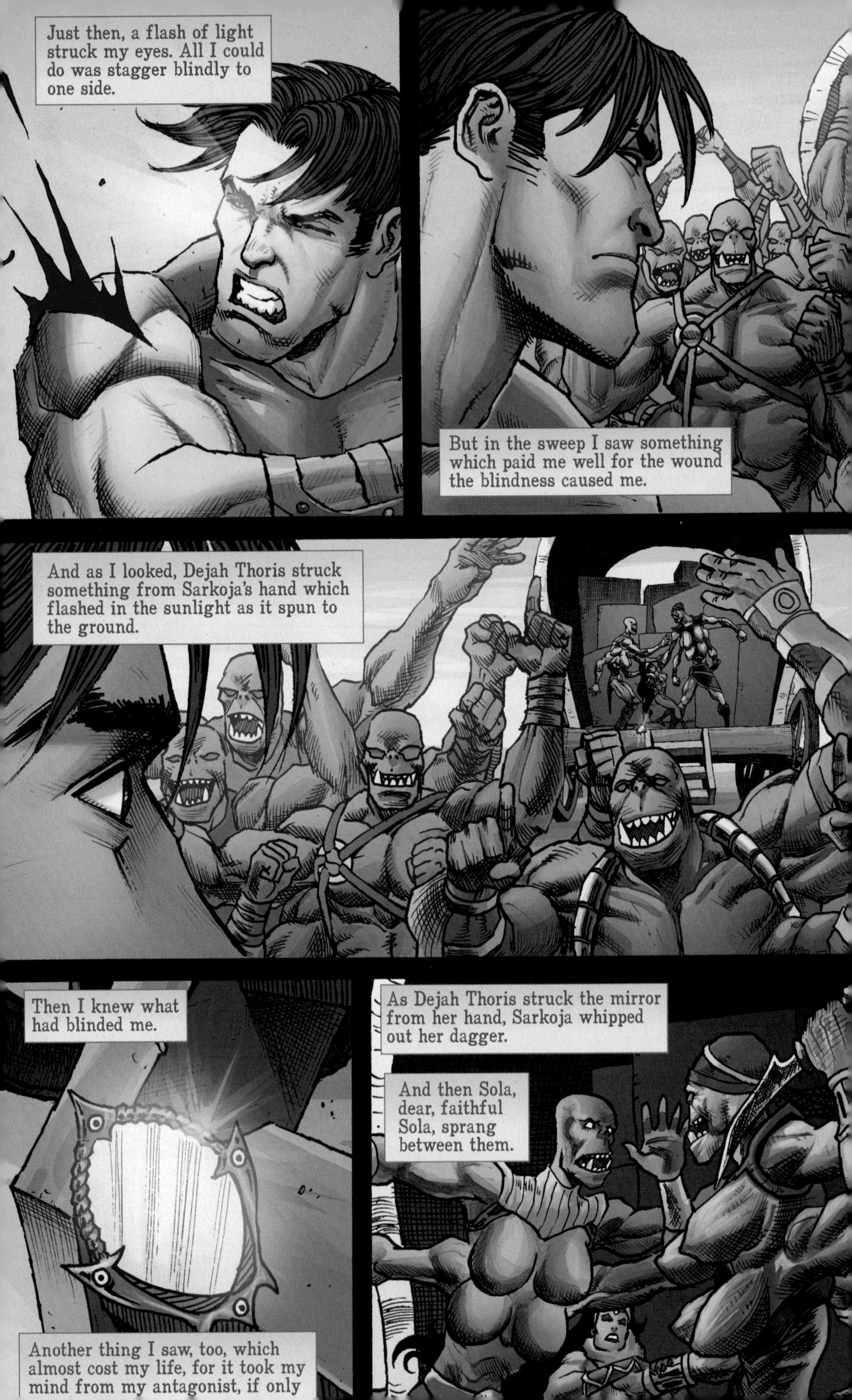
Just then, a flash of light struck my eyes. All I could do was stagger blindly to one side.
But in the sweep I saw something which paid me well for the wound the blindness caused me.
And as I looked, Dejah Thoris struck something from Sarkoja's hand which flashed in the sunlight as it spun to the ground.
Then I knew what had blinded me.
Another thing I saw, too, which almost cost my life, for it took my mind from my antagonist, if only
As Dejah Thoris struck the mirror from her hand, Sarkoja whipped out her dagger.
And then Sola, dear, faithful Sola, sprang between them.

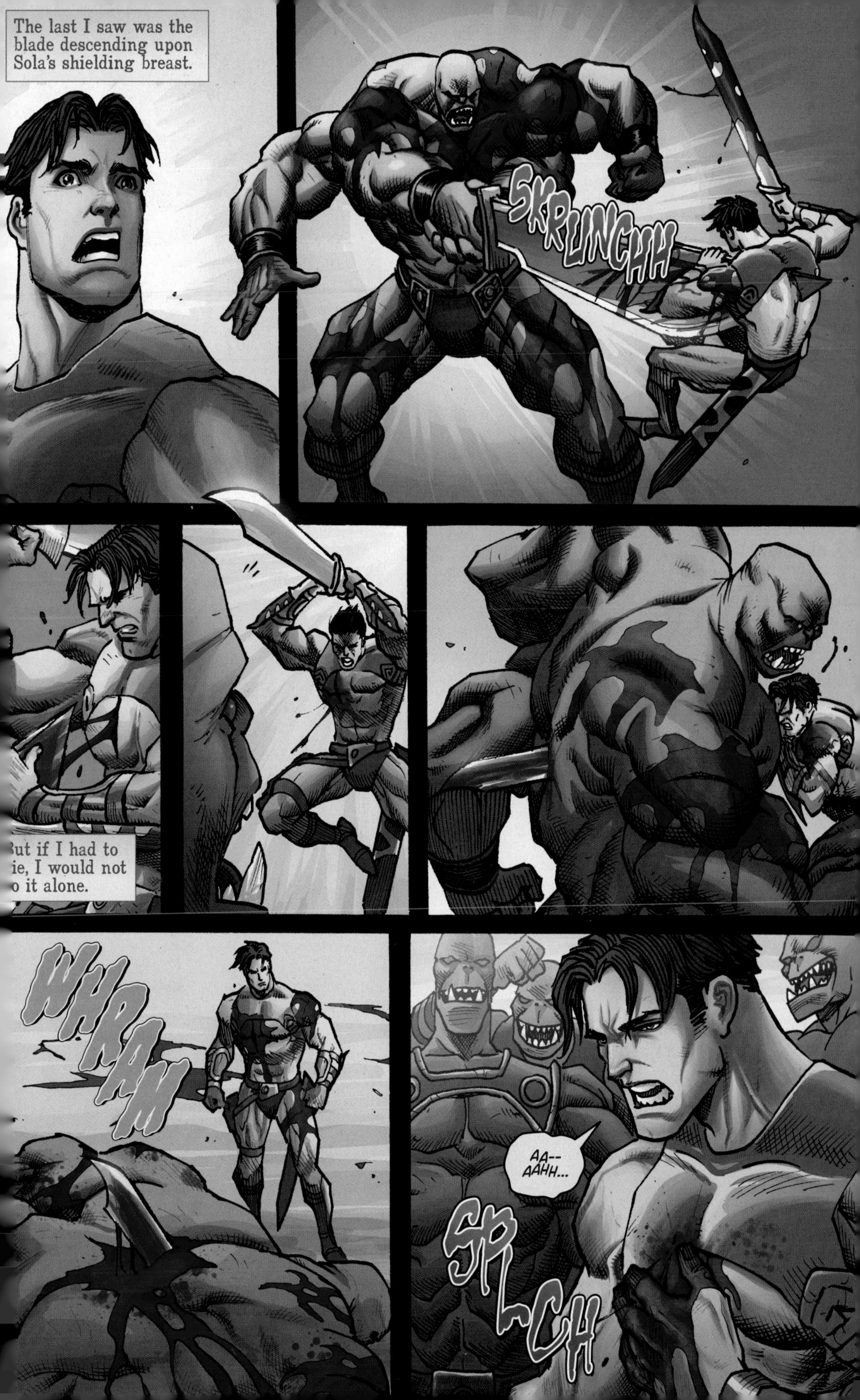
The last I saw was the blade descending upon Sola's shielding breast.
SKRUNCHH
But if I had to die, I would not do it alone.
WHRAM
AA--AAHH...
SPLCH

My head whirled in dizziness, and I felt my knees give beneath me.

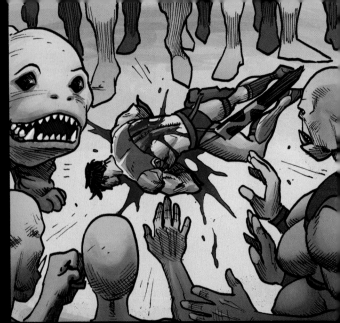

All went black before me.

SOLA. I'M... ALIVE...

YOU ARE ALIVE...

WE NEARLY COMMENDED YOU TO THE ISS, JOHN CARTER.

WHAT IS THAT... STENCH...

A POULTICE. IT MAY SMELL UNPLEASANT, BUT IT SAVED YOUR LIFE.

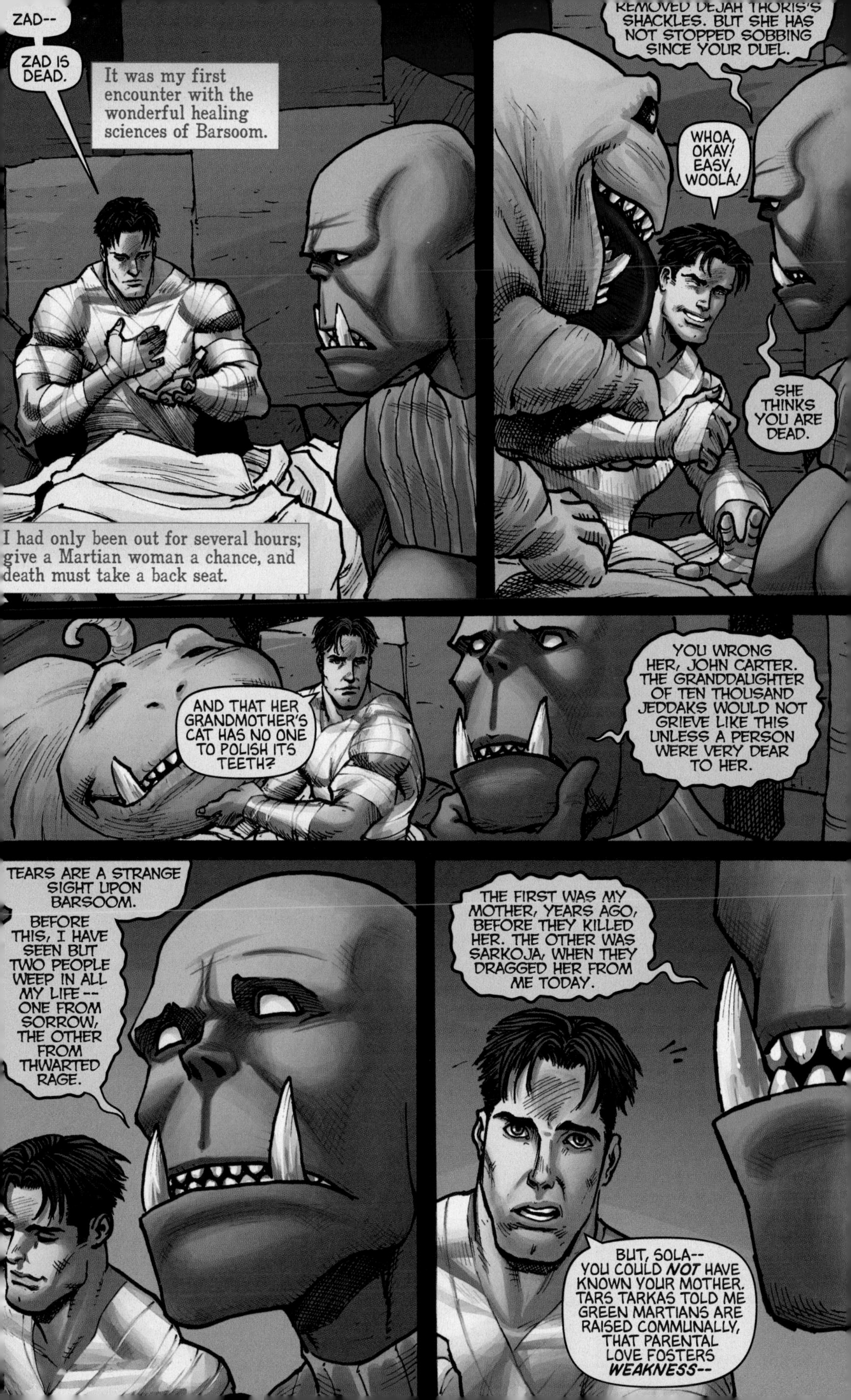
ZAD--
ZAD IS DEAD.
It was my first encounter with the wonderful healing sciences of Barsoom.
I had only been out for several hours; give a Martian woman a chance, and death must take a back seat.
REMOVED DEJAH THORIS'S SHACKLES. BUT SHE HAS NOT STOPPED SOBBING SINCE YOUR DUEL.
WHOA, OKAY! EASY, WOOLA!
SHE THINKS YOU ARE DEAD.
AND THAT HER GRANDMOTHER'S CAT HAS NO ONE TO POLISH ITS TEETH?
YOU WRONG HER, JOHN CARTER. THE GRANDDAUGHTER OF TEN THOUSAND JEDDAKS WOULD NOT GRIEVE LIKE THIS UNLESS A PERSON WERE VERY DEAR TO HER.
TEARS ARE A STRANGE SIGHT UPON BARSOOM.
BEFORE THIS, I HAVE SEEN BUT TWO PEOPLE WEEP IN ALL MY LIFE -- ONE FROM SORROW, THE OTHER FROM THWARTED RAGE.
THE FIRST WAS MY MOTHER, YEARS AGO, BEFORE THEY KILLED HER. THE OTHER WAS SARKOJA, WHEN THEY DRAGGED HER FROM ME TODAY.
BUT, SOLA-- YOU COULD *NOT* HAVE KNOWN YOUR MOTHER. TARS TARKAS TOLD ME GREEN MARTIANS ARE RAISED COMMUNALLY, THAT PARENTAL LOVE FOSTERS ***WEAKNESS--***

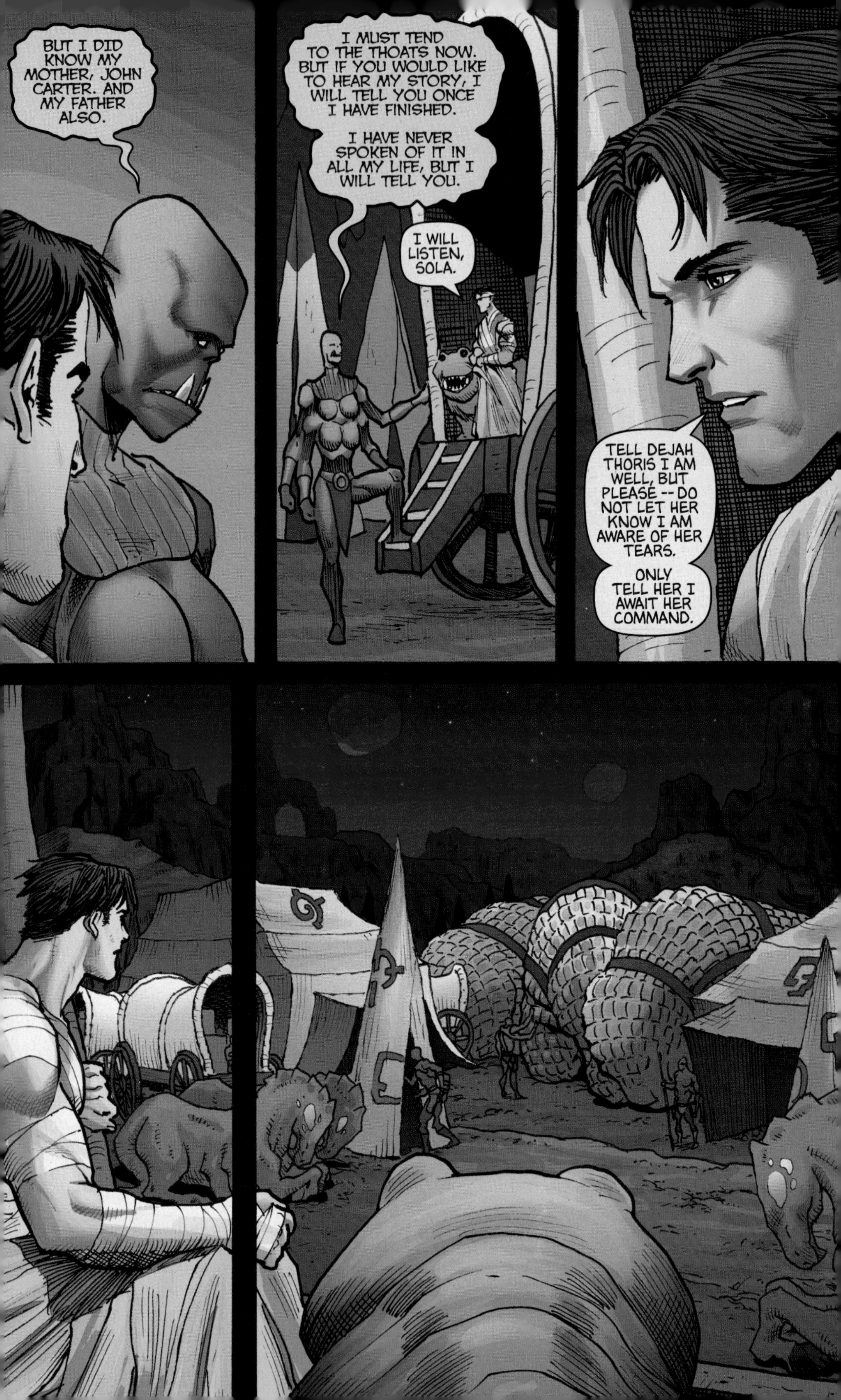
BUT I DID KNOW MY MOTHER, JOHN CARTER. AND MY FATHER ALSO.
I MUST TEND TO THE THOATS NOW. BUT IF YOU WOULD LIKE TO HEAR MY STORY, I WILL TELL YOU ONCE I HAVE FINISHED.
I HAVE NEVER SPOKEN OF IT IN ALL MY LIFE, BUT I WILL TELL YOU.
I WILL LISTEN, SOLA.
TELL DEJAH THORIS I AM WELL, BUT PLEASE -- DO NOT LET HER KNOW I AM AWARE OF HER TEARS.
ONLY TELL HER I AWAIT HER COMMAND.

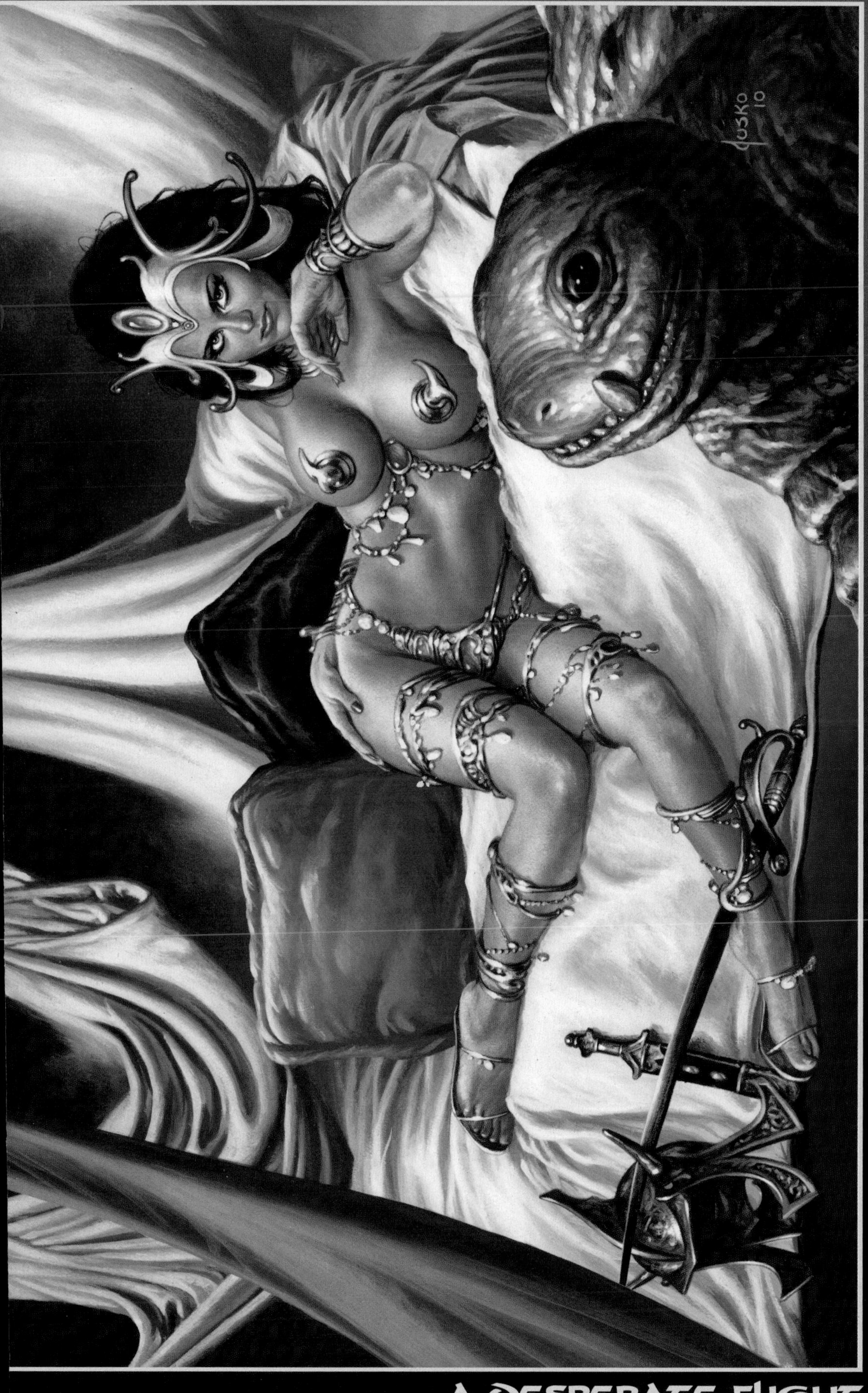

A DESPERATE FLIGHT

Issue #6 cover by JOE JUSKO

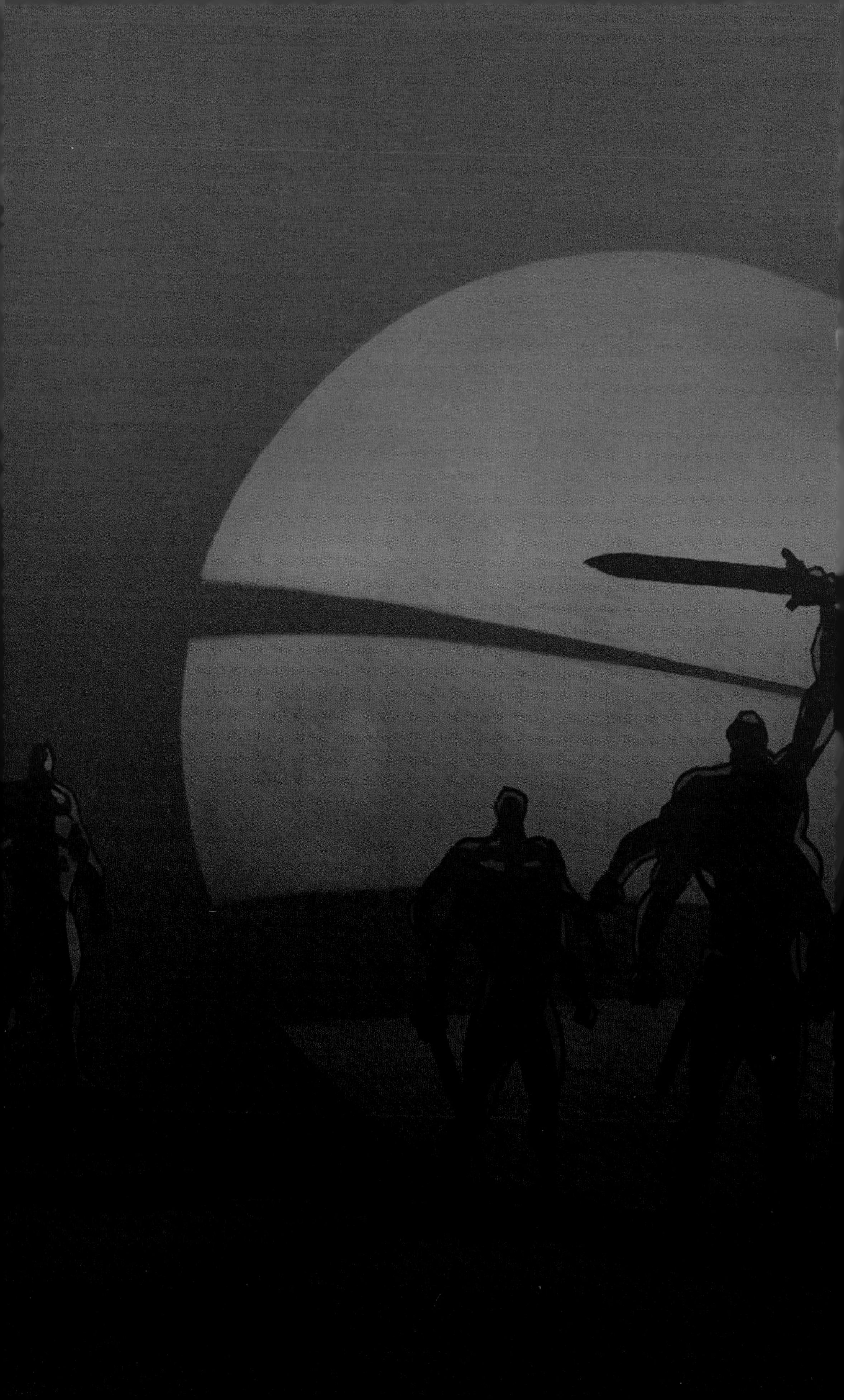

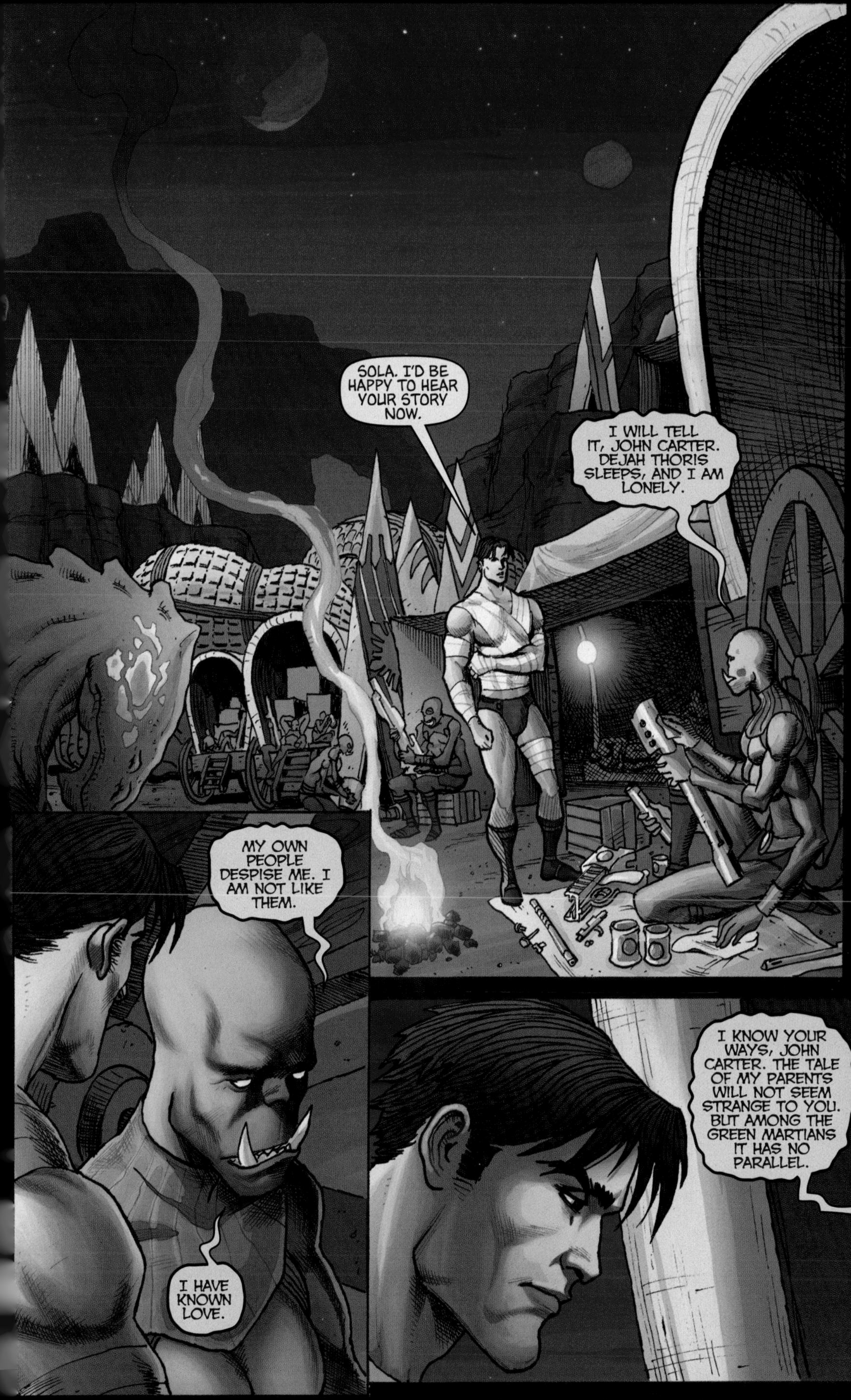

SOLA. I'D BE HAPPY TO HEAR YOUR STORY NOW.
I WILL TELL IT, JOHN CARTER. DEJAH THORIS SLEEPS, AND I AM LONELY.
MY OWN PEOPLE DESPISE ME. I AM NOT LIKE THEM.
I HAVE KNOWN LOVE.
I KNOW YOUR WAYS, JOHN CARTER. THE TALE OF MY PARENTS WILL NOT SEEM STRANGE TO YOU. BUT AMONG THE GREEN MARTIANS IT HAS NO PARALLEL.

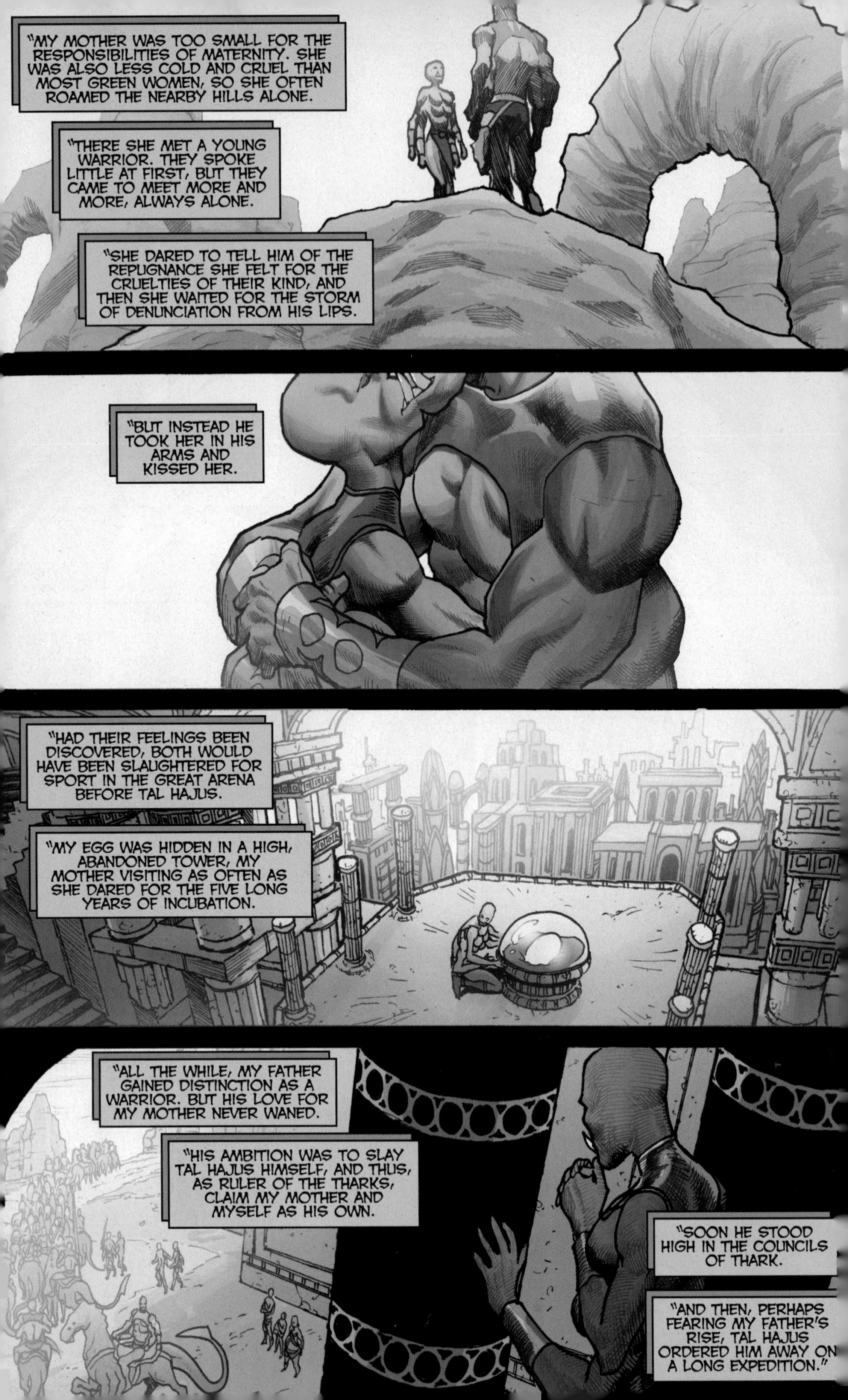
"MY MOTHER WAS TOO SMALL FOR THE RESPONSIBILITIES OF MATERNITY. SHE WAS ALSO LESS COLD AND CRUEL THAN MOST GREEN WOMEN, SO SHE OFTEN ROAMED THE NEARBY HILLS ALONE.
"THERE SHE MET A YOUNG WARRIOR. THEY SPOKE LITTLE AT FIRST, BUT THEY CAME TO MEET MORE AND MORE, ALWAYS ALONE.
"SHE DARED TO TELL HIM OF THE REPUGNANCE SHE FELT FOR THE CRUELTIES OF THEIR KIND, AND THEN SHE WAITED FOR THE STORM OF DENUNCIATION FROM HIS LIPS.
"BUT INSTEAD HE TOOK HER IN HIS ARMS AND KISSED HER.
"HAD THEIR FEELINGS BEEN DISCOVERED, BOTH WOULD HAVE BEEN SLAUGHTERED FOR SPORT IN THE GREAT ARENA BEFORE TAL HAJUS.
"MY EGG WAS HIDDEN IN A HIGH, ABANDONED TOWER, MY MOTHER VISITING AS OFTEN AS SHE DARED FOR THE FIVE LONG YEARS OF INCUBATION.
"ALL THE WHILE, MY FATHER GAINED DISTINCTION AS A WARRIOR. BUT HIS LOVE FOR MY MOTHER NEVER WANED.
"HIS AMBITION WAS TO SLAY TAL HAJUS HIMSELF, AND THUS, AS RULER OF THE THARKS, CLAIM MY MOTHER AND MYSELF AS HIS OWN.
"SOON HE STOOD HIGH IN THE COUNCILS OF THARK.
"AND THEN, PERHAPS FEARING MY FATHER'S RISE, TAL HAJUS ORDERED HIM AWAY ON A LONG EXPEDITION."

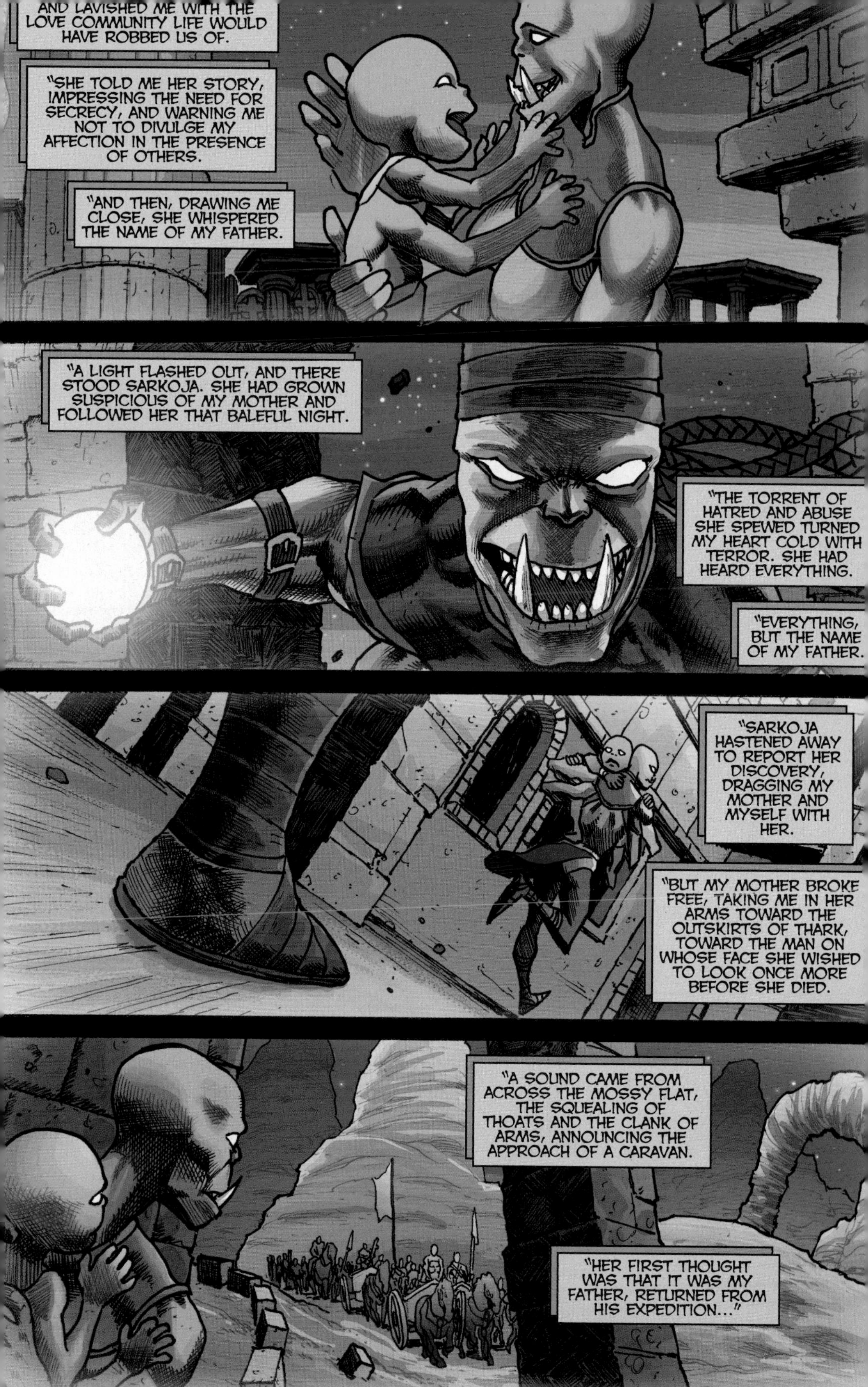
AND LAVISHED ME WITH THE LOVE COMMUNITY LIFE WOULD HAVE ROBBED US OF.
"SHE TOLD ME HER STORY, IMPRESSING THE NEED FOR SECRECY, AND WARNING ME NOT TO DIVULGE MY AFFECTION IN THE PRESENCE OF OTHERS.
"AND THEN, DRAWING ME CLOSE, SHE WHISPERED THE NAME OF MY FATHER.
"A LIGHT FLASHED OUT, AND THERE STOOD SARKOJA. SHE HAD GROWN SUSPICIOUS OF MY MOTHER AND FOLLOWED HER THAT BALEFUL NIGHT.
"THE TORRENT OF HATRED AND ABUSE SHE SPEWED TURNED MY HEART COLD WITH TERROR. SHE HAD HEARD EVERYTHING.
"EVERYTHING, BUT THE NAME OF MY FATHER.
"SARKOJA HASTENED AWAY TO REPORT HER DISCOVERY, DRAGGING MY MOTHER AND MYSELF WITH HER.
"BUT MY MOTHER BROKE FREE, TAKING ME IN HER ARMS TOWARD THE OUTSKIRTS OF THARK, TOWARD THE MAN ON WHOSE FACE SHE WISHED TO LOOK ONCE MORE BEFORE SHE DIED.
"A SOUND CAME FROM ACROSS THE MOSSY FLAT, THE SQUEALING OF THOATS AND THE CLANK OF ARMS, ANNOUNCING THE APPROACH OF A CARAVAN.
"HER FIRST THOUGHT WAS THAT IT WAS MY FATHER, RETURNED FROM HIS EXPEDITION..."

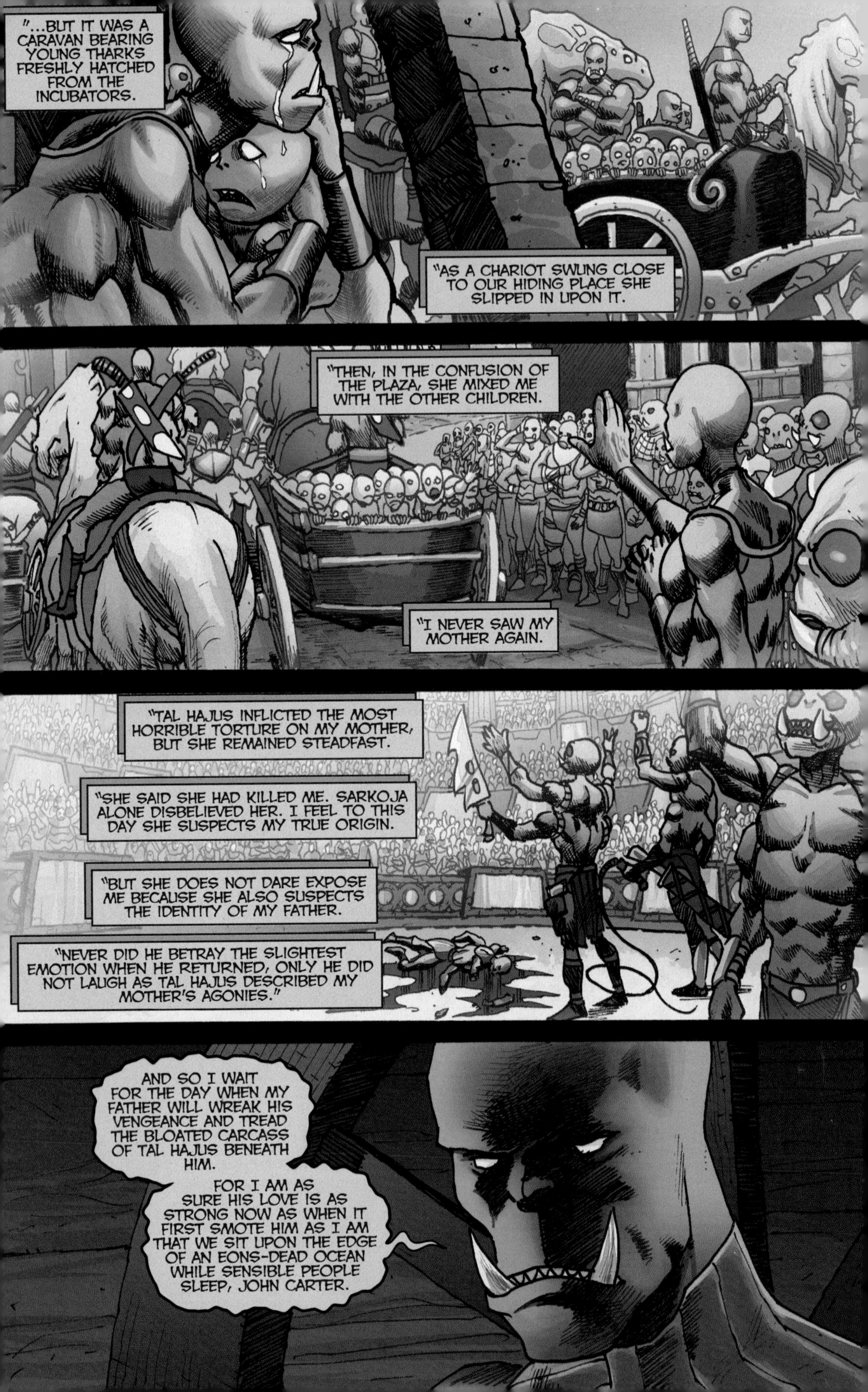
"...BUT IT WAS A CARAVAN BEARING YOUNG THARKS FRESHLY HATCHED FROM THE INCUBATORS.
"AS A CHARIOT SWUNG CLOSE TO OUR HIDING PLACE SHE SLIPPED IN UPON IT.
"THEN, IN THE CONFUSION OF THE PLAZA, SHE MIXED ME WITH THE OTHER CHILDREN.
"I NEVER SAW MY MOTHER AGAIN.
"TAL HAJUS INFLICTED THE MOST HORRIBLE TORTURE ON MY MOTHER, BUT SHE REMAINED STEADFAST.
"SHE SAID SHE HAD KILLED ME. SARKOJA ALONE DISBELIEVED HER. I FEEL TO THIS DAY SHE SUSPECTS MY TRUE ORIGIN.
"BUT SHE DOES NOT DARE EXPOSE ME BECAUSE SHE ALSO SUSPECTS THE IDENTITY OF MY FATHER.
"NEVER DID HE BETRAY THE SLIGHTEST EMOTION WHEN HE RETURNED, ONLY HE DID NOT LAUGH AS TAL HAJUS DESCRIBED MY MOTHER'S AGONIES."
AND SO I WAIT FOR THE DAY WHEN MY FATHER WILL WREAK HIS VENGEANCE AND TREAD THE BLOATED CARCASS OF TAL HAJUS BENEATH HIM.
FOR I AM AS SURE HIS LOVE IS AS STRONG NOW AS WHEN IT FIRST SMOTE HIM AS I AM THAT WE SIT UPON THE EDGE OF AN EONS-DEAD OCEAN WHILE SENSIBLE PEOPLE SLEEP, JOHN CARTER.

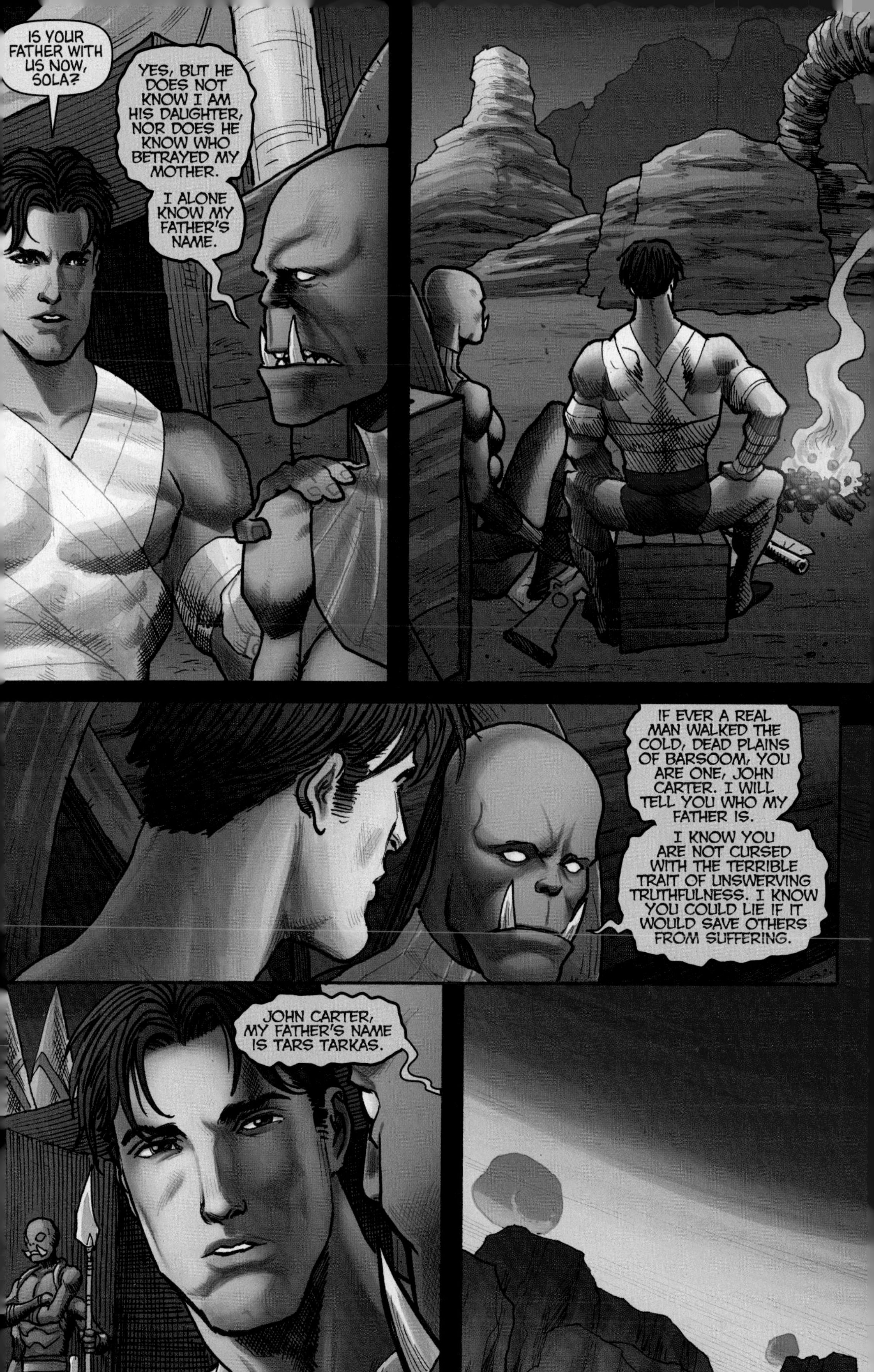
IS YOUR FATHER WITH US NOW, SOLA?
YES, BUT HE DOES NOT KNOW I AM HIS DAUGHTER, NOR DOES HE KNOW WHO BETRAYED MY MOTHER.
I ALONE KNOW MY FATHER'S NAME.
IF EVER A REAL MAN WALKED THE COLD, DEAD PLAINS OF BARSOOM, YOU ARE ONE, JOHN CARTER. I WILL TELL YOU WHO MY FATHER IS.
I KNOW YOU ARE NOT CURSED WITH THE TERRIBLE TRAIT OF UNSWERVING TRUTHFULNESS. I KNOW YOU COULD LIE IF IT WOULD SAVE OTHERS FROM SUFFERING.
JOHN CARTER, MY FATHER'S NAME IS TARS TARKAS.

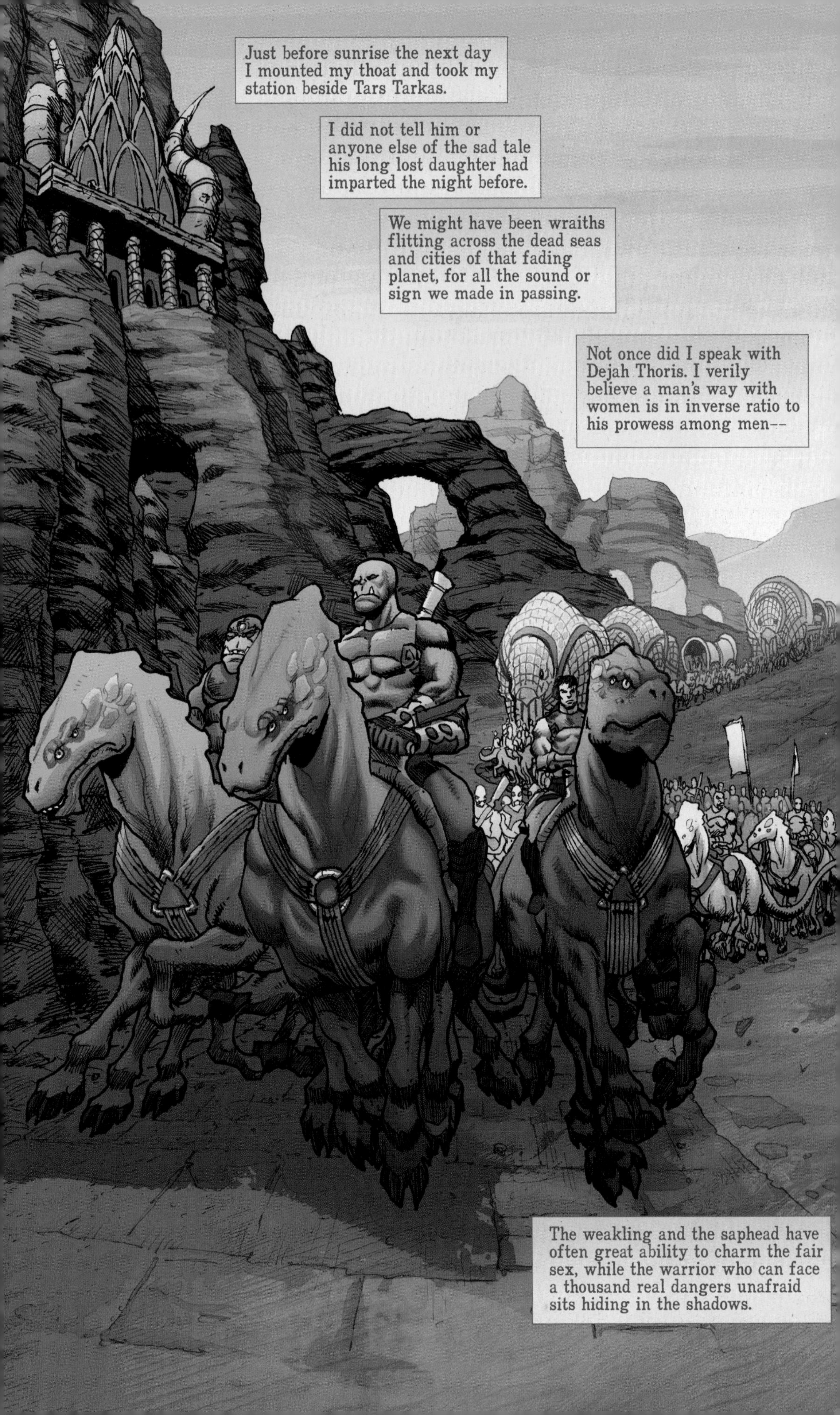
Just before sunrise the next day I mounted my thoat and took my station beside Tars Tarkas.
I did not tell him or anyone else of the sad tale his long lost daughter had imparted the night before.
We might have been wraiths flitting across the dead seas and cities of that fading planet, for all the sound or sign we made in passing.
Not once did I speak with Dejah Thoris. I verily believe a man's way with women is in inverse ratio to his prowess among men--
The weakling and the saphead have often great ability to charm the fair sex, while the warrior who can face a thousand real dangers unafraid sits hiding in the shadows.

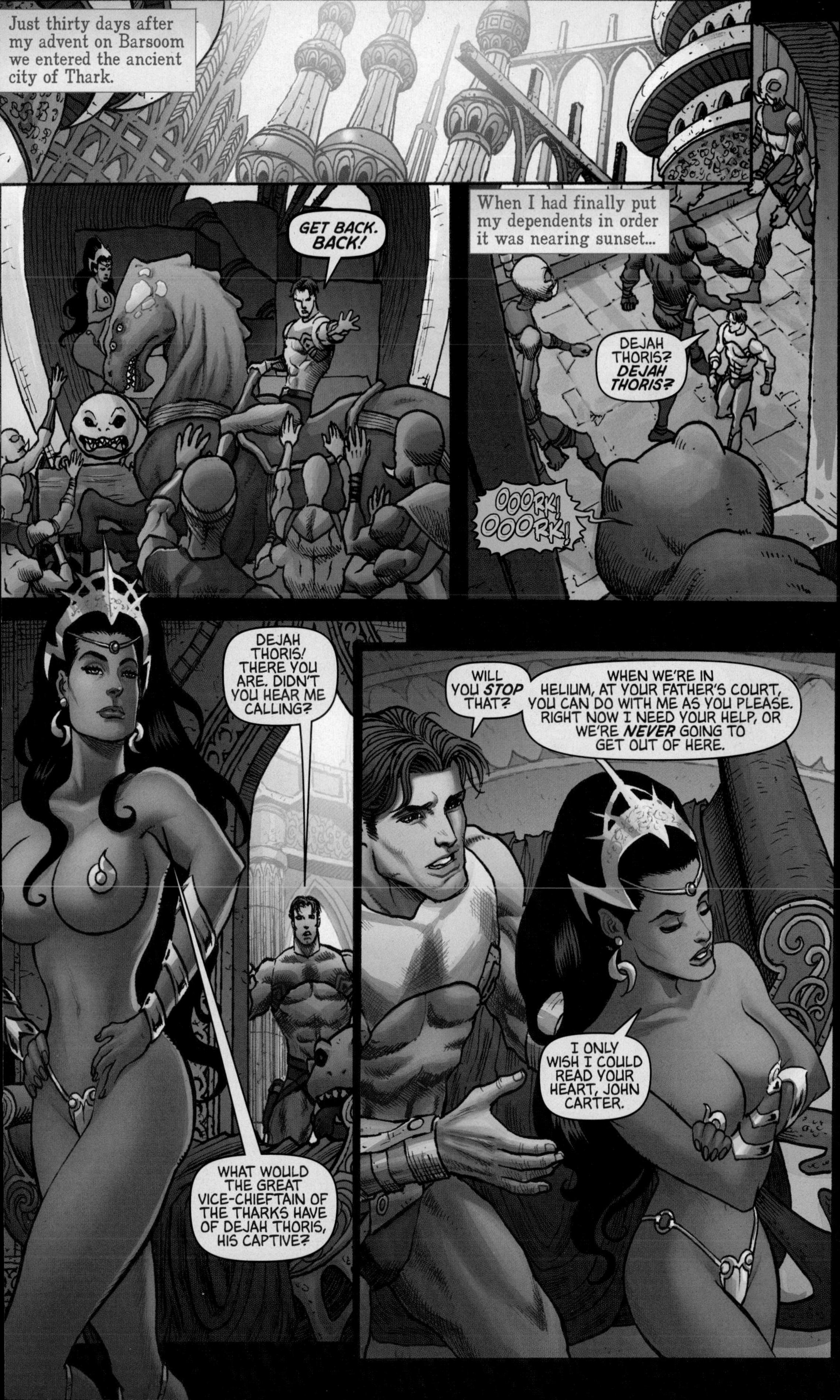
Just thirty days after my advent on Barsoom we entered the ancient city of Thark.
GET BACK. BACK!
When I had finally put my dependents in order it was nearing sunset...
DEJAH THORIS? DEJAH THORIS?
OOORK! OOORK!
DEJAH THORIS! THERE YOU ARE. DIDN'T YOU HEAR ME CALLING?
WHAT WOULD THE GREAT VICE-CHIEFTAIN OF THE THARKS HAVE OF DEJAH THORIS, HIS CAPTIVE?
WILL YOU STOP THAT?
WHEN WE'RE IN HELIUM, AT YOUR FATHER'S COURT, YOU CAN DO WITH ME AS YOU PLEASE. RIGHT NOW I NEED YOUR HELP, OR WE'RE NEVER GOING TO GET OUT OF HERE.
I ONLY WISH I COULD READ YOUR HEART, JOHN CARTER.

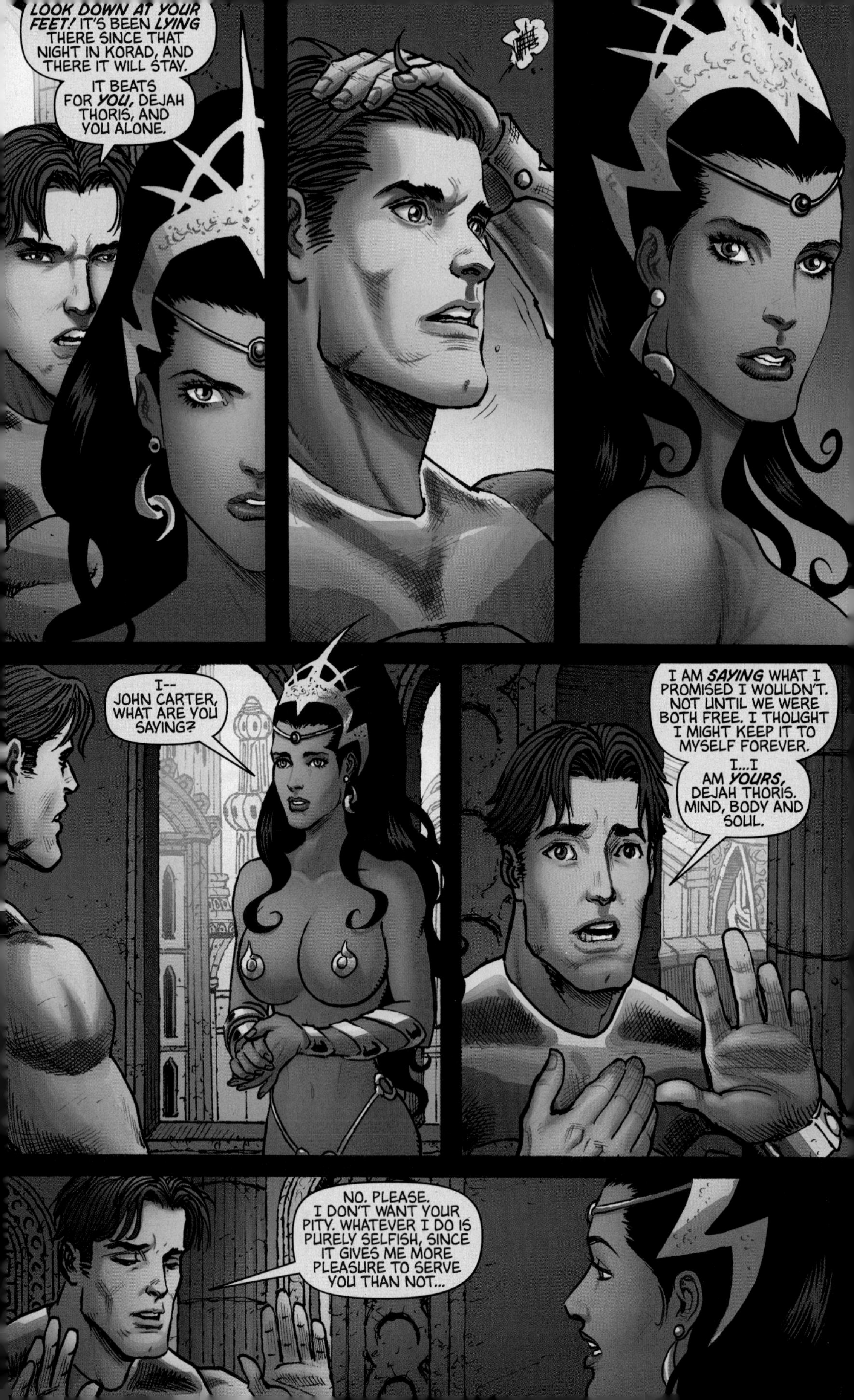
LOOK DOWN AT YOUR FEET! IT'S BEEN LYING THERE SINCE THAT NIGHT IN KORAD, AND THERE IT WILL STAY.
IT BEATS FOR YOU, DEJAH THORIS, AND YOU ALONE.
I-- JOHN CARTER, WHAT ARE YOU SAYING?
I AM SAYING WHAT I PROMISED I WOULDN'T. NOT UNTIL WE WERE BOTH FREE. I THOUGHT I MIGHT KEEP IT TO MYSELF FOREVER.
I...I AM YOURS, DEJAH THORIS. MIND, BODY AND SOUL.
NO. PLEASE. I DON'T WANT YOUR PITY. WHATEVER I DO IS PURELY SELFISH, SINCE IT GIVES ME MORE PLEASURE TO SERVE YOU THAN NOT...

SOLA! WHAT'S WRONG?

JOHN CARTER! SARKOJA HAS BEEN BEFORE TAL HAJUS.

YOU ARE TO BE THROWN TO THE WILD CALOTS IN THE GREAT ARENA FOR THE YEARLY GAMES!

ALL RIGHT. WE'RE GETTING OUT OF HERE. *RIGHT NOW.*

SOLA, COME WITH US. THIS IS YOUR CHANCE TO BE FREE.

YES, DO! YOU'VE BEEN SO KIND. THE NATION OF HELIUM WOULD WELCOME YOU MOST WARMLY.

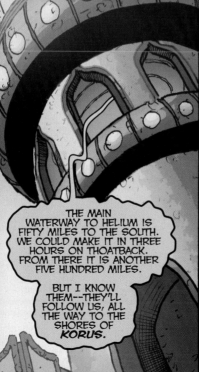

THE MAIN WATERWAY TO HELIUM IS FIFTY MILES TO THE SOUTH. WE COULD MAKE IT IN THREE HOURS ON THOATBACK. FROM THERE IT IS ANOTHER FIVE HUNDRED MILES.

BUT I KNOW THEM--THEY'LL FOLLOW US, ALL THE WAY TO THE SHORES OF *KORUS.*

THAT SOUNDS LIKE A VERY BAD IDEA, THEN.

THERE *IS* ANOTHER WATERWAY, TWO HUNDRED MILES TO THE NORTH. IT TOO LEADS TO HELIUM. THEY'D NEVER SUSPECT WE'D TRY FOR THAT.

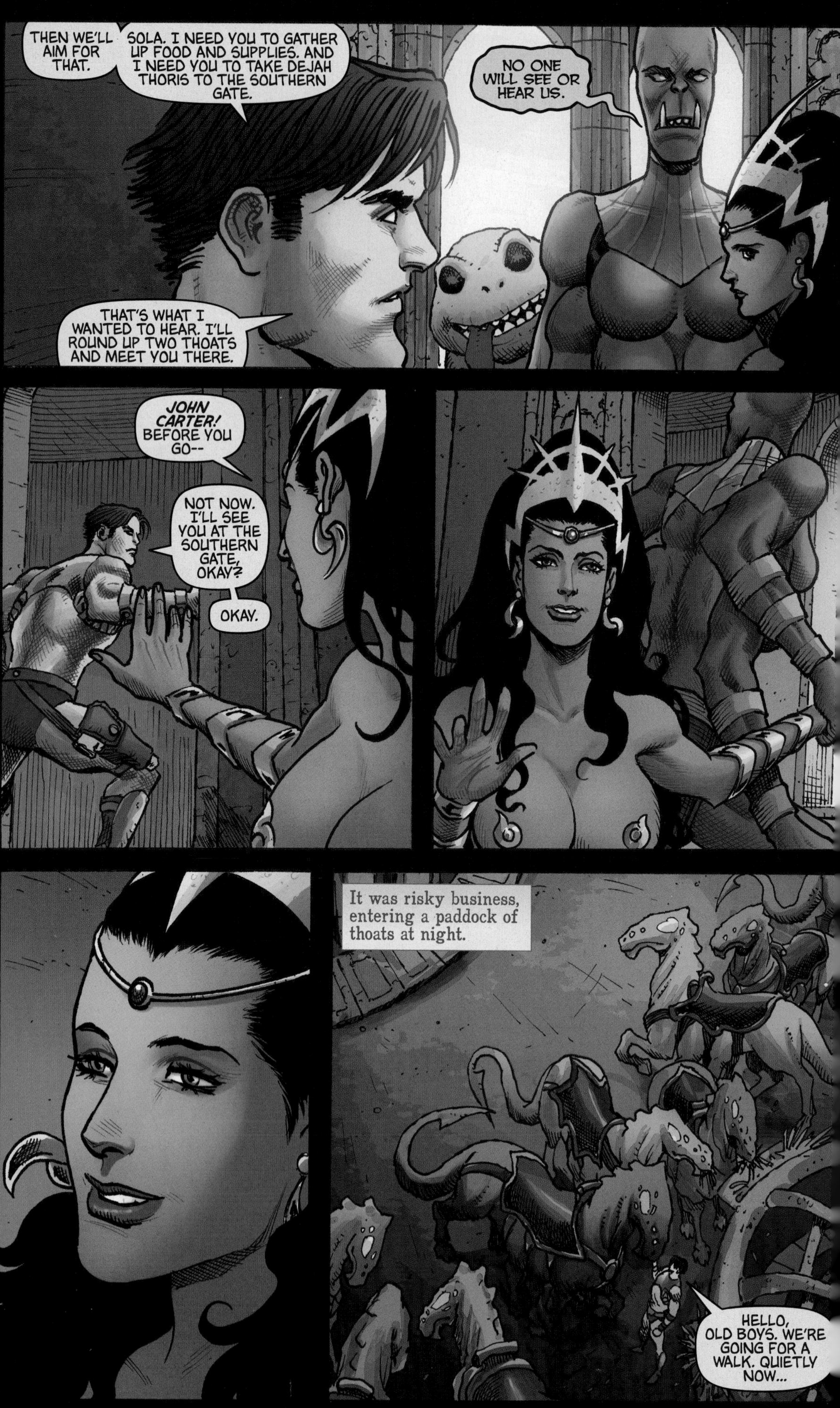
THEN WE'LL AIM FOR THAT.
SOLA. I NEED YOU TO GATHER UP FOOD AND SUPPLIES. AND I NEED YOU TO TAKE DEJAH THORIS TO THE SOUTHERN GATE.
NO ONE WILL SEE OR HEAR US.
THAT'S WHAT I WANTED TO HEAR. I'LL ROUND UP TWO THOATS AND MEET YOU THERE.
JOHN CARTER! BEFORE YOU GO--
NOT NOW. I'LL SEE YOU AT THE SOUTHERN GATE, OKAY?
OKAY.
It was risky business, entering a paddock of thoats at night.
HELLO, OLD BOYS. WE'RE GOING FOR A WALK. QUIETLY NOW...

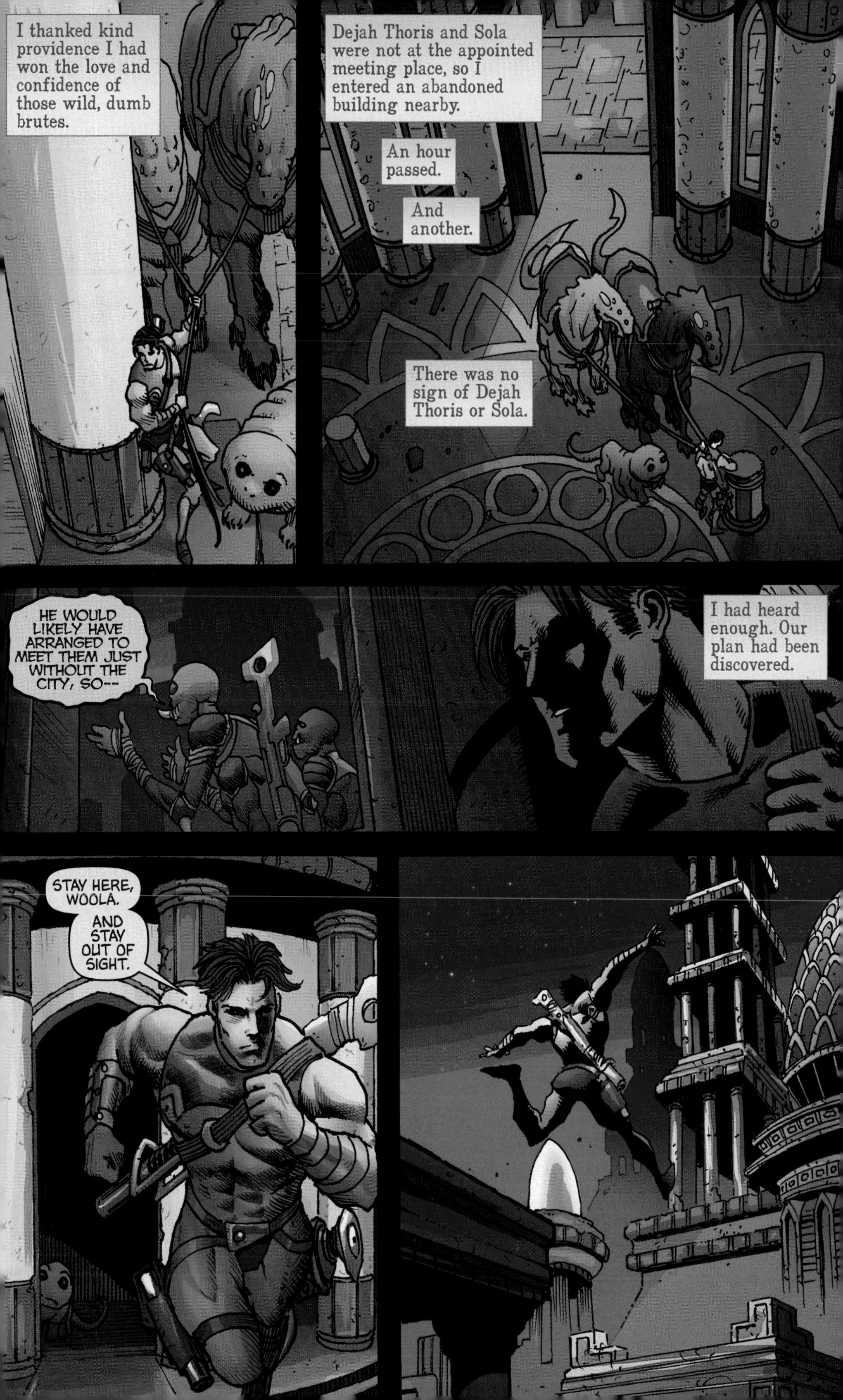
I thanked kind providence I had won the love and confidence of those wild, dumb brutes.
Dejah Thoris and Sola were not at the appointed meeting place, so I entered an abandoned building nearby.
An hour passed.
And another.
There was no sign of Dejah Thoris or Sola.
HE WOULD LIKELY HAVE ARRANGED TO MEET THEM JUST WITHOUT THE CITY, SO--
I had heard enough. Our plan had been discovered.
STAY HERE, WOOLA.
AND STAY OUT OF SIGHT.

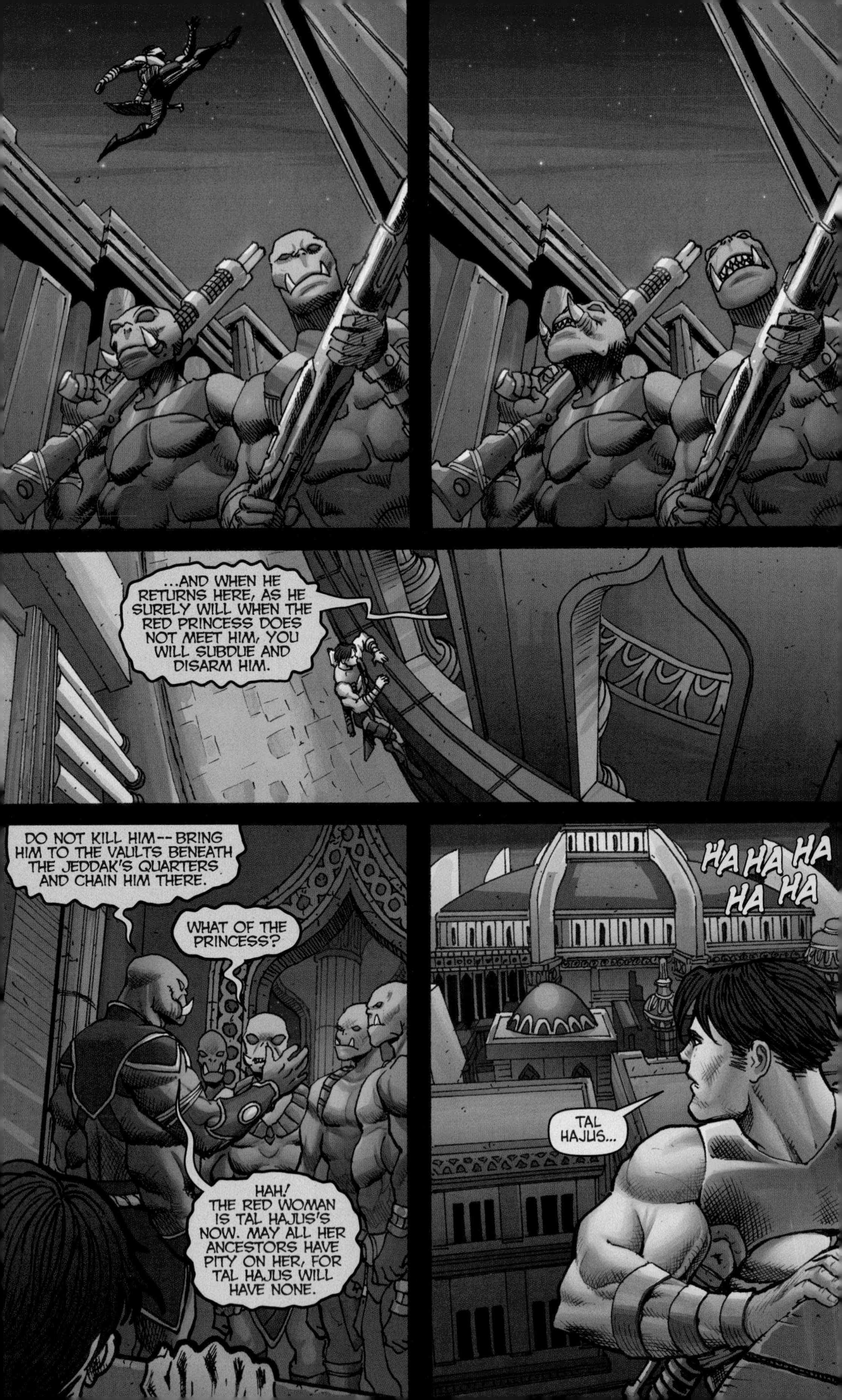

...AND WHEN HE RETURNS HERE, AS HE SURELY WILL WHEN THE RED PRINCESS DOES NOT MEET HIM, YOU WILL SUBDUE AND DISARM HIM.
DO NOT KILL HIM--BRING HIM TO THE VAULTS BENEATH THE JEDDAK'S QUARTERS AND CHAIN HIM THERE.
WHAT OF THE PRINCESS?
HAH! THE RED WOMAN IS TAL HAJUS'S NOW. MAY ALL HER ANCESTORS HAVE PITY ON HER, FOR TAL HAJUS WILL HAVE NONE.
HA HA HA HA HA
TAL HAJUS...

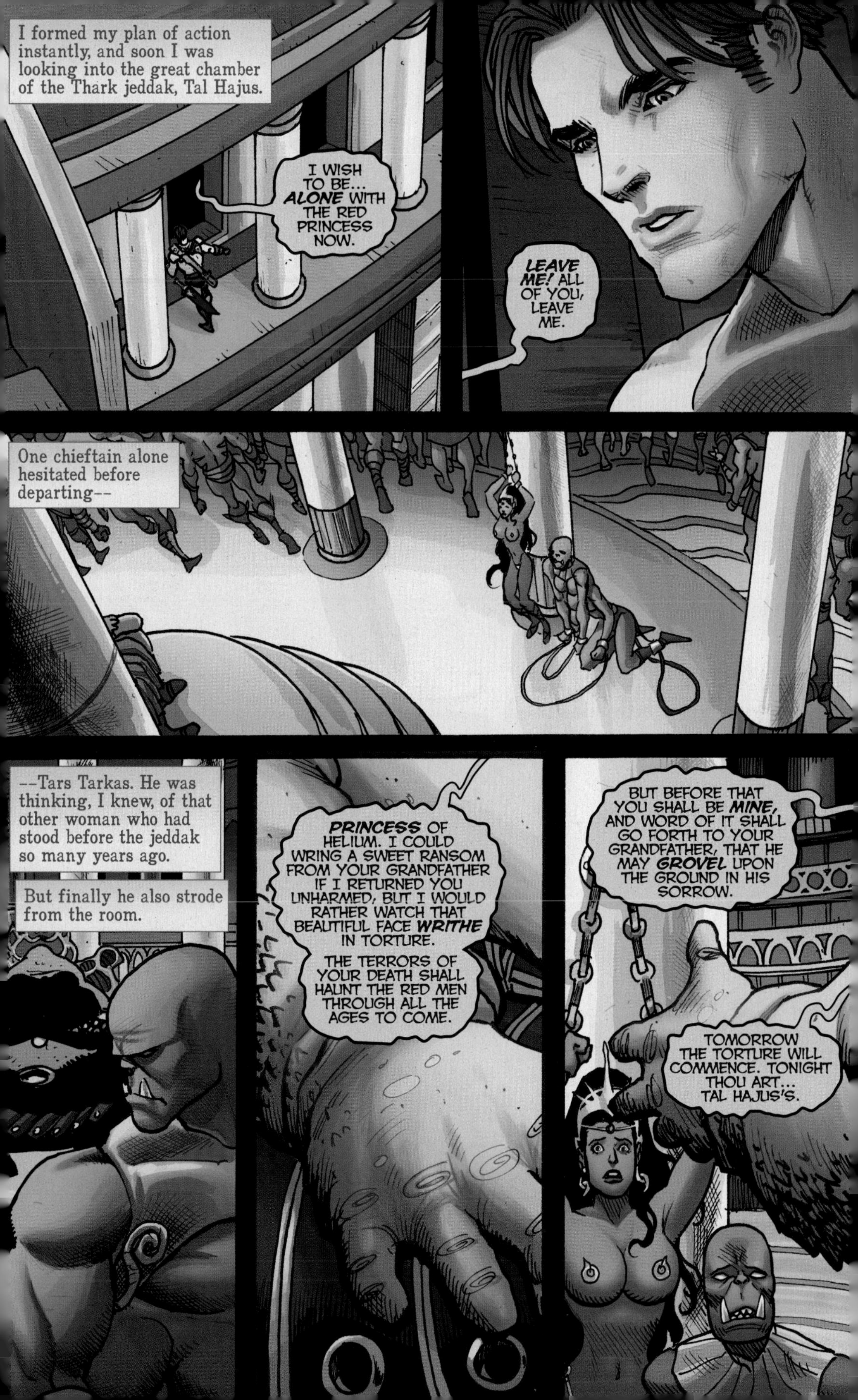
I formed my plan of action instantly, and soon I was looking into the great chamber of the Thark jeddak, Tal Hajus.
I WISH TO BE... ALONE WITH THE RED PRINCESS NOW.
LEAVE ME! ALL OF YOU, LEAVE ME.
One chieftain alone hesitated before departing--
--Tars Tarkas. He was thinking, I knew, of that other woman who had stood before the jeddak so many years ago.
But finally he also strode from the room.
PRINCESS OF HELIUM. I COULD WRING A SWEET RANSOM FROM YOUR GRANDFATHER IF I RETURNED YOU UNHARMED, BUT I WOULD RATHER WATCH THAT BEAUTIFUL FACE WRITHE IN TORTURE.
THE TERRORS OF YOUR DEATH SHALL HAUNT THE RED MEN THROUGH ALL THE AGES TO COME.
BUT BEFORE THAT YOU SHALL BE MINE, AND WORD OF IT SHALL GO FORTH TO YOUR GRANDFATHER, THAT HE MAY GROVEL UPON THE GROUND IN HIS SORROW.
TOMORROW THE TORTURE WILL COMMENCE. TONIGHT THOU ART... TAL HAJUS'S.

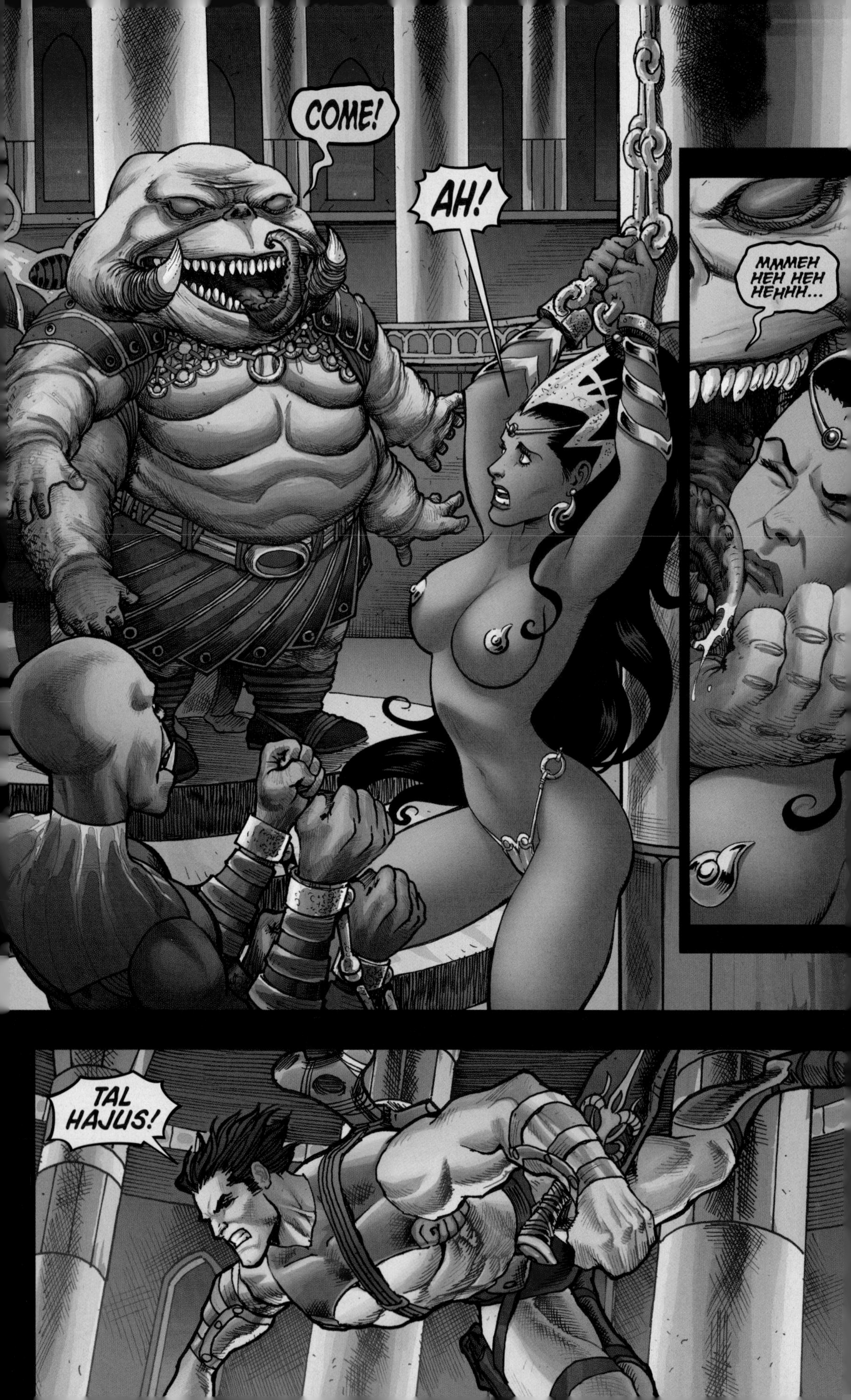
COME!
AH!
MMMEH HEH HEH HEHHH...
TAL HAJUS!

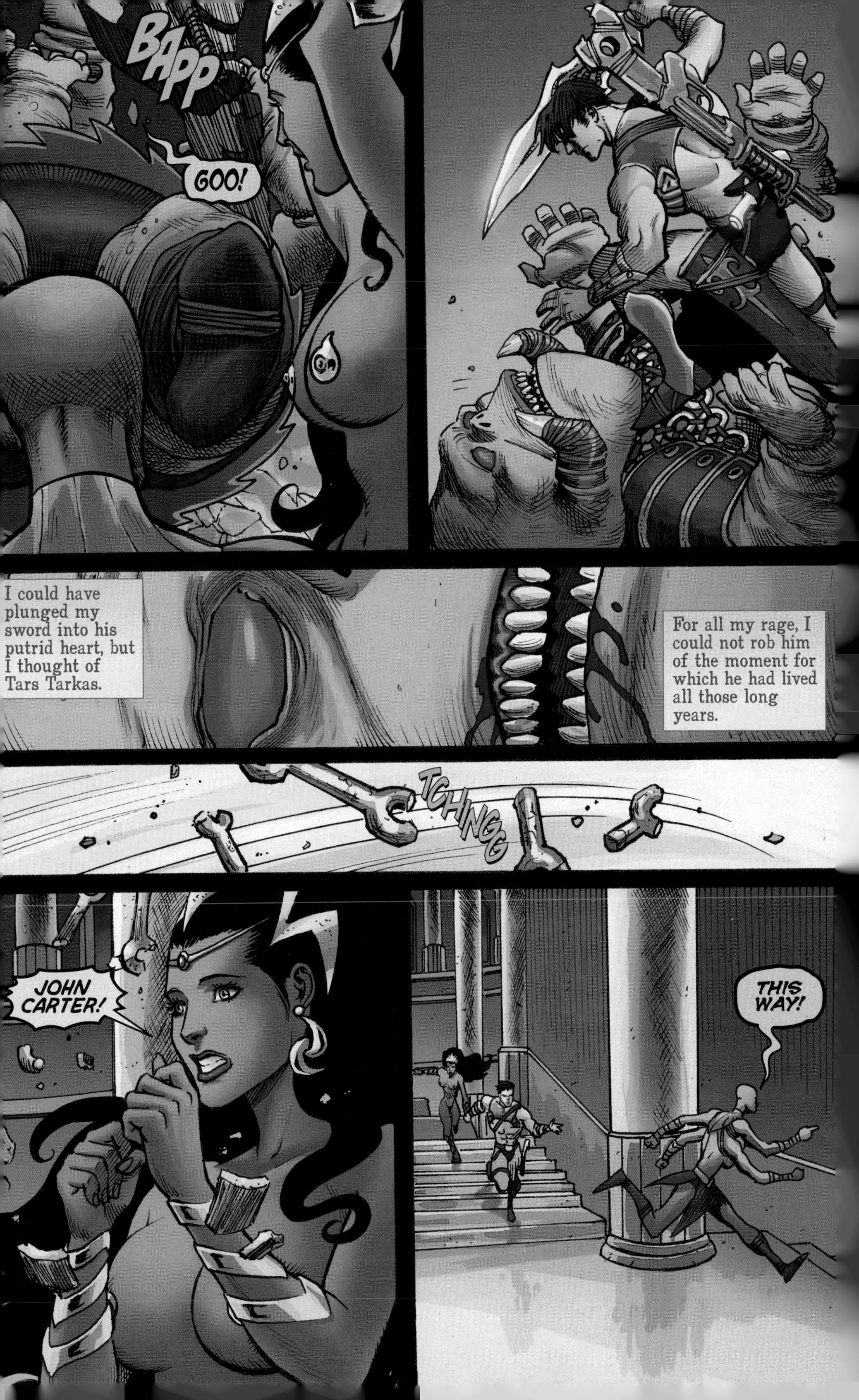
BAPP
GOO!
I could have plunged my sword into his putrid heart, but I thought of Tars Tarkas.
For all my rage, I could not rob him of the moment for which he had lived all those long years.
TCHNGG
JOHN CARTER!
THIS WAY!

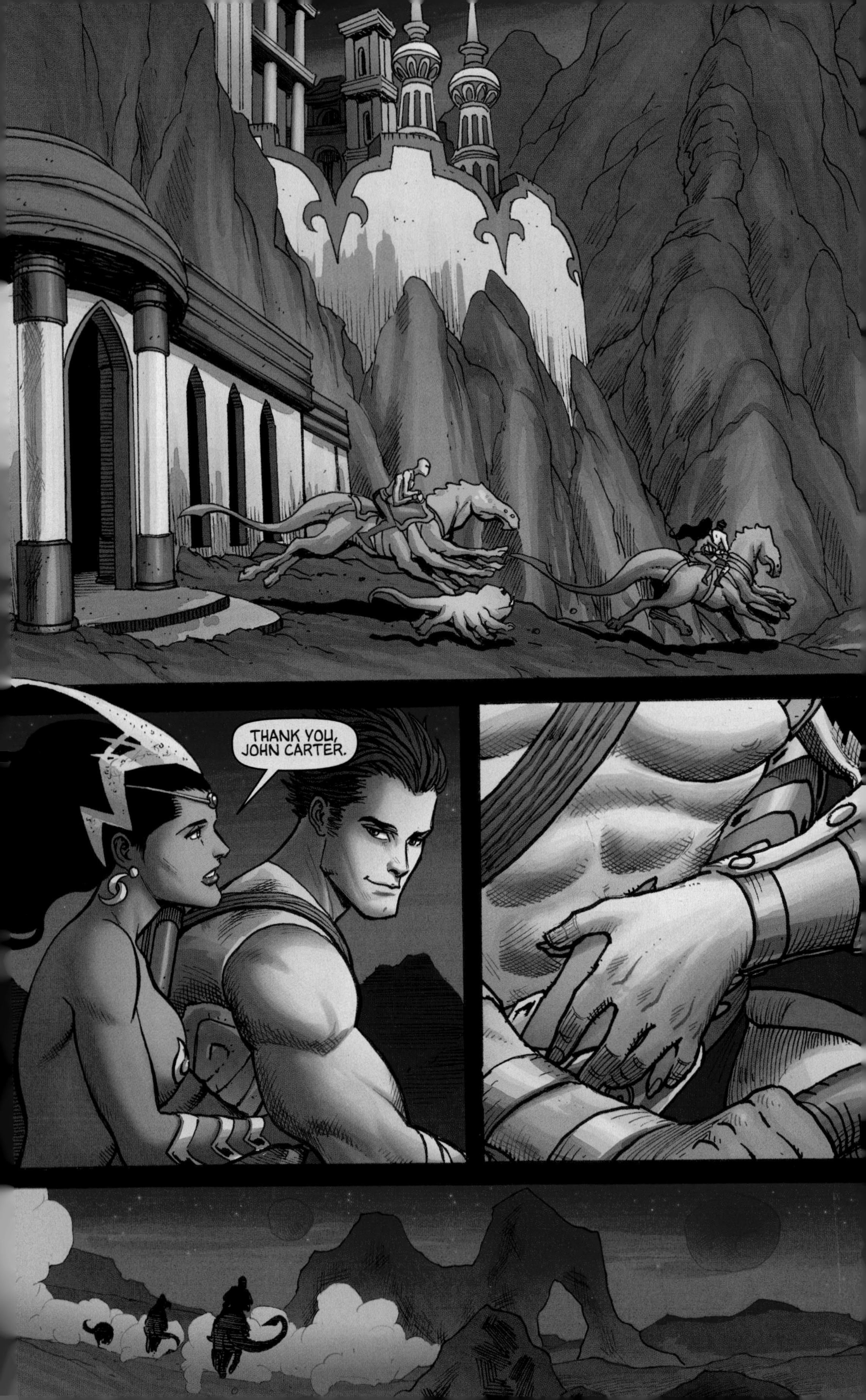
THANK YOU, JOHN CARTER.

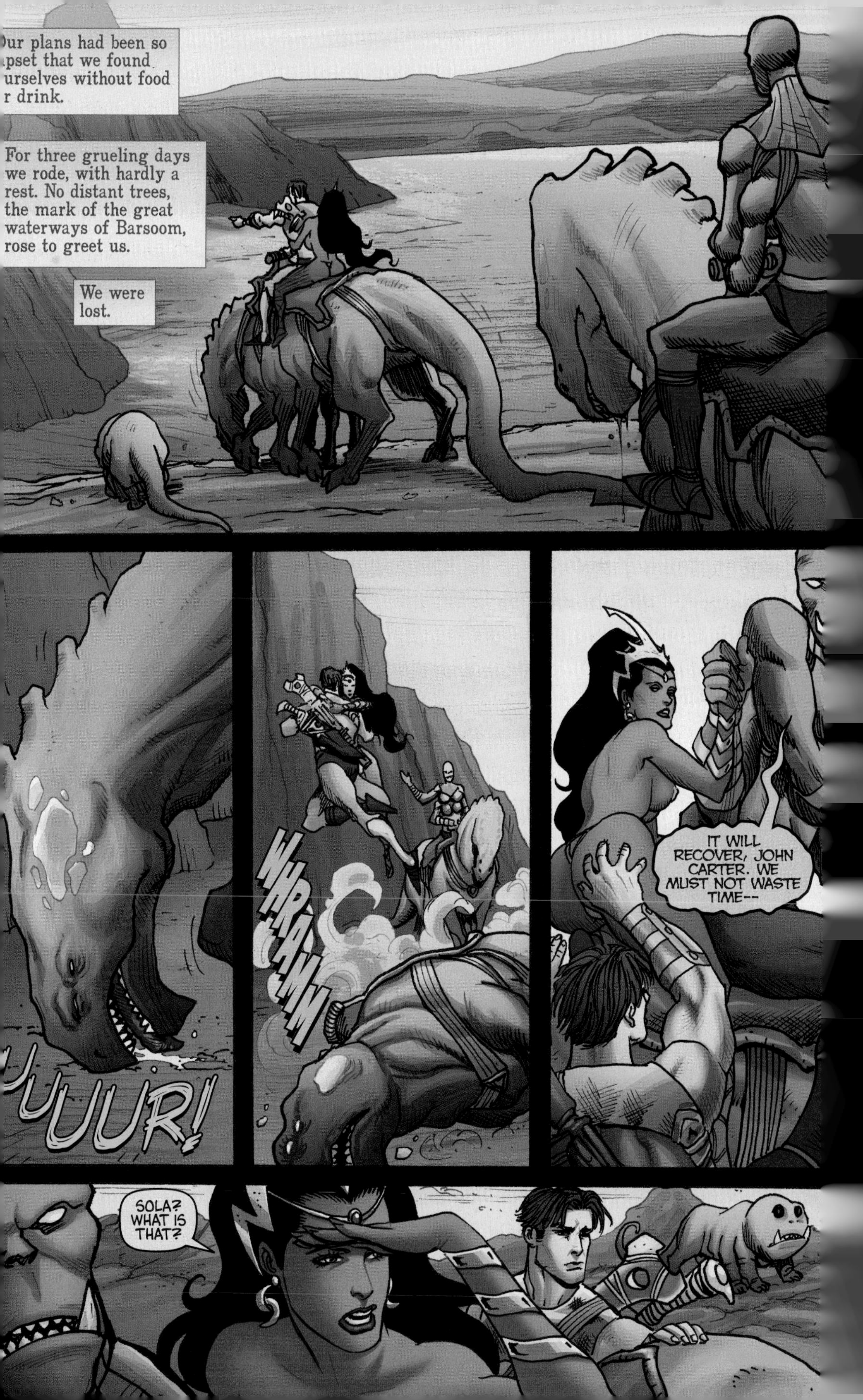
Our plans had been so upset that we found ourselves without food or drink.
For three grueling days we rode, with hardly a rest. No distant trees, the mark of the great waterways of Barsoom, rose to greet us.
We were lost.
UUUUR!
WHRAMM
IT WILL RECOVER, JOHN CARTER. WE MUST NOT WASTE TIME--
SOLA? WHAT IS THAT?

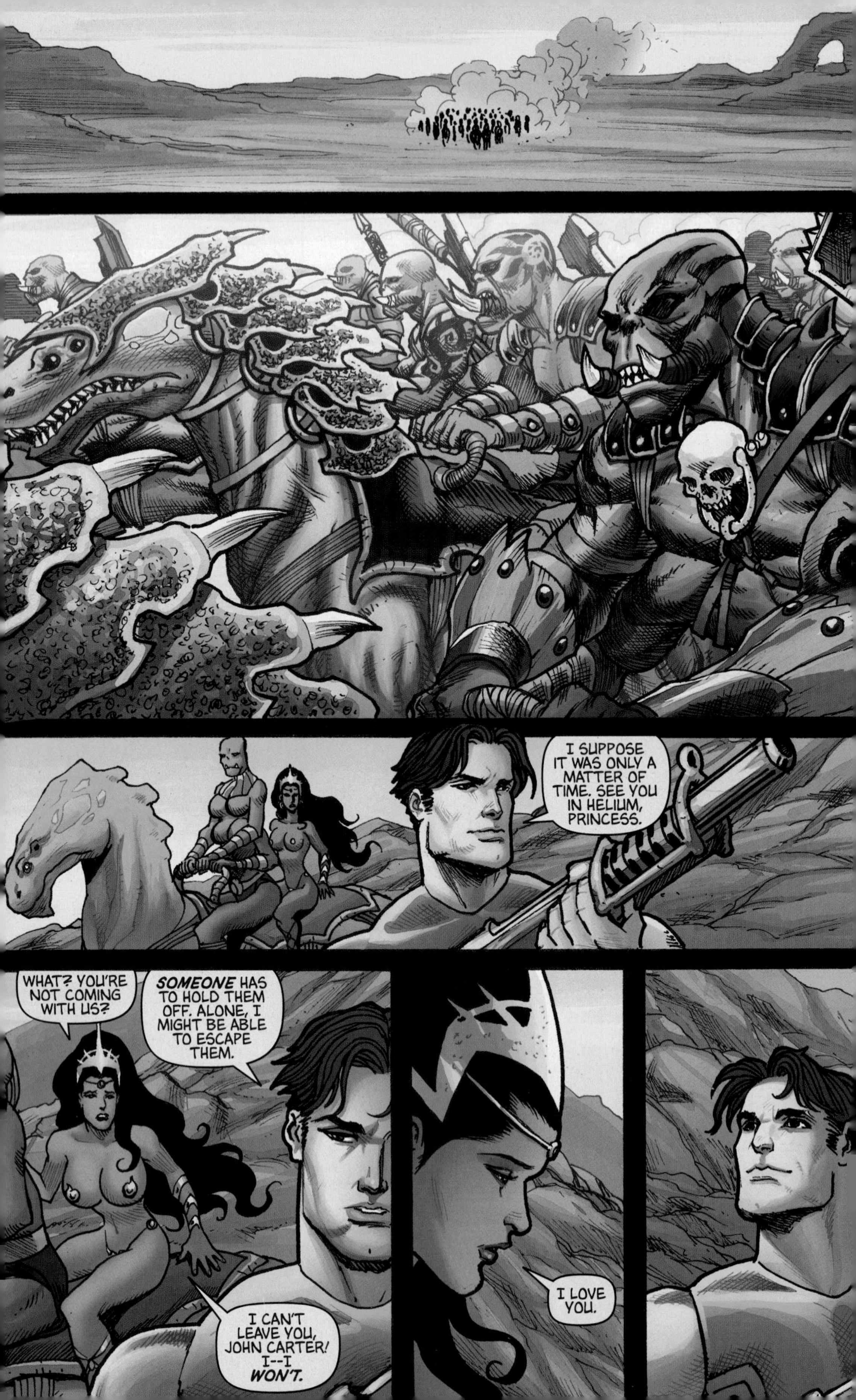
I SUPPOSE IT WAS ONLY A MATTER OF TIME. SEE YOU IN HELIUM, PRINCESS.
WHAT? YOU'RE NOT COMING WITH US?
SOMEONE HAS TO HOLD THEM OFF. ALONE, I MIGHT BE ABLE TO ESCAPE THEM.
I CAN'T LEAVE YOU, JOHN CARTER! I--I WON'T.
I LOVE YOU.

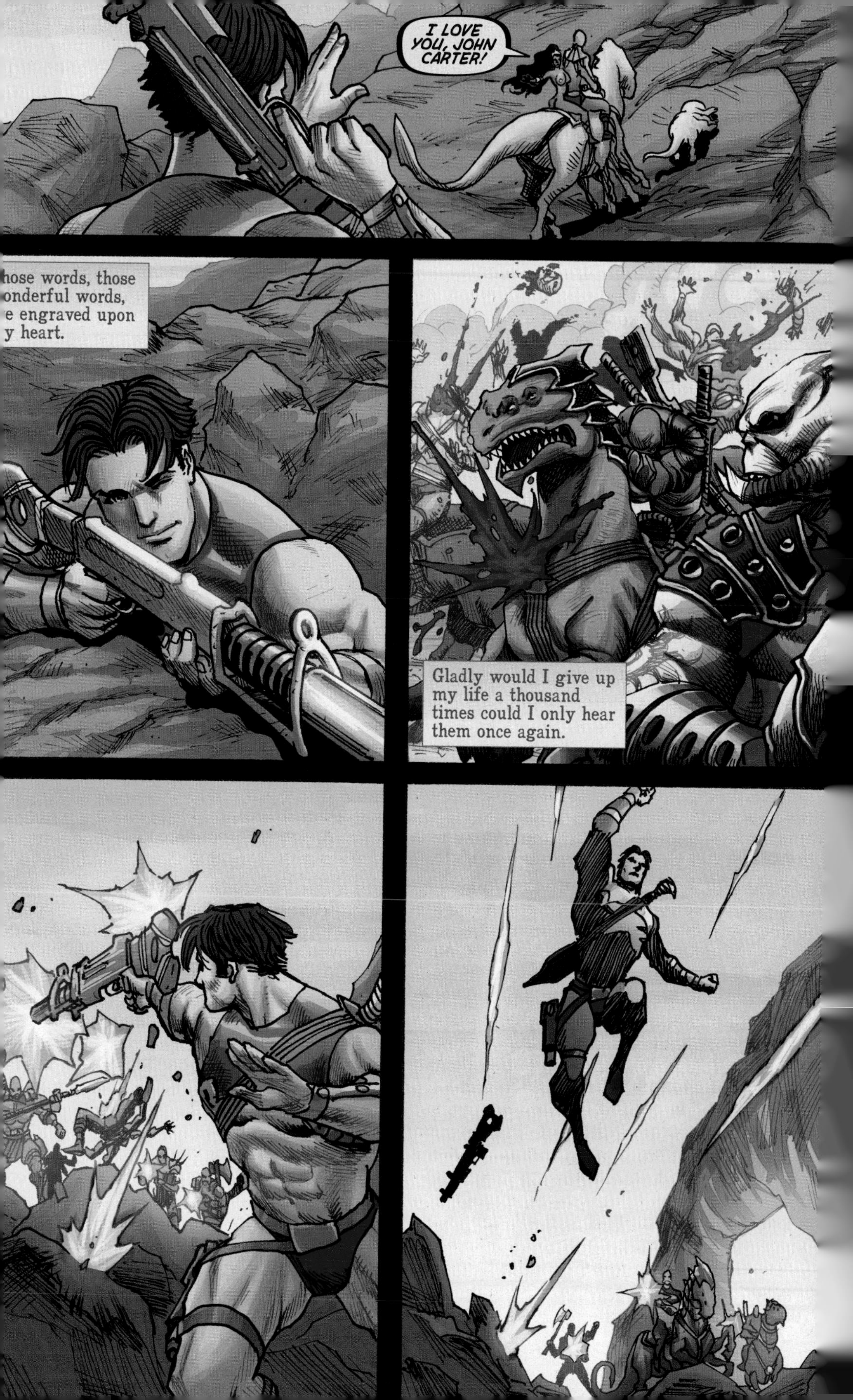

I LOVE YOU, JOHN CARTER!
hose words, those onderful words, e engraved upon y heart.
Gladly would I give up my life a thousand times could I only hear them once again.

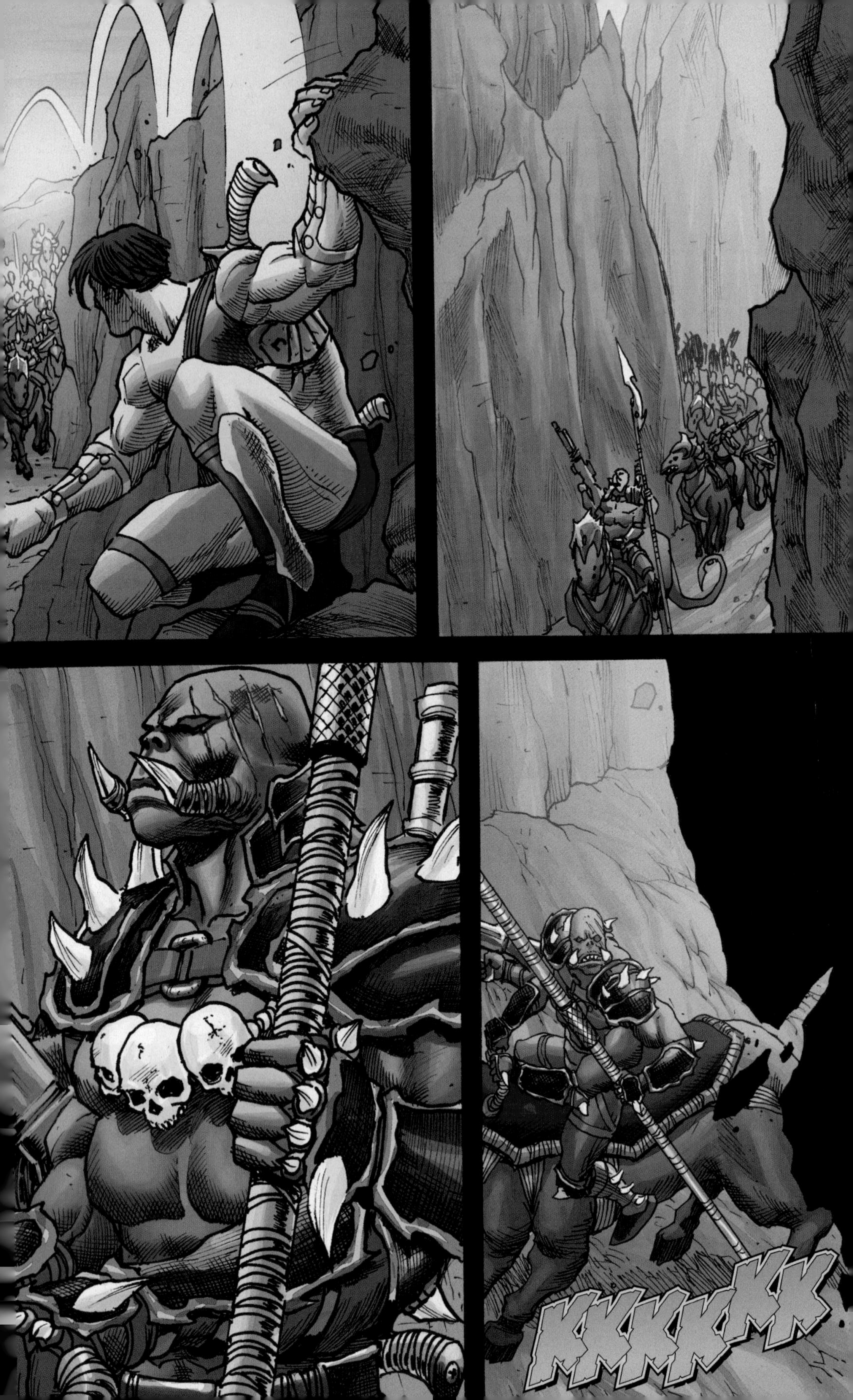
KKKKKK

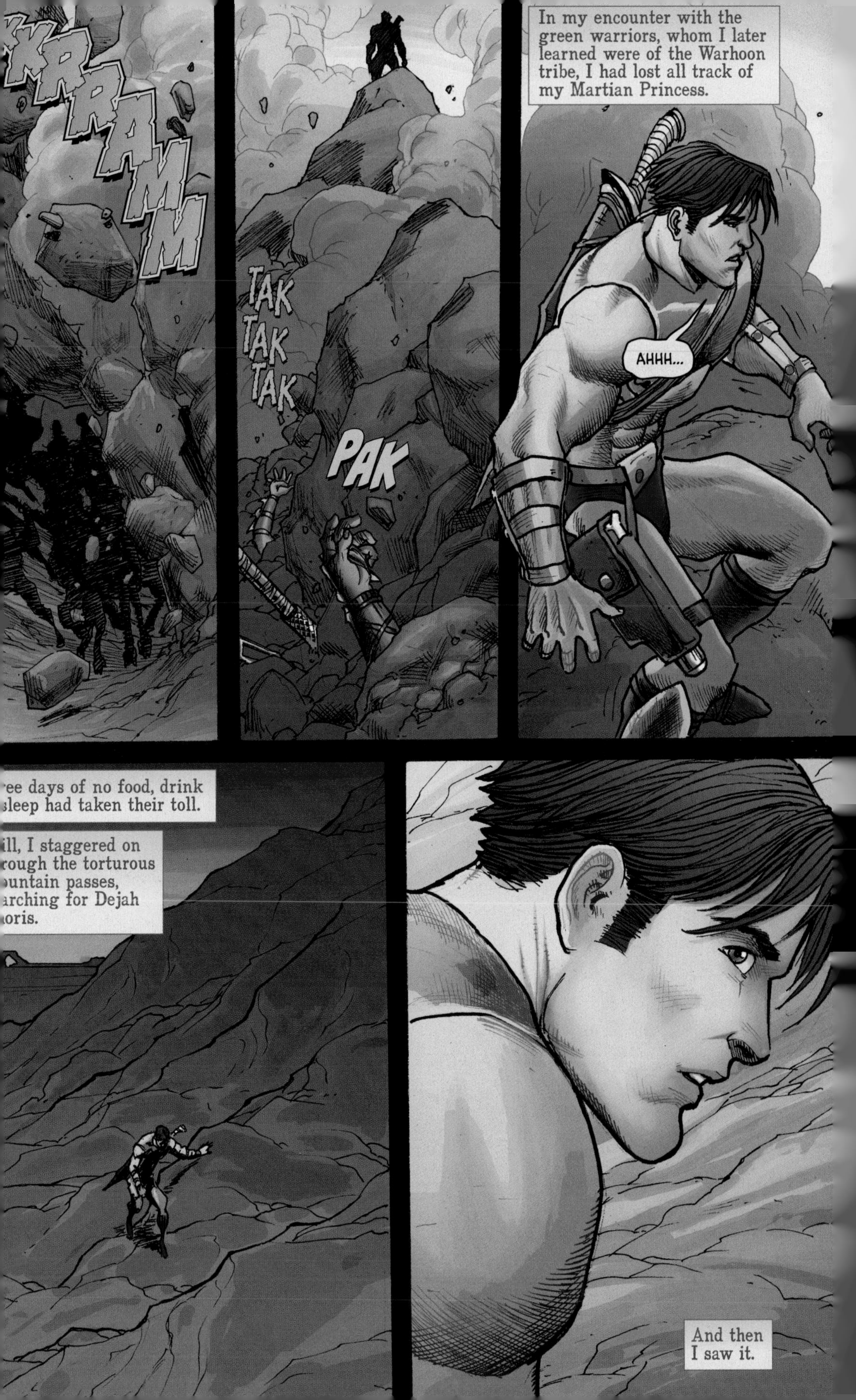
KRRAMM
TAK
TAK
TAK
PAK
In my encounter with the green warriors, whom I later learned were of the Warhoon tribe, I had lost all track of my Martian Princess.
AHHH...
ree days of no food, drink
sleep had taken their toll.
ill, I staggered on
rough the torturous
ountain passes,
arching for Dejah
oris.
And then I saw it.

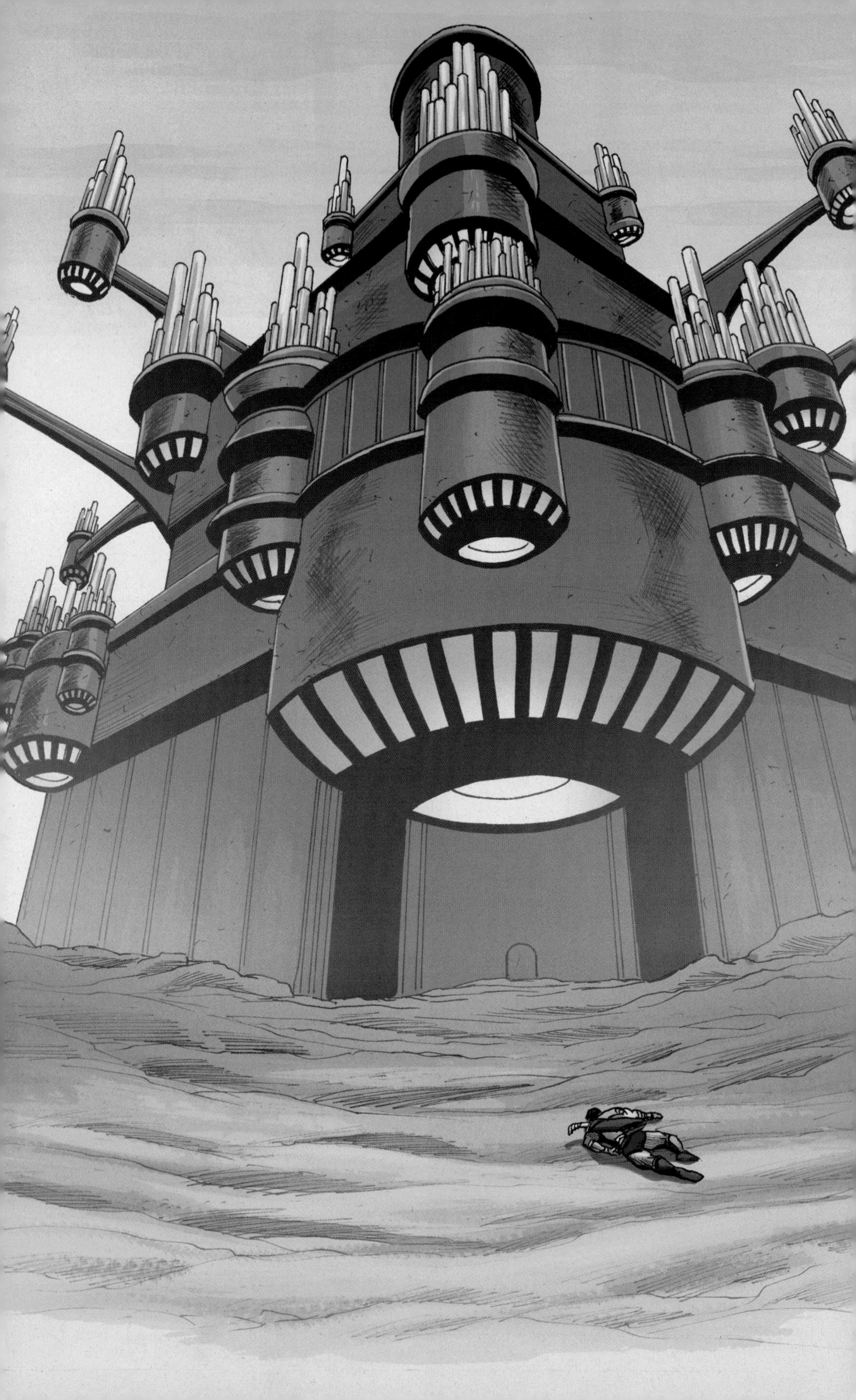

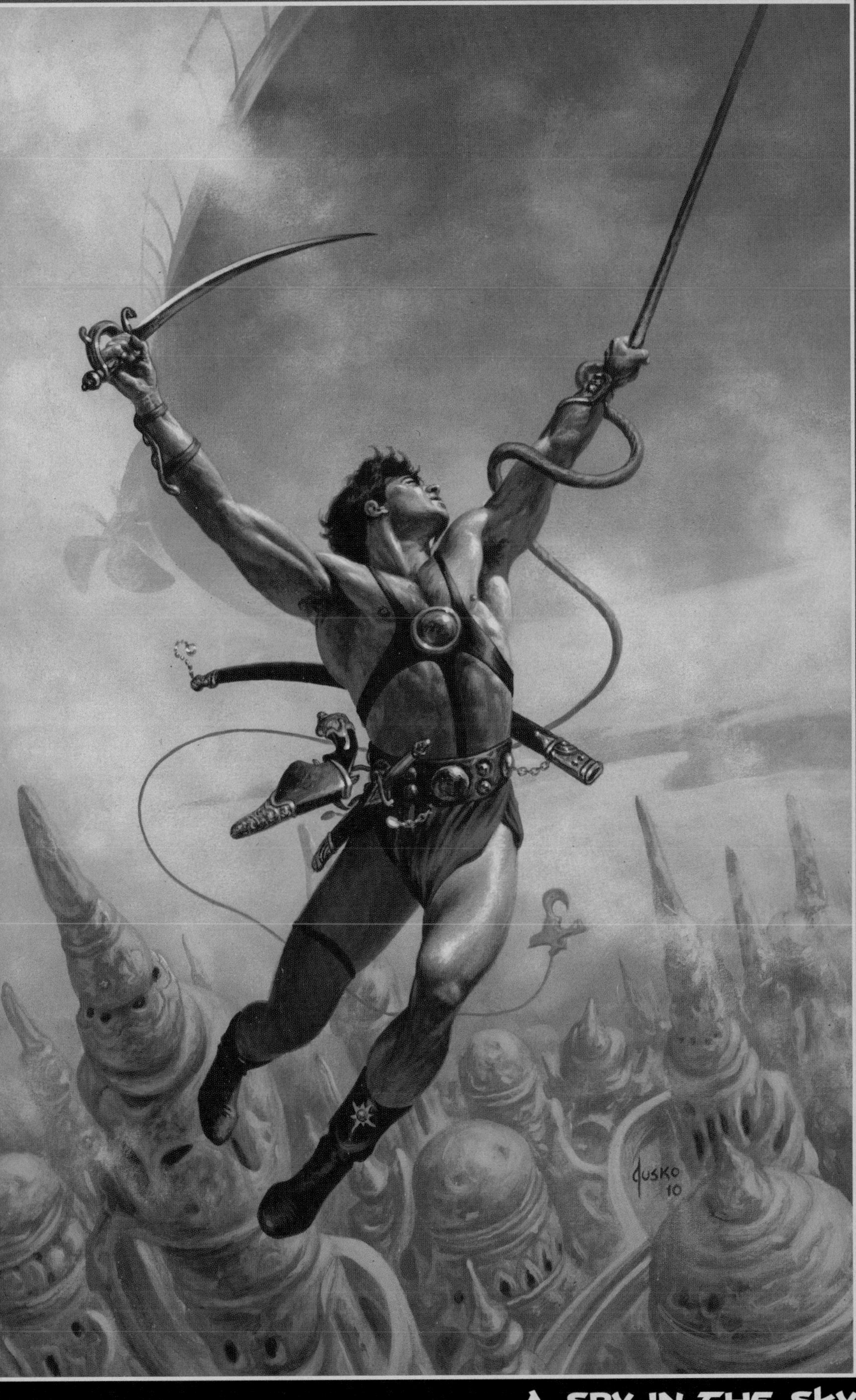
JUSKO
10

A SPY IN THE SKY

Issue #7 cover by JOE JUSKO

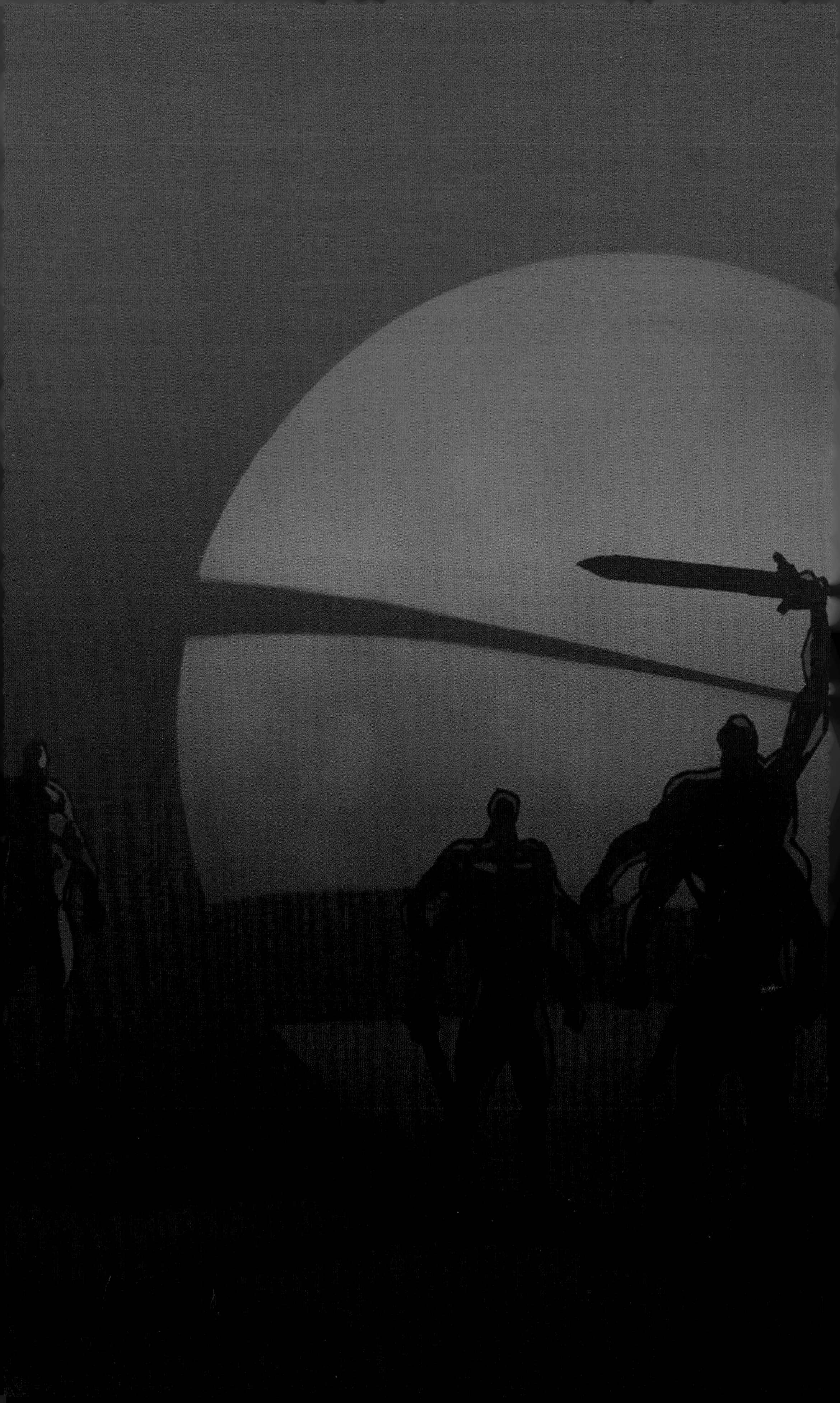

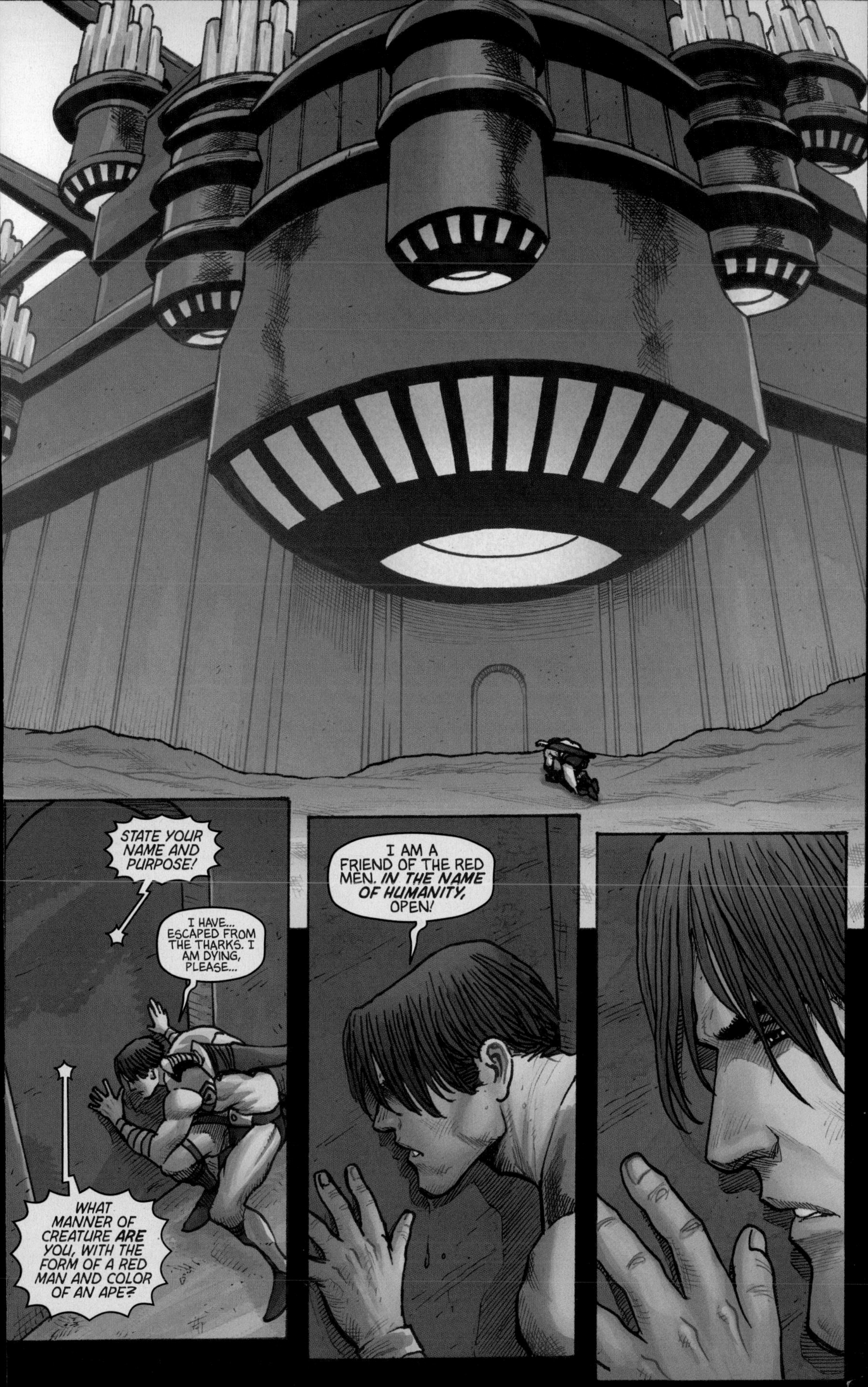
STATE YOUR NAME AND PURPOSE!
I HAVE... ESCAPED FROM THE THARKS. I AM DYING, PLEASE...
WHAT MANNER OF CREATURE ARE YOU, WITH THE FORM OF A RED MAN AND COLOR OF AN APE?
I AM A FRIEND OF THE RED MEN. IN THE NAME OF HUMANITY, OPEN!

RRRRRR

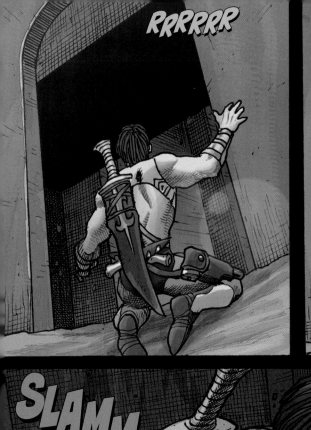

SLAMM

A second and third door opened and closed after me, just like the first.

I wasn't going anywhere.

HELP YOURSELF.

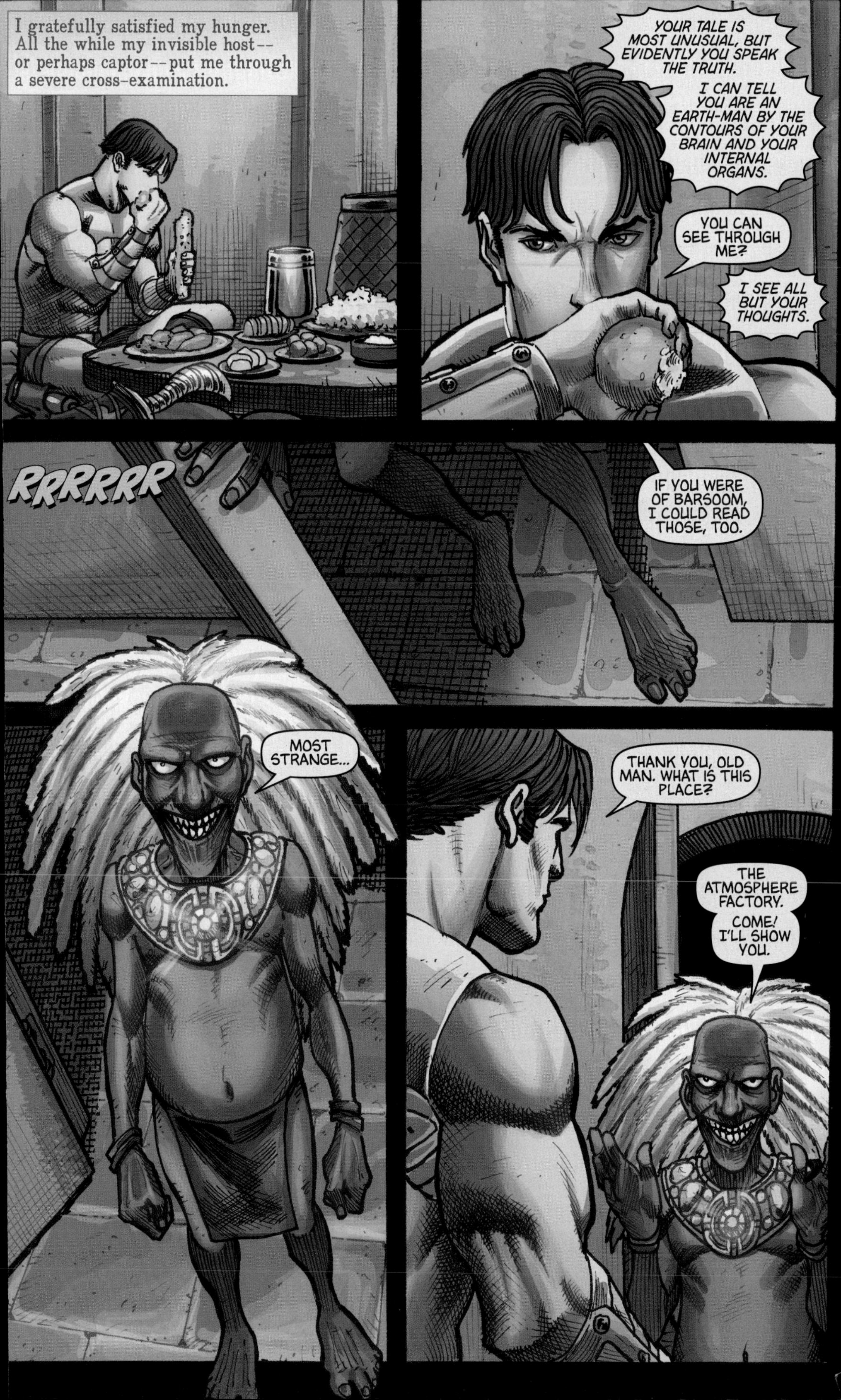
I gratefully satisfied my hunger. All the while my invisible host--or perhaps captor--put me through a severe cross-examination.
YOUR TALE IS MOST UNUSUAL, BUT EVIDENTLY YOU SPEAK THE TRUTH.
I CAN TELL YOU ARE AN EARTH-MAN BY THE CONTOURS OF YOUR BRAIN AND YOUR INTERNAL ORGANS.
YOU CAN SEE THROUGH ME?
I SEE ALL BUT YOUR THOUGHTS.
RRRRRR
IF YOU WERE OF BARSOOM, I COULD READ THOSE, TOO.
MOST STRANGE...
THANK YOU, OLD MAN. WHAT IS THIS PLACE?
THE ATMOSPHERE FACTORY.
COME! I'LL SHOW YOU.

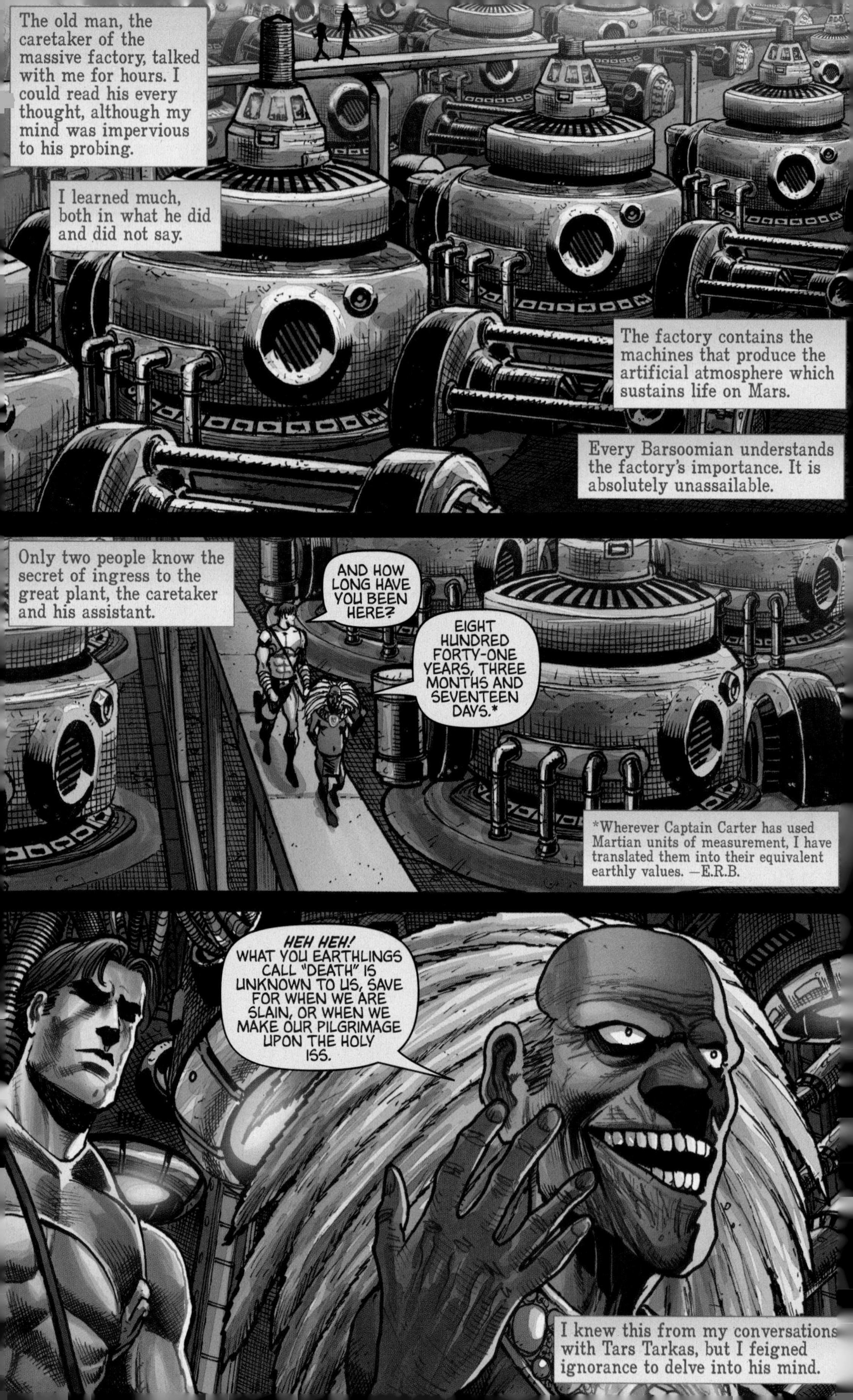
The old man, the caretaker of the massive factory, talked with me for hours. I could read his every thought, although my mind was impervious to his probing.
I learned much, both in what he did and did not say.
The factory contains the machines that produce the artificial atmosphere which sustains life on Mars.
Every Barsoomian understands the factory's importance. It is absolutely unassailable.
Only two people know the secret of ingress to the great plant, the caretaker and his assistant.
AND HOW LONG HAVE YOU BEEN HERE?
EIGHT HUNDRED FORTY-ONE YEARS, THREE MONTHS AND SEVENTEEN DAYS.*
*Wherever Captain Carter has used Martian units of measurement, I have translated them into their equivalent earthly values. —E.R.B.
HEH HEH! WHAT YOU EARTHLINGS CALL "DEATH" IS UNKNOWN TO US, SAVE FOR WHEN WE ARE SLAIN, OR WHEN WE MAKE OUR PILGRIMAGE UPON THE HOLY ISS.
I knew this from my conversations with Tars Tarkas, but I feigned ignorance to delve into his mind.

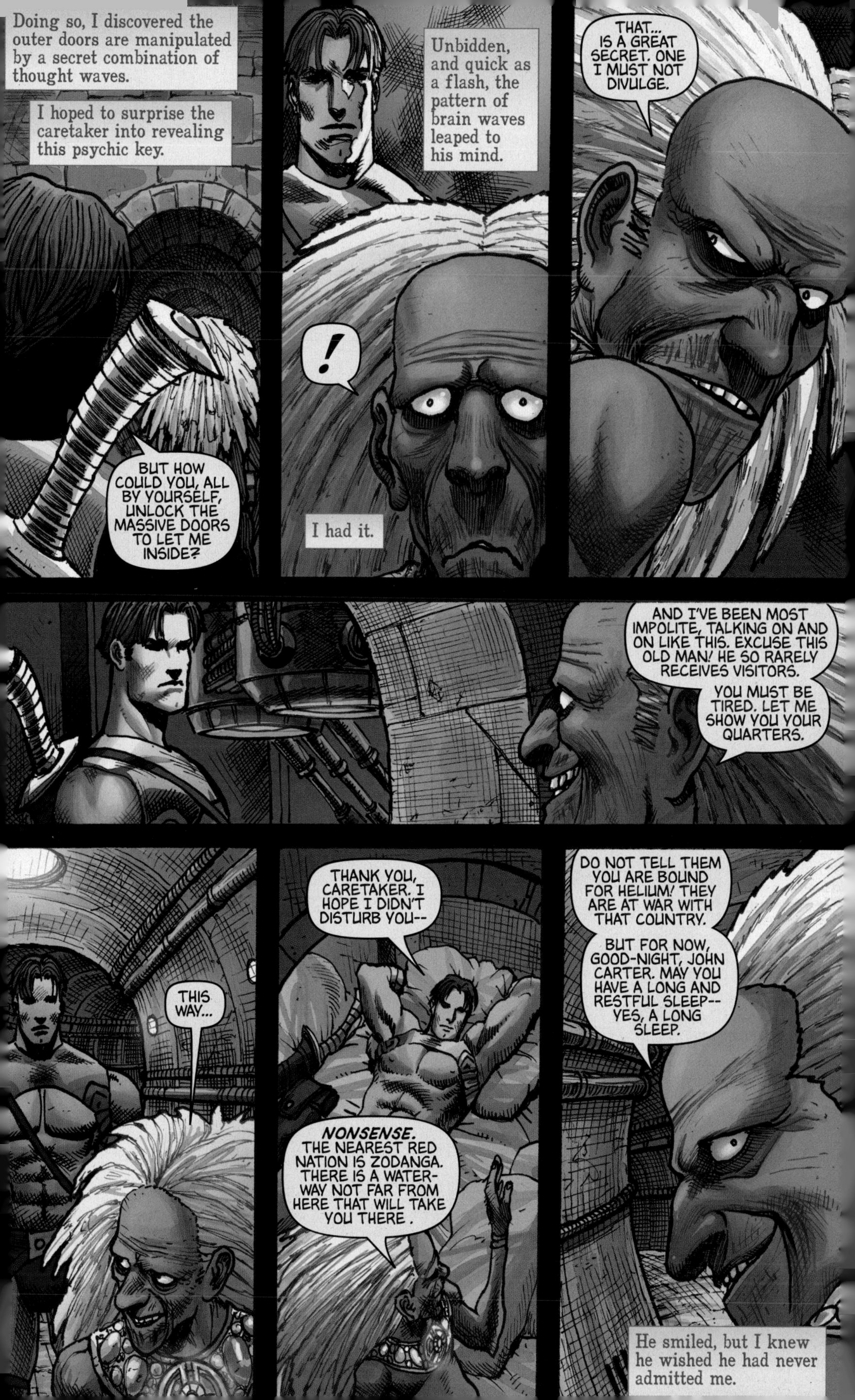

Doing so, I discovered the outer doors are manipulated by a secret combination of thought waves.
I hoped to surprise the caretaker into revealing this psychic key.
BUT HOW COULD YOU, ALL BY YOURSELF, UNLOCK THE MASSIVE DOORS TO LET ME INSIDE?
Unbidden, and quick as a flash, the pattern of brain waves leaped to his mind.
!
I had it.
THAT... IS A GREAT SECRET. ONE I MUST NOT DIVULGE.
AND I'VE BEEN MOST IMPOLITE, TALKING ON AND ON LIKE THIS. EXCUSE THIS OLD MAN! HE SO RARELY RECEIVES VISITORS.
YOU MUST BE TIRED. LET ME SHOW YOU YOUR QUARTERS.
THIS WAY...
THANK YOU, CARETAKER. I HOPE I DIDN'T DISTURB YOU--
NONSENSE. THE NEAREST RED NATION IS ZODANGA. THERE IS A WATER-WAY NOT FAR FROM HERE THAT WILL TAKE YOU THERE.
DO NOT TELL THEM YOU ARE BOUND FOR HELIUM! THEY ARE AT WAR WITH THAT COUNTRY.
BUT FOR NOW, GOOD-NIGHT, JOHN CARTER. MAY YOU HAVE A LONG AND RESTFUL SLEEP-- YES, A LONG SLEEP.
He smiled, but I knew he wished he had never admitted me.

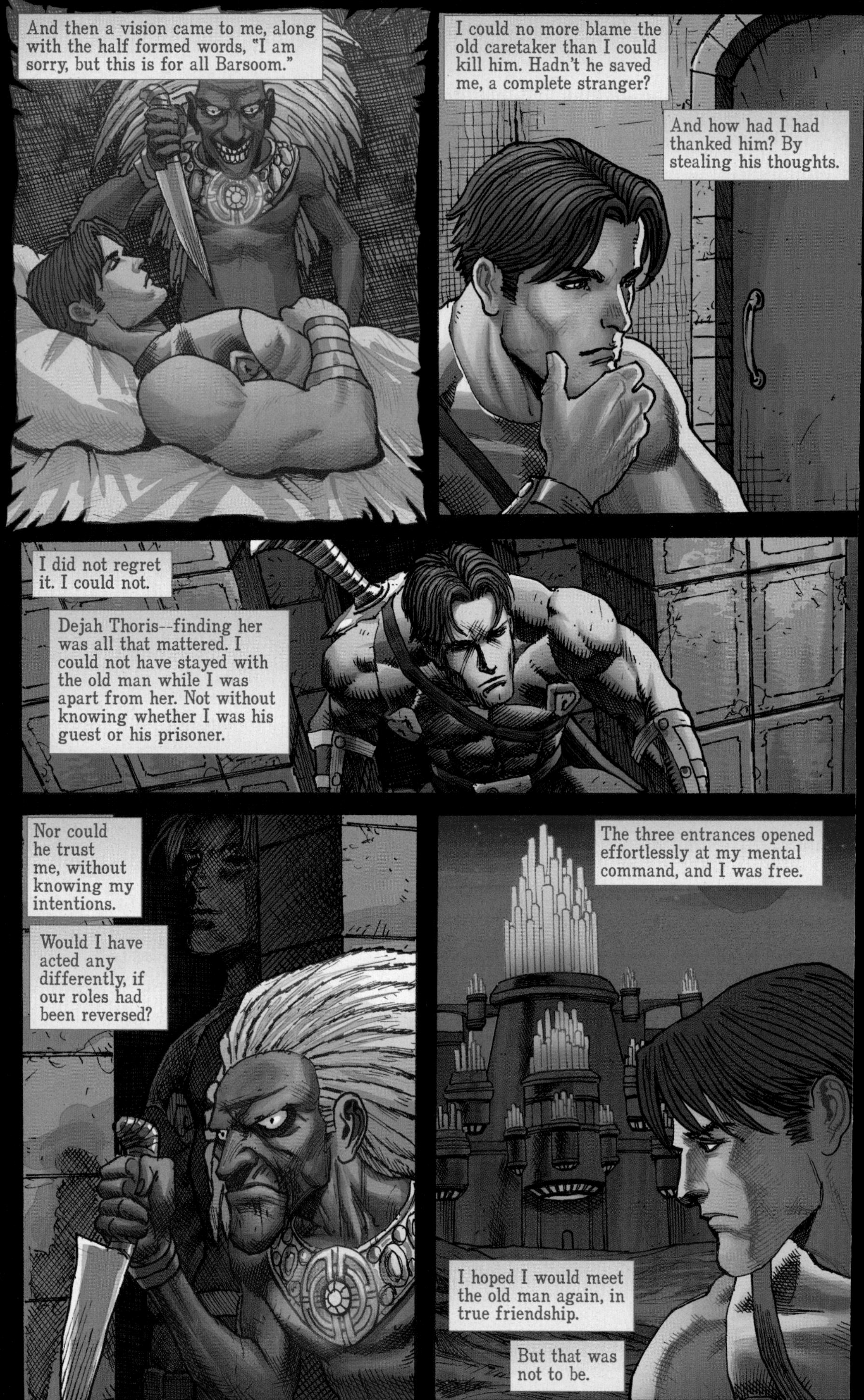
And then a vision came to me, along with the half formed words, "I am sorry, but this is for all Barsoom."
I could no more blame the old caretaker than I could kill him. Hadn't he saved me, a complete stranger?
And how had I had thanked him? By stealing his thoughts.
I did not regret it. I could not.
Dejah Thoris--finding her was all that mattered. I could not have stayed with the old man while I was apart from her. Not without knowing whether I was his guest or his prisoner.
Nor could he trust me, without knowing my intentions.
Would I have acted any differently, if our roles had been reversed?
The three entrances opened effortlessly at my mental command, and I was free.
I hoped I would meet the old man again, in true friendship.
But that was not to be.

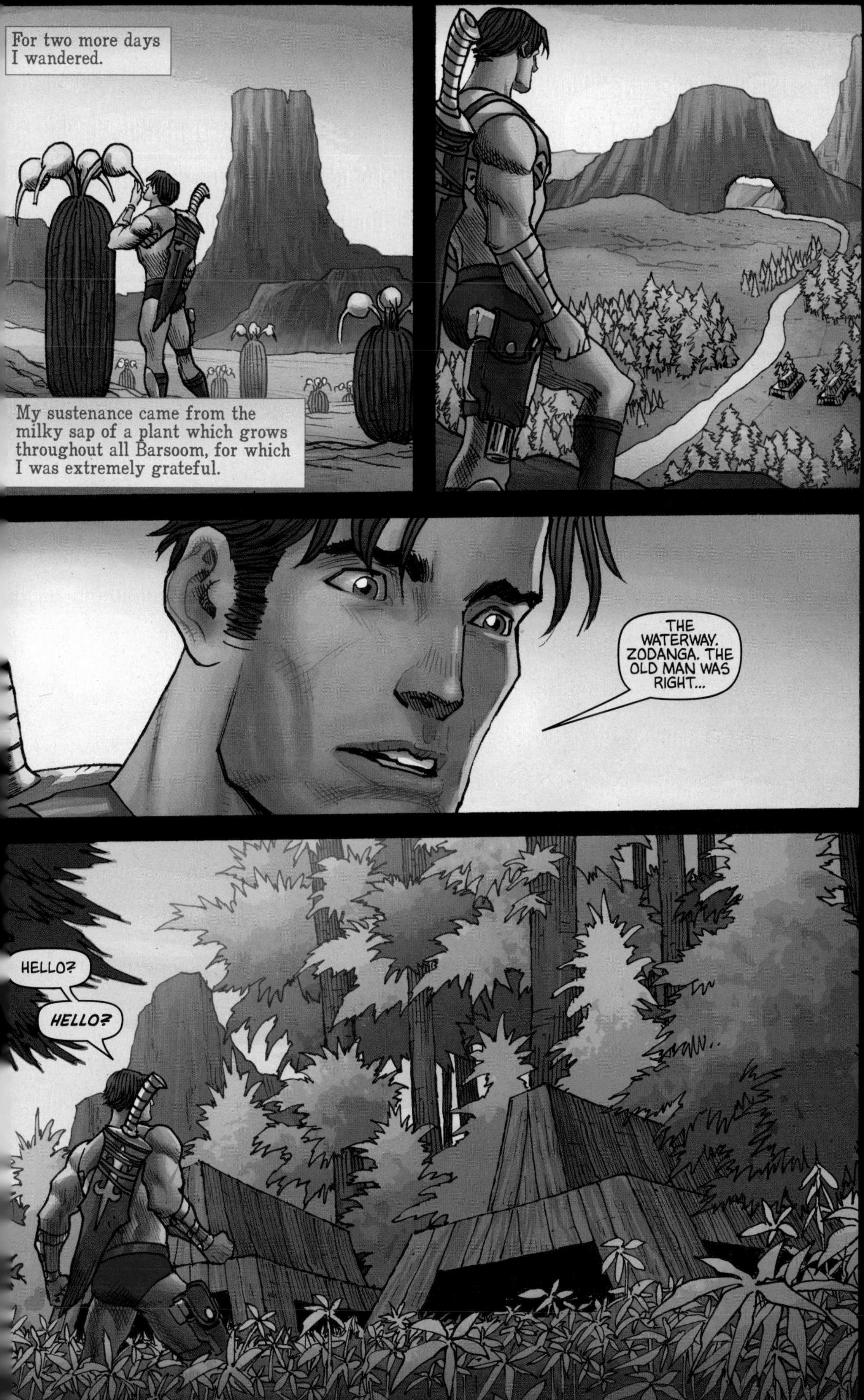
For two more days I wandered.
My sustenance came from the milky sap of a plant which grows throughout all Barsoom, for which I was extremely grateful.
THE WATERWAY. ZODANGA. THE OLD MAN WAS RIGHT...
HELLO?
HELLO?

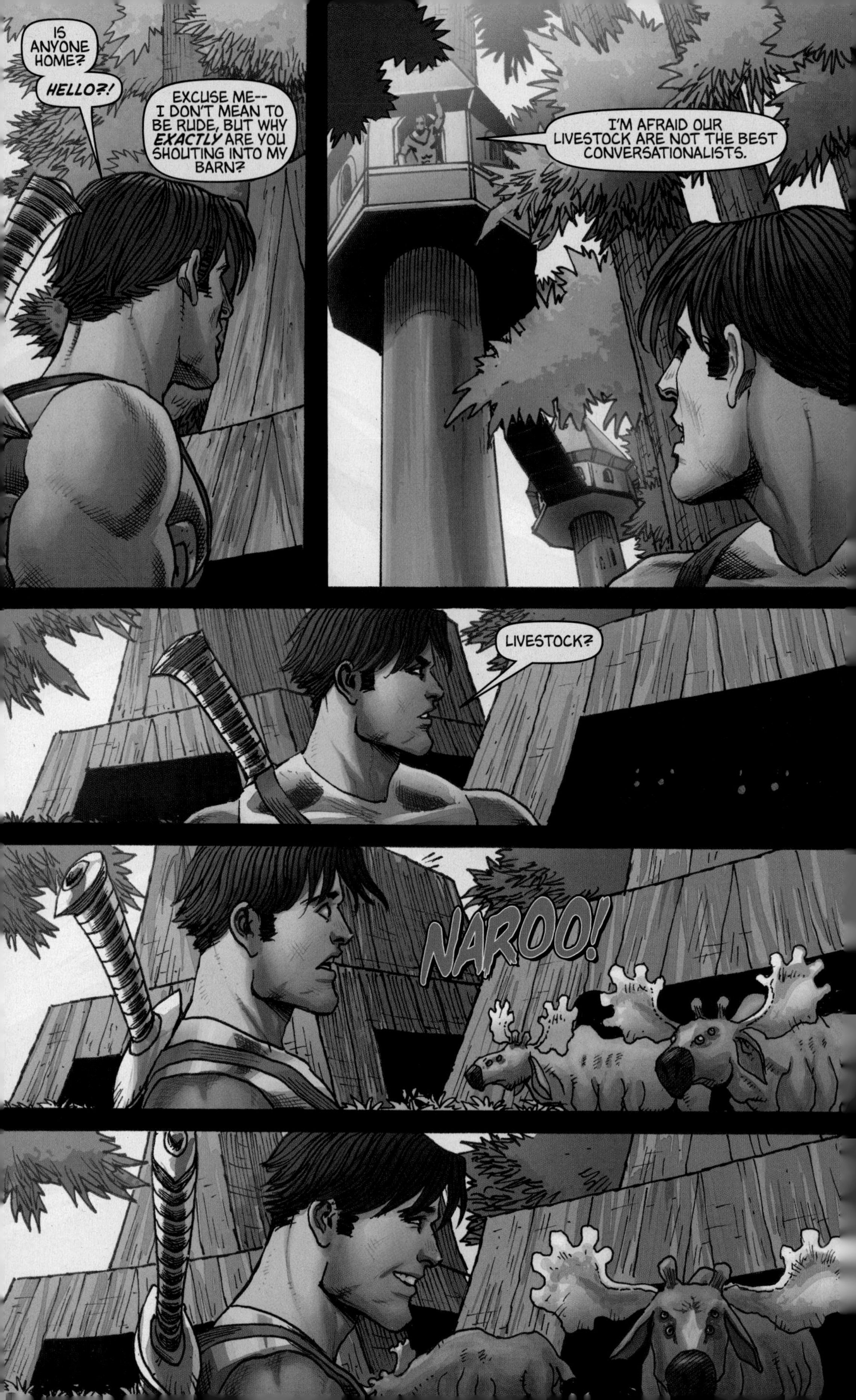
IS ANYONE HOME?
HELLO?!
EXCUSE ME-- I DON'T MEAN TO BE RUDE, BUT WHY EXACTLY ARE YOU SHOUTING INTO MY BARN?
I'M AFRAID OUR LIVESTOCK ARE NOT THE BEST CONVERSATIONALISTS.
LIVESTOCK?
NAROO!

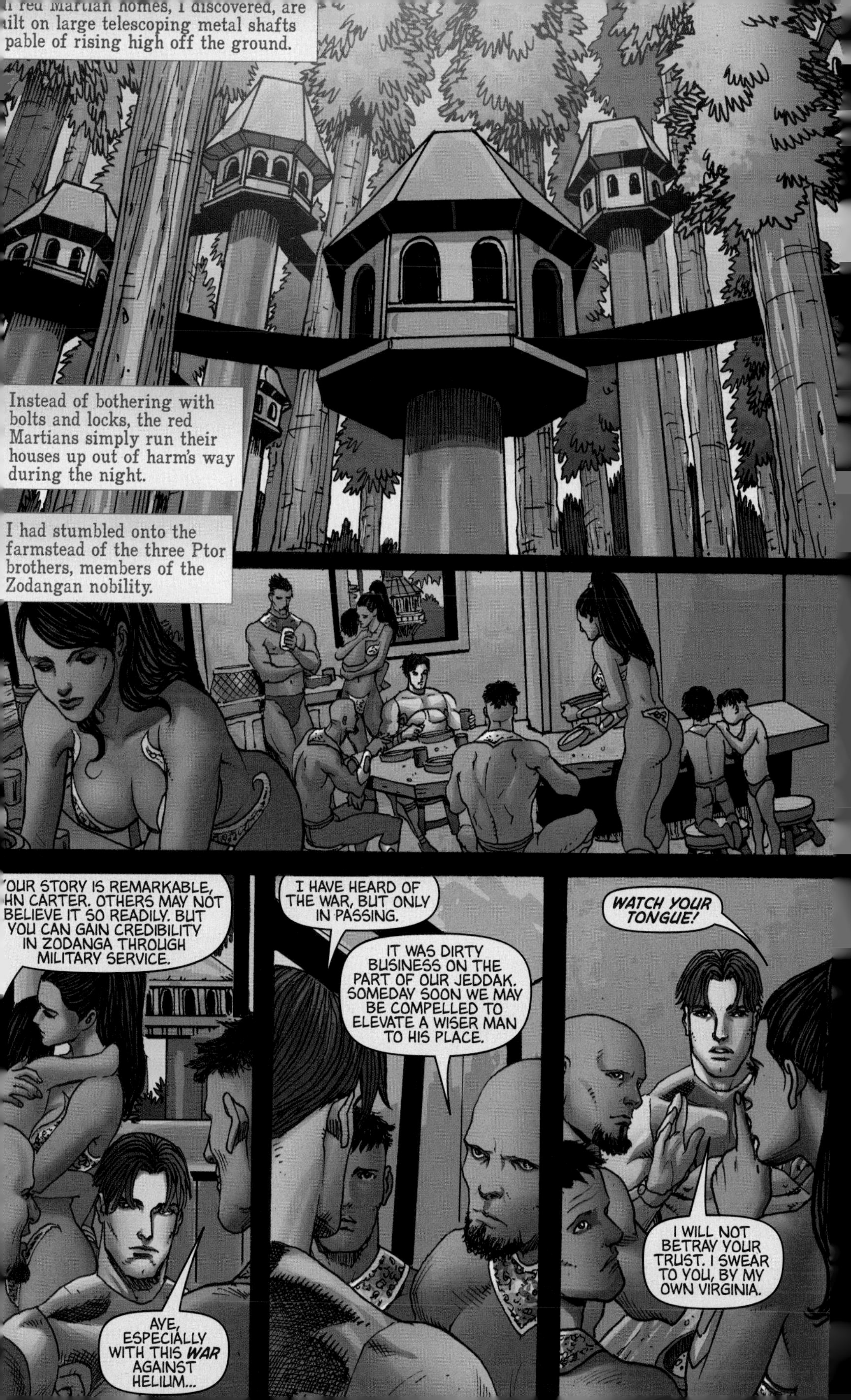

l red Martian homes, I discovered, are
ilt on large telescoping metal shafts
pable of rising high off the ground.
Instead of bothering with bolts and locks, the red Martians simply run their houses up out of harm's way during the night.
I had stumbled onto the farmstead of the three Ptor brothers, members of the Zodangan nobility.
OUR STORY IS REMARKABLE, HN CARTER. OTHERS MAY NOT BELIEVE IT SO READILY. BUT YOU CAN GAIN CREDIBILITY IN ZODANGA THROUGH MILITARY SERVICE.
AYE, ESPECIALLY WITH THIS WAR AGAINST HELIUM...
I HAVE HEARD OF THE WAR, BUT ONLY IN PASSING.
IT WAS DIRTY BUSINESS ON THE PART OF OUR JEDDAK. SOMEDAY SOON WE MAY BE COMPELLED TO ELEVATE A WISER MAN TO HIS PLACE.
WATCH YOUR TONGUE!
I WILL NOT BETRAY YOUR TRUST. I SWEAR TO YOU, BY MY OWN VIRGINIA.

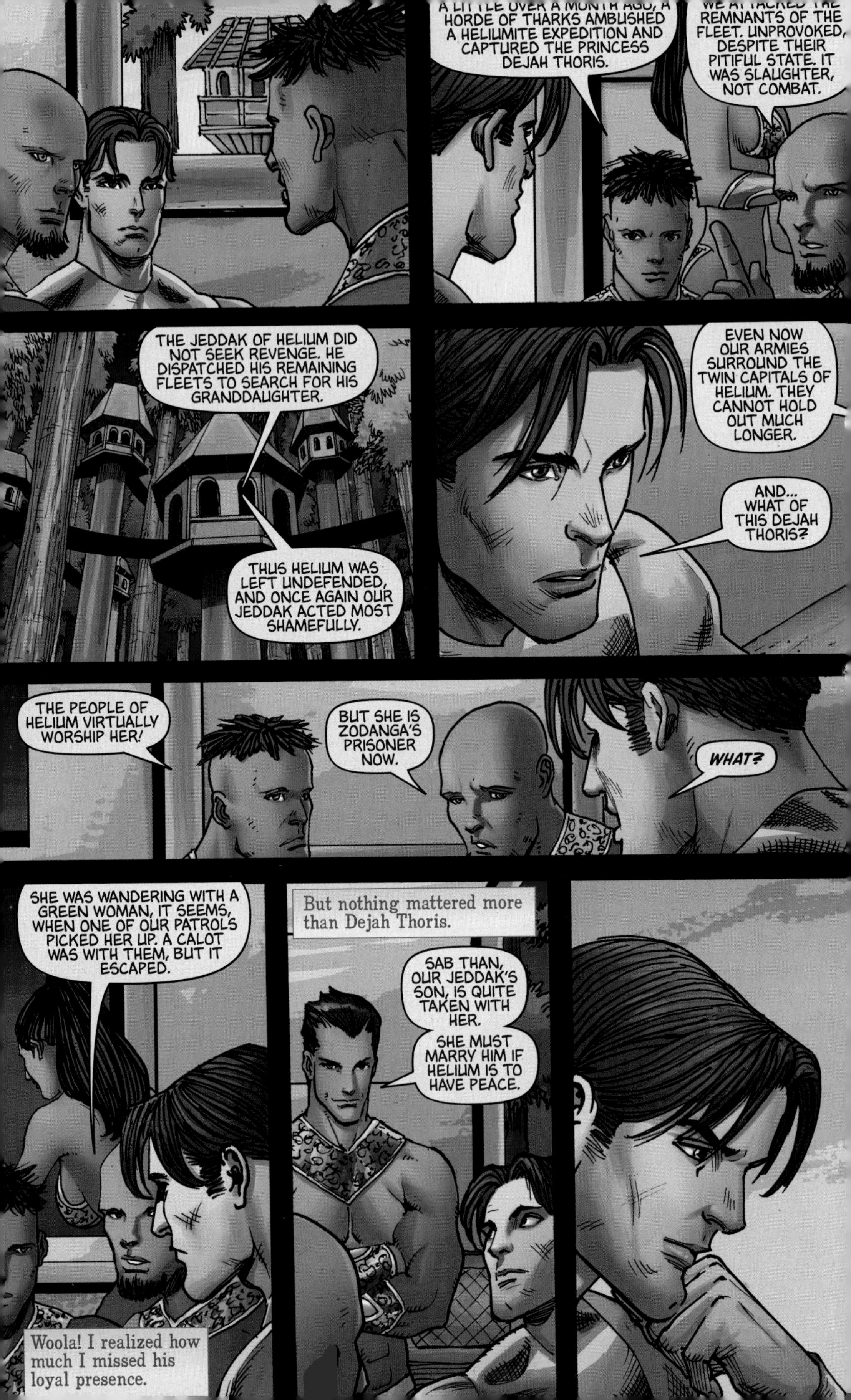
A LITTLE OVER A MONTH AGO, A HORDE OF THARKS AMBUSHED A HELIUMITE EXPEDITION AND CAPTURED THE PRINCESS DEJAH THORIS.
WE ATTACKED THE REMNANTS OF THE FLEET. UNPROVOKED, DESPITE THEIR PITIFUL STATE. IT WAS SLAUGHTER, NOT COMBAT.
THE JEDDAK OF HELIUM DID NOT SEEK REVENGE. HE DISPATCHED HIS REMAINING FLEETS TO SEARCH FOR HIS GRANDDAUGHTER.
THUS HELIUM WAS LEFT UNDEFENDED, AND ONCE AGAIN OUR JEDDAK ACTED MOST SHAMEFULLY.
EVEN NOW OUR ARMIES SURROUND THE TWIN CAPITALS OF HELIUM. THEY CANNOT HOLD OUT MUCH LONGER.
AND... WHAT OF THIS DEJAH THORIS?
THE PEOPLE OF HELIUM VIRTUALLY WORSHIP HER!
BUT SHE IS ZODANGA'S PRISONER NOW.
WHAT?
SHE WAS WANDERING WITH A GREEN WOMAN, IT SEEMS, WHEN ONE OF OUR PATROLS PICKED HER UP. A CALOT WAS WITH THEM, BUT IT ESCAPED.
Woola! I realized how much I missed his loyal presence.
But nothing mattered more than Dejah Thoris.
SAB THAN, OUR JEDDAK'S SON, IS QUITE TAKEN WITH HER.
SHE MUST MARRY HIM IF HELIUM IS TO HAVE PEACE.

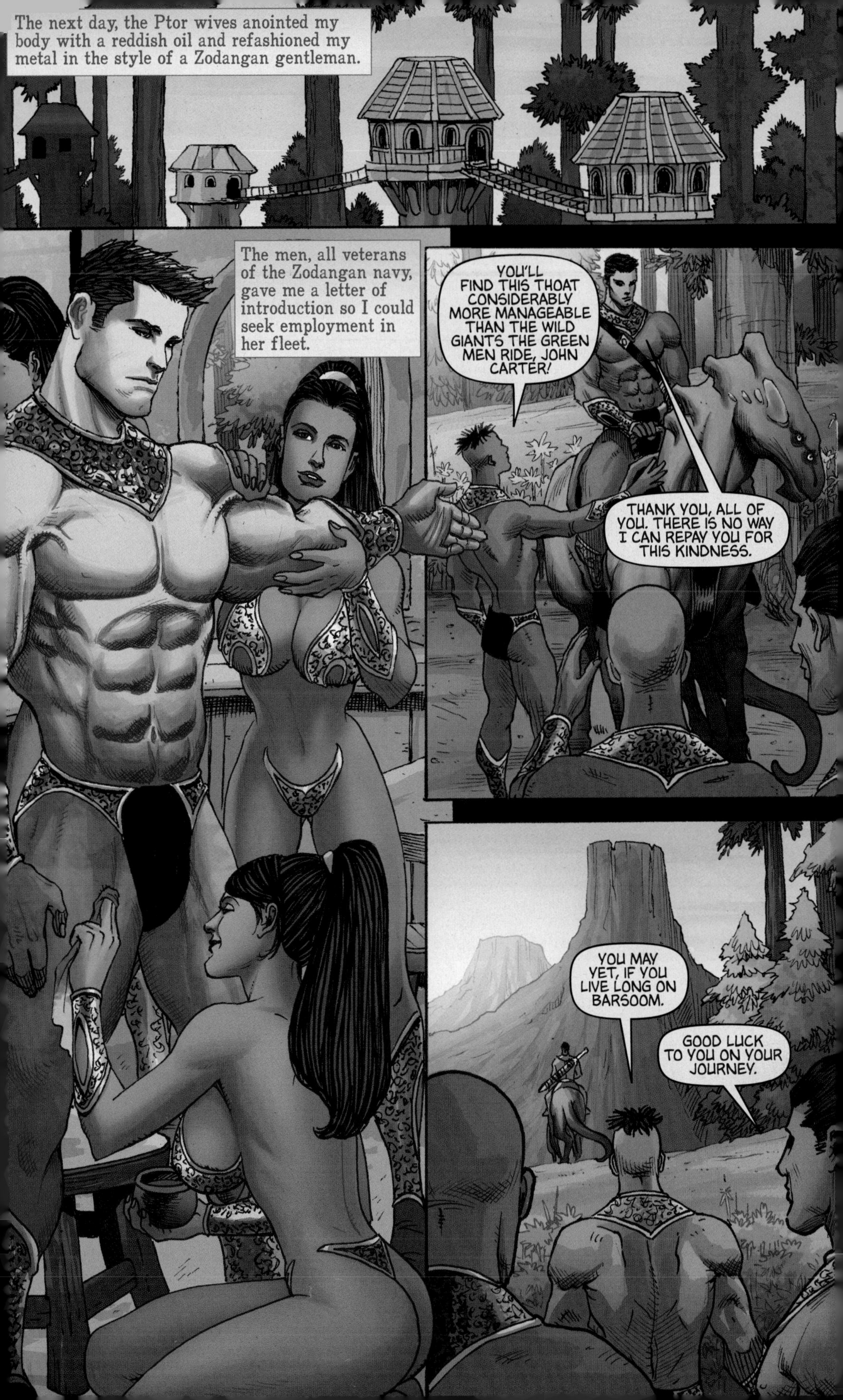
The next day, the Ptor wives anointed my body with a reddish oil and refashioned my metal in the style of a Zodangan gentleman.
The men, all veterans of the Zodangan navy, gave me a letter of introduction so I could seek employment in her fleet.
YOU'LL FIND THIS THOAT CONSIDERABLY MORE MANAGEABLE THAN THE WILD GIANTS THE GREEN MEN RIDE, JOHN CARTER!
THANK YOU, ALL OF YOU. THERE IS NO WAY I CAN REPAY YOU FOR THIS KINDNESS.
YOU MAY YET, IF YOU LIVE LONG ON BARSOOM.
GOOD LUCK TO YOU ON YOUR JOURNEY.

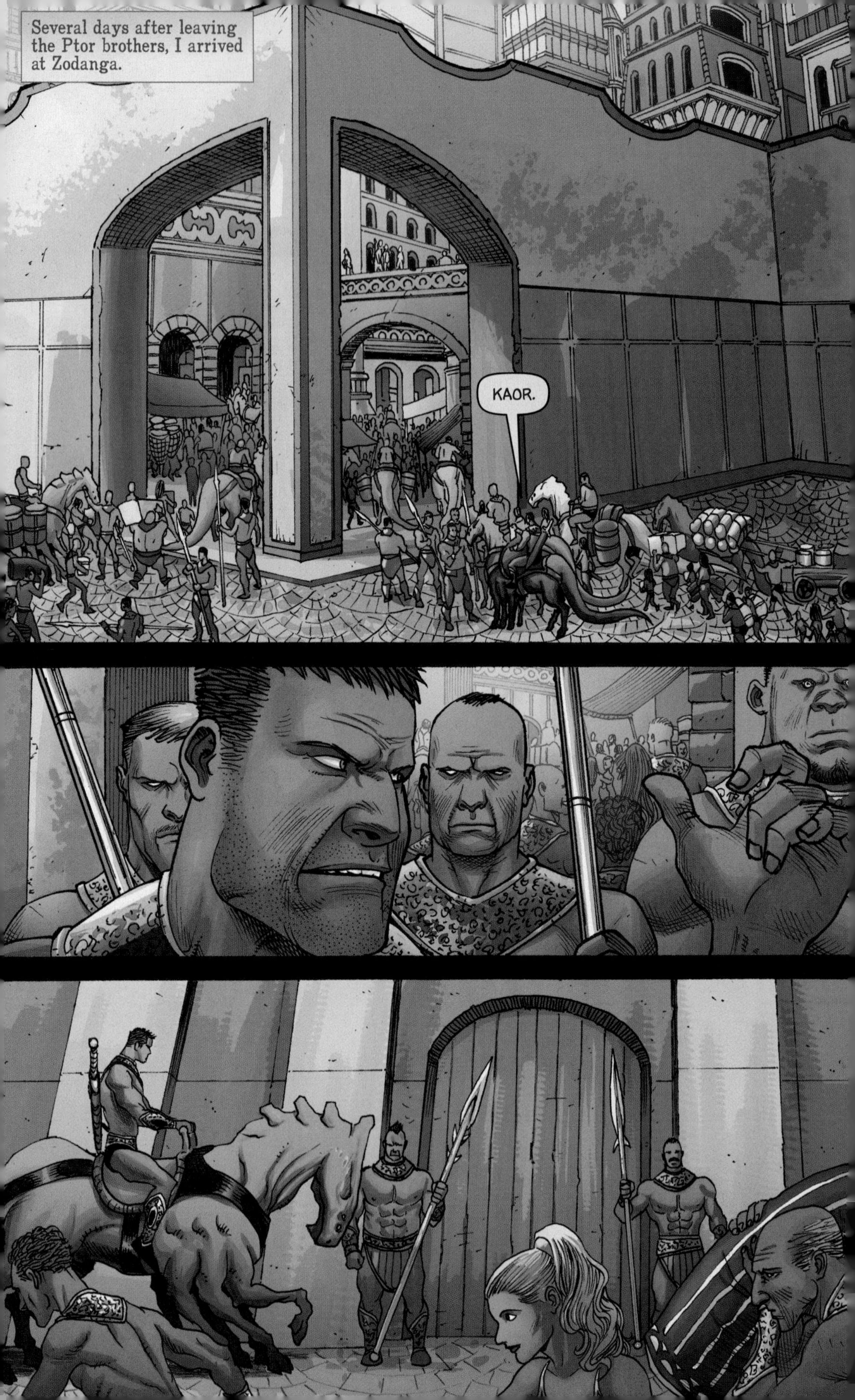
Several days after leaving the Ptor brothers, I arrived at Zodanga.
KAOR.

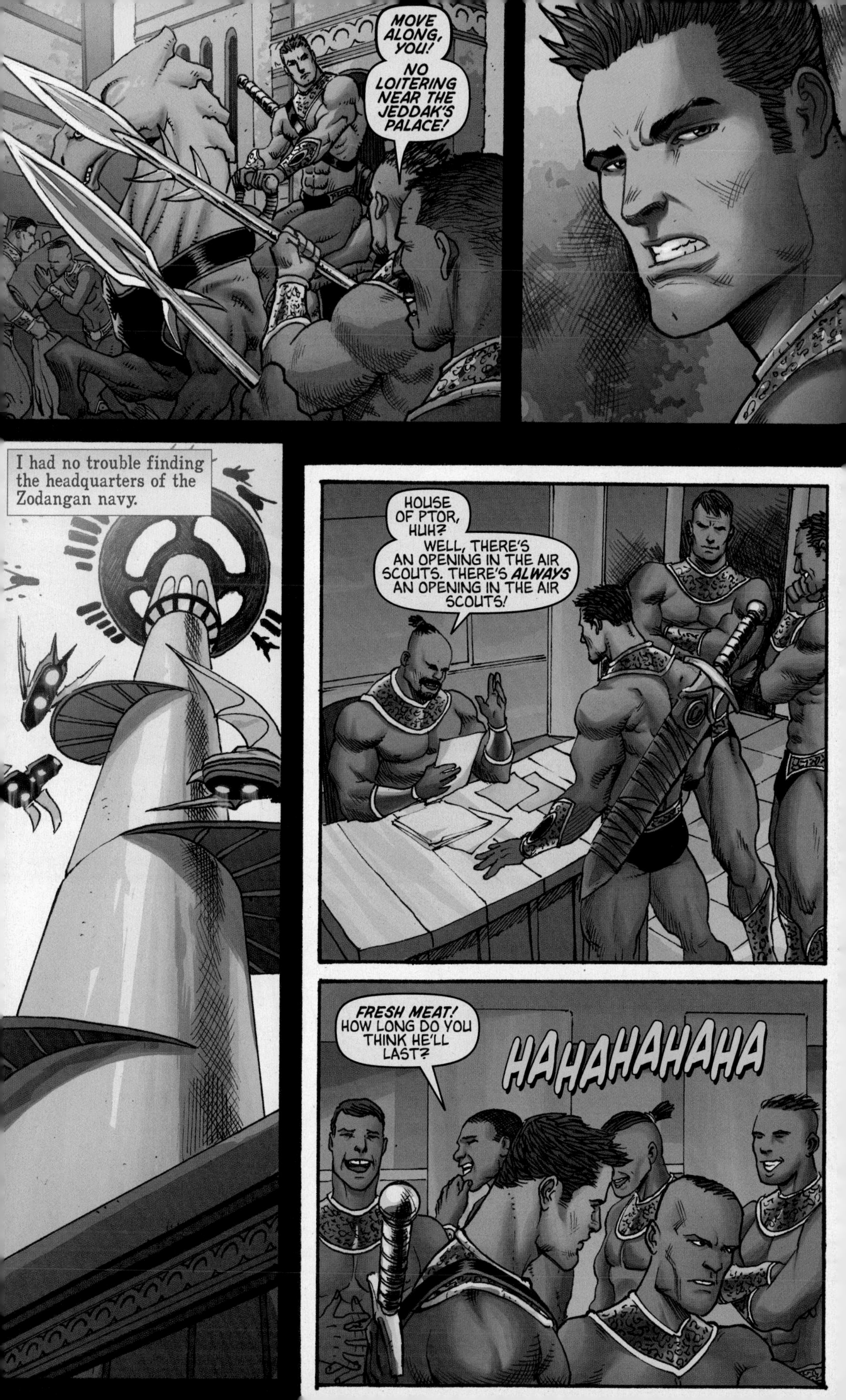
MOVE ALONG, YOU!
NO LOITERING NEAR THE JEDDAK'S PALACE!
I had no trouble finding the headquarters of the Zodangan navy.
HOUSE OF PTOR, HUH?
WELL, THERE'S AN OPENING IN THE AIR SCOUTS. THERE'S ALWAYS AN OPENING IN THE AIR SCOUTS!
FRESH MEAT! HOW LONG DO YOU THINK HE'LL LAST?
HAHAHAHAHA

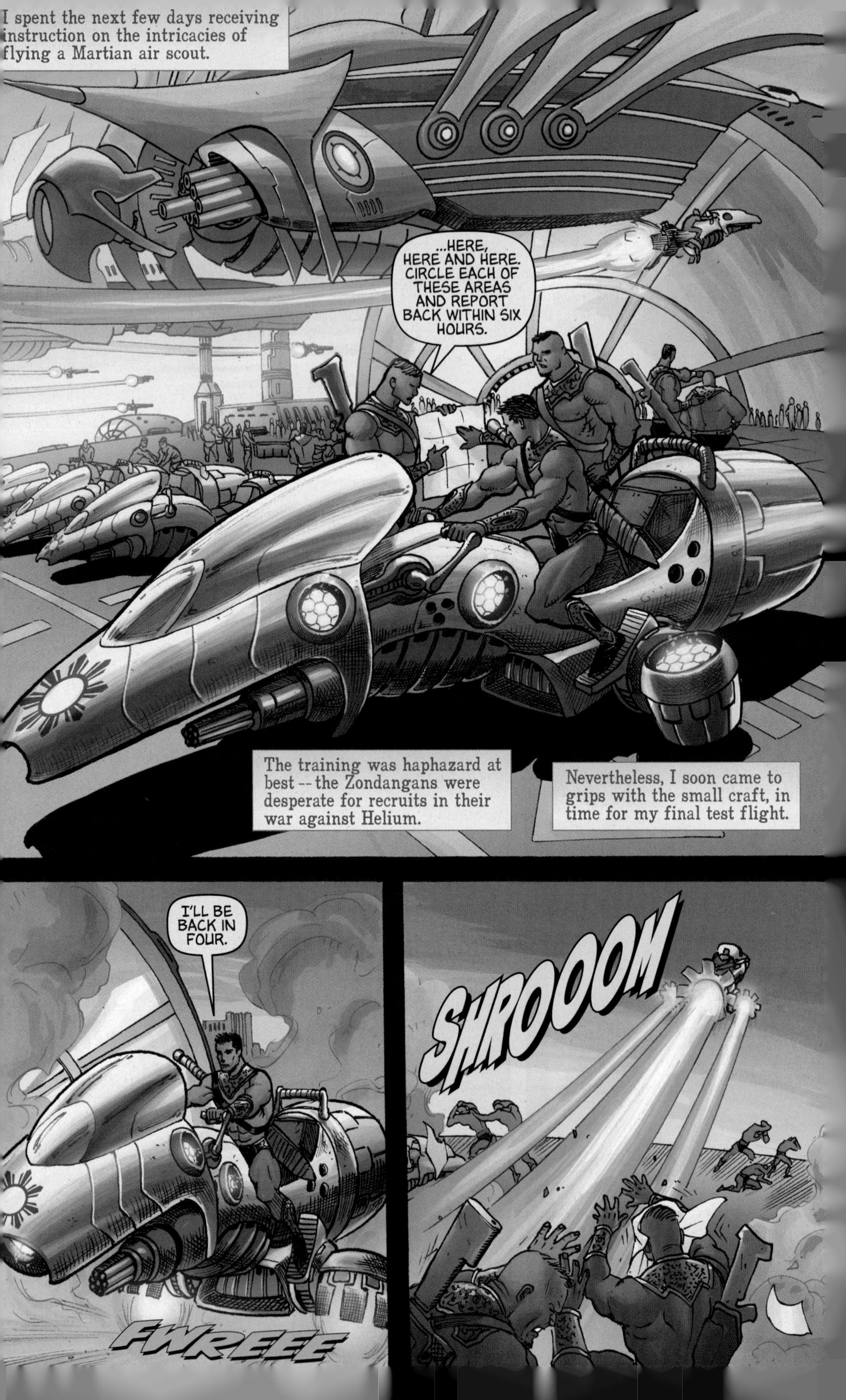

I spent the next few days receiving instruction on the intricacies of flying a Martian air scout.
...HERE, HERE AND HERE. CIRCLE EACH OF THESE AREAS AND REPORT BACK WITHIN SIX HOURS.
The training was haphazard at best -- the Zondangans were desperate for recruits in their war against Helium.
Nevertheless, I soon came to grips with the small craft, in time for my final test flight.
I'LL BE BACK IN FOUR.
FWREEE
SHROOOM

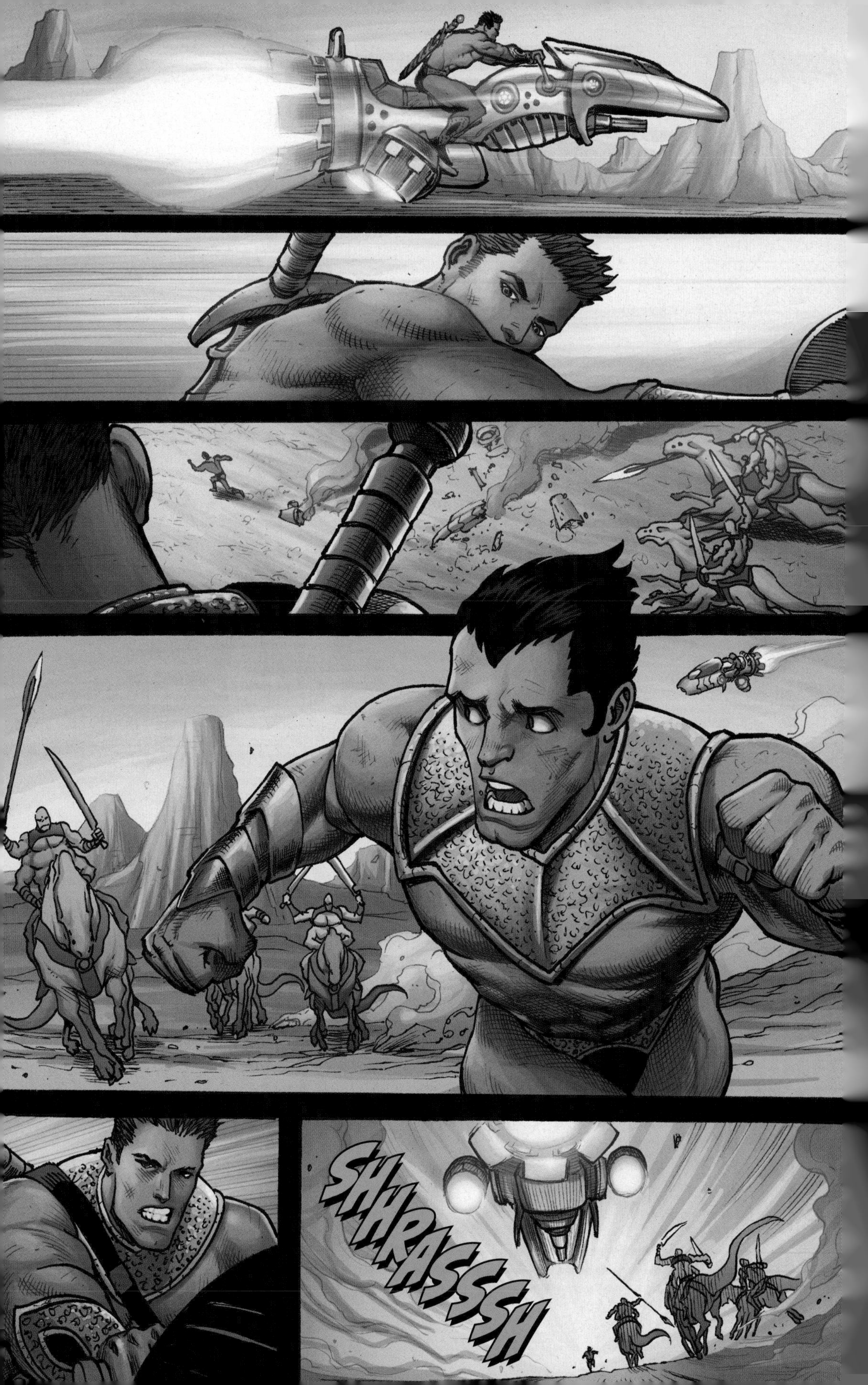
SHHRASSSH

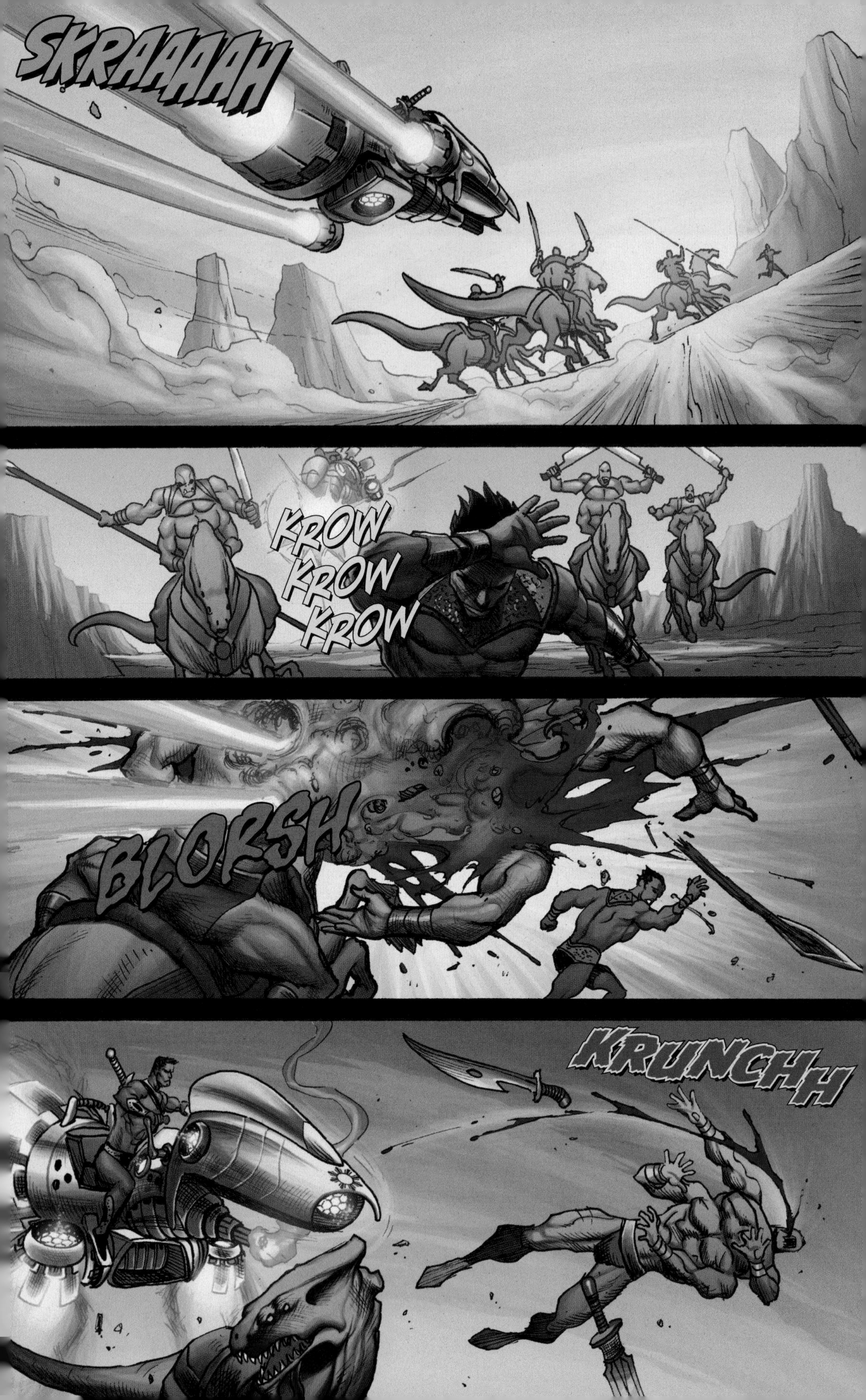
SKRAAAAH
KROW
KROW
KROW
BLORSH
KRUNCHH

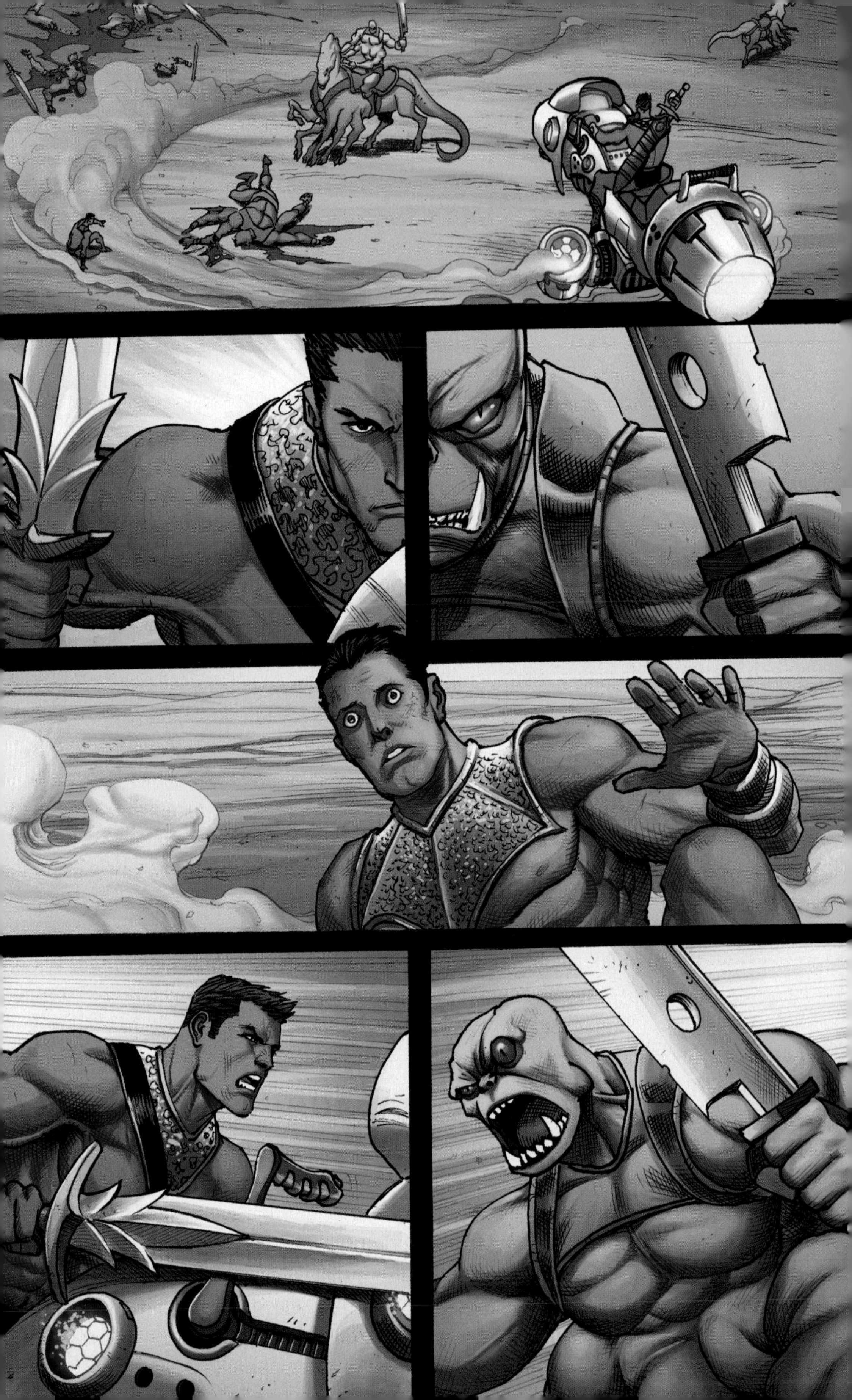

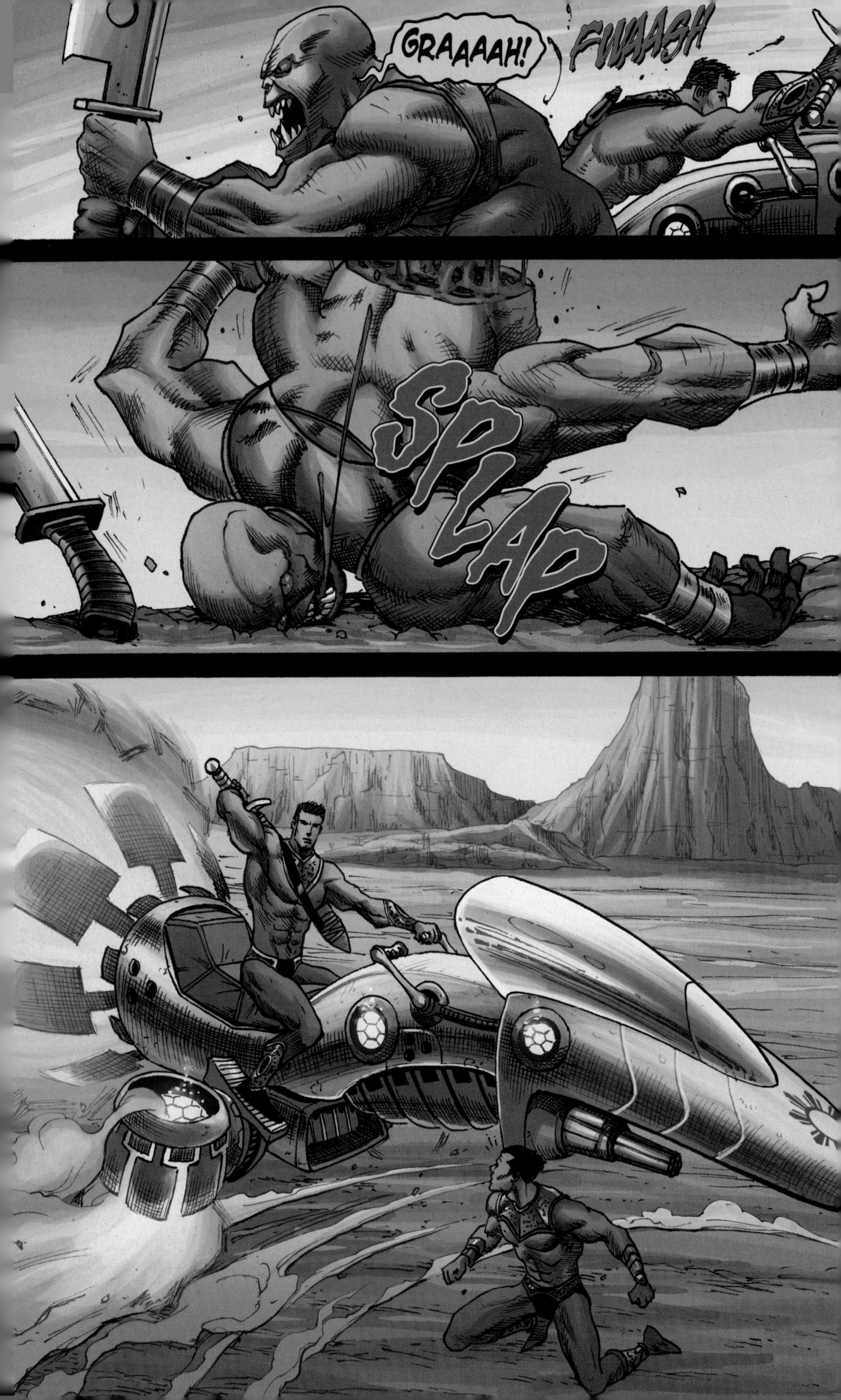
GRAAAAH!
FWAASH
SPLAP

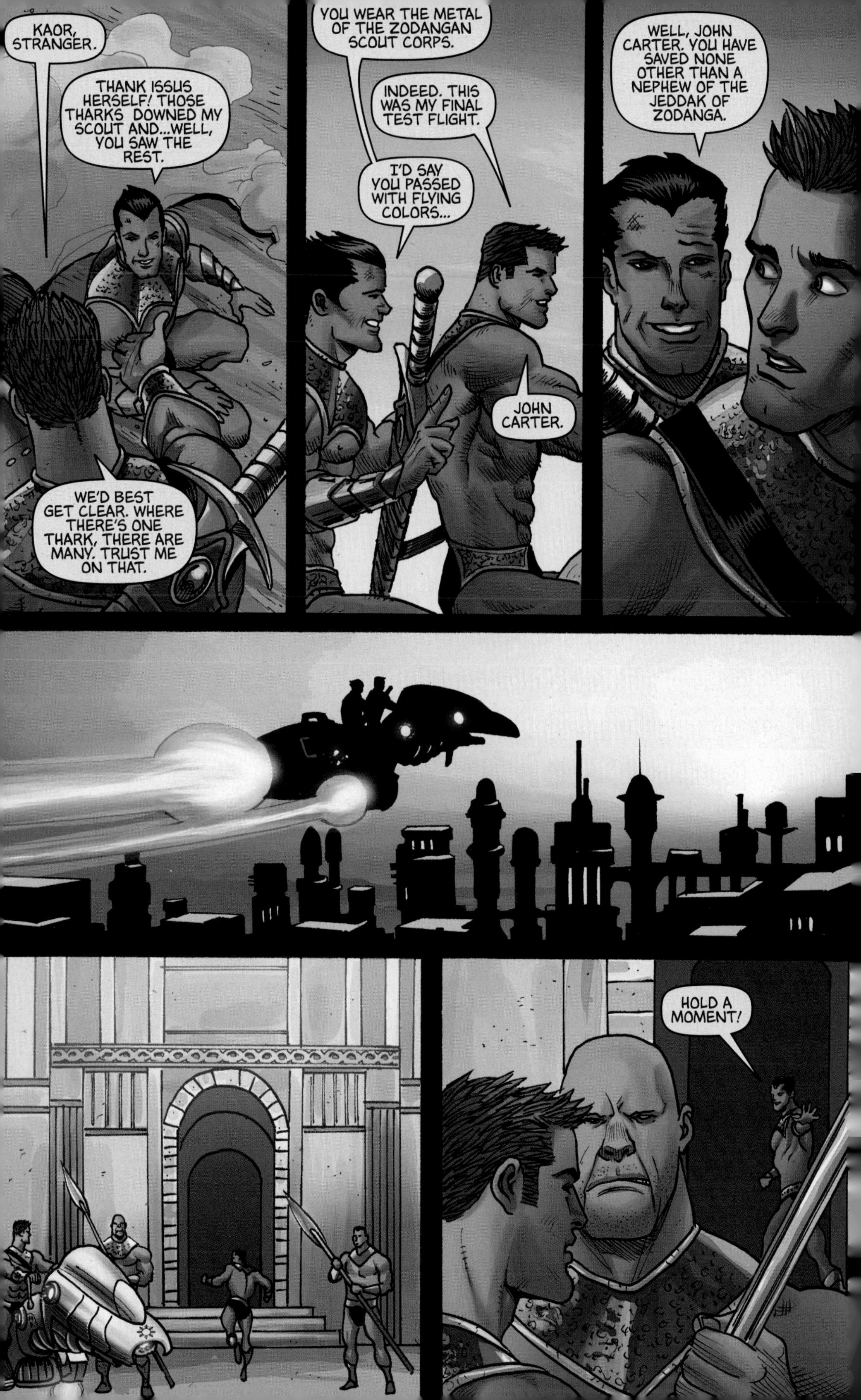
KAOR, STRANGER.
THANK ISSUS HERSELF! THOSE THARKS DOWNED MY SCOUT AND...WELL, YOU SAW THE REST.
WE'D BEST GET CLEAR. WHERE THERE'S ONE THARK, THERE ARE MANY. TRUST ME ON THAT.
YOU WEAR THE METAL OF THE ZODANGAN SCOUT CORPS.
INDEED. THIS WAS MY FINAL TEST FLIGHT.
I'D SAY YOU PASSED WITH FLYING COLORS...
JOHN CARTER.
WELL, JOHN CARTER. YOU HAVE SAVED NONE OTHER THAN A NEPHEW OF THE JEDDAK OF ZODANGA.
HOLD A MOMENT!

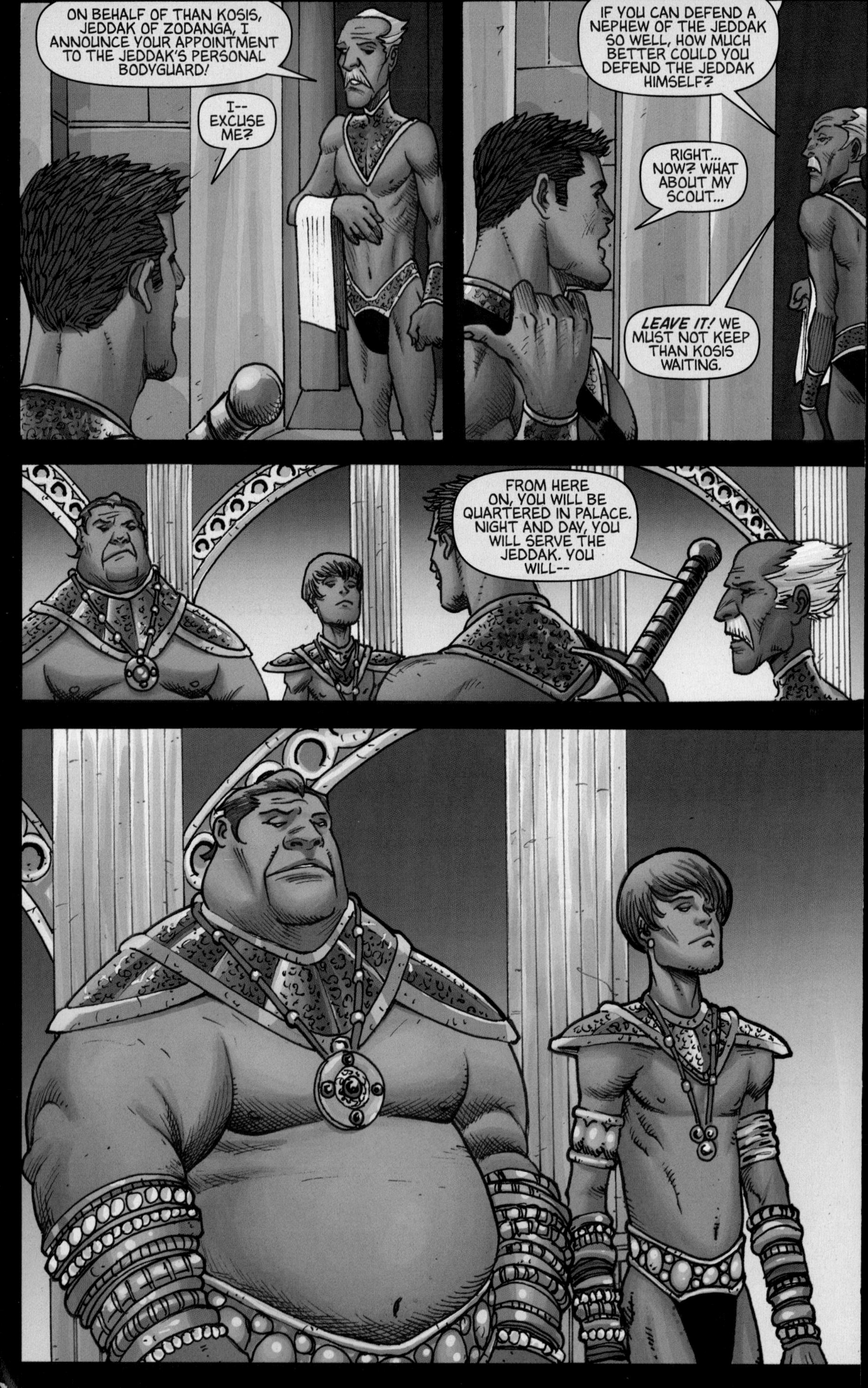
ON BEHALF OF THAN KOSIS, JEDDAK OF ZODANGA, I ANNOUNCE YOUR APPOINTMENT TO THE JEDDAK'S PERSONAL BODYGUARD!
I-- EXCUSE ME?
IF YOU CAN DEFEND A NEPHEW OF THE JEDDAK SO WELL, HOW MUCH BETTER COULD YOU DEFEND THE JEDDAK HIMSELF?
RIGHT... NOW? WHAT ABOUT MY SCOUT...
LEAVE IT! WE MUST NOT KEEP THAN KOSIS WAITING.
FROM HERE ON, YOU WILL BE QUARTERED IN PALACE. NIGHT AND DAY, YOU WILL SERVE THE JEDDAK. YOU WILL--

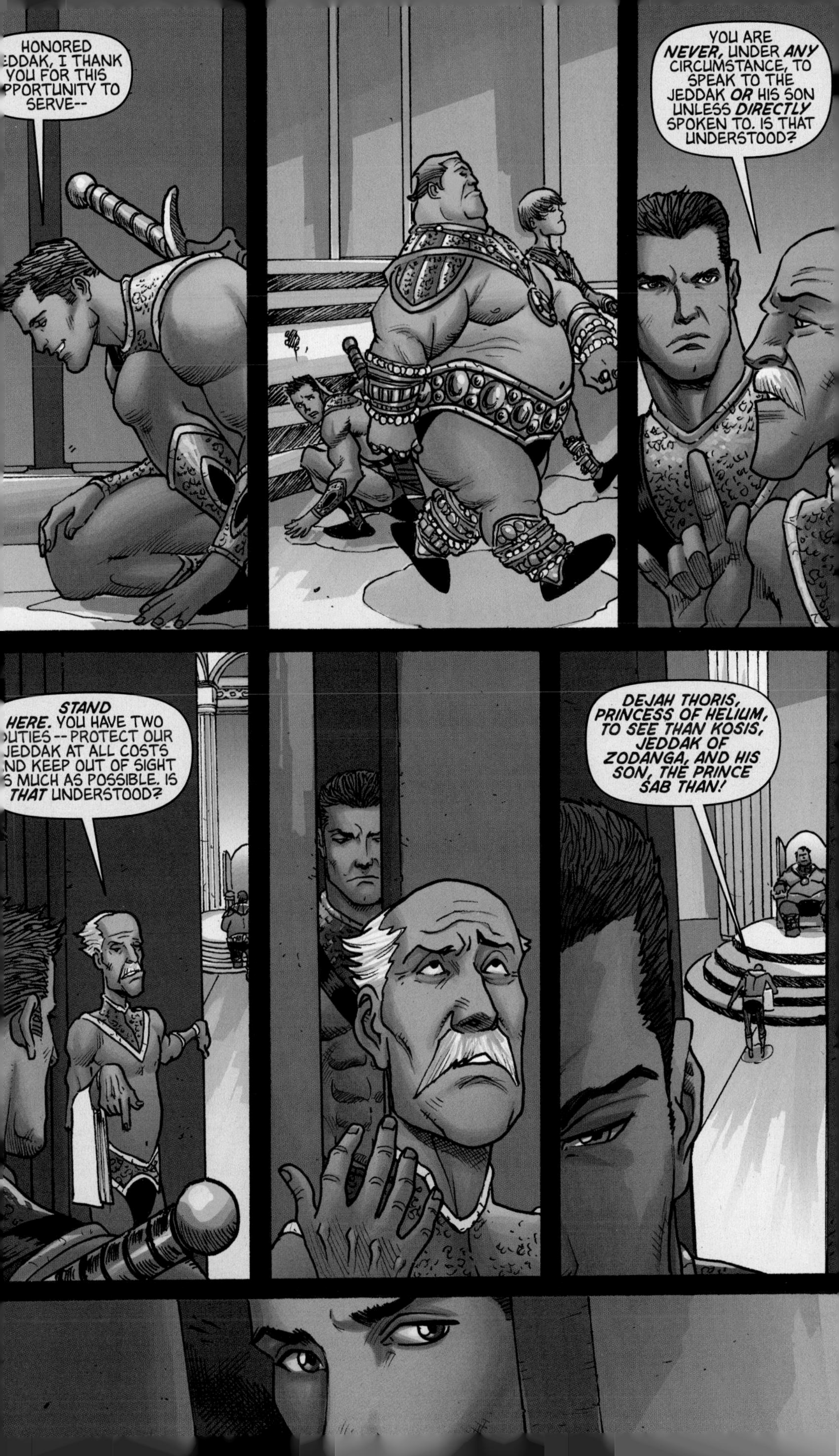
HONORED JEDDAK, I THANK YOU FOR THIS OPPORTUNITY TO SERVE--
YOU ARE NEVER, UNDER ANY CIRCUMSTANCE, TO SPEAK TO THE JEDDAK OR HIS SON UNLESS DIRECTLY SPOKEN TO. IS THAT UNDERSTOOD?
STAND HERE. YOU HAVE TWO DUTIES -- PROTECT OUR JEDDAK AT ALL COSTS AND KEEP OUT OF SIGHT AS MUCH AS POSSIBLE. IS THAT UNDERSTOOD?
DEJAH THORIS, PRINCESS OF HELIUM, TO SEE THAN KOSIS, JEDDAK OF ZODANGA, AND HIS SON, THE PRINCE SAB THAN!

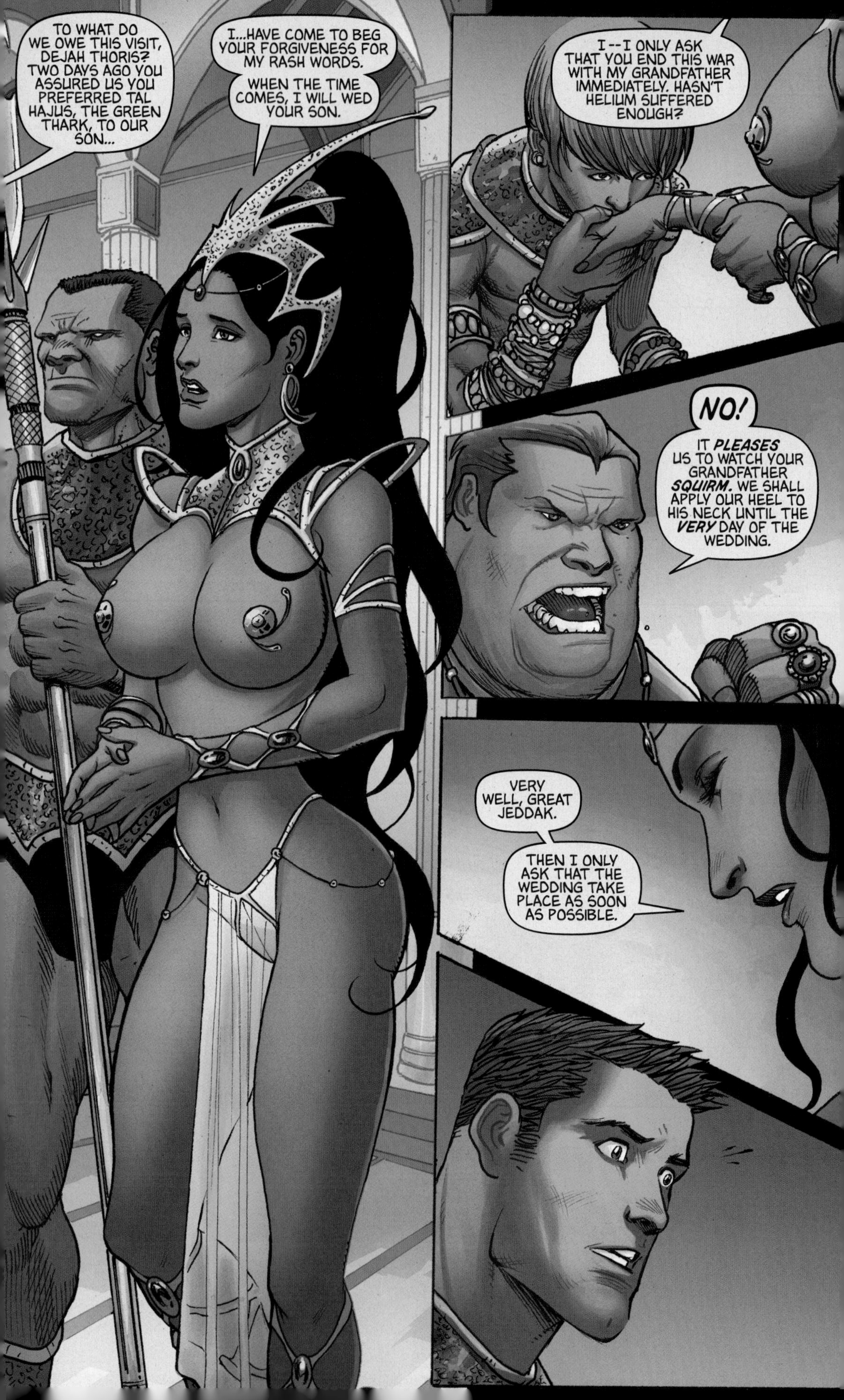
TO WHAT DO WE OWE THIS VISIT, DEJAH THORIS? TWO DAYS AGO YOU ASSURED US YOU PREFERRED TAL HAJUS, THE GREEN THARK, TO OUR SON...
I...HAVE COME TO BEG YOUR FORGIVENESS FOR MY RASH WORDS.
WHEN THE TIME COMES, I WILL WED YOUR SON.
I--I ONLY ASK THAT YOU END THIS WAR WITH MY GRANDFATHER IMMEDIATELY. HASN'T HELIUM SUFFERED ENOUGH?
NO!
IT PLEASES US TO WATCH YOUR GRANDFATHER SQUIRM. WE SHALL APPLY OUR HEEL TO HIS NECK UNTIL THE VERY DAY OF THE WEDDING.
VERY WELL, GREAT JEDDAK.
THEN I ONLY ASK THAT THE WEDDING TAKE PLACE AS SOON AS POSSIBLE.

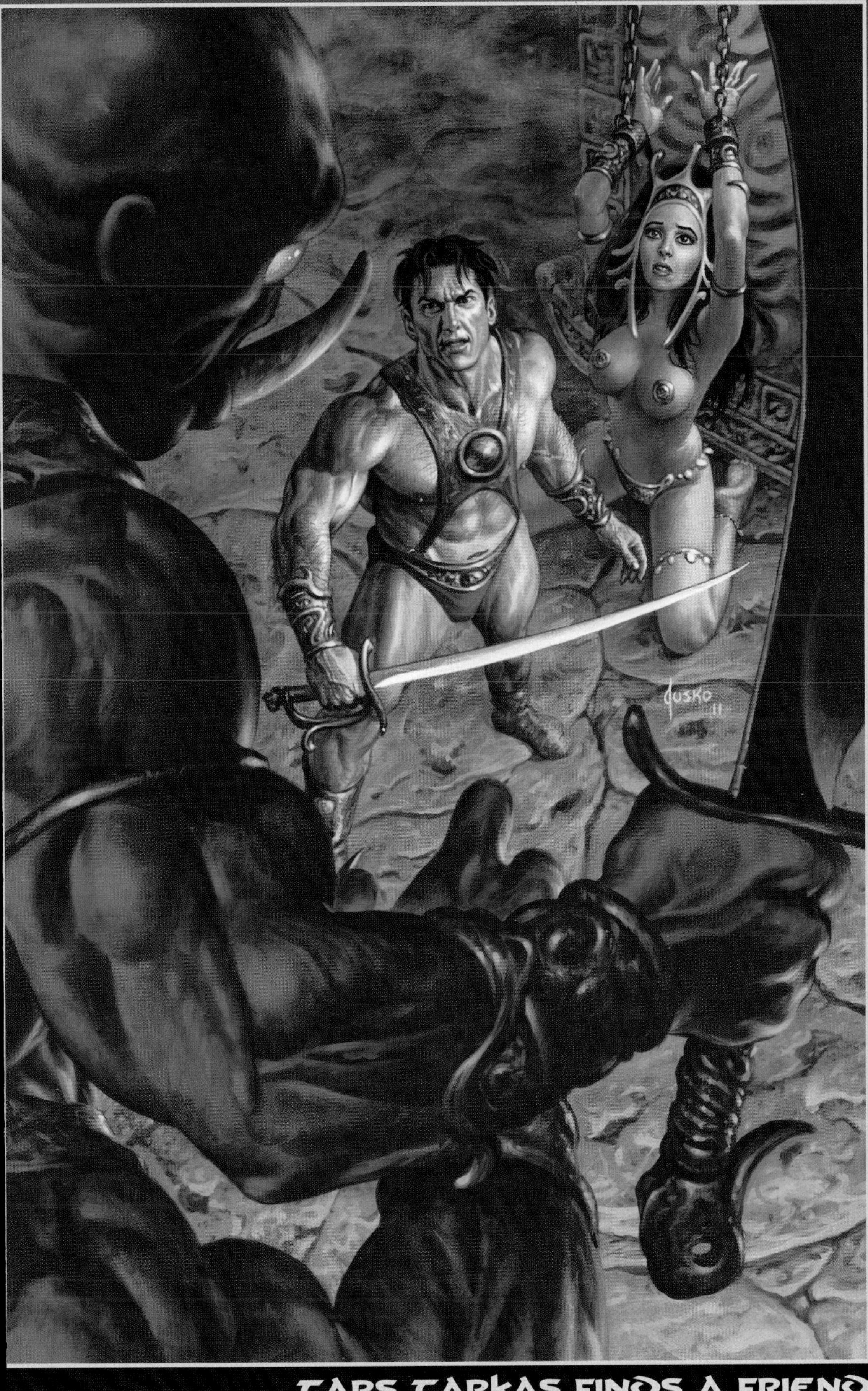
JUSKO 11

TARS TARKAS FINDS A FRIEND

Issue #8 cover by JOE JUSKO

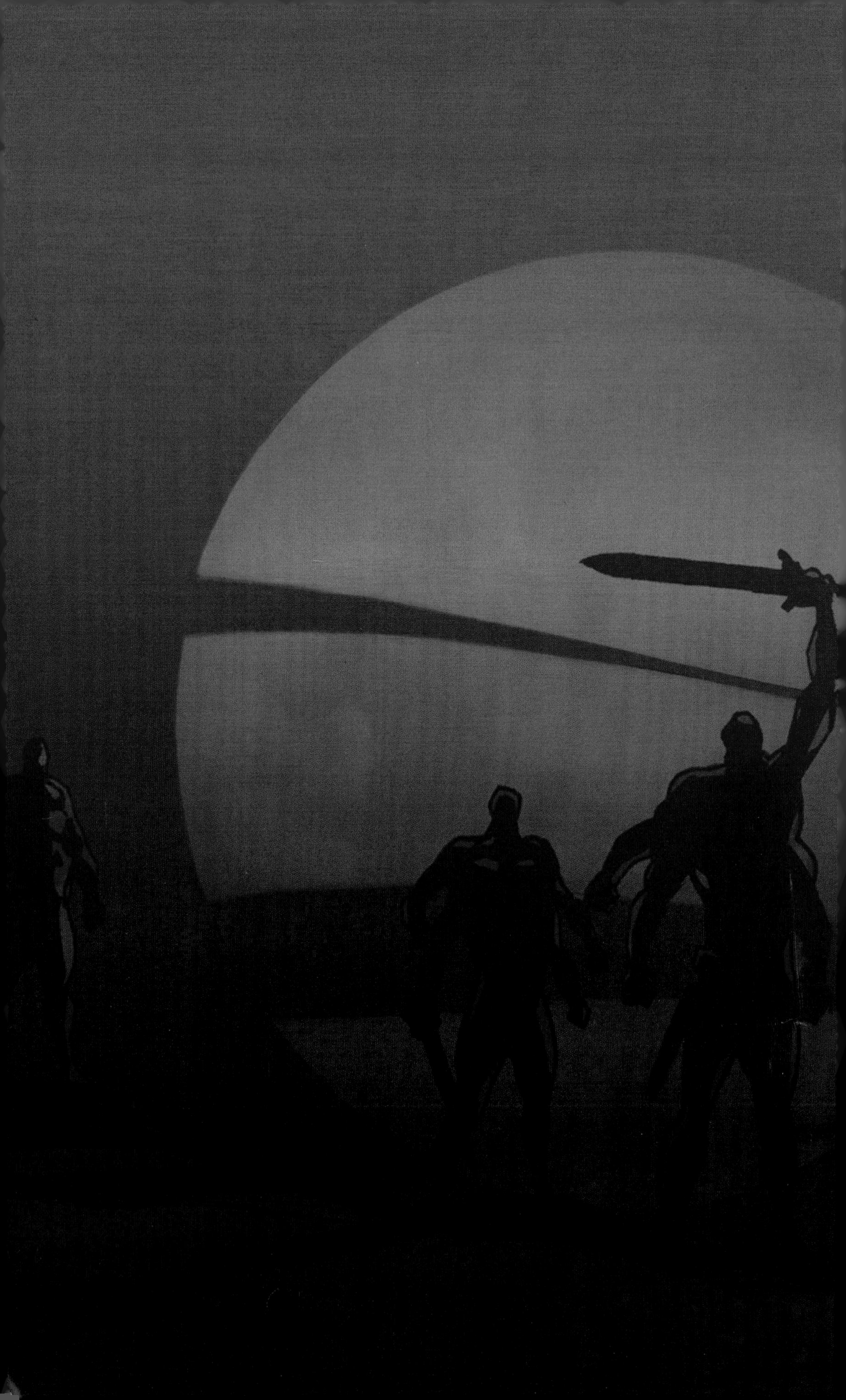

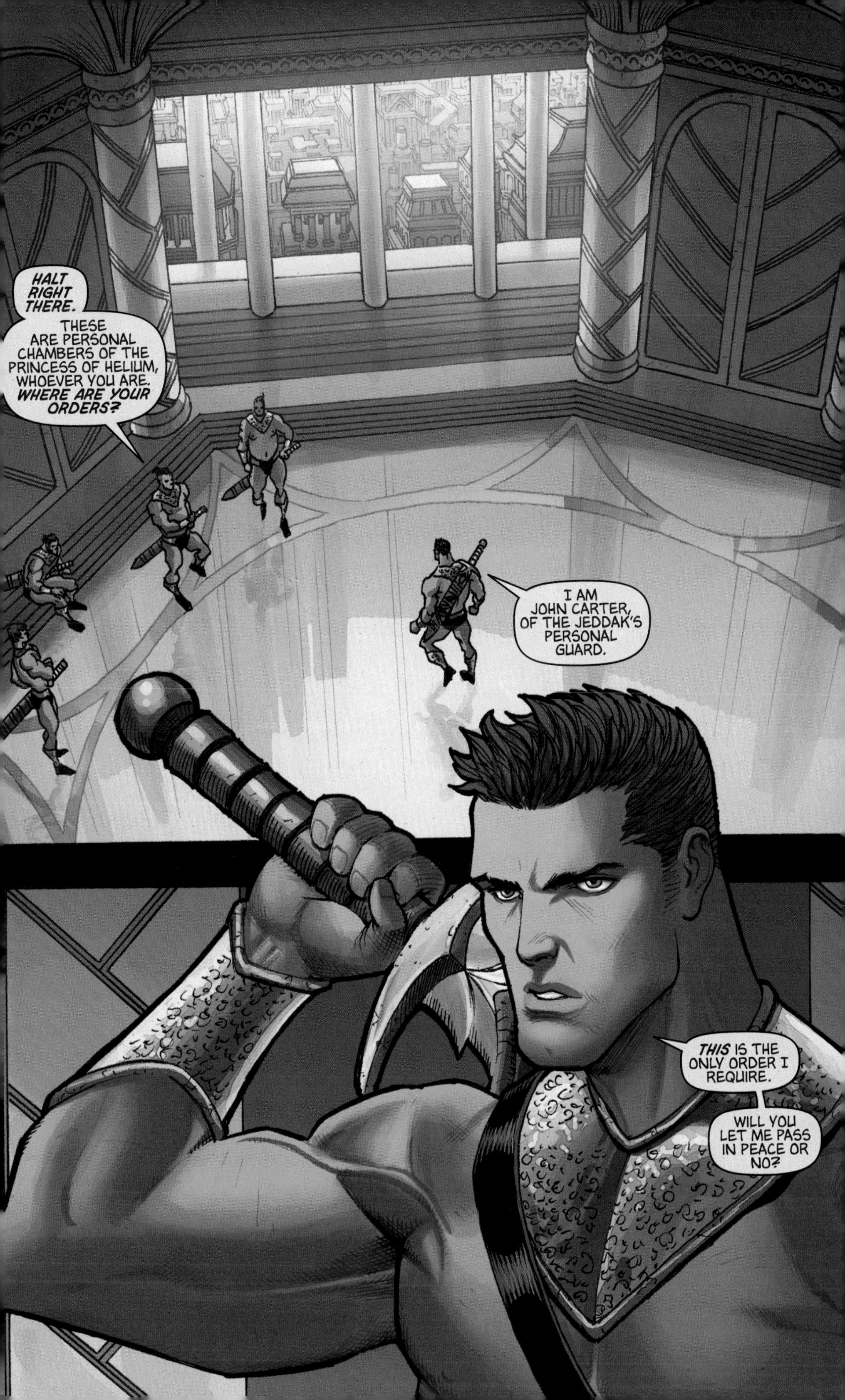
HALT RIGHT THERE.
THESE ARE PERSONAL CHAMBERS OF THE PRINCESS OF HELIUM, WHOEVER YOU ARE. WHERE ARE YOUR ORDERS?
I AM JOHN CARTER, OF THE JEDDAK'S PERSONAL GUARD.
THIS IS THE ONLY ORDER I REQUIRE.
WILL YOU LET ME PASS IN PEACE OR NO?

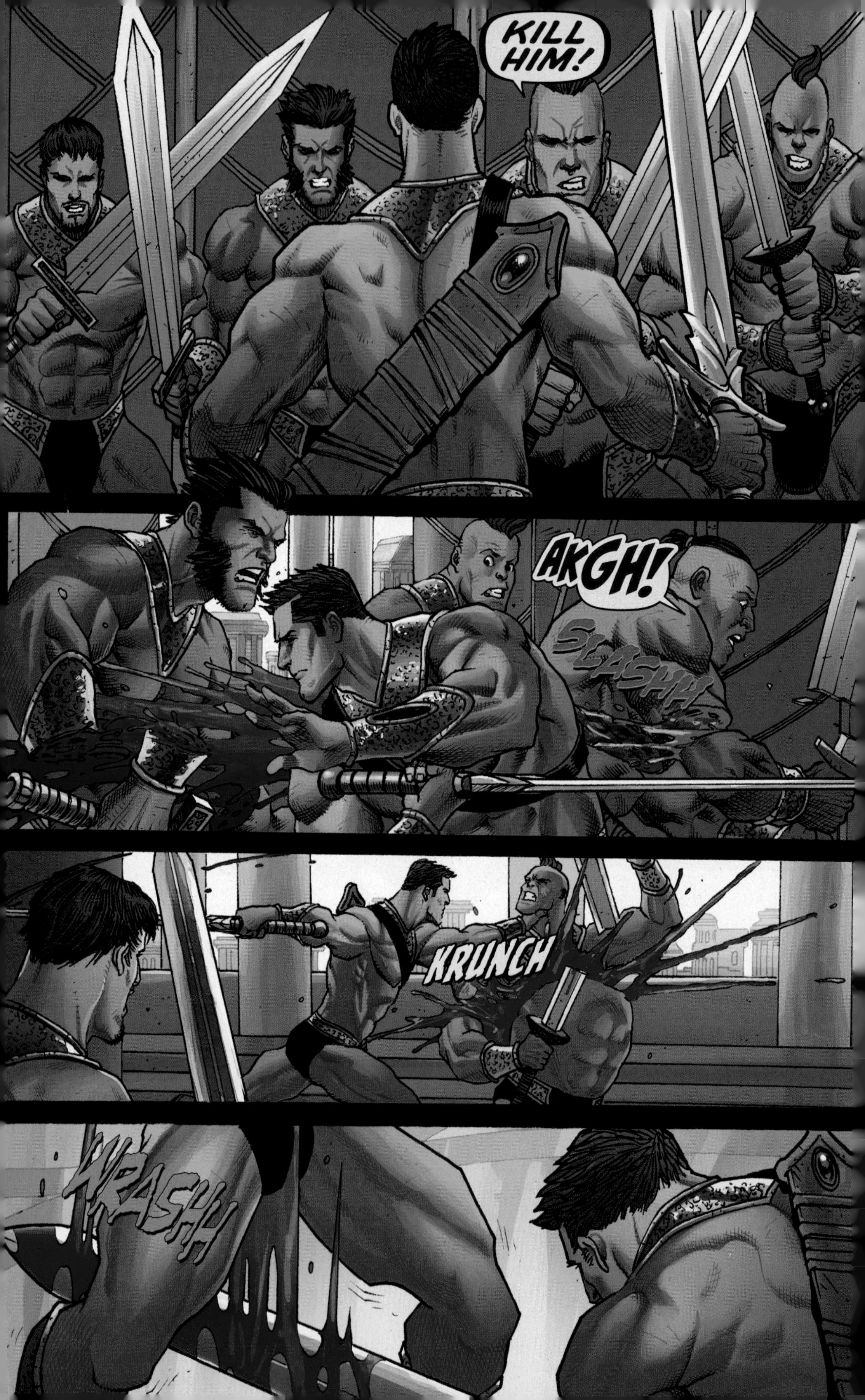
KILL HIM!
AKGH!
SLASHH
KRUNCH
WRASHH

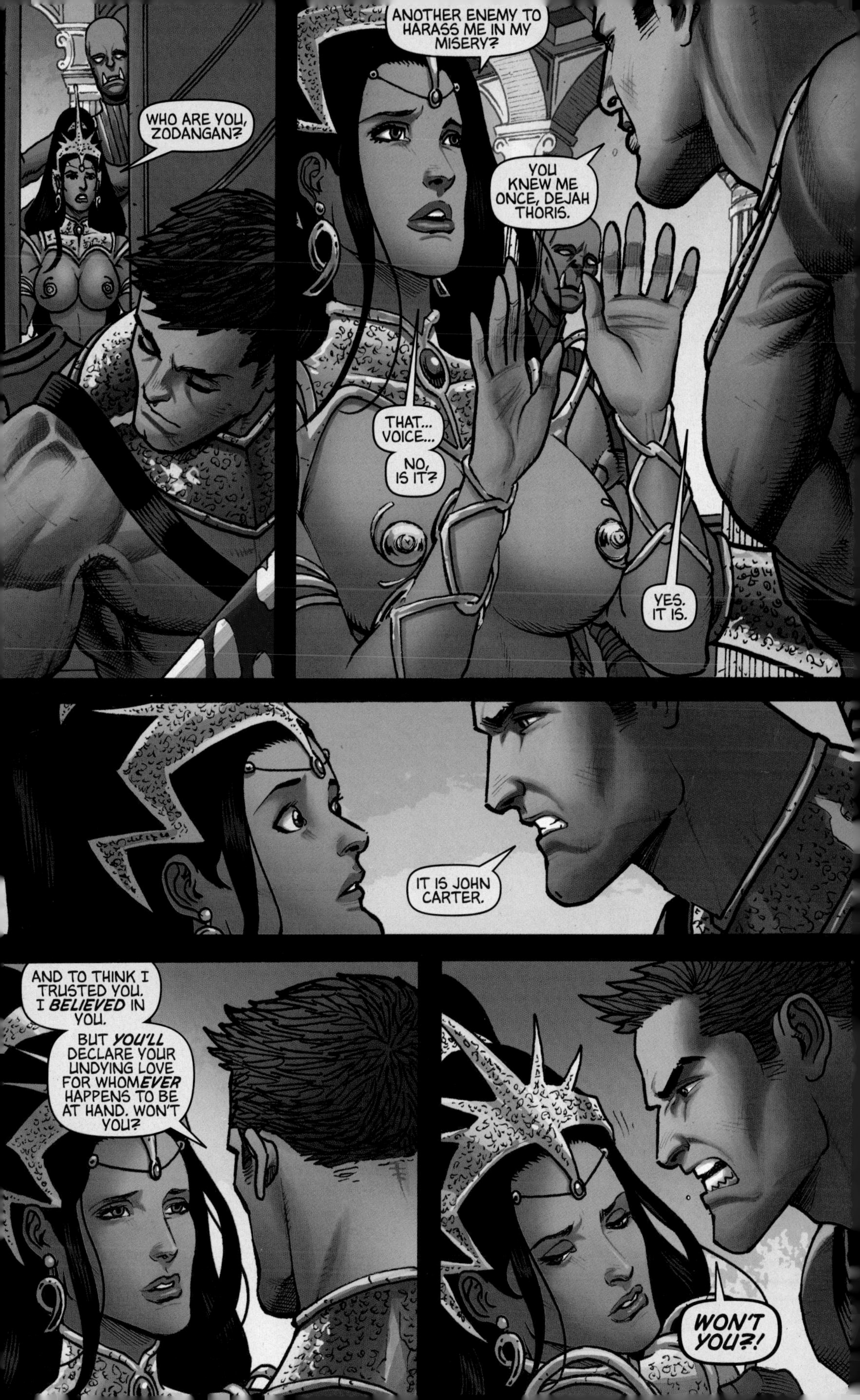
WHO ARE YOU, ZODANGAN?
ANOTHER ENEMY TO HARASS ME IN MY MISERY?
YOU KNEW ME ONCE, DEJAH THORIS.
THAT... VOICE...
NO, IS IT?
YES. IT IS.
IT IS JOHN CARTER.
AND TO THINK I TRUSTED YOU. I *BELIEVED* IN YOU.
BUT *YOU'LL* DECLARE YOUR UNDYING LOVE FOR WHOM*EVER* HAPPENS TO BE AT HAND. WON'T YOU?
WON'T YOU?!

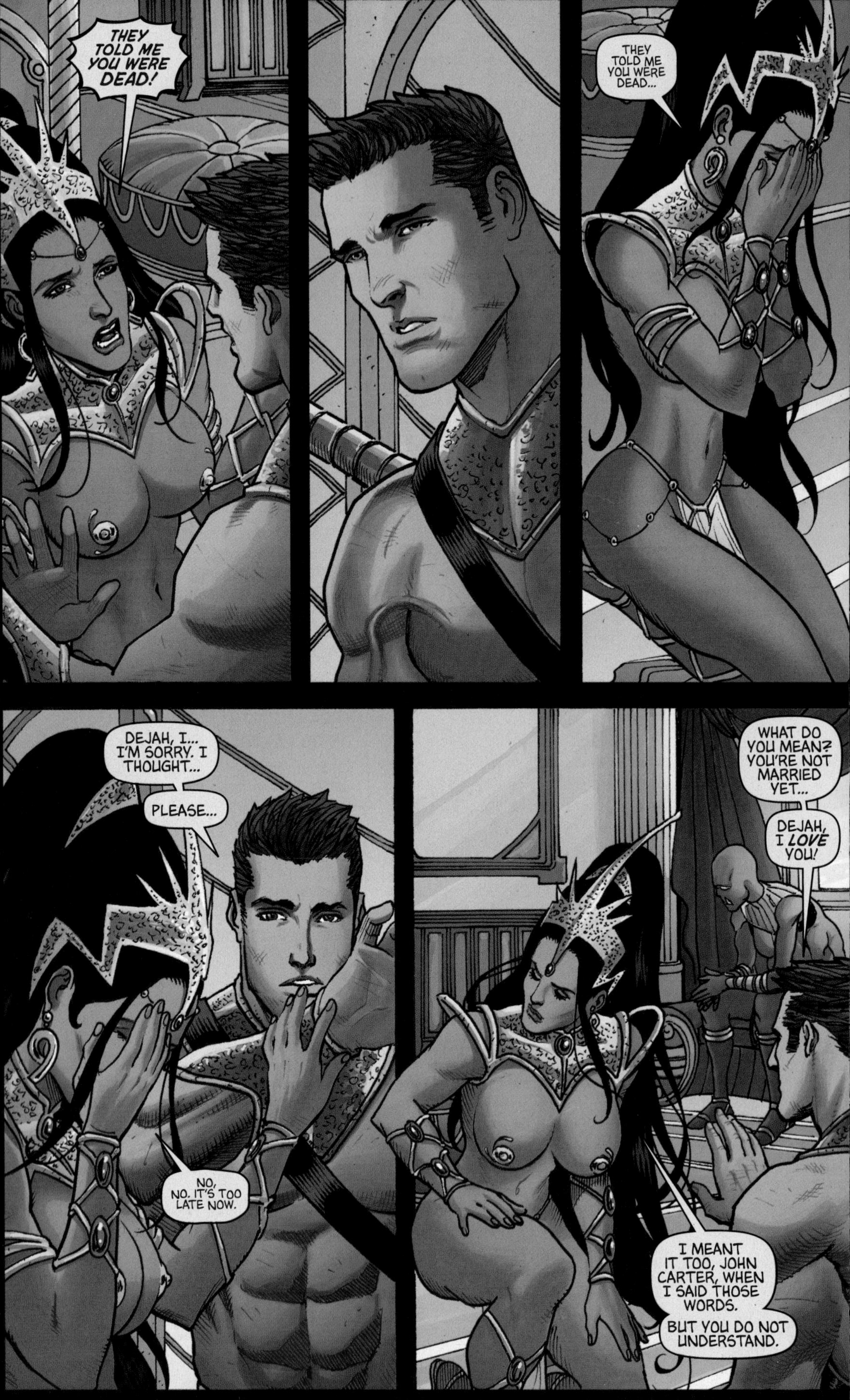
THEY TOLD ME YOU WERE DEAD!
THEY TOLD ME YOU WERE DEAD...
DEJAH, I... I'M SORRY. I THOUGHT...
PLEASE...
NO, NO. IT'S TOO LATE NOW.
WHAT DO YOU MEAN? YOU'RE NOT MARRIED YET...
DEJAH, I LOVE YOU!
I MEANT IT TOO, JOHN CARTER, WHEN I SAID THOSE WORDS.
BUT YOU DO NOT UNDERSTAND.

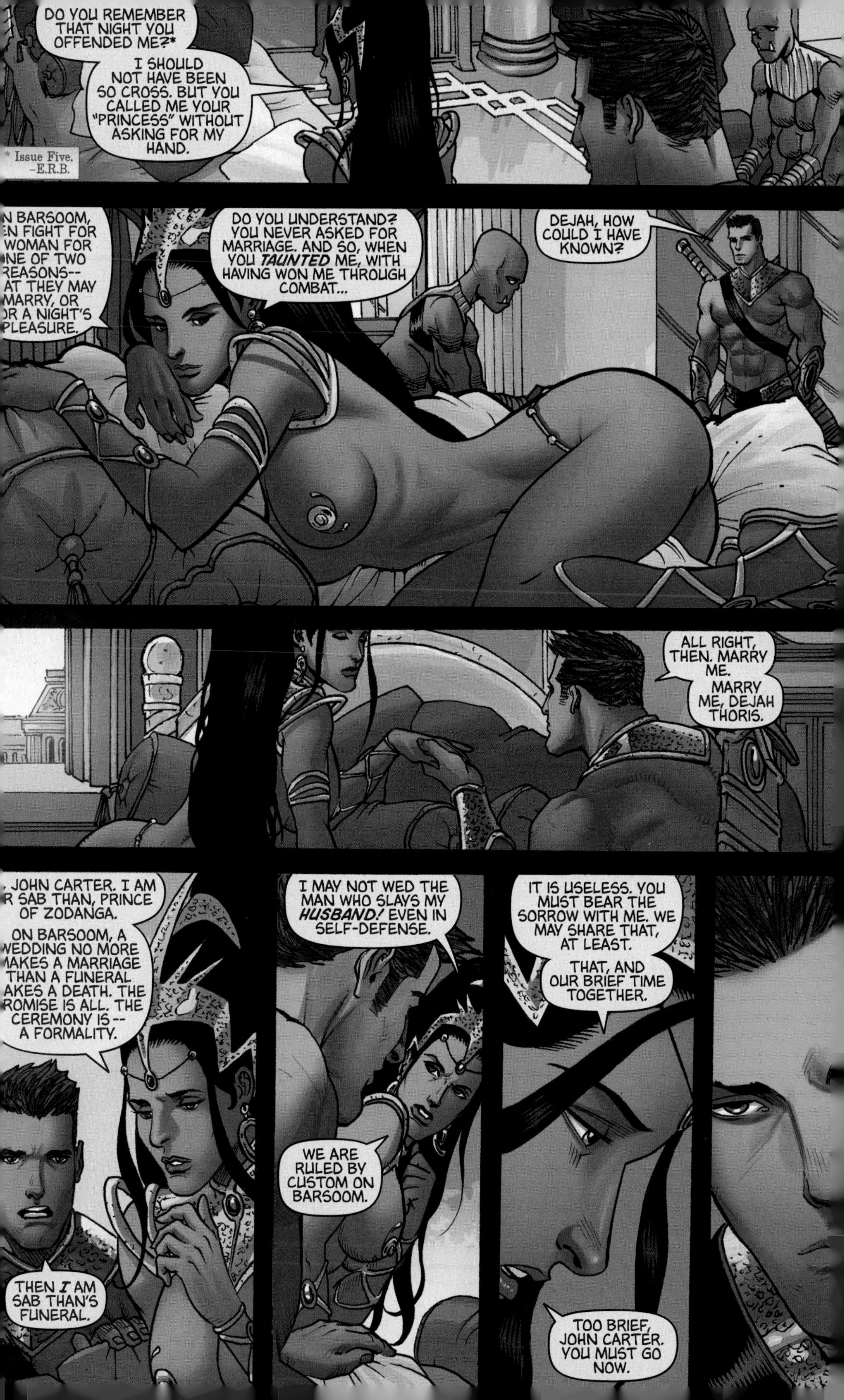
DO YOU REMEMBER THAT NIGHT YOU OFFENDED ME?*
I SHOULD NOT HAVE BEEN SO CROSS. BUT YOU CALLED ME YOUR "PRINCESS" WITHOUT ASKING FOR MY HAND.
* Issue Five. –E.R.B.
N BARSOOM, EN FIGHT FOR WOMAN FOR NE OF TWO REASONS-- AT THEY MAY MARRY, OR OR A NIGHT'S PLEASURE.
DO YOU UNDERSTAND? YOU NEVER ASKED FOR MARRIAGE. AND SO, WHEN YOU TAUNTED ME, WITH HAVING WON ME THROUGH COMBAT...
DEJAH, HOW COULD I HAVE KNOWN?
ALL RIGHT, THEN. MARRY ME.
MARRY ME, DEJAH THORIS.
JOHN CARTER. I AM R SAB THAN, PRINCE OF ZODANGA.
ON BARSOOM, A WEDDING NO MORE AKES A MARRIAGE THAN A FUNERAL AKES A DEATH. THE ROMISE IS ALL. THE CEREMONY IS -- A FORMALITY.
THEN I AM SAB THAN'S FUNERAL.
I MAY NOT WED THE MAN WHO SLAYS MY HUSBAND! EVEN IN SELF-DEFENSE.
WE ARE RULED BY CUSTOM ON BARSOOM.
IT IS USELESS. YOU MUST BEAR THE SORROW WITH ME. WE MAY SHARE THAT, AT LEAST.
THAT, AND OUR BRIEF TIME TOGETHER.
TOO BRIEF, JOHN CARTER. YOU MUST GO NOW.

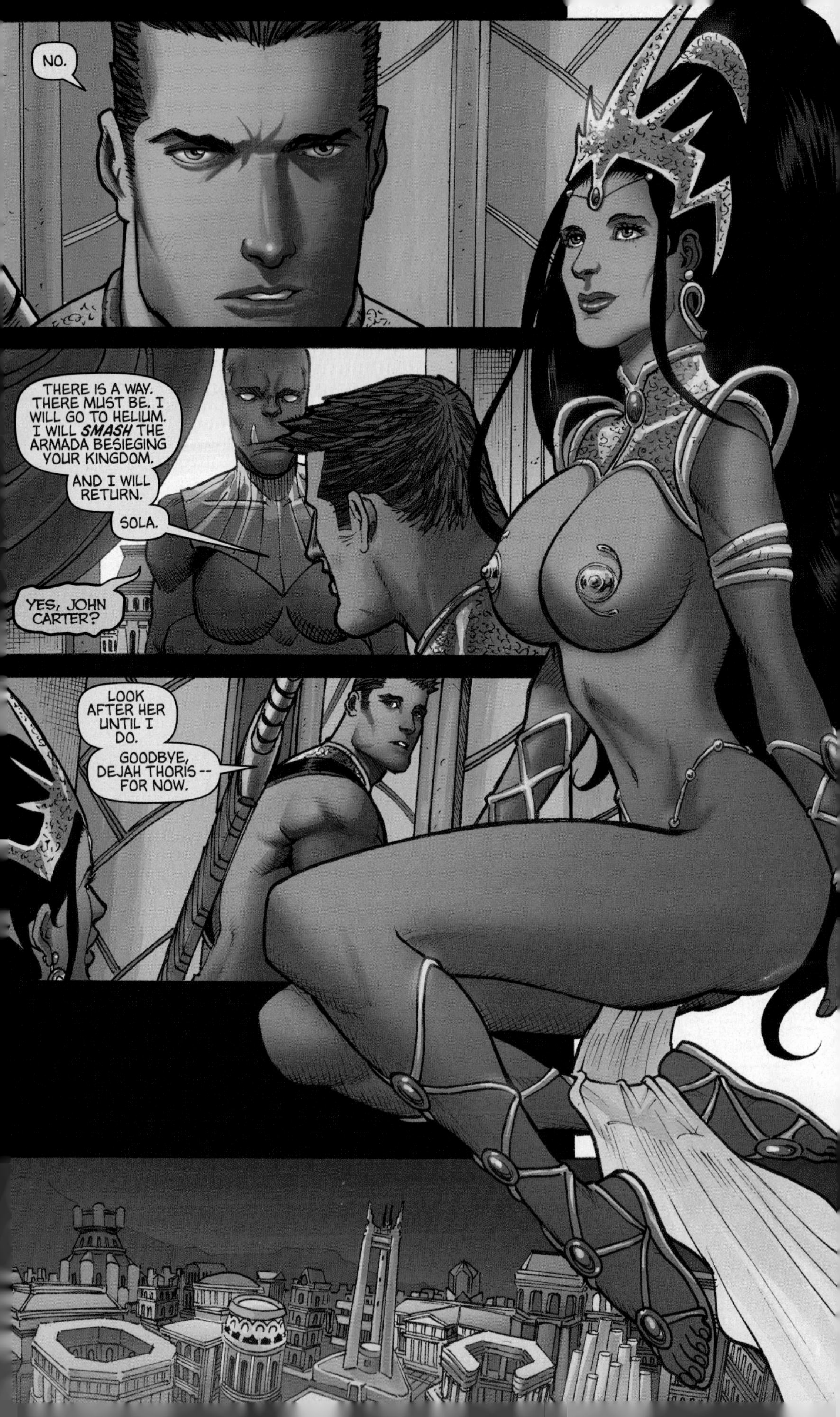
NO.
THERE IS A WAY. THERE MUST BE. I WILL GO TO HELIUM. I WILL SMASH THE ARMADA BESIEGING YOUR KINGDOM.
AND I WILL RETURN.
SOLA.
YES, JOHN CARTER?
LOOK AFTER HER UNTIL I DO.
GOODBYE, DEJAH THORIS -- FOR NOW.

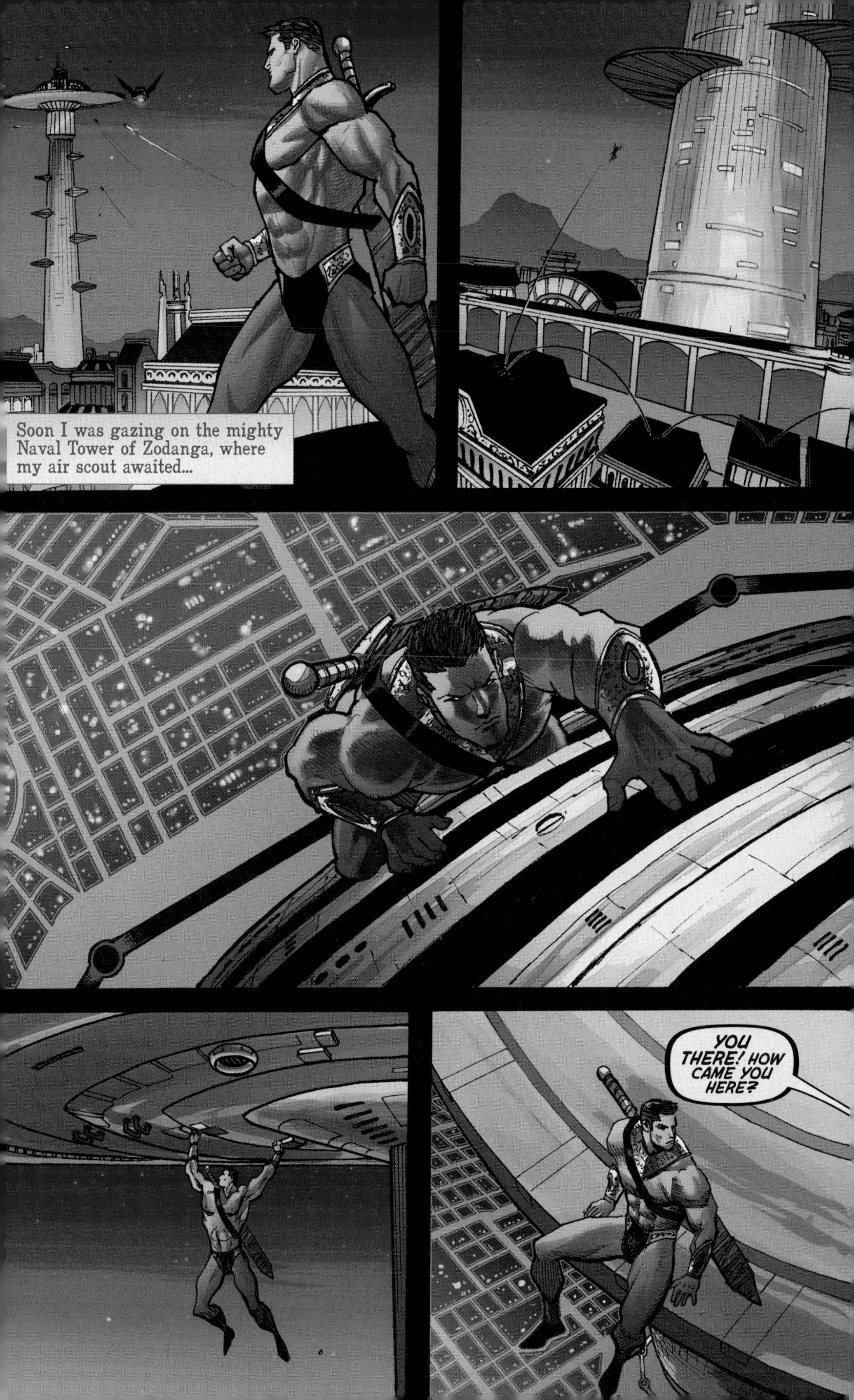
Soon I was gazing on the mighty Naval Tower of Zodanga, where my air scout awaited...
YOU THERE! HOW CAME YOU HERE?

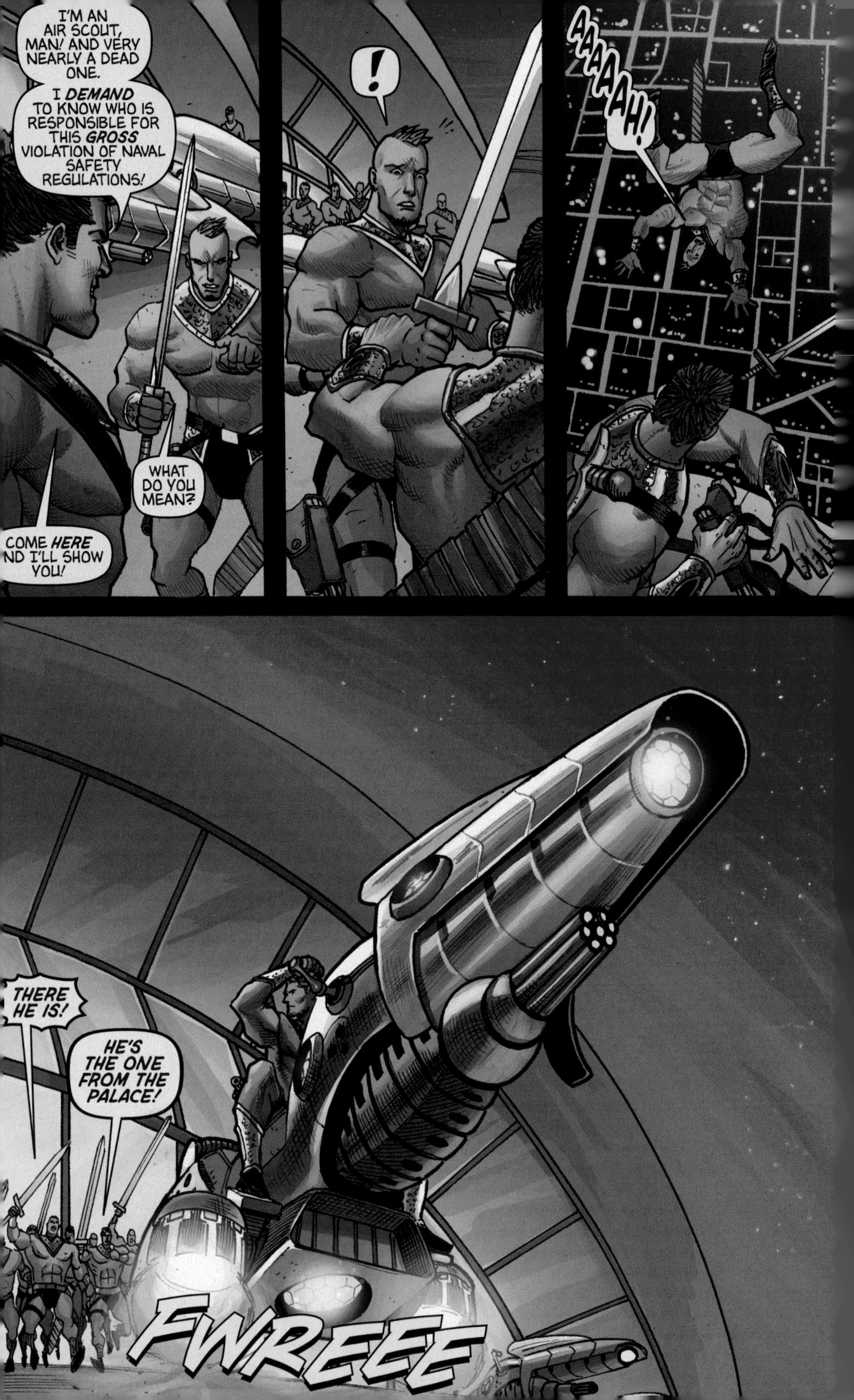
I'M AN AIR SCOUT, MAN! AND VERY NEARLY A DEAD ONE.
I DEMAND TO KNOW WHO IS RESPONSIBLE FOR THIS GROSS VIOLATION OF NAVAL SAFETY REGULATIONS!
WHAT DO YOU MEAN?
COME HERE ND I'LL SHOW YOU!
!
AAAAAAH!
THERE HE IS!
HE'S THE ONE FROM THE PALACE!
FWREEE

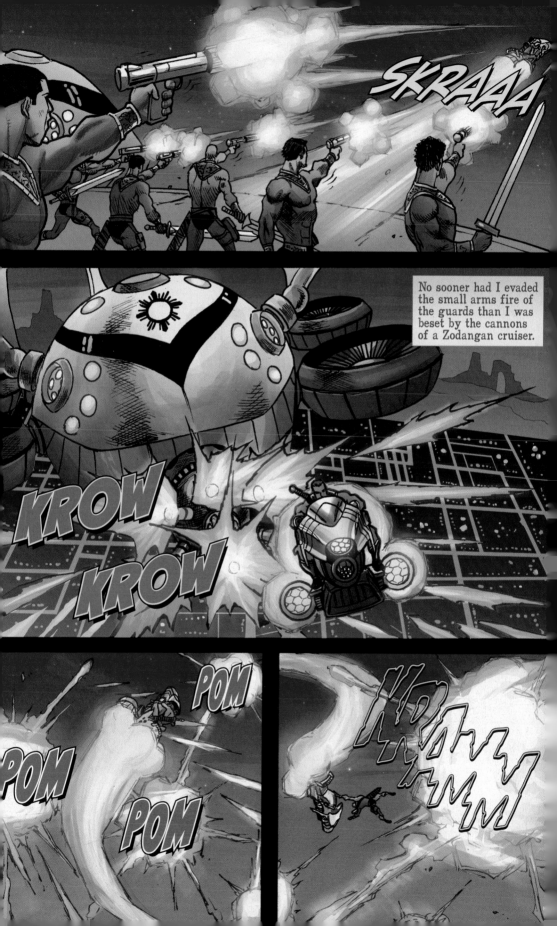

SKRAAA

No sooner had I evaded
the small arms fire of
the guards than I was
beset by the cannons
of a Zodangan cruiser.

KROW

KROW

POM

POM

POM

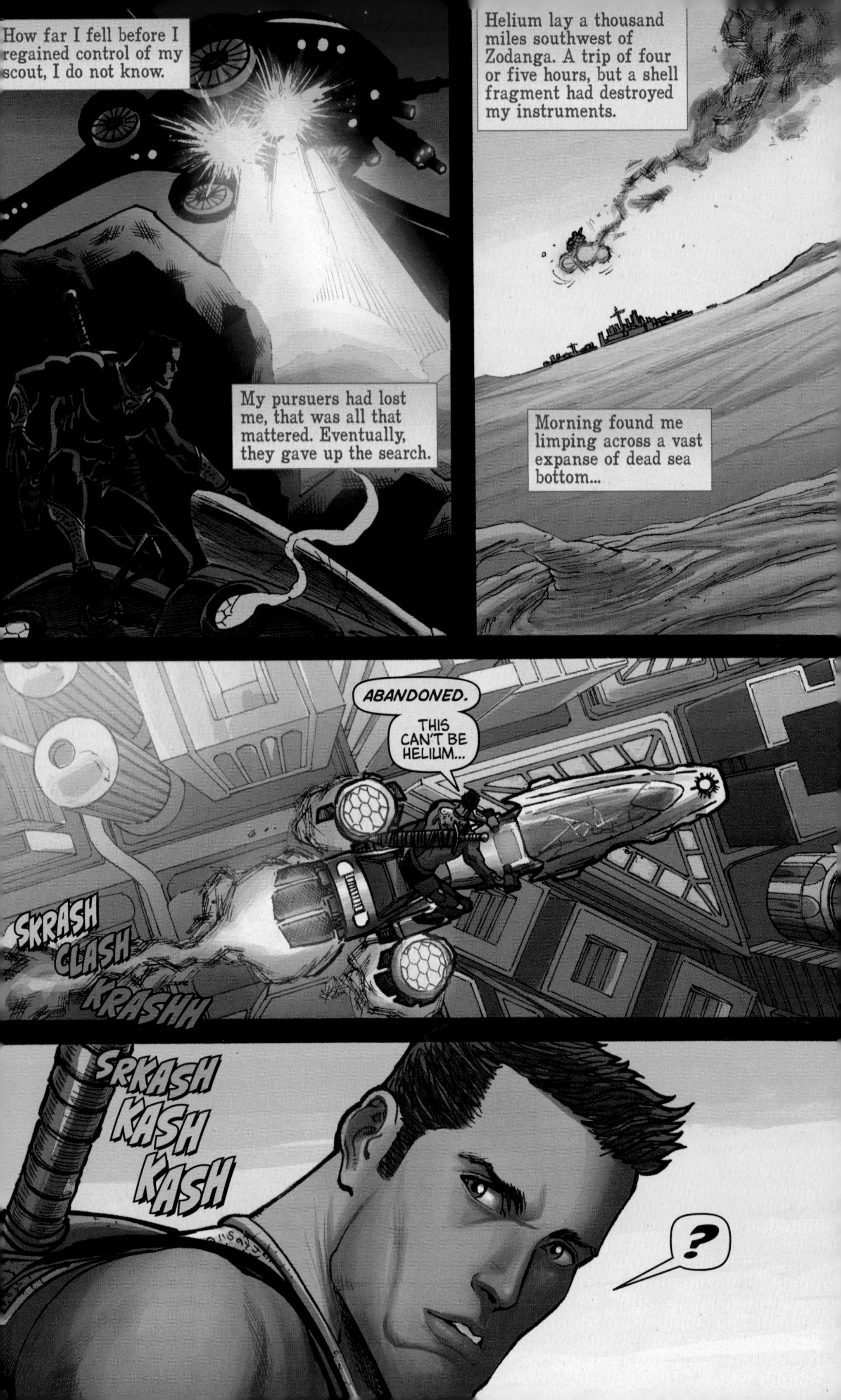
How far I fell before I regained control of my scout, I do not know.
My pursuers had lost me, that was all that mattered. Eventually, they gave up the search.
Helium lay a thousand miles southwest of Zodanga. A trip of four or five hours, but a shell fragment had destroyed my instruments.
Morning found me limping across a vast expanse of dead sea bottom...
ABANDONED.
THIS CAN'T BE HELIUM...
SKRASH
CLASH
KRASHH
SRKASH
KASH
KASH
?

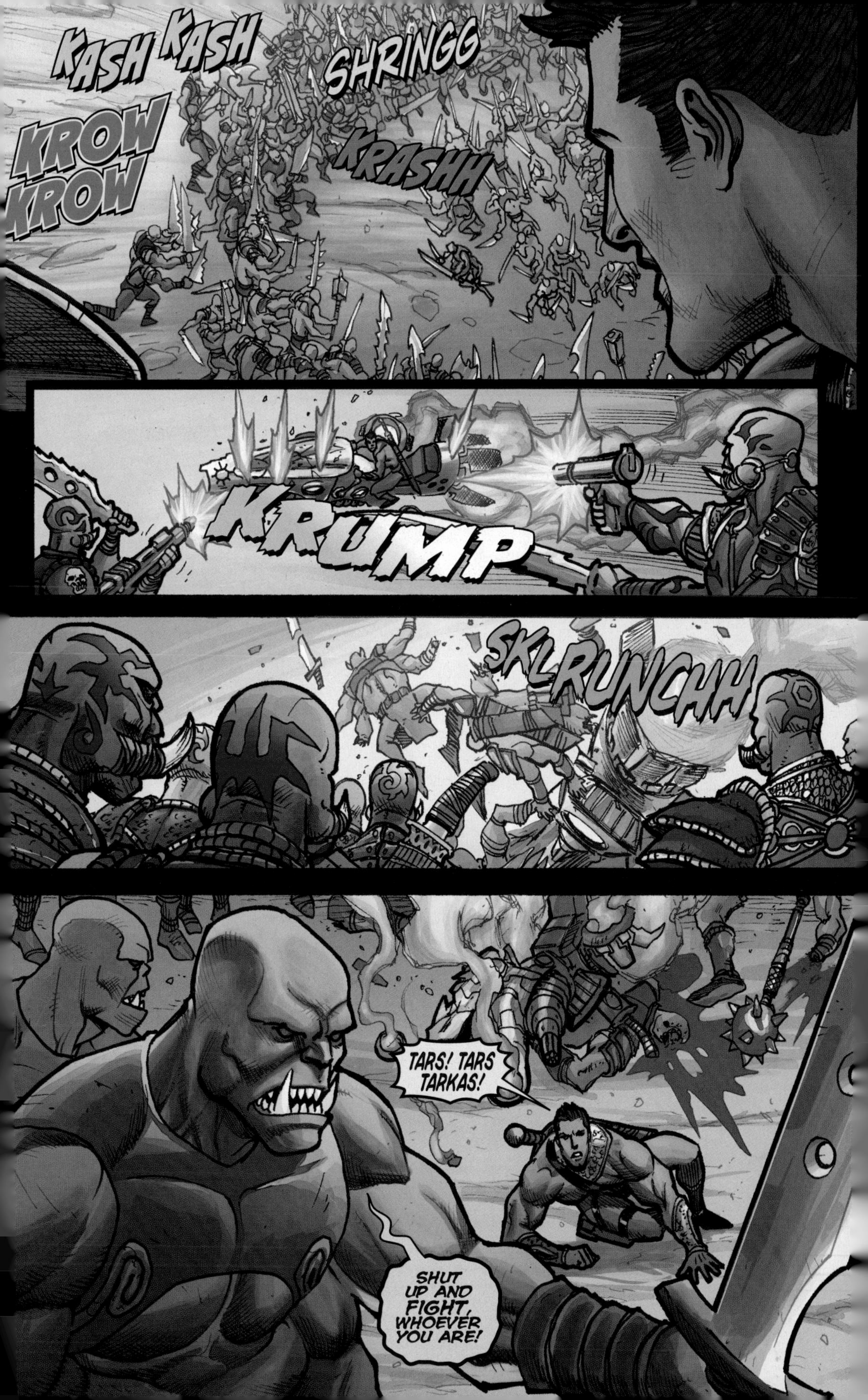
KASH KASH
SHRINGG
KROW KROW
KRASHH
KRUMP
SKLRUNCHH
TARS! TARS TARKAS!
SHUT UP AND FIGHT, WHOEVER YOU ARE!

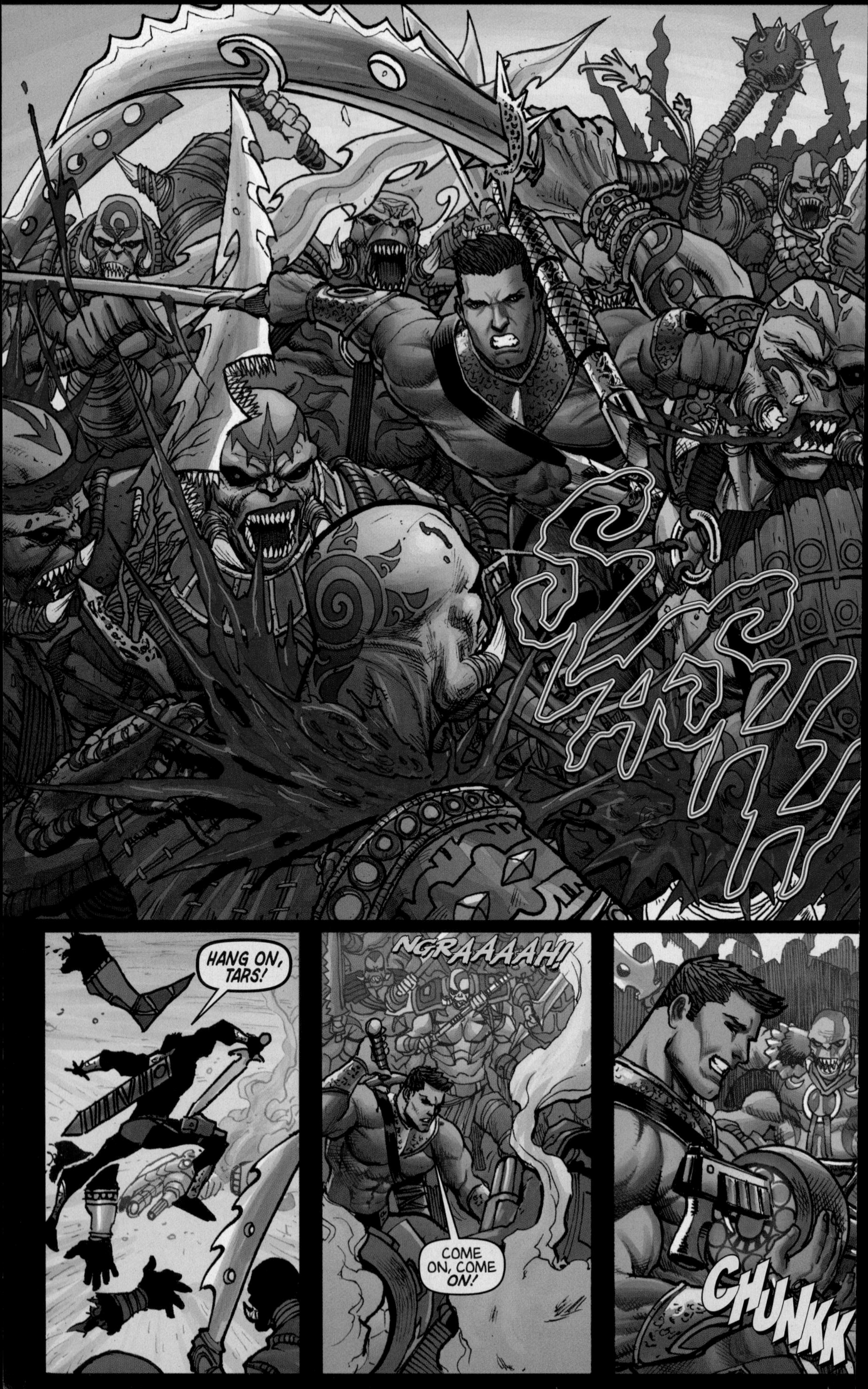
HANG ON, TARS!
NGRAAAAH!
COME ON, COME ON!
CHUNKK

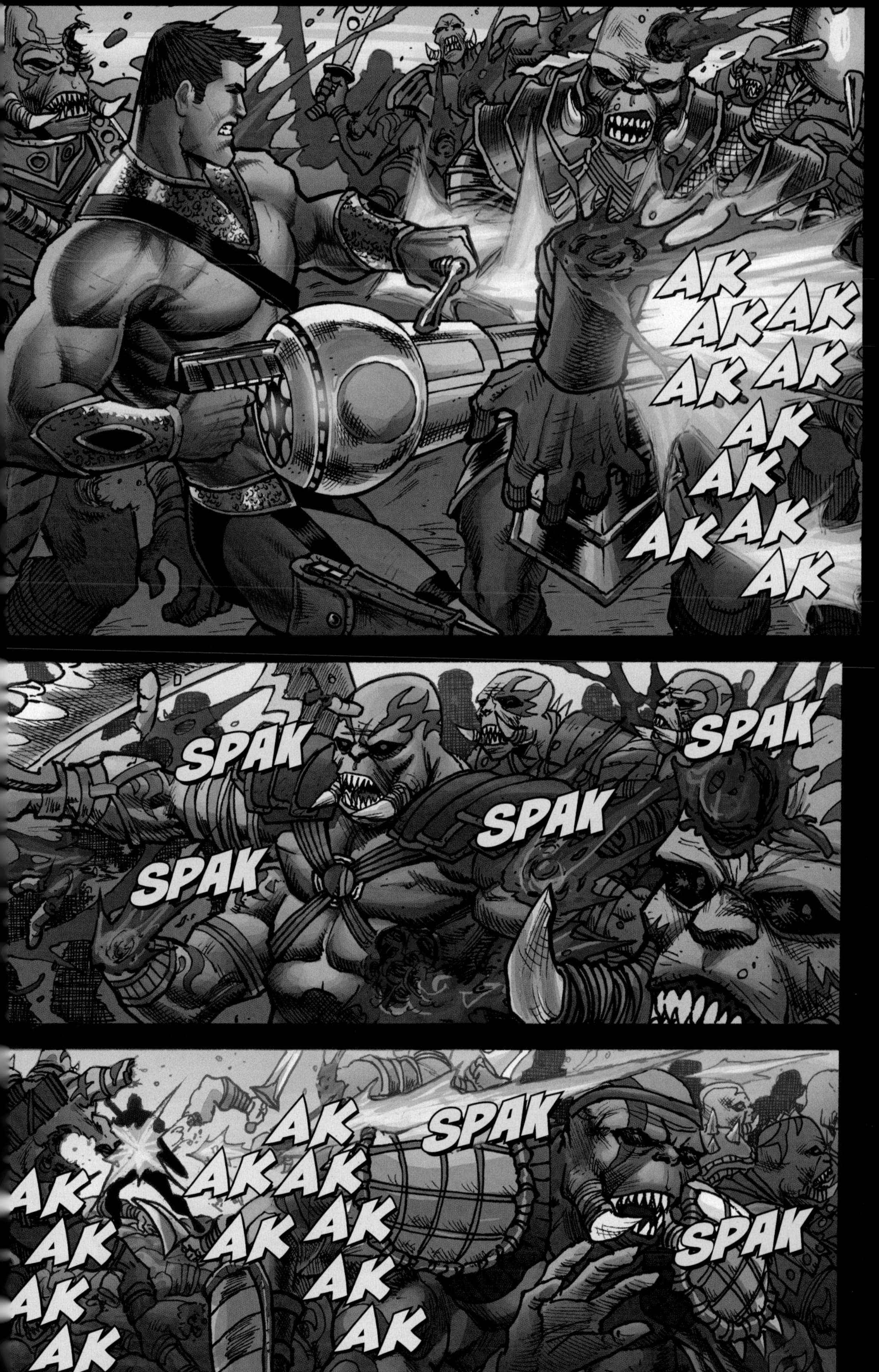
AK AK AK AK AK AK AK AK AK AK
SPAK
SPAK
SPAK
SPAK
AK AK AK AK AK AK AK AK
SPAK
AK AK AK AK
SPAK

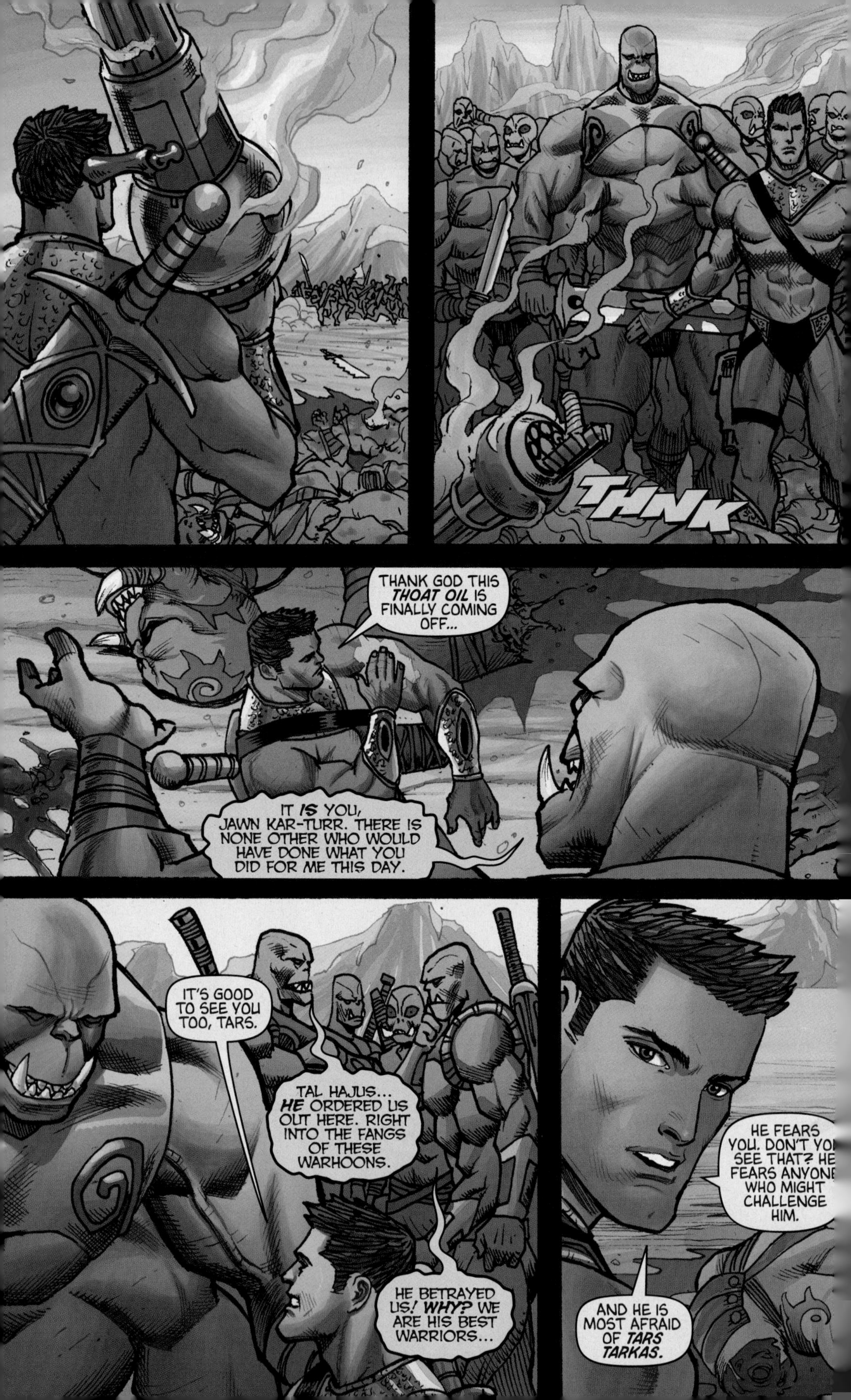
THNK
THANK GOD THIS *THOAT OIL* IS FINALLY COMING OFF...
IT *IS* YOU, JAWN KAR-TURR. THERE IS NONE OTHER WHO WOULD HAVE DONE WHAT YOU DID FOR ME THIS DAY.
IT'S GOOD TO SEE YOU TOO, TARS.
TAL HAJUS... *HE* ORDERED US OUT HERE. RIGHT INTO THE FANGS OF THESE WARHOONS.
HE BETRAYED US! *WHY?* WE ARE HIS BEST WARRIORS...
HE FEARS YOU. DON'T YOU SEE THAT? HE FEARS ANYONE WHO MIGHT CHALLENGE HIM.
AND HE IS MOST AFRAID OF *TARS TARKAS*.

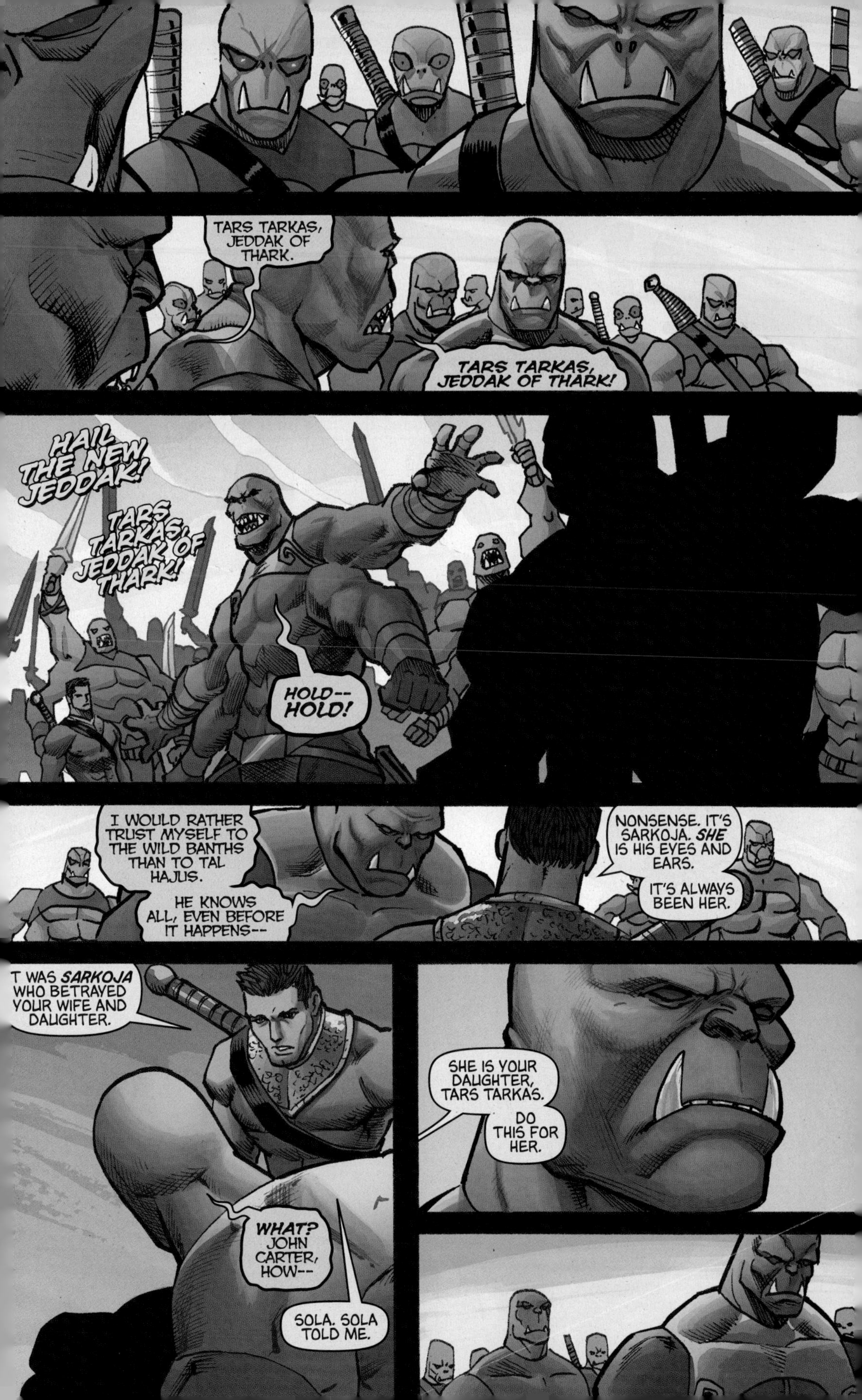
TARS TARKAS, JEDDAK OF THARK.
TARS TARKAS, JEDDAK OF THARK!
HAIL THE NEW JEDDAK!
TARS TARKAS, JEDDAK OF THARK!
HOLD-- HOLD!
I WOULD RATHER TRUST MYSELF TO THE WILD BANTHS THAN TO TAL HAJUS.
HE KNOWS ALL, EVEN BEFORE IT HAPPENS--
NONSENSE. IT'S SARKOJA. *SHE* IS HIS EYES AND EARS.
IT'S ALWAYS BEEN HER.
T WAS *SARKOJA* WHO BETRAYED YOUR WIFE AND DAUGHTER.
WHAT? JOHN CARTER, HOW--
SOLA. SOLA TOLD ME.
SHE IS YOUR DAUGHTER, TARS TARKAS.
DO THIS FOR HER.

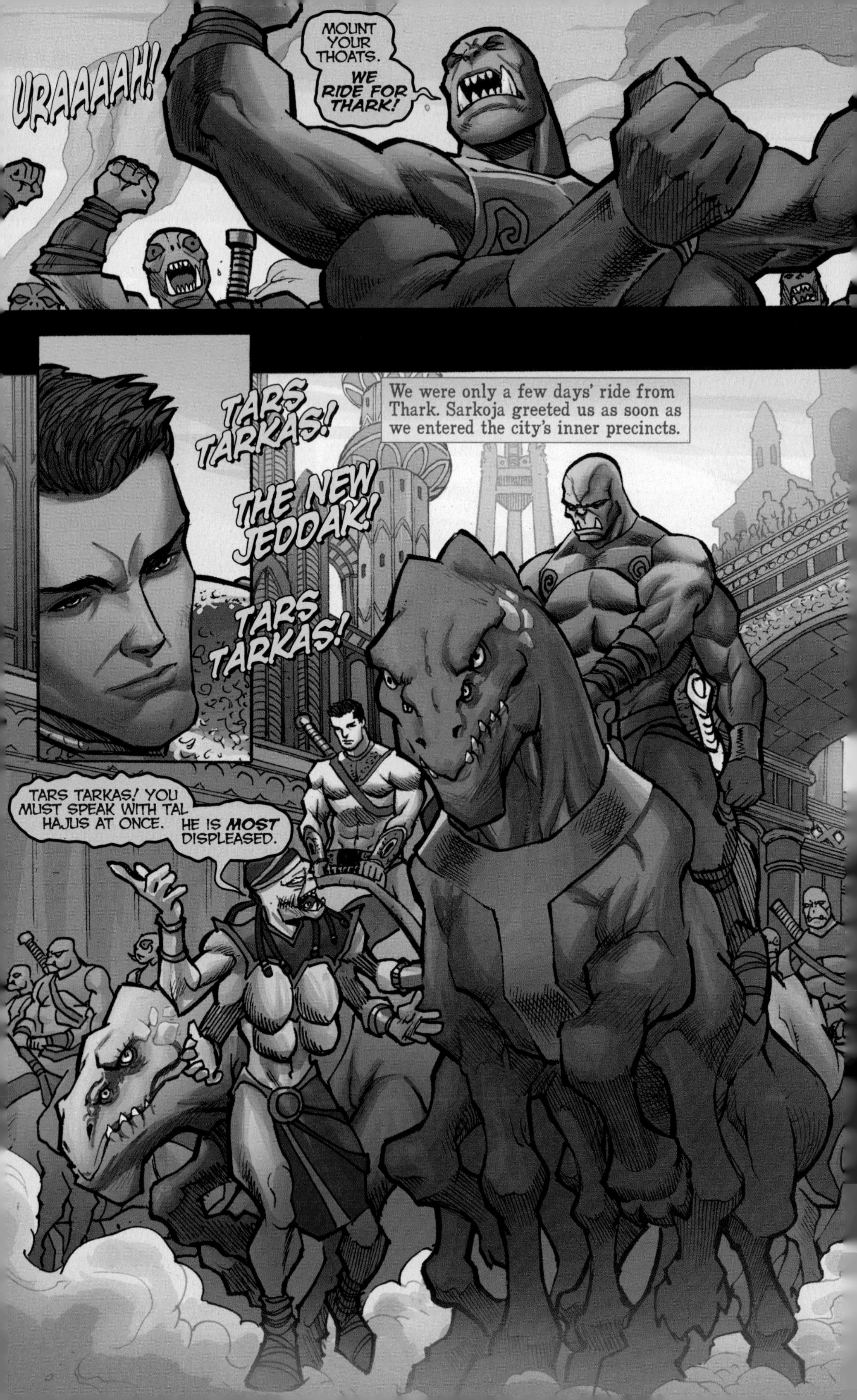
URAAAAH!
MOUNT YOUR THOATS. WE RIDE FOR THARK!
We were only a few days' ride from Thark. Sarkoja greeted us as soon as we entered the city's inner precincts.
TARS TARKAS!
THE NEW JEDDAK!
TARS TARKAS!
TARS TARKAS! YOU MUST SPEAK WITH TAL HAJUS AT ONCE.
HE IS MOST DISPLEASED.

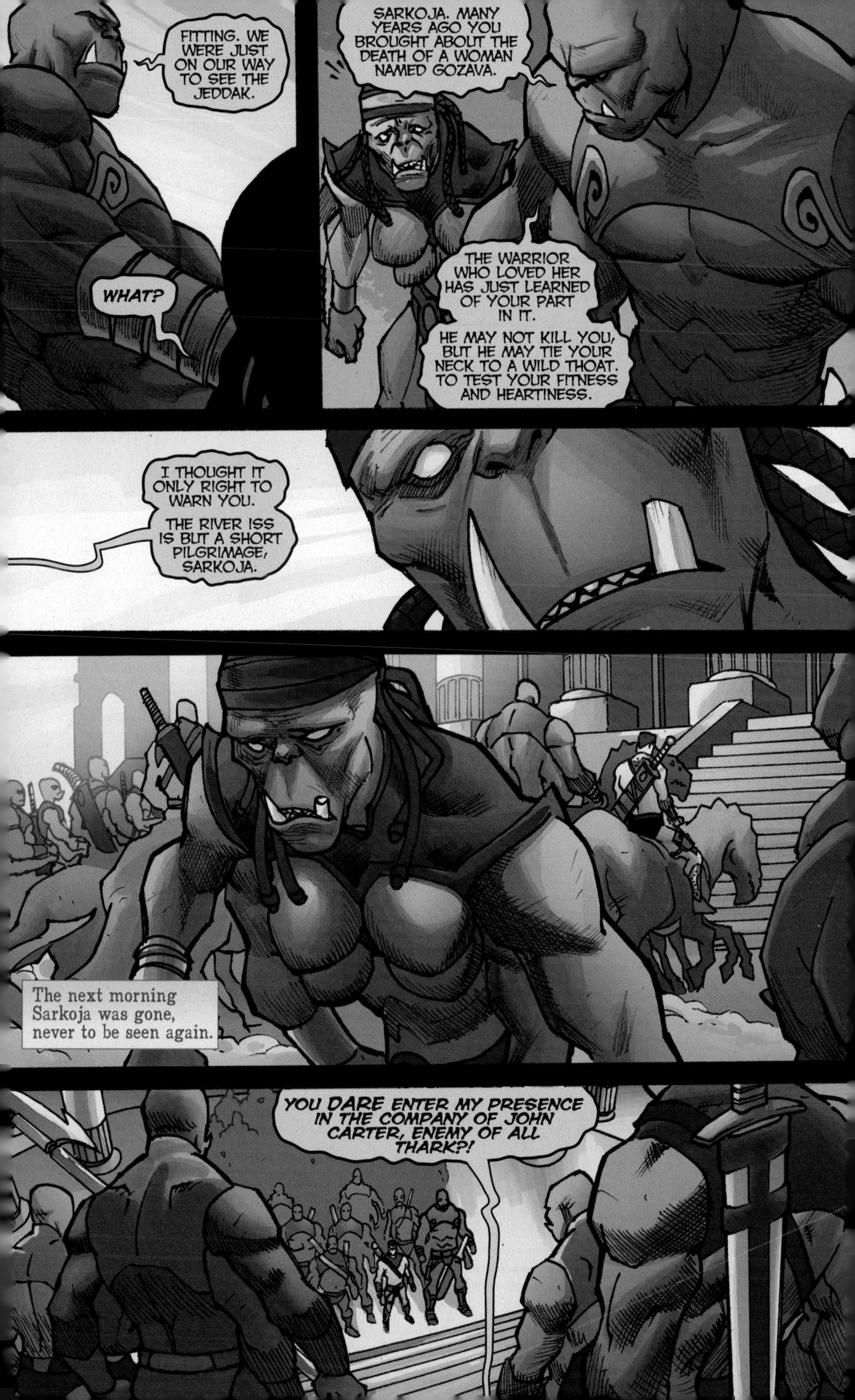
FITTING. WE WERE JUST ON OUR WAY TO SEE THE JEDDAK.
WHAT?
SARKOJA. MANY YEARS AGO YOU BROUGHT ABOUT THE DEATH OF A WOMAN NAMED GOZAVA.
THE WARRIOR WHO LOVED HER HAS JUST LEARNED OF YOUR PART IN IT.
HE MAY NOT KILL YOU, BUT HE MAY TIE YOUR NECK TO A WILD THOAT. TO TEST YOUR FITNESS AND HEARTINESS.
I THOUGHT IT ONLY RIGHT TO WARN YOU.
THE RIVER ISS IS BUT A SHORT PILGRIMAGE, SARKOJA.
The next morning Sarkoja was gone, never to be seen again.
YOU DARE ENTER MY PRESENCE IN THE COMPANY OF JOHN CARTER, ENEMY OF ALL THARK?!

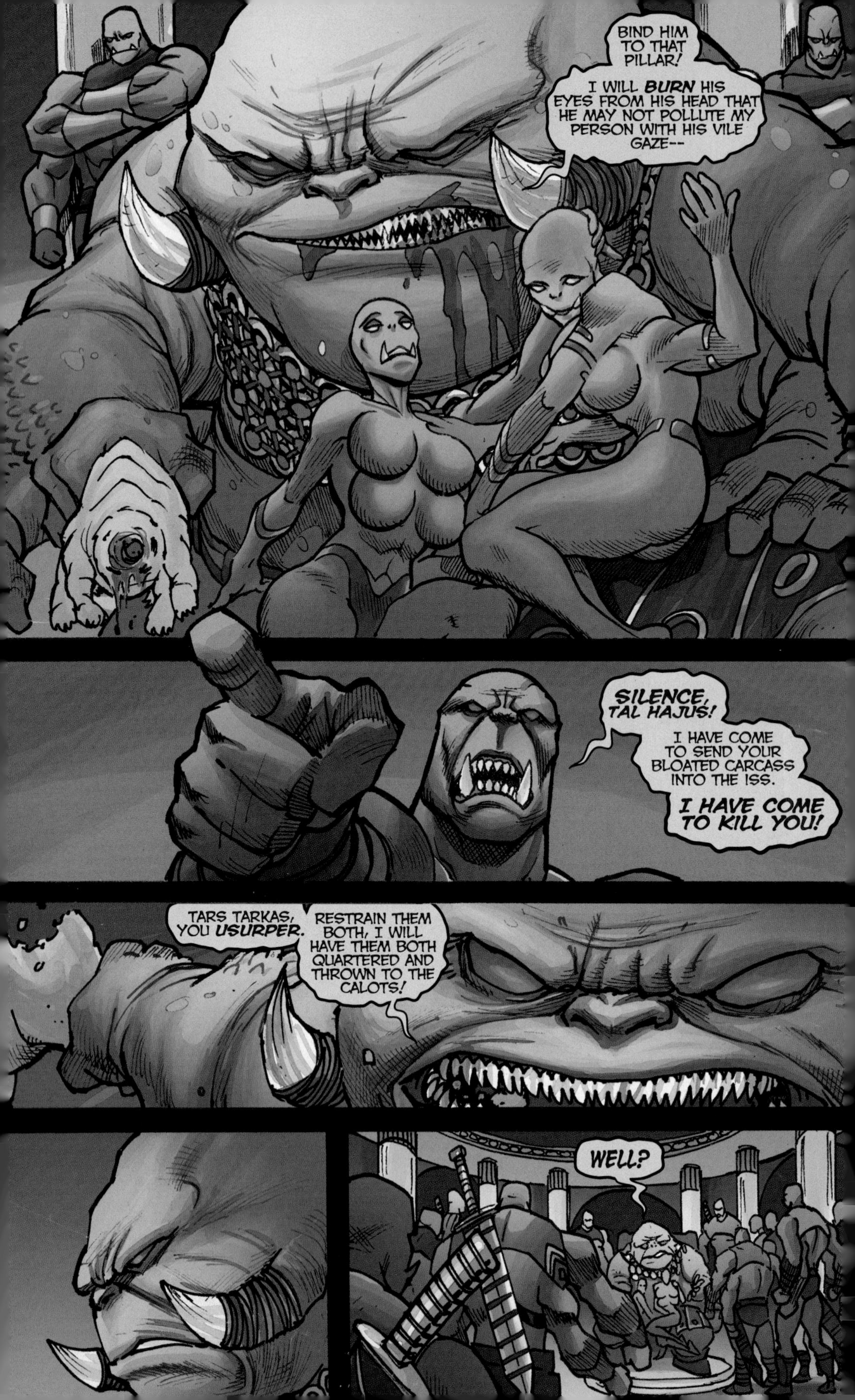
BIND HIM TO THAT PILLAR!
I WILL **BURN** HIS EYES FROM HIS HEAD THAT HE MAY NOT POLLUTE MY PERSON WITH HIS VILE GAZE--
SILENCE, TAL HAJUS!
I HAVE COME TO SEND YOUR BLOATED CARCASS INTO THE ISS.
I HAVE COME TO KILL YOU!
TARS TARKAS, YOU **USURPER**.
RESTRAIN THEM BOTH, I WILL HAVE THEM BOTH QUARTERED AND THROWN TO THE CALOTS!
WELL?

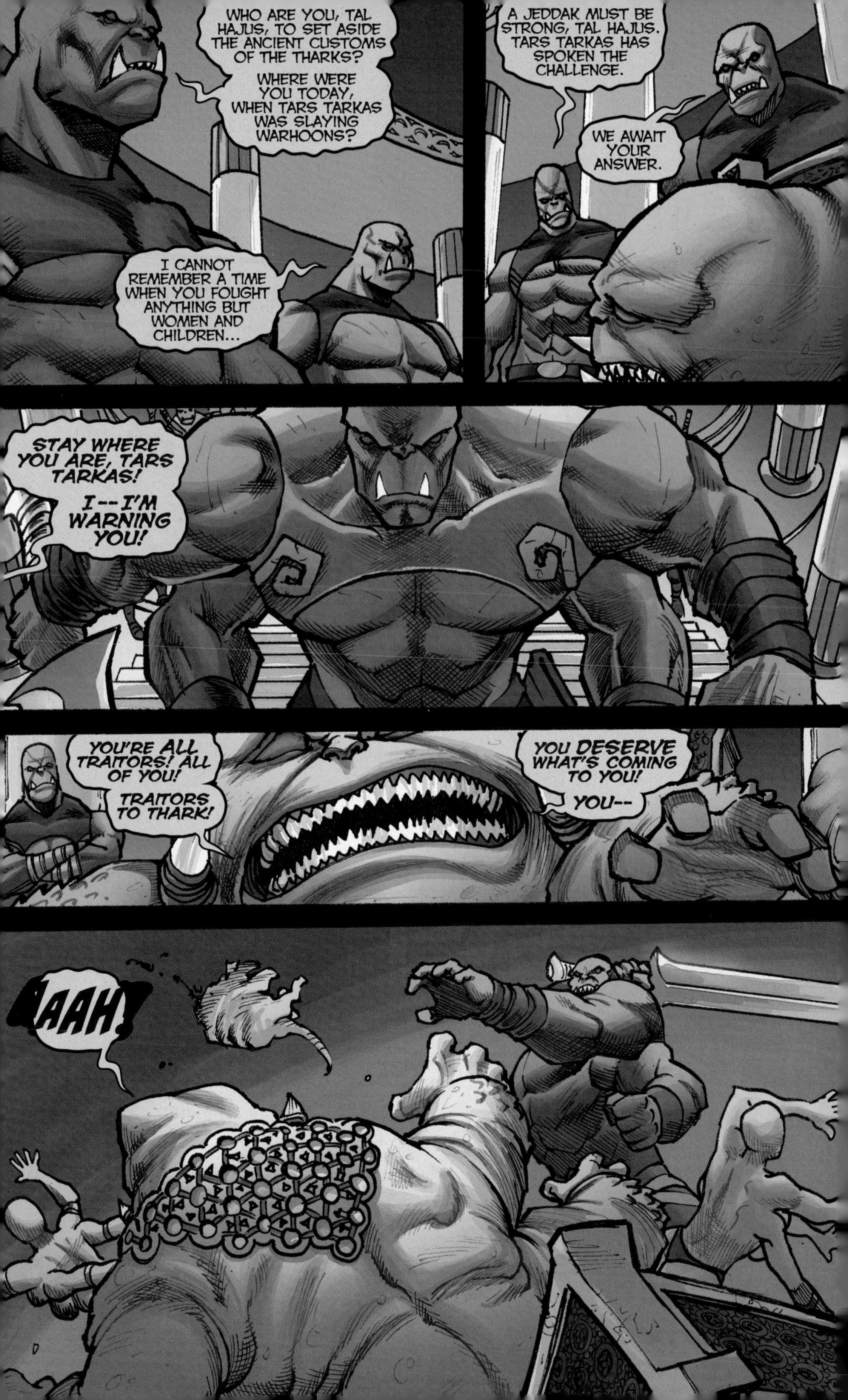
WHO ARE YOU, TAL HAJUS, TO SET ASIDE THE ANCIENT CUSTOMS OF THE THARKS?
WHERE WERE YOU TODAY, WHEN TARS TARKAS WAS SLAYING WARHOONS?
I CANNOT REMEMBER A TIME WHEN YOU FOUGHT ANYTHING BUT WOMEN AND CHILDREN...
A JEDDAK MUST BE STRONG, TAL HAJUS. TARS TARKAS HAS SPOKEN THE CHALLENGE.
WE AWAIT YOUR ANSWER.
STAY WHERE YOU ARE, TARS TARKAS!
I--I'M WARNING YOU!
YOU'RE ALL TRAITORS! ALL OF YOU!
TRAITORS TO THARK!
YOU DESERVE WHAT'S COMING TO YOU!
YOU--
AAH!

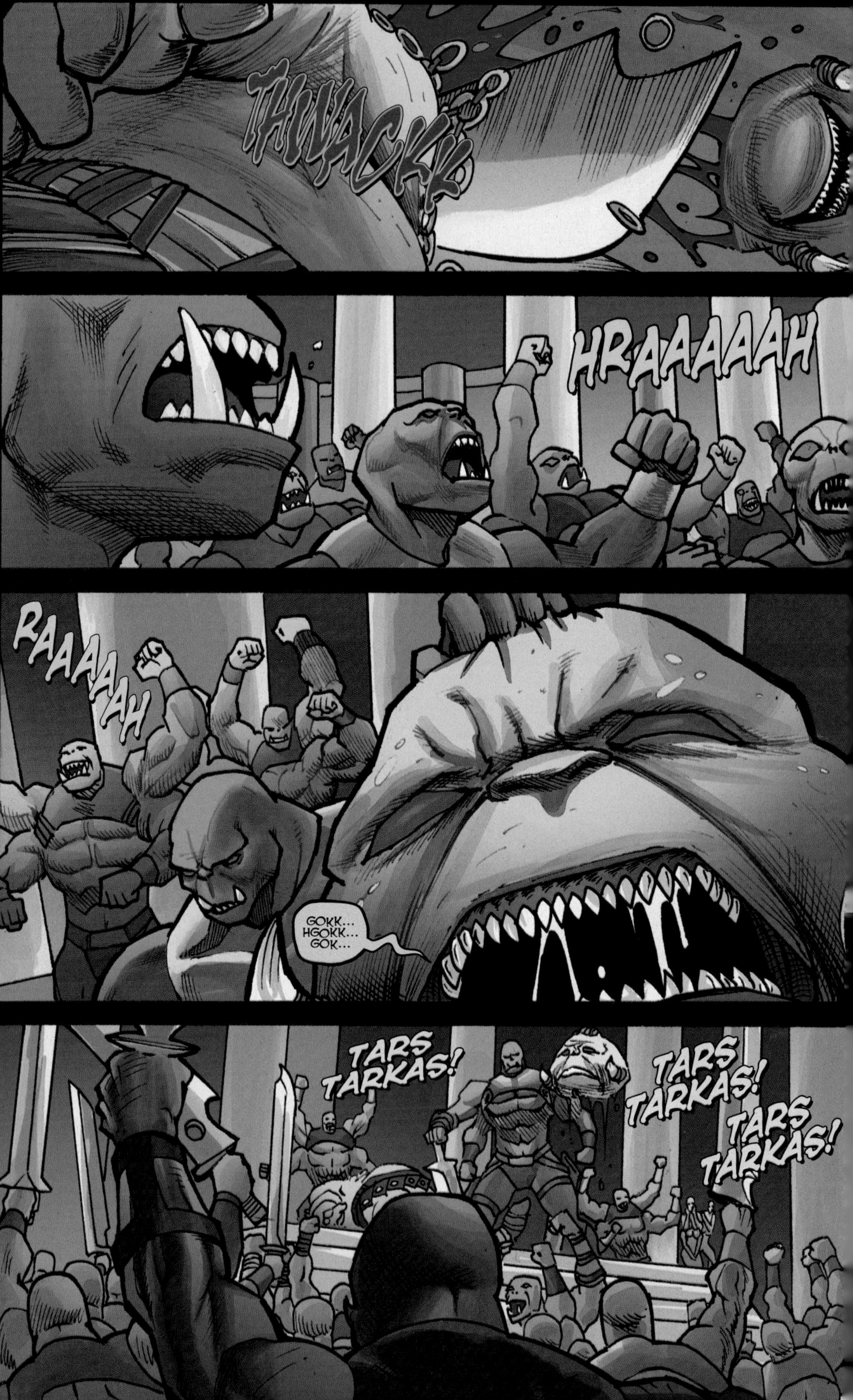
THWACKK
HRAAAAAAH
RAAAAAAH
GOKK... HGOKK... GOK...
TARS TARKAS!
TARS TARKAS!
TARS TARKAS!

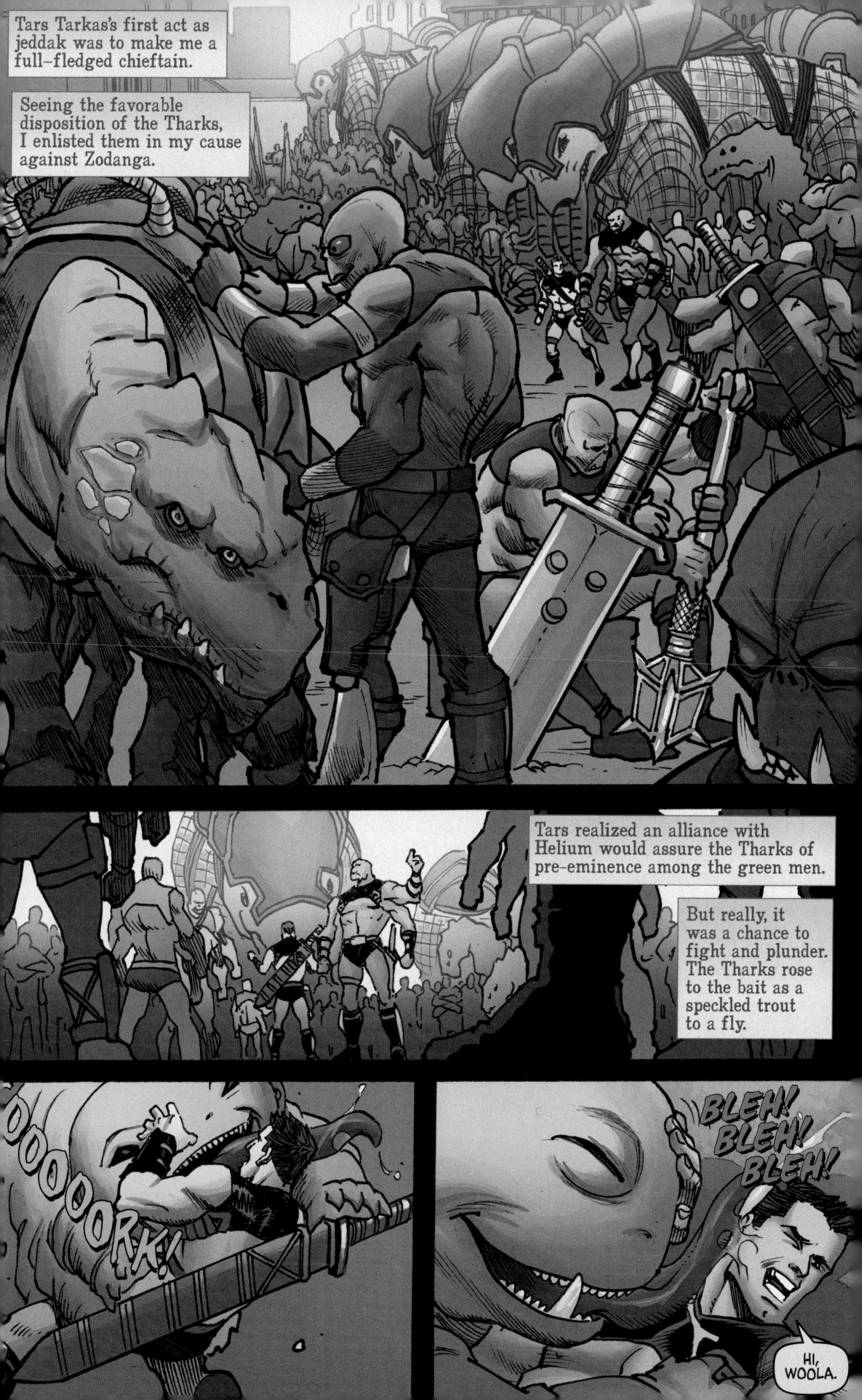
Tars Tarkas's first act as jeddak was to make me a full–fledged chieftain.
Seeing the favorable disposition of the Tharks, I enlisted them in my cause against Zodanga.
Tars realized an alliance with Helium would assure the Tharks of pre-eminence among the green men.
But really, it was a chance to fight and plunder. The Tharks rose to the bait as a speckled trout to a fly.
OOOOOORK!
BLEH! BLEH! BLEH!
HI, WOOLA.

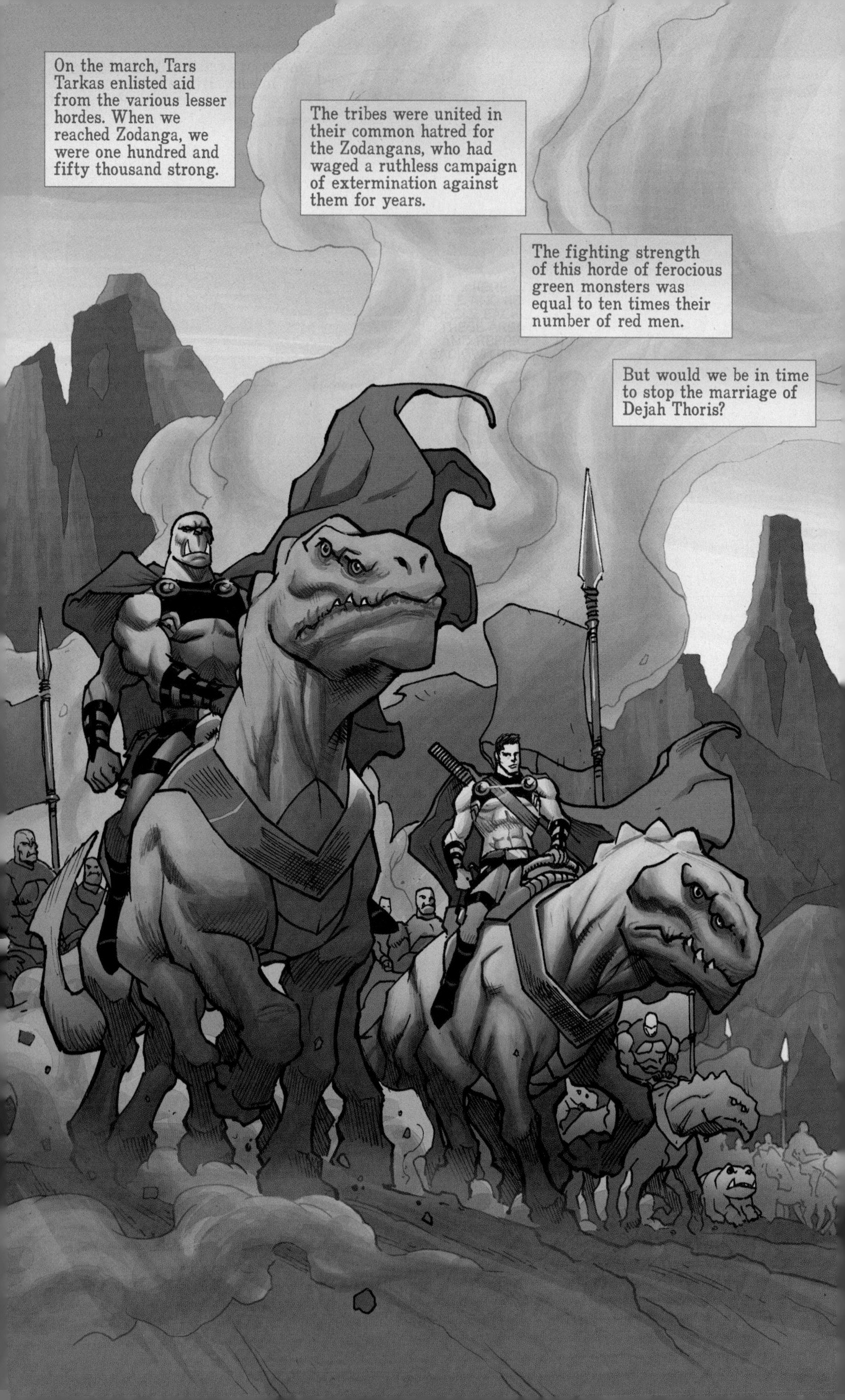
On the march, Tars Tarkas enlisted aid from the various lesser hordes. When we reached Zodanga, we were one hundred and fifty thousand strong.
The tribes were united in their common hatred for the Zodangans, who had waged a ruthless campaign of extermination against them for years.
The fighting strength of this horde of ferocious green monsters was equal to ten times their number of red men.
But would we be in time to stop the marriage of Dejah Thoris?

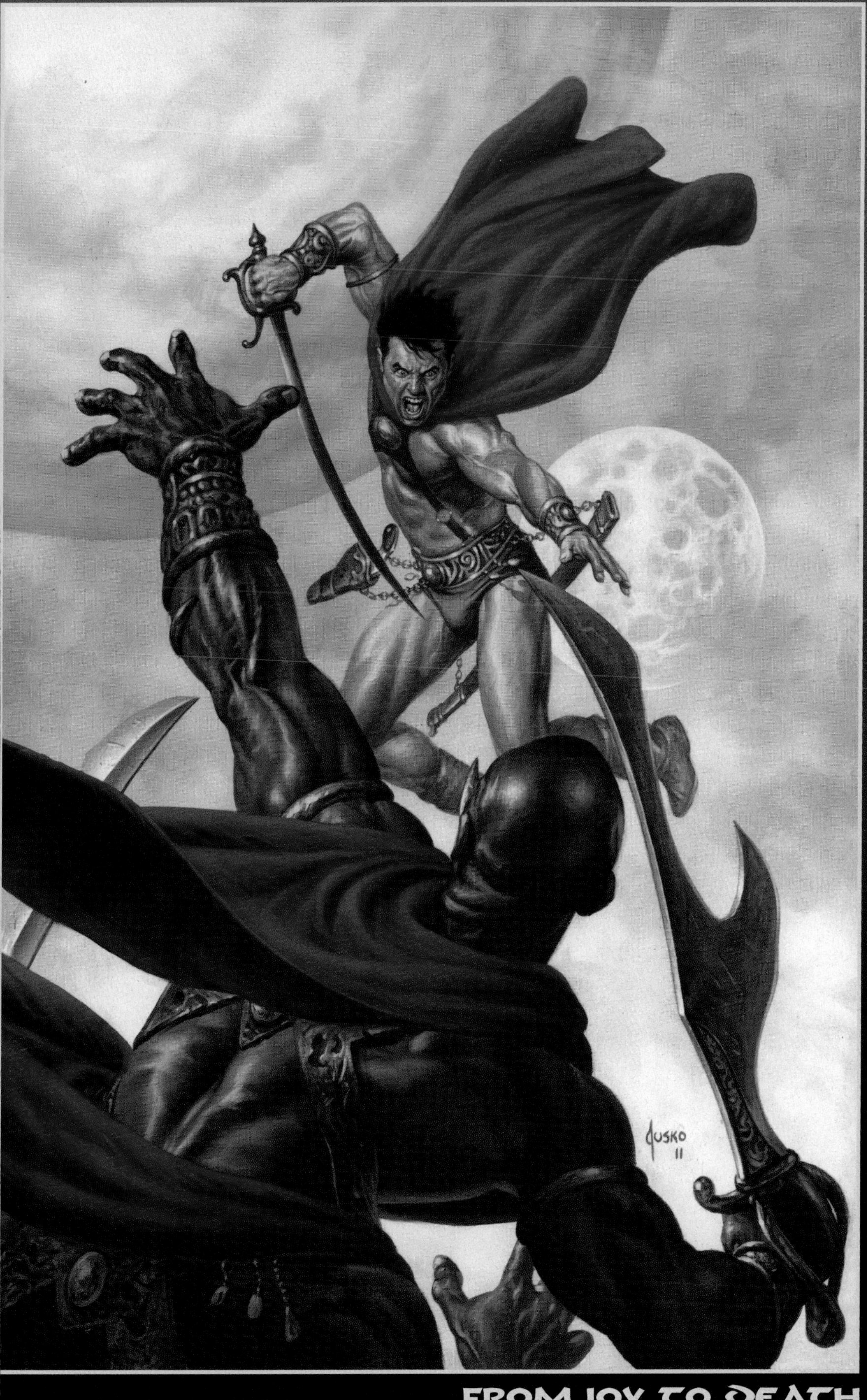
JUSKO 11

FROM JOY TO DEATH

Issue #9 cover by JOE JUSKO

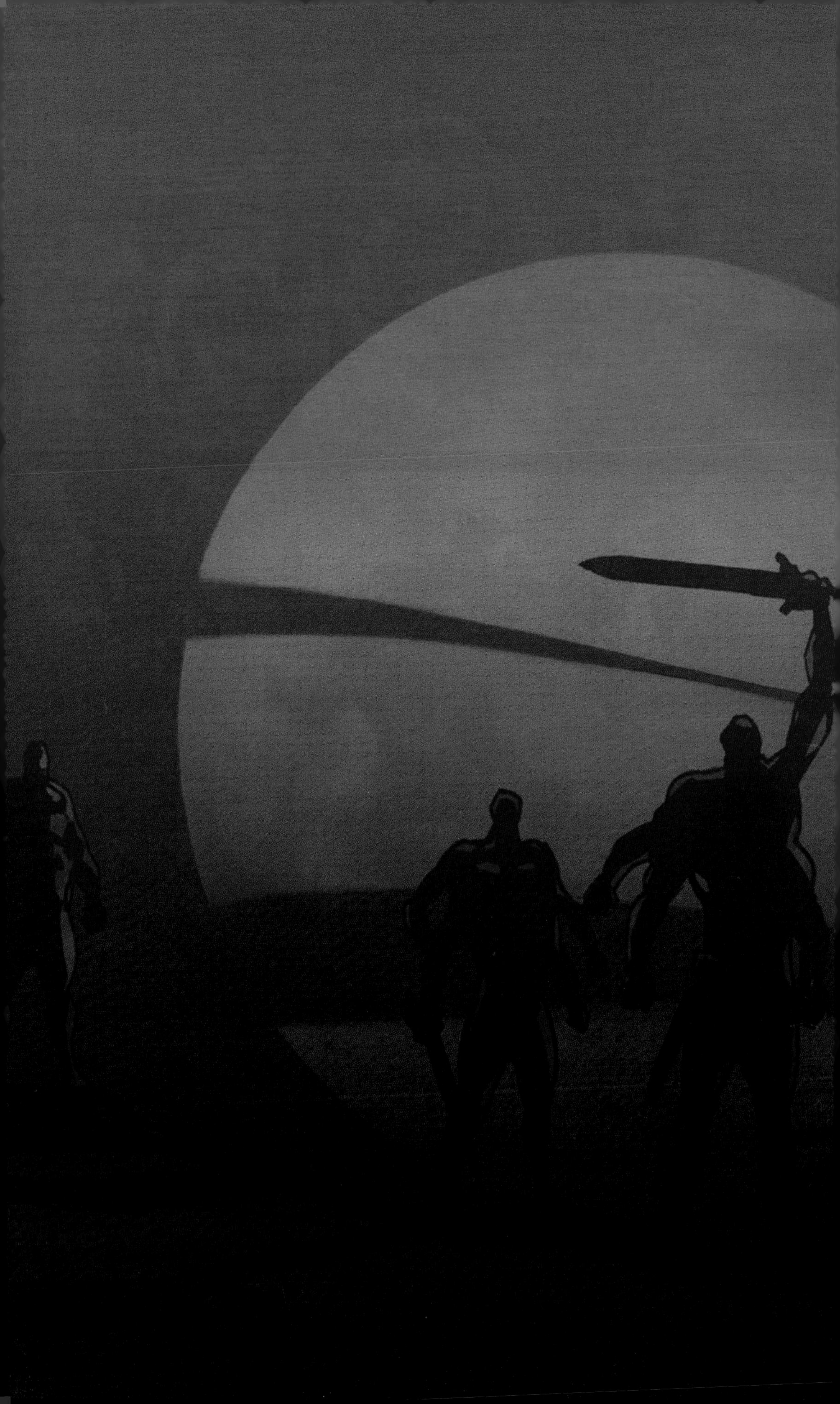

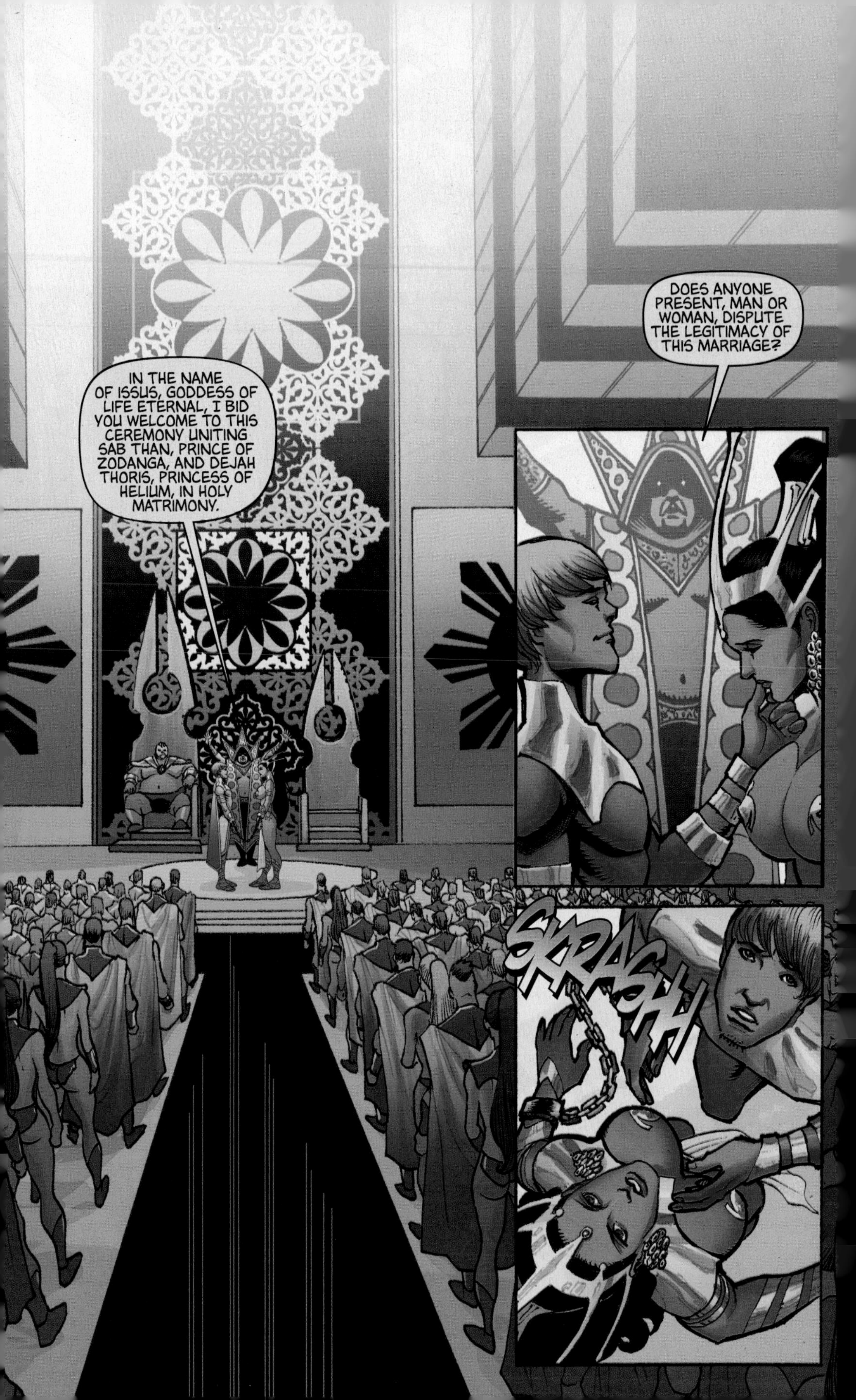
IN THE NAME OF ISSUS, GODDESS OF LIFE ETERNAL, I BID YOU WELCOME TO THIS CEREMONY UNITING SAB THAN, PRINCE OF ZODANGA, AND DEJAH THORIS, PRINCESS OF HELIUM, IN HOLY MATRIMONY.
DOES ANYONE PRESENT, MAN OR WOMAN, DISPUTE THE LEGITIMACY OF THIS MARRIAGE?
SKRASHH

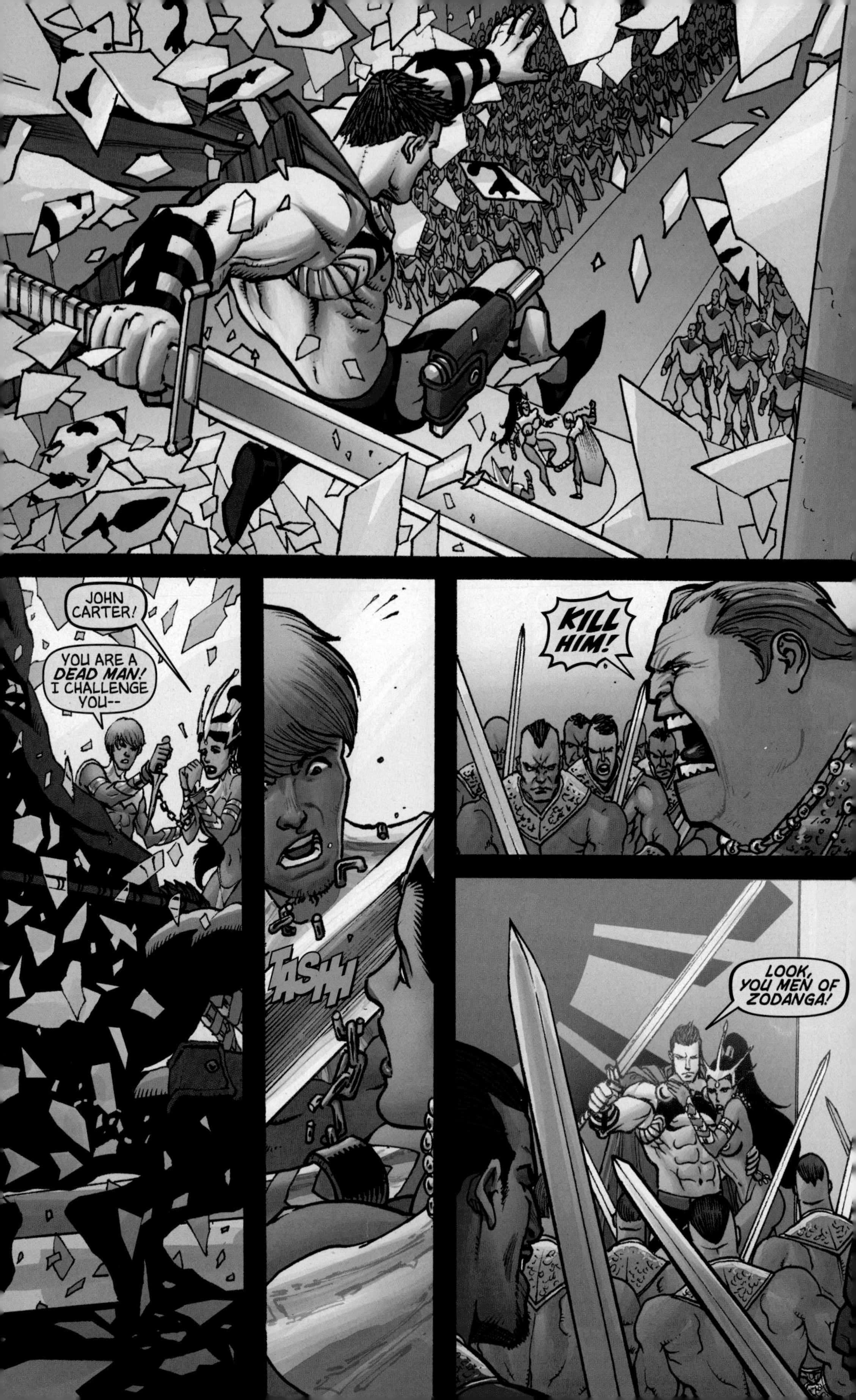
JOHN CARTER!
YOU ARE A DEAD MAN! I CHALLENGE YOU--
TASHH
KILL HIM!
LOOK, YOU MEN OF ZODANGA!

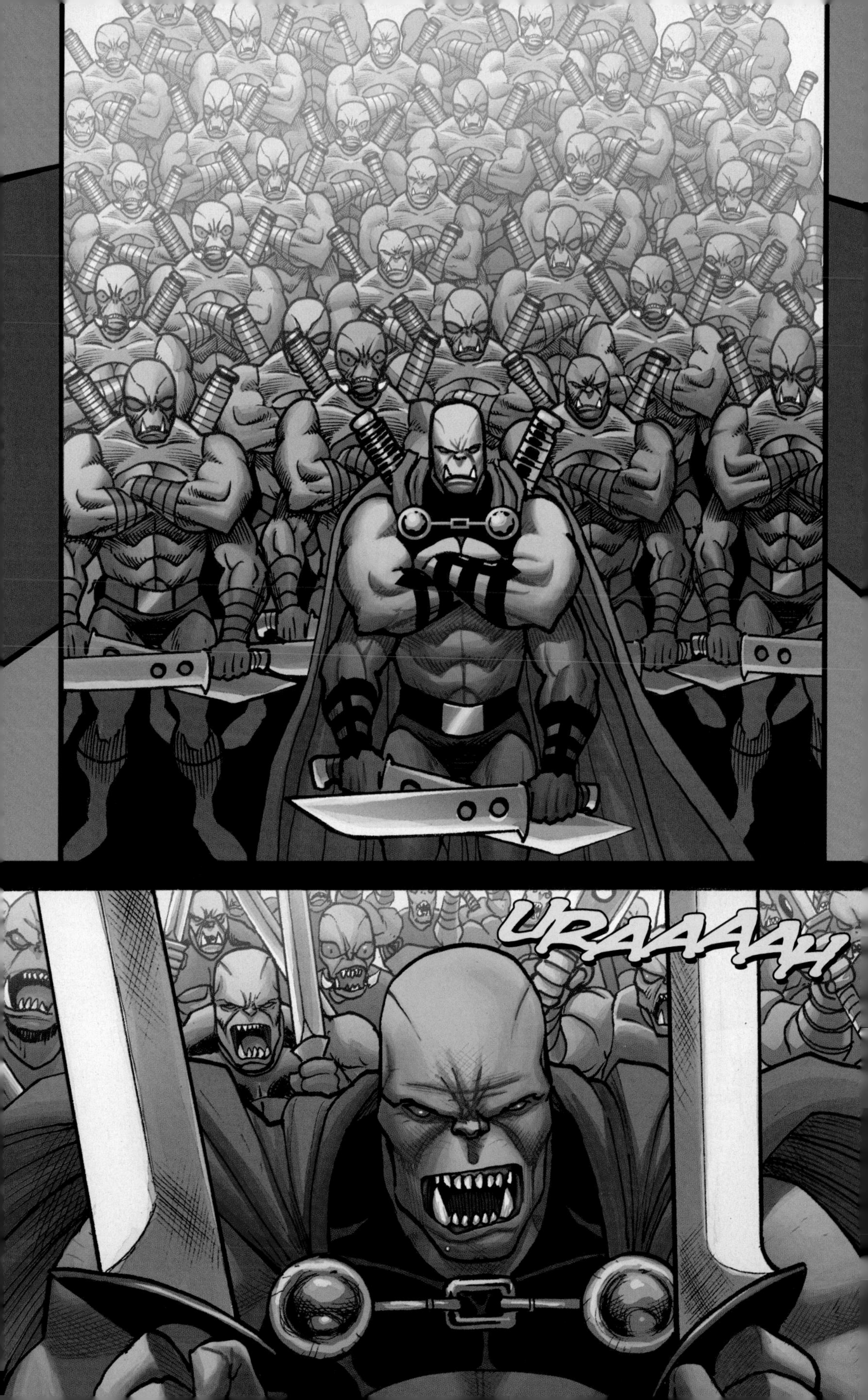
URAAAAH

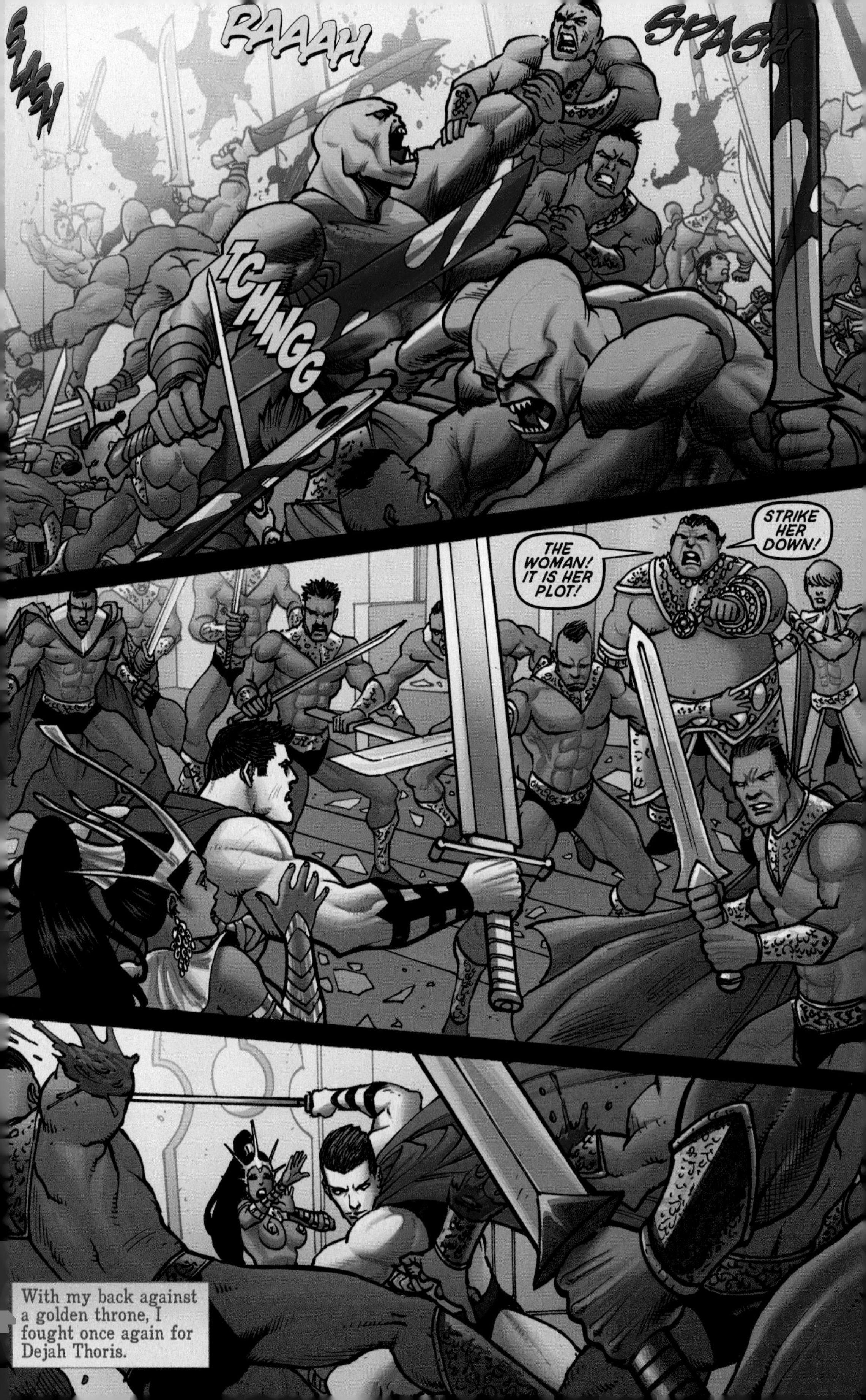
SLASH
RAAAH
SPASH
TCHINGG
THE WOMAN! IT IS HER PLOT!
STRIKE HER DOWN!
With my back against a golden throne, I fought once again for Dejah Thoris.

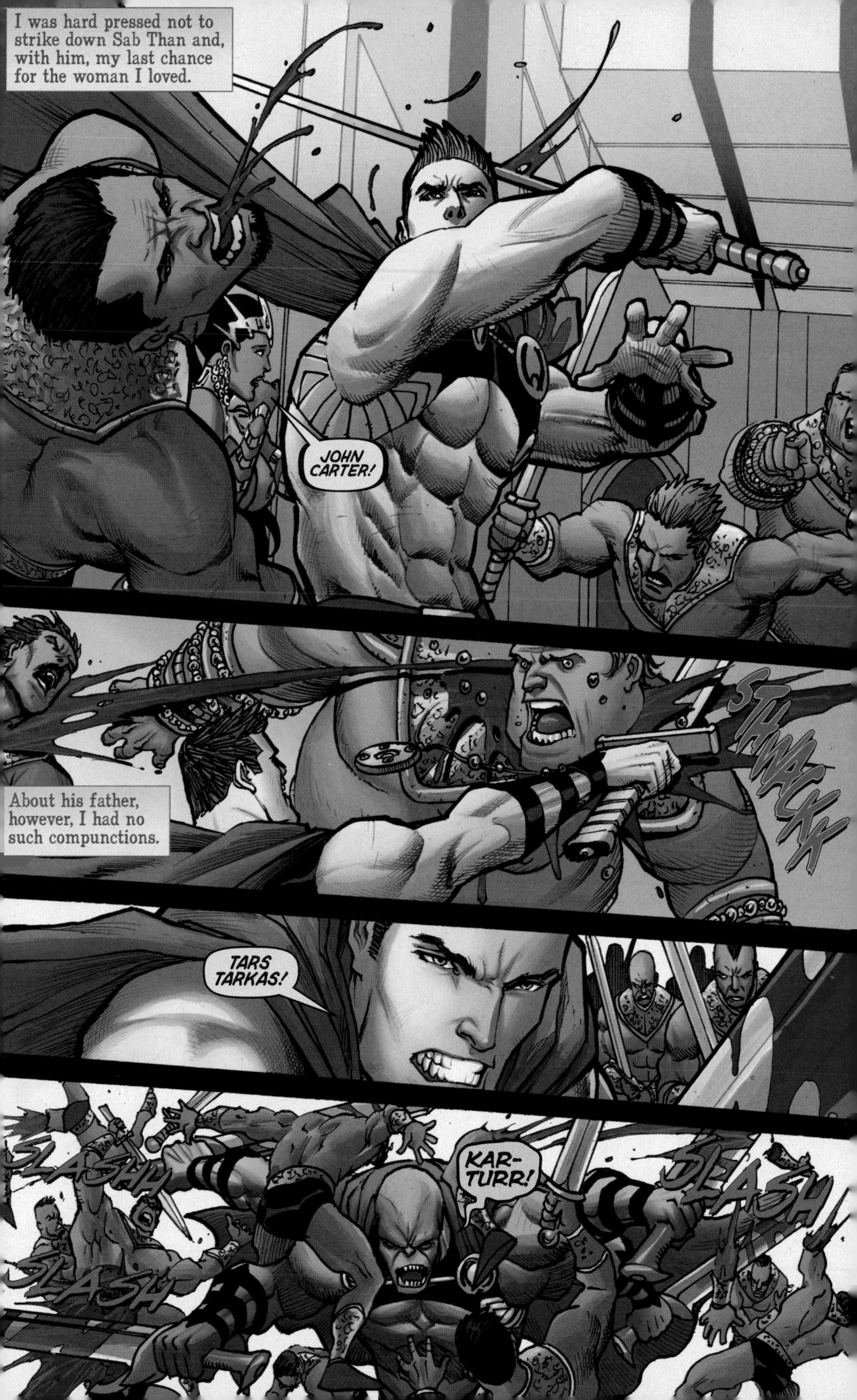
I was hard pressed not to strike down Sab Than and, with him, my last chance for the woman I loved.
JOHN CARTER!
STHWACKK
About his father, however, I had no such compunctions.
TARS TARKAS!
SLASHH
KAR-TURR!
SLASH
SLASH

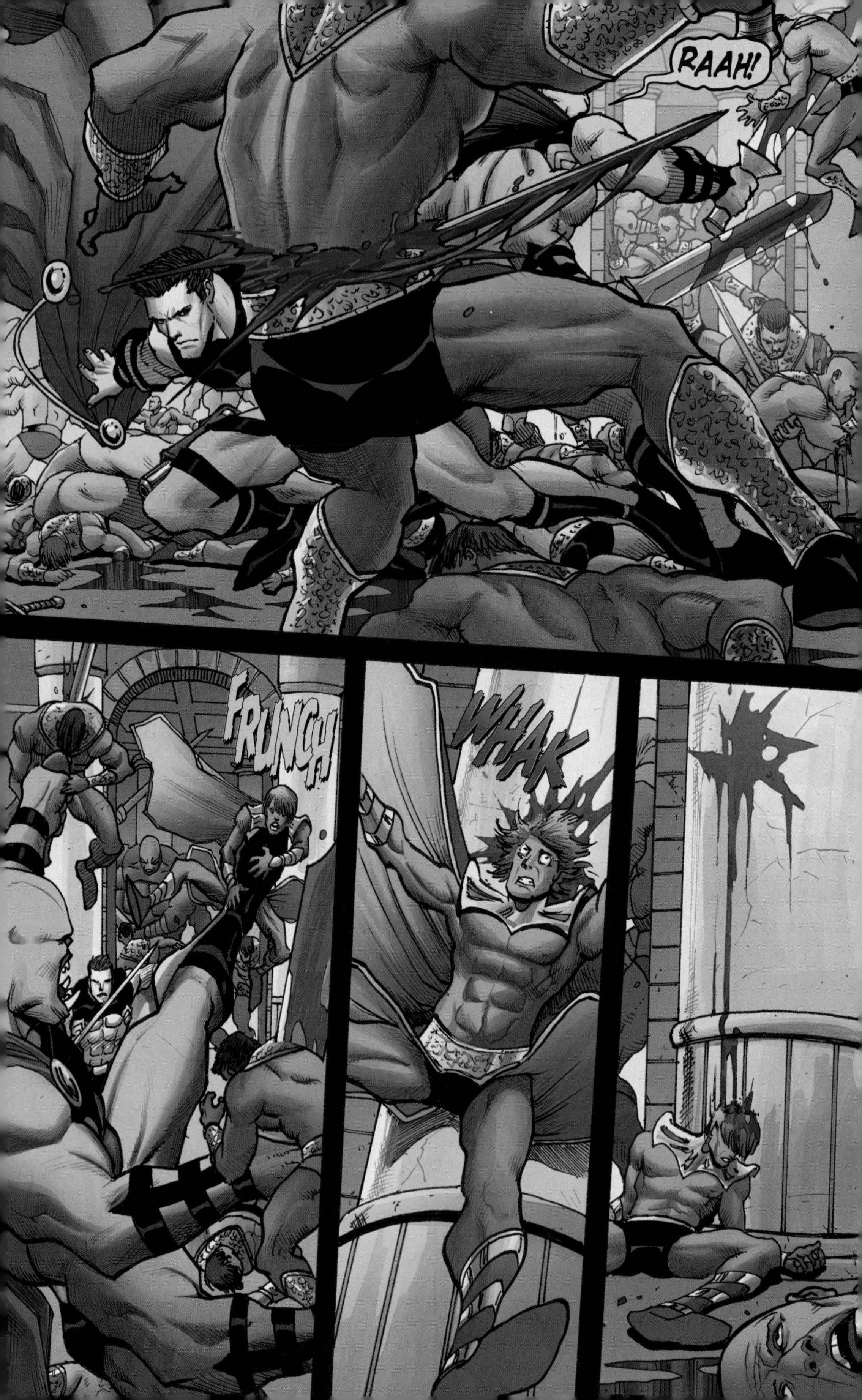
RAAH!
FRUNCH
WHAK

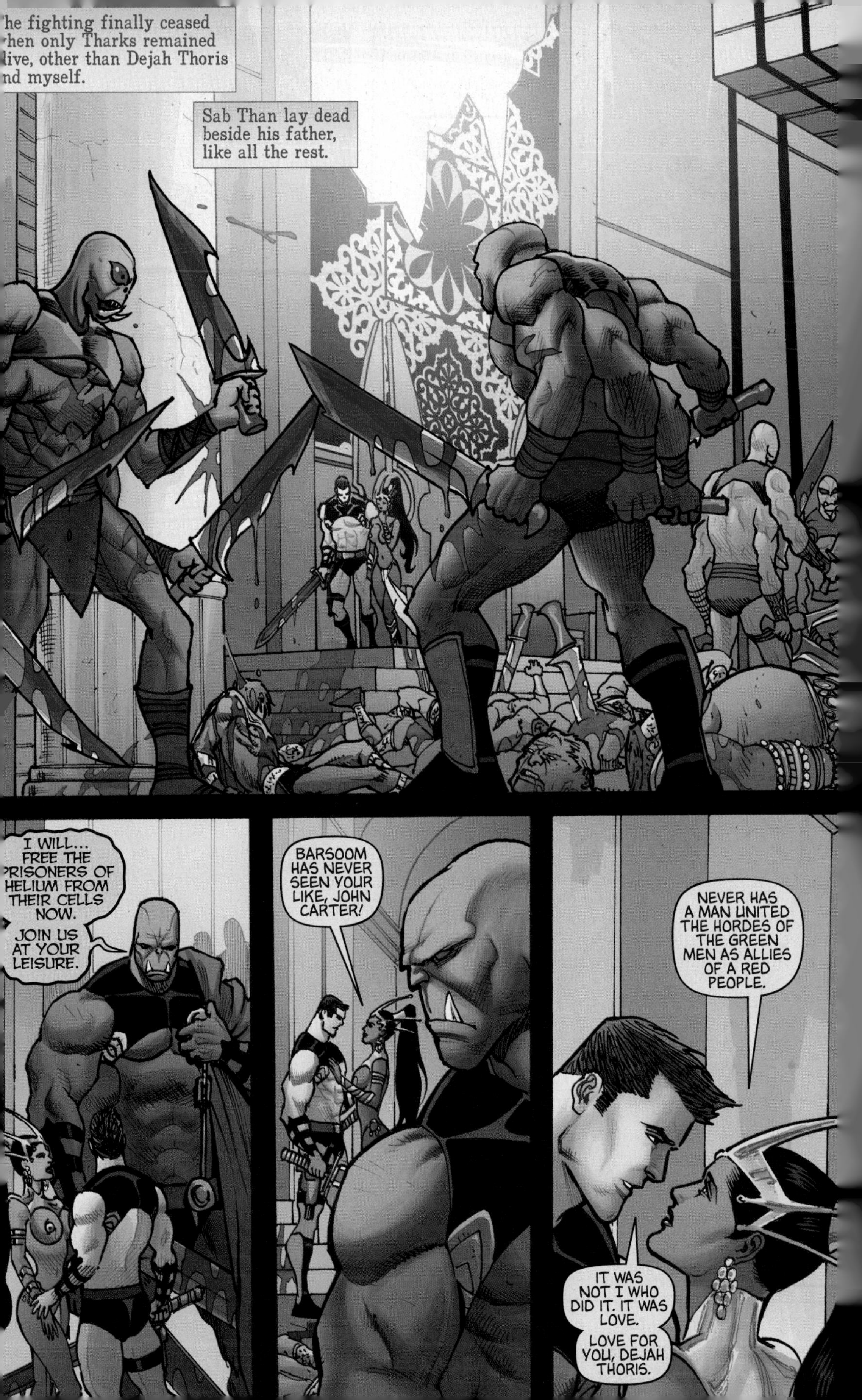
he fighting finally ceased
hen only Tharks remained
live, other than Dejah Thoris
nd myself.
Sab Than lay dead beside his father, like all the rest.
I WILL... FREE THE PRISONERS OF HELIUM FROM THEIR CELLS NOW.
JOIN US AT YOUR LEISURE.
BARSOOM HAS NEVER SEEN YOUR LIKE, JOHN CARTER!
NEVER HAS A MAN UNITED THE HORDES OF THE GREEN MEN AS ALLIES OF A RED PEOPLE.
IT WAS NOT I WHO DID IT. IT WAS LOVE.
LOVE FOR YOU, DEJAH THORIS.

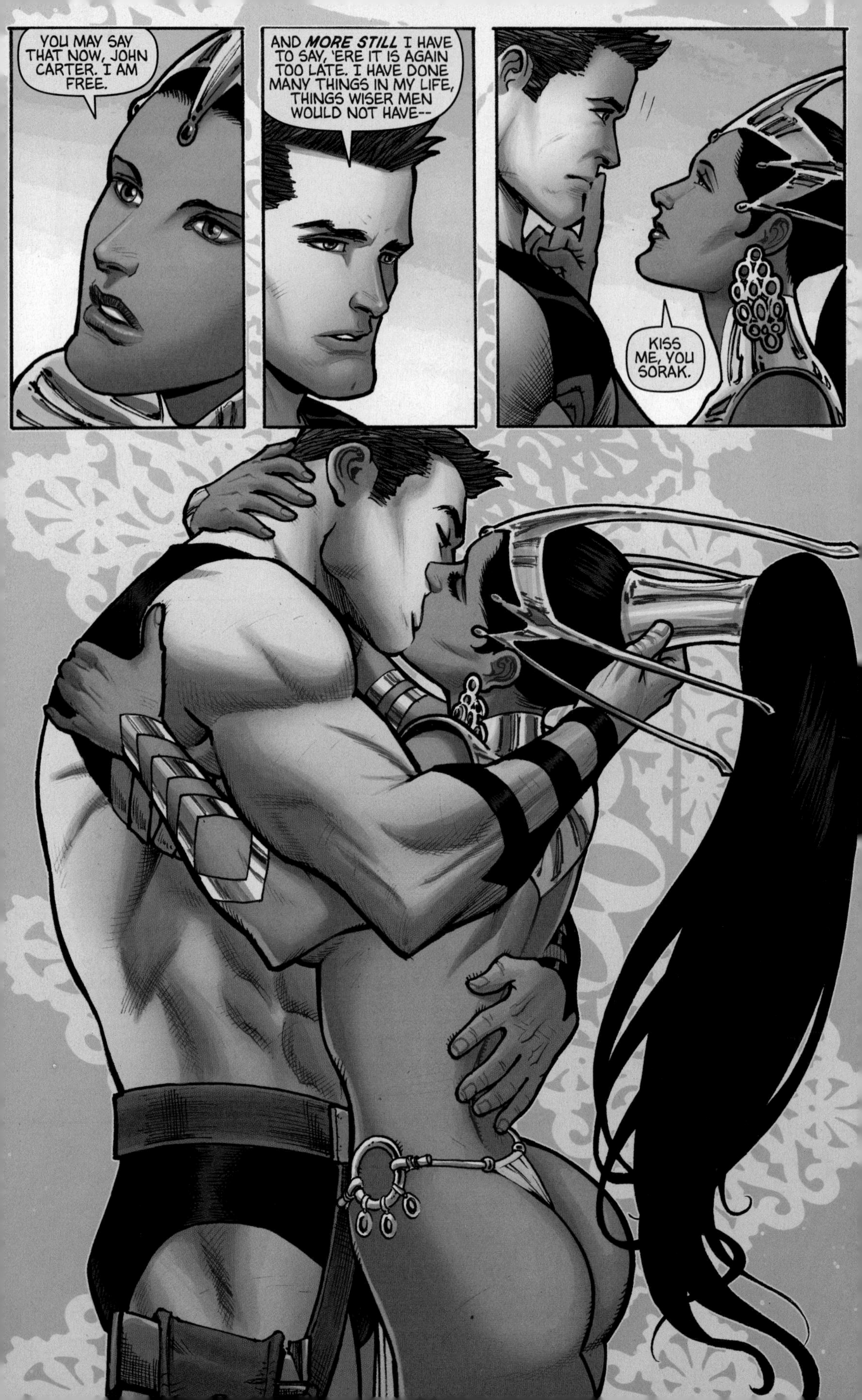
YOU MAY SAY THAT NOW, JOHN CARTER. I AM FREE.
AND MORE STILL I HAVE TO SAY, 'ERE IT IS AGAIN TOO LATE. I HAVE DONE MANY THINGS IN MY LIFE, THINGS WISER MEN WOULD NOT HAVE--
KISS ME, YOU SORAK.

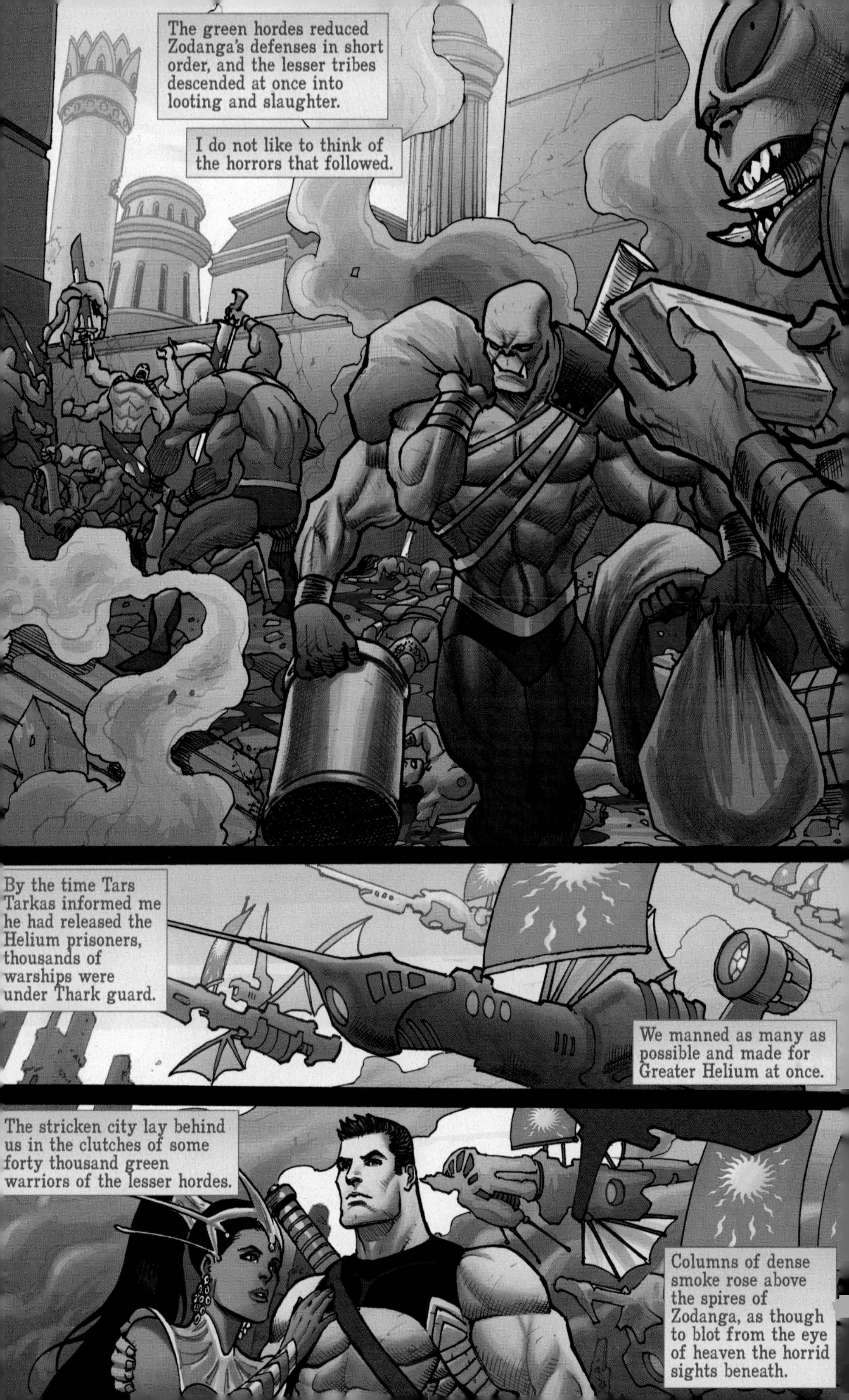
The green hordes reduced Zodanga's defenses in short order, and the lesser tribes descended at once into looting and slaughter.
I do not like to think of the horrors that followed.
By the time Tars Tarkas informed me he had released the Helium prisoners, thousands of warships were under Thark guard.
We manned as many as possible and made for Greater Helium at once.
The stricken city lay behind us in the clutches of some forty thousand green warriors of the lesser hordes.
Columns of dense smoke rose above the spires of Zodanga, as though to blot from the eye of heaven the horrid sights beneath.

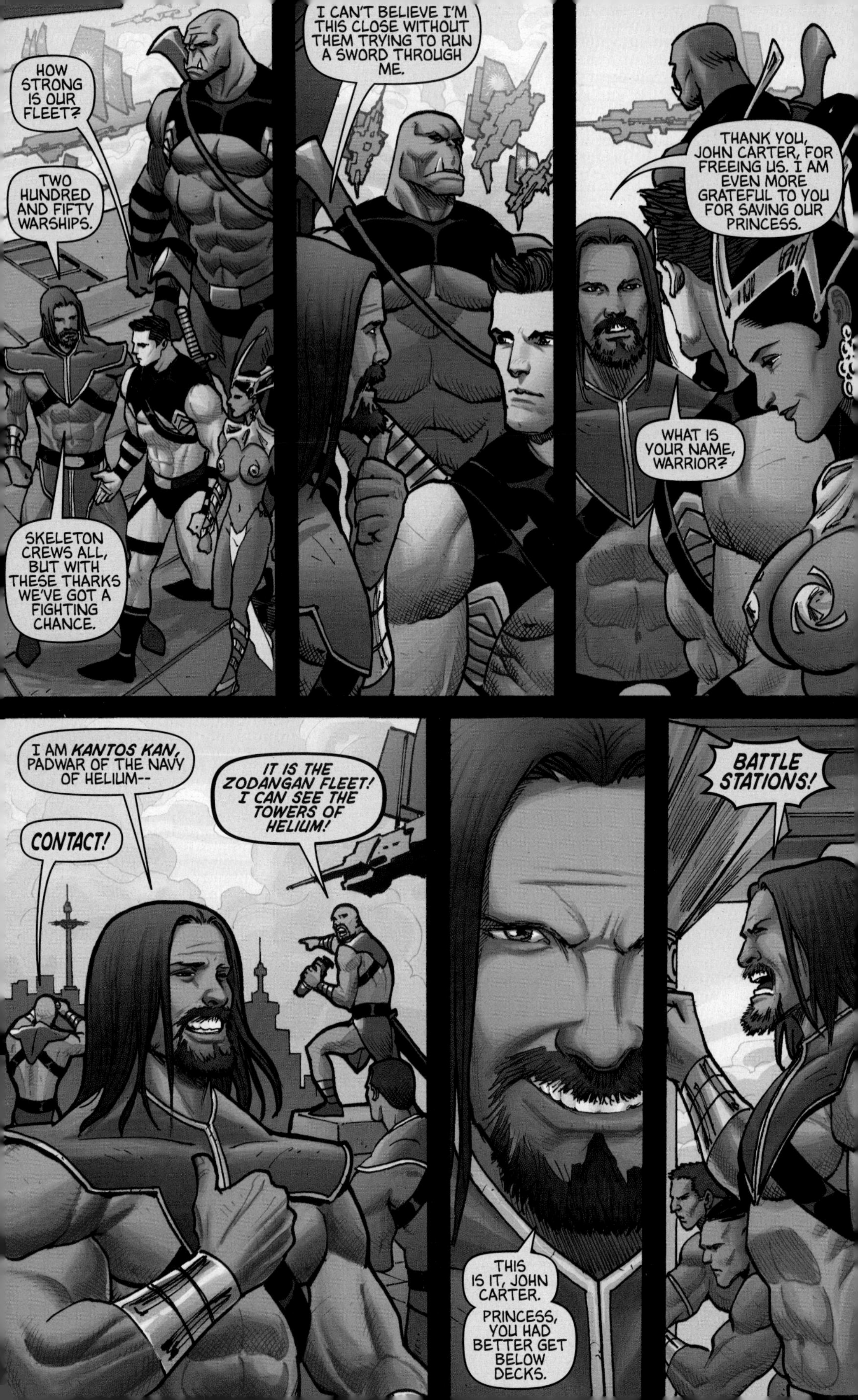
HOW STRONG IS OUR FLEET?
TWO HUNDRED AND FIFTY WARSHIPS.
SKELETON CREWS ALL, BUT WITH THESE THARKS WE'VE GOT A FIGHTING CHANCE.
I CAN'T BELIEVE I'M THIS CLOSE WITHOUT THEM TRYING TO RUN A SWORD THROUGH ME.
THANK YOU, JOHN CARTER, FOR FREEING US. I AM EVEN MORE GRATEFUL TO YOU FOR SAVING OUR PRINCESS.
WHAT IS YOUR NAME, WARRIOR?
I AM *KANTOS KAN*, PADWAR OF THE NAVY OF HELIUM--
CONTACT!
IT IS THE ZODANGAN FLEET! I CAN SEE THE TOWERS OF HELIUM!
THIS IS IT, JOHN CARTER.
PRINCESS, YOU HAD BETTER GET BELOW DECKS.
BATTLE STATIONS!

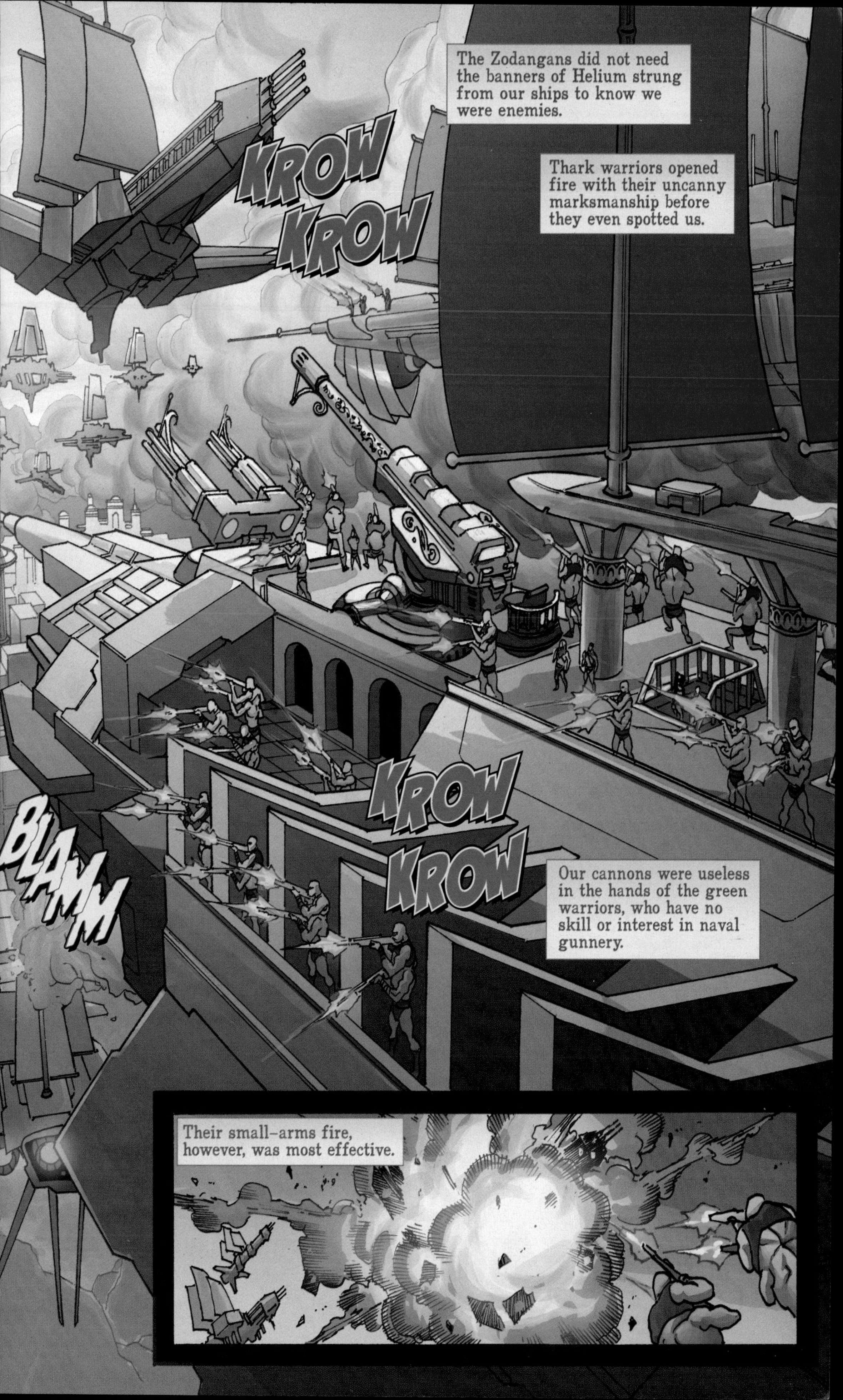
The Zodangans did not need the banners of Helium strung from our ships to know we were enemies.
KROW KROW
Thark warriors opened fire with their uncanny marksmanship before they even spotted us.
KROW KROW
BLAMM
Our cannons were useless in the hands of the green warriors, who have no skill or interest in naval gunnery.
Their small-arms fire, however, was most effective.

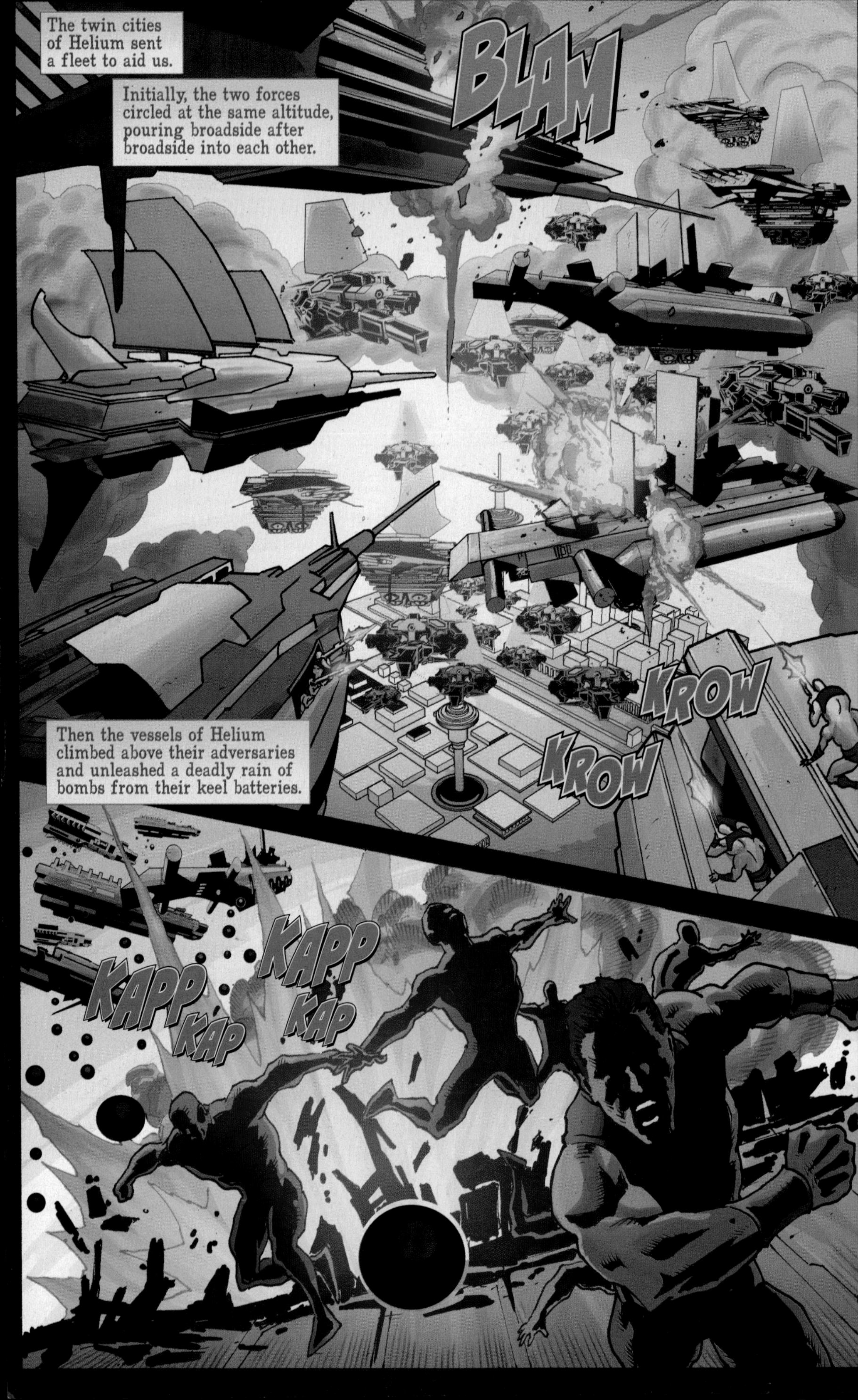

The twin cities of Helium sent a fleet to aid us.
Initially, the two forces circled at the same altitude, pouring broadside after broadside into each other.
BLAM
Then the vessels of Helium climbed above their adversaries and unleashed a deadly rain of bombs from their keel batteries.
KROW
KROW
KAPP
KAP
KAPP
KAP

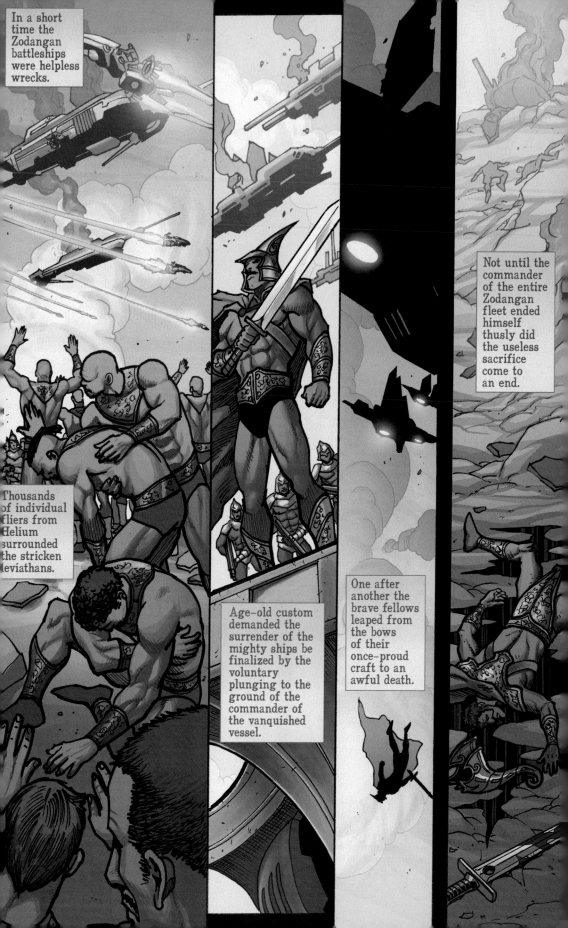

In a short time the Zodangan battleships were helpless wrecks.

Thousands of individual fliers from Helium surrounded the stricken leviathans.

Age-old custom demanded the surrender of the mighty ships be finalized by the voluntary plunging to the ground of the commander of the vanquished vessel.

One after another the brave fellows leaped from the bows of their once-proud craft to an awful death.

Not until the commander of the entire Zodangan fleet ended himself thusly did the useless sacrifice come to an end.

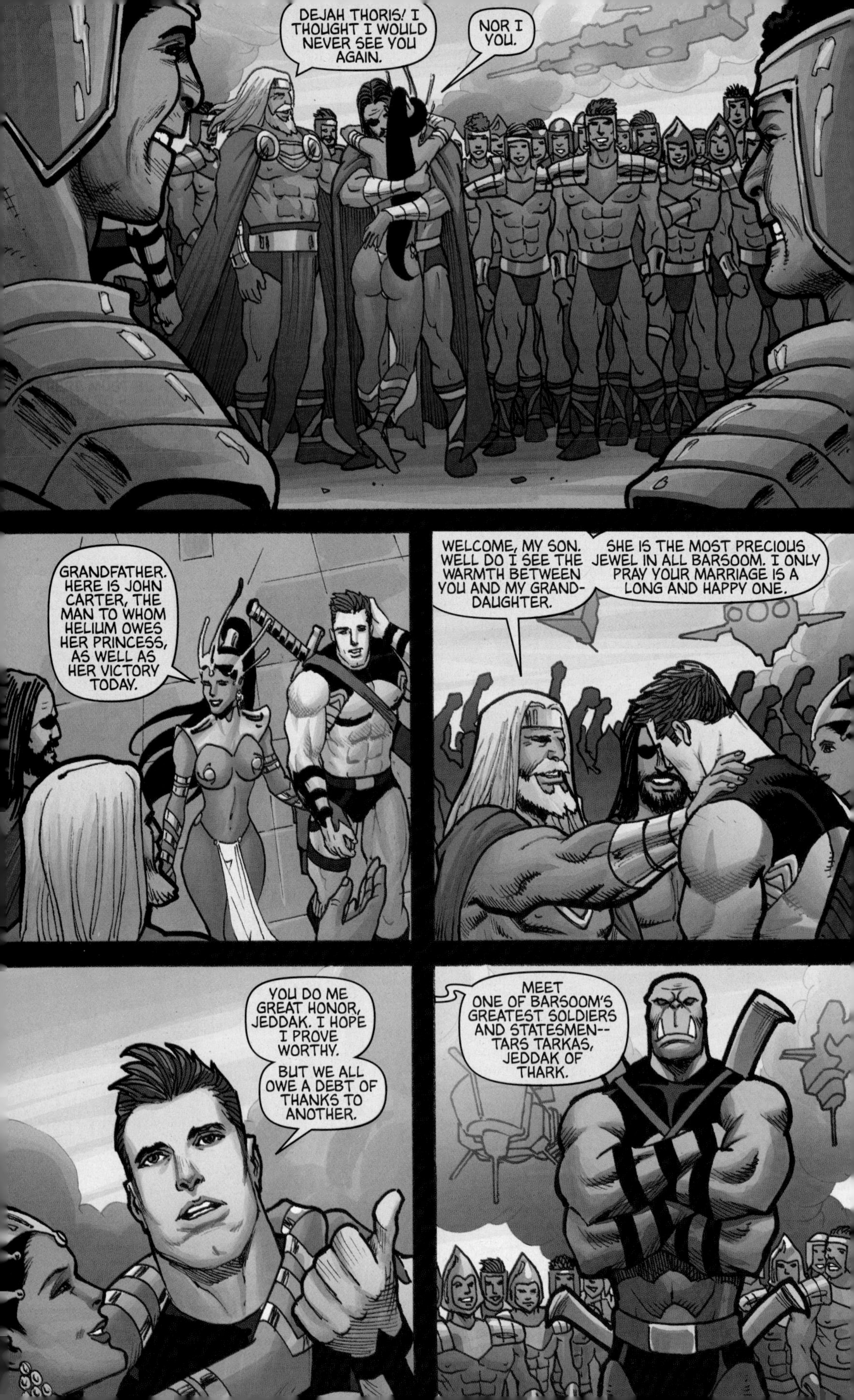
DEJAH THORIS! I THOUGHT I WOULD NEVER SEE YOU AGAIN.
NOR I YOU.
GRANDFATHER. HERE IS JOHN CARTER, THE MAN TO WHOM HELIUM OWES HER PRINCESS, AS WELL AS HER VICTORY TODAY.
WELCOME, MY SON. WELL DO I SEE THE WARMTH BETWEEN YOU AND MY GRAND-DAUGHTER.
SHE IS THE MOST PRECIOUS JEWEL IN ALL BARSOOM. I ONLY PRAY YOUR MARRIAGE IS A LONG AND HAPPY ONE.
YOU DO ME GREAT HONOR, JEDDAK. I HOPE I PROVE WORTHY.
BUT WE ALL OWE A DEBT OF THANKS TO ANOTHER.
MEET ONE OF BARSOOM'S GREATEST SOLDIERS AND STATESMEN-- TARS TARKAS, JEDDAK OF THARK.

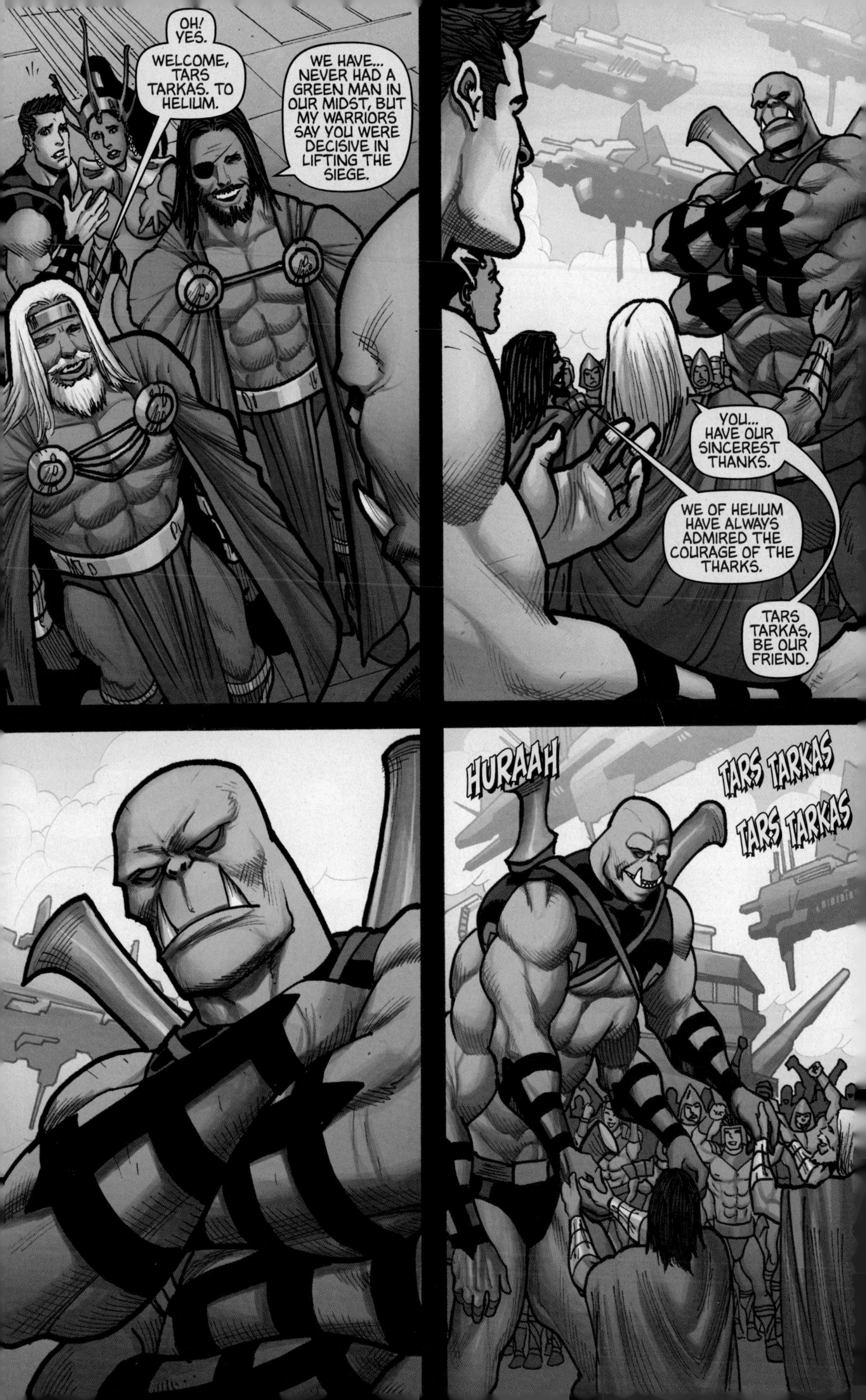
OH! YES.
WELCOME, TARS TARKAS. TO HELIUM.
WE HAVE... NEVER HAD A GREEN MAN IN OUR MIDST, BUT MY WARRIORS SAY YOU WERE DECISIVE IN LIFTING THE SIEGE.
YOU... HAVE OUR SINCEREST THANKS.
WE OF HELIUM HAVE ALWAYS ADMIRED THE COURAGE OF THE THARKS.
TARS TARKAS, BE OUR FRIEND.
HURAAH
TARS TARKAS
TARS TARKAS

For ten days, Helium feasted and celebrated with the hordes of Thark.

And, then, loaded with costly presents, the green warriors started on the journey back to their own lands.

Sola accompanied Tars Tarkas, who had acknowledged her as his daughter before all his chieftains.

For ten years I fought for Helium. The people never tired of heaping honors upon me or their beloved princess.

All the while, a snow-white egg incubated on the roof of our palace.

Vivid is the memory of my last night on Barsoom...

OH! THANK YOU.

Often Dejah Thoris and I stood before our little shrine, anticipating the day the shell should break.

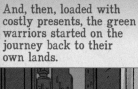

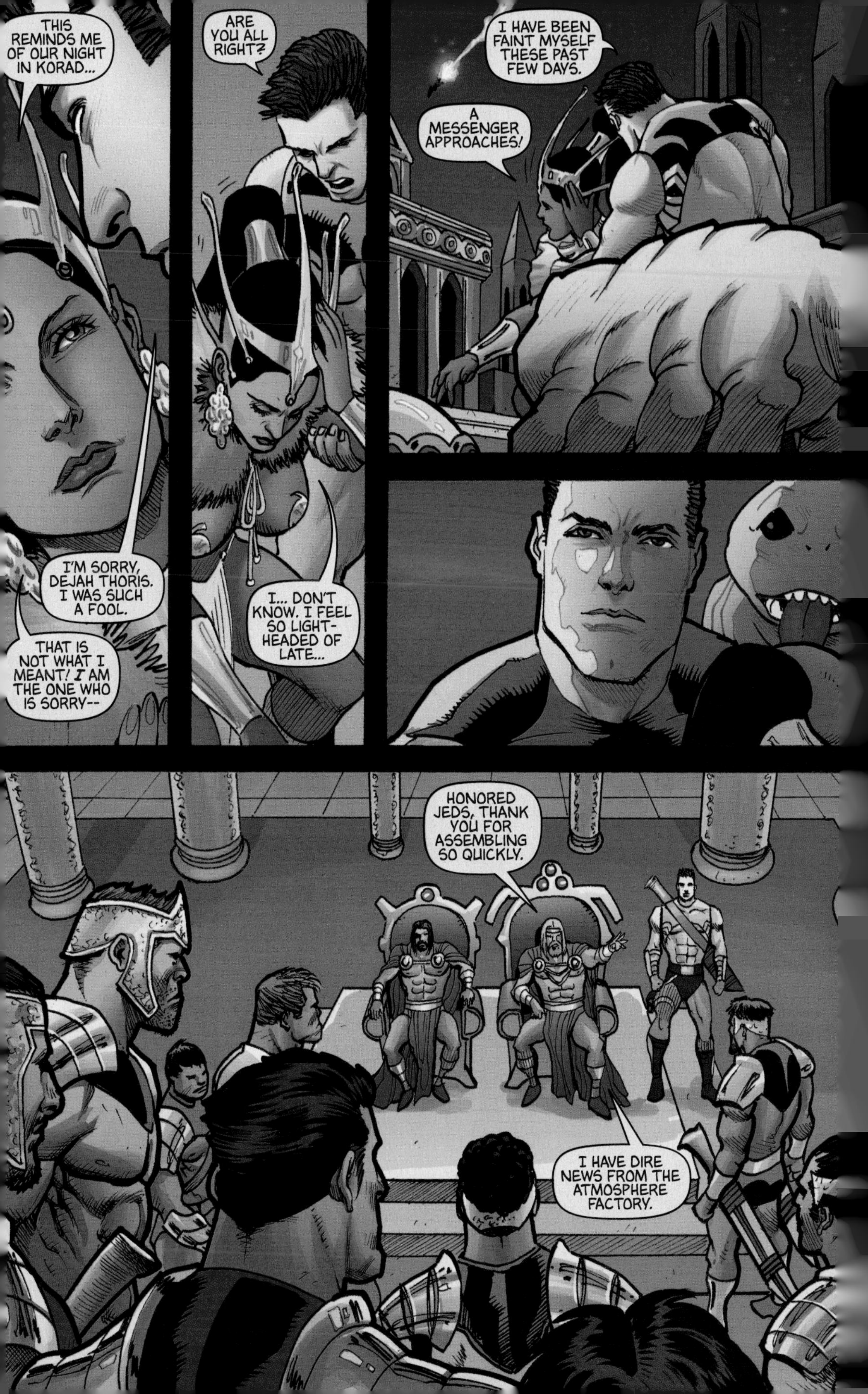
THIS REMINDS ME OF OUR NIGHT IN KORAD...
I'M SORRY, DEJAH THORIS. I WAS SUCH A FOOL.
THAT IS NOT WHAT I MEANT! I AM THE ONE WHO IS SORRY--
ARE YOU ALL RIGHT?
I... DON'T KNOW. I FEEL SO LIGHT-HEADED OF LATE...
I HAVE BEEN FAINT MYSELF THESE PAST FEW DAYS.
A MESSENGER APPROACHES!
HONORED JEDS, THANK YOU FOR ASSEMBLING SO QUICKLY.
I HAVE DIRE NEWS FROM THE ATMOSPHERE FACTORY.

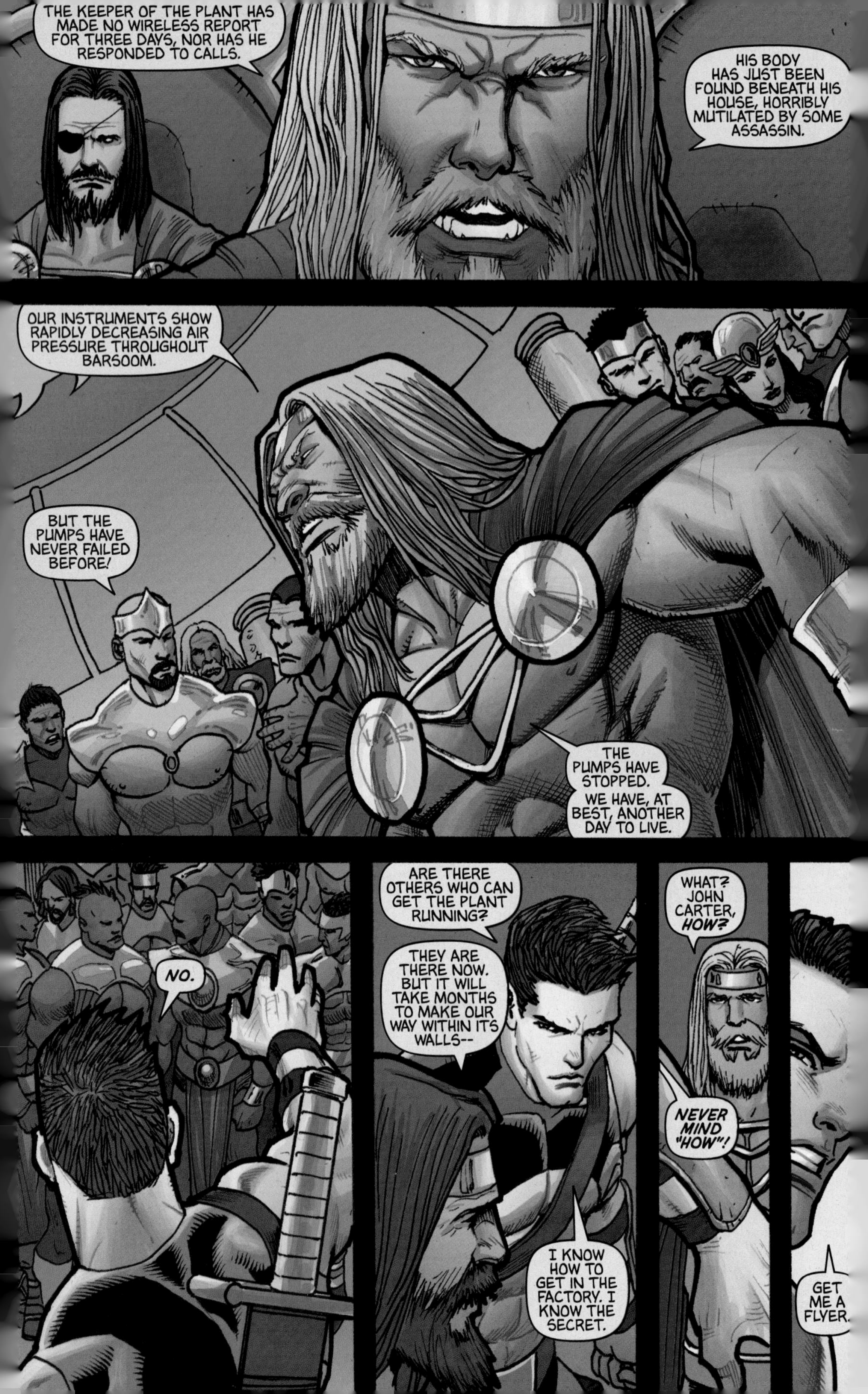
THE KEEPER OF THE PLANT HAS MADE NO WIRELESS REPORT FOR THREE DAYS, NOR HAS HE RESPONDED TO CALLS.
HIS BODY HAS JUST BEEN FOUND BENEATH HIS HOUSE, HORRIBLY MUTILATED BY SOME ASSASSIN.
OUR INSTRUMENTS SHOW RAPIDLY DECREASING AIR PRESSURE THROUGHOUT BARSOOM.
BUT THE PUMPS HAVE NEVER FAILED BEFORE!
THE PUMPS HAVE STOPPED.
WE HAVE, AT BEST, ANOTHER DAY TO LIVE.
ARE THERE OTHERS WHO CAN GET THE PLANT RUNNING?
THEY ARE THERE NOW. BUT IT WILL TAKE MONTHS TO MAKE OUR WAY WITHIN ITS WALLS--
NO.
I KNOW HOW TO GET IN THE FACTORY. I KNOW THE SECRET.
WHAT? JOHN CARTER, HOW?
NEVER MIND "HOW"!
GET ME A FLYER.

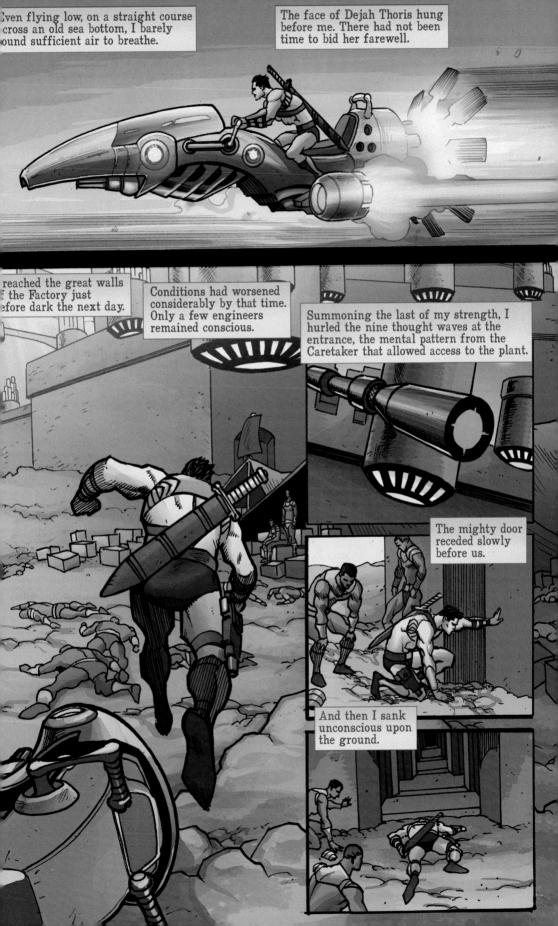

Even flying low, on a straight course across an old sea bottom, I barely found sufficient air to breathe.

The face of Dejah Thoris hung before me. There had not been time to bid her farewell.

I reached the great walls of the Factory just before dark the next day.

Conditions had worsened considerably by that time. Only a few engineers remained conscious.

Summoning the last of my strength, I hurled the nine thought waves at the entrance, the mental pattern from the Caretaker that allowed access to the plant.

The mighty door receded slowly before us.

And then I sank unconscious upon the ground.

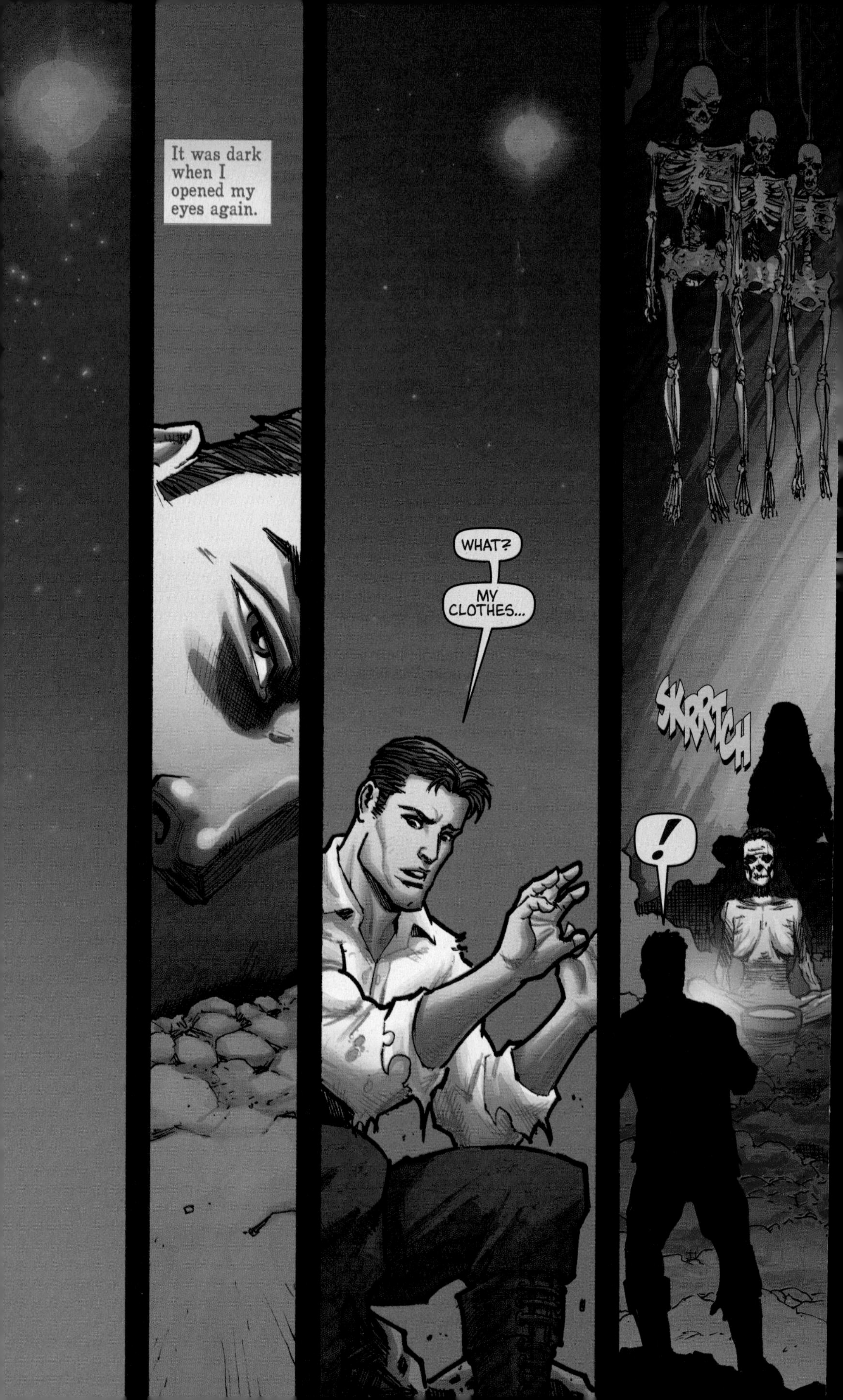
It was dark when I opened my eyes again.
WHAT?
MY CLOTHES...
SKRRTCH
!

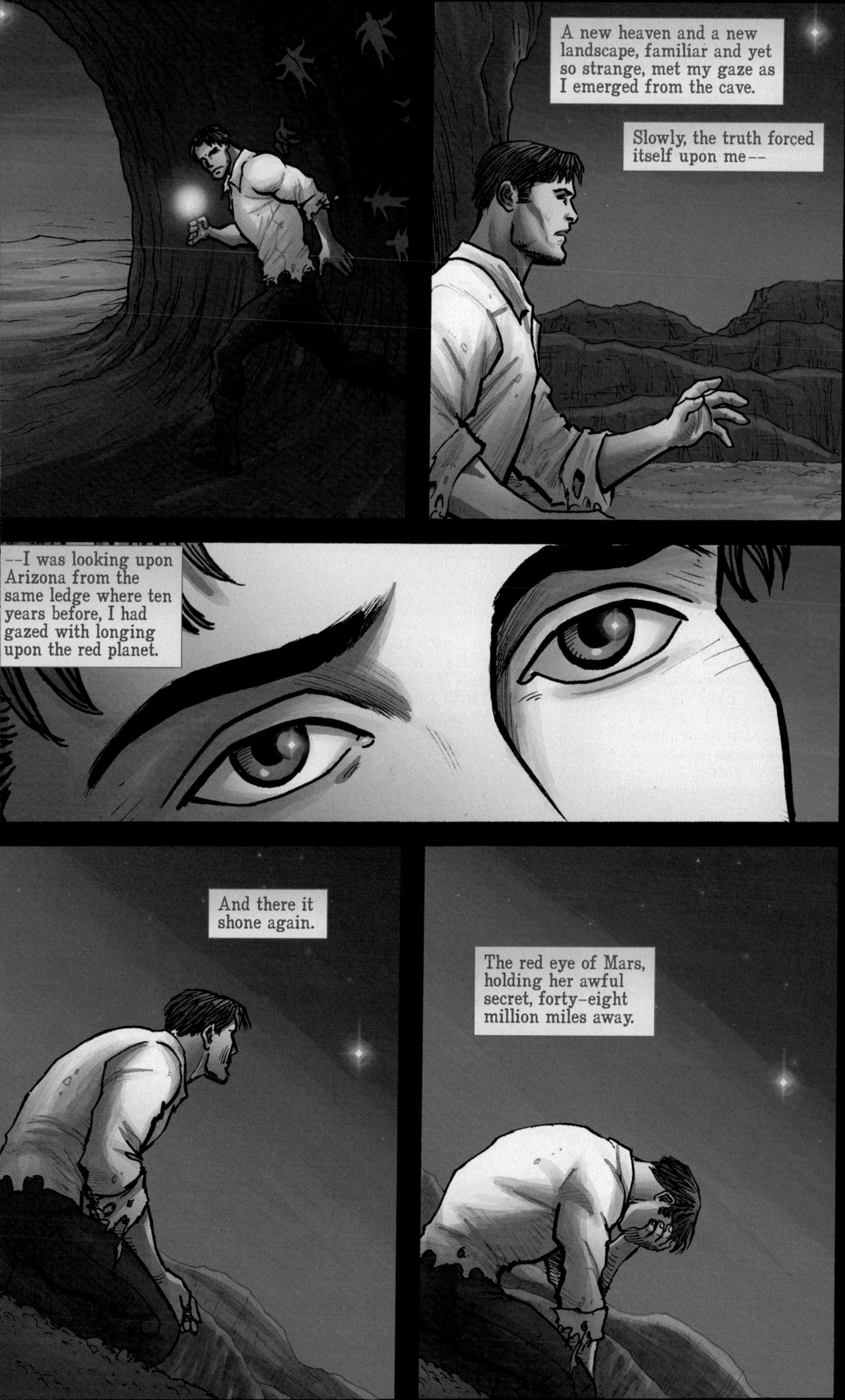
A new heaven and a new landscape, familiar and yet so strange, met my gaze as I emerged from the cave.
Slowly, the truth forced itself upon me--
--I was looking upon Arizona from the same ledge where ten years before, I had gazed with longing upon the red planet.
And there it shone again.
The red eye of Mars, holding her awful secret, forty-eight million miles away.

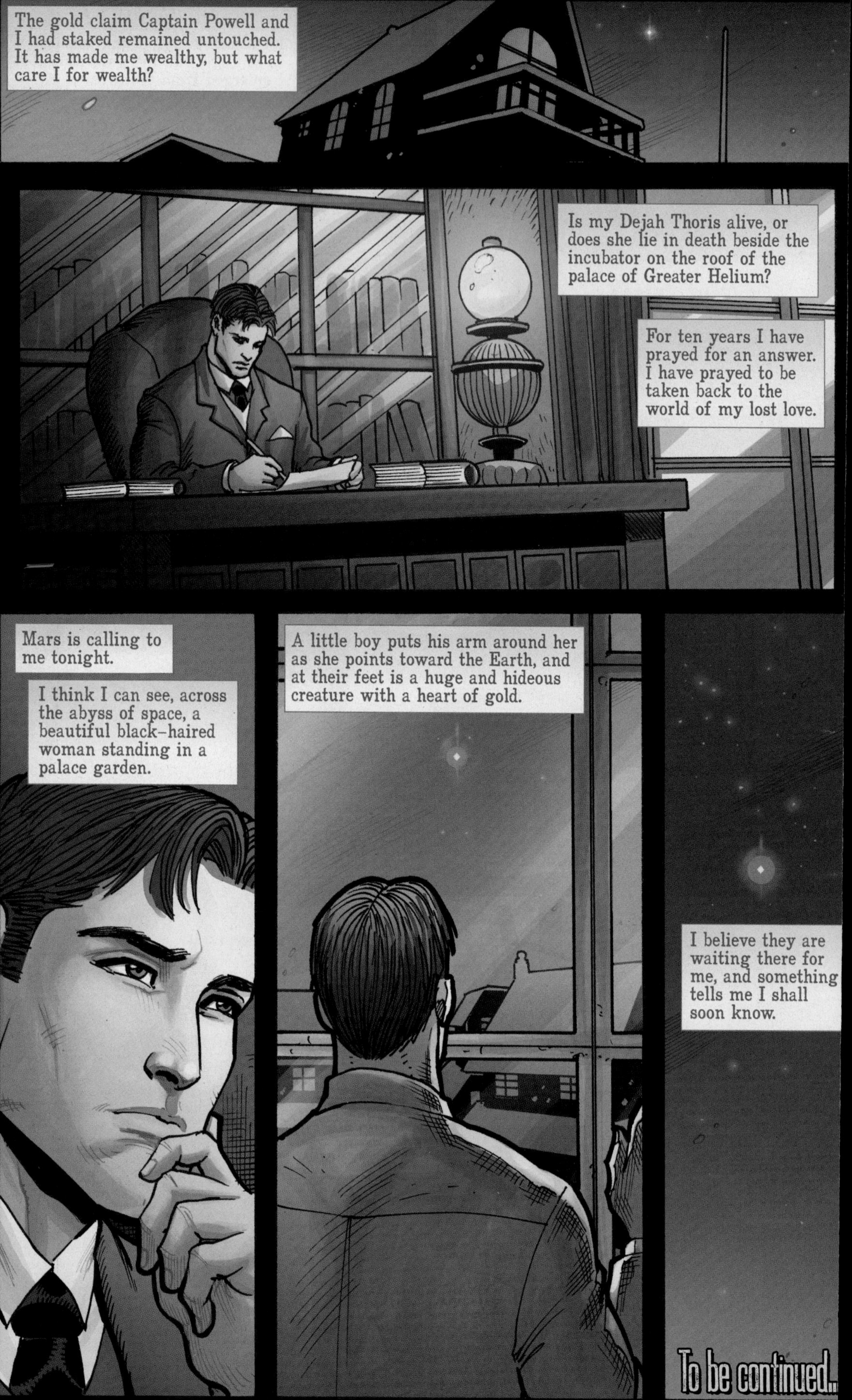

The gold claim Captain Powell and I had staked remained untouched. It has made me wealthy, but what care I for wealth?
Is my Dejah Thoris alive, or does she lie in death beside the incubator on the roof of the palace of Greater Helium?
For ten years I have prayed for an answer. I have prayed to be taken back to the world of my lost love.
Mars is calling to me tonight.
I think I can see, across the abyss of space, a beautiful black-haired woman standing in a palace garden.
A little boy puts his arm around her as she points toward the Earth, and at their feet is a huge and hideous creature with a heart of gold.
I believe they are waiting there for me, and something tells me I shall soon know.
To be continued...

Notes on Barsoom

by John Carter

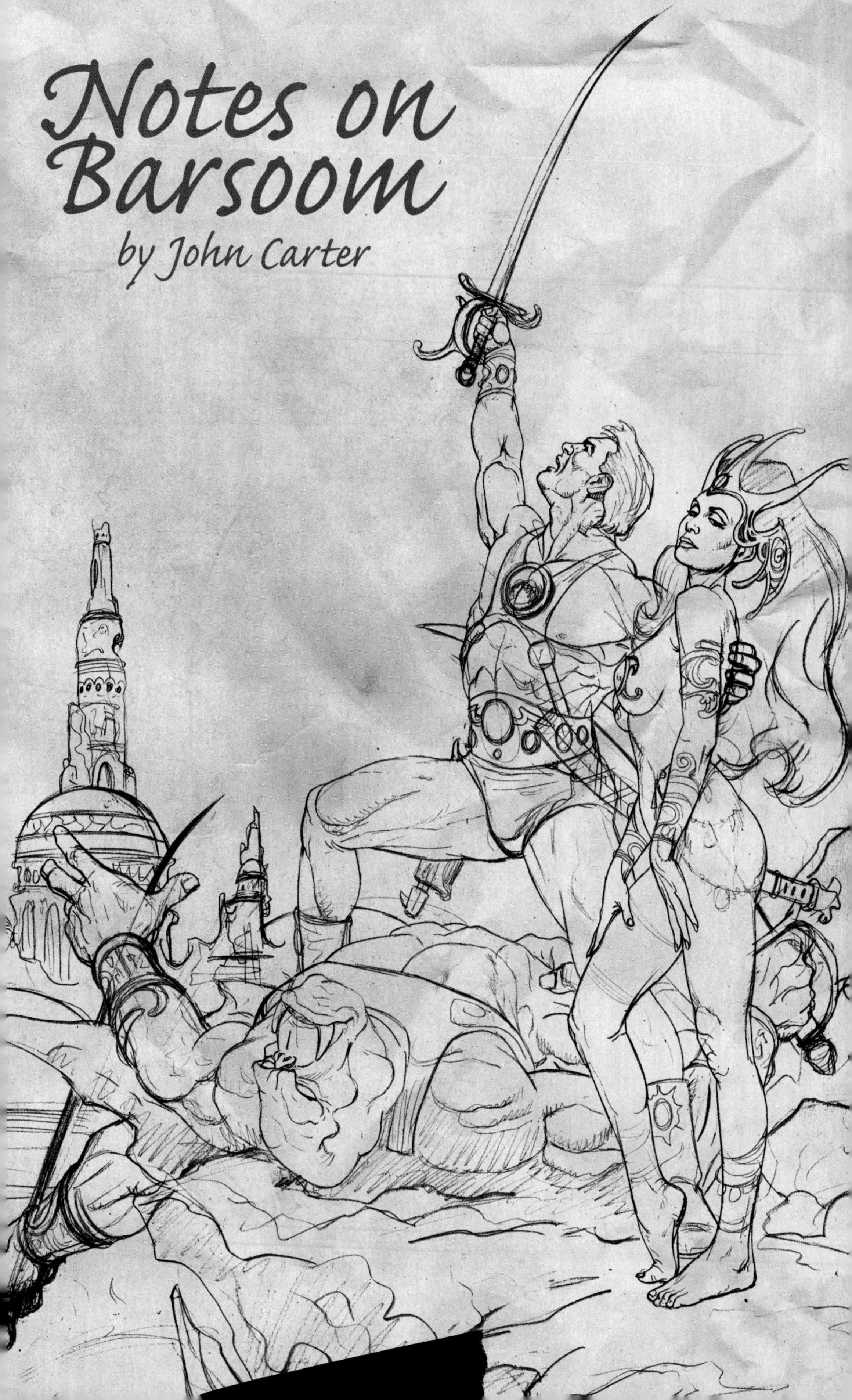

John Carter's
Natural History of Barsoom

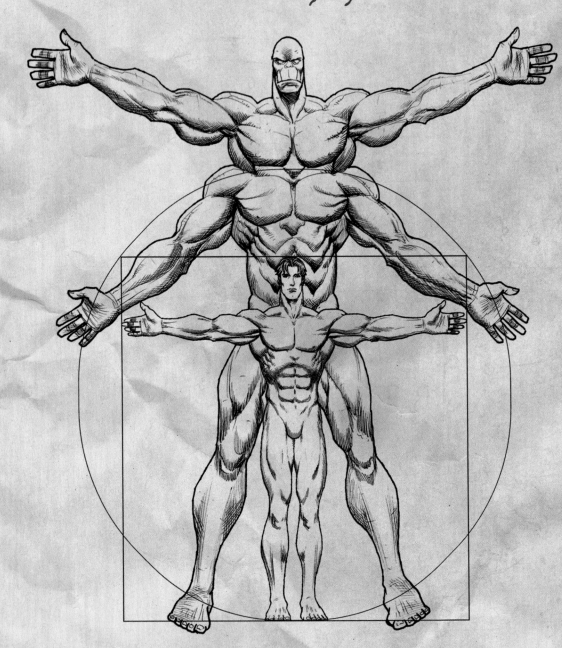

Effects of Mars on My Earthly Physiology

The lesser gravitational field of Mars, and the reduced air pressure of its greatly rarefied atmosphere, afford little resistance to my earthly muscles.

My new-found strength played mischief with me when I arrived; the mere act of rising to my feet for the first time catapulted me several yards into the air.

I therefore had to learn to walk all over again. Acclimatizing myself took several days and resulted in a multiplicity of embarrassments and injuries, although none of them mortal.

On the Green Men

While the green Martians are immense, their bones are very large, and they are muscled only in proportion to the gravitation which they must overcome.

The result is that they are infinitely less agile and less powerful, in proportion to their weight, than an Earth man. If one of them were to be transported to Earth, I doubt he could lift his own weight from the ground.

I detect no signs of extreme age amongst them, nor is there any appreciable difference in their appearance from the age of maturity, about forty, until, at about the age of one thousand years they go voluntarily upon a strange "pilgrimage" whose purpose I have not yet fathomed.

But the average life expectancy of a green Martian is closer to three hundred years. Owing to the waning resources of the planet, it evidently became necessary to counteract the increasing lifespan their remarkable medical skills produced, and so human life has come to be considered but lightly on Mars, as is evidenced by their danger-ous sports and the almost continual warfare between the various communities.

There are other and natural causes tending toward a diminution of population, but nothing contributes so greatly to this end as the fact that no male or female Martian is ever voluntarily without a weapon of destruction.

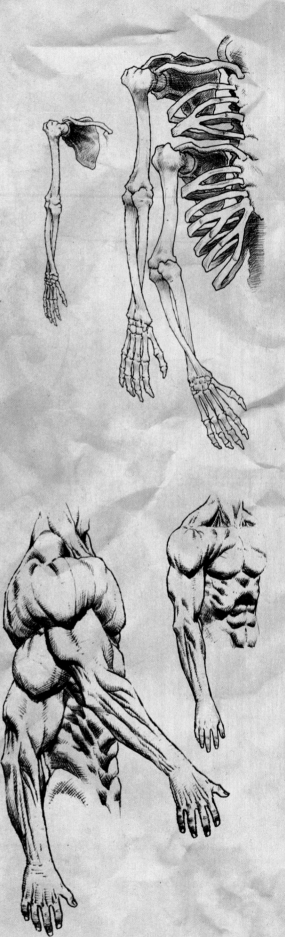

Child-raising on Mars

The green Martians regulate their birth rate to merely offset the loss by death with almost supernatural foresight.

Each adult female brings forth about thirteen eggs each year, which are then deposited in remote subterranean vaults where the temperature is too low for incubation. A council of twenty chieftains visits the vaults each year to examine the eggs. All but about one hundred of the most perfect are destroyed out of each yearly supply.

At the end of five years, the five hundred or so acceptable eggs are placed in incubators, to be hatched by the sun's rays after a period of another five years.

The incubators are built in remote fastnesses, where there is little or no likelihood of their being discovered by other tribes. The result of such a catastrophe would mean no children in the community for another five years.

Why the green men do not build their vaults and incubators nearer home is a mystery to me, and, like many other Martian mysteries, remains unsolved and unsolvable.

All but about a half-dozen eggs hatch in two days. The remaining eggs are abandoned, as their offspring might transmit the tendency to prolonged incubation, and thus upset the age-old system which permits the green Martians to calculate the proper time to return to the incubators almost to an hour.

The children emerge from their eggs perfectly developed except in size. The young are entirely unknown to their mothers, who, in turn, cannot point out the fathers with any accuracy. Their foster mothers may not even have had an egg in the incubator, but this counts for little among the green Martians.

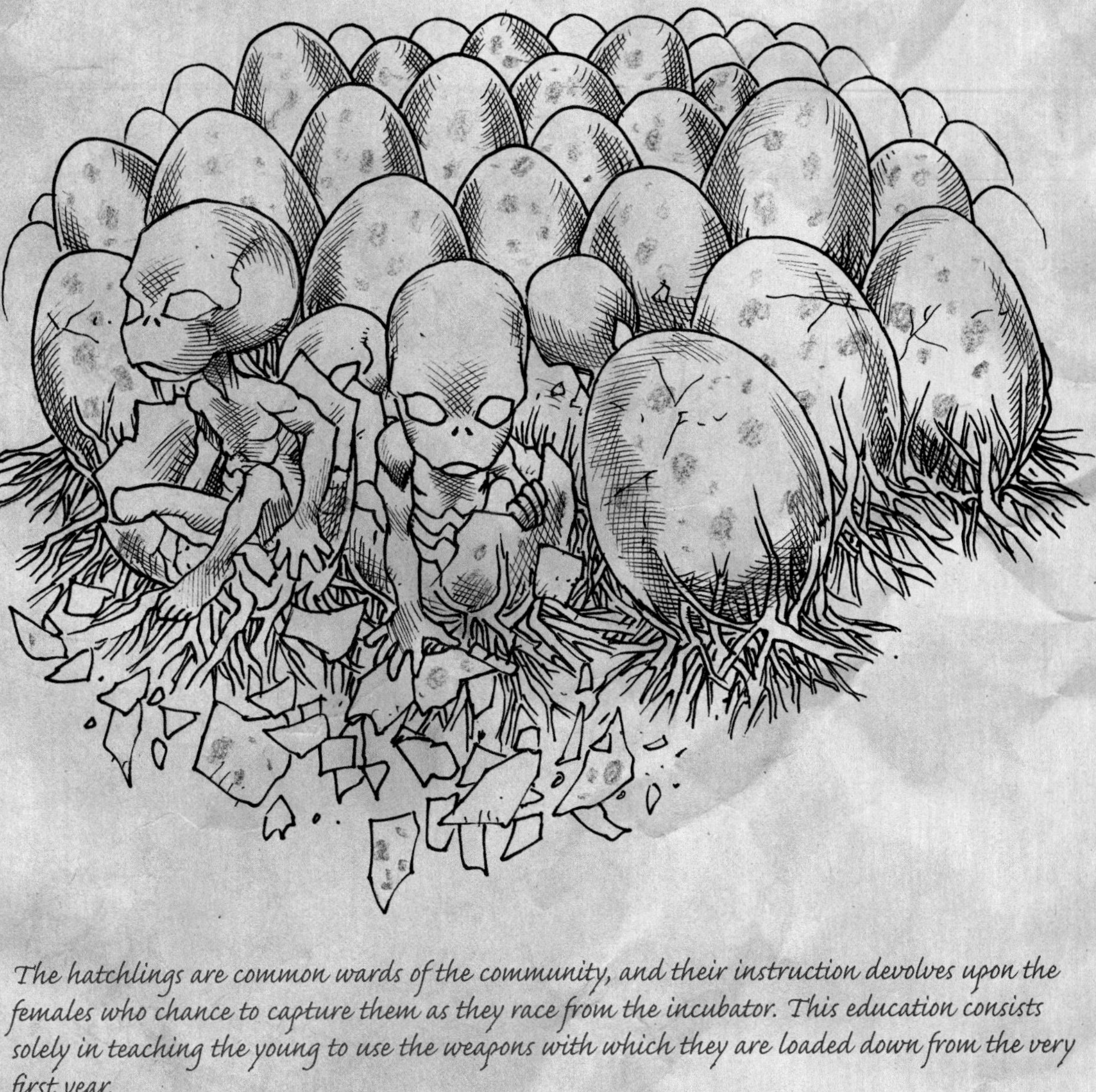

The hatchlings are common wards of the community, and their instruction devolves upon the females who chance to capture them as they race from the incubator. This education consists solely in teaching the young to use the weapons with which they are loaded down from the very first year.

I believe this horrible system, which has been carried on for ages, is the direct cause of the loss of all the finer feelings and higher instincts among these poor creatures. From birth the green Martians know no fatherly or motherly love, they know not the meaning of the word home; they are taught that they are only suffered to live until they demonstrate they are fit to do so. Any deemed deformed or defective in any way are promptly exterminated, nor do they shed a single tear for any of the cruel hardships they endure from earliest infancy.

I do not mean the green Martians are unnecessarily or intentionally cruel to their young. Theirs is a pitiless struggle for existence upon a dying planet, the natural resources of which have dwindled to a point where the support of each additional life means an added tax upon the community.

The Ancient Barsoomians

I have learned much about Mars's antiquity through my conversations with Dejah Thoris.

She informed me the people who built the abandoned cities which dot the surface of Mars had presumably flourished over a hundred thousand years ago. They were fair-skinned and flaxen-haired, but had mixed with the other great race of early Martians, who were very dark, almost black, and also with the reddish yellow race which had flourished at the same time.

These three great divisions of the higher Martians had been forced into a alliance as the drying of the seas compelled them to seek the few and always diminishing fertile areas, and to defend themselves against the wild hordes of green men.

Ages of close relationship and intermarrying had resulted in the race of red men, of which Dejah Thoris was a fair and beautiful daughter.

During the ages of hardships and incessant warring between their own various races, as well as with the green men, much of the high civilization and many of the arts of the fair-haired Martians had become lost; but the red race of today has reached a point where it feels it has made up for some of that which lies forever buried with the ancient Barsoomians.

These ancient Martians had been a highly cultivated and literary race, but during the vicissitudes of those trying centuries of readjustment to new conditions practically all their archives, records, and literature were lost.

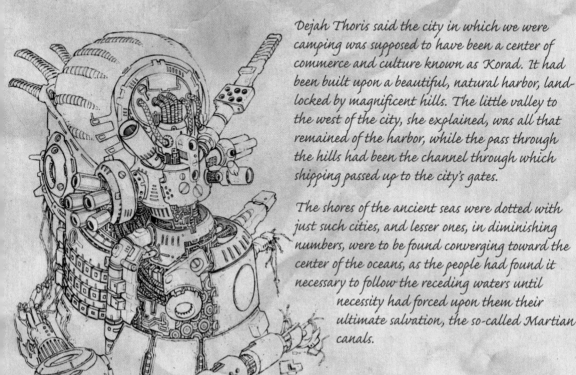

Dejah Thoris said the city in which we were camping was supposed to have been a center of commerce and culture known as Korad. It had been built upon a beautiful, natural harbor, land-locked by magnificent hills. The little valley to the west of the city, she explained, was all that remained of the harbor, while the pass through the hills had been the channel through which shipping passed up to the city's gates.

The shores of the ancient seas were dotted with just such cities, and lesser ones, in diminishing numbers, were to be found converging toward the center of the oceans, as the people had found it necessary to follow the receding waters until necessity had forced upon them their ultimate salvation, the so-called Martian canals.

Left: One of the many mysterious mechanical devices of the ancient Barsoomians, found deep within the catacombs of Korad. Purpose unknown.

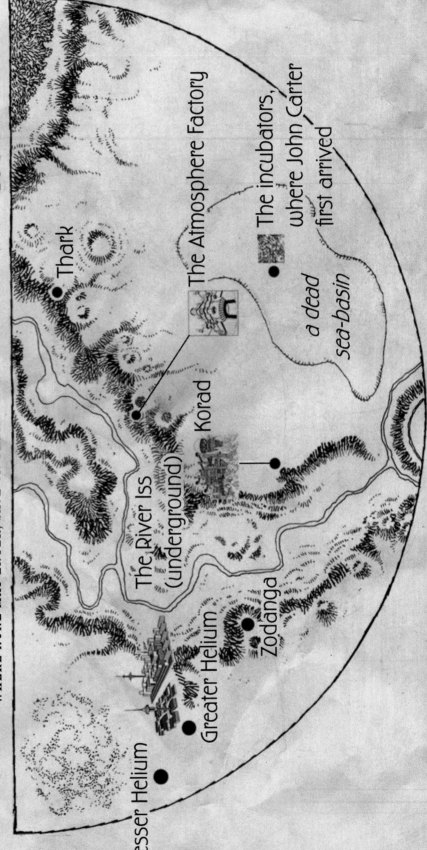

A MAP of SOUTHWESTERN BARSOOM

OMITTING the DREAD POLAR REGION

WHERE NONE MAY ENTER, SAVE ON THEIR FINAL PILGRIMAGE UPON THE "ISS"

Thark

The Atmosphere Factory

The incubators, where John Carter first arrived

a dead sea-basin

Korad

The River Iss (underground)

Zodanga

Greater Helium

Lesser Helium

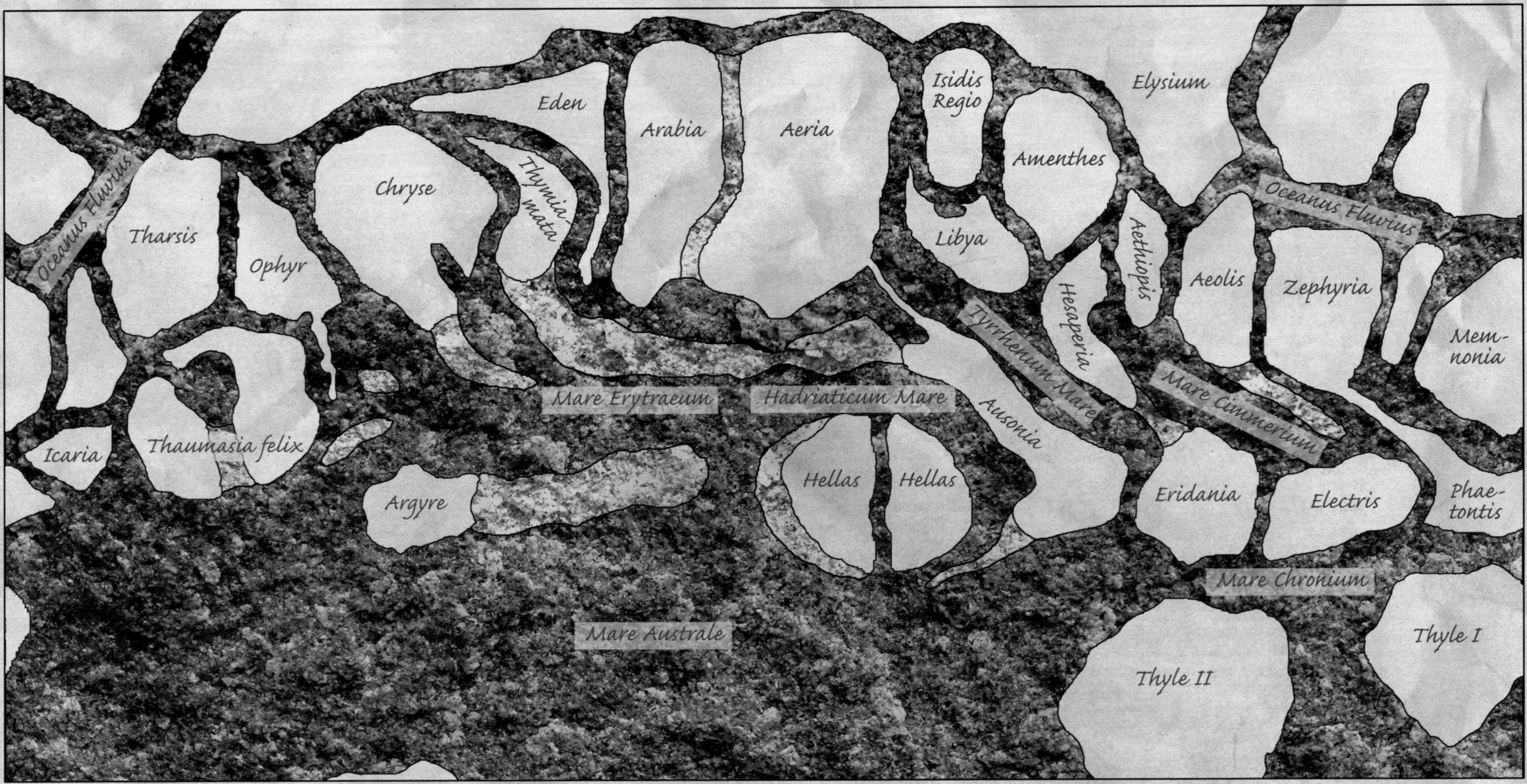
Oceanus Fluvius
Tharsis
Ophyr
Icaria
Thaumasia felix
Chryse
Eden
Thymia-
mata
Arabia
Aeria
Isidis
Regio
Libya
Amenthes
Elysium
Aethiopis
Hesaperia
Tyrrhenum Mare
Aeolis
Zephyria
Oceanus Fluvius
Mem-
nonia
Mare Cimmerium
Mare Erytraeum
Hadriaticum Mare
Ausonia
Argyre
Hellas
Hellas
Eridania
Electris
Phae-
tontis
Mare Chronium
Mare Australe
Thyle II
Thyle I

Early understanding and Earth names of select Martian canals and land masses.

The Red Planet

Mars, the fourth planet from the Sun, is named after the Roman god of war, probably because of its bloody red hue in the nighttime sky. Mars is roughly halfway between Earth and the Moon in terms of size. It is also about half again as far from the Sun as Earth.

The Martian day is just 40 minutes longer than a day on Earth, but a Martian year is much longer — about 1.88 Earth years — owing to it being further from the Sun and its slightly lesser orbital speed.

Water exists on Mars, trapped in vast sheets of ice at the poles. Whether it occurs in a liquid state is a matter of much scientific debate and conjecture.

Mars has been known to humankind since the Ancient Egyptians. The Babylonians began keeping detailed records of it, probably for astrological purposes.

But the real explosion in knowledge about our red sister came in the early 17th Century, with the invention of the telescope, which allowed European astronomers to compute the staggering distances of Mars from the Sun and from the Earth.

Now, telescopes have become so powerful astronomers can see Mars in enough detail to draw maps of its surface. In 1877, Giovanni Schiaparelli, a pioneering Martian cartographer, was among the first people to view the surface of Mars with these new telescopes, and among the first to record the large grooves he saw on the planet's surface. The Italian word for "grooves," "canali," became permanently ensconced in the English language as the famous "canals" of Mars.

Much of the scientific establishment scoffed at Schiaparelli's observations, but several decades later the American visionary Percival Lowell took up the cause of Mars at the observatory he founded in Flagstaff, Arizona.

In his most recent book, published just nine years ago, Lowell claims he can observe these canals quite clearly, as well as dark patches on Mars's surface that grow and contract with the seasons — swaths of vegetation, in his view. The canals, he claims, are the product of an advanced Martian civilization, designed to tap the precious, dwindling water resources at the planet's poles. Mars, Powell claims, is a dying planet, and as it dies, so too will its mysterious, intelligent inhabitants.

Lowell's telescopes are not large enough to prove any of his startling theories. But time will tell if his views are correct, as technological progress marches onwards, and we develop ever more precise and powerful instruments of astronomical observation.

Science and Technology on Barsoom

The Ninth Ray and the Atmosphere Plant

The secret of the process by which the Barsoomians manufacture their atmosphere hinges on the use of the "ninth ray." This "ray," or portion of the electromagnetic spectrum, is separated from the other rays of the sun by means of finely adjusted instruments. This product is then incorporated with certain quantities of refined electric vibrations. As it is released, contact with the ether of space transforms it into breathable atmosphere.

The Eighth Ray and the Barsoomian Airships

This ray, like the ninth ray, is unknown on Earth, but it is an inherent property of all light. The Barsoomians have learned it is this "eighth ray" which compels light to radiate outwards. When separated, amplified and stored, this ray constitutes a force of repulsion able to lift enormous weights from the surface of the ground. It is this ray which has enabled the red Martians to build their great fleets of airships.

Many accidents occurred during the early years of the discovery of this ray. In one instance, some nine hundred years before my arrival, the first great battleship built with this technology was stored with too great a quantity of the ray. She had sailed up from Helium into outer space with five hundred officers and men, never to return.

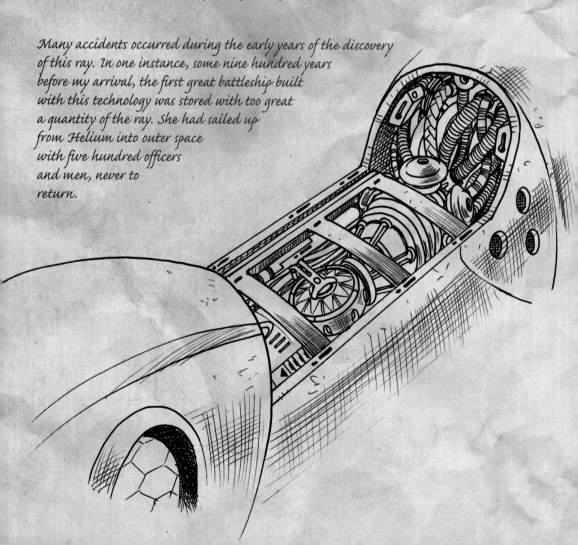

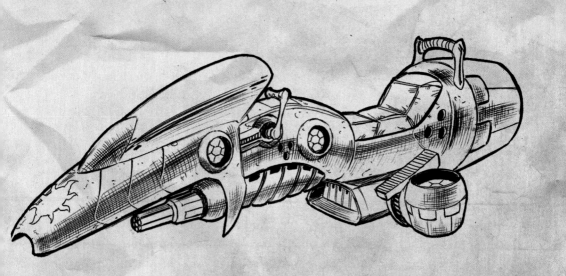

Hydrology, Agriculture and the Martian "Canals"

Out of sheer necessity, the red Martians have instituted a system of planet-wide irrigation for their cities and crops. Water is collected in immense underground reservoirs at either pole from the melting ice caps and is then pumped through conduits, the so-called "canals," to population centers. Along either side of these conduits, and extending their entire length, lie the cultivated districts. These are divided into tracts, each tract being under the supervision of one or more government officers.

Instead of flooding the surface of the fields, and thus wasting immense quantities of water by evaporation, the precious liquid is carried underground through a vast network of small pipes directly to the soil.

Martian "Skytower" Homes

All red-Martian homes are raised high above the ground at night on a large round metal shaft which slides up and down upon a sleeve sunk in the ground. The mechanism is operated by a tiny radium engine, located in the entrance hall of most domiciles. They also have a portable, wireless device for lowering or raising their homes remotely, a sort of "remote control."

Assassination is the ever-present fear of all Barsoomians, and for this reason alone their homes are raised at night, or in times of danger, as theft is completely unknown on Barsoom.

Martian Projectile Weaponry

It had never been given to me to see such deadly aim as is possessed by the green Martians. Their unfailing accuracy more than makes up for their utter lack of the vast air battleships of the red Martians.

Martian rifles are stocked with a very light and intensely hard wood, much prized on Mars and entirely unknown to denizens of Earth. The metal of the barrel is an alloy composed principally of aluminum and steel which they have learned to temper to a hardness far exceeding that of the steel with which we are familiar.

The weight of these rifles is comparatively little, and with the small caliber, explosive projectiles which they use, and the great length of the barrel, they are deadly at ranges which would be unthinkable on Earth. When equipped with a wireless finder and sighter, a green marksman can hit a target a trifle over two hundred miles downrange.

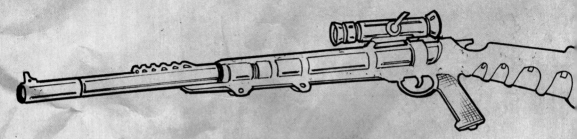

The rifles fire radium* shells, which must be manufactured by artificial light, as exposure to sunlight results in an explosion. The opaque outer coating of a shell is broken on impact, exposing the radium powder.

The moment the sunlight, even though diffused, strikes this powder it explodes with considerable violence. Night battles are marked by the absence of these explosions, while the following sunrise will be filled with the detonations of missiles fired the preceding night.

The red Martians have perfected the engineering of the radium firearm to a high degree, and they have developed a compound that detonates even in darkness. The same basic firing mechanism is at work on a much greater scale in the massive cannons that adorn the battleships and cruisers of their navies.

Smaller, rapid-fire cannons fortify the one-man speeders that scout ahead for the slow-moving leviathans of the air. The cannons on the scout ships are not powerful enough to breach the hull of a capital ship, but against unarmored targets the effects are devastating, as I learned when I stumbled onto Tars Tarkas after my escape from Zodanga.

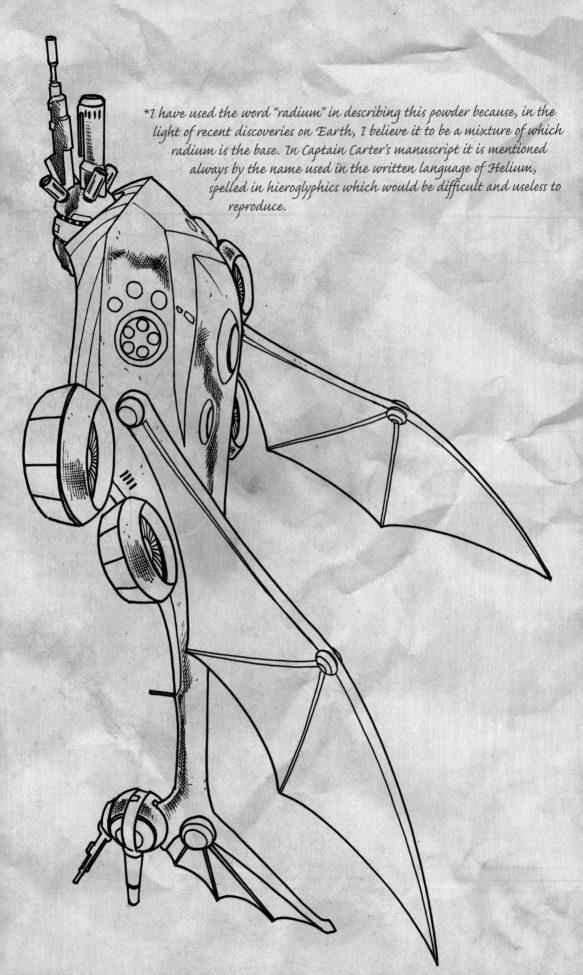

*I have used the word "radium" in describing this powder because, in the light of recent discoveries on Earth, I believe it to be a mixture of which radium is the base. In Captain Carter's manuscript it is mentioned always by the name used in the written language of Helium, spelled in hieroglyphics which would be difficult and useless to reproduce.

Martian Naval Warfare

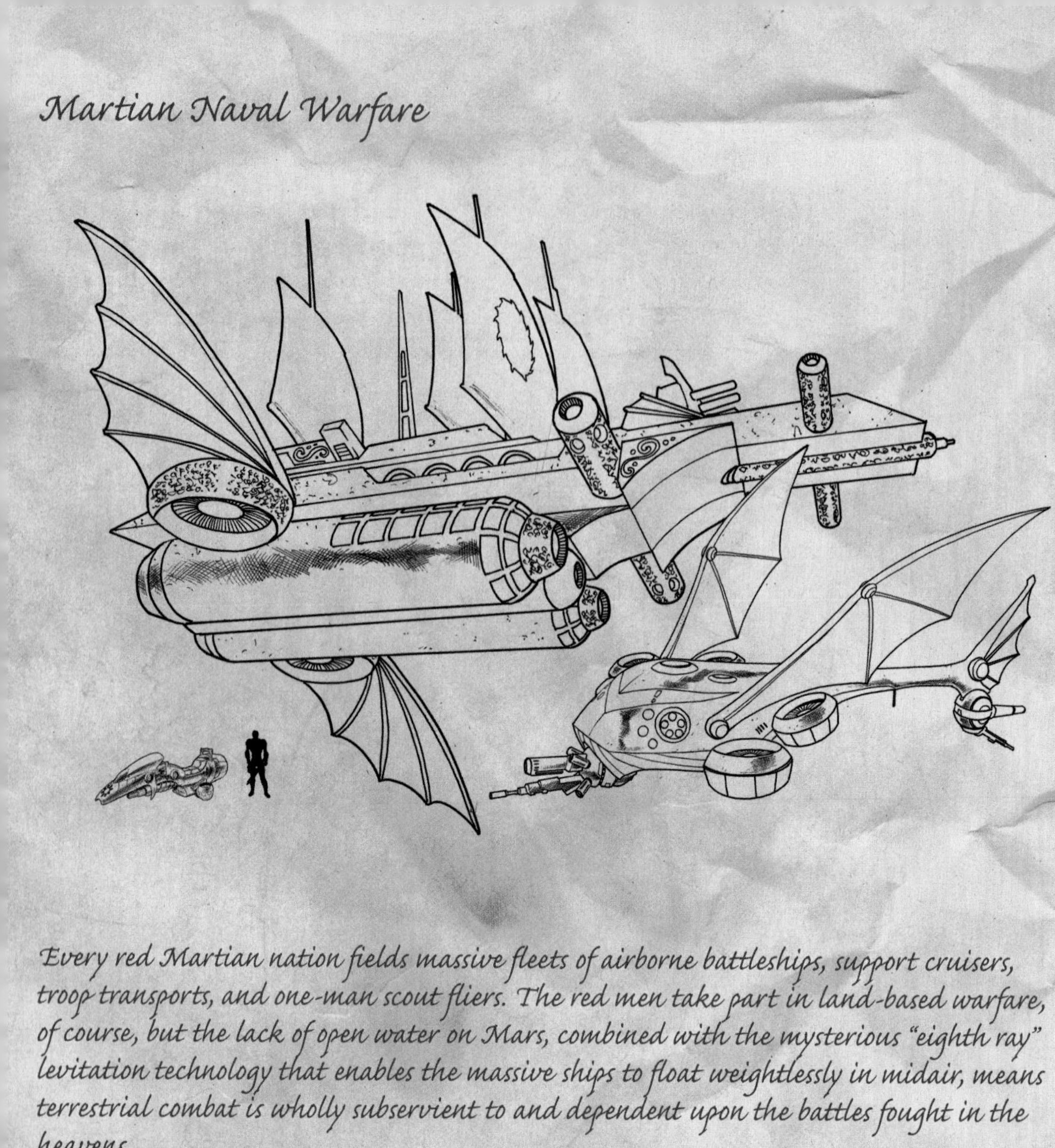

Every red Martian nation fields massive fleets of airborne battleships, support cruisers, troop transports, and one-man scout fliers. The red men take part in land-based warfare, of course, but the lack of open water on Mars, combined with the mysterious "eighth ray" levitation technology that enables the massive ships to float weightlessly in midair, means terrestrial combat is wholly subservient to and dependent upon the battles fought in the heavens.

The cruisers primarily play a defensive role, staving off the attacks of one-man fighters against the decks of the massive battleships, which are possessed of truly awesome firepower. The cruisers are armed only with cannons; they lack the devastating bomb batteries of the battleships that so often prove decisive in aerial engagements.

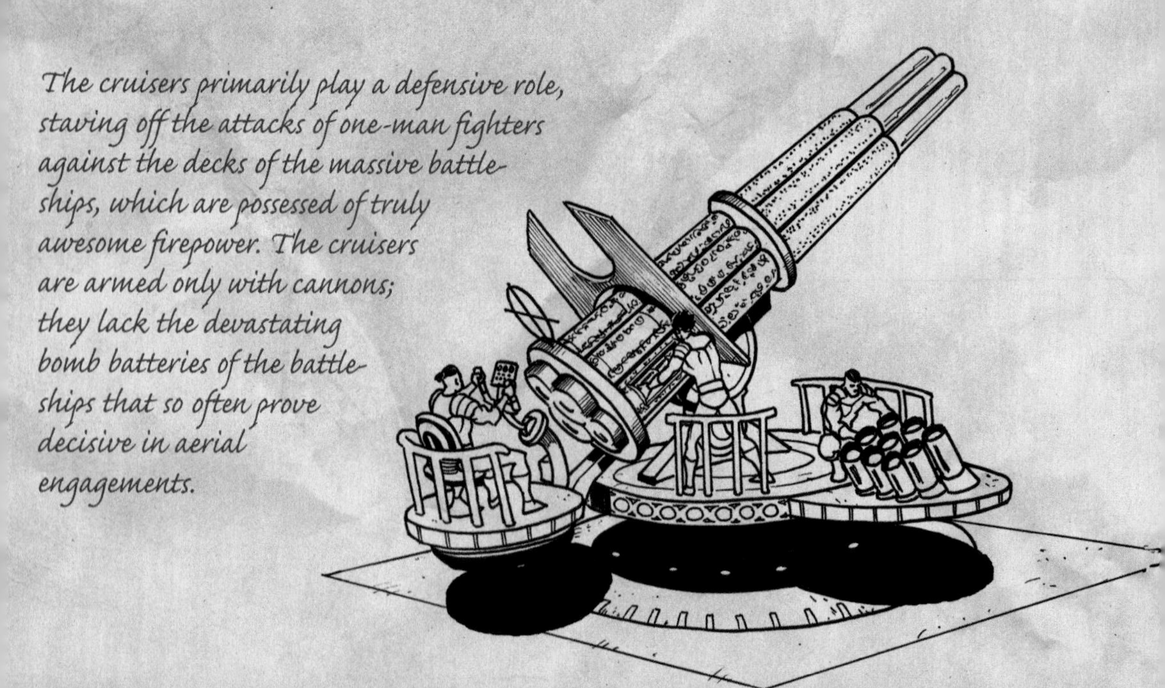

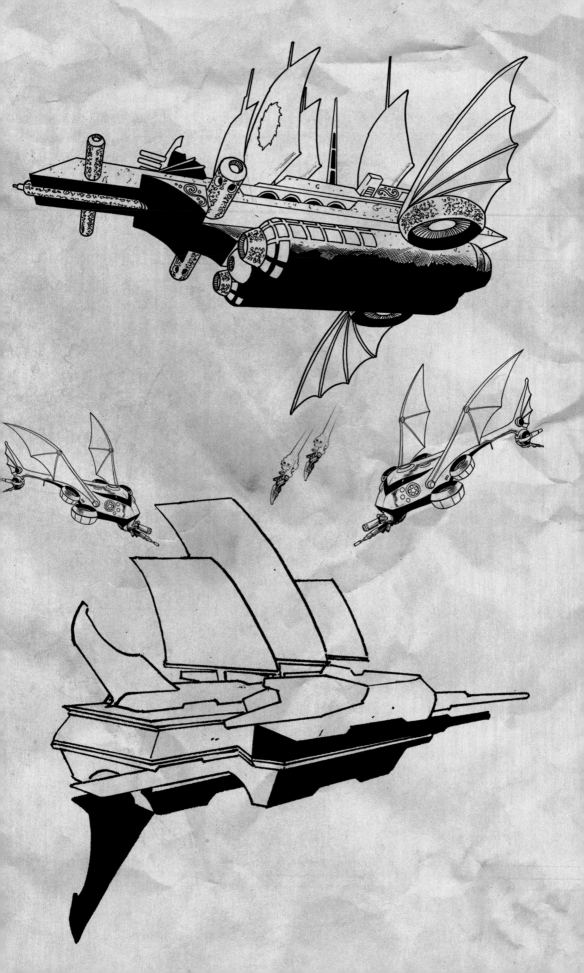

Naval service is a requirement for all red Martian males of age, but the duty is seen as a privilege rather than a burden. Service aboard one of the great battleships that dominate Martian aerial warfare is considered a great mark of distinction, but there is no greater glamour than that attached to the pilots of one-man fliers, which variably act as scouts and direct assault craft. Piloting a scout flier is especially dangerous, but the small, agile vessels often have a disproportionate effect on the outcome of hostilities between two fleets.

Standard naval doctrine prescribes maneuvering above one's enemy, so the deadly bomb compliments of the battleships can be unleashed. Once a fleet has been out—or rather "under"—maneuvered, it generally spells great disaster and impending defeat. The bombs have terrible effects on population centers, though ages of Martian custom and honor prevent naval vessels from taking part in the direct bombardment of cities.

As was the case during the Age of Sail on Earth, Martian honor dictates "a captain must go down with his ship"..On Mars, this applies not just for ships that are foundering, but also to those which have been forced to surrender. Martian air battles thus assume a deadly ferocity unparalleled in Earthly warfare.

—Captain John Carter of Virginia

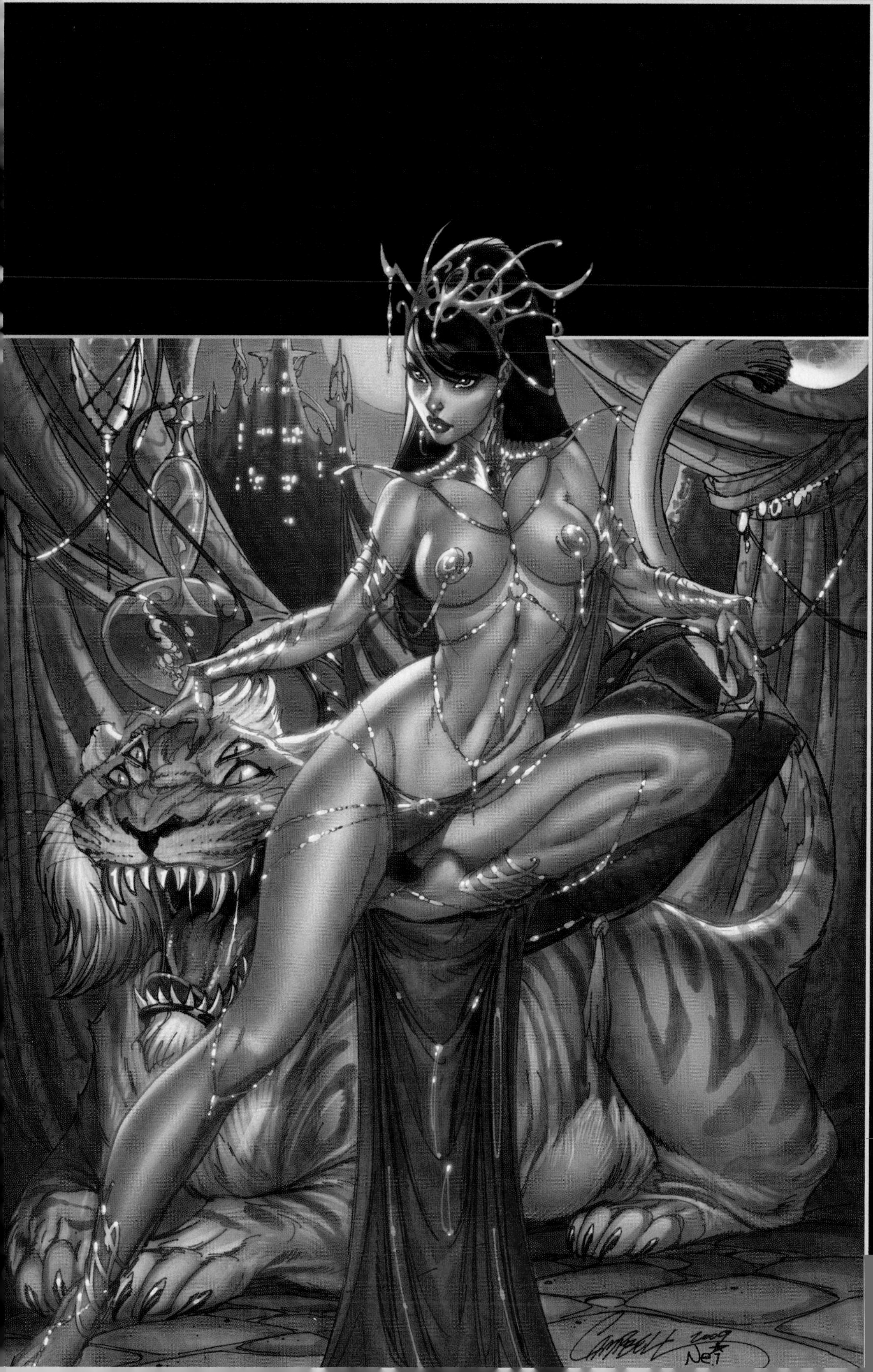

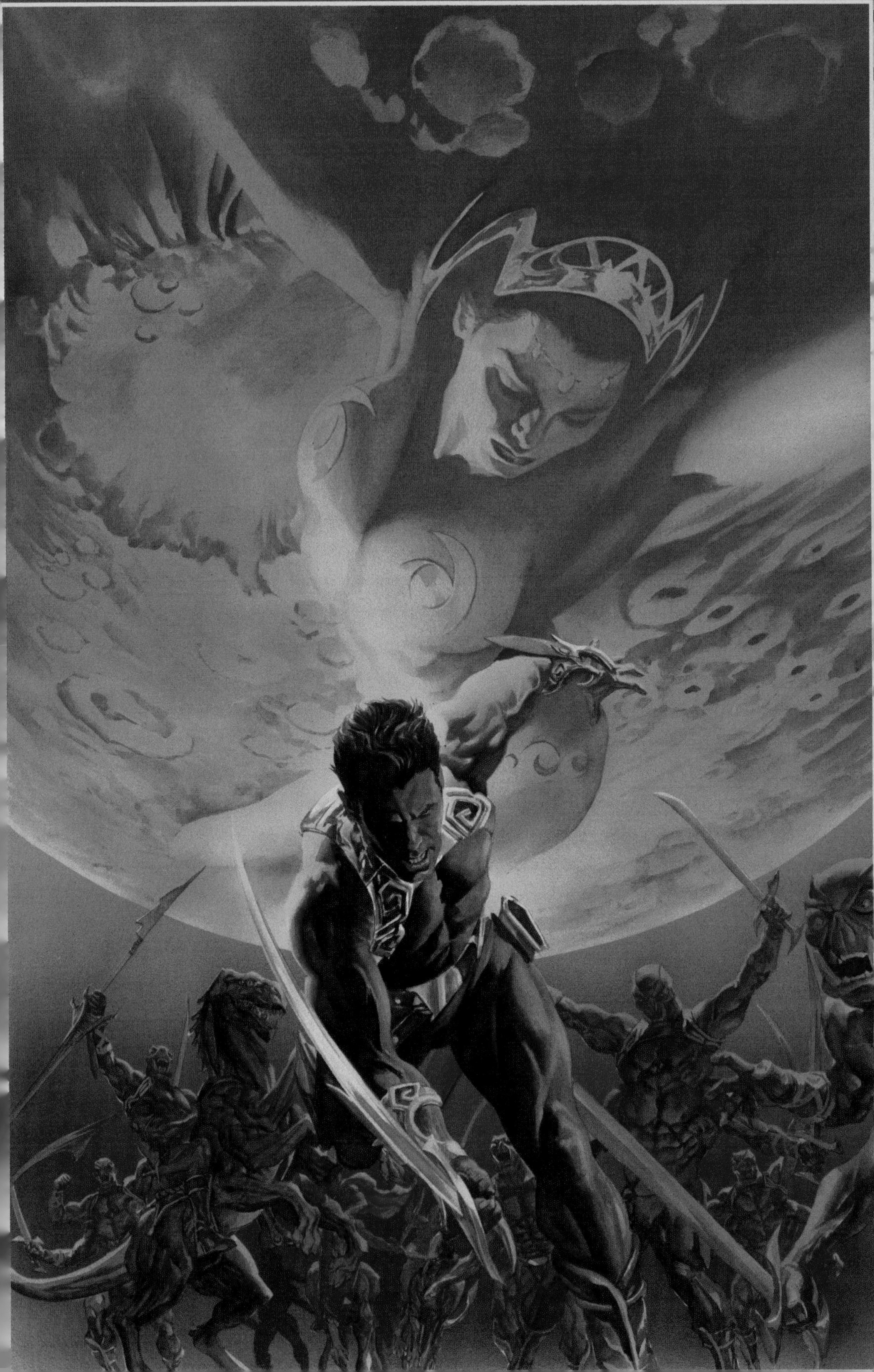

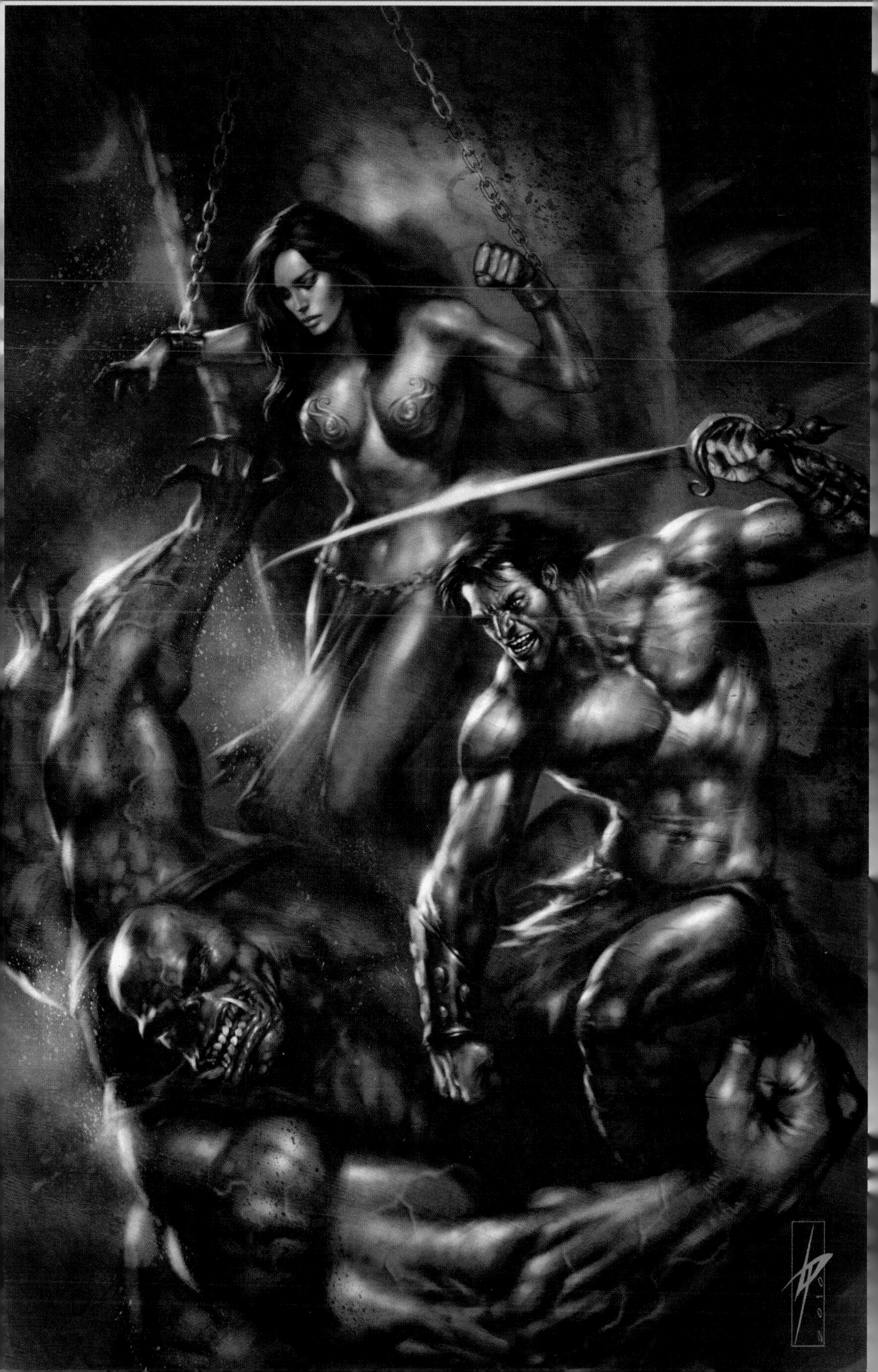

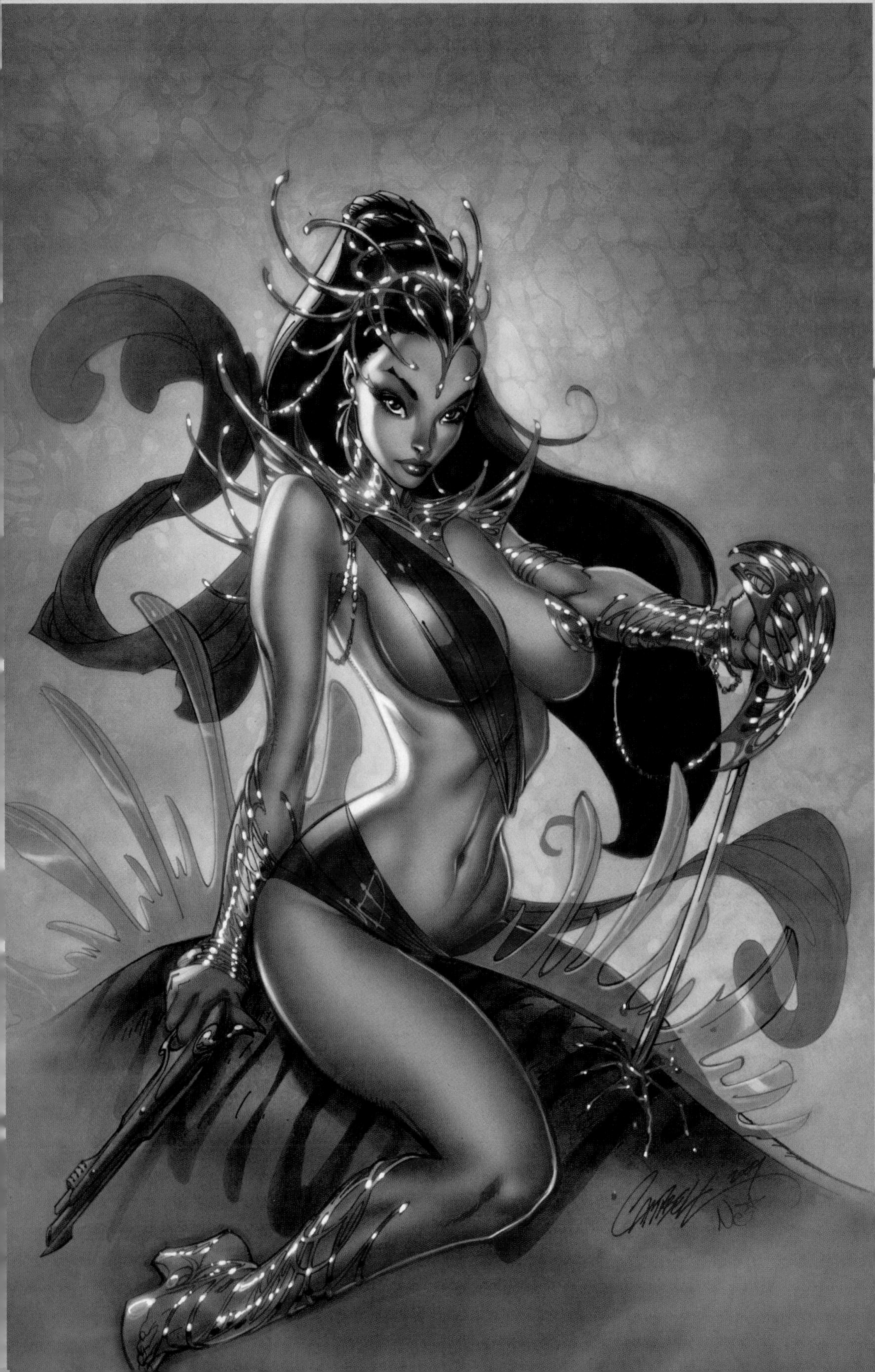

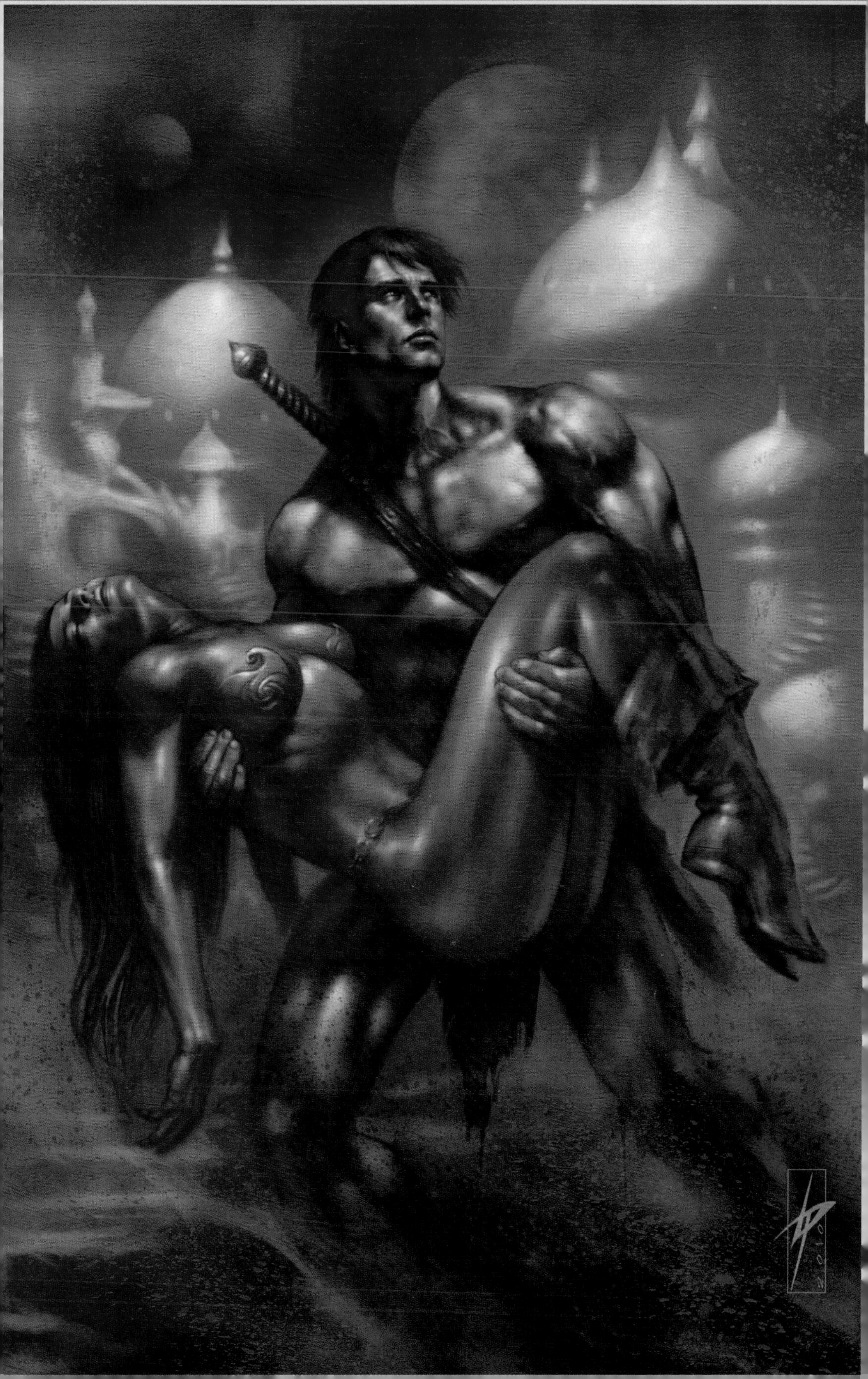

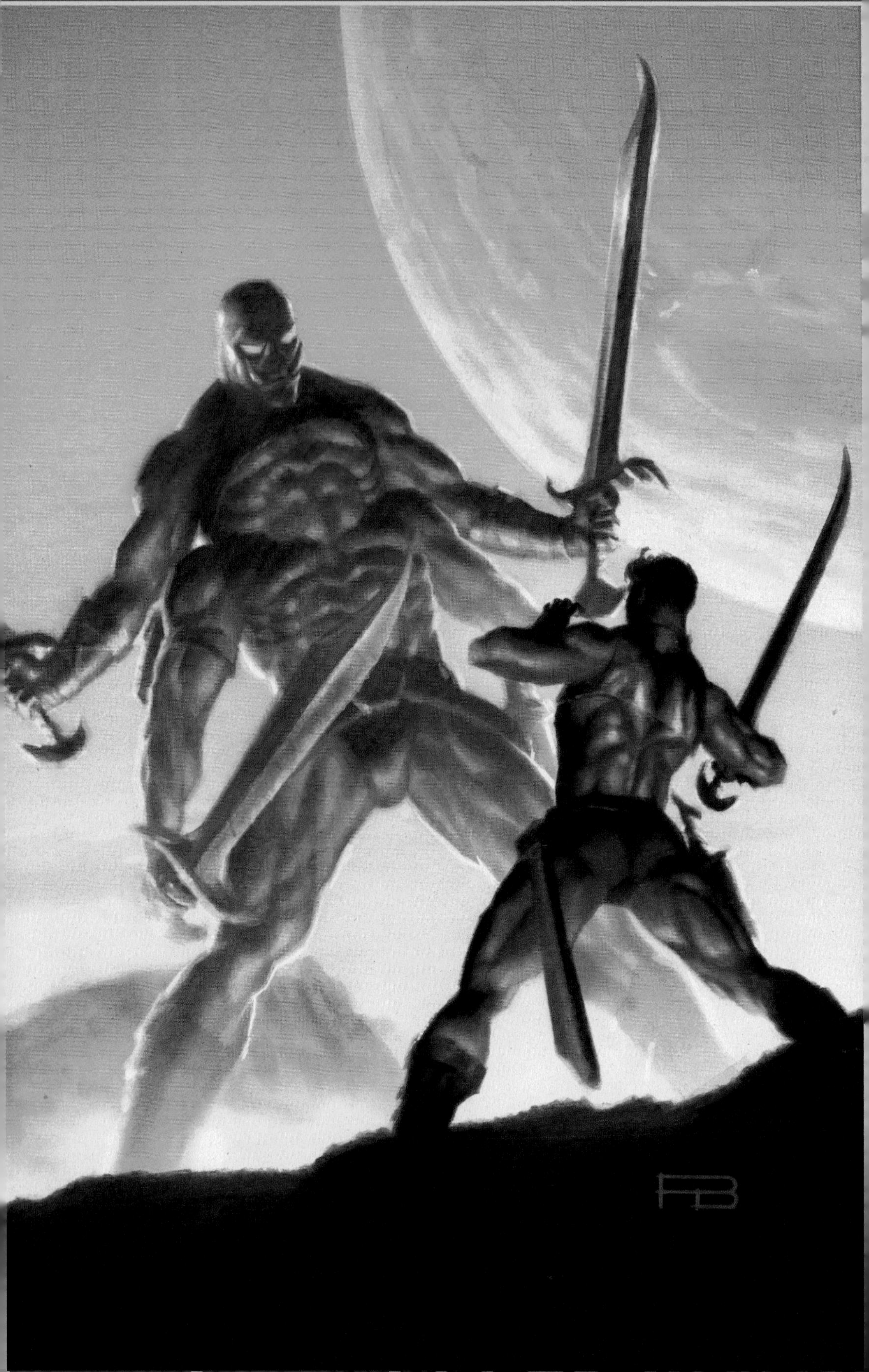

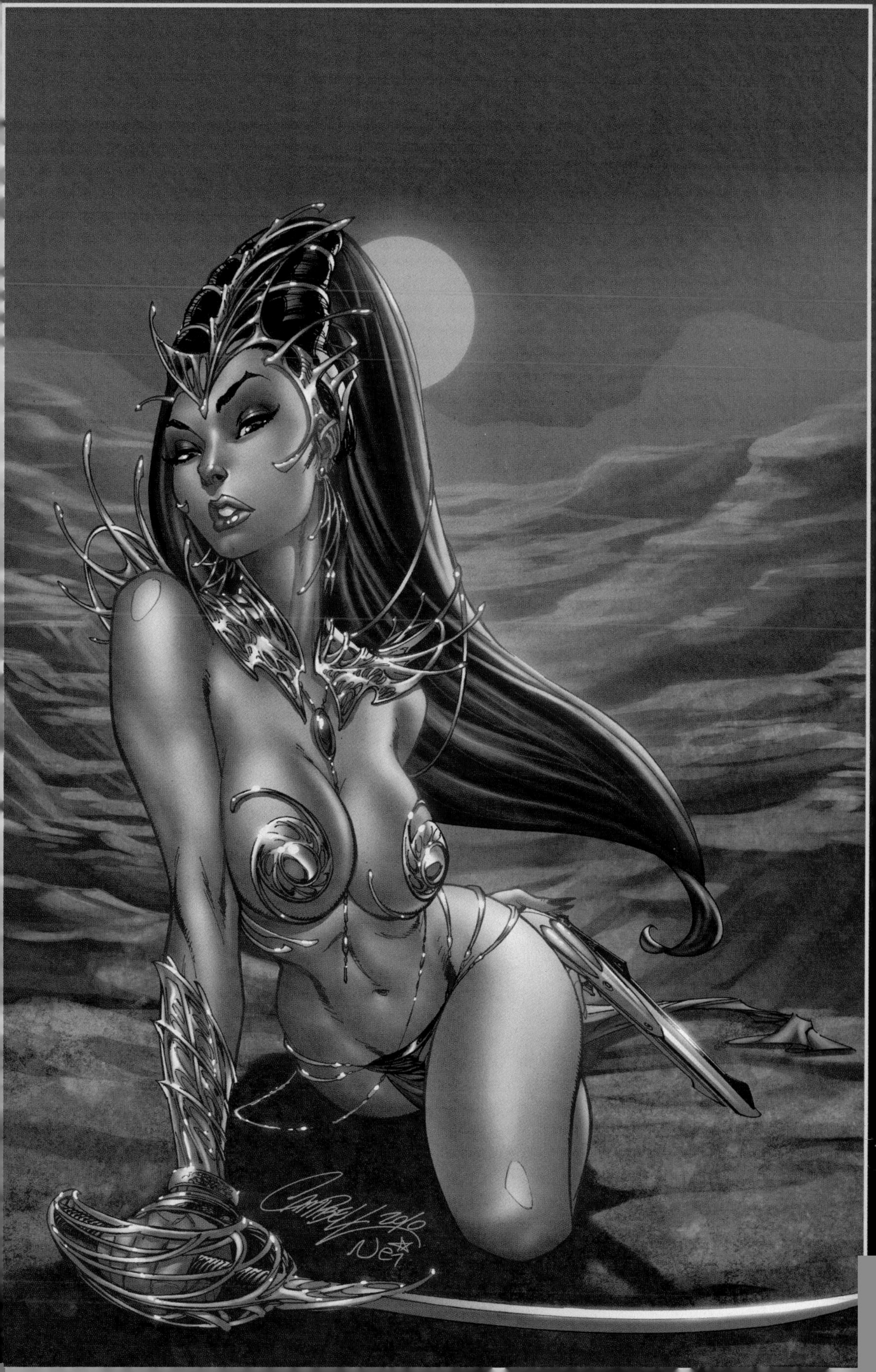

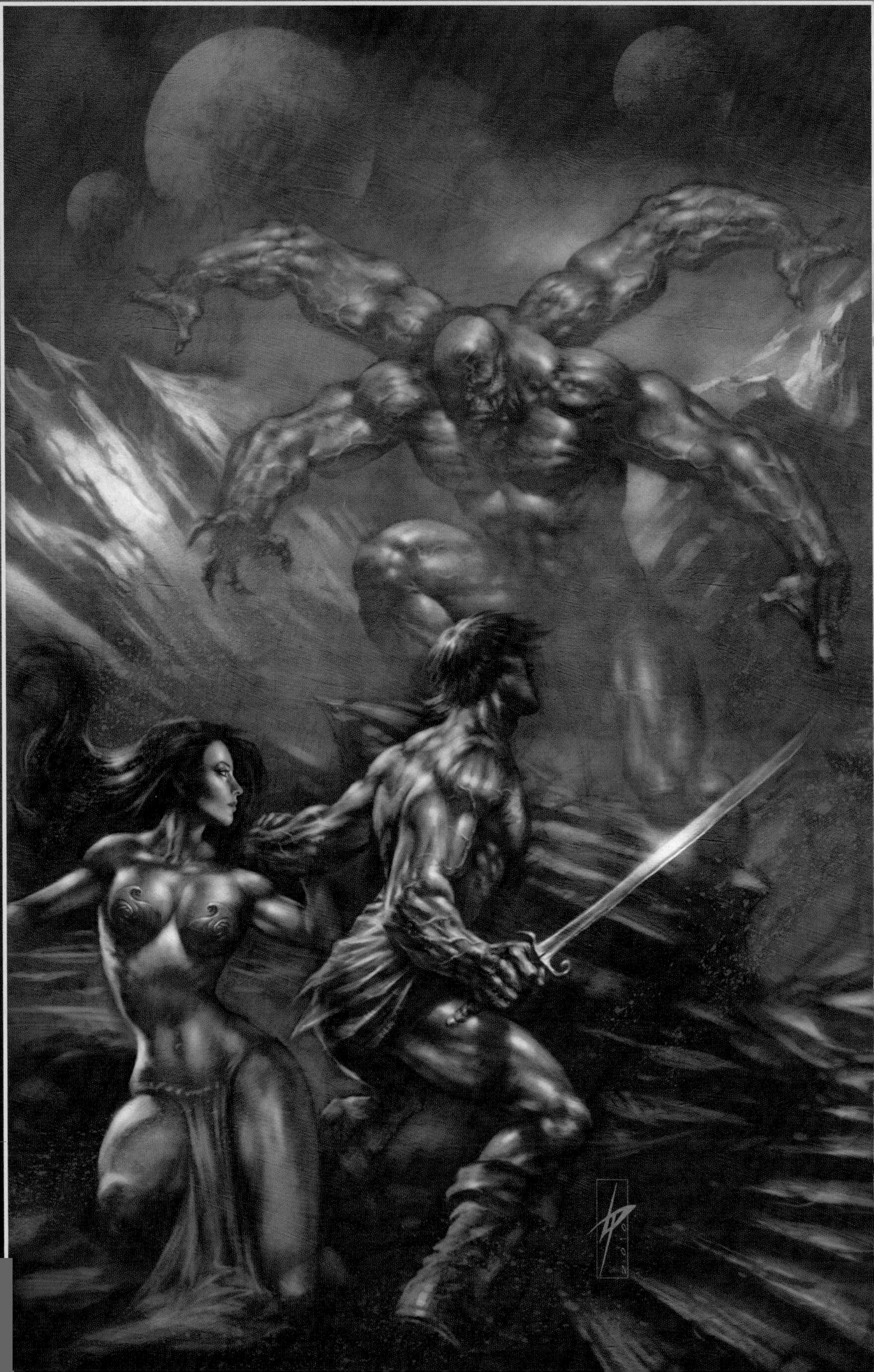

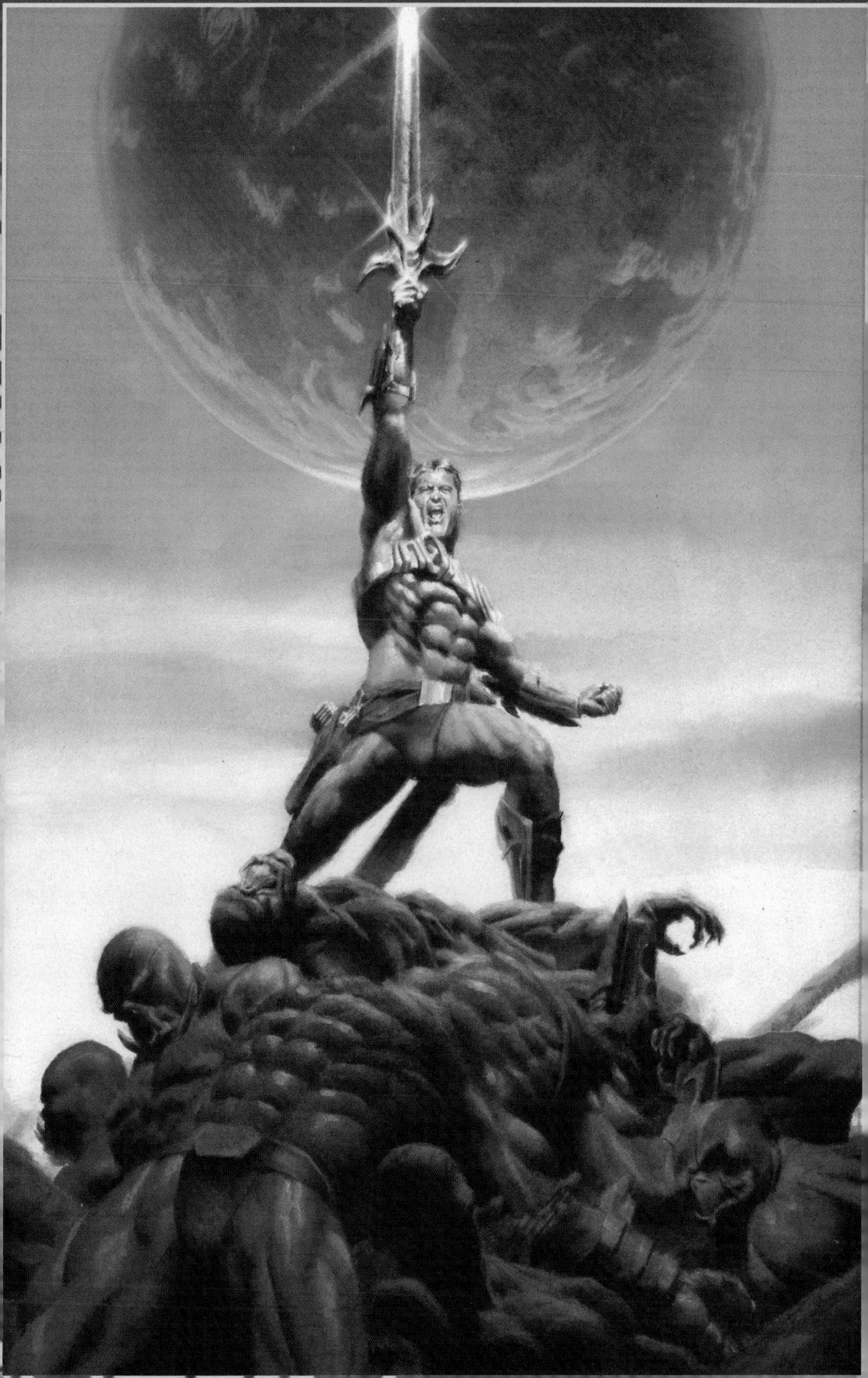

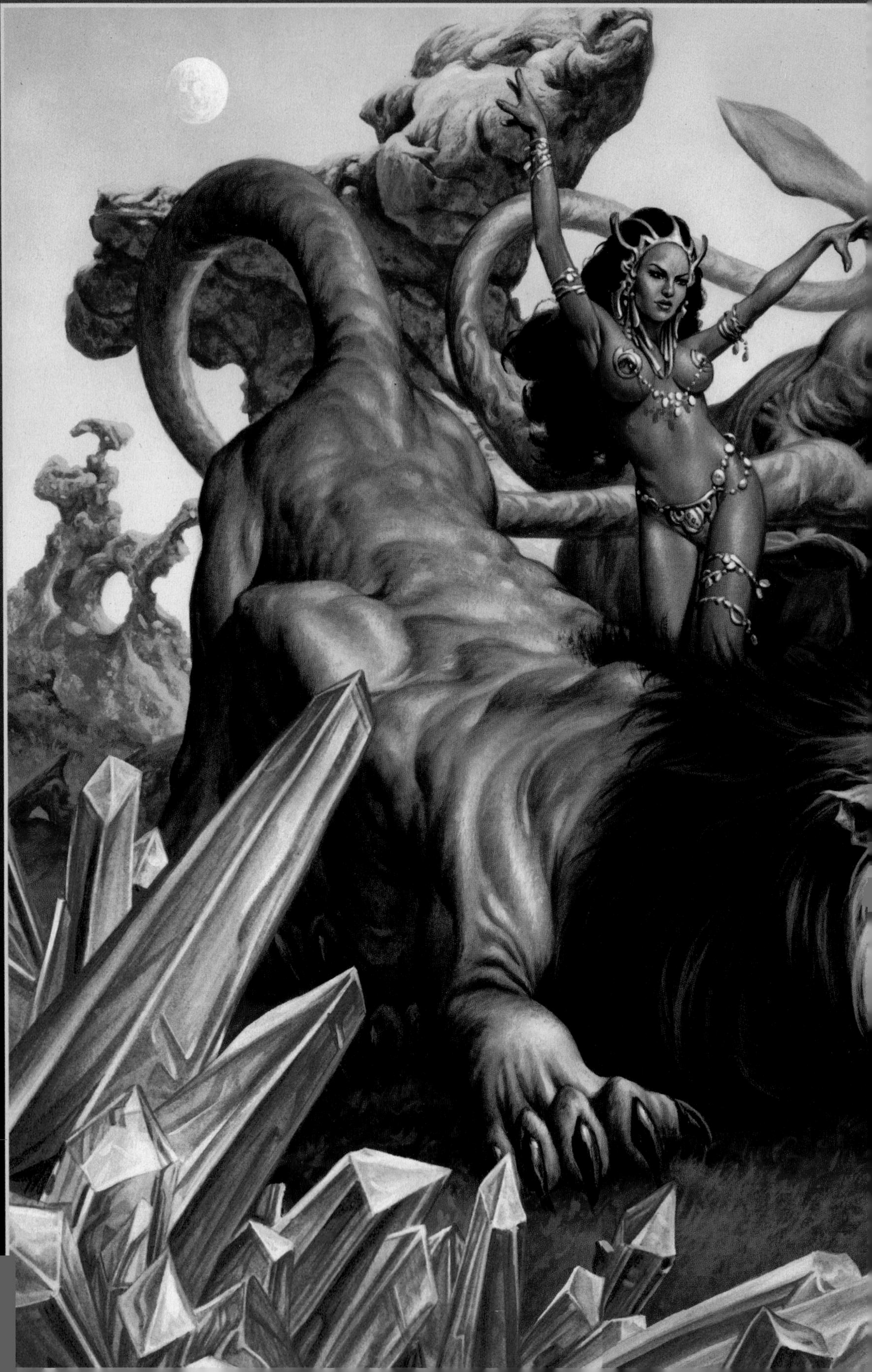

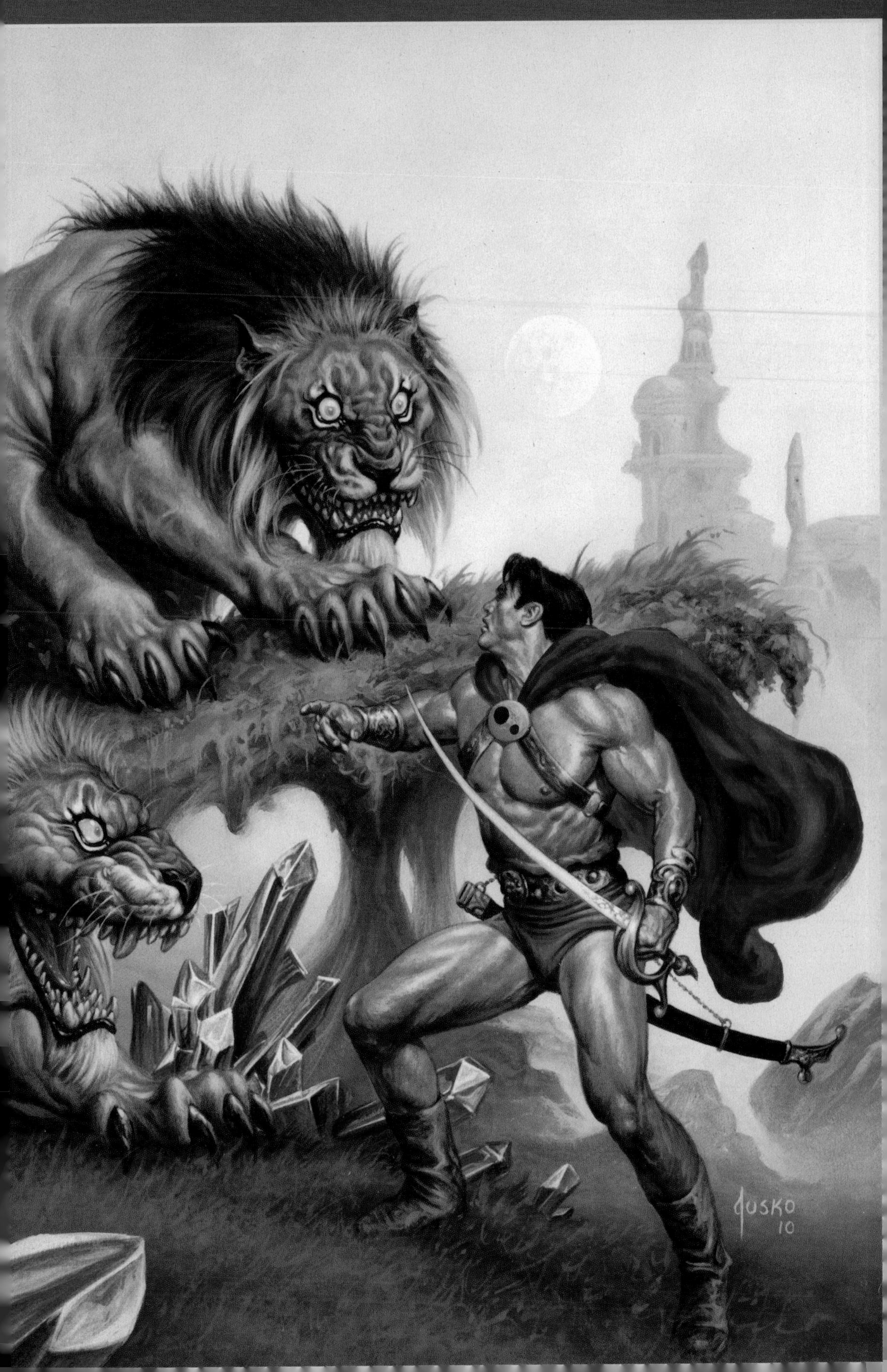
JUSKO
10

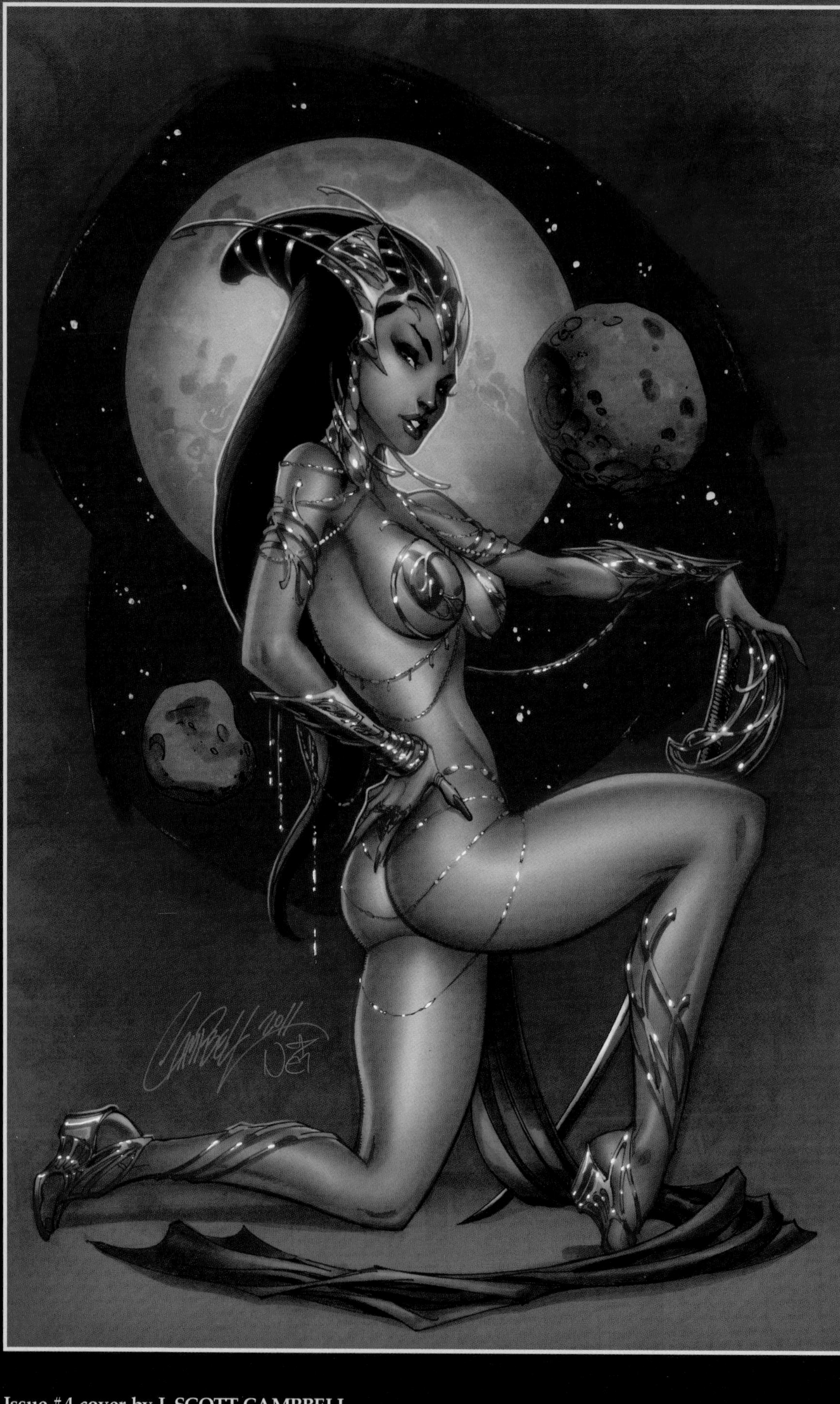

Issue #4 cover by J. SCOTT CAMPBELL

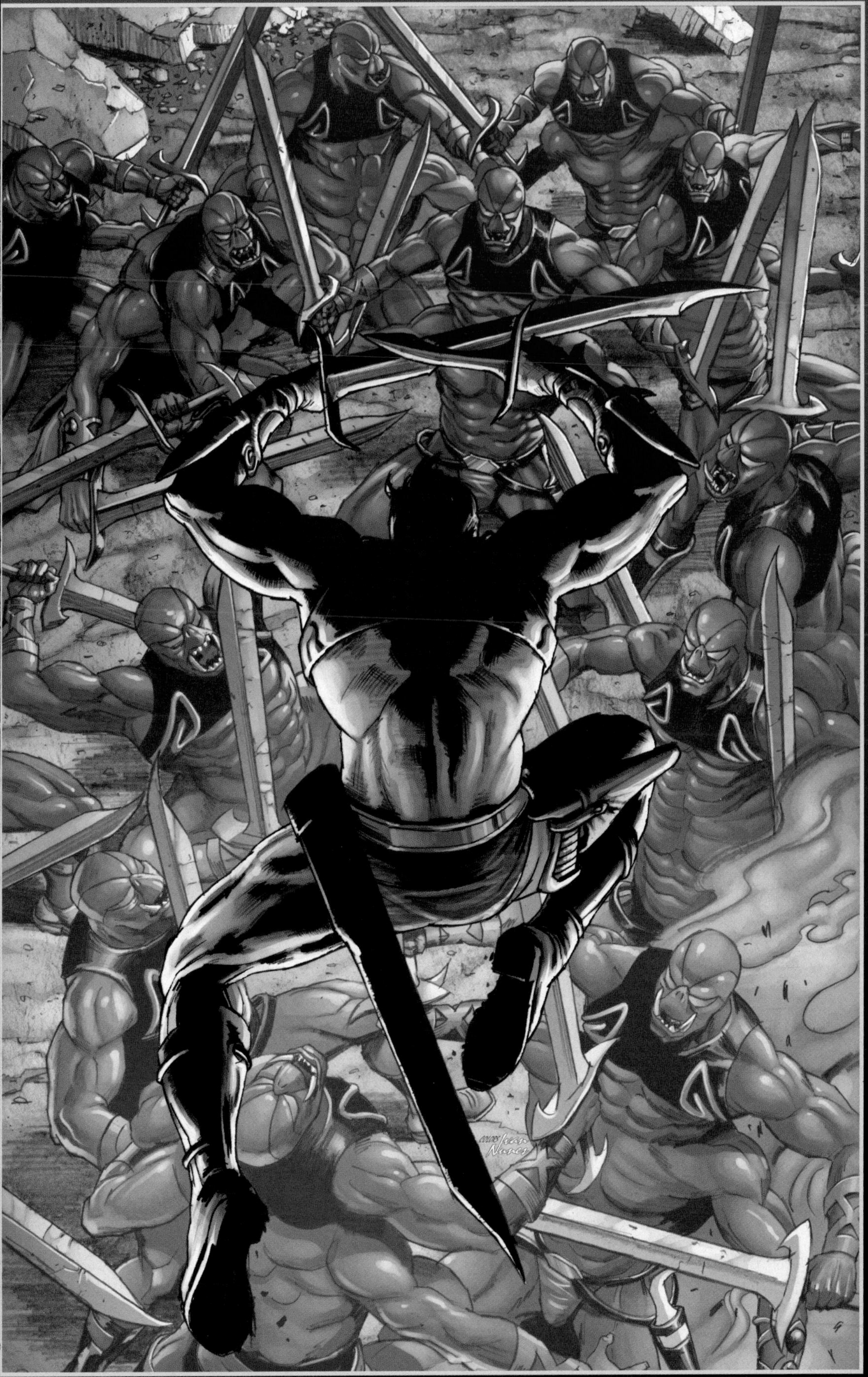

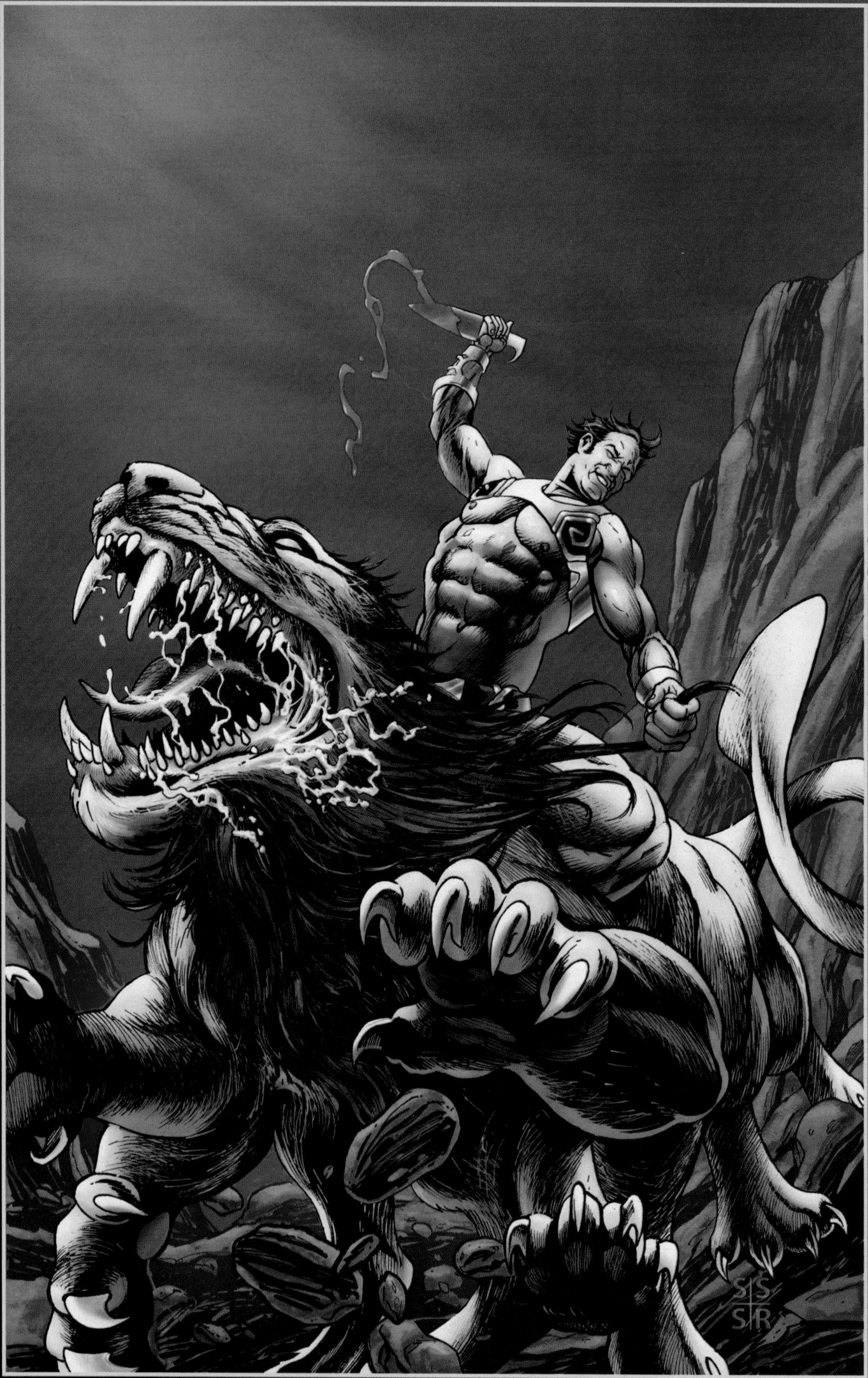

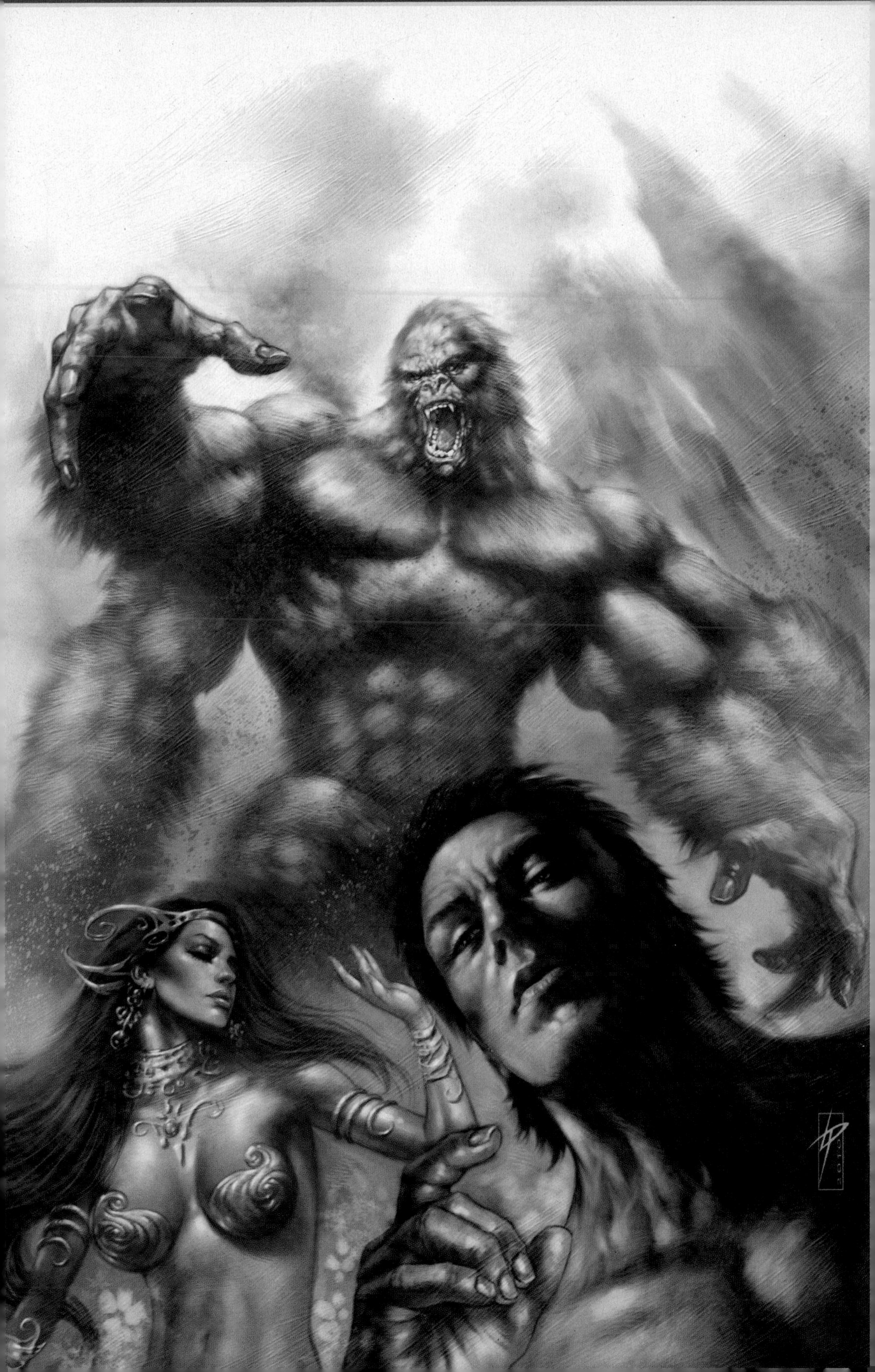

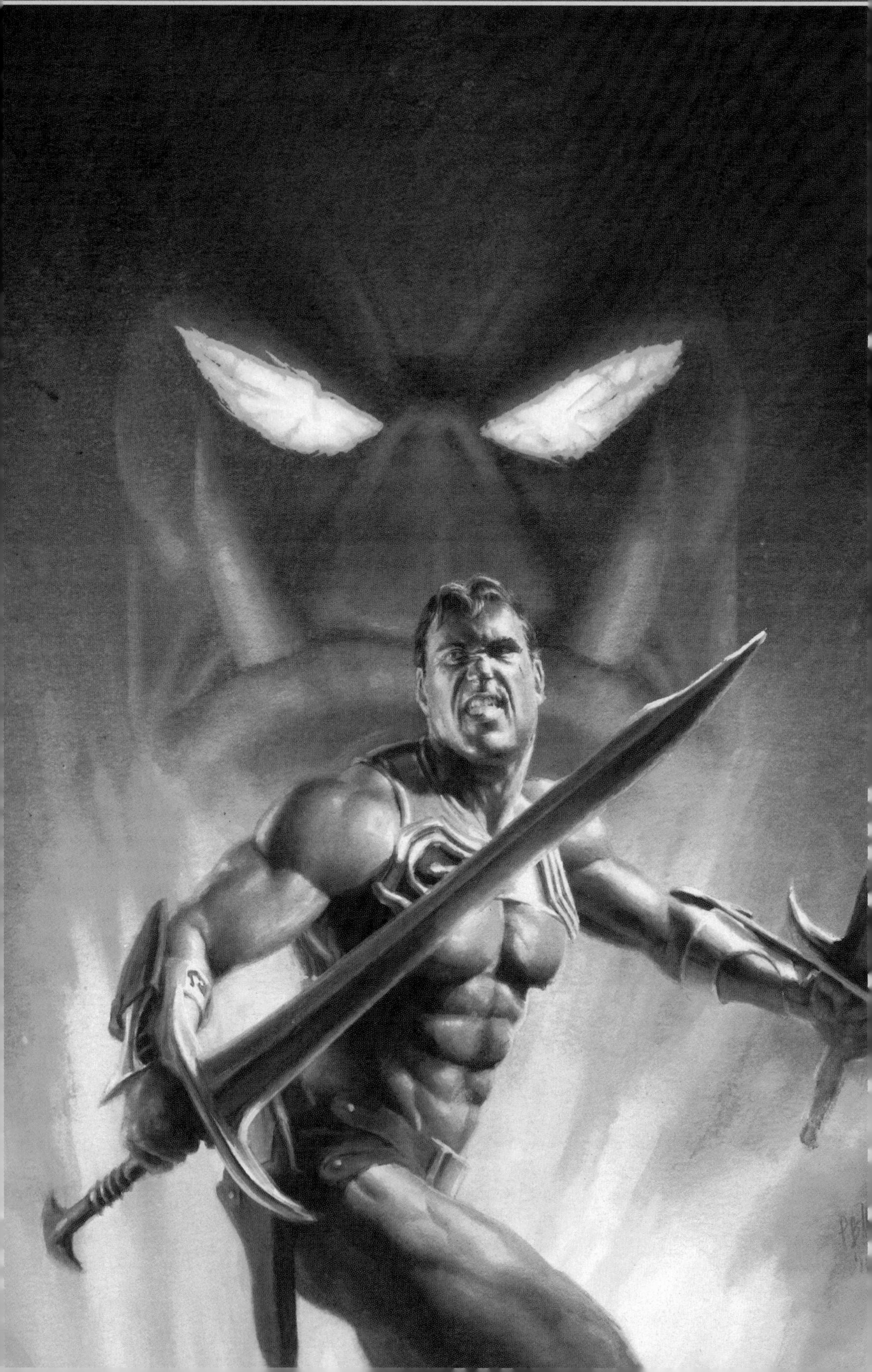

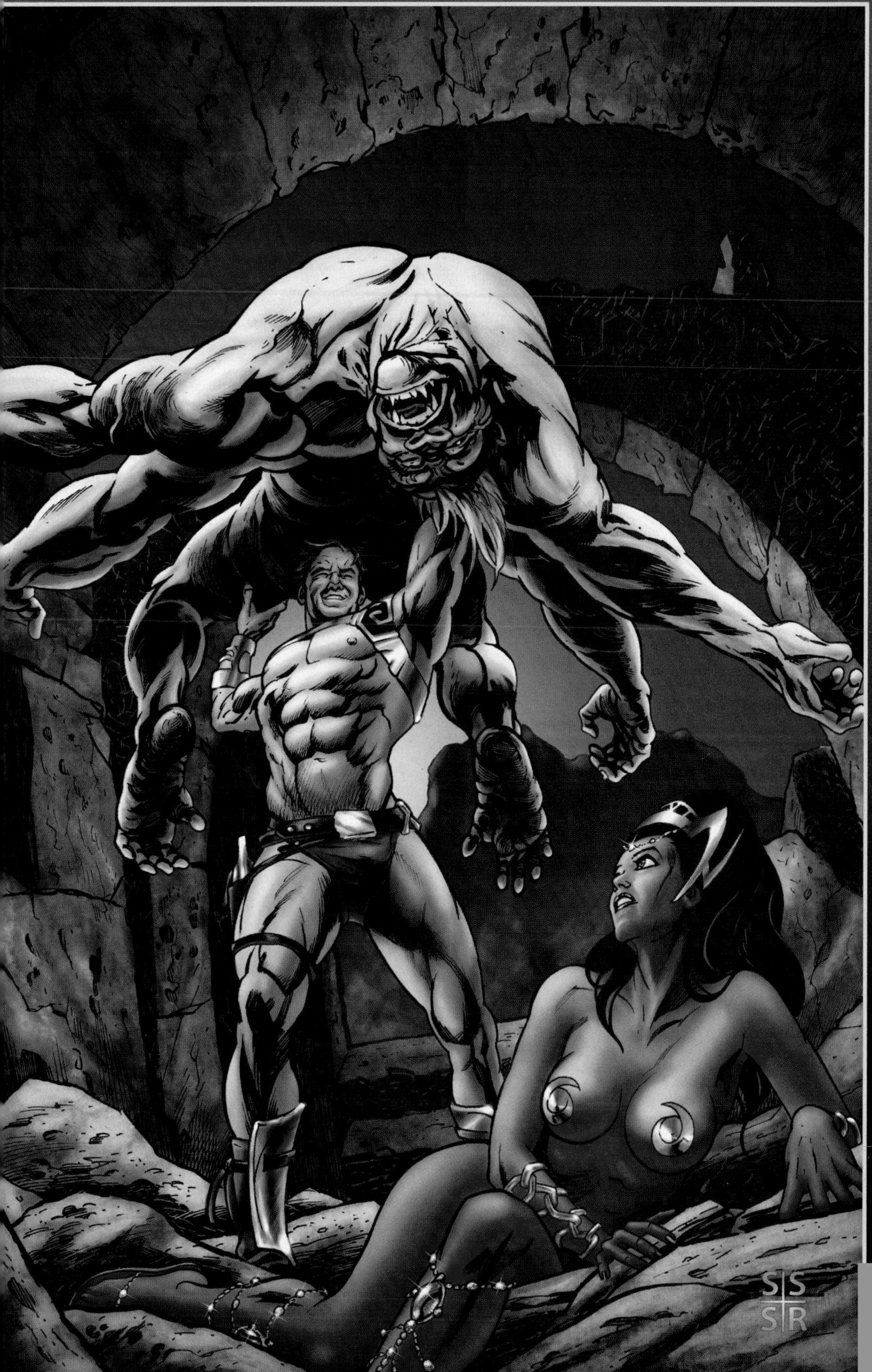

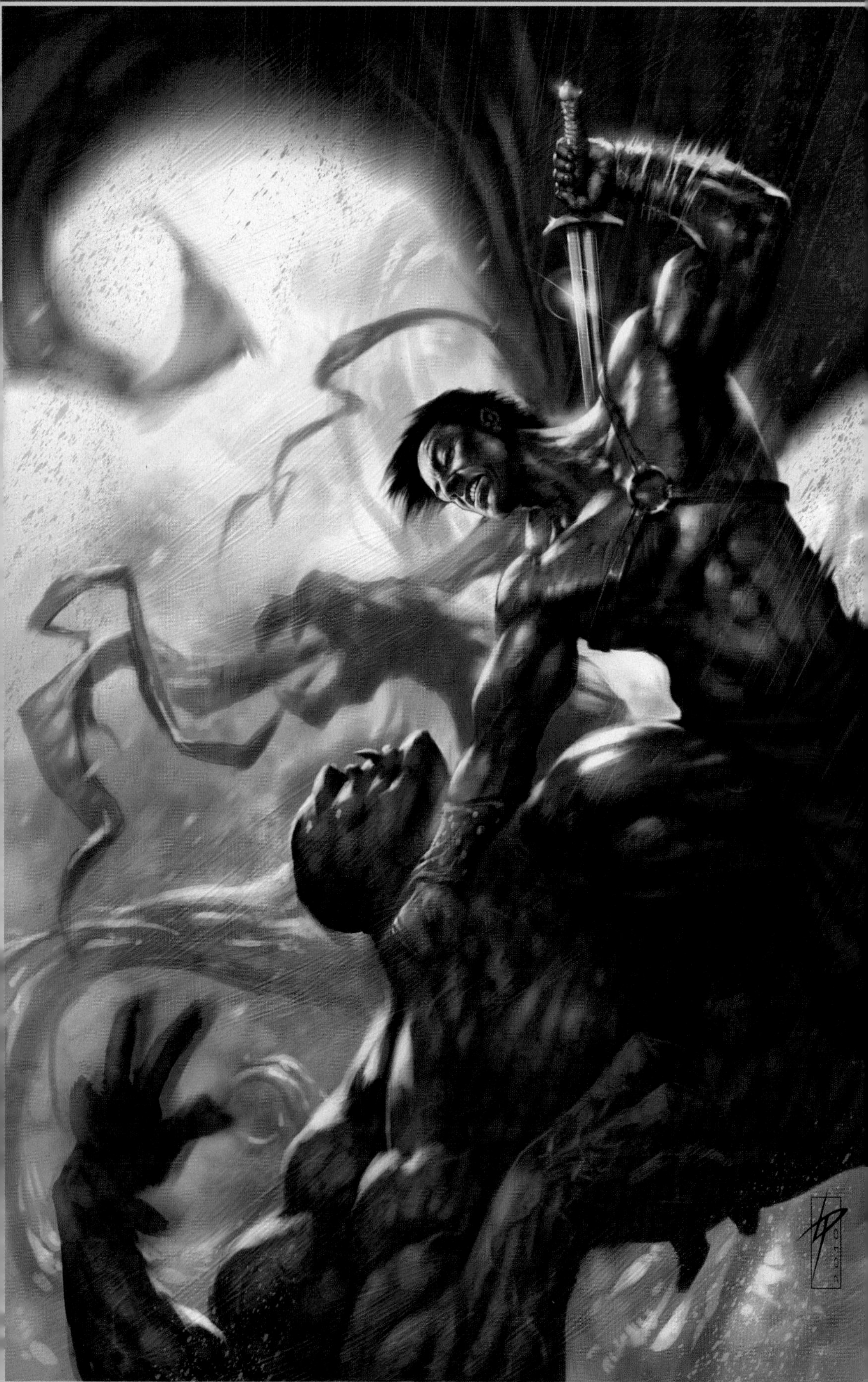

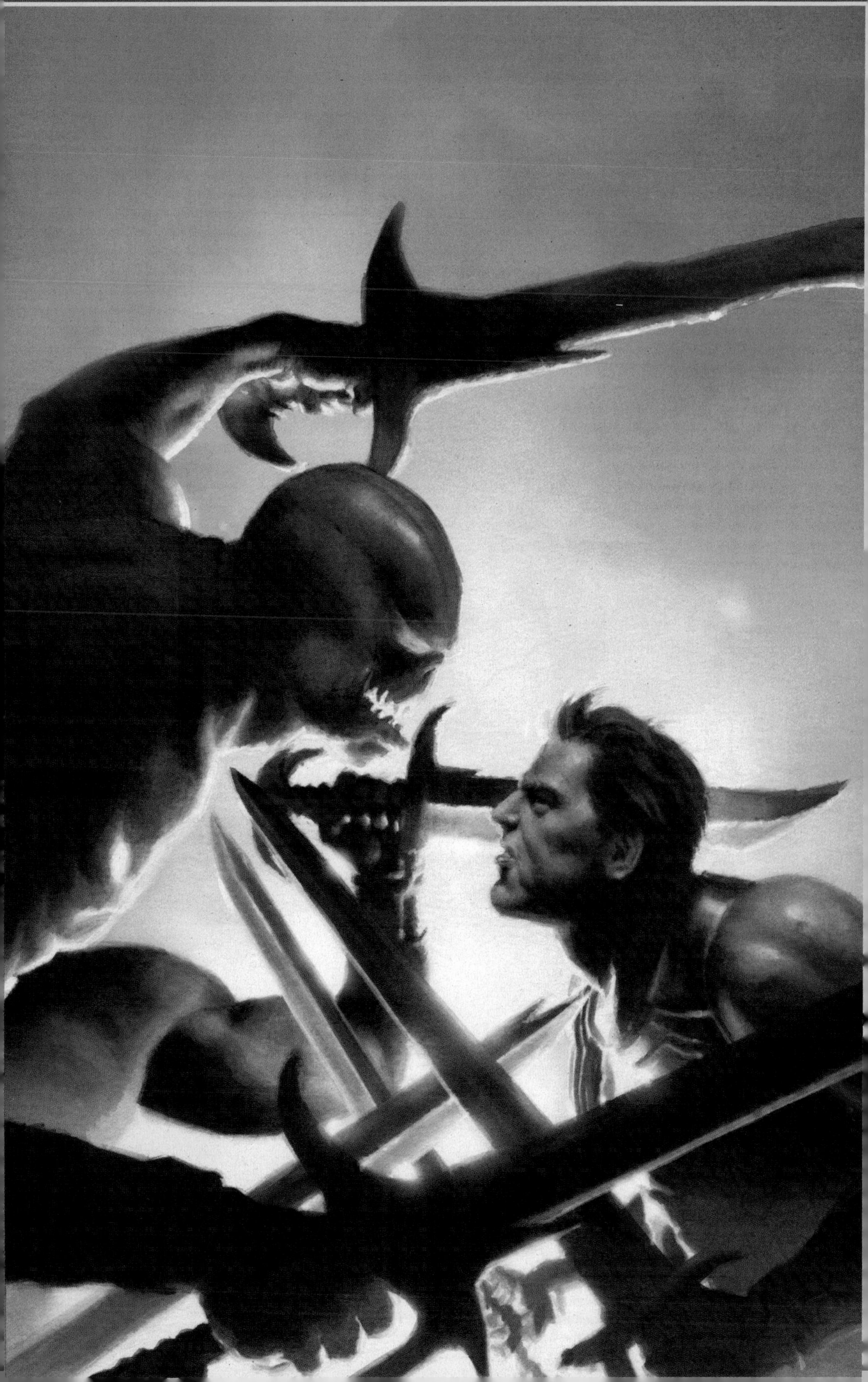

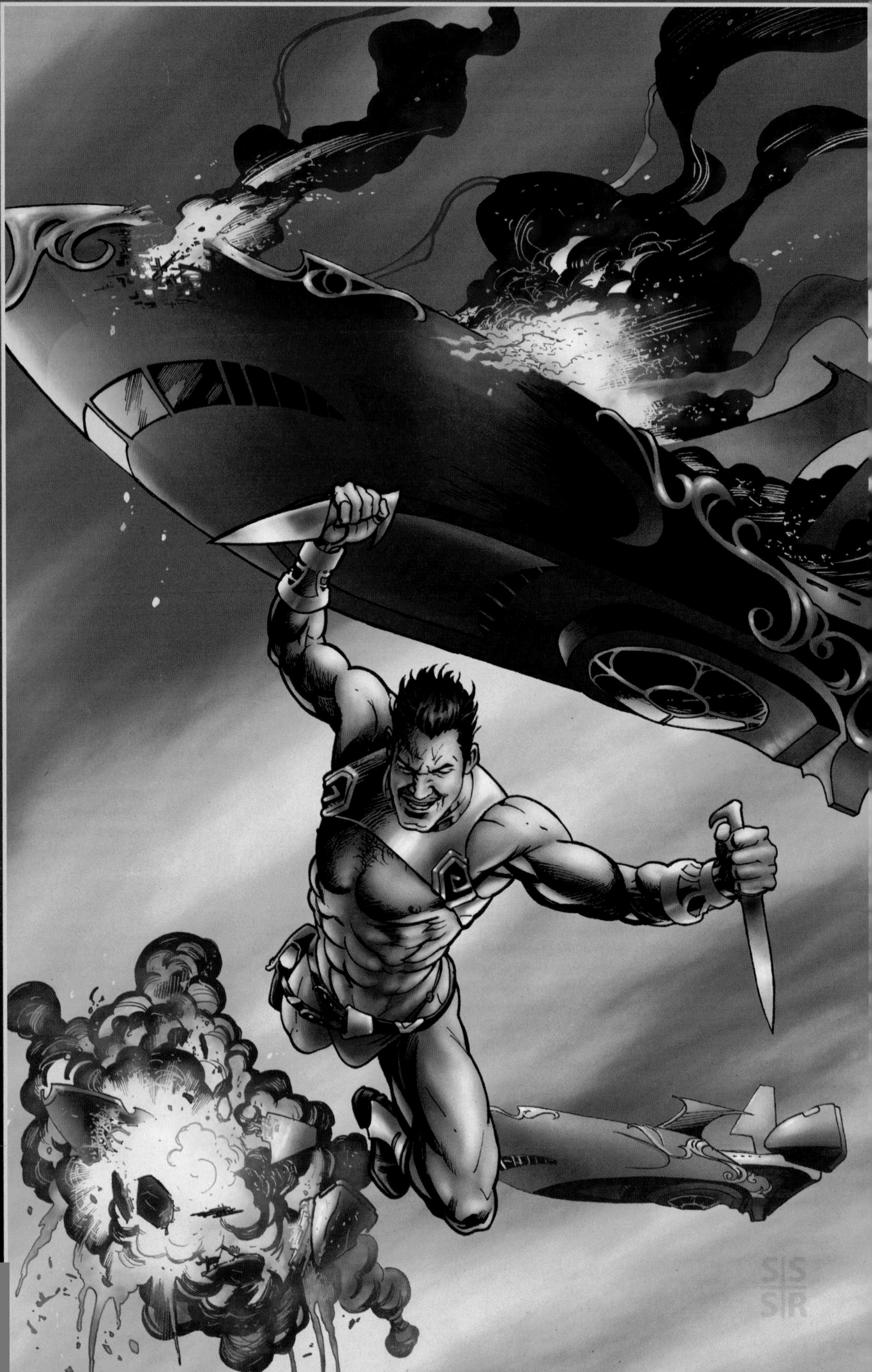

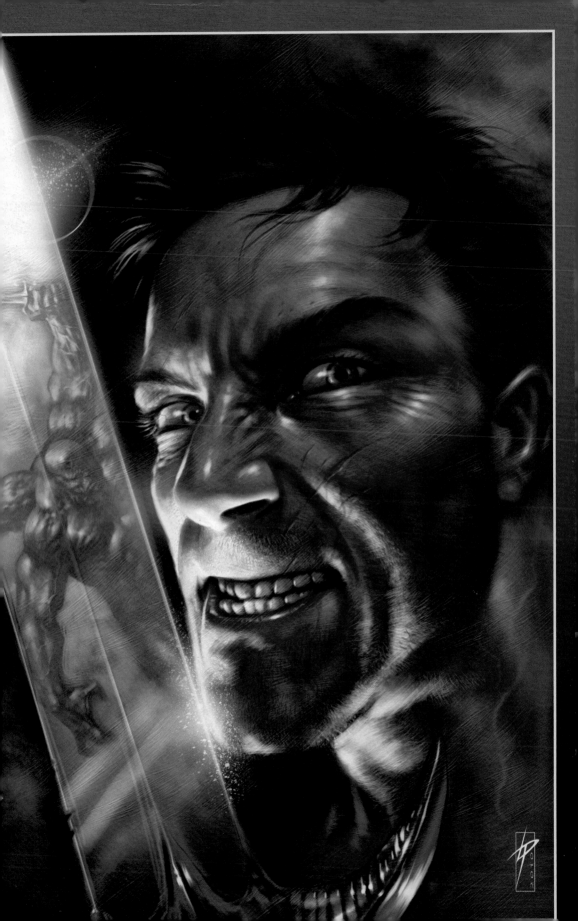

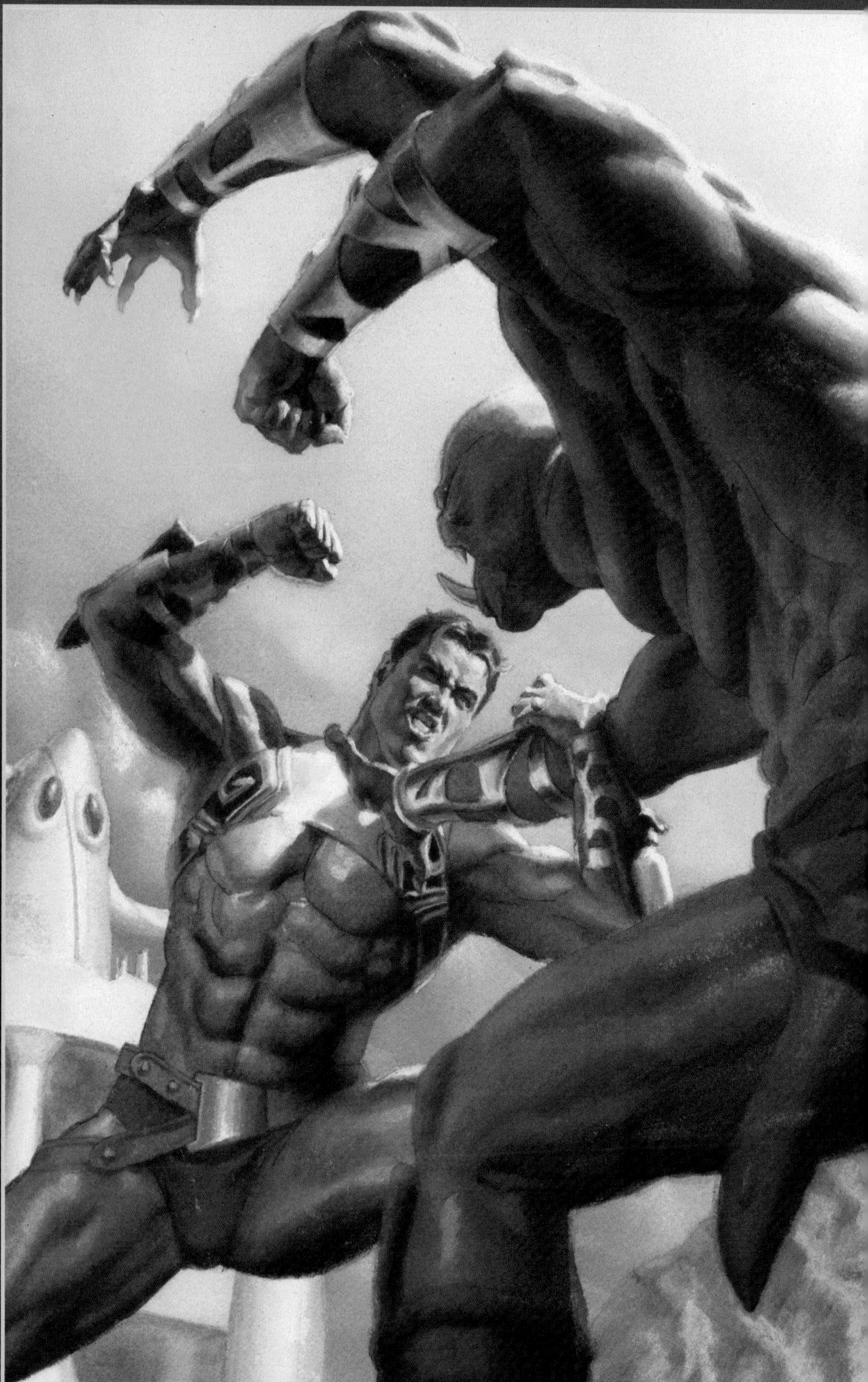

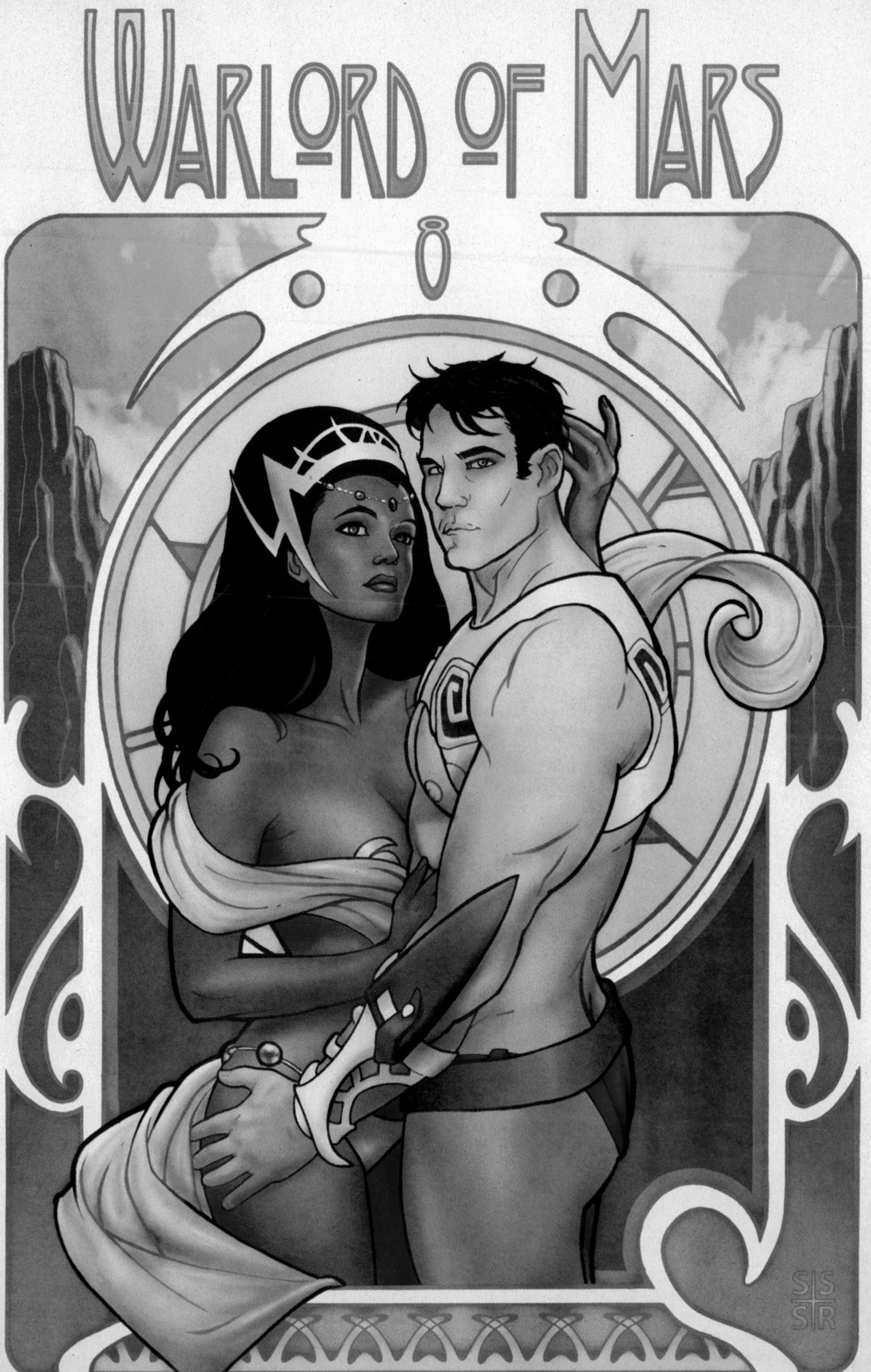
WARLORD OF MARS
8
SS
SR

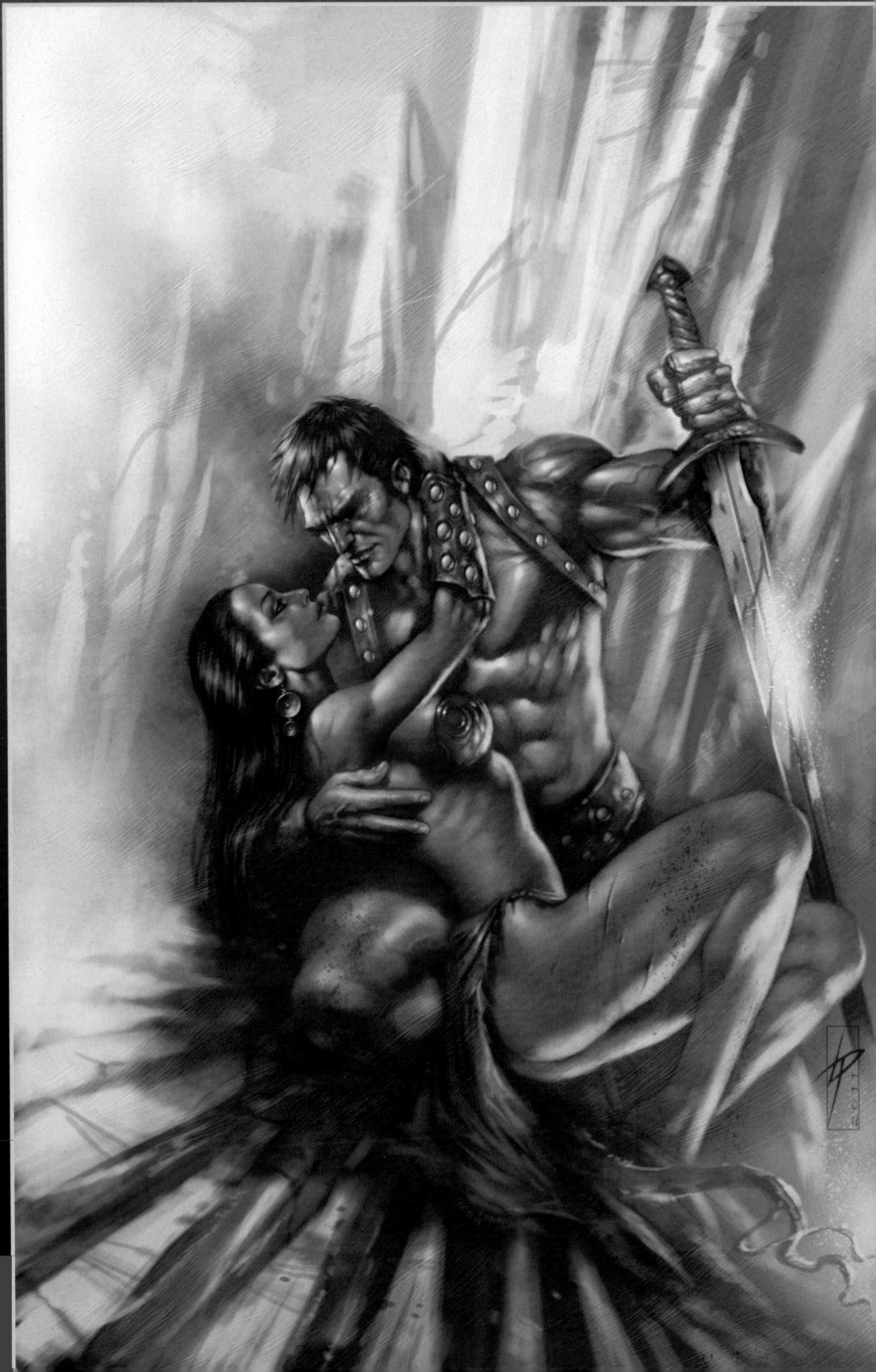

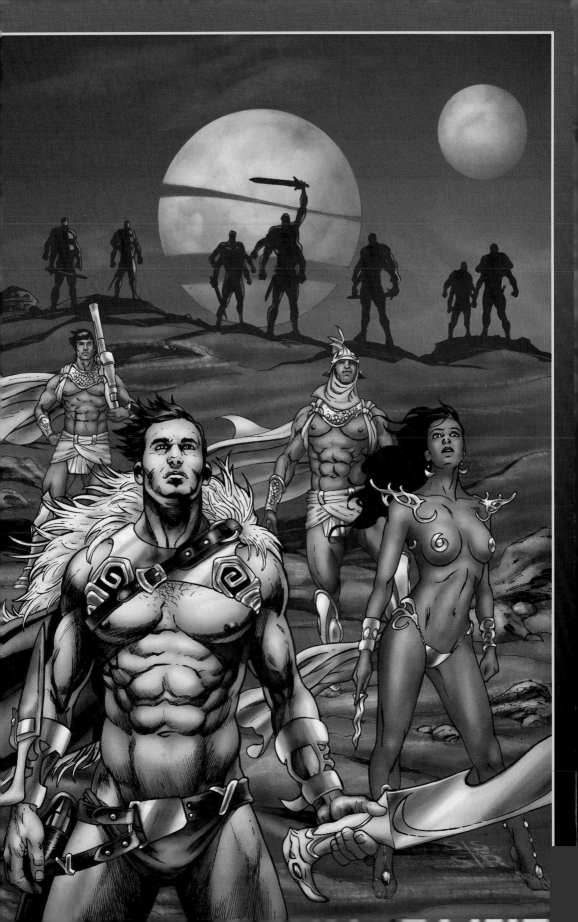

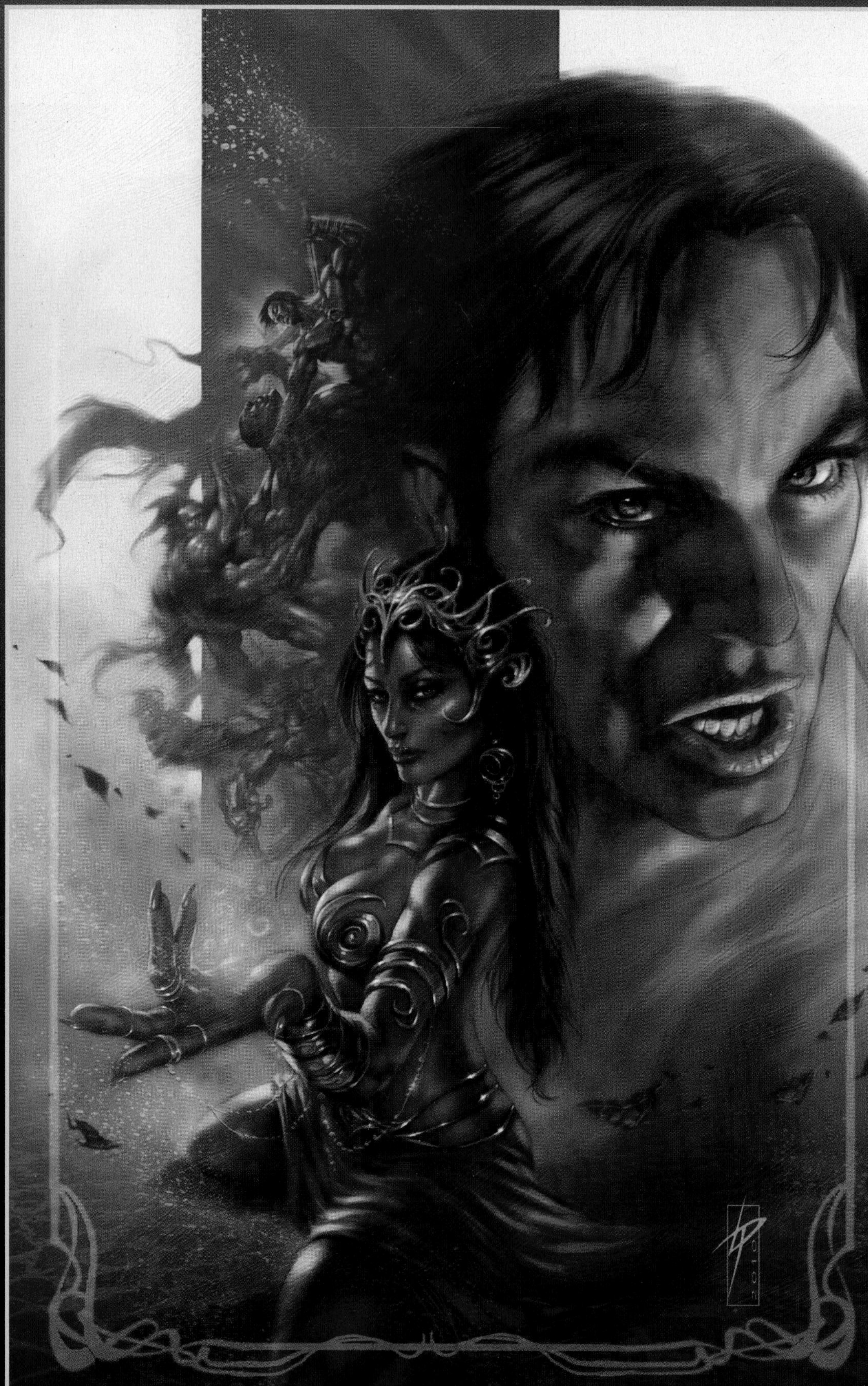

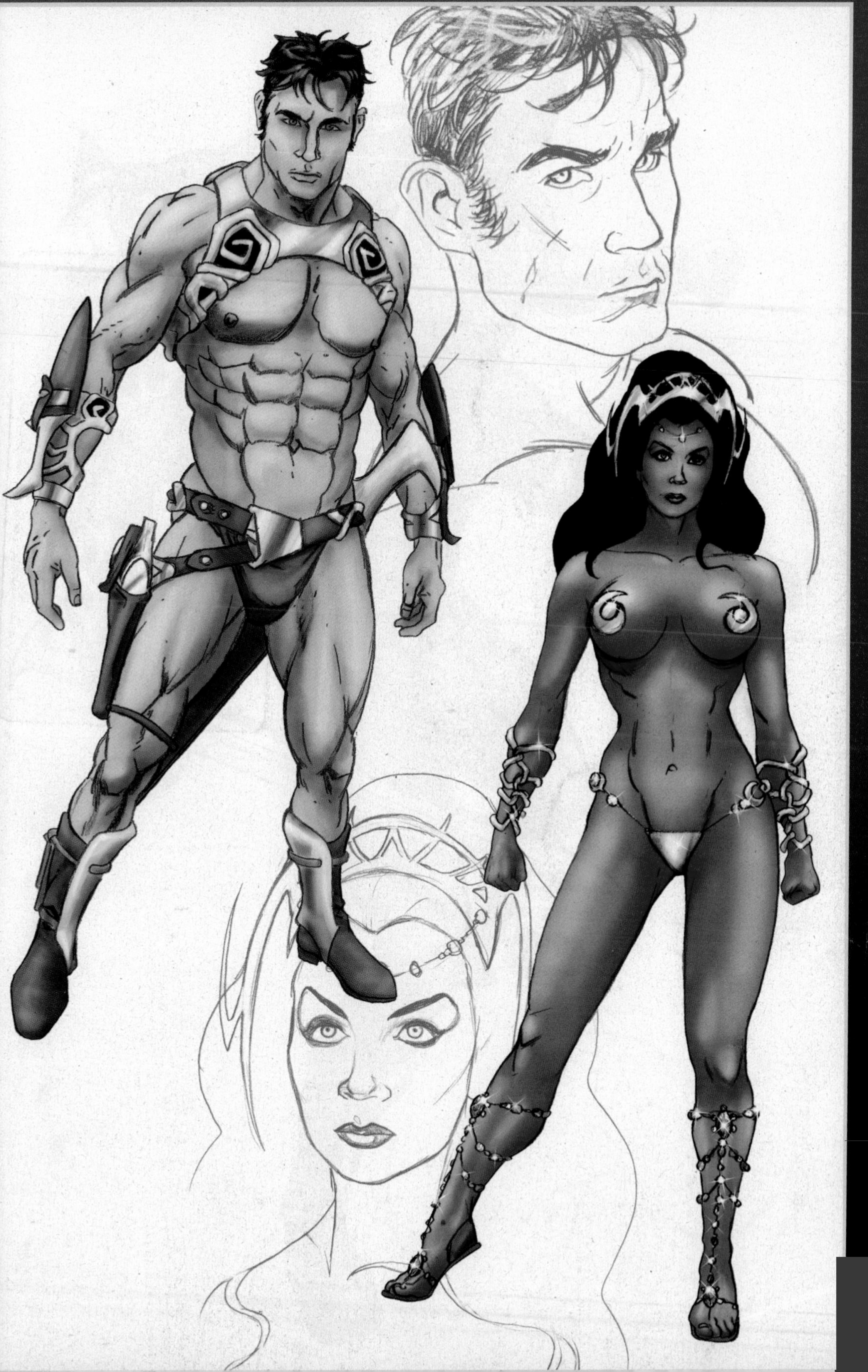

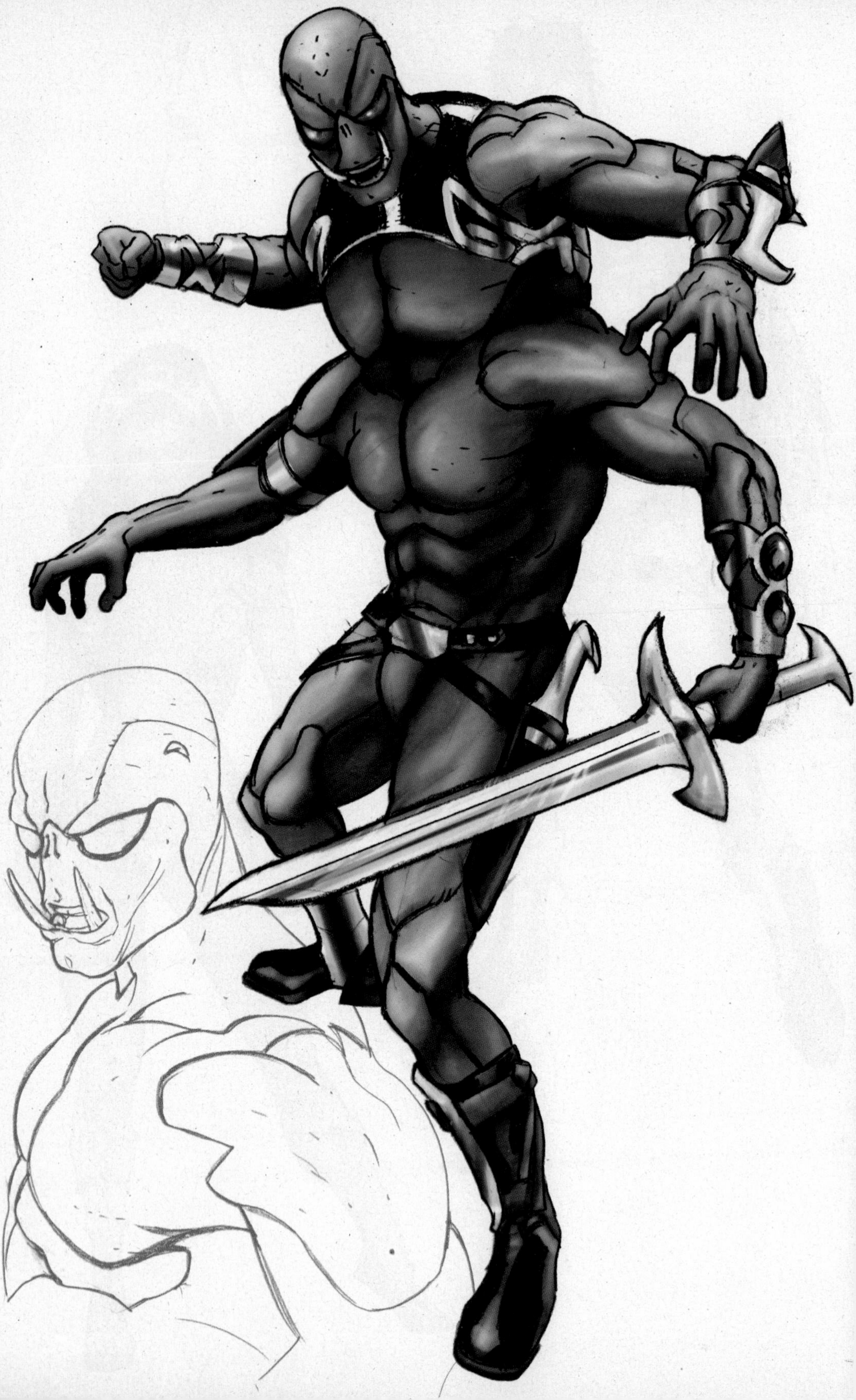